DATE DUE

May 11, 2010	

Studies in Development Economics and Policy

General Editor: **Anthony Shorrocks**

UNU WORLD INSTITUTE FOR DEVELOPMENT ECONOMICS RESEARCH (UNU-WIDER) was established by the United Nations University as its first research and training centre and started work in Helsinki, Finland, in 1985. The purpose of the institute is to undertake applied research and policy analysis on structural changes affecting the developing and transitional economies, to provide a forum for the advocacy of policies leading to robust, equitable and environmentally sustainable growth, and to promote capacity strengthening and training in the field of economic and social policy-making. Its work is carried out by staff researchers and visiting scholars in Helsinki and through networks of collaborating scholars and institutions around the world.

UNU World Institute for Development Economics Research (UNU-WIDER)
Katajanokanlaituri 6B, FIN-00160 Helsinki, Finland

Titles:

Tony Addison and Alan Roe (*editors*)
FISCAL POLICY FOR DEVELOPMENT
Poverty, Reconstruction and Growth

Tony Addison, Henrik Hansen and Finn Tarp (*editors*)
DEBT RELIEF FOR POOR COUNTRIES

George J. Borjas and Jeff Crisp (*editors*)
POVERTY, INTERNATIONAL MIGRATION AND ASYLUM

Ricardo Ffrench-Davis and Stephany Griffith-Jones (*editors*)
FROM CAPITAL SURGES TO DROUGHT
Seeking Stability for Emerging Economies

Basudeb Guha-Khasnobis (*editor*)
THE WTO, DEVELOPING COUNTRIES AND THE DOHA DEVELOPMENT AGENDA
Prospects and Challenges for Trade-led Growth

Aiguo Lu and Manuel F. Montes (*editors*)
POVERTY, INCOME DISTRIBUTION AND WELL-BEING IN ASIA DURING THE TRANSITION

Robert J. McIntyre and Bruno Dallago (*editors*)
SMALL AND MEDIUM ENTERPRISES IN TRANSITIONAL ECONOMIES

Vladimir Mikhalev (*editor*)
INEQUALITY AND SOCIAL STRUCTURE DURING THE TRANSITION

E. Wayne Nafziger and Raimo Väyrynen (*editors*)
THE PREVENTION OF HUMANITARIAN EMERGENCIES

Matthew Odedokun (*editor*)
EXTERNAL FINANCE FOR PRIVATE SECTOR DEVELOPMENT
Appraisals and Issues

Laixiang Sun (*editor*)
OWNERSHIP AND GOVERNANCE OF ENTERPRISES
Recent Innovative Developments

Studies in Development Economics and Policy
Series Standing Order ISBN 0–333–96424–1
(*outside North America only*)

You can receive future titles in this series as they are published by placing a standing order. Please contact your bookseller or, in case of difficulty, write to us at the address below with your name and address, the title of the series and the ISBN quoted above.

Customer Services Department, Macmillan Distribution Ltd, Houndmills, Basingstoke, Hampshire RG21 6XS, England

Poverty, International Migration and Asylum

Edited by

George J. Borjas

and

Jeff Crisp

in association with the United Nations
University – World Institute for Development
Economics Research

First published 2005 by
PALGRAVE MACMILLAN
Houndmills, Basingstoke, Hampshire RG21 6XS and
175 Fifth Avenue, New York, N.Y. 10010
Companies and representatives throughout the world

PALGRAVE MACMILLAN is the global academic imprint of the Palgrave Macmillan division of St. Martin's Press, LLC and of Palgrave Macmillan Ltd. Macmillan® is a registered trademark in the United States, United Kingdom and other countries. Palgrave is a registered trademark in the European Union and other countries.

ISBN 1–4039–4365–6

This book is printed on paper suitable for recycling and made from fully managed and sustained forest sources.

A catalogue record for this book is available from the British Library.

Library of Congress Cataloging-in-Publication Data
Poverty, international migration, and asylum / edited by
George J. Borjas and Jeff Crisp.
    p.   cm. — (Studies in development economics and policy)
"In association with the United Nations University World Institute for Development Economics Research."
Includes many of the studies presented at a UNU-WIDER sponsored conference held in Helsinki in September 2002.
Includes bibliographical references and index.
ISBN 1–4039–4365–6 (cloth)
1. Emigration and immigration—Economic aspects—Congresses.
2. Asylum, Right of—Economic aspects—Congresses.   3. Illegal aliens—Economic aspects—Congresses.   4. Alien labor—Economic aspects—Congresses.   5. Immigrants—Economic conditions—Congresses.   I. Borjas, George J.   II. Crisp, Jeff.   III. World Institute for Development Economics Research.   IV. Series.
JV6217.P68 2005
304.8—dc22   2004061051

10   9   8   7   6   5   4   3   2   1
14   13   12   11   10   09   08   07   06   05

Printed and bound in Great Britain by
Antony Rowe Ltd, Chippenham and Eastbourne

Contents

List of Tables

List of Figures

ix

Foreword*

The list of participants, the scope of topics and wide range of background papers for this conference is an impressive academic effort vested in the very important and timely theme of Poverty, International Migration and Asylum. Or should I rather say the three themes, each of which is indeed challenging in its own right, and even more so in combination.

International migration is not a problem in itself. Mobility of labour may in some circumstances be beneficial for the economies of both the source and destination countries. For the migrants themselves, having an option to change labour market is clearly an opportunity. Yet migration may become a problem where there is a mismatch between the push factors in source countries and the policies of destination countries. This seems to be increasingly the case in our times, to a point where migrational pressures are perceived as security threats.

The trend towards increased international migration appears to result from all aspects of the globalization process in combination and of continued huge income gaps between different countries. Globalization clearly boosts the pull factors of migration through increased flows of knowledge, media coverage, ideas and cultural values as well as through increased mobility of tradable goods and services as well as capital. Increased travelling and familiarity with opportunities in foreign countries triggers increased mobility of people. In addition, poverty, environmental degradation, political instability and human rights abuses clearly fuel the 'push factors' for migration from some regions of the world.

A direct link between poverty and migration is particularly obvious in some situations. Unexpected disasters, such as droughts, floods or conflicts may deprive people of their means of subsistence and force impoverished populations to move. We may at times lose sight of the large numbers of poor displaced populations hosted in neighbouring developing countries. The efforts of these countries deserve our sincere recognition and support.

Destination countries can and should contribute to the management of migration through cooperation with source countries in combating poverty, environmental degradation and discrimination. The need to prevent mass exoduses is yet another reason to recommit ourselves to the global millennium goals for development (MDGs), especially the goal of reducing by half the

---

*From the opening address to the UNU–WIDER conference on 'Poverty, International Migration and Asylum'.

number of people living in absolute poverty by the year 2015. Appropriations for development cooperation need to be adjusted with a view of meeting the internationally agreed goal. Key exports of developing countries should be ensured more fair conditions on the global market.

Poverty and asylum are an odd couple. Poverty is among the reasons causing persons to migrate but poverty as such is excluded from accepted grounds for protection. I assume it is not a coincidence that the two words are separated in the title of the conference. Under international refugee law, asylum may not be sought for reasons other than certain forms of persecution. Even under human rights law a prohibition to return somebody to their own country may be sought only from treatment deemed as inhuman or degrading. A clear distinction between managing migration for the purpose of work and protecting the right of everyone to seek asylum is essential.

At the same time, it should be noted that poverty and human rights problems often occur together in poor social conditions and in connection with humanitarian problems. Disadvantaged minorities may face situations of poverty which are both the results of and causes for discrimination, if not persecution. Large income inequalities or humanitarian emergencies may involve human rights problems relevant to asylum applications.

The prevention of unmanageable migrational pressure is a common international concern. Destination countries may want to include such considerations in their development cooperation strategies. They must in that event conform with the overriding goal of reducing poverty and the development goals of partner countries. They must also respect the right of everyone to leave their country of residence, enshrined in international human rights law. Finland was very active in the European summit in Seville to ensure that development cooperation was used only as a positive incentive in these respects.

An important question under discussion is the question of gender-based discrimination which at times amounts to persecution or inhuman treatment in the sense of international law. Recent examples, such as the sentencing to death by stoning of Amina Lawal in Nigeria, have drawn attention to discriminatory cultural practices that violate the human rights of women. In Sweden, killings of young minority women in the name of perceived honour have had a similar awareness-raising effect. Violence against women, including female genital mutilation, is a severe form of discrimination in many parts of the world. For me, it seems important to acknowledge in any proper asylum regime that persecution in the meaning of the Geneva Convention may occur solely on the grounds of gender.

In order to retain the treaty-based asylum system functional and legitimate, we need to have a correct understanding of the threats against it. An abundance of unfounded or abusive asylum application is one significant threat, as it overburdens the system. On the other hand, the criteria for presuming an asylum request manifestly unfounded should not put in jeopardy the right to individual inquiry. Another threat that may under-mine public support for the asylum system is the stereotyping of asylum seekers. Labelling asylum seekers collectively as so-called 'economic migrants' or 'economic refugees' not only stigmatizes the asylum seekers but in practice also the refugees already in the country and indirectly all ethnic minorities of migrant origin. Stereotyping in these terms also seems for many to imply an assumption that refugees are more of a burden than a human resource to the host country.

Poverty is fuelling the supply of victims for traffickers in human beings. Most victims of this contemporary slave trade are women and girls, criminal organizations make them indebted and dependant and control their economic exploitation in the destination country. The victims of trafficking live in fear of violence and of being revealed to the authorities. In order to be able to fight these traffickers it is essential that victims of trafficking are treated primarily as victims rather than accomplices to the crime and be offered appropriate witness protection measures.

Trafficking may often be carried out using legal means of entering the destination country. It is never sufficient to combat trafficking through fighting clandestine smuggling of persons. International cooperation against trafficking in human beings needs to be comprehensive and address not only measures against people smuggling and crime prevention but also the root causes related to poverty and the status of women and girls in countries of origin as well as rehabilitation victims. The prompt ratification by all states of the trafficking protocol to the UN Convention against transna-tional organized crime and the protocol on the sale of children to the UN Child Convention are important first steps, which Finland is preparing to take.

At the Johannesburg Summit, the world leaders reiterated their commitment to poverty eradication based on a broad agenda for sustainable develop-ment. Economic development is closely interlinked with social and environ-mental policies and must be based on democracy and respect for human rights. The world community needs to address also the migration issues, not only as a matter of border control but as an aspect of pursuing sustainable development.

SUVI-ANNE SIIMES
Member of the Parliament of Finland
and former Minister for Development Cooperation

Acknowledgements

This volume is an outcome of a UNU-WIDER research project on 'Poverty, International Migration and Asylum' and a related conference which took place in Helsinki in 2002. The project and conference were organized by George Borjas of Harvard University and Jeff Crisp of UNHCR, whom I heartily thank for their contribution to the work of UNU-WIDER. Special thanks are also due to Janis Vehmaan-Kreula, who handled both the conference administration and preparation of this volume, and to Suvi-Anne Siimes, former Finnish Minister for Development Cooperation, for her opening remarks to both the conference and to this volume.

Discussion at the conference ranged widely over the challenges and dilemmas for policy-makers posed by the increase in migration and refugee movements and their impact (both positive and negative) on development and human well-being. Many conference participants made valuable contributions to these discussions; others later acted as manuscript referees providing comments on individual chapters. I offer thanks to the individual authors for their help in preparing the final manuscript, and to all the other people involved in the project, including the staff at UNU-WIDER.

UNU-WIDER gratefully acknowledges the support of UNHCR through the work of Jeff Crisp, and the financial contributions to the 2002–03 research programme provided by the governments of Denmark (Royal Ministry of Foreign Affairs), Finland (Ministry for Foreign Affairs), Norway (Royal Ministry of Foreign Affairs), Sweden (Swedish International Development Cooperation Agency – Sida) and the United Kingdom (Department for International Development).

ANTHONY SHORROCKS
Director, UNU-WIDER

List of Abbreviations

ACM	Australian Correctional Management
CBA	cost-benefit analysis
CES	constant elasticity of substitution
CMA	Canadian Metropolitan Areas
DAC	Development Assistance Committee (OECD)
DSS	Department of Social Security (United Kingdom)
ECRE	European Council for Refugees and Exiles
EEA	European Economic Area
ERF	European Refugee Fund
EIU	Economist Intelligence Unit
EU	European Union
FDI	foreign direct investment
FY	financial year
GATT	General Agreement on Tariffs and Trade
GDP	gross domestic product
GLA	Greater London Authority
GNP	gross national product
GNI	gross national income
GTMO	Guantanamo Bay (US military base)
HDI	Human Development Index
HHD	high human development
IADB	Inter-American Development Bank
ICMPD	International Centre for Migration Policy Development
IDP	internationally displaced person
ILO	International Labour Office
IMF	International Monetary Fund
IMSS	Mexican pension system
IOM	International Organization for Migration
INS	Immigration and Naturalization Service (United States)
IRCA	Immigration Reform and Control Act
ISPA	Pre-accession Instrument for Structural Policies
IT	information technology
JHA	Justice and Home Affairs
LDC	less developed countries
LHD	low human development
LTTE	Liberation Tigers of Tamil Eelam
MDG	Millennium Development Goals
MHD	medium human development

MPL	marginal productivity of labour
NAFTA	North American Free Trade Agreement
NATO	North Atlantic Treaty Organization
NGO	non-governmental organization
ODA	official development assistance
OECD	Organisation for Economic Co-operation and Development
PKK	Kurdish Workers' Party
PPP	purchasing power parity
RCOA	Refugee Council of Australia
RSC	Refugees Studies Centre (Oxford)
S&E	science and engineering
SAC	Special Assistance Category
SAW	Special Agricultural Worker (programme)
SAPARD	Special Accession Programme for Agricultural and Rural Development
SHP	Special Humanitarian Program
SIS	Schengen Information System
SLBFE	Sri Lanka Bureau of Foreign Employment
SSA	sub-Saharan Africa
STC	safe third country
TANF	temporary assistance for needy families
TPV	temporary protection visa
UFW	United Farm Workers
UNDP	United Nations Development Programme
UNHCR	United Nations High Commissioner for Refugees
UNPD	United Nations Population Division
USCR	United States Committee for Refugees
WTO	World Trade Organisation

Notes on the Contributors

Kræn Blume is a researcher at the Institute for Local Government Studies, AKF, Copenhagen, working in the areas of immigration, poverty and income mobility.

George J. Borjas is the Robert W. Scrivner Professor of Economics and Social Policy at the John F. Kennedy School of Government, Harvard University, and is also a Research Associate at the National Bureau of Economic Research. He has published extensively on the economics of immigration, including *Heaven's Door: Immigration Policy and the American Economy* (Princeton University Press, 1999).

Stephen Castles is Professor of Migration and Refugee Studies, and Director of the Refugee Studies Centre at the University of Oxford. He has carried out research on migration, ethnic relations and citizenship in Europe, Australia and Asia, and is the author of many books and articles on these topics.

Géraldine Chatelard is a Marie Curie Fellow at the Robert Schuman Centre for Advanced Studies, European University Institute in Florence. Her current work focuses on migration and mobility in the Middle East and the Sahara.

Jeff Crisp is Director of Policy and Research with the Global Commission on International Migration. Previously he was Head of Evaluation and Policy Analysis of the United Nations High Commissioner for Refugees (UNHCR).

Riccardo Faini is Professor of Economics at the University of Rome Tor Vergata. He is co-director (with Thierry Verdier) of the International Trade Programme at the CEPR and has worked as a consultant for the World Bank, UNIDO, UNCTAD, the OECD, UNDP and the IMF.

David Fisher is an international lawyer supporting the mandate of the Representative of the UN Secretary-General on Internally Displaced Persons at the Office of the UN High Commissioner for Human Rights.

Matthew J. Gibney is University Lecturer in Forced Migration at the Refugee Studies Centre, Queen Elizabeth House, University of Oxford, and Official Fellow, Linacre College, Oxford.

Björn Gustafsson is Professor in the Department of Social Work, Göteborg University, working in the areas of social assistance, poverty, the distribution of economic well-being, and the welfare state and immigrants.

Randall Hansen holds a Professorial Chair in Politics at the University of Newcastle upon Tyne and was previously Fellow and Tutor in Politics at Merton College, University of Oxford.

Timothy J. Hatton is Professor and Head of Economics at the Australian National University, Professor of Economics at the University of Essex, and Research Fellow at the CEPR and IZA.

Ana María Iregui is a Research Economist at the Banco de la Republica, Colombia.

Khalid Koser is Lecturer in Human Geography and a member of the Migration Research Unit at University College London.

Bjørn Letnes is a PhD student of Political Science at the Norwegian University of Science and Technology (NTNU), Trondheim, Norway.

Sean Loughna is a Research Officer at the Refugee Studies Centre and Co-Director of Forced Migration Online. His research has largely focused on forced migration and civil society in Latin America.

Philip Martin is Professor of Agricultural and Resource Economics at the University of California, Davis and chair of the University of California's Comparative Immigration and Integration Program. He edits the newsletters *Migration News* and *Rural Migration News*, which provide timely and non-partisan summaries of significant migration developments.

Susan Martin is the Director of the Institute for the Study of International Migration (ISIM) at Georgetown University's School of Foreign Service. She also co-directs, with Andrew I. Schoenholtz, the Certificate Program in Refugees and Humanitarian Emergencies.

Jonathon W. Moses is Professor of Political Science at the Norwegian University of Science and Technology (NTNU), Trondheim, Norway.

Peder J. Pedersen is Professor of Economics, University of Aarhus and Danish National Institute of Social Research, working in the areas of labour economics, retirement and migration.

Catherine Phuong is Lecturer in Law at the University of Newcastle (UK). She has published widely in the area of international refugee law, including *The International Protection of Internally Displaced Persons* (Cambridge University Press, 2004).

Andrew I. Schoenholtz is the Deputy Director of the Institute for the Study of International Migration (ISIM) at Georgetown University's School of Foreign Service. He also co-directs, with Susan Martin, the Certificate Program in Refugees and Humanitarian Emergencies.

Andrés Solimano is Regional Adviser, United Nations Economic Commission for Latin America and the Caribbean (ECLAC), Santiago, Chile.

Claudia Tazreiter is a Lecturer in the School of Sociology and Anthropology at the University of New South Wales, Sydney. She teaches and researches in the areas of migration, in particular, the causes of and responses to forced migration in the context of human rights, inequality and violence.

Elizabeth Thomas-Hope holds the James Seivright Moss-Solomon (Snr.) Chair of Environmental Management, and is Head of the Department of Geography and Geology at the University of the West Indies. She is the author of *Caribbean Migration* (University of the West Indies Press, reprinted 2002) as well other works on migration, Caribbean social issues and the environment.

Nicholas Van Hear is a Senior Researcher at the Centre on Migration, Policy and Society (COMPAS), University of Oxford. He has worked on forced migration, development and related issues for more than twenty years, with research in Africa, the Middle East and South Asia.

Raimo Väyrynen is President of the Academy of Finland. A political scientist, he has previously worked as Professor of International Relations at the Universities of Helsinki and Notre Dame, and as Director of the Helsinki Collegium for Advanced Studies. His main areas of interest include international political economy and security studies.

Mette Verner is Associate Professor of Economics, Aarhus School of Business, working in the areas of labour economics, family-friendly policies, economics of migration and integration.

Jeffrey G. Williamson is Laird Bell Professor of Economics and ex-Chair at Harvard University, Faculty Fellow at Harvard CID and Research Associate at NBER.

1
Poverty, International Migration and Asylum: Introduction

George J. Borjas and Jeff Crisp

In recent years, substantial numbers of people have migrated – or sought to migrate – from regions that are afflicted by poverty and insecurity to more prosperous and stable parts of the world. By the year 2002, the United Nations estimated that about 180 million persons – or roughly 3 per cent of the world's population – were living in a country where they were not born. Nearly 12.5 per cent of the population in Austria, 19.3 per cent in Canada, 10 per cent in France, 22.4 per cent in Switzerland and 12.3 per cent in the United States was foreign-born. Even Japan, which is thought of as being very homogeneous and geographically immune to immigrants, now reports major problems with illegal immigration.

Such population flows, involving increasingly tortuous and dangerous long-distance journeys, have been both prompted and facilitated by a variety of factors associated with the process of globalization: a growing disparity in the level of human security to be found in different parts of the world; improved transportation, communications and information technology (IT) systems; the expansion of transnational social networks; and the emergence of a commercial (and sometimes criminal) industry devoted to the smuggling of people across international borders.

These population movements have been a cause for growing concern in the industrialized states. Such states are ready to acknowledge the positive value of international migration when it meets the needs of their labour markets, and when it takes place in a controlled and predictable manner. But when it involves the irregular and 'spontaneous' arrival of people from other parts of the world, and when those migrants appear to bring little financial or social capital with them, the countries react with alarm.

As a result of these huge population flows, the impact of immigration is now being heatedly debated globally, in both host and source countries. The political discussion is typically focused around three substantive questions:

- First, how do immigrants perform in the host country's economy?
- Second, what impact do immigrants have on the economic opportunities of workers in the host country and what impact do they have on the economic opportunities of the workers who remain behind in the source country?
- Finally, which set of immigration policies should countries pursue?

The policy significance of these questions is self-evident. For example, immigrants who have high levels of productivity can make a significant contribution to economic growth in the host country, but adversely impact economic growth in the source country. Similarly, the debate over immigration policy has long been fuelled by the widespread perception that immigrants may have an adverse effect on the employment opportunities of natives. Which native workers are most adversely affected by immigration, and how large is the decline in the native wage? Conversely, how do large outflows of workers affect the economic opportunities of workers who remain behind?

Finally, there is great diversity in immigration policies across countries. Some countries, such as the United States, award entry visas mainly to applicants who have relatives already residing in the country. Other countries, such as Australia and Canada, award visas to persons who have a desirable set of socioeconomic characteristics, and still other countries, such as Germany, encouraged the migration of 'temporary' guest workers in the 1960s, only to find that the temporary migrants became a permanent part of the German population. The choice of the 'right' immigration policy can obviously have a significant impact on economic activity and social conditions, in both the short run and in the long run.

The concerns over the resurgence of large-scale immigration have been exacerbated by the fact that a significant proportion of new arrivals in the industrialized states establish a foothold there by lodging claims to refugee status – an act that normally prevents them from being deported and which allows them to remain in a country for months or even years while their asylum applications are being processed. In the perception of many politicians and the general public, seeking asylum has become a means of circumventing legitimate immigration controls. And a very expensive means, too, given the costs involved in the administration of asylum procedures, as well as the provision of social welfare, public services and legal advice to refugee claimants.

Confronted with this phenomenon, the industrialized states have in recent years introduced a barrage of measures intended to obstruct or dissuade people from gaining access to and seeking asylum on their territory. While such measures have in some respects achieved their intended objectives, they have also had some unintended consequences. There is now good reason to believe that the imposition of restrictive asylum practices has had the effect of diverting migrants to alternative destinations and of prompting them to resort to clandestine forms of movement. Measures that were intended to control a relatively visible and measurable flow of asylum seekers have contributed to a boom in human smuggling which is far more difficult to detect and quantify.

The UNU–WIDER project on International Migration, Refugees and Poverty consisted of two related sub-projects, one examining the economic consequences of immigration and the other examining issues associated with asylum migration. Each of these partner projects commissioned a number of studies, as well as issuing a more general call for papers. The conference, held in Helsinki in September 2002, attracted a wide array of scholars and policy-makers. This volume contains many of the studies that were presented at that conference.

The joint themes of 'regular' migrants and refugees dominated the discussion. Concurrent with the resurgence of large-scale immigration, a large literature has developed that analyses the economic impact of immigration on host countries, particularly the United States. To a large extent, this literature has focused on documenting the labour market and fiscal impacts of immigration on United States-born workers and on expenditures in welfare programmes by federal, state, and local governments in the United States. Given the global nature of large-scale population flows, the project aimed to expand the focus of the studies of economic consequences of legal and illegal immigration to other host countries, to source countries, as well as to place the economic study of immigration in a global context. In doing so, we encouraged authors to examine whether the economic consequences that are now being perceived in source and host countries had a historical parallel in earlier waves of immigration. This type of analysis will surely help increase our understanding of the economic, social, and political forces that shape how immigration alters the economic well-being of populations, as well as provide some insights into how the shaping of immigration policy reacts to the perceived economic consequences. Similarly, the authors were encouraged to examine the economic consequences of immigration in the context of the increasing globalization of world trade – in particular, what do current patterns of globalization and migration imply about convergence in economic conditions across countries?

There was a similar concern about analysing illegal immigration. After all, an important aspect of the large-scale migration flows in the world today is the prevalence of large flows of illegal migrants. These large flows may well become more important in the future, and affect a wider set of industrialized economies. Finally, the project contains a number of case studies, detailing immigration consequences and policies in various parts of the world, including such wide-ranging experiences as those of the EU, as well as Argentina, the Caribbean and Iraq.

Regarding asylum migration, it is worth noting that the increasing size of refugee flows has given rise to a voluminous literature, produced not only by the academic community, but also by international organizations, regional bodies and human rights agencies, not to mention the growing number of research and policy institutes focusing on what has become known as 'the migration–asylum nexus'.

At this risk of excessive generalization, it can be argued that the recent literature on the migration–asylum nexus is skewed in several respects. While much has been written about the way states have responded to the issues of irregular migration and asylum migration, the changing size, direction and composition of such population movements has been subject to far less scrutiny. The existing literature has a strong institutional focus, but reveals relatively little about irregular and asylum migrants themselves – and even less about those people who are unable or unwilling to find a way out of countries where the conditions of life would appear to be intolerable. In disciplinary terms, recent writing on the migration–asylum nexus has not generally been informed by economics or development economics, especially when compared with the literature on other forms of migration.

The UNU-WIDER project was designed to enhance our understanding of those migratory movements which are undertaken for the purpose or with the consequence of seeking asylum in another state. More specifically, the project focused specifically on a number of important dimensions of asylum migration. A key component of the volume provides a historical, empirical and statistical overview of the phenomenon, focusing on the changing nature of asylum migration:

- Where do asylum migrants come from?
- Where do they go to?
- What routes do they take to get there?
- What is the demographic and socioeconomic profile of such migrants?
- And what does this data tell us about the causes of and motivation for asylum migration?

In addition, the authors were encouraged to establish a *typology of asylum migration*, focusing especially on the modes and methods by which people move from one country and region to another. This typology examines the information which people use in making their decision to migrate; the methods used to mobilize resources for the journey, as well as the role of human smuggling in the process of asylum migration. In this respect, the project will provide a critical appraisal of the widespread assumption that human smuggling involves the deception and exploitation of migrants by organized criminal syndicates.

The authors were similarly encouraged to analyse the impact of asylum immigration for *both* receiving and sending states. The authors examined whether asylum migration, from the receiving countries' perspective, can be usefully analysed in terms of the 'costs' and benefits' which it brings to receiving states. The authors also looked more generally at the consequences of asylum migration for those countries, focusing on issues such as economic activity, social structure, popular culture, ethnic relations and foreign relations. Similarly, the project examined an issue that has received relatively little attention in the existing literature: the impact of asylum migration on countries of origin. Among the questions asked are:

- To what extent does asylum migration involve the departure of skilled and educated people, and what impact does this have on a country's labour market and potential for economic development?
- How and with what consequences does asylum migration affect household and community structures in countries of origin?
- How is asylum migration associated with the development of transnational social networks, and what functions do these networks perform?
- What remittances do asylum migrants send back to their own country, and how are such remittances used?

Finally, no discussion of asylum migration is complete without an analysis of the *public policy response*. How do states and other actors (regional bodies, international and non-governmental organizations, for example) respond to the phenomenon of asylum migration? What considerations have determined the response of such actors? How effective have these responses been (and in this context, what does 'effectiveness' mean anyway?) To what extent is there a consensus among these actors with regard to policy responses? And, looking to the future, can alternative responses to the asylum migration be anticipated?

We now turn to a more detailed discussion of the individual projects. The book begins with Part I, containing four chapters that analyse, from a global perspective, various issues in asylum and immigration policy. Timothy J. Hatton and Jeffrey G. Williamson (Chapter 2) offer a quantitative assessment of the economic and demographic fundamentals that have driven and are driving world migration, across different historical epochs and around the world. The chapter is organized around three questions:

1. How do the standard theories of migration perform when confronted with evidence drawn from more than a century of world migration experience?
2. How do inequality and poverty influence world migration?

3. Is it useful to distinguish between migration pressure and migration *ex post*, or between the potential demand for visas and the actual use of them?

Hatton and Williamson usefully consider the implications of their discussion for the future of world migration. They conclude that even if migration pressures increase but policy regimes harden then *ex post* world migration could be lower despite greater migration pressure. Under such conditions, we would see a further increase in illegal migration and an escalation of policies aimed at combating it. By identifying future migration pressures, we can inform those policies. Hatton and Williamson specifically examine the demographic trends on migration pressure in Africa's future and conclude that the demographic forces that drive African migration will serve as a powerful force raising emigration pressure over the next twenty years.

Stephen Castles and Sean Loughna (Chapter 3) provide a detailed examination in the trends of asylum migration over the entire twentieth century. Castles and Loughna outline trends and patterns in movements of asylum seekers to Western so-called industrialized countries from 1990 to 2001. They identify three distinct phases of asylum migration since the end of the Second World War:

- Treating refugees as migrant workers;
- Migrants with mixed motivations claiming asylum; and
- Asylum seekers moving as undocumented migrants.

They note that there is now an increasing perception that asylum seekers are really economic migrants who are abusing the asylum process. This has led to increasingly restrictive entry rules. The feedback effect of such policies is that many genuine refugees are unable to make claims, because they cannot enter a potential country of asylum. This in turn has caused some asylum seekers to enter illegally, often using the services of people smugglers. The result is that the distinction between asylum seekers and undocumented migrants has become blurred, leading to the notion of the 'asylum–migration nexus'.

Matthew J. Gibney and Randall Hansen (Chapter 4) continue the global study of asylum policy by noting that for much of the post-war period, asylum and immigration were distinct concepts and processes. Throughout the west, asylum was bound up with the Cold War, with refugees mainly originating in Communist countries. As for immigration, it meant different things in different countries: in the settler societies of Canada, Australia and New Zealand, it was a permanent movement of people who sought to try their luck in the new world. In the traditional emigration countries of Europe, it referred to the putatively temporary movement of guest workers who were expected to feed the European economic machine for a few years before returning home. The important point is that, in both cases, the two movements were everywhere separate. Gibney and Hansen note that these two processes have merged in recent decades, particularly in Europe, where 'immigration' and 'asylum seeking' are now referred to interchangeably. They note that the result is that in most Western countries asylum applications are at levels where they generate deep political controversy and are likely to remain there; that public policy reform has not enabled states to reduce these numbers and is not likely to in the future; and that the costs associated with asylum rise with non-return and non-labour market incorporation.

Part II of the book contains six chapters that address various aspects of the consequences of immigration and asylum policy. Susan Martin, Andrew Schoenholtz and David Fisher (Chapter 5) provide a detailed examination of the impact of asylum policies on receiving countries. They stress the important point that government policies for handling asylum affect the impact of asylum seekers. For example, complex application systems will inevitably increase the fiscal cost of implementing asylum policy. Impacts will also vary by post-adjudication treatment of asylum applicants. In some countries, a high proportion of asylum seekers are granted asylum, as is the case in the United States and Canada, whereas in other countries the vast majority of asylum applicants are rejected. Some of those rejected for asylum are nevertheless eligible for complementary forms of protection, particularly if they cannot be returned to a country undergoing conflict. Policies on return of rejected asylum seekers, as well as individuals granted temporary protection who are no longer in need of such protection, also profoundly influence the ways in which asylum affects receiving countries. If governments find themselves unable or unwilling to repatriate rejected asylum seekers, their domestic impact will be more long-reaching than if the asylum seekers return home. Finally, the socioeconomic and demographic characteristics, including the skill composition, age distribution and family structure of asylum seekers, will further influence the impact of asylum on receiving countries. Martin, Schoenholtz and Fisher conclude that the number of asylum seekers, government policies and socioeconomic characteristics all determine the impacts of asylum. The impacts of asylum can thus differ significantly from country to country.

The analysis of Khalid Koser and Nicholas Van Hear in Chapter 6 provides a mirror-image analysis to the Martin–Schoenholtz–Fisher study by examining the impact of asylum migration on the countries of origin. Their study not only provides a review of the literature, but also reports many new empirical findings. They specifically consider three distinct questions: the impact of refugees on the countries of origin, with a specific emphasis on such variables as the scale of the movement and the characteristics of the refugees; they review the evidence about the continuing influence of asylum seekers and refugees once they reach their country of destination; and, finally, they examine the implications for countries of origin of the return of asylum seekers and refugees. An important conclusion of their study is the emphasis that exiled communities are not necessarily isolated communities. Many asylum seekers and refugees maintain links with their countries of origin and try to engender change there, and at least some have considerable potential to effect change. They also stress that physical return is not the only way to integrate refugees in post-conflict reconstruction. In particular, refugees can contribute to democratization, reconciliation and reconstruction from a distance. It is a truism of the modern world that money, goods, ideas and votes can cross international borders more easily than people.

Raimo Väyrynen in Chapter 7 examines a crucial question in the immigration debate: human trafficking and illegal immigration. He stresses the important point that the illegal and clandestine movement of people across national borders cannot be separated from issues of governmental control and enforcement. Although states have the authority to criminalize specific transnational activities, they are typically not willing fully to fund capabilities that might realistically enforce such restrictions. This creates particular problems in those countries where the market demand for illicit entry is high. The Väyrynen study also provides an important perspective to human smuggling: this activity exists because people benefit from moving to higher-income countries and the smuggler benefits because start-up costs in the business are small and profit margins are high.

Riccardo Faini in Chapter 8 examines the theoretical underpinnings and empirical evidence about the link between skilled migration, education and remittances. He argues that, even after accounting for substantial remittances, the concerns in sending countries about the economic impact of skilled migration are warranted. First, a higher skilled content of migration is found to be associated with a lower flow of remittances. He interprets this surprising result as indicating that skilled migrants tend to loosen their links with their home country, are more likely to bring their family to the host country and, therefore, have a lower propensity to remit. Second, he finds little evidence suggesting that raising the skill composition of migration has a positive effect on the educational achievements in the home country. In short, the outmigration of skilled workers is unlikely to provide many benefits to the remaining population in the source countries.

Chapters 9 and 10 examine the economic consequences of more freedom of movement by persons across countries. According to recent estimates, up to 25 per cent of the world's population lives on less than US$1 a day. It is a well-known theorem in economic theory that greater freedom of movement (whether in goods or people) increases economic efficiency and world income. In particular, the unhampered movement of persons from low-income to high-income countries could significantly improve the well-being of many persons in the world. Jonathon Moses and Bjørn Letnes examine two specific questions: First, what sort of economic gains might the world expect to reap by liberalizing world labour markets? And, second, how realistic is the underlying framework used for estimating these gains? The simplest model examined by Moses and Letnes yields the remarkable results that the removal of restrictions on international migration would yield both large-scale migration flows and large-scale economic gains.

Ana María Iregui in Chapter 10 continues the analysis of these important questions by examining a more general economic framework that permits various feedbacks among the economic actors. Chapter 10 computes the worldwide efficiency gains from the elimination of restrictions on labour mobility. A distinctive feature of Iregui's analysis is the introduction of a segmented labour market (i.e. skilled and unskilled labour), which allows for the introduction of non-homogeneous labour. According to Iregui's calculations, the elimination of global restrictions on labour migration generates worldwide efficiency gains ranging from 15 per cent to 67 per cent of world gross domestic product (GDP). Iregui also considers various restrictions on the type of migration that the receiving countries would allow, such as an immigration policy that allows only the migration of skilled workers. Even in this very restrictive case, worldwide efficiency gains would range from 3 per cent to 11 per cent of world GDP.

Part III of the book contains eight case studies that examine immigration and asylum in particular geographic settings. George J. Borjas in Chapter 11 examines the factors that determine economic integration of immigrants in the United States. He stresses that there is an important link between the notion of economic assimilation stressed in studies of the economic consequences of immigration and the cultural issues that are traditionally emphasized in the debate over assimilation in many host countries. In particular, to experience economic assimilation, an immigrant will often have to acquire skills that are valued by employers in the host country, such as learning the language and adopting the norms of the new workplace. Each of these decisions helps weaken the link between the immigrant's foreign past and his or her future in the new country. Borjas also points out that the economic integration experienced by a particular immigrant wave is strongly dependent on historical circumstances. As a result, the historical experience of past waves of immigrants provides little guidance for predicting the future integration prospects of current waves.

Andrés Solimano in Chapter 12 examines the case of international migration in Argentina, a country that during the twentieth century changed from being a net importer to a net exporter of labour. At the beginning of the twentieth century, a large number of Europeans, mostly from Italy and Spain, left their homelands and headed to the shores of Argentina in response to the good economic opportunities, fertile land and hopes for a better future that were to be found there. At the time, Argentina was one of the most vibrant world economies. European migration to Argentina virtually stopped in the 1950s and in the next thirty years or so the country became a net exporter of professionals who were fleeing economic decline, poor opportunities and authoritarian regimes. Argentinians are still leaving in large numbers, to Spain, Italy and other destinations. This outmigration is associated with the collapse of the country's currency experiment of the 1990s which left a legacy of massive output decline, high unemployment, financial crisis and lost hopes. Solimano investigates the impact of lagging economic growth and modest development performance on the direction of migration flows to and from Argentina. The empirical evidence summarized in his chapter shows that two key factors help explain the pattern of labour flows to and from Argentina: the *per capita* income differential between Argentina and the potential source and destination countries, and the presence of authoritarian regimes.

Philip Martin in Chapter 13 examines the case of Mexico, the country that is now responsible for the largest-volume migration relationship in the world. About 9 million of the 109 million persons born in Mexico have migrated to the United States. Martin examines the expected impact of the North American Free Trade Agreement (NAFTA) on Mexico–United States migration flows. NAFTA lowered barriers to trade and investment in Canada, Mexico and the United States, and was expected to spur job and wage growth in the three member countries. Most of the benefits of this freer trade were expected to accrue to Mexico, and most of the adjustments to freer trade were also expected there. Virtually all of the available evidence concludes that most of the additional jobs due to NAFTA would be in Mexico. Martin's examination of NAFTA's likely impacts on Mexican migration implies that the flow of Mexicans to the United States, running at about 200,000 settlers and 1–2 million sojourners a year in the early 1990s, would likely increase by 10–30 per cent for five–fifteen years, producing a 'migration hump'. However, Mexico–United States migration should then decline for demographic and economic reasons. Martin's chapter provides a valuable description of the evolution and effects of Mexico–United States migration, and highlights the NAFTA approach to economic integration – namely, free up trade and investment while stepping up efforts to prevent unauthorized migration.

Elizabeth Thomas-Hope in Chapter 14 focuses on migration in the Caribbean region. She stresses that present-day Caribbean societies were largely formed through immigration, both forced migration and free migration. In more recent decades, outmigration from Caribbean countries has played an increasingly important role, with continuing and overlapping episodes of emigration within the wider Caribbean, and also to other regions, notably Europe and North America. The policy concerning most Caribbean irregular migrants is typically based on the needs of the potential destination countries, and typically stresses the perspective that the migrants are economic immigrants. Irregular migration and the issue of asylum from Caribbean countries typically reflect various aspects of poverty and the vast economic disparities that exist within the region. Thomas-Hope stresses that irregular migration and the question of asylum greatly affect diplomatic relations between Caribbean countries of migration source and destination.

Krœn Blume, Björn Gustafsson, Peder J. Pedersen and Mette Verner in Chapter 15 examine the well-being of immigrants in Denmark and Sweden. They begin by noting that low-skill immigration to the rich Organization for Economic Co-operation and Development (OECD) countries has been of increasing importance in recent years. Many of the European OECD countries were open to immigration of people from outside the rich OECD area until the first oil price shock in the mid-1970s. At that time, many countries, including Denmark and Sweden, enacted legislation to stop the flow of guest workers, and these have been in effect since then. Immigrants in these countries have had a difficult time in integrating into the labour market. The chapter uses a comparable panel data set of immigrants in Denmark and Sweden to examine the problem of low income and poverty in the immigrant population. For example, the ratio of the unemployment rates for immigrants and natives hovers around 2–3 in a number of European countries, including Denmark and Sweden, as compared to a ratio of roughly 1.0 for the United States and Canada. Blume *et al.* argue that these differences are the net outcome of differences not only of labour market institutions, but also of immigration policies.

Géraldine Chatelard in Chapter 16 examines the process of migration for Iraqis into Jordan. In 1996, 4 million Iraqis were reported to live abroad, of whom over 600,000 were recognized as refugees. Following a first wave of forced migration during the Iran–Iraq war (1980–88), the majority of Iraqis currently living abroad as refugees or asylum seekers fled their country during the 1991 Gulf War or in the following decade. Most left Iraq in 1991–92, mainly because of two episodes of failed uprising against the regime of Saddam Hussein. In 1991, the Kurds in the Northern provinces and the Shiites in the central area revolted and both uprisings where crushed. Chatelard describes the case of Iraqis who arrived in Jordan in the 1990s as forced migrants, and continued to Western Europe or Australia as asylum migrants. She argues that this pattern in asylum migration cannot be understood without looking at a set of interrelated issues in the countries of *first* reception of the forced migrants: reception standards, the migrants' poor socioeconomic conditions, further violations of their human rights and the functioning of the migrants' social networks and of human smuggling rings.

Claudia Tazreiter in Chapter 17 examines asylum policy in Australia, a country that because of its relative geographic isolation has not experienced the large-scale influxes of asylum seekers seen in many parts of the world. Nevertheless, the Australian government has implemented harsh policy and administrative measures directed at asylum seekers with a substantial measure of public support. In August 2001, for example, an incident involving

433 asylum seekers was branded in popular discourse an 'asylum crisis'. Tazreiter argues that the implications of the Australian response to asylum seekers are significant not only in the Asia/Pacific region, but further afield, as policy responses toward asylum seekers by receiving states have converged in the recent past. The 'security state' remains central in driving the political and social construction of refugees and in particular of asylum seekers as 'irregular' arrivals. In particular, irregular (illegal) arrivals are perceived as a threat to the cohesion of the nation, while also providing a focus for resentment, readily exploited by politicians searching for simplistic ways of communicating about complex social and political problems to their constituents. The issue of people smuggling and the illegal status of arrivals, has caused enormous tension, particularly as this form of entry is perceived as a security threat. In addition, refugee entry causes local anxiety due to the perceived change it causes in the receiver society culturally, and in terms of the resources needed to administer the claims of such entrants.

Catherine Phuong in Chapter 18 examines the impact of accession on the candidate countries' asylum and immigration laws and policies. Phuong examines the ways in which candidate countries are responding to increasing asylum migration from the east and argues that recent changes in asylum and immigration laws in candidate countries have been largely affected by current EU efforts to devise a common immigration policy and a possible common asylum system. Instead of devising their own response to asylum migration, candidate countries are merely aligning their asylum policies with EU practice and expectations. Because of their geographical location, the new member states will be responsible for policing the new eastern border of the EU and receiving asylum seekers travelling from further east.

As this diverse set of chapters illustrates, the debate over poverty, international migration and asylum raises issues of fundamental policy importance, not only for the sending and receiving countries but also for the larger global community. The chapters collected in this book illustrate that a greater understanding of the underlying issues can be attained by systematically applying the thought processes of various disciplines to a common set of questions.

Part I

Global Aspects of Immigration and Asylum

2
What Fundamentals Drive World Migration?*

Timothy J. Hatton and Jeffrey G. Williamson

Introduction

Stories about foreign migrants – legal, illegal and asylum seekers – appear almost daily in the news. Governments in Europe, North America and Australia note these events with alarm and grapple with policy reforms aimed at selecting certain migrants and keeping out others. Economists appear to be well armed to advise the debate since they are responsible for an impressive literature that examines the characteristics of individual immigrants, their absorption and the consequences of their migration on the sending and receiving regions involved. Economists are, however, much less well armed to speak to the determinants of the migration flows that give rise to public alarm.

This chapter offers a quantitative assessment of the economic and demographic fundamentals that drive world migration, not just in one country or at one point in time but across different historical epochs and around the world. The chapter is organized around three questions:

- How do the standard theories of migration perform when confronted with evidence drawn from more than a century of world migration experience?
- In an effort to reverse the causal direction that has become so common in modern debate about the impact of trade and immigration on unskilled workers in rich countries, how do inequality and poverty influence emigration from poor countries?
- Is it useful to distinguish between migration *pressure* and migration *ex post*, or between the potential demand for visas and the actual use of them?

The next section provides some background motivation. We then outline a basic theoretical framework to guide us through the specification and interpretation of models that explain rates of international migration. Drawing on our previous research, we examine the key economic and demographic fundamentals that drove the European mass emigration in the half-century before 1914. Having identified the fundamentals that drove world migration in an era when potential migrants were relatively unconstrained by policy intervention, we turn to US immigration since the 1970s, when policy intervention has been a fact of life. These two examples raise issues about emigration from very poor countries, and so we next turn to migration from and within Africa. Finally, we explore the determinants of migration on a global database and conclude with speculations about the future trends in world migration.

Themes surrounding world migration

There is widespread agreement that globalization has been on the rise in the half-century since the Second World War. 'Rising globalization' is interpreted to mean that the mobility of goods and factors across international borders has reached new and unprecedented heights. However, the international mobility of goods and capital is probably no greater than it was a century ago (O'Rourke and Williamson, 1999; Findlay and O'Rourke, 2003; Lindert and Williamson, 2003; Obstfeld and Taylor, 2003; Hatton and Williamson, 2004). In contrast, what used to be 'free' world migration has become tightly constrained by tough immigration policies that undoubtedly suppress a vast amount of potential migration that might otherwise have taken place (Chiswick and Hatton, 2003).

Evidence compiled by the United Nations suggests that the number of people around the world who were living in a country other than the one in which they were born rose from 75 million in 1965 to 120 million in 1990. Although these absolute numbers have certainly increased, world migrants represented just 2.3 per cent of world population at both dates (Zlotnick, 1998: 431). Even if the share increased a bit during the 1990s, these statistics hardly speak of a dramatic increase in globalization as it applies to world migration. Part of the reason that these figures seem inconsistent with common perception is that migrant (foreign-born) stocks in less developed countries have fallen. In any case, the more relevant point is that migrant stocks in the developed world increased from 3.1 to 4.5 per cent between 1965 and 1990. In North America, western Europe and Australasia combined, the increase has been even more pronounced, rising from 4.9 to 7.6 per cent over the same twenty-five years, an increase of 2.7 percentage points. This measure of the rising globalization of world labour markets is certainly impressive, but the rise in these migrant stock shares is still smaller than the rise in the trade/GDP ratio (Findlay and O'Rourke, 2003) or the foreign capital/world capital stock ratio (Obstfeld and Taylor, 2003). Another reason why the rise in migrant stock shares has been smaller is that temporary and return migration has become much more common: thus, gross flows have increased faster than net flows.

No matter how the *ex post* world migration figures are interpreted, migration *pressure* seems to have been on the increase. One indicator is the long queues of applicants for immigration to developed countries. In 1994 the waiting list for admission to the United States totalled 3.6 million (Smith and Edmonston, 1997: 45). Another obvious symptom of this pressure is the surge in illegal immigration, most prominently across the southern border of the United States and into Western Europe from the east and the south. About 300,000 illegal immigrants enter the United States every year while 400,000–500,000 enter the countries of Western Europe. It is estimated that illegals add 10 or 15 per cent to the stock of foreign-born in OECD countries. Another symptom is the rise in those seeking asylum in developed countries. According to UNHCR statistics there were 560,000 asylum applications to twenty-eight industrialized countries in 2000, with about a million awaiting decision. These figures have soared since the 1980s and it seems clear that the demand for asylum has increased far faster than the supply of visas offered to these refugees.[1]

So why has the pressure on world migration been on the rise? What economic and demographic fundamentals have been at work? Do we expect those fundamentals to rise even more in the future, or to abate?

There exists a wide variety of approaches to these questions (Massey *et al.*, 1993), but the underlying theory used in seeking answers often has its shortcomings. We have tried to improve the quality of the answers in three ways. First, most of the theories of migration which all of us find useful deal with a world *without immigration controls*. This serious shortcoming can be repaired only if we can figure out how to integrate policy into migration models, and then to estimate what difference it would make to our predictions. What makes this agenda so difficult is that immigration policy is itself endogenous, probably influenced by the same forces that drive world migration pressure. One way to get useful answers to this question about fundamentals is to compare the experience in the age of 'free' migration before 1914 with 'constrained' migration of more recent times.

Second, the recent empirical literature has focused extensively on the effects of migration selectivity on immigrant outcomes. This literature examines the qualifications and labour market quality of immigrants upon arrival, and their subsequent economic assimilation relative to the native-born. Assimilation experience is seen as reflecting the effects of economic incentives and immigration policy on the selectivity of immigrants by individual attributes and country of origin. This literature has been long on examining immigrant labour market performance but short on verifying the underlying model of migration by which this performance is interpreted.

Third, it is often observed that emigration from poor countries *increases* as economic development takes place in the source country. This was certainly true of the nineteenth century (Hatton and Williamson, 1998: ch. 3), and a glance at the immigration statistics of OECD countries today confirms that the poorest countries typically generate fewer emigrants than those that are further up the *per capita* income ladder. This common observation does not seem to be consistent with the notion that migration is driven by the gap between income at home and abroad. Instead, observers have detected a 'hump-shaped' relationship between economic development at home and emigration (Massey, 1988; Hatton and Williamson, 1998: ch. 3; Stalker 2000: ch. 7): emigration rates out of really poor countries are thus very low, while they are much higher out of moderately poor countries. One possible explanation for the paradox is that the structural and demographic changes coincident with industrialization generate more migration in its early stages than later on. Another, not necessarily competing, explanation is that poverty constrains migration since financing investment in a long-distance move is difficult for the very poor. Thus, any 'catching up' increase in incomes at home serves to relax the poverty constraint on emigration, and this positive effect may dominate the negative effect associated with any narrowing of the income gap between home and abroad.

Migration theory

The application of theory to world migration provides a useful guide to the variables that might be expected to influence migration pressure and *ex post* migration quantities. Important contributions have been made by Sjaastad (1962), Borjas (1987, 1989), and others.[2] In the simplest framework, the decision of individual i ($i=1\ldots n$) in source country h to migrate to destination country f can be expressed as:

$$d_i = w_{f,i} - w_{h,i} - z_i - c > 0 \tag{2.1}$$

where $w_{f,i}$, $w_{h,i}$ are the earnings of that individual in destination (f for foreign) and source (h for home) countries, respectively, z_i is the individual's compensating differential in favour of h and c is the direct cost of migration. This comparison can be viewed in terms of utility if, for example, utility is logarithmic and the variables are expressed as natural logs. Clearly, individual i is more likely to migrate the higher is the destination wage and the lower are the home wage, the compensating differential and the fixed migration cost. If the first three terms are interpreted as present values then the likelihood of migration will decline with the age of individual i as the remaining working life becomes shorter. Thus, for a given incentive, migration will be higher the more the source population is skewed towards the younger working ages.

The recent literature has focused on other elements of selectivity in migration. Let individuals in the source country have skill levels indexed by $s_{h,i}$, with mean μ_{sh} and variance σ_{sh}^2. Incomes at the destination and the source are represented, respectively, as:

$$w_{f,i} = \alpha_f + \beta_f s_i; \qquad w_{h,i} = \alpha_h + \beta_h s_i; \tag{2.2}$$

with means and variances, respectively, μ_{wf}, μ_{wh}, σ_{wf}, σ_{wh}. Substituting into (2.1):

$$d_i = \alpha_f - \alpha_h + (\beta_f - \beta_h)\, s_i - z_i - c \qquad (2.3)$$

Migration will thus increase with skill level (migrants will be positively selected) if the return to skills is greater in the destination than the source ($\beta_f > \beta_h$), and migration will decrease with skill level (migrants will be negatively selected) if the return to skills is greater in the source.

Following Borjas (1989), if s_i and z_i are normally distributed the migration rate from the source country to the destination can be expressed as:

$$D = 1 - \Phi \frac{(-\mu_{wf} + \mu_{wh} + \mu_z + c)}{\sigma_d} \qquad (2.4)$$

where μ_z is the mean of z_i, σ_d is the standard deviation of d_i and Φ is the cumulative distribution function of the standard normal. Because σ_d is a function of the variances of the source and destination wage distributions, σ_{wf} and σ_{wh} (and therefore of the underlying parameters β_f and β_h), the migration rate depends on the wage distributions as well as on their means, with an effect that will be non-monotonic. If the destination is 'richer' than the source (in the sense that $\mu_{wf} > \mu_{wh} + \mu_z + c$), it can be shown that the migration will be an inverse 'u' shaped function of σ_h / σ_f^3.

Note that there is no separate effect for the average skill level (μ_{sh}) in this model, unless it appears for reasons not considered so far. However, the destination wage or income variable often used in empirical studies is typically the average for all workers at the destination; not the average wage that would be received by the source country workforce, if employed in the destination. The former can be written as:

$$\mu_{wf} = \mu^*_{wf} - \beta_f (\mu_{sf} - \mu_{sh}) \qquad (2.5)$$

where μ^*_{wf} is the mean wage of the destination workforce and μ_{sf} is their mean skill level. If (2.5) is substituted into the migration equation (2.4) then relative skill levels will matter with an effect that reflects the return to skills at the destination.

Much of the literature suggests that non-economic factors are important in migration decisions. Such effects are represented here in the individual-specific compensating differential z_i. One important influence on z_i is the stock of previous migrants from the source country living in the destination – the so-called 'friends and relatives' effect. Consider two economic interpretations of this effect. One is that it increases destination-specific utility, perhaps also reducing the loss of ethnic capital that might otherwise be incurred in migration. The second interpretation is that immigrant networks reduce migration costs directly, implying an individual-level reduction in c. The immigrant network can relax the poverty constraint on potential migrants by providing access to loans or outright gifts.

A key feature of migration decisions is the presence of policies that restrict immigration to destination countries. They can be thought of as two types: quotas that restrict *numbers* (by source country or in total) or policies that select immigrants according to certain *characteristics* (with or without a cap on numbers). Both can be seen as raising the costs of immigration. In the former, competition for visas raises costs both directly and through queuing. In the latter, the costs are those associated with the acquisition of the relevant characteristics. Two key elements of immigration policy are family reunification and selection by skill. Adding these policy-related components of costs, the individual's decision can be represented as:

$$d_i = w_{f,i} - w_{h,i} - z_i - c^* + v_i \qquad (2.6)$$

Here the fixed cost of migration c has been modified (now denoted c^*) to include the costs imposed by immigration policy and the additional term v_i reflects the lowering of immigration costs associated with individual characteristics. If the individual has close relatives at the destination then this will raise the value of v_i. If immigration policy is skill-selective then v_i will be a function of the individual's skill level. Thus the aggregate migration rate will depend on average skill-level independently of the effects operating through source and destination earnings.[4]

In the presence of high migration costs – imposed by policy or otherwise – potential migrants in poor countries may be constrained by their poverty. For a given (fixed and appropriately normalized) cost threshold $\hat{c}$, the proportion of the population who are constrained would be:

$$P = \Phi\left(\frac{-\mu_s + \hat{c}}{\sigma_s}\right) \qquad (2.7)$$

Thus the higher is mean income and the lower is the standard deviation of income, the smaller the proportion of potential migrants that will be poverty-constrained. Clearly the poverty constraint is not independent of the migration decision and it would be mitigated by the relaxation of credit constraints, but the most important channel for relaxing the credit constraint it likely to be through *remittances from previous migrants*.

The age of European mass emigration

The age of mass migration before the First World War gives us an opportunity to look at the economic and demographic fundamentals that drove international migration in a period of relatively free and unrestricted immigration.

More than 50 million migrants departed from Europe for the New World between 1820 and 1913. About three-fifths went to the United States and the remainder to Canada and to South America, Australasia, and southern Africa. In the first half of the century, Britain was the dominant source of the migrants. These were joined in mid-century by a stream of emigrants from Germany followed by a rising tide from Scandinavia and elsewhere in northwestern Europe. Emigration surged from southern and eastern Europe from the 1880s – accounting for most of the increase in total European emigration. It came first from Italy and parts of the Austro-Hungarian Empire and then from the 1890s it included Poland, Russia, Spain and Portugal.

After mid-century the migrants were typically young and single and about two-thirds of them were male. More than three-quarters of the immigrants entering the United States were aged 16–40, at a time when 42 per cent of the United States population was in this age group. They were also relatively (and increasingly) unskilled, a fact that largely reflects shifts in the origin-country composition of the flow. And, once the mass migration took hold, a large proportion moved through migrant networks to join friends and relatives who had previously migrated to the same destination. Although some moved in response to famines, persecution and political upheaval, the characteristics of the migrants reinforce the premise that the vast majority moved in response to *economic incentives* – maximizing the gains and minimizing the costs.

Emigration rates varied widely across Europe in the late nineteenth century. The highest rates were from Ireland, averaging 13 per 1,000 per annum between 1850 and 1913. Norway and Sweden had emigration rates approaching 5 per 1,000 from 1870 to 1913, while those from Germany were under 2 per 1,000 and France was close to zero. These emigration rates also display different trends. Emigration from Ireland declined from the 1860s, and from Germany and Norway it declined from the 1880s. Almost at the same time emigration from Italy and Spain began a steep ascent, a trend that was halted only by the outbreak of war. A challenge to any theory of migration is to explain not only the differences in average rates of emigration across countries, but also the different trends in these rates.

In Hatton and Williamson (1998: ch. 3), we explained decade-average emigration rates pooled across twelve European countries between 1860 and 1913 as a function of four key fundamentals (Table 2.1). The share of the labour force in agriculture is interpreted as a measure of differential mobility between urban and rural populations. The effect is weakly negative providing a little support for the view that rural populations were less internationally mobile. More important is the wage gap as represented by the purchasing power parity (PPP) adjusted real wage in the source country relative to that for a weighted average of destinations. Note that these wage data are for homogeneous occupations across countries, so there is less need to add a measure of average education or skills. The effect of the wage ratio is

Table 2.1   Regression estimate for emigration from Europe, 1860–1913

MigRate = − 6.08 − 4.57 AgShare − 6.86 LnWRatio + 0.37 LagBirth
            (3.3)   (1.3)   (4.4)   (3.5)
         + 0.22 MigStock + 5.64 Dum;   Adj. R^2 = 0.69
            (8.4)   (4.7)

Note: *t*-statistics in parentheses.
Sample: Decade-average observations for an unbalanced panel comprising: Belgium 1860–1913; Denmark 1880–1913; France 1870–1913; Germany 1870–1913; Great Britain 1860–1913; Ireland 1860–1913; Italy 1880–1913; Netherlands 1860–1913; Norway 1880–1913; Portugal 1870–1913; Spain 1890–1913; Sweden 1860–1913.
Variable definitions: MigRate = gross emigration rate per 1,000 population per decade to all foreign destinations; AgShare = share of labour force in agriculture; LnWRatio = log of the ratio of PPP adjusted wage rates, source country to a weighted average of destination countries; LagBirth = source country birthrate lagged twenty years; MigStock = stock of previous immigrants in destination countries at beginning of decade per 1,000 of source country population; Dum = dummy for Belgium, Italy, Portugal and Spain.
Method: Pooled OLS regression on forty-eight country/period observations.
Source: Hatton and Williamson (1998), table 3.3, col. 4, p. 39.

strongly negative and the coefficient implies that, in the long run, a 10 per cent increase in the wage ratio raised the annual emigration rate by 0.7 per 1,000. The birthrate lagged twenty years stands as a proxy for the young adult cohort size. Its effect is positive, and it is large – suggesting that up to half of additional births ultimately spilled over into emigration. Of course, demographic forces can have two effects on emigration: *directly*, by raising the young adult share; and *indirectly*, by glutting the home labour market and thus worsening employment conditions there. Finally, a bigger stock of previous emigrants raised current emigration as the friends and relatives effect would predict: for every 1,000 previous emigrants, 20 more were 'pulled' abroad every year.

Some observers have suggested that the typical European country went through an emigration cycle that followed an inverted 'U'-shape (Massey, 1988; Hatton and Williamson, 1998). As industrial and demographic revolutions unfolded, emigration rates first rose and then fell. Such a pattern can be detected in our data, although for a number of countries it was abruptly ended by the First World War and the immigration restrictions that followed. This stylized pattern can be explained as follows. Demographic effects, aided by urbanization and the growing migrant stock, were important forces in the upswing of the cycle. Later on, these forces weakened and were more than offset by strong convergence of European real wages on those in the New World.

It has been argued that instead of, or in addition to, the forces just mentioned, European emigration patterns were driven by the progressive relaxation of the poverty constraint as economic development raised living standards. Industrialization spread from west to east, as did emigration. Faini and Venturini (1994) found that the sharp rise in Italian emigration from the 1880s could be explained by rising real wages at home – an effect which dominated the negative influence of the rising home to foreign wage ratio. In contrast, we could find only very weakly positive home wage effects in our cross-country panel, probably because it was dominated by observations from the relatively prosperous European northwest where the poverty constraint was less binding than in Italy and where it was also mitigated by loans from friends and relatives who had previously emigrated.

What drives immigrants to the United States?

In the age when world migration has become severely constrained by policy, the United States has remained the leading destination country. After falling to a low in the 1930s, immigration grew from an annual average of 252,000 in the 1950s to 916,000 in the 1990s. This growth was accompanied by a radical shift in the source-country composition. In the 1950s, Europeans accounted for more than half of all immigrants and these were overwhelmingly from Western Europe (Table 2.2). The proportion from relatively rich Western Europe declined sharply to a mere 5.7 per cent in the

Table 2.2 Source area composition of US immigration, 1951–99 (per cent of total)

Region of origin	1951–60	1961–70	1971–80	1981–90	1991–9
Europe	52.7	33.8	17.8	10.3	14.9
Western	47.1	30.2	14.5	7.2	5.7
Eastern	5.6	3.6	3.3	3.1	9.2
Asia	6.1	12.9	35.3	37.3	30.8
Americas	39.6	51.7	44.1	49.3	49.7
Canada	15.0	12.4	3.8	2.1	2.1
Mexico	11.9	13.7	14.2	22.6	25.3
Caribbean	4.9	14.2	16.5	11.9	10.8
Central America	1.8	3.1	3.0	6.4	5.6
South America	3.6	7.8	6.6	6.3	5.9
Africa	0.6	0.9	1.8	2.4	3.8
Oceania	0.5	0.8	0.9	0.6	0.6
Total (000s)	2,515	3,322	4,493	7,338	7,605

Notes: Immigrants classified by country of last residence. Percentages exclude the category 'origin not specified'. Western Europe is defined as the countries of the EU, excluding Finland but including Norway and Switzerland. Eastern Europe includes the category 'Other Europe'.
Source: United States Department of Justice (2002), table 2.

1990s while that from relatively poor Eastern Europe nearly doubled. The counterpart to the decline in the European share was the rise in the Asian share which exceeded a third in the 1970s and 1980s – another shift from rich to poor immigrant source – and a rise in the share from the American continent which increased from 40 per cent in the 1950s to 50 per cent in the 1990s. Within the Americas the decline in the proportion from rich Canada was more than compensated by increases from poor Central America, the Caribbean and especially Mexico. The poorest continent, Africa, accounts for only a small share of United States immigrants although that share has grown rapidly.

Policy has been important. The dominance of Europe was reinforced by national origins quotas until the 1960s. They were originally introduced in 1921 and 1924, and they strongly favoured the countries that dominated the inflow during the nineteenth century, particularly Britain, Ireland and Germany. The 1965 amendments to the Immigration Act abolished the national origins criteria, replacing it with separate quotas for the western and eastern hemispheres, and with a system of preferences that emphasized family reunification. The hemispheric ceilings were combined into a world-wide quota in 1979. The Immigration Reform and Control Act of 1986 introduced mass legalization of immigrants who had resided in the United States since 1982. Finally, the 1990 Immigration Act (effective 1992) raised the overall immigration quota and introduced a new system of preferences that allocated a larger share of available visas by occupational attributes rather than by family reunification.

There has been considerable debate about the changing composition of US immigrants and its impact. It has been forcefully argued that the labour market quality of successive cohorts of immigrants, as reflected in education levels, entry wages and rates of assimilation, declined between the 1950s and the 1980s (Borjas, 1987, 1994, 1999). That trend is seen largely as the result of the 1965 Amendments that abolished the quotas. Opening the door to poorer parts of the world produced a much larger pool of potential immigrants for whom the income gains far outweighed compensating differentials favouring the home country. As a result of their lower skill levels, the new immigrants were located further down the US income distribution than were previous immigrants. More speculatively, to the extent that the return to skills (as reflected in income inequality) was greater in source countries than in the United States, there would be negative selection from within each source country,[5] reinforcing the downward trend in the skills of the average US immigrant. Earlier post-war waves of European immigrants, coming from countries with income distributions more equal than the United States, should have been positively selected. Finally, an immigration policy which favoured family reunification, gradually lowered the costs of immigration for successive cohorts of migrants from these 'new' source countries. Thus, US immigration policy had exactly the opposite impact intended: it served to hasten the switch in immigrant source towards poorer countries.

The most lively debate on US immigration has been about *assimilation outcomes*. Although the framework used in these studies is underpinned by the migrant selection model, the determinants of the immigration flow itself have been comparatively neglected. Thus, it is unclear to what degree the forces that drive US immigration are consistent with the interpretations placed on assimilation outcomes. Existing studies of the determinants of immigration by source country have failed to test properly the specification implied by the theoretical discussion above. Nevertheless, these studies have provided some useful insights. For a cross-section of source-country average emigration rates to the United States for 1951–80, Borjas (1987) found that migration was negatively related to source-country income *per capita* and to source-country inequality. Yang (1995) confirmed the negative source-country income effect in a cross-section of emigration rates to the United States for the shorter period 1982–86, but found that the stock of previous immigrants was the single most important determinant. More recently, Kamemera, Oguledo and Davis (2000) used panel data for the decade 1976–86, including a wide range of variables both for the United States and source countries. Distance, relative income and United States unemployment all mattered, but migration was also positively related to measures of political rights and individual freedom in source countries and negatively related to political instability.

In recent (and ongoing) work with Ximena Clark we have developed a model that attempts to explore these issues more directly. Our data set is a panel of immigration rates into the United States from eighty-one countries over the years 1971–98. One variant of this model appears in Table 2.3. The relative income variable is PPP adjusted *per capita* income and, for that reason, relative skill levels are also included as proxied by years of education. These variables produce significant coefficients with negative and positive signs, respectively, and they matter quantitatively. For example, the net effect of lower levels of income and education in South America compared to Western Europe is to raise the typical South American country's migration rate by 25 per cent over that of Western Europe. The coefficients on the return to skills, as proxied by relative inequality, also strongly support the Roy model for the case where the destination country is relatively rich. The quadratic peaks with relative inequality at 1.33, and with an effect that raises immigration from the typical South American country by 46 per cent over that of the typical Western European country. The share of source-country population in the 15–29 age range has a positive effect but its impact is more modest. It raises migration rates from South America by 11 per cent over those from Western Europe.

Other variables also have strong effects in the expected direction. Adding a thousand miles to distance from Chicago reduces the migration rate from a country by about a fifth, being landlocked reduces it by more than a third, while being predominantly English-speaking raises it by a factor of three. The stock of previous immigrants from a source country residing in the United States per 1,000 of the source country population has a significant effect. Evaluated at the mean, the coefficients imply that an addition of 1,000 to the migrant stock increases the annual flow of immigrants by 26 – an order of magnitude comparable with that found for nineteenth-century Europe. The coefficients imply that the stock of previous migrants raises South American migration by 49 per cent (high stock to population ratio) compared with East Asia (low stock to population ratio). This difference is itself the result of cumulative differences in past migration rates.

What about poverty? Here we use a trickling-down proxy for the source-country poverty rate – the ratio of the country's Gini coefficient of household income to the square of its income *per capita*. At a given mean income, a rise in inequality increases the poverty rate, whereas for a given level of inequality, a rise in mean income reduces the poverty rate.[6] This proxy variable has a negative effect (Table 2.3) so that absolute poverty reduces migration

Table 2.3   Regression estimate for US immigration, 1971–98

LnMigRate = $-11.95 - 1.80$ Ypc(f/h) $+ 2.61$ Sch(f/h) $+ 4.17$ Gini(f/h)
$\quad$ (35.9) (9.5) $\quad\quad$ (12.7) $\quad\quad\quad$ (7.1)
$\quad\quad - 1.57$ (Gini(f/h))$^2 - 2.71$ Sp15–29 $- 0.18$ Dist $+ 1.11$ Englp $- 0.31$ Landlk
$\quad\quad\quad$ (6.5) $\quad\quad\quad\quad$ (2.7) $\quad\quad\quad$ (12.3) $\quad\quad$ (15.4) $\quad\quad$ (7.0)
$\quad\quad + 42.91$ ImStck $- 182.94$ (ImStck)$^2 - 0.36$ Pov $+ 0.06$ WH71–6
$\quad\quad\quad$ (10.7) $\quad\quad\quad\quad$ (6.5) $\quad\quad\quad\quad$ (3.9) $\quad\quad$ (0.8)
$\quad\quad - 0.42$ EH71–6 $- 0.01$ D92–8 $+ 0.14$ D92–8*Sch $+ 0.05$ IRCA; $R^2 = 0.77$
$\quad\quad\quad$ (6.3) $\quad\quad\quad\quad$ (0.1) $\quad\quad\quad$ (0.8) $\quad\quad\quad\quad$ (2.9)

Note: Robust *t*-statistics in parentheses.

Sample: Balanced panel of number of immigrants to the United States, by country/year 1971–98.

Variable definitions: LnMigRate = log of the ratio of immigrants admitted by country of birth per 1,000 of source-country population; Ypc(f/h) = ratio of GDP *per capita* at 1985 PPP, source country to United States; Sch(f/h) = ratio of years of schooling for those aged 15 and over, source country to United States; Sp15–29 = share of source-country population aged 15–29; Gini(f/h) = ratio of Gini coefficient of household income, source country to United States; Dist = great circle distance from Chicago in 1,000 miles; Englp = dummy equals 1 if source country is predominantly English-speaking; Landlk = dummy equals 1 if source country is landlocked; ImStck = stock of immigrants in the United States from source country per 1,000 of source-country population; Pov = source-country Gini coefficient/source country income *per capita* squared; WH71–6 = dummy equals 1 for Western hemisphere countries times dummy equals 1 for 1971–76; EH71–6 = dummy equals 1 for Eastern hemisphere countries times dummy equals 1 for 1971–76; D92–8 = dummy equals 1 for 1992–98; D92–8*Sch = D92–8 times years of schooling ratio; IRCA = estimated number of illegal immigrants residing in the United States in 1980 per 1,000 of source-country population times dummy = 1 for 1989–91.

Method: Pooled OLS regression on 2,268 country/year observations. Dummies for Canada, Mexico and eight regions (with Western Europe as the excluded group) included but not reported.

Source: This is a variant of the model presented in Clark *et al.* (2002).

to the United States. Thus, a rise in source-country *per capita* income has two effects on US immigration: a negative effect operating through the relative income variable, and a positive effect operating through the poverty variable. Furthermore, these effects depend on the initial income level. For a typical West European country, a 10 per cent rise in GDP *per capita* (holding education constant) reduces migration to the United States by 12.6 per cent. A 10 per cent rise in income would reduce migration from the typical East Asian country by 4.3 per cent and from the typical South American country by 3.7 per cent. But for the typical African country, a 10 per cent rise in income *per capita increases* migration to the United States by 0.3 per cent. Looking at the poverty effect alone (that is, assuming income also rose by 10 per cent in the United States) there would be virtually no effect on the west European country but a 2 per cent rise in migration from the African country.

It should be stressed, however, that all of these effects are measured in the presence of a quota on total immigration. Thus while they may be a reasonable guide to the effect of changes in domestic conditions in a single source country, they would be a misleading guide to the effect of worldwide changes that would tighten the constraint imposed by the quota. US immigration policy is represented by the variables in the fourth line of Table 2.3 (plus WH71–6 in the third line). Merging the eastern and western hemispheres after 1976 sharply relaxed the constraint on immigration from eastern hemisphere countries. By contrast the 1990 Immigration Act had marginal effects, even when interacted with relative schooling levels to reflect the shift towards positive selection on skills. Finally the effects of the IRCA legalization programme over the years 1989–91 is captured by a variable reflecting the estimated number of source country illegal immigrants residing in the United States in 1980. This effect doubled the Mexican immigration rate during those years.

Migration in and from Africa

By far the world's poorest continent, Africa has generated remarkably few migrants to the major labour-scarce countries despite the massive gains that it would bring to the migrants. True, migration pressure, as reflected by illegal flows between North Africa and southern Europe, has often hit the headlines. The share of Africans in legal immigration to the United States has increased. Yet, real incomes in Africa are a tiny fraction of those in Europe and North America so the incentive to emigrate should be huge. Indeed, the gaps are many times larger than those that gave rise to the mass emigrations from Europe a century ago.

There are three possible explanations for this apparent paradox. First, OECD immigration policies that stress family reunification or skills impose high hurdles that serve to screen out potential African migrants. This explanation is consistent with the finding that migrant stock effects are large at very low levels. Second, the poverty constraint is sufficiently large to offset the effect of large income gaps for most poor Africans. Third, Africans are simply less mobile than populations elsewhere. We will start with the third of these possible explanations for the paradoxically low African emigration rates to the labour-scarce OECD.

There is, of course, abundant evidence of *coerced* African migration. Large numbers travelled as slaves across the Atlantic to the Americas from the seventeenth to the nineteenth century. More recently, Africa has become notorious for its refugees. While Africa accounts for a little more than a tenth of world population, it typically accounts for more than a third of the world's stock of refugees living in foreign countries. Typically, these displaced Africans return to their homelands as soon as possible (Rogge, 1994) because of political motives, tribal and kinship ties and the loss of cultural identity (Makanya, 1994). Does this suggest an unwillingness to migrate? Probably not, since there is a more important force at work: African refugees, often displaced into rural parts of bordering states, experience even greater deprivation than they do at home.

The literature on migration within Africa suggests no lack of mobility. It is worth citing a few examples. One study of rural Botswana found a highly elastic and positive migration response to wage rates and employment probabilities in the urban sector and a negative response to local wage rates and employment probabilities (Lucas, 1985). Another study found that rural–urban migration in Kenya is strongly related to the wage gap and to the individual's education, selecting those with higher education as a result of the greater economic return to education in the cities (Agesa, 2001). But such is not always the case: emigration from Egypt to the Gulf states selected those with few skills and without land. And there is little evidence to suggest that the poorest labourers were constrained from migrating by poverty (Adams, 1993: 162).

In recent research, we estimated the determinants of net migration to and from countries across sub-Saharan Africa (SSA). The migration rates are inferred by demographic accounting where net migration was simply calcu-lated as a residual. Thus, we do not know where emigrants went or where immigrants came from, but the vast bulk of the movements across African borders are not overseas. Still, we have explained these net migration rates, illustrated by the regression in Table 2.4. The net outward movement of refugees is, of course, an important component of total African cross-border movement although the estimated coefficient is less than one, perhaps because refugees crowd out potential emigrants that would have moved for employment reasons in the absence of the refugees. The share of the home country population aged 15–29 also has a positive effect, indicating that a rise of 5 percentage points in the share of young adults increases annual outmigration by one per 1,000.

Table 2.4   Regression estimate for African net migration, 1977–95

NetMigRate = − 58.45 + 0.47 NetRef + 10.02 LnWRatio(f/h) + 2.11 Sp15–29
(2.4)   (3.1)   (2.9)   (2.4)
− 0.53 grY(h) + 0.04 grY(f) − 1.46 Pov $R^2 = 0.53$
(2.0)   (0.2)   (1.7)

Note: Robust *t*-statistics in parentheses.

Sample: Unbalanced panel of country/years comprising: Angola 1982–95; Burundi 1980–85; Cameroon 1980–95; Central African Republic 1989–95; Chad 1980–95; Côte d'Ivoire 1989–95; Gabon 1977–90; Ghana 1977–95; Lesotho, 1981–95; Malawi 1987–95; Mali 1987–95; Nigeria 1977–95; Rwanda 1979–95; Senegal 1989–95; Sierra Leone 1991–95; Sudan 1984–95; Swaziland 1978–95; Togo 1982–93; Zambia 1981–95; Zimbabwe 1983–95.

Variable definitions: NetMigRate = net outmigration per 1,000 of population; NetRef = net outflow of refugees per 1,000 of population; LnWRatio = ratio of real unskilled wage rates at 1990 PPP, foreign to home, where the foreign index is a weighted average regional (0.9) and OECD (0.1) wage rates; grY(h) = growth rate of real GDP *per capita* in home country; grY(f) index of growth rate of GDP in the region, where the African regions are west, east, middle and south; Pov = inverse of home real wage squared.

Method: Pooled OLS regression on 265 country/year observations. Dummies for Ghana 1983 and 1985 and Nigeria 1983 and 1985 included but not reported.

Source: This is a variant of the model presented in Hatton and Williamson (2003).

The relative income variable is the PPP adjusted unskilled wage rate and hence there is no need to adjust for differences in education. The foreign to home wage ratio has a strong positive coefficient implying that a 10 per cent rise in the wage ratio increases net outmigration by about one per 1,000 of the population, an impact similar to that for European emigration a century ago. While the growth of domestic output has a negative effect on outmigration, the effect of the growth of output in other economies in the region seems to have little impact. Finally, the poverty constraint, captured here by the inverse of the squared home real wage, has a negative influence, but only significant at the 10 per cent level, implying that the poverty constraint is weak. At the mean wage rate a 10 per cent increase in the real wage increases outmigration by 0.2 per 1,000, an effect that only partially offsets the one per 1,000 negative effect operating through the wage ratio. This contrasts with the finding for immigration from Africa to the United States where the poverty constraint effect more than offsets the relative income effect.[7] But since most of the net migration reported in Table 2.4 is within Africa, it makes sense that the poverty constraint would be a smaller impediment for cross-border movements than it would be for trans-Atlantic migration.

Although these estimates are based on very crude macro data, they do seem to be consistent with micro studies. Findlay and Sow (1998) studied rural households in the Senegal River valley in Mali. They found that the poorer the family, the more likely its migrants would remain in Africa – suggesting that poverty constraints were more important for migration out of Africa. They also found that households with previous emigration experience in France were more likely to send new migrants to France – suggesting that the 'friends and relatives' effect influenced the direction of those migrations. But immigration policy and economic conditions in overseas destinations mattered, too.

World migration

Despite the disproportionate attention that has been given to immigration pressures on the United States and other OECD countries, there have been other major migration streams around the world. These, too, have been driven by a combination of demographic and economic trends as well as by political upheavals. In Eastern Europe, the collapse of the Soviet regime led to large westward flows in the early 1990s from countries such as Romania, Bulgaria, Poland and Russia itself. By 1993 the number of migrants from Central and Eastern Europe in the EU (excluding the German *Aussiedler*) had risen to nearly 2 million (Bauer and Zimmermann, 1999: 6). These pressures had abated somewhat by the late 1990s as the backlog cleared and conditions in these countries began to improve. Later in the decade, civil war in the former Yugoslavia led to mass outflows, although many of the refugees ultimately returned (OECD, 2001a: 68–86).

In Asia, there have also been major currents of migration driven by demographic pressures and growing income disparities. Until the middle of the 1980s one of the most important magnets for migrants within Asia were Kuwait, Saudi Arabia and the other Gulf states. Mass migration came from neighbouring countries such as Lebanon, Palestine and Jordan that were also influenced by wars and instability in the region (Shami, 1999). The oil-rich states increasingly drew migrants from further afield including East Asia and the Indian subcontinent – a trend that was halted by the Gulf War in 1991. Elsewhere, the economic miracles in the 'Asian tiger' economies also resulted in major migration movements. In countries such as Korea and Malaysia persistent net emigration was replaced by two-way streams with falling outflows of natives and rising inflows of foreigners. Such trends as there were halted at least temporarily by the financial crisis of 1997 that was followed by sharp clampdowns on immigration (OECD, 2001b).

Similar combinations of forces seem to have been shaping migration, within and between regions, the world over and it is tempting to see how far a simple migration model can explain them. Our results using net migration inferred from demographic reconstructions are sufficiently encouraging to suggest it would be worthwhile to apply the technique more widely. The United Nations calculates annual average net immigration rates over five-year intervals for most countries. We have used these data to form

Table 2.5   Regression estimate of net immigration for eighty countries, 1970–2000

NetMigRate = 2.65 – 0.18 Sp15–29 + 0.23 ImStck – 2.05 CivWar
    (1.3) (2.3)   (7.1)   (2.7)
    + 0.89 (YpcW – SchW)(h/f) + 0.72 (YpcR – SchR)(h/f) + 1.49 Pov
    (3.0)   (4.8)   (2.2)
    $R^2 = 0.26$

Note: *t*-statistics in parentheses.
Sample: Balanced panel of five-year averages 1970–75 to 1995–2000 for eighty countries.
Variable definitions: NetMigRate = net immigration per 1,000 of the population per annum, five-year average; Sp15–29 = percentage of population aged 15–29, five-year average; ImStck = percentage of foreign-born in the country, beginning of period; CivWar = proportion of civil war years in period; (YpcW – SchW)(h/f) = five-year average of ratio of county GDP *per capita* at 1985 ppp divided by the weighted average GDP *per capita* of all other countries, *minus* five-year average of ratio of country years of education for those aged 15 and over divided by the weighted average years of education of all other countries; (YpcR – SchR)(h/f) = five-year average of ratio of country GDP *per capita* at 1985 PPP divided by the weighted average GDP *per capita* of other countries in the same region, *minus* five-year average of ratio of country years of education for those aged 15 and over divided by the weighted average years of education of other countries in the region; Pov = average ratio of country Gini coefficient divided by *per capita* income squared.
Method: Pooled OLS regression on 480 country/period observations.
Source: A variant of the model presented in Clark *et al.* (2002).

a panel of five-year periods 1970–75 to 1995–2000 for eighty countries. The results of this exercise appear in Table 2.5.

The share of population aged 15–29 in a country has a negative effect on immigration, consistent with our findings for immigration to the United States and cross-border migration in Africa. The coefficient implies that a decrease in the youth share from, say 30 per cent to 25 per cent, would increase the net immigration rate by 0.9 per 1,000 of the population. The magnitude of the demographic effect is very close to what we found for emigration in SSA. The immigrant stock has a positive effect on net immigration and its size is consistent with the estimates presented earlier. The coefficient implies that an increase of a 1,000 in the immigrant stock increases net immigration by about twenty-three per annum. Refugee movements are captured by a variable measuring the share of years during which the country was embroiled in civil war. This was found to be the most important variable determining refugee displacements across borders in Africa (Hatton and Williamson, 2003). Here the effect of a civil war reduces annual immigration (chiefly though refugee outflows) by about 2 per 1,000 of the population.

Income effects are captured by two education adjusted relative income terms, one relative to the world as a whole and one relative to the region in which the country is located. These variables are defined as GDP *per capita* for the country divided by a population-weighted average for the world or the region *minus* the ratio of education years for the country relative to the world or the region. The restriction that the GDP *per capita* ratios take equal and opposite signs to the years of education ratios is comfortably accepted by the data.[8] These two variables represent the effects on total net migration of income gaps relative to the world as a whole and within the region. Both are positive so that a rise in domestic income relative to the world and relative to the region both increase a country's net immigration. A 10 per cent increase in education adjusted income raises immigration for the typical country by 0.12 per 1,000 from the worldwide effects and by 0.09 per 1,000 for the regional effect. These combined effects are somewhat smaller than those we found previously.

What about the poverty constraint? Here again the poverty constraint is proxied by the Gini coefficient of household income divided by the square of GDP *per capita*. Its effect should be positive on net immigration if greater poverty leads to lower emigration and therefore higher net immigration than otherwise. As before, because of the non-linearity, an increase in mean income has different effects at different income levels. For a typical African country, a 10 per cent increase in education adjusted income increases net immigration by 0.10 per 1,000 through the two relative income effects but it also reduces net immigration by 0.16 per 1,000. Thus, as was suggested earlier, the effect of increasing incomes at home for the poorest countries is to increase net emigration (and therefore to reduce net immigration). Africa is the only region where the overall effect of a rise in home income is negative for net immigration. The poverty constraint effect is very small in Western Europe, and thus the overall effect of a rise in home income is to increase immigration by 0.31 per 1,000. In other regions, the poverty constraint effect is bigger. Thus, for South America the impact of a rise in home income is to increase immigration by 0.13 per 1,000; for the Caribbean 0.22 per 1,000; and for East Asia 0.20 per 1,000.

The future for South–North and South–South migration

Can we use our estimates to project a pattern of world migration over the next two or three decades? Probably not, since future trends are likely to be determined largely by policy. Indeed, the *ex post* migration streams that we have analysed have been conditioned by immigration policies that serve as a filter between the desire to migrate and the actual moves that take place. Economic and demographic variables strongly influence world migration, but that fact does not diminish the importance of policy, and since we cannot project policy, we cannot project world migration either.

Still, it may be valuable to use our estimates to say something about future migration *pressures*. If migration pressures increase but policy regimes harden then *ex post* world migration could be lower despite greater migration pressure. Under such conditions, we would see a further increase in illegal migration and an escalation of policies aimed at combating them. By identifying future migration pressures, we can inform those policies.

Our previous work examined the effects of demographic trends on migration pressure in Africa's future. It used UN forecasts of the population size and age structure to predict net migration rates for African countries into the future, taking account also of their effects on real wage rates. Those projections suggested that migration pressure over the next twenty years would increase for demographic reasons alone. Assuming that a mere 5 per cent of that additional predicted migration spilled out from SSA, projected annual emigration would increase by nearly a million per annum between 1995 and 2025. While any prediction must deal with the uncertainties associated with the future course of the HIV/AIDS epidemic, it still seems unambiguously clear that the demographic forces that drive African migration will serve as a powerful force raising emigration pressure over the next twenty years.

In contrast, the demographic component of migration pressure seems likely to abate in other key immigrating regions. Table 2.6 reports past and future demographic projections for selected regions using the UN medium variant forecasts. Between 1970 and 1995 the share of population aged 15–29 increased significantly in East Asia and SSA and dramatically in Central America. But the projections suggest that, in contrast to SSA, there will be a dramatic population ageing in three of the low-wage regions that have been such important immigrant sources for high-wage parts of the world. This implies either modest increases or actual declines in the absolute size of migration-age cohorts. Thus, while demographic forces will ease migration pressure in aggregate, they will alter the *sources* of the South–North migrations, and will probably also lead to growing South–South migrations.

Economic developments are likely to reinforce these trends. While OECD economies have experienced a convergence in living standards, there has

Table 2.6 UN population estimates and projections

	Change in percentage aged 15–29		Growth of population aged 15–29 (% p.a.)	
	1970–95	*1995–2020*	*1970–95*	*1995–2020*
Eastern Asia	2.27	−8.63	1.80	−0.85
Central America	4.47	−4.54	3.05	0.82
Eastern Europe	−1.27	−5.41	0.23	−1.65
SSA	1.34	1.93	3.00	2.67

Source: United Nations (2001).

been continued divergence for the world as a whole (Pritchett, 1997). In the quarter-century after 1970, spectacular growth in East Asia dramatically increased the ratio of its *per capita* income relative to the world average, while Central America, Eastern Europe and SSA suffered relative declines. The same was true for education adjusted *per capita* incomes. Should those trends continue, then migration pressure from these three lagging regions will increase. Still, the catching up on the OECD by the largest labour surplus parts of the world – China and India (Lindert and Williamson, 2003) – would probably reduce aggregate migration pressure, although an unrequited demand for emigration, which past policy restrictions choked off but left latent, might persist.

Even if convergence between low-wage and high-wage parts of the world took place over the next quarter-century, migration pressure might still increase. Successful development and poverty eradication in the Third World (Dollar and Kraay, 2000; Chen and Ravallion, 2001; Sala-i-Martin, 2002; Lindert and Williamson, 2003) will most certainly release the poverty constraint on potential emigrants from the poorest parts of the world. Those effects seem to be greatest for Africa where, as we have seen, increases in living standards at home (all else the same) tend to increase the pressure for intercontinental migration, but they are also likely to play a role in China, South Asia and the Asian interior.

Furthermore, the growing numbers of emigrants from the poorest countries establishing beach heads in the developed world serves to ensure that changes in the fundamentals will persist into the future, just as they have in the past. That is, the progressive reductions in poverty that led to the upswing of the emigration cycle observed a century ago in Europe, and more recently in other poor parts of the world, tend to cumulate through a rising immigrant stock. The 'friends and relatives' effect that worked so powerfully in the age of free migration operates just as strongly today, reinforced by immigration policies that include a major family reunification component.

We end with a final question. How long will it be before successful development shifts target from the emigrating poor from OECD labour markets to those which have recently arrived, or shortly will arrive, on the industrial scene? After all, there may be more skills to learn in a newly industrial country's manufacturing job, which is also closer to the poor sending region, than in a post-industrial country's domestic service job, which is also further away. These opportunities will most assuredly change the direction of South–North flows in a more South–South direction, easing the pressure on the OECD immigration, but creating new problems for the newly industrial country. The future rise of South–South migration will, no doubt, take those analysts who ignore history by surprise. It will not take economic historians by surprise. After all, when those 50 million Europeans left home before 1914, there were at the same time far more than 50 million who left China and India for jobs elsewhere in the periphery. South–South migration is not new. It is just ignored by economists.[9]

Notes

* We are grateful for the contributions from previous collaborations with Ximena Clark as well as for the comments made by participants at the UNU-WIDER conference on 'Poverty, International Migration and Asylum', held in Helsinki on 27–28 September 2002. Timothy Hatton would like to acknowledge financial support through a British Academy Research Readership and Jeffrey G. Williamson would like to do the same for the National Science Foundation SES-0001362.
1. For seventeen countries in Western Europe there were a total of 650,450 asylum applications in 1982–86, rising to 1,931,900 in 1997–2001. For the same periods, the number granted refugee status under the 1951 Geneva Convention rose from 183,550 to 221,200, while those granted humanitarian status outside the Convention rose from 27,200 to 206,050. Thus acceptances under these two headings accounted for a third of applications in 1982–86 but only a quarter in 1997–2001.
2. One important strand of theory considers migration as a *household decision* rather than an individual decision; for example, Mincer (1978), Stark (1991). That strand of the literature is not considered here, partly to maintain simplicity and partly because the empirical sections that follow deal with aggregate migration, not distinguishing between households and individuals.
3. In the case where s_i and z_i are independently distributed the maximum occurs at the point where $\sigma_h/\sigma_f = 1$. The effects of income distribution have rather different effects in the analysis of Stark and Taylor (1991). They posit that migration is positively related to the degree of relative deprivation among potential migrants at the source. In this case, only income inequality at the source should matter and it should have a monotonically positive effect on the probability of migration. For migration within and from Mexico (to the United States) Stark and Taylor obtained an inverse 'U'-shaped relation between their relative deprivation index and the probability of migration to the United States – a result they attribute to the poverty constraint (see further below).
4. The aggregate migration equation (2.4) can be easily modified to incorporate immigration policy (Clark, *et al.* 2002: appendix 1). This alters the (non-monotonic) effects of income distribution on migration such that the maximum occurs where $\sigma_h/\sigma_f > 1$ in the case where policy is positively skill-selective. For an analysis of the effects of skill-selective immigration policy in a household context, see Cobb-Clark (1998).
5. Ramos (1992) finds evidence for negative selection among migrants to the United States from Puerto Rico and for positive selection among return migrants. However Chiswick (2000) has argued that a fixed migration cost will be larger in proportion to the prospective gains for low-skilled migrants, leading to positive selection. Funkhouser (1992) finds this to be the case for prospective illegal immigrants from El Salvador: given the high fixed cost, the net gains are greater for those with higher education.
6. Ravallion (2001) reports an elasticity of the change in the share in poverty with respect to the change in mean private consumption expenditure of around –2 across a set of less developed countries.

7. The evidence from Germany also suggests that the poverty trap effect is strong for international migrants from the poorest countries (Rotte and Vogler, 2000).
8. The computed F-statistic for this restriction is 2.09 compared to the 5 per cent critical value of 3.0.
9. W. Arthur Lewis (1978) had plenty to say about South–South migration, but not many other economists have followed his lead. However, the two of us are starting a project on South–South migration since 1850, which we hope will redress the balance. See also Hatton and Williamson (2004: ch. 7).

References

Adams, R. H. (1993). 'The Economic and Demographic Determinants of International Migration in Rural Egypt', *Journal of Development Studies*, 30(1): 146–67.

Agesa, R. U. (2001). 'Migration and the Urban to Rural Earnings Difference: A Sample Selection Approach', *Economic Development and Cultural Change*, 49(4): 847–65.

Bauer, T. and K. F. Zimmermann (1999). 'Assessment of Migration Pressure and its Labour Market Impact following EU Enlargement to Central and Eastern Europe', IZA Research Report, No. 3.

Borjas, G. J. (1987). 'Self-Selection and the Earnings of Immigrants', *American Economic Review*, 77(4): 531–53.

Borjas, G. J. (1989). 'Economic Theory and International Migration', *International Migration Review*, 23(3): 457–85.

Borjas, G. J. (1994). 'The Economics of Immigration', *Journal of Economic Literature*, 32(4): 1667–1717.

Borjas, G. J. (1999). *Heaven's Door: Immigration Policy and the American Economy*, Princeton, NJ: Princeton University Press.

Chen, S. and M. Ravallion (2001). 'How Did the World's Poorest Fare in the 1990s?', *Review of Income and Wealth*, 47: 283–300.

Chiswick, B. R. (2000). 'Are Immigrants Favorably Self-Selected? An Economic Analysis', in C. D. Brettell and J. F. Hollifield (eds), *Migration Theory: Talking Across Disciplines*, New York: Routledge.

Chiswick, B. R. and T. J. Hatton (2003). 'International Migration and the Integration of Labor Markets', in M. Bordo, A. M. Taylor and J. G. Williamson (eds), *Globalization in Historical Perspective*, Chicago: University of Chicago Press.

Clark, X., T. J. Hatton and J. G. Williamson (2002). 'Where Do US Immigrants Come From? Policy and Sending Country Fundamentals', NBER Working Paper, 8998, Cambridge, MA: National Bureau of Economic Research.

Cobb-Clark, D. A. (1998). 'Incorporating United States Policy into a Model of the Immigration Decision', *Journal of Policy Modeling*, 20(5): 621–30.

Dollar, D. and A. Kraay (2000). 'Trade, Growth, and Poverty', Washington, DC: World Bank (October), unpublished paper.

Faini, R. and A. Venturini (1994). 'Italian Emigration in the Pre-War Period', in T. J. Hatton and J. G. Williamson (eds), *Migration and the International Labor Market, 1850–1939*, London: Routledge.

Findlay, R. and K. H. O'Rourke (2003). 'Commodity Market Integration 1500–2000', in M. Bordo, A. M. Taylor and J. G. Williamson (eds), *Globalization in Historical Perspective*, Chicago: University of Chicago Press.

Findlay, S. and S. Sow (1998). 'From Season to Season: Agriculture, Poverty and Migration in the Senegal River Valley, Mali', in R. Appleyard (ed.), *Emigration Dynamics in Developing Countries, Vol. 1: Sub-Saharan Africa*, Aldershot: Ashgate.

Funkhouser, E. (1992). 'Mass Emigration, Remittances and Economic Adjustment: The Case of El Salvador', in G. J. Borjas and R. B. Freeman (eds), *Immigration and the Workforce: Economic Consequences for the United States and Source Areas*, Chicago: University of Chicago Press.

Hatton, T. J. and J. G. Williamson (1998). *The Age of Mass Migration: Causes and Economic Impact*, New York: Oxford University Press.

Hatton, T. J. and J. G. Williamson (2003). 'Demographic and Economic Pressure on Emigration Out of Africa', *Scandinavian Journal of Economics*, 105: 465–86.

Hatton, T. J. and J. G. Williamson (2004). *World Mass Migration: Two Centuries of Policy and Performance*, Cambridge, MA: MIT Press (forthcoming).

Kamemera, D., V. I. Oguledo and B. Davis (2000). 'A Gravity Model Analysis of International Migration to North America', *Applied Economics*, 32(13): 1745–55.

Lewis, W. A. (1978). *The Evolution of the International Economic Order*, Princeton, NJ: Princeton University Press.

Lindert, P. H. and J. G. Williamson (2003). 'Does Globalization Make the World More Unequal?', in M. Bordo, A. M. Taylor and J. G. Williamson (eds), *Globalization in Historical Perspective*, Chicago: University of Chicago Press.

Lucas, R. E. B. (1985). 'Migration among the Batswana', *Economic Journal*, 95: 358–82.

Makanya, S. T. (1994). 'The Desire to Return', in T. Allen and H. Morsink (eds), *When Refugees Go Home*, London: Africa World Press.

Massey, D. S. (1988) 'Economic Development and International Migration in Comparative Perspective', *Population and Development Review*, 14(3): 383–413.

Massey, D. S., J. Arrango, G. Hugo, A. Kouaouci, A. Pellegrino and J. E. Taylor (1993). 'Theories of International Migration: A Review and Appraisal', *Population and Development Review*, 19(3): 431–66.

Mincer, J. (1978). 'Family Migration Decisions', *Journal of Political Economy*, 86(5): 749–73.

Obstfeld, M. and A. M. Taylor (2003). 'Globalization and Capital Markets', in M. Bordo, A. M. Taylor and J. G. Williamson (eds), *Globalization in Historical Perspective*, Chicago: University of Chicago Press.

OECD (2001a). *Trends in International Migration*, Paris: OECD.

OECD (2001b). *International Migration in Asia: Trends and Policies*, Paris: OECD.

O'Rourke, K. H. and J. G. Williamson (1999). *Globalization and History*, Cambridge, MA: MIT Press.

Pritchett, L. (1997). 'Divergence, Big Time', *Journal of Economic Perspectives*, 11(3): 3–17.

Ramos, F. A. (1992). 'Out-Migration and Return Migration of Puerto Ricans', in G. J. Borjas and R. B. Freeman (eds), *Immigration and the Workforce: Economic Consequences for the United States and Source Areas*, Chicago: University of Chicago Press.

Ravallion, M. (2001). 'Growth, Inequality and Poverty: Looking Beyond Averages', unpublished paper, Washington, DC: World Bank.

Rogge, J. R. (1994). 'Repatriation of Refugees', in T. Allen and H. Morsink (eds), *When Refugees Go Home*, London: Africa World Press.

Rotte, R. and M. Vogler (2000). 'The Effects of Development on Migration: Theoretical Issues and New Empirical Evidence', *Journal of Population Economics*, 13(3): 485–508.

Sala-i-Martin, X. (2002). 'The Disturbing "Rise" of Global Income Inequality', NBER Working Paper, 8904, Cambridge, MA: National Bureau of Economic Research.

Shami, S. (1999). 'Emigration Dynamics in Jordan, Palestine and Lebanon', in R. Appleyard (ed.), *Emigration Dynamics in Developing Countries: Vol. IV: The Arab Region*, Aldershot: Ashgate.

Sjaastad, L. (1962). 'The Costs and Returns of Human Migration', *Journal of Political Economy*, 70(5) (Part 2): S80–S93.

Smith, J. P. and B. Edmonston (1997). *The New Americans: Economic, Demographic and Fiscal Effects of Immigration*, Washington, DC: National Academy Press.

Stalker, P. (2000). *Workers Without Frontiers: The Impact of Globalisation on International Migration*, London: Lynne Rienner.

Stark, O. (1991). *The Migration of Labour*, Oxford: Blackwell.

Stark, O. and J. E. Taylor (1991). 'Migration Incentives, Migration Types: The Role of Relative Deprivation', *Economic Journal*, 101: 1163–78.

United Nations (2001). *World Population Prospects: The 2000 Revision*, New York: United Nations.

United States Department of Justice (2002). *1999 Statistical Yearbook of the Immigration and Naturalization Service*, Washington, DC: US GPO.

Yang, P. Q. (1995). *Post-1965 Immigration to the United States: Structural Determinants*, Westport, CT: Praeger.

Zlotnick, H. (1998). 'International Migration, 1965–96: An Overview', *Population and Development Review*, 24(3): 429–68.

3
Trends in Asylum Migration to Industrialized Countries, 1990–2001*

Stephen Castles and Sean Loughna

Introduction

This chapter outlines trends and patterns in movements of asylum seekers to Western, industrialized countries from 1990 to 2001. The receiving countries covered are the United States, Canada, Australia and Western Europe (which here comprises the Member States of the EU in 2002, Norway and Switzerland). Other industrialized states such as Japan and New Zealand have not been included since the numbers of asylum seekers involved are relatively small. All sending countries are included in the data, but our discussion will focus mainly on the countries of origin of the largest numbers – generally the 'top ten' sending countries for each receiving area. The aims of the desk study reported here are largely descriptive, and its main substance is contained in the tables and charts (the latter are in the Appendix). However, the chapter also has analytical aspects, as it is not possible to describe the evolution of the movements without examining the causes of migratory patterns and the factors responsible for change.

In this chapter 'asylum migration' is used as shorthand for 'migratory movements undertaken for the purpose of, or with the consequence of, seeking asylum in another state'. This follows Jeff Crisp's definition for the purposes of the UNU-WIDER conference. It is a pragmatic usage, based on the recognition that it is often impossible to tell at the time of movement whether an asylum-seeker is actually a 'refugee' in the sense of the 1951 United Nations Refugee Convention. Determining this frequently requires a lengthy and complex process. Moreover, many asylum seekers will be permitted to stay on humanitarian or other grounds, even if denied refugee status.

In recent years, some politicians and other observers have claimed that many asylum seekers are really economic migrants who are abusing the asylum process. This has led to increasingly restrictive entry rules. The feedback effect of such policies is that many genuine refugees are unable to make claims, because they cannot enter a potential country of asylum. This in turn has caused some asylum seekers to enter illegally, often using the services of people smugglers. The result is that the distinction between asylum seekers and undocumented migrants has become blurred, leading to the notion of the 'asylum–migration nexus'. Ideally, therefore, this study should present data both on asylum seeker movements and undocumented migration, and then seek to disentangle the two. However, the availability and quality of data on undocumented migration make it extremely difficult to find the empirical information needed for this type of analysis. The data presented are thus mainly concerned with asylum seekers.

The chapter starts by discussing the development of asylum migration, and then provides background material on global refugee and asylum movements. The data for the various Western asylum countries are discussed, followed by some remarks on changing routes used by asylum seekers. Finally, we examine some of the causal factors behind asylum migration.

The three phases of asylum migration

All Western European countries, as well as Australia, Canada and the United States are signatories to the 1951 United Nations Refugee Convention and/ or its 1967 Protocol. This obliges them to provide protection to persons who qualify under the Convention definition, according to which a refugee is a person residing outside his or her country of nationality, who is unable or unwilling to return because of a 'well-founded fear of persecution on account of race, religion, nationality, membership in a particular social group, or political opinion'. States party to the Convention undertake not to return refugees to their country of origin against their will (the principle of *non-refoulement*). This may require states to grant entry and/or to provide temporary or permanent residence status.

The international refugee regime is based on the principle of different treatment for refugees compared with economic migrants. This worked very well for the classical refugees of the Cold War: the dissidents who voted with their feet against the repressive regimes of the Soviet Union and its satellites. They were welcomed with open arms in the West, as a living proof of the superiority of democracy. Since relatively few got out through the Iron Curtain, the costs of hospitality were limited. The situation became more problematic with the struggles against colonialism and authoritarian regimes from the 1960s onwards. It became extremely difficult to make clear distinctions between asylum seekers and economic migrants from countries undergoing rapid change and crisis. Political upheavals, economic difficulties and violent conflicts tend to occur simultaneously, so that many migrants have multiple motivations for moving. Governments, too, may have multiple motivations for admitting migrants.

The migration–asylum nexus is not a new dilemma. Although some people entering Western countries are clearly refugees while others are clearly economic migrants, there have always been people who could not be easily categorized. Often migrants respond to migration rules and policies of receiving states in deciding on their mode of migration. From the migrants' perception such rules and policies can be seen as *opportunity structures*, rather than absolute definitions. It is possible to identify three distinct phases in the development of the migration asylum nexus.

Phase one: *treating refugees as migrant workers*. At the end of the Second World War there were over 40 million displaced persons in Europe. The preferred solution was repatriation to their home countries, but many had both political and economic reasons for not wanting to return to countries taken over by Stalinist regimes. Countries such as Australia and Canada offered refuge because they needed labour for economic growth and people for demographic growth. Similarly, many of the migrant workers who came to France and Germany in the 1960s and 1970s were escaping authoritarian regimes in Spain, Portugal, Greece and Turkey. However, they were admitted because the receiving countries needed labour, and no one bothered to examine their need for protection. They were treated as migrant workers and if they lacked passports and visas, regularization programmes were set up (notably in France) to give them a secure status.

Phase two: *migrants with mixed motivations claiming asylum*. This followed the 1973 oil crisis, when Western European countries stopped labour recruitment and redefined themselves as 'zero immigration countries'. For many people, claiming asylum became the only legal route to entering and settling in the industrialized world. For instance, when Germany stopped entry of Turkish workers in 1973, the migratory process continued through family reunion and asylum. This does not imply that the asylum seekers were not genuine: Turkey was beset by political instability, military coups and ethnic conflict. The point is that people who had previously been admitted as workers now had to claim asylum.

Phase three: *asylum seekers moving as undocumented migrants*. While the right under international law to claim asylum continued to be generally respected by Western states, they also began to restrict entry to eliminate bogus claims. By the early 1990s, many industrialized states, including Western European countries, Australia and the United States (although not Canada) had introduced policies aimed at restricting access to asylum including: temporary protection regimes, non-arrival policies (such as imposing visa requirements on travellers and 'carrier sanctions' on airlines), diversion policies (such as declaring some transit countries as 'safe third countries'), and deterrence policies (such as detention and prohibition of employment). Increasingly during the 1990s, and as an apparent response to tougher rules and regulations, those seeking asylum fled to industrialized countries through ever more sophisticated 'illegal' means, often with the assistance of people smugglers.

Global refugee and asylum-seeker movements

According to the United Nations High Commissioner for Refugees (UNHCR), the global refugee population grew from 2.4 million in 1975 to 10.5 million in 1985 and 14.9 million in 1990. A peak was reached after the end of the Cold War with 18.2 million in 1993. By 2000, the global refugee population had declined to 12.1 million (UNHCR, 1995, 2000a).[1] Refugees came mainly from countries affected by war, violence and chaos. Globally, the ten main places of origin of refugees in 1999 were Afghanistan (2.6 million), Iraq (572,000), Burundi (524,000), Sierra Leone (487,000), Sudan (468,000), Somalia (452,000), Bosnia (383,000), Angola (351,000), Eritrea (346,000) and Croatia (340,000) (UNHCR, 2000b: 315).

Annual asylum applications in Western Europe, Australia, Canada and the United States combined rose from 90,400 in 1983 to 323,050 in 1988, and then surged again with the end of the Cold War to peak at 828,645 in 1992 (UNHCR, 1995: 253). Altogether, 5 million asylum seekers entered Western countries from 1985 to 1995 (UNHCR, 1997: 184). Applications fell sharply to 480,000 in 1995, but began creeping up again to 534,500 in 2000 (OECD, 2001: 280).[2] Nearly the whole of the decline can be explained by falls in asylum applications following changes in refugee law in Germany (438,200 applications in 1992, but only 127,900 in 1995) and Sweden (84,000 in 1992; 9,000 in 1995). The United Kingdom had relatively few asylum seekers in the early 1990s, with 32,300 in 1992, but numbers increased at the end of the decade to 55,000 in 1998, and 97,900 in 2000 (OECD, 2001: 280).

This rise in asylum applications led to considerable concern in Western countries. It became a major policy issue within the EU. Western leaders called for greater burden sharing between countries of asylum. In fact, however, only a small proportion of asylum seekers and refugees actually come to the highly developed countries. Table 3.1 shows the top ten refugee hosting countries in 2000 according to three different criteria. The first column shows the total refugee population. Pakistan and Iran had by far the largest refugee populations – mainly from Afghanistan. Africa figures prominently in the table, but the United States is also in the list, together with two European countries: Germany and the Federal Republic of Yugoslavia (FR Yugoslavia). However, to understand the weight of the 'refugee burden', it is more useful to relate refugee population to overall population in host countries. This is shown in the second column of Table 3.1, which consists mainly of very poor countries, with the sole exceptions of FR Yugoslavia and Sweden. Even more instructive is to relate refugee populations to the wealth of the receiving country (third column). This list does not include a single highly developed country. Refugees are overwhelmingly concentrated in the poorest countries.

Table 3.1   Top ten refugee-hosting countries, 2000

Total refugee population		Refugees per 1,000 inhabitants		Refugee population relative to GDP	
Country	No. of refugees (000s)	Country	No. of refugees	Country	No. of refugees per US$1 million of GDP
Pakistan	2 002	Armenia	79.7	Armenia	172.4
Iran	1 868	Guinea	58.5	Guinea	119.9
Germany	906	FR Yugoslavia	45.7	Tanzania	86.0
Tanzania	681	DR Congo	42.5	Zambia	74.9
United States	507	Djibouti	36.3	DR Congo	62.9
FR Yugoslavia	484	Iran	27.6	Cen. African Rep.	52.7
Guinea	433	Zambia	27.3	DR Congo	47.7
Sudan	401	Liberia	21.7	Uganda	35.6
DR Congo	333	Tanzania	20.3	Pakistan	31.3
China	294	Sweden	17.7	Ethiopia	30.1

Source: UNHCR (2001: 28).

Asylum migration to industrialized countries

This section describes asylum migration flows to the various industrialized countries. Appendix Figures 3A.1–3A.4 (see pp. 65–6) show flows to the United States, Canada, Australia and Western Europe from the 'top five' countries of origin of asylum seekers for the twelve-year period. Annual figures often show fluctuations, with increases in numbers from certain countries, which are not sustained. Appendix Figure 3A.5 compares flows to the various receiving areas. Tables 3.2–3.5 in the text below show the 'top ten' countries of origin for the four selected countries or regions for the years 1990 and 2001. This enables us to compare the most significant countries of origin at the beginning of the period with those at the end. It also allows us to see certain regional differences and similarities.

We start with the so-called 'classical immigration countries' and then move on to Western Europe. The United States, Canada and Australia have long histories of immigration, welcoming both refugees and economic migrants. Today, these three are among only about ten countries in the world, which have regular programmes for resettlement of refugees in collaboration with the UNHCR. However, these countries have also experienced growing inflows of asylum seekers since the 1980s. By contrast, most Western European countries have not had resettlement programmes, with the exception of short-term ones for particular emergencies such as in Indochina or Kosovo.

Table 3.2 United States: top ten countries of origin of asylum seekers, 1990, 2001, 1990–2001

1990		2001		1990–2001	
Country of origin	*Asylum seekers*	*Country of origin*	*Asylum seekers*	*Country of origin*	*Asylum seekers*
El Salvador	22 271	Mexico	8 747	El Salvador	223 887
Nicaragua	18 304	China	8 008	Guatemala	178 047
Guatemala	12 234	Colombia	7 144	Mexico	66 338
Cuba	3 925	Haiti	4 938	China	60 926
Romania	1 593	Armenia	2 147	Haiti	51 308
Liberia	1 572	India	1 894	Nicaragua	34 411
Iran	1 550	Indonesia	1 671	India	30 985
Ethiopia	1 532	Ethiopia	1 467	Russia	20 913
China	1 287	Albania	1 425	Pakistan	16 700
Honduras	1 097	Liberia	1 281	Cuba	16 600
Total top 10	**65 365**	**Total top 10**	**38 722**	**Total top 10**	**700 115**
Total asylum seekers	**73 637**	**Total asylum seekers**	**59 432**	**Total asylum seekers**	**997 696**
Top 10 as share of total (%)	**89**	**Top 10 as share of total (%)**	**65**	**Top 10 as share of total (%)**	**70**

Source: UNHCR, Population Data Unit, PGDS/DOS, Geneva.

United States

Between 1975 and 2000 the United States provided permanent resettlement to over 2 million refugees, including some 1.3 million people from Indochina. The United States accepted more people for resettlement during this period than the rest of the world put together (UNHCR, 2000b). The total number of asylum applications rose from 75,600 in 1990 to a peak of 148,700 in 1995, then declined to 32,700 in 1999 before rising again to 59,400 in 2001. In 2001, the United States hosted 396,000 pending asylum applicants, 28,0000 persons granted asylum during the year and 68,500 newly resettled refugees (USCR, 2001: 275).

Appendix Figure 3A.1 shows asylum-seeker flows from the top five countries of origin to the United States. Large numbers of persons fleeing conflict and persecution in Central American countries began arriving in the United States in the 1980s. Many of these did so 'illegally' as the United States did not recognize all Central American countries as refugee producing countries. The 'open door' policy towards Cubans fleeing to the United States, in place since 1959, began to be restricted in the 1980s, and interdiction at sea commenced in the 1990s. Large numbers of Haitians attempting to come to the United States during the 1980s and 1990s were generally prevented in doing so.

As Table 3.2 shows, at the beginning of the 1990s the top three countries of origin of asylum seekers coming to the United States were all Central American states experiencing civil war: El Salvador, Guatemala and Nicaragua. In 1990, asylum seekers coming from El Salvador were falling in numbers and continued to do so until 1992 when they began to rise again, peaking in the mid-1990s at the highest number coming from a single country during the decade. Their numbers dropped equally dramatically in 1996 and remained at relatively low levels for the remainder of the decade.

Asylum-seekers from Guatemala peaked in the early 1980s during the civil war, but were again increasing in the early 1990s. However, the number of Guatemalans seeking asylum in the United States began to fall significantly in 1992 and particularly from 1994 onwards. Although significant numbers continued to arrive for the remainder of the decade, they were at much abated levels. This drop may reflect the ceasefire and significant moves towards accountable government in Guatemala in 1992, followed by a lengthy peace process which advanced significantly in 1994 and culminated in a final agreement in 1996.

Flows of asylum seekers to the United States from Nicaragua were dropping in 1990 and did not rise again significantly during the remainder of the decade. Nicaraguans had been fleeing to the United States in significant numbers throughout the 1980s. Then in 1988, in the wake of the Iran–Contra affair, the United States Congress banned all aid to the contras. Later that year, the Sandinista government and the opposition began a national dialogue which culminated in a series of agreements the following year and ultimately to a cessation to the conflict.

For the 1990–2001 period as a whole, six out of the top ten sources of asylum seekers were Latin American or Caribbean countries, which are relatively close to the United States. However, there were substantial fluctuations over the period. As Table 3.2 shows, in 1990, the great majority of asylum seekers came from Latin America. In 2001 by contrast, the top country of origin was Mexico, followed by China, while the rest of the top ten included a wide range of areas of origin. Moreover the top ten in 2001 made up only 65 per cent of all applications, compared with 89 per cent in 1990, indicating a greater level of diversity in origins. The asylum approval rate for Mexicans was only 7 per cent, compared with 64 per cent for Chinese and 57 per cent for asylum seekers overall (USCR, 2001: 275). Asylum seekers from Colombia were not coming to the United States in large numbers in 1990, but were by 2001. This appears to reflect the intensification of the armed conflict there. Although this conflict has been going on for close to four decades, with large-scale displacement of the civilian population, the situation has become significantly worse since the late 1990s. The widening of the conflict across the country has meant that the displaced population is increasingly unsafe remaining within the borders of their country.

Entry routes have also changed. Most Central Americans come to the United States by land via Mexico, whereas Cubans and Haitians frequently come by boat. However, numbers have declined due to interdiction programmes of the United States Coast Guard. Quite large numbers of Chinese were brought in illegally by ship in the mid-1990s, but the number interdicted in 2001 was only 53, compared with 1,092 in 1999. This indicates a shift to other means of entry, especially by air using tourist visas.

After the terrorist attacks of 11 September 2001, the United States halted its refugee resettlement programme. Resumption was authorized in November 2001, but the United States admitted only 800 refugees in the last three months of that year. The USA Patriot Act of October 2001 introduced much stronger detention powers for non-citizens suspected of terrorist activities. Although these measures were not directed specifically against asylum seekers, it was feared that they might lead to an increase in the already substantial use of detention: an average of 3,000 asylum-seekers were in detention during 2001 (USCR, 2001: 279).

Operation Gatekeeper and similar operations were introduced in 1994, in an attempt to tighten security along the US–Mexico border and reduce the numbers of people entering the United States illegally. The United States Immigration and Naturalization Service (INS) has introduced double steel fences, helicopters, high-intensity searchlights and high-tech equipment. The number of agents enforcing the border has tripled over the same period. To fund all of this, the INS has seen its budget triple since 1994, to US$5.5 billion. However, there has been no decline in the number of illegal border crossings – indeed official figures suggest an increase. The number of people dying as they attempt to cross the border has also increased as people take ever-greater risks: in 1994, twenty-three people died trying to cross and this figure has increased every year since then. In 2000, at least 499 died attempting to cross. The cause of death has also altered as people move ever further eastward in attempting to cross the border; they usually now die from dehydration, hypothermia, sunstroke or drowning as they attempt to swim the All American Canal. Finally, the average cost of hiring a 'coyote' – who smuggles people across the border – has risen from US$143 to US$1,500 in six years (Cornelius, 2001).

The Chinese immigrants on the east coast of the United States, particularly in New York, are largely from Fujian province on the southeast coast of China. Snakeheads (smugglers) play an important role in facilitating their migration out of China. Smugglers of Chinese migrants are particularly sophisticated and have access to advanced communications technology and the ability to make false passports and visas. Most Chinese travel to the United States by air, whether directly or through transit countries and possibly with some passage by land. According to a study by Chin (1999) on Fujianese Chinese, 47 per cent entered the United States by air, 41 per cent by land, and only about 12 per cent by sea. A more recent strategy of transporting undocumented Chinese to the United States, as well as to Canada and European countries, has been to smuggle them on aeroplanes and in cargo ships and trucks. According to one study, more than forty-three countries have played a transit role in airborne and seaborne smuggling of Chinese (Myers, 1997: 117). Given the variety of transit routes, no attempt has been made to map the individual pathways used. However, it has been reported that Thailand and Mexico are particularly important transit countries (Kyle and Liang, 2001).

As well as tougher border control measures in the United States, new legislation was also introduced in China in 1999, which allows the government to put illegal migrants in prison for one year plus impose a heavy fine. Prior to that, China's policy was to mainly punish only the smugglers. Despite efforts by law enforcement officials in both countries, the flow of undocumented workers from China to the United States does not seem to have abated. The smuggling fee, however, is reported to have risen from US$28,000 in the early 1990s to US$60,000 in 2001 (Kyle and Liang, 2001). One of the most frequently used justifications for the basis of asylum claims of Chinese in the United States is China's 'One Child Policy'. The practice of the outlawed Falun Gong has also more recently been used as a basis for claims of asylum.

Canada

Like the United States, Canada accepted large numbers of people from Indochina: some 200,000 between 1975 and 1995. During the 1980s, Canada offered resettlement to an average of 21,000 refugees per year. Between 1989 and 1998, resettlement admissions fell from 35,000 to under 9,000. However, they rose to 17,000 in 1999 as a result of the humanitarian evacuation programme for refugees from Kosovo (UNHCR, 2000b). The resettlement figure for 2001 was 10,900 (USCR, 2001: 263).

As Table 3.3 shows, the number of asylum seekers coming to Canada declined from 36,700 in 1990 to 20,300 in 1993, increased again to 39,400 in 1999, and then reached its highest annual level ever of 44,000 in 2001.

In contrast to the United States, only one out of the top ten countries of origin for the 1990–2001 period was a Latin American country: Mexico. Most asylum seekers in Canada are from the Indian subcontinent or China, with Sri Lanka consistently near the top of the list. The general picture is one of considerable and increasing diversity over the whole period. Again, a change over time can be seen. The large numbers of asylum seekers from Hungary (which Canada did not recognize as a refugee-producing country) and Zimbabwe in 2001 were new developments in response to unusual circumstances, leading Canada to impose visa restrictions for both countries. This trend has since reversed and it seems to have been exceptional to Canada. See Appendix Figure 3A.2 for asylum migration flows from the top five countries of origin.

Table 3.3   Canada: top ten countries of origin of asylum seekers, 1990, 2001, 1990–2001

1990		2001		1990–2001	
Country of origin	*Asylum seekers*	*Country of origin*	*Asylum seekers*	*Country of origin*	*Asylum seekers*
Sri Lanka	4 548	Hungary	3 895	Sri Lanka	40 009
Somalia	3 856	Pakistan	3 192	Somalia	21 120
China	3 086	Sri Lanka	3 001	Pakistan	18 680
Bulgaria	2 514	Zimbabwe	2 653	China	17 651
Lebanon	2 316	China	2 413	Iran	15 590
El Salvador	2 137	Colombia	1 831	India	14 106
Iran	2 101	Turkey	1 755	Mexico	8 940
Argentina	1 175	Mexico	1 669	Hungary	8 915
Ghana	1 149	Argentina	1 456	Israel	8 527
Pakistan	988	India	1 300	DR Congo	8 229
Total top 10	**23 870**	**Total top 10**	**23 165**	**Total top 10**	**161 767**
Total asylum seekers	**36 735**	**Total asylum seekers**	**44 038**	**Total asylum seekers**	**355 425**
Top 10 as share of total (%)	**65**	**Top 10 as share of total (%)**	**53**	**Top 10 as share of total (%)**	**46**

Source: UNHCR, Population Data Unit, PGDS/DOS, Geneva.

In 2001, Canada made decisions upon 22,887 refugee claims, with an approval rate of 58 per cent. The highest approval rates were for Afghanistan (97 per cent), Somalia (92 per cent), Colombia (85 per cent), Sri Lanka (76 per cent) and Democratic Republic of Congo (DR Congo) (76 per cent). The lowest success rates were for Hungary (27 per cent) and Mexico (28 per cent) (USCR, 2001: 261).

Claims for asylum in Canada from people originating from the Indian subcontinent remained consistently high between 1990 and 2001. In the United States, numbers of asylum seekers from Central America have reduced and those from Mexico and Colombia had increased significantly during the same period. Asylum seekers from the Americas tend to come by land. But most asylum seekers coming to Canada come much larger distances and by necessity travel by sea or air. It is difficult with the information available to make generalizations and identify patterns about many such asylum seekers. A factor seems to be Canada's programme of resettlement of refugees and asylum seekers. Many asylum seekers going to Canada appear to be from the elite sectors of their societies of origin and they frequently fly there.

Australia

Australia has a Humanitarian Program, designed to bring in refugees from overseas, with fairly constant targets of around 12,000 per year since the early

1990s. Until 1999–2000 the Humanitarian Program had three components: *Refugees* as defined by the 1951 UN Refugee Convention, to resettle refugees in collaboration with the UNHCR; the *Special Humanitarian Program* (SHP) for people who suffer gross human rights violations but would not qualify under the 1951 Convention; and the *Special Assistance Category* (SAC) which was established to allow people displaced by violence in such countries as FR Yugoslavia to join relatives in Australia. In 2000–01 the SAC was phased out. In recent years an additional non-Program category has grown in importance: *Onshore Protection Visa Grants*, for people who claim asylum after arriving in Australia.

The Humanitarian Program arrival figures show an apparent decline in recent years, falling from 13,824 in 1995–96 to 8,779 in 1997–98 and 7,625 in 2000–01 (DIMIA, 2002). This is due to the increase in Onshore Protection Visas from 1,588 in 1997–98 to 1,834 in 1998–99, 2,458 in 1999–2000 and 5,577 in 2000–01. Some of these visas were granted to people who arrived by air on a visitor visa and then claimed asylum, but increasing numbers have gone to boat people. The number of persons arriving in Australia by boat without permission averaged only a few hundred per year up to the late 1990s, but went up to 920 in 1998–99, 4,175 in 1999–2000 and 4,141 in 2000–01 (Crock and Saul, 2002: 24). Although these numbers are low compared with other parts of the world, the growth is seen as undermining the tradition of strict government control of entries, which has hitherto been possible because of Australia's remote location.

The illegal entrants fell into two main groups: Chinese people smuggled in mainly for purposes of undocumented work; and asylum seekers from the Middle East and South Asia (Iraqis, Iranians, Afghans and others) brought in from Indonesia, usually on fishing boats chartered by people smugglers. In 1999, the Australian government introduced a number of deterrent measures, including a three-year temporary protection visa (TPV), which confers no right to permanent settlement or family reunion. Another deterrent is to stop boat people from landing on Australian shores, and to try to send them back to Indonesia. Those who do land are detained – sometimes for years – in remote camps, where they are isolated from lawyers, the media and supporters. Hunger strikes, riots, self-inflicted injuries and even suicide have become commonplace. The government has also introduced legal measures to limit the power of the courts in asylum matters (Crock and Saul, 2002: Chapter 5).

Matters got even worse in August 2001, when the Norwegian freighter MV *Tampa* picked up over 400 asylum seekers (mainly from Afghanistan and Iraq) from a sinking boat off Northern Australia. The government refused the captain permission to land, and the *Tampa* anchored near the Australian territory of Christmas Island. This was the start of a saga involving inter-national diplomacy, heated public debates in Australia and feverish political activity. In the 'Pacific Solution', Australia tried to export the asylum seekers

Table 3.4   Australia: top ten countries of origin of asylum seekers, 1996, 2001, 1996–2001

1996		2001		1996–2001	
Country of origin	*Asylum seekers*	*Country of origin*	*Asylum seekers*	*Country of origin*	*Asylum seekers*
Philippines	1 630	Afghanistan	2 161	Indonesia	7 529
Indonesia	1 420	Iraq	1 784	China	6 649
Sri Lanka	1 096	China	1 176	Iraq	5 378
China	1 007	Indonesia	897	Philippines	4 665
India	339	Fiji	799	Afghanistan	4 241
Turkey	269	India	650	Sri Lanka	4 025
Lebanon	262	Iran	559	India	2 873
Thailand	253	Sri Lanka	397	Fiji	2 134
Fiji	221	Malaysia	261	Iran	1 910
Iran	215	Bangladesh	261	Thailand	1 263
Total top 10	6 712	**Total top 10**	8 945	**Total top 10**	40 667
Total asylum seekers	9 758	**Total asylum seekers**	12 366	**Total asylum seekers**	62 153
Top 10 as share of total (%)	69	**Top 10 as share of total (%)**	72	**Top 10 as share of total (%)**	65

Source: UNHCR, Population Data Unit, PGDS/DOS, Geneva.

to its neighbours, Nauru and New Guinea – and was willing to spend vast sums of money to do so. Asylum became the central issue in the November election, giving victory to Liberal-National prime minister Howard. Before the *Tampa* affair, a Labor victory had been predicted. The 2002–03 Federal Budget included A\$2.8 billion for border control measures – an increase of A\$1.2 billion over the previous year. Even stricter border control legislation was introduced in 2002 (Castles and Vasta, 2003).

Table 3.4 shows the top ten countries of origin of asylum seekers in 1996 and 2001, while Appendix Figure 3A.3 shows the flows for the top five countries from 1996–2001.

In the case of Australia, comparable figures are not available for the 1990–95 period. Asylum-seekers were more numerous in the early 1990s than later on – probably due to arrivals from the FR Yugoslavia. Some 12,100 asylum seekers arrived in 1990 and 16,700 in 1991. The numbers dipped to 6,000–7,000 annually in the mid-1990s. Despite the recent asylum panic, the number of asylum seekers only rose to 13,100 in 2000 and 12,400 in 2001.

Western Europe

The data presented for Western Europe refer to asylum seekers making applications in the fifteen member countries of the EU in 2002, as well as Norway and Switzerland, from 1990–2001.[3] Table 3.5 presents figures on the

Table 3.5 Western Europe: top ten countries of origin of asylum seekers, 1990, 2001, 1990–2001

1990		2001		1990–2001	
Country of origin	*Asylum seekers*	*Country of origin*	*Asylum seekers*	*Country of origin*	*Asylum seekers*
Romania	62 194	Iraq	42 834	FR Yugoslavia	935 973
Turkey	48 771	Afghanistan	39 756	Romania	412 326
FR Yugoslavia	33 216	Turkey	29 458	Turkey	392 867
Lebanon	29 881	FR Yugoslavia	27 169	Iraq	272 918
Afghanistan	21 420	Russia	14 380	Afghanistan	192 581
Sri Lanka	19 279	Iran	12 802	Bosnia & Herzegovina	184 005
Iran	18 451	Somalia	11 320	Sri Lanka	169 666
Vietnam	13 466	Sri Lanka	10 858	Iran	143 651
Bulgaria	13 020	Bosnia & Herzegovina	10 623	Somalia	142 148
Somalia	12 296	Algeria	10 056	DR Congo	123 441
Total top 10	**271 994**	**Total top 10**	**209 256**	**Total top 10**	**2 969 576**
Total asylum seekers	**441 711**	**Total asylum seekers**	**402 399**	**Total asylum seekers**	**5 052 783**
Top 10 as share of total (%)	**62**	**Top 10 as share of total (%)**	**52**	**Top 10 as share of total (%)**	**59**

Source: UNHCR, Population Data Unit, PGDS/DOS, Geneva.

top ten countries of origin of asylum seekers for Western Europe. Again the figures are ranked by size for 1990, 2001 and for the aggregate of the twelve years. The top ten countries of origin for the period 1990–2001 were FR Yugoslavia, Romania, Turkey, Iraq, Afghanistan, Bosnia and Herzegovina, Sri Lanka, Iran, Somalia and the Democratic Republic of the Congo (DR Congo). The flows for the top five countries for the period are to be seen in Appendix Figure 3A.4.

The data shows the dominance of the FR Yugoslavia as a country of origin with almost 936,000 asylum seekers over the period. The two peaks of asylum seekers from the FR Yugoslavia coincide with the wars in Croatia and Bosnia in 1991–93 and the war in Kosovo in 1998–99. The next country of origin is Romania, with a total of over 400,000 concentrated overwhelmingly in the early part of the 1990s, at a time of marked persecution of Roma and other ethnic minorities. Next comes Turkey, with over 392,000 asylum seekers quite evenly distributed across the period. Most appear to be Kurds, fleeing violent conflicts involving government forces in areas of supposed support for the Kurdish separatist party, the PKK.

All the countries of origin in Figure 3A.4 show considerable fluctuations, linked to the development of internal conflicts and civil wars in the countries concerned. Together the top ten countries of origin accounted for almost 3 million asylum seekers entering Western Europe from 1990–2001. This is 59 per cent of the total number of asylum seekers in the period. Just over one-third of these asylum seekers came from three European countries: FR Yugoslavia, Romania and Bosnia and Herzegovina.

An earlier study conducted by the same authors (Castles *et al.*, 2003), shows that in some individual years during the period 1990–2000, other countries of origin also appear in the top ten: for example China, Vietnam, Algeria and Nigeria. The next ten countries of origin for this period (after those listed in Table 3.5) were Bulgaria, Pakistan, India, Nigeria, Russia, Vietnam, Algeria, China, Albania and Lebanon. Together they accounted for about 18 per cent of all asylum seekers. Of these just under a quarter were from European countries, if Russia is not included. If Russia is included, the share goes up to one-third. The top twenty countries together make up 77 per cent of all asylum seekers entering Western Europe during this eleven-year period.

There is no space for a detailed analysis of the figures for each Western European country here. In general, the top ten countries of origin for asylum seekers coming to Western Europe as a whole also usually appear in the top fifteen countries of origin for each individual country in the region. However, there are significant national variations, apparently linked to a number of factors. The first is *geographical position* (or proximity): countries towards the eastern borders of Western Europe are more likely to receive asylum seekers from Eastern Europe, such as Russians and Bulgarians in Finland and Austria. Southern European countries, such as Greece, are more likely to receive asylum seekers from South-eastern Europe (Albania, Romania) or the Middle East (Iraq, Iran). Other factors include *pre-existing links*, especially through a former colonial presence, and a *common language*. Belgium is host to many asylum seekers from the DR Congo, its former colony of the Congo; France has many asylum seekers from Mali and Mauritania.

Routes used by asylum-seekers

Increasingly in recent years, much asylum migration is conducted clandestinely, often with the assistance of smugglers. By necessity, these routes are often complex, kept as secret as possible and are ever-changing. For example, in the case of Chinese travelling to the United States, the use of air, sea and land-based forms of transport through over forty-three transit countries makes it difficult to generalize in any meaningful way about the routes used.

In 1990, most people seeking asylum in the United States, and significant numbers in Canada, were from Central America (El Salvador, Guatemala and Nicaragua) and Cuba (see Tables 3.2 and 3.3). These are all neighbouring countries from which asylum seekers could travel to the United States by land or by a relatively short sea crossing. Many Central Americans travelled up to the United States via Mexico. Although many Mexican immigrants (documented and undocumented) went to the United States, relatively few sought asylum until a few years later. By 2001, comparatively large numbers of Colombians and Mexicans were seeking asylum in the United States and Canada, also largely travelling by land. However, by this time a much larger proportion of asylum seekers to North America were coming from a greater diversity of countries and from much further afield.

While concrete evidence is often difficult to come by, most people seeking asylum in Western Europe from other European countries (such as the FR Yugoslavia, Romania, Bosnia and Herzegovina) and West Asian countries (Iraq, Iran, Afghanistan) arrive by land, often following long and sometimes indirect transit routes. For those travelling longer distances, particularly from SSA and Latin America, strong colonial links and direct flights often go hand-in-hand. Mode of transportation is often clearly influenced by economic status. The better off are more likely to fly, and to go to a country of their own choosing. The poor may be smuggled in boats and trucks, and the smugglers may strongly influence the choice of destination.

Many asylum seekers pass through other countries before arriving in Western Europe. Some of these transit countries, which are often very poor, host large refugee populations of their own. For some forty years, Tanzania has received some of the largest refugee inflows in Africa from its troubled neighbours, including at various times the Republic of South Africa, Mozambique, Malawi, Zimbabwe, Uganda, Burundi, Rwanda and the DR Congo. Today Tanzania – one of world's poorer nations – still has the largest refugee population of the continent: at least 500,000. Other important transit countries include Guinea, Kenya, Indonesia, Iran, Pakistan, Thailand and Turkey. In what are already impoverished countries, the refugees live in cramped conditions without access to legal rights and basic services, placing huge burdens upon their host states. While EU states have increasingly resisted resettling refugees from these 'safe third countries', they have also provided insufficient support to the states hosting them. This was recognized in a European Commission report in 2000 (European Parliament, 2000).

Most asylum seekers going to Australia seem to have been doing so by often-perilous voyages on fishing boats and similar craft across the Timor Sea or the Indian Ocean. The adoption of very tight monitoring and interdiction policies by the Australian authorities since 2000 seems to have considerably restricted such flows.

Causes of asylum-seeker movements to Western countries

To explain the changes in asylum migration flows for the various receiving areas, it is important to understand their causes. The following section is based on an analysis of causal factors for main source areas for the EU from 1990–2000 (Castles *et al.*, 2003). To get a full picture it would be necessary to examine causes in all significant countries of origin. However, for reasons of time and resources, our discussion focuses on just the top ten. It is our view that the diverse profiles of the top ten are reasonably representative of the sending countries as a whole; we also assume that the factors relevant for asylum migration to the EU apply reasonably well to the other destination countries. We distinguish here between 'push factors', 'pull factors' and 'intermediate factors and migration mechanisms'. This distinction is useful for a discussion of the various factors, but it is important to realize that specific migratory processes are always shaped by a combination of these factors. The main emphasis in our account is on 'push factors'.

Push factors

We identified the following as possible key push factors:

(1) Repression of minorities or ethnic conflict;
(2) Civil war;
(3) High numbers of internally displaced persons (IDPs) relative to total population;
(4) Poverty as reflected in low *per capita* income;
(5) Low position on the Human Development Index (HDI);
(6) Low life expectancy;
(7) High population density; and
(8) High adult literacy rate.

Factors (1), (2) and (3) relate directly to *persecution and conflict*. We should expect these to be significant, since flight is generally a survival strategy in the face of threats to life and personal safety. Factors (4), (5) and (6) are indicators of *underdevelopment*, and would be important if migration were mainly economically motivated. Factor (7) needs to be considered, as some analysts claim that both economic and forced migration are linked to *high population density*. Factor (8) relates to the importance of *human capital* in giving people the ability to migrate. It is obviously significant for economic migration, but should be less so for forced migration.

Factor (1): repression of minorities or ethnic conflict

There is no single statistical indicator for this type of conflict. We have used reports produced by the Immigration and Nationality Directorate of the United Kingdom's Home Office, the US Department of State, and the US Committee for Refugees. These show that issues of persecution of minorities or ethnic conflicts exist in all the top ten countries of origin. This is indeed the only common factor in all the cases. In several cases, these have taken the form of all-out internal war. In other cases, there has been persecution of ethnic or religious minorities by dominant groups, or by leaders using ethnicity as a way of consolidating their own power.

Most asylum seekers from Romania belong to the Roma (or gipsy) minority. Intense persecution of this group after the collapse of the pro-Soviet Ceaucescu regime in 1989 led to a mass exodus, mainly to Germany. The improvement of the human rights situation in the late 1990s led to reduced emigration. Many asylum seekers from Turkey, Iraq and Iran belong to the Kurdish minority, which experiences discrimination and persecution in all three countries. Violent repression of Shi'a Muslims by the Sunni Muslim ruling group is also a cause of flight from Iraq. Identifying ethnic conflict as a key factor does not imply that we see ethnicity itself as an explanation for conflict. Ethnic conflict is often a surrogate for other problems: political entrepreneurs have used ethnicity in the post-Cold War period as an effective tool of mobilization, but the underlying aims are often economic or political (Gallagher, 1997; Turton, 1997).

Factor (2): civil war

Major internal wars occurred or continued in the period 1990–2001 in the FR Yugoslavia, Afghanistan, Bosnia and Herzegovina, Iraq, Sri Lanka, Somalia and the DR Congo. Some of the conflicts were at least in part hangovers from the proxy wars of the Cold War period. The conflicts in Eastern and South-Eastern European countries were linked to problems of transition following the collapse of the Soviet bloc. Some of these conflicts have in the meantime been resolved or reduced in intensity.

In the post-Cold War period, ideological conflict has been replaced by more localized conflicts connected with identity struggles, ethnic divisions, problems of state formation and competition for economic assets. Internal wars are simultaneously transnational as they are linked to international economic and political interests, and draw in a range of international actors, both military and humanitarian. The means of warfare have also changed. The protagonists are not large standing armies but irregular forces. The aim is not control of territory, but political control of the population. Mass population expulsion is often a strategic goal, which is why the 'new wars' have led to such an upsurge in forced migration (Kaldor, 2001), 90 per cent of those killed are civilians. Both government forces and insurgents use exemplary violence including torture and sexual assault as means of control. Genocide and ethnic cleansing are systemic elements of the new form of warfare, rather than expressions of 'age-old hatreds' (Summerfield, 1999).

Factor (3): high numbers of IDPs in the country

A large population of IDPs in a country can provide a reservoir of people seeking to escape misery at home through finding asylum in industrialized countries. All the top ten source countries of asylum seekers going to the

Table 3.6   IDPs, 2000

Country of origin	Total no. of IDPs	No. of IDPs per 1,000 of population
FR Yugoslavia	480 000[a]	45
Romania	0[b]	n.a.
Turkey	400 000–1 000 000[a]	6–16
Iraq	700 000[a]	31
Afghanistan	375 000	14
Bosnia and Herzegovina	518 000	133
Sri Lanka	600 000	32
Iran	0[b]	n.a.
Somalia	300 000	32
DR Congo (Zaire)	1 800 000[a]	36

Notes: [a] These figures are rough estimates.
[b] The figure zero here does not mean that there are no IDPs at all in the country concerned, but rather that they are not present in significant numbers.
Source: US Committee on Refugees (2001), *World Refugee Survey 2001*, Washington, DC: USCR.

EU, except Romania and Iran, have substantial IDP populations. Clearly there is a link between IDPs and asylum-seeking, although an IDP population is not a root cause, but rather a symptom of conflict within a country. IDP populations alone cannot explain asylum-seeking in the EU, for there are many countries with huge IDP populations, which do not move to the EU or other industrialized countries in significant numbers (Table 3.6).

Factor (4): standard of living as shown by low per capita income

Politicians and the media often assert that many asylum seekers are in fact *economic migrants*, who misuse the asylum system to circumvent immigration restrictions. If this were the case, one might expect migrants to come primarily from poor countries with large unemployed populations. One way of testing this is to look at the GDP *per capita* of the main sending countries. The figures in Table 3.7 are based on 'purchasing power parities' (PPP) – that is, they are corrected to indicate relative living standards. Unfortunately, data is not available for all ten countries.

These figures appear to offer no support for a simple connection between low income and propensity to seek asylum in the EU. Asylum-seekers come from both middle-income countries such as Turkey and Iran, and from low-income countries such as Afghanistan, Somalia and the DR Congo. However, the figures should not be read as indicating the absence of a link between the economic situation and forced migration. Rather the link appears to be more complex. For instance, *relative deprivation* might be more relevant than absolute income levels: where income has declined or inequality

Table 3.7   GDP *per capita*, 1992, 1999

Country of origin	GDP per capita (PPP in US$)	
	1992	*1999*
FR Yugoslavia	–	–
Romania	2 840	6 041
Turkey	5 230	6 380
Iraq	3 413	–
Afghanistan	819	–
Bosnia-Herzegovina	–	–
Sri Lanka	2 850	3 279
Iran	5 420	5 531
Somalia	1 001	–
DR Congo (Zaire)	523	801

Sources: UNDP (1995, 2001).

increased due to economic problems this might lead to outmigration, even if absolute income is at relatively high levels. The figures for Romania show a strong growth in income from 1992 to 1999, which coincided with a decline in outmigration. This indicates that economic improvement may be linked to reduced forced migration.

Factor (5): low position on HDI

A more sophisticated measurement of development and social well-being is provided by the UN Development Programme's (UNDP) Human Development Index (HDI), which assigns countries a HDI value on the basis of a range of indicators including: longevity, as measured by life expectancy at birth; educational attainment; and standard of living. We have used figures for 1995, when 174 states were included in the HDI, and for 1999, when 162 states were included (UNDP, 1995, 2001) (Table 3.8).

Again, Table 3.8 shows no simple link between HDI scores and forced migration to the EU. None of the sending countries are high on the HDI, but several are at an intermediate level, notably Romania, Turkey, Iran and Sri Lanka. Somalia, Afghanistan and DR Congo are very low on the HDI. But there are many countries with low HDI scores which are not significant source countries for asylum seekers. Underdevelopment in itself does not appear to be a major 'push factor' for forced migration. Again, we would speculate that there are links, but that they are more complex in nature. It is well established in migration theory that most economic migrants do not belong to the very poorest strata in the lowest-income countries. Rather migrants tend to come from intermediate groups, who have the *economic and cultural capital* needed for mobility (Massey *et al.*, 1998; Chiswick, 2000;

Table 3.8   Human Development Index (HDI) values and rankings, 1995, 1999

Country of origin	HDI value		HDI ranking	
	1995	*1999*	*1995*	*1999*
FR Yugoslavia	–	–	–	–
Romania	0.703	0.772	98	58
Turkey	0.792	0.735	66	82
Iraq	0.617	–	106	–
Afghanistan	0.228	–	170	–
Bosnia and Herzegovina	–	–	–	–
Sri Lanka	0.704	0.735	97	81
Iran	0.770	0.714	70	90
Somalia	0.246	–	166	–
DR Congo (Zaire)	0.384	0.429	143	142

Sources: UNDP (1995, 2001).

Martin and Taylor, 2001). By contrast, refugees and IDPs often include the very poorest people from very poor countries. Such people are likely to remain in the region of displacement, as they lack the resources to move further. This explains why relatively few refugees from some of the world's largest displaced populations – such as Burundi, Sierra Leone, Sudan and Angola – have come to the EU (Schmeidl, 2001).

It is helpful to separate between why people leave their countries, and why they come to industrialized countries. Refugees and asylum seekers flee their countries of origin because of persecution or threats to their very existence. They often seek immediate protection in neighbouring countries. However, many countries of first asylum cannot offer effective protection or assistance, due to their own political and economic difficulties. The displaced people may therefore continue their flight. In this process, a certain selection takes place: those with the greatest financial resources and human capital are more likely to move onwards, and a small proportion of these will seek protection in the developed world.

Factor (6): low life expectancy

We now turn to demographic and social indicators thought by some to show possible causes of forced migration. Table 3.9 presents data for the next three indicators.

Low life expectancy can be taken as indicative of poor health conditions, poor nutrition and similar social ills. However, the figures presented in Table 3.7 show no clear pattern. Life expectancy ranges from very low in Afghanistan, Somalia and DR Congo to quite high in the FR Yugoslavia, Romania, Turkey, Bosnia-Herzegovina, Sri Lanka and Iran. High mortality

Table 3.9 Population density, illiteracy and life expectancy at birth, 1992–99

Country of origin	Population density (1999)	Adult illiteracy (% of pop.)		Life expectancy at birth	
		1992	1999	1992	1999
FR Yugoslavia	104	–	–	–	72
Romania	97	3	2	70	70
Turkey	84	19	16	67	70
Iraq	52	45	46	66	59
Afghanistan	40	71	65	44	46
Bosnia and Herzegovina	76	–	–	–	73
Sri Lanka	294	11	9	72	73
Iran	39	35	26	68	71
Somalia	15	73	–	47	48
DR Congo (Zaire)	22	26	41	52	51

Sources: UNDP (1995); World Bank (2001).
Definitions: Population density represents the total number of inhabitants per km² of the surface area. Life expectancy at birth represents the number of years a new-born infant would live if prevailing patterns of mortality at the time of birth were to stay the same throughout the child's life. Adult illiteracy represents the percentage of people aged 15 and above who cannot, with understanding, both read and write a short, simple statement on their everyday life.

and low life expectancy could obviously be a result of protracted conflict, as is probably the case in the countries mentioned, but it is interesting to see how relatively high life expectancy has been maintained in certain conflict areas.

Factor (7): high population density

The figures on population density show considerable variation, ranging from high density in Sri Lanka, through intermediate levels in most of the countries, to low density in DR Congo and Somalia. Population density in itself seems to have no explanatory value. However, it might be argued that it is not population density itself, but rather *population growth* that is important. Some analysts claim that rapid population growth is leading to resource competition, economic decline and conflict in many less developed countries (Zolberg, 2001). To test this relationship, Kritz carried out a quantitative analysis of demographic indicators in countries of origin of migrants to the United States. She found: 'no support for the claim that population growth drives United States immigration. Indeed migrants are more likely to come from countries with low to moderate population growth rates rather than ... from countries with the highest growth rates' (Kritz, 2001: 36). She also found no link between total fertility rates or population density and migration. This analysis concerns all migrants, but is likely to be valid for forced migrants, too.

Factor (8): adult illiteracy rate

A high degree of literacy might be seen as conducive to economic migration as it helps potential migrants obtain the 'cultural capital' (that is the knowledge of opportunities and mechanisms of migration) needed for mobility. It should not in principle be relevant for asylum seekers who move out of sheer necessity. The figures presented on adult illiteracy in Table 3.9 show considerable fluctuations, from very low in Sri Lanka and Romania, to very high in Iraq, Afghanistan and Somalia. However, most of the countries have reasonably high rates of literacy – defined here as illiteracy rates of less than 25 per cent of the population.

Relative importance of the push factors

Table 3.10 summarizes which push factors are present or absent in each country of origin. A number of assumptions have been made for indicators for which we have no hard data (such as GDP in the FR Yugoslavia). HDI scores are not included in this table, as they are a composite of other factors.

It is quite obvious that indicators of conflict are far more significant than indicators of development. Repression of minorities and ethnic conflicts are the only factor present in all the top ten sending countries. Civil wars are present in seven cases. A high number of IDPs is also to be found in seven cases. Low income is to be found in only half the countries, while high population density exists in only one – Sri Lanka. Low life expectancy is to be found only in three of the top ten countries of origin. The only social indicator of any real significance seems to be the relatively high literacy

Table 3.10 'Push factors' in top ten countries of origin of asylum seekers coming to EU countries, 1990–2000

Push factors	FRY	ROM	TUR	IRQ	AFG	BOS	SRL	IRA	SOM	DRC
1. Repression of minorities/ ethnic conflicts	X	X	X	X	X	X	X	X	X	X
2. Civil war	X	0	0	X	X	X	X	0	X	X
3. High no. of IDPs	X	0	0	X	X	X	X	0	X	X
4. Low *per capita* income	0	0	0	X	X	0	X	0	X	X
6. Low life expectancy	0	0	0	0	X	0	0	0	X	X
7. High population density	0	0	0	0	0	0	X	0	0	0
8. High literacy rates	X	X	X	X	0	X	X	0/X	0	0

Notes: X = significant factor; 0 = not a significant factor.
Sources: Data from Tables 3.6–3.9.

levels (over 75 per cent of the population) found in six cases, with Iran on the borderline.

A factor not addressed in this study is the importance of *gender-related* violence and persecution for forced migration. Gender-based violence plays a major part in many ethnic conflicts and internal wars. Systematic rape of women on the basis of ethnic group belonging or minority status took place in Bosnia, Rwanda and many other places in the 1990s. Domestic violence and female genital mutilation are on-going phenomena in many societies – often closely linked to underdevelopment, absence of the rule of law and deprivation of human rights. Gender-based persecution has been recognized in refugee jurisprudence as a grounds for granting asylum, usually on the basis of the 1951 Convention category of membership of a specific social group. There is a need for detailed research on the links between gender-based persecution and the other factors dealt with here.

'Pull factors'

In the context of this chapter, 'pull factors' refers to factors which influence forced migrants to seek asylum in a given country or region. Despite the fact they are fleeing violence or persecution, some asylum seekers may have a degree of control over where they go and how they travel. In general, people seek asylum in industrialized countries mainly because they hope to obtain protection and security for themselves and their families. The high level of peace and public order, democratic institutions and the rule of law constitute attractions for people who have been persecuted by their own governments or by insurgent forces. Economic factors play a part, too, even for refugees. Strong economies and developed welfare and health systems offer the chance of reasonable living standards for people originating in countries with high degrees of inequality, corrupt administrations and war-devastated economies.

These are constant factors, which make industrialized countries attractive. However, most asylum seekers come from a fairly small number of countries. Other countries, which generate large numbers of IDPs and refugees, are not the source of major flows to Western Europe, North America and Australia. Clearly there are selective factors at work. *Geographical proximity* is clearly very important: asylum seekers from Eastern and South Eastern Europe tend to go to Austria and Germany, while North Africans are more likely to go to France, Italy or Spain. Central Americans mainly go to the United States. By contrast, Canada and Australia seem to attract asylum seekers from a wide range of origins.

Past colonial links, common language and diaspora communities are very important. For instance, asylum seekers from the DR Congo tend to go to

Belgium, while Nigerians appear to favour the United Kingdom. The lack of proximity in these cases is often compensated for by direct airline connections. Another factor is past labour recruitment: for instance, the high proportion of Turks and people from FR Yugoslavia coming to Germany is linked to the 'guest worker' recruitment of the 1960s and 1970s. The presence of an existing ethnic community can thus be an important pull factor for others from the same country of origin. It is important to realize that asylum seeking is part of the dynamic social process of migration: once a migratory flow is established it tends to continue even if policies change. This does not imply that the quest for asylum is not genuine, but rather that it is part of a broader process of social transformation.

Intermediate factors and migration mechanisms

The distinction between push and pull factors is useful for descriptive purposes, but is too schematic to be maintained in an analysis of any specific migratory movement. The decision to migrate – even for purposes of seeking asylum – is the result of consideration of a wide range of factors by the potential migrants, their families and their communities (Bissell and Natsios, 2001). Typically, refugees are forced to flee by violence and persecution and have no time to plan their departure. However, as they move on from the initial place of refuge, people consider conditions and opportunities in both sending and receiving areas, as well as the costs and risks of the travel. This is why *intermediate factors* are important in deciding where forced migrants go. The presence of a pre-existing ethnic community in a potential destination was discussed above as a pull factor, but it can also be seen as the basis for a transnational migrant network – and thus as an intermediate or facilitating factor. Communication with previous migrants can be seen as a type of social capital, since it can provide the means of obtaining advice and support to enable a person to move, and of finding shelter, work and protection on arrival.

Such networks take on a more formal shape in the so-called 'migration industry'. This term embraces the many people who earn their livelihood by organizing migratory movements as travel agents, bankers, labour recruiters, brokers, interpreters and housing agents. Such people range from lawyers who give advice on immigration law, through to human smugglers who transport migrants illegally across borders. Some migration agents are themselves members of a migrant community, helping their compatriots on a voluntary or part-time basis: shopkeepers, priests, teachers and other community leaders often take on such roles. Others are unscrupulous criminals, out to exploit defenceless migrants or asylum seekers by charging them extortionate fees for non-existent jobs. Yet others are police officers or bureaucrats, making money on the side by showing people loopholes in regulations. In many cases, it is the people smugglers who decide where people will go – the migrants themselves may have little choice, and may not even know where they are going. Government attempts to crack down on illegal operators, are not likely to have much success as long as there are powerful reasons to move. Facilitating migration has become a major international business partly as a result of attempts at border control and regional restriction. By making it harder for people to move legally to meet an existing labour demand, opportunities for alternative modes of migration have been expanded (Castles and Miller, 2003: ch. 5).

Conclusions

There is nothing new about the blurring of distinctions between economic migration and refugee movements, but this asylum–migration nexus has gained added significance in the current climate of concern about the possibility of controlling cross-border flows in an epoch of globalization. Our description of asylum migration to the main industrialized receiving countries shows a high degree of fluctuation in numbers and source countries, as well as trends towards increasing diversity in areas of origin. However, there are also some constants, such as the importance of proximity, prior linkages (such as colonial presence or cultural affinities) and diasporas (or migration networks). Many of the principles of migration theory, though based on the experience of economic migration, are also relevant for analysing asylum migration.

In comparing migration asylum flows to Western Europe the United States, Canada and Australia for the period 1990–2001, we found that Western Europe is the destination of most asylum-seekers going to industrialized countries. The next most significant destination is the United States, followed by Canada and finally Australia. To a greater or lesser extent, asylum migration to Western Europe, the United States and Canada have all followed a similar pattern in annual volumes of flows during the period. This pattern involved an upsurge in total numbers in the early 1990s, followed by a levelling off and a reduction around the mid-1990s. Beginning in 1996 in Western Europe, and 1998–99 in the United States and Canada, these numbers were rising again at the decade's end.

A comparison of the numbers of asylum seekers coming to individual industrialized countries relative to the populations of these receiving countries is informative. For example, while the United States receives more asylum seekers in absolute numbers than any other country included in this study, it receives a relatively low number in proportion to its overall population.

For most countries of asylum in this study the numbers of asylum seekers from the top ten countries of origin as a proportion of the total numbers coming to these countries had reduced significantly in 2001 compared with 1990 (from 1996 to 2001 in the case of Australia). This indicates that there was an increasing diversity in countries of origin of asylum seekers during this period.

Finally, as the countries of origin in the tables indicate, asylum migrants generally came from further afield in 2001 compared with 1990. Although asylum migration from neighbouring countries, often travelling by land, remained significant for many receiving countries, it was less so in 2001 compared with 1990. There has been a trend to ever-more sophisticated and expensive ways and means of travelling from countries of origin to countries of asylum. Increasingly people have been travelling by air, using false visas and passports and using intermediaries, including people smugglers. There appears to be much more diversity and complexity in routes used, involving the use of more people to guide, transport and shelter migrants.

The policies of receiving countries, though not analysed in detail here, are important in shaping asylum migration. Attempts to control migration or to stop certain flows may have unforeseen results in changing the direction and characteristics of mobility. Migration rules should be seen not as rigid barriers but as elements in *opportunity structures* which help influence how, and where, people move.

The analysis of the causes of forced migration to the EU shows the complex relationship between push, pull and intermediate factors. The main focus was on causes in the countries of origin. We found that indicators of conflict (repression of minorities or ethnic conflict, internal wars and IDP populations) were the best predictors of outflows of forced migrants. However, to explain why most migrants remained within the region while others went to specific EU countries, it was necessary to look at pull and intermediate factors as well. In fact, the separation into these types of causal factors, although useful for analysis, cannot be sustained in practice, for every migratory movement is the result of a *dynamic interaction* between a multitude of factors. Economic and political causes form not a pair of opposites but a continuum. Similarly, the distinction between conflict and development indicators needs to be questioned, because conflicts are often the expression of failure to bring about economic and social development, to introduce democratic institutions and to safeguard human rights. Multiple causes for migratory movements and multiple motivations on the part of migrants are very frequent.

Appendix

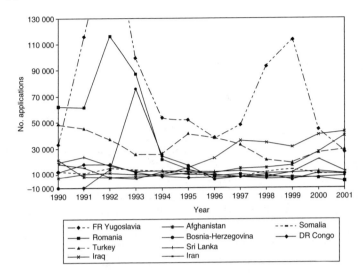

Figure 3A.1 Annual asylum applications submitted in Western European countries from ten most significant countries of origin, 1990–2001

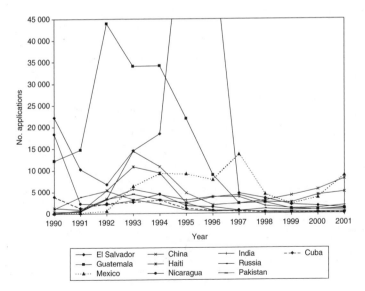

Figure 3A.2 Annual asylum applications submitted in the United States from ten most significant countries of origin, 1990–2001

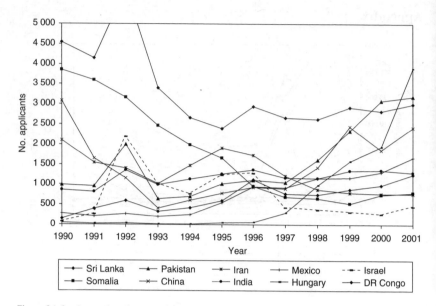

Figure 3A.3 Annual asylum applications submitted in Canada from ten most significant countries of origin, 1990–2001

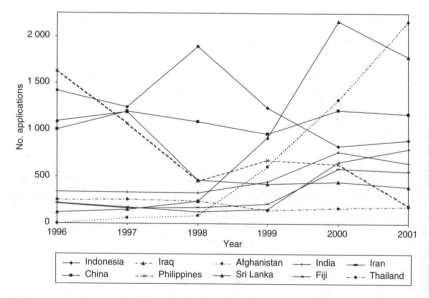

Figure 3A.4 Annual asylum applications submitted in Australia from ten most significant countries of origin, 1990–2001 (no country data, 1990–95)

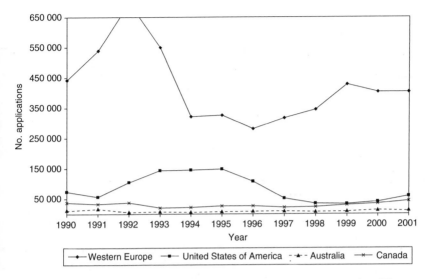

Figure 3A.5 Total annual asylum applications submitted in Australia, Western Europe, Canada and the United States, 1990–2001

Notes

* The authors would like to thank Béla Hovy, Head of UNHCR's Population Data Unit, Population and Geographic Data Section (PGDS/DOS) in Geneva for his assistance in providing much of the data in this chapter. We would also like to thank Kate Prudden of the RSC for her assistance in preparing Figures 3A.1–3A.5.
1. The broader category of 'people of concern to the UNHCR' (which includes refugees, some internally displaced persons and some returnees) peaked at 27.4 million in 1995, and was down to 21.1 million in 2000.
2. Figures for selected OECD countries, including the European Economic Area (EEA), United States, Canada, Australia and New Zealand.
3. Some of the material presented in Western Europe in this chapter is based on a study carried out by the authors together with Heaven Crawley for the Institute of Public Policy Research (London) on behalf of the European Commission. See Castles *et al.* (2003).

References

Bissell, R. E. and A. S. Natsios (2001). 'Development Assistance and International Migration', in A. R. Zolberg, and P. M. Benda (eds), *Global Migrants, Global Refugees: Problems and Solutions*, New York and Oxford: Berghahn: 297–321.

Castles, S. and M. J. Miller (2003). *The Age of Migration: International Population Movements in the Modern World*, Basingstoke: Palgrave Macmillan.

Castles, S., H. Crawley and S. Loughna (2003). *States of Conflict: Causes and Patterns of Forced Migration to the EU and Policy Responses*, London: Institute of Public Policy Research.

Castles, S. and E. Vasta (2003). 'Australia: New Conflicts Around Old Dilemmas', in W. Cornelius, P. L. Martin and J. F. Hollifield (eds), *Controlling Immigration: A Global Perspective*, Stanford, CA: Stanford University Press.

Chin, K.-L. (1999). *Smuggled Chinese: Clandestine Immigration to the United States*, Philadelphia: Temple University Press.

Chiswick, B. R. (2000). 'Are Immigrants Favorably Self-selected? An Economic Analysis', in C. B. Brettell, and J. F. Hollifield (eds), *Migration Theory: Talking Across Disciplines*, New York and London: Routledge: 61–76.

Cornelius, W. A. (2001). 'Death at the Border: Efficacy and Unintended Consequences of US Immigration Control Policy', *Population and Development Review*, 27(4): 661–85.

Crock, M. and B. Saul (2002). *Future Seekers: Refugees and the Law in Australia*, Sydney: Federation Press.

DIMIA (2002). *Immigration Update, Special Edition 2000–1*, Canberra: Department of Immigration, Multicultural and Indigenous Affairs.

European Parliament (2000). *European Commission High Level Working Group Report on Asylum Seekers and Migrants – Action Plans for Countries of Origin or Transit*, Brussels: Committee on Citizens' Freedoms and Rights, Justice and Home Affairs, 29 February, a5–0057/2000.

Gallagher, T. (1997). 'My Neighbour My Enemy: The Manipulation of Ethnic Identity and the Origins and Conduct of War in Yugoslavia', in D. Turton (ed.), *War and Ethnicity: Global Connections and Local Violence*, New York: Rochester University Press.

Kaldor, M. (2001). *New and Old Wars: Organized Violence in a Global Era*, Cambridge: Polity.

Kritz, M. M. (2001). 'Population Growth and International Migration: Is There a Link?', in A. R. Zolberg, and P. M. Benda (eds), *Global Migrants, Global Refugees: Problems and Solutions*, New York and Oxford: Berghahn: 19–41.

Kyle, D. and Z. Liang (2001). 'Migration Merchants: Human Smuggling from Ecuador and China', in V. Guiraudon, and C. Joppke (eds), *Controlling a New Migration World*, London and New York: Routledge.

Martin, P. L. and J. E. Taylor (2001). 'Managing Migration: the Role of Economic Policies', in A. R. Zolberg, and P. M. Benda (eds), *Global Migrants, Global Refugees: Problems and Solution*, New York and Oxford: Berghahn: 95–120.

Massey, D. S., J. Arango, G. Hugo, A. Kouaouci, A. Pellegrino and J. E. Taylor (1998). *Worlds in Motion, Understanding International Migration at the End of the Millennium*, Oxford: Clarendon Press.

Myers, W. H. (1997). 'Of Qinqing, Qinshu, Guanxi, and Shetuo: The Dynamic Elements of Irregular Population Movement', in P. Smith (ed.), *Human Smuggling, Chinese Migrant Trafficking and the Challenge to America's Immigration Tradition*, Washington, DC: Centre for Strategic and International Studies: 93–133.

OECD (2001). *Trends in International Migration: Annual Report 2001*, Paris: OECD.

Schmeidl, S. (2001). 'Conflict and Forced Migration: A Quantitative Review, 1964–95', in A. R. Zolberg, and P. M. Benda (eds), *Global Migrants, Global Refugees: Problems and Solutions*, New York and Oxford: Berghahn: 62–85.

Summerfield, D. (1999). 'Sociocultural Dimensions of War, Conflict and Displacement', in A. Ager (ed.), *Refugees: Perspectives on the Experience of Forced Migration*, London and New York: Pinter: 111–35.

Turton, D. (1997). 'War and Ethnicity: Global Connections and Local Violence in North East Africa and Former Yugoslavia', *Oxford Development Studies*, 25(1): 77–94.

UNDP (1995). *Human Development Report 1995*, Oxford: Oxford University Press.

UNDP (2001). *Human Development Report 2001*, Oxford: Oxford University Press.

UNHCR (1995). *The State of the World's Refugees: In Search of Solutions*, Oxford: Oxford University Press.

UNHCR (1997). *The State of the World's Refugees 1997–98: A Humanitarian Agenda*, Oxford: Oxford University Press for United Nations High Commissioner for Refugees.

UNHCR (2000a). *Global Report 2000: Achievements and Impact*, Geneva: United Nations High Commissioner for Refugees.

UNHCR (2000b). *The State of the World's Refugees: Fifty Years of Humanitarian Action*, Oxford: Oxford University Press.

UNHCR (2001). *Global Report 2000: Achievements and Impact*, UNHCR: Geneva.

USCR (2001). *World Refugee Survey 2001*, Washington, DC: US Committee for Refugees.

World Bank (2001). *World Development Report 2000/2001: Attacking Poverty*, Washington, DC: World Bank.

Zolberg, A. R. (2001). 'Introduction: Beyond the Crisis', in A. R. Zolberg, and P. M. Benda (eds), *Global Migrants, Global Refugees: Problems and Solutions*, New York and Oxford: Berghahn: 1–16.

4
Asylum Policy in the West: Past Trends, Future Possibilities*

Matthew J. Gibney and Randall Hansen

Introduction

For much of the post-war period, 'asylum' and 'immigration' were distinct concepts and processes. Throughout the West, asylum was bound up with the Cold War: 'protection' meant protection from Communism, and the terms 'refugee' and 'defector' were synonymous. When the public thought about refugees, to the extent it thought about them at all, it associated them with Hungarian freedom fighters or Soviet ballet dancers, both of whom were popular figures. As for immigration, it meant different things in different countries: in the settler societies of Canada, Australia and New Zealand, it was a permanent movement of people who sought to try their luck in the New World. In the traditional emigration countries of Europe, it referred to the putatively temporary movement of guest workers who were expected to feed the European economic machine for a few years before returning home. The important point is that, in both cases, the two movements were everywhere separate.

In the 1980s and 1990s, they have merged. This fusion is most complete in Europe, where politicians and the public speak of 'immigration' and 'asylum seeking' interchangeably. Where immigration becomes politicized and subject to far-right exploitation, as it has in Denmark, France, the Netherlands and Italy, asylum seekers are the focus of this hostility. Other contributors to this volume focus on why immigration has folded into asylum; in this chapter, we focus on how politicians have responded to this development. Our focus is on Northern countries in general – Western and Central Europe, the United States, Canada and Australasia – but we accord somewhat disproportionate attention to the countries of the EU. The justification for this focus is two-fold: first, it is in these countries that the intermingling of asylum and immigration is most complete; and, second, EU member states have gone furthest in coordinating their policies in order to restrict access to asylum.

Observers of asylum in Europe have interpreted hostility to asylum as hostility to immigration *tout court*. This represents a misunderstanding; in fact, all European countries have expanded access for primary immigrants at the same time as they have sought to reduce asylum applications. One way of interpreting this two-fold development is as an effort to sustain the distinction between the two movements while maintaining control over both: nation states, not only in Europe but particularly in Europe, are attempting to retain the capacity to limit asylum seekers' entry, and they are resisting the conclusion that asylum is a form of uncontrolled immigration. In all likelihood, they will fail. As we illustrate in the first section, EU Member States have restricted access to asylum as much as they can while still respecting the 1951 Geneva Convention and their own national constitutions. Indeed, in some instances they have violated the spirit (and, in some cases, even the letter) of both. Despite these efforts, asylum applications remain high by post-war standards, and there is no let-up in the pressures that fuel them. Indeed, North–South wealth disparities and continuing violence and instability mean that, if anything, they may increase. At the same time, legal, moral and practical restraints mean that only a fraction of asylum seekers whose applications are rejected are returned; expanded deportation for unsuccessful claimants is thus not an effective policy way of dealing with the challenges associated with making asylum regimes more effective. These two developments, combined with asylum seekers' difficulty in adapting to western labour markets and restrictions on their right to work, lead to sharply increasing costs, above all in Europe.

The result is that in most Western countries asylum applications are at levels where they generate deep political controversy and are likely to remain there; that public policy reform has generally not enabled states to reduce these numbers and is not likely to in the future; and that the costs associated with asylum rise with non-return and non-(labour market) incorporation. Moreover, even those few states that have seen rates of asylum seeking drop in recent years (such as Germany and the United States) can, we will argue, have little confidence that their success in taming asylum flows will continue. After developing these arguments, we turn in the last section to outline possible paths future asylum policy might take.

Context: the politicization of asylum

Since the 1980s, there has been a proliferation of asylum policy reforms designed to reduce, deter and rationalize asylum claims and processing. Few if any policy-makers in the 1970s would have predicted the complex battery of asylum measures, and their emergence requires explanation. The short and easy answer is numbers: as asylum applications increased in the late 1980s, and skyrocketed in the early 1990s, policy-makers sought ways to reduce them. A sharper answer requires explaining two aspects of the change: why did numbers increase so sharply, and why did states view high numbers as so undesirable? The latter is less obvious than it might seem, as Canada, the United States and Australia define themselves as countries of immigration, and Northern Europe welcomed millions of unskilled migrants in the 1950s and 1960s.

The root causes of increased asylum applications can only be examined briefly, but five developments were crucial:

- In 1967, a Protocol was added to the UN Convention on Refugees expanding the application of the Convention to refugees who emerged as a result of events occurring after 1951 and came from countries outside Europe (Suhrke, 1997: 218–19).
- The spread of film, television and telecommunications made differences in income, employment and lifestyles across countries better advertised than ever before, while cheaper transcontinental transport made mass movement possible.
- By the early 1960s, France, Germany, Switzerland, Scandinavia and the United Kingdom had all ended policies that encouraged or tolerated labour migration from Southern Europe and former colonies/the third world (Castles and Kosack, 1973; Hollifield, 1992). Around the same time, even countries of permanent settlement, such as Australia, found themselves cutting back on immigration, in part due to rising unemployment.
- From the 1960s, refugee-producing events in the South – and, after 1989, in the Balkans – escalated.
- A global industry in the smuggling and, in some cases, trafficking of people enabled asylum seekers to evade immigration control measures imposed by Western nation states.

These developments have led to a sharp rise in asylum seekers since the 1980s. Table 4.1 summarizes this movement.

Governments viewed the increased numbers flowing from these developments as undesirable for reasons bound up with domestic constitutions, legal jurisprudence and social policy. Referring to Germany, but with implications for almost all OECD states, Arthur Helton suggested that the 'dirty little secret' of asylum is that while many people apply, few are granted refugee status (Helton, 2002: 169). In Europe, only a fraction of those arriving receive refugee status; in settler societies, only a minority. Whereas Germany received 95,100 applications for asylum in 1999, only 10,940, or 8.6 per cent, were recognized as refugees in that year; in France, the figures were 30,910 applications, 4,460 or a 14 per cent recognition rate; in the United Kingdom a total of 71,100 applicants for refugee status were received in 1999, with some 6,200 or 8.7 per cent receiving refugee status. Even Canada, praised by UNHCR as an 'exemplar' in refugee recognitions, has a recognition rate of less than 50 per cent, with 13,000 grants of refugee status and 30,100

Table 4.1 Asylum seekers in select Western countries, 1985–2000 (000s)[a]

Country	1985	1986	1987	1988	1989	1990	1991	1992	1993	1994	1995	1996	1997	1998	1999	2000
Austria	6.7	8.7	11.4	15.8	21.9	22.8	27.3	16.2	4.7	5.1	5.9	7.0	6.7	13.8	20.1	18.3
Australia	–	–	–	–	–	–	–	6.1	7.2	5.1	7.6	9.8	9.3	8.2	9.5	13.1
Belgium	5.3	7.7	6.0	5.1	8.1	13.0	15.2	17.8	26.9	14.3	11.4	12.4	11.8	22.0	35.8	42.7
Canada	8.4	23.0	35.0	45.0	19.9	36.7	32.4	37.8	20.3	22.0	26.0	26.0	22.6	23.8	29.3	37.9
Denmark	8.7	9.3	2.8	4.7	4.6	5.3	4.6	13.9	14.4	6.7	5.1	5.9	5.1	5.7	7.0	12.2
Finland	–	–	–	–	0.2	2.5	2.1	3.6	2.0	0.8	0.8	0.7	1.0	0.4	3.1	3.2
France	25.8	23.4	24.8	31.6	60.0	56.0	46.5	28.9	27.6	26.0	20.2	17.2	21.0	22.4	31.0	38.6
Germany	73.9	99.7	57.4	103.1	121.0	193.0	256	438.2	322.6	127.2	127.9	116.4	151.7	98.6	95.1	78.8
Greece	1.4	4.3	6.3	9.3	6.5	4.1	2.7	2.0	0.8	1.3	1.4	1.6	4.4	3.0	1.5	3.0
Ireland	–	–	–	–	–	0.1	0.0	0.0	0.1	0.4	0.4	1.2	3.9	4.6	7.7	10.1
Italy	5.4	6.5	11.0	1.3	2.2	4.7	31.7	2.6	1.6	1.8	1.7	0.6	1.9	11.1	33.4	15.6
Luxembourg	–	–	–	–	–	0.1	0.2	0.1	0.2	0.1	0.2	0.3	0.4	1.7	2.9	0.6
Netherlands	5.7	5.9	13.5	7.5	14.0	21.2	21.6	20.3	35.4	52.5	29.3	22.9	34.4	45.2	39.3	44.0
Norway	0.9	2.7	8.6	6.6	4.4	4.0	4.6	5.2	12.9	3.4	1.5	1.8	2.3	8.4	10.2	10.1
Portugal	0.1	0.3	0.5	0.4	0.2	0.1	0.3	0.7	2.1	0.6	0.5	0.3	0.3	0.4	0.3	0.2
Spain	2.3	2.3	2.5	3.3	4.0	8.6	8.1	11.7	12.6	12.0	5.7	4.7	5.0	6.6	8.4	7.0
Sweden	14.5	14.6	18.1	19.6	32.0	29.0	27.3	84.0	37.6	18.6	9.0	5.8	9.7	12.8	11.2	16.3
Switzerland	9.7	8.6	10.9	16.7	24.4	36.0	41.6	18.0	24.7	16.1	17.0	18.0	24.0	41.3	46.0	17.6
United Kingdom	6.2	5.7	5.9	5.7	16.8	38.2	73.4	32.3	28.0	42.2	55.0	27.9	32.5	46.0	71.2	99.0
United States	–	–	–	–	–	–	–	150.1	207.5	209.6	216.2	155.3	75.7	52.1	46.0	59.3
Totals[b]	–	–	–	–	320.3	438.7	563.2	695.5	554.2	329.1	293.1	244.5	338.7	367.8	453.5	455.2

Notes: [a] Rounded figures.
[b] Totals exclude Australia and United States.
Sources: UNHCR (1995); ECRE (1998); Salt (1999); *World Refugee Survey* (1999).

applications in 1999.[1] In the United States in the same year, the recognition rate stood at 22 per cent.[2]

Another 'little secret' is that while few are granted asylum status, fewer still leave. Yearly removal rates hover at most in the 10–20 per cent range.[3] The result is a gradually expanding population of rejected asylum seekers remaining within Europe and North America. In Germany alone, Interior Minister Otto Schily told the then-British Home Secretary Jack Straw, that there were some 400,000 rejected asylum seekers in 2000 that Germany could not remove.[4] A report by the Greater London Authority (GLA) estimated that more than 75,000 people rejected for asylum or exceptional leave to remain (a non-Convention status) are residing illegally in London. The figure, moreover, rises to 100,000 if dependents are included (Wintour, 2001). Generalizations across countries are difficult to make, but in the OECD countries somewhere between 50 and 70 per cent of asylum seekers receive neither refugee nor a non-Convention status but nonetheless remain.

Removal rates are so low because of a series of moral, financial, legal and political constraints.[5] In the West, asylum seekers enter not any state, but a particular type of state: a *liberal democracy founded on a rights culture* expressing itself in two ways. First, the whole asylum system revolves around processing individual claims. Except in 'fast-track' cases, the process is time-consuming and expensive. Moreover, once the process is completed, the state must still embark on a new range of costly and difficult procedures: tracking down the individual to be deported, detaining him or her pending removal, finding (or chartering) an airline or carrier willing to remove the individual, and providing an escort to ensure the safety of the deportee – and, in some cases, other passengers. In Canada, for instance, the non-salary costs of removal fluctuated between C\$5,480,567 in 1991–92 and C\$6,205,068 in 1994–95 (Tassé, 1996). Second, and closely related, rights are linked with *residence*: the longer individuals spend on national territory, the stronger the claim they can make against removal. The process is thus self-reinforcing: the same rights culture that facilitates longer stays makes them the basis of a legitimate claim to remain. Domestic constitutions and international treaties, interpreted by national courts, sharply constrain the capacity of states to use return. Within Europe, the process is compounded by *social policy*: national legislation and judicial interpretation not only prevents the return of many rejected asylum seekers but obliges states to provide housing, medical and subsistence-level welfare support. In the United Kingdom alone, asylum seeker support in 2000 cost £835 million, or £34 per United Kingdom household (BBC, 2001). Once processing is added, the total bill is said to approach £2 billion (*Guardian*, 2002).

The flip side of asylum seekers' dependence on welfare is their *non-participation in the labour market*. In many countries, including France and (since 1997) Germany, legislation prohibits asylum seekers from seeking work. Yet, in countries like the United Kingdom where, until 2002, work was allowed after six months, there was little evidence that asylum seekers integrated into the legal market. They lack the professional accreditation, linguistic ability or occupational skills (for instance, in high-tech industries) requisite to labour market participation. In an era in which Western nations used mass, low-skilled immigration to fill positions within booming 'old economy' industries, an intermingling of the asylum and immigration queues would have posed no difficulties. Today, these jobs are either gone (the United Kingdom) or rarer and obtained only following highly competitive apprenticeship programmes (Germany). That said, there is anecdotal evidence of incorporation into the illegal labour market – as a visit to a London bar or a Berlin construction site attests – but often under precarious conditions and substandard wages.[6] If there is a labour shortage at the low end of the occupational hierarchy, politicians, especially in Northern Europe, are largely unwilling to admit it.

In short, the ending of primary immigration to Europe and the expansion of asylum numbers, when interacting with constraints on removal and (European) social policy commitments, have led asylum deep into political controversy. The symptoms are high and in some cases spiralling costs, long delays for asylum seekers and growing public opposition to asylum. As gaining access to national territory triggers the asylum process and its attendant costs and obligations, policy-makers have sought to erect barriers to this access. The restrictionist policy framework is arguably most developed in Europe, but Australia and the United States have at times been prepared to use the harshest measures.

State responses

In response to the rising numbers and changed international and domestic contexts outlined above, Western governments have introduced a range of policy measures to prevent, deter, limit the stay of and manage the settlement of asylum seekers and refugees since the mid-1980s. Though numerous and varied, the goals behind these policies are more easily summarized: preventing asylum seekers from accessing state territory; deterring potential asylum claims; limiting the amount of time asylum seekers and refugees spend in the state; and, finally, imposing order on the inward movement of refugees and, to a lesser extent, asylum seekers.

Measures to prevent access to state territory

Since the early 1990s, all Western states have embraced as a chief policy goal (arguably the chief goal) the prevention of asylum seekers' arrival at their frontiers or territory. They have done so largely to avoid incurring responsibilities under the 1951 Refugee Convention (and other domestic and international legal instruments), and by so doing to escape the expenses of asylum processing and the possibility of political backlashes caused by the arrival of large numbers of entrants.

Beginning in the early 1980s a number of traditional immigration policy measures, notably visas and carrier sanctions, were either re-tooled or initiated to prevent the arrival of asylum seekers. Notwithstanding talk of wanting simply to prevent the movement of economic migrants, all Western countries now use *visa regimes*, more or less explicitly, to prevent the movement of people from refugee source countries (such as Iraq and Afghanistan) to their territory. There are, to be sure, variations across states. Australia, for example, requires visas for all foreign nationals wishing to enter its territory; whereas Canada, the United States and EU Member States require visas only for the nationals of countries deemed to produce large numbers of asylum seekers or overstayers (for example, Morocco, Nigeria, Rwanda). Member countries of the EU have, under the Schengen agreement, harmonized visa requirements, resulting in a situation where the citizens of some 120 countries now require visas to enter EU states. While visa regimes have purposes other than stopping asylum flows, the linkage with asylum was evidenced in the imposition of visa requirements for Sri Lankans by the British government in 1986; for Algerians by the French in the same year; and for Hungarians by the Canadian government in 2001. In almost all cases, asylum seekers wishing to travel to the West have to apply for visas; in almost all cases Western states deny visas to those believed to be seeking asylum.

Carrier sanctions – the levelling of fines on sea, air and land carriers that bring foreign nationals (for example, asylum seekers) without proper documentation or visas to state territory – are now a part of the immigration control armoury of almost all states. Australia, Austria, Belgium, Canada, Denmark, France, Germany, Italy and the United States all use such sanctions, though the penalties they impose vary between approximately €100 for each individual brought to state territory (in the case of Italy) to a maximum fee of €10,000 (for complicit carriers in Germany, 1997 figures). In July 2002, the French presidency of the EU proposed a directive harmonizing carrier sanctions (NoborderZone, 2002).

Pre-inspection regimes in foreign countries to prevent unwanted arrivals are another, more innovative, example of migration policy by 'remote control'.[7] By the end of the 1990s, the United Kingdom, Canada, the United States, Sweden and France had employed an advance guard of immigration staff, commonly referred to as 'airport liaison officers', in selected foreign airports to detect potential illegal entrants. Australia, the Netherlands and Norway, on the other hand, have sent immigration officials abroad to train airline staff at foreign airports to recognize fraudulent or incomplete documentation. The United States goes one step further, posting its immigration gates abroad; travellers from Dublin, Montreal and Toronto pass through immigration control and enter the United States while physically still in Ireland or Canada.[8] The primary goal of visa regimes, carrier sanctions and pre-inspection is to prevent the arrival of unwanted and illegal entrants.

While pre-inspection regimes *extend* migration boundaries, some states have also contracted their boundaries to evade asylum claims. Switzerland, France, Germany and Spain have all declared parts of their airports *international zones*. Such zones are established to function as areas in which officials are not obliged to provide asylum seekers or foreign individuals with some or all of the protections available to those officially on state territory (for example, the right to legal representation, or access to a review process) in order to enable speedy removal from the country. In a similar vein, the United States has used Guantanamo Bay for the processing of Haitian and Cuban asylum claims in order to obviate the need to grant them the constitutional protections held by foreigners on United States sovereign territory.[9] Arguably the most radical development along these lines was the Australian government's redefinition of the status of its island territories for immigration purposes. A 2001 law 'excised' Christmas Island, Ashmore Reef, the Cocos Island and other territories from its migration zone, so that the landing of asylum seekers on these territories did not engage most of the country's protection obligations. While Australia's obligations under the 1951 Refugee Convention still applied, the more extensive protections and entitlements associated with the country's domestic asylum laws, including the right to seek review of negative decisions, were no longer available to individuals on these territories (USCR, 2002a).

Finally, states have resorted to *interdiction* to prevent asylum seekers from accessing national territory. While all interdiction aims to prevent asylum seekers from reaching the territory (or waters) of the repelling country, the implications for asylum seekers differ between cases. In some cases, asylum seekers are indiscriminately turned back to the country from which they departed; in others, some attempt is made to separate out refugees through a preliminary screening procedure, thus reducing the chances of *refoulement*. Throughout the first half of the 1990s, United States policy towards Haitian boat people moved back and forth between these two responses (Perusse, 1995). In other cases still, interdicted asylum seekers are taken to an offshore territory or to a safe third country with or without the intention of resettlement in the interdicting country if determined to be refugees. Australia used the latter response during the *Tampa* incident of 2001. The island nation of Nauru was enlisted to host asylum seekers while their eligibility for refugee status was assessed (Perusse, 1995).

All interdiction increases the risk of *refoulement*; indeed, it arguably violates any reasonable interpretation of the principle.[10] Nonetheless, interdiction appears to be becoming more acceptable. In a scene worthy of Jean Raspail's *Camp of Saints*, the United Kingdom, faced with rising numbers of asylum seekers in 2001, announced that it was considering deploying naval carriers in the Mediterranean to prevent illegal migrants from arriving in Europe

(Milne, 2002). The announcement had, to be sure, the flavour of a publicity stunt for the consumption of the highly restrictionist British electorate. But the government's willingness even to float the idea illustrates the extent to which the bounds of acceptable discourse and practice have shifted.

Measures to deter arrivals

Whereas preventative measures directly impede the entry of asylum seekers, deterrent measures operate more indirectly. They attempt to discourage asylum seekers from seeking asylum in a particular state by making the costs of entry so high (or the benefits so low) that arrival is not attempted. While analytically distinguishable, there is an obvious overlap in practice between preventative and deterrent measures because many policies that prevent entry also deter others from arriving (for example, interdiction policies increase the chance of being refused entry in a particular country and can thus act to dissuade people from seeking asylum there). The deterrent policies commonly used by states have focused on reducing the privileges and entitlements available to asylum seekers.

These policies have recently included:

- *Limitations on employment.* In order to discourage economic migrants entering via the asylum route, most Western countries restrict the right of asylum seekers to gain paid employment while their claims are processed. In France, the United Kingdom (since 2002), the United States and Germany (since May 1997), asylum seekers may not work at any time during processing. In the Netherlands and Belgium, there is a delay of twelve weeks and during initial processing, respectively. In Austria, they may work only in auxiliary services directly related to their accommodation (for example, cleaning). Canada is one of the few exceptions to this rule: an asylum claimant is eligible for a nine-month work authorization after a medical examination.
- *Limitations on welfare.* At the same time as limiting work, governments have also restricted access to state funds, ostensibly to reduce the 'pull factor' of welfare payments. Asylum seekers are typically offered welfare either at a reduced level relative to permanent residents, or under more stringent conditions (for example, the United States, France, Australia, Italy, Spain); or are, pocket money aside, eligible only to receive in-kind benefits rather than cash payments (the United Kingdom, Germany). The United Kingdom has also tried to deny welfare to individuals who do not apply for asylum immediately after arrival. In the United States, asylum seekers are expected to rely on family and charity.
- *Detention and restrictions on residency.* While newly arrived asylum seekers (like immigrants) typically desire to congregate in cities close to previous waves of their conationals and to immigrant services, recent government policies have attempted to restrict where asylum seekers reside. Asylum

seekers in EU states are usually required to live in special accommodation centres often outside major cities.[11] To prevent asylum seekers from residing in London, United Kingdom officials have made housing and welfare benefits dependent upon applicants moving to other areas of the country, including the North. As well as supposedly deterring economic migrants, restrictions on where asylum seekers live are seen as making it easier for officials to keep track of applicants and more difficult for individuals to disappear into the community. In Australia, the United States and Canada asylum seekers not in detention are more likely to have access to traditional forms of public housing and thus to greater choice in their place of residence.

All of the restrictions on work, welfare and accommodation outlined above have rationales other than deterrence. Geographical dispersal policies, for example, may spread the social cost of housing new arrivals between different communities or provinces; this is the basic practice in Germany. But over the 1990s deterring new asylum claims has increasingly come to be part of the public rationale for such restrictions. This is particularly apparent in the case of another key public policy, arguably the severest: detention.

While all of Western states detain asylum seekers for at least some reasons, the extent and length of detention varies widely. Detention is resorted to least in continental European countries (notably France, Sweden, Germany), and in Canada, where constitutional law typically limits detention to individuals who are deemed likely to abscond or whose identity has not yet been ascertained.[12] The United Kingdom government, by contrast, faces relatively few domestic legal constraints on its use of detention (an important House of Lords' judicial ruling decision overturned a lower court decision that detention for the sake of administrative convenience was unlawful) (Travis, 2002). Yet, as discussed above, practical and moral considerations, compounded by a lack of available detention places, mean that only a relatively small percentage of all asylum seekers is detained. Detention is used mostly freely in Australia and the United States. In the United States, under 1996 legislation, all asylum applicants without a right to remain on a valid visa are at a minimum detained until they can establish that they have a 'credible fear of persecution'. In Australia, all asylum seekers arriving in the country without a valid visa or other documentation are subjected to mandatory detention for the period during which their claims are processed (in some cases, over a year). The location of detention centres far from the major cities in isolated, outback areas of the country merely increases the deterrent effect of the government's policy.

Measures to limit stay

Through preventative and deterrent measures, governments have been able to avoid some of the social, economic and political costs of asylum. However, in spite of these measures, historically large numbers of asylum seekers continue to arrive in Western states claiming protection. The key policy issue involved with these arrivals over the 1990s has been how to limit the period of time they spend in the state. In particular, governments have grappled with the question of how to ensure that individuals with failed asylum claims and refugees no longer in need of protection are removed. This policy priority grows out of the recognition that the removal of unwanted foreigners becomes more difficult – legally, politically and morally – the longer that they have been resident. Moreover, the failure to remove rejected asylum applicants is widely believed not only to bring the integrity of asylum determination systems into question, but to encourage abuse of asylum systems by economic migrants (Van Kessel, 2001).

As we shall now show, policies aimed at limiting residence and hastening departures have been introduced in all aspects of the asylum process in recent years. They now run the gamut from initial admission to final removal.

- *Exclusion from the asylum process.* Western states have used a range of policy measures to exclude asylum seekers from determination procedures making them eligible for return. Most significantly, countries have invoked, with limited success, safe third country (STC) measures. The STC principle links asylum applications with first destination; asylum seekers are expected to apply in the first safe country they reach.[13] It has reached its most developed form in the Dublin Convention, signed by EU states, which came into force in 1997. Despite difficulties in facilitating return amongst Dublin signatory states, countries outside Europe have shown increasing interest in STC agreements. Since 1995, Australia has treated China as a STC for Sino-Vietnamese asylum applicants,[14] and Canada and the United States have also negotiated such an agreement (USCR, 2002b). In addition to STC agreements, states, such as the United States have limited access to asylum systems by introducing penalties on the future re-entry for asylum seekers who are found not to have a valid claim for asylum.[15] Many states, including the United States and the United Kingdom, have also legislated in recent years to exclude individuals from asylum systems on the grounds of 'non-compliance' – that is, failing to submit application forms on time or attend required hearings. This is not a minor development. In the United Kingdom in 2000, a full 27 per cent of all asylum applications were refused on the grounds of this category of technicality alone (Scottish Refugee Council website).
- *Speeding the process of determination.* In addition to reducing the number of asylum claims, Western states have also attempted to boost the judicial and administrative efficiency of asylum processing. Many asylum systems (Germany, the United Kingdom, Canada, the United States) faced large backlogs in asylum applications in the 1990s due to a combination of rising numbers of applicants and inadequate funding (see Table 4.1).

These backlogs encouraged the creation of fast-track procedures. In Canada, such procedures enable individuals from well-known countries of persecution to be quickly admitted to Refugee Convention or humanitarian status. In the United States, the post-1996 system of expedited removals ensured the immediate departure of individuals entering without proper documentation not deemed to have a 'credible fear'. In the United Kingdom and most other European countries those deemed to be from a safe country of origin have their claims determined through a pared-down asylum process. The increasing judicialization of refugee decision-making has posed another challenge for officials as appeals to the law courts invariably slow down the decision. In response, governments in Australia, the United States and the United Kingdom have engaged (with mixed results) in legislative attempts to cut off avenues for legal appeals of asylum decisions.[16]

- *Restricting grants of permanent residence.* Traditionally, Convention refugee status has been a ticket to long-term residence or even citizenship in Western states. Since the mid-1990s, however, the connection between refugee status and permanent residence has become looser. States have increasingly linked the admittance of refugees for resettlement with a requirement of return when conditions in the country of origin improve. EU member states (including Austria, Germany, the United Kingdom and the Netherlands) have used various forms of temporary protection during the conflicts in the former Yugoslavia and/or Kosovo. Outside Europe, Canada and the United States were more reluctant to use the status, though Australia took Kosovan refugees on a temporary basis. Refugees admitted under temporary schemes have usually received new and often ad hoc forms of status rather than Geneva Convention protection. The end of temporary protection regimes has proven a controversial business, especially when refugees have been reluctant to return. In response, states have devised a number of supplementary policy measures: 'look and see' visits (the United Kingdom, Germany, Nordic states), start-up payments upon return (the United Kingdom, Germany, Nordic countries), and, more punitively, the withdrawal of welfare assistance (Germany) and the threat of removal to new locations (Australia) have all been used to boost the likelihood of departure.[17] Temporary protection is not new (the United States employed temporary schemes for Central American refugees in the 1980s and 1990s).[18] However, the spread of such schemes during the 1990s and the (albeit gradual) emergence of an EU legal infrastructure for temporary protection are novel. Moreover, the uses of temporary protection appear to be changing. The Australian government has used it in a punitive fashion to discourage asylum seekers. According to 1999 legislation, 'unauthorized' arrivals later determined to be refugees may not be granted permanent residence visas. They are eligible only for temporary protection visas, a status that denies them family reunion rights and the ability freely to travel overseas, as well as security of status.[19]

- *Removals and deportations.* Despite the moral, practical and financial constraints on deportation, states have adopted a range of measures designed to encourage departure. The United States, for example, expanded use of detention in a 1996 Act, thus expediting the process of return for failed applicants; Canada has increased its technological resources for tracking the status of asylum seekers to coordinate swift return after unsuccessful asylum decisions; 2003 legislation in Britain aims to create a more 'holistic' asylum process that will ensure that asylum seekers are kept under the eye of the state from initial entry to final departure; finally, Germany, along with many other countries, has, since the early 1990s, entered into a range of aid, trade and immigration bargaining with asylum source countries to ensure the readmission of rejected asylum applicants and undocumented migrants.[20] Notwithstanding these initiatives, human rights and practical constraints seem likely to ensure that the gap between those eligible for deportation and those actually removed remains a feature of Western asylum systems for some time to come.

Measures to manage arrival

Beyond prevention and deterrence, Western states have engaged in a range of somewhat more positive ways to make the arrival of asylum seekers more orderly and equitable. Reform of refugee decision-making and the use of resettlement programmes have been two such areas.

Refugee decision-making

In the midst of constructing measures to limit asylum seeker numbers during the 1980s and 1990s, many states put more thought, energy and resources into refugee determination procedures, resulting in general to improvements in the quality and professionalism with which asylum decisions are made. This has been clear, for example, in Canada, where a highly regarded body, independent of the immigration department, the Immigration and Refugee Board, has been established to make decisions on refugee status. In the United States, a professional corps of asylum decision-makers was created at the beginning of the 1990s, thus enabling the disentanglement of determination decisions from foreign policy and immigration enforcement pressures (Joppke, 1999: 119; Martin and Schoenholtz, 2000). It is perhaps no coincidence that both the United States and Canada have some of the highest rates of grants of refugee status of any Western countries. Over the last decade, a range of countries, including Canada, Australia and the United States have also radically improved the quality of country of origin information used in making asylum decisions, enabling greater accuracy in the assessment of claims (Martin and Schoenholtz, 2000).

Resettlement programmes

During the period of rising asylum numbers in the 1990s, traditional immigration countries, such as Australia, the United States and Canada, operated annual resettlement programmes for refugees. These programmes, which have served as a kind of adjunct to skilled migration schemes, have allowed pre-screened refugees from first countries of asylum to enter for resettlement. Well over 1 million refugees (and people in humanitarian need) entered under these schemes during the 1990s.

By contrast, EU states, such as Germany, the Netherlands and the United Kingdom, have traditionally provided (both permanent and temporary) resettlement places on an *ad hoc* basis in response to specific refugee crises. Nonetheless, in 2002 the United Kingdom government announced its intention to follow the lead of countries like Australia and the United States and implement an annual resettlement scheme (beginning with a modest annual intake of 500) ostensibly in order to allow legitimate refugees a legal way of reaching Britain; other Northern European countries are already operating similar schemes. While these schemes may represent a positive development, a range of concerns remain. Some worry that resettlement will be offered as an alternative to protection for asylum seekers; that governments will choose for entry only refugees with desired labour market or language skills; and that the provision of new places for pre-screened refugees will legitimate even harsher preventative practices towards claimants at the frontiers. Linkages of this sort are hardly beyond the realms of possibility. The practice of the Australian government has been to reduce the number of refugees it settles annually by the number of onshore asylum applicants the country receives in order to balance its overall refugee intake.[21]

While new unilateral measures in the area of resettlement are beginning to emerge, *burden (or responsibility) sharing* remains, despite many EU-level proposals, relatively undeveloped. In the 1990s, Germany was a strong supporter of responsibility sharing, while France and especially the United Kingdom were generally hostile (Thielemann, 2002). Unsurprisingly, when asylum applications to the United Kingdom trebled in the late 1990s, its policy-makers began to see the benefits of cooperating with other EU countries. The various proposals for burden sharing slot into one of two broad schemes: financially compensating Member States receiving disproportionate numbers or devising formulas for fairly distributing refugees between states in situation of mass influx, such as Kosovo. The most promising is clearly a system of financial recompense. Indeed in the late 1990s, the EU established the European Refugee Fund (ERF) to create a financial pool (so far a fairly paltry one) to 'create an equitable mechanism for sharing financial responsibility for supporting refugees between Member states' (ECRE, 2001: 12). Agreeing to share actual refugees between states has proven more difficult.

The kind of solidarity among member states that would enable them to transcend a cost-benefit analysis (CBA) of their interest in specific refugee situations has thus far been lacking.[22]

In summary, the responses put in place by states are remarkable both for the vast array of different policy measures involved and for the speed of their development. Policy measures that touch upon all aspects of the asylum seeking (and migration) processes have been assembled by states in little over a decade. The story is one of *learning and convergence*: while there is no doubt that some states operate stricter measures than others, the main elements of state policies (visa regimes, carrier sanctions, STC agreements, fast-tracking schemes, readmission arrangements, etc.) are essentially very similar. It is also one in which the harshest policy developments towards asylum seekers – those that come closest to violating the 1951 Convention or international human rights obligations – have been pioneered by traditional immigration countries, notably the United States and Australia.[23] A history of receptiveness and experience with economic migration in no way guarantees that a welcome will be extended to asylum seekers. Finally, while the bulk of restrictive policy measures developed have been legitimated publicly by the desire to disentangle mixed flows (by the aim to preserve asylum for 'real' refugees), most policy measures are completely indiscriminate in their effects. That is, they are as likely to prevent, deter or punish the entry of legitimate refugees as economic migrants. Equally however, such measures are likely to remain, and in the next section we offer an evaluation of their effects.

Effects

To what extent has the raft of policy measures implemented to deal with rising numbers of asylum seekers been effective? The question of whether particular policies are effective cannot be disentangled from the question of *whom* they are effective for. There are at least three different perspectives: those of Western governments, those of people in need of protection, and those of the international community. Each reflects a different interest in relation to asylum and, consequently, generates a different standard for evaluating current practices. In what follows, we will briefly outline these different perspectives and consider, in broad terms, the extent to which the current amalgam of policies can be considered effective.

The Western government perspective

What have governments been trying to achieve through the array of public policy measures they have implemented since the 1980s? While there are difficulties in generalizing across states and in seeking too much coherence in their purposes, Western governments appear to have been struggling to put in place systems that achieve the following goal: *a manageable flow of asylum seekers and refugees that is stable in that it does not fluctuate dramatically upwards over time.*

Two points are worth clarifying. First, the requirement of a *manageable flow* assumes that states do have reasons for accepting refugees and asylum seekers. These reasons emerge from the desire of states to be seen domestically and internationally as respectful of humanitarian goals, given the requirements of inherited legal commitments (notably, the 1951 Refugee Convention) and, in some cases, pressure by internal interest groups, both economic and ethnic, and external actors, such as other states. The intepretation of a manageable flow will vary, in numerical terms, between states depending on their size, migration history, integrative capability, etc.: a manageable flow for Ireland is going to be different than one for the United States. Second, the requirement of *stability* (that is, that entrants not rise dramatically over time) stems from the desire by governments to be seen as in control of the inward movement of foreigners. Large short- or long-term rises in asylum seeker arrivals are viewed as politically intolerable.[24] In sum, Western states have attempted to purge asylum seeker movements of their unruly and unpredictable characteristics. The aim of policy-making has generally been to impose on asylum movements the kind of predictability and manageability associated with quota-based refugee resettlement schemes.

If the combination of manageability and stability is an accurate way of describing government aspirations, then very few Western states could, by 2001, be said to be operating effective asylum policies. Taking the criterion of stability, only in five out of twenty-one countries (Australia, Canada, Germany, the Netherlands and Spain) was the difference between the highest annual intake of asylum seekers and the lowest annual intake between 1995 and 2000 less than 100 per cent. Indeed, in eleven countries it was greater than 200 per cent. In terms of overall trends, only three Western states (Germany, Portugal and the United States) received fewer asylum applications in the three years between 1998 and 2000 than in the years between 1995 and 1997. Two other countries (Australia and Spain) experienced only a small increase. In the rest, the volume of asylum seekers rose substantially and often dramatically. While Portugal and Spain have rarely experienced substantial asylum flows, all the other states with falling (or fairly stagnant) numbers were at the forefront of restrictive measures over the 1990s. Germany pioneered 'STC procedures' and readmission agreements in an attempt to insulate itself from asylum claims; Australia and the United States have both used interdiction and tough detention policies.[25]

According to these criteria, we have a complicated story: only a small number of states appear to have asylum application volumes that have not fluctuated dramatically in recent years; fewer still appear to have applications on a downward trend.[26] The ineffectiveness of the policy responses of most states is reflected in widespread public dissatisfaction. The success of the far right in elections in Austria, Denmark and the Netherlands (joining the governing coalition in all three), and the success of Jean Marie Le Pen in France (which was stunning from a political point of view, less so from a psephological one) all came on the back of anti-immigrant sentiment. The Howard government in Australia snatched electoral victory from the jaws of defeat by playing up public concerns over boat people claiming asylum. Finally, much is beyond the control of national policy. The United States and Germany, the United Kingdom and most other Western states have substantial levels of illegal migration that do not enter into asylum statistics. It is possible that tough asylum policies have deflected potential asylum seekers into a life underground. It is also impossible to know whether low asylum applications in a country reflect the success of its policy or its relative unattractiveness to other asylum seekers *vis-à-vis* other destinations. The case of the United Kingdom, which in the late 1990s could have been described as operating successful policies, suggests that harsh policy measures deter only while other countries operate more inclusive measures (Hansen, 2002). If all states scramble to implement tough policies, any relative advantage in avoiding asylum seekers accruing to restrictive states is lost.

The perspective of those seeking protection

How might those in need of protection judge the effectiveness of recent asylum policies? It seems reasonable to assume that refugees would do so on the basis of whether the policies respected the basic human rights of asylum seekers and increased the likelihood that those in need of protection would receive it.

The interests of those in need of protection yield straightforward standards for assessing recent policy developments. First, do they make it easier or harder for refugees to gain the protection of asylum? Over a five-year period, the number of refugees (as determined by the UNHCR) has fallen, as has the number of asylum applications across Western states. Importantly, however, the fall in the proportion gaining access to Western asylum systems has outstripped the decrease in the volume of the world's refugees. In 1995, there were 14.5 million refugees, and 695,500 asylum applications in Europe; in 2000, the figures were 12 million (a 17 per cent drop) and 455,000 (a 25 per cent drop).[27] While this does not prove that asylum is becoming more difficult for refugees to access, it makes such a claim highly plausible, particularly given that restrictive measures have fallen indiscriminately on genuine refugees as well as economic migrants.

Second, do recent policy measures respect the human rights of asylum seekers? The position of asylum seekers has unquestionably deteriorated as a result of recent policies. First, the proliferation of preventative measures has driven asylum seekers into taking greater and greater risks (being sealed in lorries, jumping moving trains and so on) to enter Western states. The increasing sophistication of barriers to entry has also meant that many asylum seekers must rely on traffickers to enter, a reliance that can lead to enslavement in an immigration underworld (Gibney, 2000b). Second, deterrence measures used by states increasingly undermine the rights of asylum seekers (to work, to live where they choose, to welfare, to freedom, etc.) in order to deter the arrival of others. Not only are these deprivations ethically dubious in themselves, but by reducing the gap between the rights the state offers and the relative freedom of living outside the law as an illegal, they may, as we have noted, encourage legitimate refugees to abandon the asylum system altogether (Gibney, 2000b; Morrison and Crosland, 2001). In sum, there is a strong, if not overwhelming, case that policy changes in the West have harmed the interests of refugees; for scholars working in the area, this conclusion will come as no surprise.

The perspective of international society

The perspective of international society refers to something more nebulous than the other perspectives we have discussed. Here we mean to denote a long-term or enlightened interest that all states (Western and non-Western) have in ensuring the survival of the institution of asylum. Asylum is both valuable in itself and linked to other common interests, such as humane governance, solidarity between states and international stability. While it may be in the short-term interests of Western governments to reduce the number of asylum seekers they receive, their actions can have hidden costs both for other actors and, in the long term, for themselves. For example, policies that deflect or contain refugees can generate regional instability or corrode international norms on refugee protection by creating great inequalities in the burdens between states.

Considered from this perspective, recent policies enacted by Western governments certainly fall short of being effective. Given that such policies are not aimed at maximizing protection, this conclusion is unremarkable. The bulk of energy has gone into implementing practices that deter and prevent movement with little regard for the stability of the states or regions that asylum seekers attempt to move from. A number of observers have pointed out that Western policies effectively contain refugees in the southern hemisphere, and to the poorest countries therein; see, for example, Chimni (1998) and Helton (2002). Furthermore, many recent Western practices come close to corroding fundamental refugee norms, notably the principle of *non-refoulement*. The practice of interdiction is the clearest example, but the general movement to shift border control measures outwards is, at its worse, an attempt by Western states to escape 1951 Convention responsibilities at the expense of other states.[28] Even when their actions do not undermine the *non-refoulement* norm directly, the employment of non-arrival measures by Western states has served to underwrite the increasing reluctance of countries in the South to take in or to continue to host refugees (Loescher, 1993). Finally, when they are successful, current policies aimed at deterrence and prevention discourage cooperation by states to deal with the long-term economic and political causes of refugee and asylum seeker movements. Those states that manage to escape large refugee flows are sapped of any motivation to ameliorate the factors that give rise to refugees.

These deterrent and preventative policies do not, however, simply find their motivation in state malice and ill will. The public, particularly in Europe but also in Canada and Australia, is suspicious of current levels of asylum seekers. That suspicion turns to hostility when numbers suddenly increase or arrivals generate media attention, as they did in Germany in 1992, the United Kingdom in 2000 and Australia in 2001. In all cases, the convergence of a series of factors places liberal democratic governments in an acute dilemma. Long first-determination processing times (ranging from several months to several years) and appeal rights mean that even 'illegitimate' asylum seekers may remain for several years once they have reached national territory. Costs associated with asylum seekers – for housing, medical care, subsistence and legal costs – are high, and they are compounded by asylum seekers' exclusion from the labour market and/or their poor performance within it. Finally, limits on deportation mean that, despite low recognition rates, the entry of asylum seekers correlates highly with the likelihood of their stay. In short, governments have turned to exclusionary measures in part because of the liberal and inclusionary nature of the liberal democratic polity itself. The relative liberality with which asylum seekers are treated once they reach the soil of Western states is closely related to the complex of exclusions designed by states to keep them from doing so.[29] With this basic dilemma in mind, we turn in the next section to possible future directions for asylum policy in the West. Of the four proposals, the first is most consistent with the current asylum regime; the last three would involve departures, possibly substantial ones, from it.[30] Space limitations present a full treatment of this suggestion; we outline it in the spirit of a thought-piece rather than a comprehensive programme.

Future directions

Expanded immigration

One possible way of relieving pressure on asylum systems, often proposed by activists and scholars, is expanding possibilities for *legal immigration*. Doing so would seem to have the great advantage of calling states' bluff. The claim that large numbers of asylum seekers are 'bogus' economic migrants is made frequently; if there were any truth in the claim, expanding economic migration would take pressure off asylum queues. If there were little in the claim, then allowing new forms of legal migration would have no effect on asylum applications, exposing states' arguments as untenable. In practice, the matter is unlikely to be that simple. Western states face two sorts of labour shortages: an avowed high-skilled shortage, particularly in high-tech industries, and a concealed, low-skilled shortage for precarious, badly paid and unappealing jobs. An expansion of high-skilled migration is occurring in Europe: in the last decade, Germany and the United Kingdom have expanded opportunities for high-skilled immigration, and there is pressure for France to follow suit. In these countries, illegal migrants, some of whom are undoubtedly asylum seekers, now fill low-skill shortages. In Southern Europe, Spain and Italy have gone a step further, regularizing low-skilled migrant labour in 1993 and 1998.[31] As yet, these changes have had little impact on movements of asylum seekers. In Northern Europe, those gaining access to the high-skilled labour market are highly educated individuals in either professional employment or education in their countries of origin; they are often selected directly by the companies themselves. In Southern Europe, the numbers accepted – some 30,000 in Spain – are too low to have any broader impact on asylum flows to Europe. It is true that asylum applications to Spain and Italy are modest, possibly suggesting some local effect. Yet, it might also be the case that asylum seekers and traffickers view these countries as transit countries on the way to Northern Europe.

In short, expanding immigration categories might have some influence on asylum applications, but it is by no means certain and would require an ambitious programme for accepting large numbers of low-skilled migrants. There is little evidence to suggest that European publics would support such a move – and, even if an enlightened elite led them, trade unions would offer stiff resistance to low pay and poor working conditions. Such a programme might also have to be linked with limitations on access to welfare if such benefits were greater than the market wage.

Expanded resettlement

A second way of ensuring a future for asylum in the West would be through a greater focus by these countries on the *resettlement of refugees*. Resettlement, once a major tool of asylum policy in the West, has declined in a more or less direct relationship with increases in asylum applications over the 1990s. In 2001, only five EU countries (Sweden, Ireland, Finland, Denmark and the Netherlands) took part in the UNHCR refugee resettlement programme with a miserly quota of 2,652 refugees between them. Canada alone accepted three times as many – 7,500 in 2000 – and the United States set a 2001 quota for the resettlement of 80,000 refugees.[32] The United Kingdom, in an effort to compensate for its restrictive attitude to refugees over the 1990s, offered to resettle a risible 500.

The current unpopularity of resettlement belies the fact that it could be a useful tool for managing asylum pressures. Resettlement programmes enable states to admit refugees in a way likely to minimize political controversy. By enabling the number of refugees arriving in any particular year to be publicly determined and announced in advance, present public concerns that the arrival of asylum seekers reflects policy failure on the part of governments could be defused. The benefits for advancing refugee protection are obvious. By opening up new avenues for asylum in Western states, resettlement programmes could be used to discourage refugees from using irregular (and often expensive and highly dangerous) routes to gain the protection they need. The effects on asylum pressures would, moreover, grow in proportion to the number of states that agreed to operate such programmes or to increases in the number of people coming under current ones. A new and concerted commitment to resettlement might also strengthen the institution of asylum internationally. While the deterrent and preventative practices of Western countries are currently eroding the traditional willingness of Southern countries to accept refugees, greater use of resettlement in the West might well encourage a renewed faith in the institution of asylum and a greater willingness to host refugees.

Important challenges would, of course, still remain. A greater number of refugees accepted through resettlement schemes might reduce flows of refugees arriving 'spontaneously' in Western states, but it would not reduce such arrivals entirely, nor affect the volume of economic migrants. Moreover, for resettlement to have any real affect on asylum pressures, it would need to be embraced by a substantial number of states. Yet states have proven themselves notoriously reluctant to embark upon cooperative schemes in the refugee realm when the possibilities of 'free riding' (opting out of providing asylum in the knowledge that other countries would continue to take their fair share of refugees) would be high. Some kind of international legal agreement, such as an additional protocol to the 1951 Refugee Convention, which could enshrine the resettlement obligation of states in law might be necessary in order to encourage compliance.

Asylum without welfare: a market-based approach

Another way in which asylum might be reformed would involve leaving the processing machinery untouched and instead reforming the social policies accompanying it. This would involve the radical step of ending the incorporation of asylum seekers into the welfare state; such a reform would have its greatest application in Europe. Asylum seekers would be processed as they currently are, but they would not be entitled to income support and housing benefits (they would retain access to health care and education). If granted refugee status, the right to such support would then follow. While their claims were being processed, asylum seekers would be entitled to work. It would be delusional to claim that such a radical step would not lead to considerable misery for asylum seekers, and perhaps discomfort in the form of crime and street violence for Europeans. But it would have the great advantage of undercutting one far-right argument against asylum seekers, and it would definitively resolve the debate about whether asylum seekers are fleeing violence or simply seeking social support. It would in effect involve accepting that asylum and migration are not distinct movements, and allowing the market to determine asylum movements.

Such a step is emphatically not a turn to open borders. Western states would continue to control their borders and, at least in the short term, to maintain the panoply of restrictive measures currently in place. If asylum seekers were able to integrate into labour markets with relative ease and/or if numbers of asylum seekers fell to a more manageable rate, states could then look to dismantling these measures – with relative security from populist backlash. The asylum procedure system itself would be maintained, but efforts should be concentrated on speeding application decisions, as it would generally be accepted that the difference between recognition and rejection is one between residence with or without social rights, and not between residence and return. After a determined period of time, asylum seekers who remained in the Western states could be granted full social entitlements. Welfare incorporation would follow labour market incorporation rather than preceding it.

Expanded possibilities for return

A fourth possibility faces serious political constraints and is morally dubious, but it deserves mention if only for analytical purposes. If nation states' desire to restrict access flows from limits on removal, it follows that policy-makers and the public might be more willing to tolerate large numbers of asylum seekers if they could be confident that there would be a clearer relationship between rejection and return. Even if expanded return were morally acceptable, it would be difficult to implement in practice, as it would require much shorter processing times, further limits on rights to appeal and resort to mass deportations, probably with military carriers. It is hard to imagine such a regime being consistent with either national jurisprudence or liberal-democratic norms. It would require moving the entire asylum system away from its individualist and legalist foundation to a much more utilitarian one. There would be many more false negatives (that is, genuine refugees would be denied protection) that would have to be set against greater ease of access to national territories for the thousands, if not hundreds of thousands, of legitimate asylum seekers who have no hope of reaching Western soil. The fact that it is so difficult to imagine the implementation of such a regime is partly a reflection of how alien it is to our principles, and partly a reflection of the basic dilemma that renders the current asylum crisis so difficult to resolve: the battery of exclusionary measures adopted by Western states are closely related to the asylum standards the West seeks to maintain.

There is, in the end, a final alternative, namely the status quo. However inadequate in the face of raw state power, there are national and international constraints on restrictive asylum legislation. Despite the battery of measures instituted, states have little choice but to process and accept the majority of asylum seekers reaching their shores, with the aid of the idealistic and the unscrupulous. Perhaps the Geneva Convention is preferable to any conceivable alternative; if it is, however, it is not because its original provisions and intent are being respected. Reinforcing the status quo requires acceptance of situation in which many of the most deserving will never reach Western shores; in which the use of traffickers be widespread and increasing and in which the distinction between migrant and refugee – in some sense the whole point of the Convention – becomes even more attenuated. This is hardly a glowing endorsement, but it is perhaps a sufficient one. In making it, however, we should not delude ourselves into thinking that the asylum crisis can be solved through tinkering. Only dramatic developments – an unlikely resolution of the economic equality, political instability and violence that leads to asylum movements – or drastic changes – a major overhaul of the current asylum system – would move us beyond the impasse.

Notes

* A first draft of this chapter was presented at the WIDER International Conference on 'Poverty, International Migration and Asylum', Helsinki, 27–28 September 2002. We owe our thanks to George Borjas, Jeff Crisp and Janis Vehmaan-Kreula for organizing the conference, and to Susan Martin, Timothy Hatton and the other participants for comments.
1. The figures are from UNHCR (2000: 321–4).
2. In most Western countries, the number actually given a right to stay is boosted significantly by grants of humanitarian status.
3. At most because statistics on removal include cases in addition to asylum seekers and because in some countries, such as Germany, they include airport turnarounds.
4. Confidential source.
5. For a discussion of these, see Gibney and Hansen (2003).
6. On illegal migrants in Berlin's construction industry, see Hadji-Ristic (n.d.).
7. We borrow this term from Aristide Zolberg.
8. US officials, it is important to note, have sometimes tended to justify the use of pre-inspection as a way of easing the movement of people from favoured countries (for example, Ireland and Canada) rather than as a way of boosting control *per se.*
9. In 1994, the Eleventh Circuit Court of Appeals determined that these aliens 'had no legal rights under the domestic law of the US or under international law' because such rights were available only to persons on US territory. The court found that Guantanamo Bay, while under US 'jurisdiction and control', was not US sovereign territory. See Jones (1995).
10. The US Supreme Court has demurred, however. In *Sale* v. *Haitian Centers Council (1994)* it ruled eight to one in 1994 that interdicting Haitian boats before they reached US territorial waters and returning the occupants to Haiti, without assessment of their asylum claim, was not a violation of domestic US or international law.
11. The United Kingdom is one country where this has traditionally not been true. However, plans outlined in the government's White Paper on asylum and immigration

(Home Office 2002), and included in legislation, foreshadow a move to establish new accommodation centers to house asylum seekers.

12. In Sweden, for example, 'illegal migrants', applying for asylum, may be held in detention only until their identity has been established. This process takes around two weeks to two months (*Migration News*, 2001).

13. In addition, the Dublin Convention adds further criteria: family members and past receipt of a visa.

14. http://www.immi.gov.au/facts/74unauthorised.htm.

15. 1996 legislation in the United States makes an alien found to have filed a 'frivolous application' permanently ineligible for any immigration benefits.

16. US legislation in 1996 limited judicial review on a range of decisions to lift bans on an individual's ability to apply for asylum (for example, for reasons of changed circumstances in an asylum seeker's country of origin). Successive Australian governments have legislated to limit the powers of the judiciary in asylum matters. 1992 legislation, for example, said that the courts were not to release asylum seekers detained for arriving without valid visas. (See USCR, 2002c). The hostility of the current Howard government is, if anything, stronger, see the *Sydney Morning Herald* (2002). The former British Home Secretary, David Blunkett, has also been publicly critical of judicial decisions that threaten the government's liberty to make policy in the area of asylum. (See *Guardian*, 2003).

17. For a broader discussion of the practice of and the issues raised by Temporary Protection, see Gibney (2000a). On the methods used by the Australian government in relation to the Kosovans, see USCR (2000).

18. Although the concept is understood differently in the United States: it is granted only to individuals already in the United States when home circumstances change.

19. The scope of those to whom these restrictions applied was increased further and made more punitive by legislation in 2001. For more details, see USCR (2000).

20. See Lavenex (1999). For a fuller discussion of removals and deportation, see Gibney and Hansen (2003).

21. USCR (2002c: 6). The Howard government has pursued this practice with alacrity, but the practice of linking the two has its roots in the 1980s.

22. For a helpful analysis of some of the difficulties facing attempts by EU states to burden share, see Thielemann (2003).

23. Some argue that the drop in asylum applications in the US, following 1990 and 1995 policy changes, reflects not the deterrence of genuine asylum seekers but rather the weeding out of ill-founded applicants. See Martin (2003).

24. This aspect of the politics of asylum is discussed in greater depth in Gibney (2003).

25. The statistical conclusions reached in this paragraph are based on the statistics in Table 4.1. On Australia, see Chapter 17 (in this volume).

26. In contrast to most other countries, the United States has seen a large fluctuation in asylum numbers because it managed to reduce its asylum numbers so dramatically in the final years of the 1990s.

27. Statistics taken from http://www.proasyl.de/g-world1.htm and http://www.unhcr.org/ (accessed 1 September 2002).

28. See Gibney (2003).

29. We develop this idea in greater detail in Gibney and Hansen (2003).

30. In the suggestions for future directions that follow we do not discuss solutions that address the causes of forced and voluntary migration movements, not least because we focus here on more short-term policy responses. None the

less, it is important to note that policy interventions by Western states in the areas of trade, international development and debt relief to boost the economic prosperity and security of poorer states could help alleviate current migration pressures.

31. For a more detailed discussion, see Favell and Hansen (2002).
32. http://www.ecre.org/factfile/realfacts.shtml#origin (accessed 14 August 2002).

References

BBC (2001). 'Councils "Overspend on Asylum Seekers"', 5 April, http://news.bbc.co.uk/1/hi/uk_politics/1261116.stm (accessed 13 August 2002).
Castles, S. and G. Kosack (1973). *Immigrant Workers and Class Structure in Western Europe*, Oxford: Oxford University Press.
Chimni, B. S. (1998). 'The Geopolitics of Refugee Studies: A View From the South', *Journal of Refugee Studies*, 11(4): 350–74.
ECRE (1998). Country Reports websites: http://www.unhcr.ch/statist/99profiles/can.pdf, http://www.unhcr.ch/statist/rsd220601.pdf, '2000 Global Refugee Trends. Analysis of the 2000 Provisional UNHCR Population Statistics, May 2000': http://www.unhcr.ch/statist/2000provisional/trends.pdf (accessed 19 September 2001).
ECRE (2001). *The Promise of Protection: Progress Towards a European Asylum Policy Since the Tampere Summit 1999*, November.
Favell, A. and R. Hansen (2002). 'Markets Against Politics: Migration, EU Enlargement and the Idea of Europe', *Journal of Ethnic and Migration Studies*, 28(4): 581–601.
Gibney, M. J. (2000a). 'Between Control and Humanitarianism: Temporary Protection in Contemporary Europe', *Georgetown Immigration Law Journal*, 14(2) 2: 689–709.
Gibney, M. J. (2000b). 'Outside the Protection of the Law: Irregular Migration in Europe', *Refugee Studies Centre Working Paper*, No. 6, University of Oxford, December.
Gibney, M. J. (2003). 'The State of Asylum: Democratization, Judicialization and the Evolution of Refugee Policy', in S. Kneebone, (ed.), *The Refugees Convention 50 Years On: Globalisation and International Law*, Aldershot: Ashgate.
Gibney, M. J. and R. Hansen (2003). 'Deportation and the Liberal State', *UNHCR New Issues in Refugee Research Working Paper*, No. 77, Geneva, February.
Guardian (2002). 'Blunkett Concedes Asylum Overspend Could Top £1bn'. 3 June. http://society.guardian.co.uk/asylumseekers/story/0,7991,727599,00.html (accessed 13 August 2002).
Guardian (2003). 'Blunkett Hits Out at Power of Courts', 21 February, http://politics.guardian.co.uk/Print/0,3858,4610781,00.html (accessed 13 August 2002).
Hadji-Ristic, P. (n.d.). 'Migrant Labour Exploited, but Helps Build Economy', Gemini News, London, http://www.oneworld.org/gemini/freebies/GN34799.html (accessed 20 August 2003).
Hansen, R. (2002). 'Commentary' (on Zig Layton Henry), in W. Cornelius, P. L. Martin and J. F. Hollified, *Controlling Immigration: A Global Perspective*, Stanford, CA: Stanford University Press.
Helton, A. C. (2002). *The Price of Indifference: Refugees and Humanitarian Action in the New Century*, Oxford: Oxford University Press.
Hollifield, J. F. (1992). *Immigrants, Markets and States: The Political Economy of Immigration in Postwar Europe*, Cambridge, MA: Harvard University Press.
Home Office (2002). 'Secure Borders, Safe Haven', Home Office, UK.

Jones, T. D. (1995). 'A Human Rights Tragedy: The Cuban and Haitian Refugee Crises Revisited', *Georgetown Immigration Law Journal*, 9(3): 479–523.

Joppke, C. (1999). 'Asylum and State Sovereignty', in C. Joppke (ed.), *Challenge to the Nation State*, Oxford: Oxford University Press.

Lavenex, S. (1999). *Safe Third Countries. Extending EU Asylum and Immigration Policies to Central and Eastern Europe*, Budapest: Central European University Press.

Loescher, G. (1993). *Beyond Charity: International Cooperation and the Global Refugee Crisis*, Oxford: Oxford University Press.

Martin, S. (2003). 'The Politics of US Immigration Reform', *Political Quarterly* (special issue on immigration), 74(s1): 132–49.

Martin, S. and A. Schoenholtz (2000). 'Asylum in Practice: Successes, Failures and Challenges Ahead', *Georgetown Immigration Law Journal*, 14(3).

Migration News (2001). Vol. 8, No. 2.

Milne, S. (2002). 'Declaration of War on Asylum', *Guardian*, 23 May.

Morrison, J. and B. Crosland (2001). *The Trafficking and Smuggling of Refugees: The End Game in European Asylum Policy?* UNHCR New Issues in Refugee Research Working Paper, 39, Geneva.

NoborderZone (2002). see http://zone.noborder.org/x11/templ/artikel_det.php?itemid=7 (accessed 22 August 2002).

Perusse, R. I. (1995). *Haitian Democracy Restored: 1991–1995*, Lanham, MD: University Press of America.

Salt, J. (1999). 'Current Trends in International Migration in Europe', Strasbourg: The Council of Europe (CDMG (99) 10).

Scottish Refugee Council (n.d.), 'UK Figures', http://www.scottishrefugee council.org.uk/Documents/Facts.PDF (accessed 22 September 2003).

Suhrke, A. (1997). 'Uncertain Globalization: Refugee Movements in the Second Half of the Twentieth Century', in W. Gungwu (ed.), *Global History and Migrations*. Boulder, CO: Westview Press.

Sydney Morning Herald (2002). 'Even as "Good Cop" Howard Beats up on the Judiciary', 13 August, www.smh.com.au (accessed 10 September 2002).

Tassé, R. (1996). *Removals: Processes and Peoples in Transition*, Ottawa: Citizenship and Immigration Canada.

Thielemann, E. R. (2002). 'Does Policy Matter? On Governments' Attempts to Regulate Asylum Flows', Paper prepared for presentation at the UNU-WIDER conference on 'Poverty, International Migration and Asylum', Helsinki, 27–28 September.

Thielemann, E. R. (2003). 'Between Interests and Norms: Explaining Burden-Sharing in the European Union', *Journal of Refugee Studies*, 16(3): 253–73.

Travis, A. (2002). 'Law Lords Clear Asylum Fast Track', *Guardian*, 1 November, http://society.guardian.co.uk/asylumseekers/story/0,7991,823728,00.html (accessed 22 September 2003).

UNHCR (1995). *The State of the World's Refugees 1995: A Humanitarian Agenda*, Oxford: Oxford University Press.

UNHCR (2000). *The State of the World's Refugees 2000*, Oxford: Oxford University Press.

USCR (US Committee for Refugees) (2000). 'Country Report: Australia, 2000', http://www.refugees.org/world/countryrpt/eastasia_pacific/2000/australia.htm.

USCR (US Committee for Refugees) (2002a). 'Country Report: Australia, 2002', http://www.refugees.org/world/countryrpt/eastasia_pacific/australia.htm.

USCR (US Committee for Refugees) (2002b). 'Country Report: Canada, 2002', http://www.refugees.org/world/countryrpt/amer_carib/canada.htm (accessed 22 September 2003).

USCR (US Committee for Refugees) (2002c). *Sea Change: Australia's New Approach to Asylum-Seekers*, Washington, DC, February: 6.

Van Kessel, G. (2001). 'Global Migration and Asylum', *Forced Migration Review*, 10: 10.

Wintour, P. (2001). 'Deportation Raids "Will Harm Race Relations"', *Guardian*, 11 July, www.guardianunlimited.co.uk (accessed 12 April 2002).

World Refugee Survey (1999). US Committee for Refugees, Washington, DC.

Part II

Consequences of Immigration and Asylum

5
The Impact of Asylum on Receiving Countries

Susan Martin, Andrew I. Schoenholtz and David Fisher

Introduction

The number of long-term international migrants (that is, those residing in foreign countries for more than one year) has grown steadily since the 1960s. According to the UN Population Division, in 1965, only 75 million persons fitted the definition, rising to 84 million by 1975 and 105 million by 1985. There were an estimated 120 million international migrants in 1990. As of 2000 there are 175 million international migrants (UNPD, 2002).

Between 1965 and 1975, the growth in international migration (1.16 per cent per year) did not keep pace with the growth in global population (2.04 per cent per year). However, overall population growth began to decline in the 1980s while international migration continued to increase significantly. During the period from 1985 to 1990, global population growth increased by about 1.7 per cent per year, whereas the total population of international migrants increased by 2.59 per cent per year (IOM, 2000).

The industrialized countries belonging to the Organisation for Economic Co-operation and Development (OECD) experienced significant growth in their immigrant population during the 1990s. In 1986–87, about 36 million international migrants (some of whom subsequently naturalized) lived in the United States, France, Germany, Canada, Australia and the United Kingdom (OECD, 2001). As of 2000, more than 63 million international migrants were reported to be living in these same countries, a 75 per cent increase (UNPD, 2002).

These international migrants include both voluntary and forced migrants. Whereas international migration overall has shown a steady increase in the industrialized countries, the number of asylum seekers ebbed and flowed over the course of the 1980s and 1990s. According to the UN High Commissioner for Refugees (UNHCR), asylum applications showed a progressive increase during the 1980s (beginning with less than 200,000 in 1980), reached a peak in 1992, with almost 900,000 applications in the industrialized countries, then saw a reduction to less than 415,000 in 1997, and a subsequent increase to more than 600,000 in 2001 (UNHCR, 2001, 2002). The pattern varied by country, however. Germany saw a relatively steady decline during the latter part of the 1990s, from more than 400,000 in 1992 to about 90,000 in 2002, whereas the United Kingdom experienced a steady increase during this period, from a little more than 32,000 in 1992 to almost 100,000 in 2000 (UNHCR, 2002). These fluctuations are explained, at least in part, by the origins of the asylum seekers. Germany was the principal destination of asylum seekers from the FR Yugoslavia, and hence experienced significant inflows during the height of the conflict in Bosnia and subsequent declines after the Dayton Peace Accord. Government policies also affect flows, as do the assumptions made by smuggling and trafficking groups about vulnerabilities in migration control in individual countries.

Whereas asylum seekers and the systems for adjudicating their claims to refugee status in developed countries have garnered considerable attention and, often, have been at the centre of political controversy, there has been relatively little research on their actual impact on receiving countries. Many studies do not seek to distinguish between asylum seekers and other types of migrants. Other studies examine legal changes in asylum policies rather than the impact of asylum seekers and those granted asylum. Still others focus on specific nationalities, but even when the nationality is closely associated with asylum, the statistics do not permit an analysis of the experiences and impact of those who come through the asylum system versus other migration routes.

Given the paucity of research and data that can be used in assessing the impact of asylum on receiving countries, this chapter does not attempt to address the question through extensive empirical analysis. Rather, the next section discusses the factors that determine whether asylum, as distinct from other forms of migration, is likely to have specific enough impacts to be worth assessing on its own. The following sections summarize the research that exists on the impact of asylum and attempts to tease out of research on international migration more generally what the potential effects of asylum seekers are likely to be.

Factors influencing the impact of asylum

The impact of asylum, as distinct from other forms of migration, will be greater in those countries in which asylum accounts for a higher share of migration. There is considerable variation from country to country in the proportion of total international migration attributable to asylum seekers. In the United States, for example, asylum applicants account for a small portion of the total number of new arrivals. Asylum applications averaged about 60,000 cases per year from 1997–2001, accounting for perhaps 87,000 persons (assuming 1.45 applicants per case), whereas most experts estimate that the number of long-term foreign residents increased by more than

1 million persons per year (counting both legal immigrants and unauthorized migrants who remain in the country for more than one year) (UNHCR, 2002). Asylum has also been a small part of other humanitarian movements to the United States; refugee resettlement and temporary protected status for victims of conflict and natural disasters represent far larger numbers (INS, 2003: table 4). By contrast, in many European countries, asylum applicants are 25 per cent or more of the annual inflow of international migrants (OECD, 2001).

The impact will also vary depending on the proportion of the total population who are international migrants. In the traditional immigration countries, the foreign-born/foreign-national population account for upwards of 10 per cent of the total population; among non-traditional states, this is the case in Sweden and Switzerland. By contrast, the foreign-born/foreign-national population in other countries is below 4 per cent (for example, the United Kingdom, Ireland, Italy, Netherlands and Spain) (OECD, 2001). Even if asylum seekers account for a significant share of international migrants, they are unlikely to have significant demographic, labour market or other generalized impact on the society as a whole. Asylum seekers may, however, affect greatly public opinion about immigration if they are perceived as a growing population, even if not yet a significant one in numerical terms.

Government policies for handling asylum affect the impact of asylum seekers. First, governments make choices as to the systems used for adjudicating applications. If there are complex procedures with multiple levels of appeal, the fiscal costs of implementing the asylum systems will be higher. At the same time, the system may benefit from greater protection of the rights of the asylum seekers from forced return to persecution. If the government detains asylum seekers during lengthy adjudications, the fiscal costs will also be higher than if asylum seekers are released into the community and find their own housing and support networks. On the other hand, it may be more difficult to deport rejected asylum seekers if they are released from detention, creating another type of impact. And, if the government provides housing stipends and otherwise assists the asylum seekers during adjudications, the costs can be as high as detention. By contrast, if the government grants work permits, the fiscal impact may be lower (and in fact may become a net benefit through tax revenues), but again, it may be more difficult to remove a working asylum seeker if his or her application is rejected, and the work permit may be an incentive for abuse of the asylum system. If the asylum seeker obtains asylum, however, the work experience during the application stage may enable longer-term economic integration that will benefit the receiving society.

Impacts will also vary by post-adjudication treatment of asylum applicants. In some countries, a high proportion of asylum seekers are granted asylum, as is the case in the United States and Canada, whereas in other countries, the vast majority of asylum applicants are rejected. Some of those rejected for asylum are nevertheless eligible for complementary forms of protection, particularly if they cannot be returned to a country undergoing conflict. The fiscal, economic and other impacts of asylum will vary depending on the eligibility of those granted some type of status to work, reside permanently, become citizens, obtain access to public assistance, enrol in language and other training programmes, reunify with families, etc. Depending on the nature and effectiveness of some of these policies, those granted asylum or complementary protection may become quickly self-supporting or languish for lengthy periods of time on public assistance rolls.

Policies on return of rejected asylum seekers, as well as individuals granted temporary protection who are no longer in need of such protection, also profoundly influence the ways in which asylum affects receiving countries. If governments find themselves unable or unwilling to repatriate rejected asylum seekers, the domestic impact of the asylum system will be more far-reaching than if the asylum seekers return home. If they are returned too soon, however, particularly to a fragile post-conflict country, the policies may negatively affect not only the asylum seeker but the potential stability of the country of origin as well. Post-conflict Central American countries, for example, asked the United States to permit their nationals to remain in the United States because their remittances were considered essential to the reconstruction of their home communities (*Migration News*, 2001). By contrast, other post-conflict countries have encouraged early return of their diasporas to participate in elections and to help in reconstruction. In this respect, the policies of the source countries can be as influential as the policies of the receiving countries themselves in determining the impact of asylum on the destination countries.

The socioeconomic and demographic characteristics of asylum seekers will further influence the impact of asylum on receiving countries. Impacts will vary depending on the age, marital status and family structure of the asylum seekers. A large number of unaccompanied minors requiring assistance from public authorities will pose greater fiscal costs than a large number of working-age asylum seekers who hold jobs. Impacts will also differ based on the education and skill level of those applying for asylum. Education and skills affect not only employment patterns but also earnings and income, particularly for those granted asylum and/or work permits.

This analysis of the factors influencing asylum patterns and outcomes demonstrates that there is no single way in which the presence of asylum seekers will affect a receiving country. The number of asylum seekers, government policies and socioeconomic characteristics all determine the impacts of asylum. The impacts of asylum can thus differ significantly from country to country. Even within the same country, one could expect to see varied impacts depending on the age, education and skill level of individual asylum seekers.

Fiscal impact of asylum

The most readily measurable impact of asylum is the cost to taxpayers to maintain an asylum adjudication process and to detain and/or care for and maintain asylum seekers. Governments complain of these costs but relatively little documentation is available of the actual numbers. The most comprehensive study of fiscal impact is a 1995 study by the International Centre for Migration Policy Development (ICMPD) entitled *Structure and Costs of the Asylum Systems in Seven European Countries* (Jandl, 1995). Focusing on Austria, Denmark, Finland, Germany (partial data), Norway, Sweden and Switzerland, the study estimated that the total annual state costs, including both processing and care and maintenance, amounted to almost US$2.7 billion (not counting Germany).

Care and maintenance costs accounted for 93 per cent of the total costs, according to the ICMPD study. These costs included the cost of reception centres established to house asylum seekers until (i) a decision was made on their case; or (ii), if granted status, they moved into their own accommodation. They generally also included social assistance and health care. Total care and maintenance costs varied greatly by country, depending on the number and characteristics of asylum seekers and those granted some other form of protection. Average costs also varied, generally by the type and duration of aid. The duration was in turn dependent on the average processing time, the potential for those who were granted status to continue to remain in reception centres or otherwise receive assistance, work authorization and other similar factors.

The processing costs accounted for US$167 million, or 6 per cent of total costs, the study showed. These costs included the funding of admissibility procedures (first-instance and subsequent appeals), legal representation of asylum seekers and return of rejected applicants. The proportion of costs attributable to processing varied by country, with Norway spending 13 per cent of its costs on processing and Denmark and Finland spending less than 3 per cent on these activities.

Because the study was conducted in 1994–95, the findings were skewed by the large number of persons from the FR Yugoslavia who were granted temporary protection without going through an adjudication of an asylum application. Those granted temporary protection were generally eligible for the same benefits as native residents of the countries. Even in countries where they were eligible for work permits, unemployment remained high.

A more recent study of fiscal impact came from the Swedish government, which estimated the *per capita* costs of reception in 2001 at 214 SEK per day, which was significantly down from the 340 SEK figure cited in the ICMPD study for 1990–91 (*Migrationsverket*, 2002). Measured costs included food and accommodation, health and medical care, education and other similar costs. Sweden received 23,515 asylum seekers in 2001. Unfortunately, the study does not indicate average number of days that an applicant received reception services, nor the total cost to the government.

The UK costs for providing support to indigent asylum seekers was £536 million in the 1999/2000 fiscal year and £747 million in 2000/2001 (Home Office, 2001). A separately published study projected future costs (Home Office, 2002), taking into account cost savings projected from changes in government policies. With a shift to voucher payments for some of the assistance then provided by the Department of Social Security (DSS), the study projected a reduction in total costs to £448 million.

These studies demonstrate the extent to which fiscal costs vary according to government policies regarding both adjudications and care and maintenance. While there has not been a similar study of the costs of asylum in the United States, one could posit a far different picture than these European studies show. Asylum seekers in the United States are not eligible for any federally funded public assistance, except for emergency medical care.[1] They are also not eligible for work permits, unless the government takes more than six months to adjudicate their applications (rare for more recent applicants).[2] As a result, the cost to the federal taxpayer is minimal for the type of care and maintenance provided in Europe. However, the United States detains a larger number of asylum seekers than is true in most other industrialized countries, particularly those who enter with fraudulent or missing documents. Used as a deterrence measure, detention costs have been large and growing. Further, the costs of care and maintenance for those at liberty may well be shifted to family members, community groups and local authorities. Alternatively, the asylum seekers are working illegally, presenting a still different type of impact – this time undermining the credibility of the immigration work restrictions. It is important to note, however, that asylum seekers constitute a small proportion of undocumented workers in the United States.

The shift, or at least allocation, in costs from central to state and local authorities is a factor in a number of countries. Generally, central authorities are responsible for adjudicating asylum claims, in keeping with national law as well as international commitments. However, asylum seekers are often distributed around the country, with state or local authorities having responsibility for their care and maintenance. In Germany, for example, the states (*Länder*) have principal responsibility for the reception and care of asylum seekers and those granted temporary protection, as is the case in Austria, Switzerland and other federal states (Jandl, 1995). Some national governments (for example, Sweden) compensate municipalities for some of the costs incurred on behalf of asylum seekers (Jandl, 1995). Even when asylum seekers work and pay taxes, states and localities may still bear a disproportionately high share of the fiscal costs. United States studies of the fiscal costs of immigration in general repeatedly show that tax revenues generally accrue to the federal government (particularly from payments into the social security pension system) whereas many of the costs of education, housing, and health care are felt at the state and local level (National Research Council, 1997).

The studies on the fiscal impact of asylum adjudications generally focus on gross expenditures, not taking into account possible contributions of asylum seekers and asylees to tax revenues. Work conducted in the United States and the United Kingdom on overall fiscal impacts of migrants suggest that such an equation for asylum seekers and asylees would vary substantially, based largely on government policies regarding work authorization and the demographic and socioeconomic characteristics of the asylum seekers. Younger immigrants with relatively high levels of education tend to be net contributors during the course of their lifetime, whereas older, less educated immigrants tend to remain a public cost (National Research Council, 1997; Gott and Johnston, 2002).

ICMPD has compared the costs of adjudication and care and maintenance for asylum seekers with the contributions of industrialized countries towards assistance and protection for the far larger number of refugees in developing countries. In 1993, for example, ICMPD estimated the total cost of asylum systems in thirteen OECD countries to amount to US\$11.6 billion, whereas those same states contributed only US\$670 million to the UNHCR (Jandl, 1995). Clearly, the cost of caring for refugees in highly industrialized countries exceeds greatly the cost of maintaining refugee camps in developing countries. The implication is that states would spend more money on refugees overseas if they had fewer asylum seekers at home. However, government budgets are not necessarily fungible in that way. The costs at home are generally paid by ministries responsible for social security and social services, or by Ministries of Interior (formerly Justice Department, now Homeland Security, in the US case). By contrast, funding for UNHCR generally comes from ministries responsible for development aid or foreign affairs. The ability to shift funding from one stream and agency to another is often very limited in government budgets.

Economic impact

The impact of asylum on the broader economic life of a receiving country is affected by such factors as government policies regarding eligibility for employment and welfare benefits, the education and skills character- istics of the asylum seekers and the capacity and willingness of labour markets to absorb new entrants. While there has been much study, particularly in the traditional immigration countries, of the economic integration and effects of new immigrants, the literature often does not distinguish among labour migrants, family migrants, asylum seekers and resettled refugees. In fact, most of the economic integration and impact research conducted in the United States, Canada and Australia focuses on resettled refugees, with little attention to the experiences of those entering through the asylum system.

Generally, the literature assumes that labour migrants will have better economic outcomes than asylum seekers and resettled refugees, with family migrants fitting in between the two other groups. *Labour migrants* are generally chosen because of their skills or come spontaneously because they know of employment. Hence, a higher proportion is assumed to be employed and wage earning. Empirical evidence often, but not inevitably, supports this contention (Borjas 1994; Fix and Passel 1994; Blos, *et al.* 1997). *Family migrants* come to receiving countries through family and community networks that are often able to place the newcomers into employment as well. Moreover, many governments allow family reunification only in those cases in which the applicants have sufficient financial resources to support the newcomers.

By contrast, *refugees* are more strongly motivated by the 'push factors' of conflict and repression, even though they may choose to claim asylum in a particular country because of their networks or perceived economic opportunities. Successful applicants for asylum are not chosen for their skills or family connections, but rather they are granted refugee or complementary status based on their well-founded fear of persecution or conflict. Their education and employment in their home country may well have been disrupted by the very circumstances that make them deserving of humanitarian protection.

Government policies may also work against early engagement in employment. Asylum seekers are often barred from working, at least until they obtain asylum or a complementary status. They may be isolated in reception centres or detention centres during the application process, or they may be dispersed throughout the country in order to avoid excessive burden on a few communities that would otherwise likely receive the majority of asylum seekers. If the settlement sites are chosen for their remoteness, rather than the economic opportunities available, the refugees may well find it difficult to obtain jobs even when authorized to do so. When refugees have few transferable skills, they may find it difficult to obtain jobs that pay as well as the welfare system. In many cases, refugee families are larger than the average receiving country's families, making it even more difficult to replace the income derived from welfare benefits with wages. Many may take jobs in the informal economy rather than risk the total loss of social benefits.

Over time, however, the problems experienced by refugees may be overcome, leading to higher employment and income than other immigrants with similar educational background. Borjas (1982) has pointed out that 'refugees face higher costs of return immigration than do economic immigrants, and therefore the former have greater incentives to adapt rapidly to the US labor force'.

Empirical evidence appears to support this picture, although there are too few studies of the economic situation of those entering through the asylum system to state the case definitively. A study of employment and wage assimilation of male first-generation immigrants in Denmark showed that 'the initial employment probability of refugee immigrants is much lower than that of non-refugee immigrants'. Refugees from Africa and Palestine had lower rates of employment than those from Europe, Vietnam and the Americas. Refugees also started at much lower wage levels than non-refugee immigrants. Yet, after five–ten years in Denmark, 'the employment probability of refugees seems to approach the level of non-refugee immigrants and Danish born individuals'. With longer attachment to the labour market, the refugees would be able to close the wage gap as well, but it continued to be difficult for refugees to maintain full time employment over a ten-year period (Husted *et al.*, 2000).

Brink (1997) found very high rates of unemployment for refugees in the Netherlands. She cites estimates from the Dutch Interdisciplinary Demographic Institute that more than 50 per cent of refugees in the Netherlands were unemployed, with more than 75 per cent of more recent arrivals (less than three years) without jobs. Her own small sample of refugees from the FR Yugoslavia, Iran and Somalia also showed extremely low rates of employment (10 per cent) upon the grant of asylum (they were ineligible until the grant). Over the next eighteen months, the employment rate grew to 30 per cent. The type of employment became more secure as well, with a majority holding contract jobs. Most of the unemployed refugees were following a course of Dutch-language instruction. By the end of eighteen months, only 2 per cent of the sample did not speak any Dutch (compared to 22 per cent at the beginning of the project). Some respondents also pursued vocational training programmes, generally at the recommendation of the employment services. Courses were sometimes at a lower level than the former work or educational experiences in the home country. If the refugees found jobs after vocational training, the employment was often at an even lower level of skill. It appeared that the human resources with which the refugees entered the Netherlands were not well utilized.

A study in the United Kingdom also found under-utilization of refugee skills. Bloch (1999) cites statistics from the Refugee Council that 70 per cent of refugees in London were unemployed in the early 1990s; a survey conducted by the Home Office at about the same time found that 56 per cent of the refugees had never been in paid employment and 30 per cent had only had sporadic employment in Britain. Factors influencing the dismal employment outcomes include lack of skills transferable to an urban environment, lack of English ability, lack of networks and personal ties to employers, lack of information about how to find a job, difficulty in providing references or evidence of former employment experience and propensity for the refugees to see themselves as guests rather than long-term residents. Women refugees face particular barriers related to lack of skills, English ability and child care provisions.

Bloch surveyed 180 refugees and asylum seekers from Somalia, Sri Lanka and Zaire (DR Congo) who had been employed in a diverse range of jobs in their home countries. The refugee men held such jobs as teachers, engineers and shopkeepers, whereas the women had been working as cashiers, market traders and secretaries. Almost a quarter had university degrees, and more than half had at least a secondary education. Only 16 per cent had only a primary education or no education at all. All of these were Somalis. At the time of the survey, however, only 14 per cent were working in Britain. Immigration status affected employment, with those already granted asylum or extraordinary leave to remain having higher rates than those with temporary permits or appealing a negative decision. Length of residence was also important in explaining employment, with a third of those who arrived in Britain before 1990 working but less than 10 per cent of those arriving in 1995 or later. The jobs were of a significantly lower skill level than the educational background of the refugees would indicate. The refugees cited such factors as racial discrimination and discrimination against refugees, along with their own lack of experience and English literacy skills, as major factors preventing them from getting a more suitable job.

Higher-than-average unemployment has also been found among refugees resettled in receiving countries. The likelihood of employment appears related to education, skills and government policies. According to Bach and Carroll-Seguin (1986), Southeast Asian refugees in the 1980s were persistently 10–15 percentage points less likely to be in the labour force than the United States population, and once in the labour force were likely to experience considerably higher levels of unemployment. Foreign education was the most significant predictor of labour force participation. Residence in California was also a strong predictor of unemployment, holding other factors constant, explained by the relatively more generous public assistance system in that state that permitted refugees to meet their household income needs through welfare rather than work.

Hauff and Vaglum (1993) found a similarly poor labour force participation and unemployment experience among Vietnamese refugees in Norway. Unemployment was higher for refugees with low formal education. Wooden (1991) found that labour force participation rates among the largely Southeast Asian population of refugees in Australia were similar or higher than other immigrants, but their unemployment rates were much higher and they persisted over time. Although he cites discrimination against refugees and long-term 'scarring' arising from the initial high levels of unemployment as two possible reasons for the persistence in unemployment, Wooden emphasizes the importance of lower levels of English-language skills as the more likely explanation of the poor labour market outcomes.

Even more highly educated resettled refugees find difficulties in adapting to the labour markets in their new countries. A comparison of Soviet Jews resettled in the United States and Germany showed similar patterns of underemployment among refugees unable to transfer their academic and scientific credentials to new professional positions (Tress, 1998). Krahn *et al.* (2000) found that refugees in Alberta who were in professions and managerial positions pre-resettlement experienced much higher rates of unemployment, part-time employment and temporary employment than did Canadian-born individuals. Unfamiliarity with the Canadian job market, limited English skills, and controls over entry into professions in Canada (including certification and credentialing requirements) all affected employment.

Given these high rates – and, in some but not all cases, a persistent pattern of unemployment among refugees – it is unlikely that they are having negative impact on the employment, wages or working conditions of other residents of the destination countries. Again, this is an area that has not been extensively researched. One of the few studies to examine this issue is Card's (1990) study of the impact of the Mariel boatlift on the labour market in Miami. He found that the Mariel Cubans increased the Miami labour force by 7 per cent, and the unskilled labour force even more, but he found little negative effect on the wages or employment of lesser-skilled workers, including Cubans who had migrated in earlier years. He pointed to the absorptive capacity of the Miami labour market that had repeatedly adjusted to the large waves of Cuban refugees. He did find, however, that the net migration of natives and other immigrants into Miami from elsewhere in the United States slowed down after the boatlift.

Card's findings are at odds with most economic theory about the effects of immigration on employment and earnings. Generally, immigrants are believed to have a net positive impact on native populations who differ from them in education and skills, and a net negative impact on those with similar characteristics (National Research Council, 1997). In other words, when immigrants are *complements* (rather than competitors) to the native population, the impact of immigration is largely beneficial. On the other hand, if immigrants are substitutes for the native population, or any part of it, the impact is negative for those who are in direct competition. In the United States, to take an example, the educational level of the native-born population can be described as a 'diamond shape' – few Americans have less than a high school education and few have more than a university education; most are in the middle. On the other hand, the educational level of the foreign-born population can be described as an 'hourglass' – about 40 per cent of the immigrants have less than a high school education and more than 25 per cent have a university education or higher. Most immigrants are therefore complements to the United States population. However, the foreign-born are substitutes for those at the top and bottom of the educational ladder, where one might expect the greatest competition for jobs. Theory also dictates that immigrants will have the greatest impact on the immigrants already in the country since they are the most likely substitutes for their labour (National Research Council, 1997).

To the extent that asylum seekers and refugees are complements to the prevailing population in destination countries, the impact of asylum should be beneficial, particularly if refugees are able to enter the workforce. On the other hand, asylum seekers may have negative impact on other immigrants if they arrive with similar educational and skill characteristics.

How the economic impacts will play out over time will be determined in large part by the receptivity of the receiving countries to integrating refugees into the labour market. In this regard, the demographic trends unfolding, particularly in Europe, may play an important role. In most developed countries, fertility levels are well below replacement rates – that is, couples are having fewer than two children (UNPD, 2000). These countries can foresee a time in which total population will decrease, leading some demographers to refer to a looming population implosion. They can also expect an ageing population. According to UNPD projections, the number of persons aged 60 or older will increase from 600 million in the late 1990s to 2 billion in 2050 (UNPD, 1999). The population of older persons will exceed that of children for the first time in history. At the same time, the number of working-age persons per each older person will decline.

Some commentators already see refugees and asylum seekers as potential contributors to the economy if they are able to fill positions that would otherwise be unfilled. For example, a study conducted by the National Institute of Adult Continuing Education in the Leicester area of the United Kingdom concluded that about one-third of the asylum seekers in the vicinity had a higher-education diploma and could help solve shortages in such areas as teaching, medicine and engineering (Aldridge and Waddington, 2001). At the same time, an Assistant Commissioner in Scotland Yard recommended recruitment of refugees and asylum seekers as special constables who could work with ethnic communities, noting 'there are some real professionals [among] refugees and asylum-[seekers] ... They could do lots of roles – Special Constables, mediation, break down some of the bureaucracy, reduce criminality' (Bennetto, 2001). Whether such sentiments proliferate as demographic pressures increase is still to be seen.

Impact on social, cultural and community relations

Asylum has been one of the most controversial migration issues facing many destination countries, affecting public perception of newcomers as well as social and community relations between asylum seekers and other residents. The controversy appears to have little relationship to the actual number of asylum seekers or their fiscal or economic impact on the receiving society. Rather, small numbers of asylum seekers even to such traditional immigration countries as Australia have precipitated extensive public back-lash, often fuelled by political leaders who hope to benefit at the voting booths from a tough stance on unauthorized arrivals. On the other hand, very large groups of asylum seekers have been welcomed in receiving countries (Bosnians and Kosovars, for example), particularly when the situations they are fleeing are well known to the public and accepting them as refugees meets other priorities.

Negative public reactions may derive as well from basic cultural and linguistic differences between the asylum seekers and already resident populations. There may be intergroup misunderstandings concerning practices that are viewed as offensive or upsetting by natives. In the United States, community tensions tend to arise among minority groups, whereas, in Europe, the tensions appear to be strongest between the majority population and the newcomers (Christian and Martin, 1999). The tensions are not generally related to asylum *per se*, but asylum seekers and refugees often come from countries whose traditions are far different from those found in the receiving society. For example, from the perspective of established residents, the presence of large, extended families in immigrant households produces overcrowded housing. In some cases, social and cultural practices of the newcomer groups, such as domestic violence, underage marriages and female genital mutilation, are in violation of the laws of the host country.

Receiving countries have adopted a number of different strategies to address these community tensions. The most effective ones appear to fall into the following broad categories: promoting tolerance through educational programmes, empowering migrants to participate in civic affairs, orienting new immigrants to the communities in which they live, mediating conflicts, prosecuting offences against racial and ethnic communities, establishing trust between migrant groups and law enforcement agencies and reducing anti-immigrant discrimination. In addition to government efforts, non-profit groups and faith-based organizations have been particularly active in educating the public about asylum seekers and educating asylum seekers about the laws and values of the destination countries.

Impact on foreign relations and national security

Asylum seekers – *en masse* or individually – can impact a state's foreign policy and national security. In the extreme, mass movements of those fleeing persecution or conflict can precipitate military intervention by a receiving country. Significant populations of asylees may play a major role in shaping a receiving country's foreign policy towards a sending country. With respect to individual security threats, asylum systems subject to abuse can impact national security.

Since the end of the Cold War, receiving states concerned about mass movements of asylum seekers have occasionally intervened in sending states in order to address the root causes of the movements. In 1994, the United States removed a military regime and restored a democratically elected President in Haiti in large part to quell the number of Haitians who had taken to rafts and boats to escape the effects of repression in Haiti (Schwartz, 2002). The United States interdicted those who fled by boat and took them to Guantanamo Naval Base (GTMO) as a safe haven. Interestingly, a similar exodus in 1992 following the overthrow of President Aristide resulted in a completely different foreign policy. In terms of foreign policy, the US government relied on diplomatic attempts to restore democracy in 1992, and interdicted and refouled asylum seekers rather than provide them with a safe haven.

A more serious threat to peace involved ethnic conflict in the FR Yugoslavia. The Serbian special forces of the Milosevic regime terrorized and displaced ethnic Albanians in Kosovo as part of a crackdown on Kosovo's separatist movement, particularly after early 1998. Prior to the seventy-eight-day bombing campaign by NATO that began on 24 March 1999, the Milosevic regime had already displaced some 260,000 Kosovar Albanians within Kosovo and an additional 200,000 in the rest of the FR Yugoslavia. Milosevic's forces then conducted a massive campaign of ethnic cleansing, uprooting nine-tenths of Kosovo's Albanians from their homes. During the forced exodus of some 465,000 Kosovar Albanians to Albania, 360,000 to Macedonia and 70,000 to Montenegro, the Macedonians closed their borders at different times out of concern that the refugees would adversely impact a delicate demographic balance of ethnic groups (USCR, 2000).

Ambassador Warren Zimmerman wrote about the spillover of asylum seekers as a threat to regional security in 1994 during the Bosnian civil war:

> If, by accident or design, violence broke out in Kosovo, the historic area of Serbia 90 percent populated by Albanians, spillover could become a reality. Albanians could flee to Albania, already militantly anti-Serb, and to Macedonia, whose population is about 30 percent disgruntled Albanians. The moderate government of Macedonia could easily become destabilized, leaving the field to a match-up between the Albanians and the Macedonian nationalists who form a major political force in Macedonia. Interested neighbors could come into play: Serbia, which ruled Macedonia between the wars; Bulgaria, which has traditionally claimed that Macedonians are really Bulgarians; Greece, which has been waging a fierce economic war against Macedonia on the absurd assumption that Macedonia was threatening it; and Turkey, whose interest would derive from the involvement of its traditional enemy, Greece. (Zimmerman, 1995: 107–8)

Those granted asylum (asylees) may develop significant influence on a state's foreign policy once they make roots in the receiving country. The most salient case of this is the Cuban community in the United States, particularly those in the Miami area. Once naturalized, these Cuban refugees exercised considerable power as a voting block during the Cold War. Even after the Cold War ended and the Cuban community developed differing perspectives on the appropriate foreign policy towards Castro's Cuba, the community remained influential in setting US policy.

Interestingly, that influence was seriously challenged in the summer of 1994 when 32,000 Cubans fled the island for south Florida. While some in the Cuban community had questions about the anti-Castro *bona fides* of those who took to rickety rafts and tyres to escape, most wanted the United States to continue to open its arms to these asylum seekers. In contrast with the US policy towards Haitian asylum seekers which was to interdict and return (or, starting in the spring of 1994, to interdict and provide safe haven at GTMO in Cuba), about 5,000 Cuban rafters had been picked up by the US Coast Guard and brought to the United States during the first six months of 1994. That all changed on 19 August 1994. The Governor of Florida, Lawton Chiles, believed that perceived and actual impact of a mass influx on southern Florida communities would seriously erode his re-election bid that year. When the numbers of rafters significantly increased in August 1994, Governor Chiles informed President Clinton that he would declare a state of emergency to handle the situation himself if the President didn't take action to stop the influx. On 19 August, Clinton reversed a three-decade policy of welcome for Cubans seeking asylum in the United States and announced that the Coast Guard would bring any rafters to GTMO where they would be held and screened. That interdiction policy continues today (Martin *et al.*, 1998).

Another important impact that those granted asylum or temporary protection may have on a state regards reconstruction and development aid or its equivalent to a sending country emerging from conflict. During the Bosnia civil war, for example, Germany provided temporary protection to some 350,000 Bosnians. Once the war ended in December 1995, the German government and certain of its states (*Länder*) with concentrated populations of Bosnians were anxious for the return of these refugees to Bosnia. Germany had provided the civil war refugees with support for food, shelter, clothing, etc. and the fiscal impact of hosting this population was high in the minds of certain politicians. The timing of return was a major issue, as the country was devastated by the war, with homes destroyed unemployment very high, about 1 million Bosnians internally displaced, and communities ethnically cleansed and towns inhabited by new populations. The new Bosnian Federation government wanted at some point to receive these predominantly Bosniak (Muslim) refugees from Germany, but urged the German government not to rush their return. The Bosnian Federation asked for reconstruction aid from Germany and the EU in order to rebuild the country, resettle the internally displaced, and receive the returnees. Within the EU, Germany felt that it had spent considerable funds supporting the civil war refugees and that other European governments or the EU as a whole should shoulder the reconstruction burden. But individual German communities with Bosnian populations provided limited reconstruction aid and ultimately Germany responded (along with the EU and several individual European govern-ments) at least partially to the significant reconstruction needs (Martin and Schoenholtz, 1999).

The significance of remittances transmitted by civil war refugees has also played a key role in the foreign relations of certain governments. In the aftermath of conflict in Central America, Presidents of Central American countries such as El Salvador asked the President of the United States to allow the sending state's refugees to remain in the United States so that they could continue to send remittances to help rebuild the war-torn country. Similar requests followed natural disasters. In early 2001, following a major earthquake, the president of El Salvador met with President Bush with two requests. First, he asked that the United States let Salvadorans stay and continue to send monies home. He also asked for some assistance to address the consequences of the natural disaster, but these monies were considerably less than the estimated US$2 billion that Salvadorans in the United States send back home every year (IADB, 2002). For many reasons including pro-business and pro-immigrant values as well as a desire to attract Hispanic votes, President Bush granted both requests.

With regard to national security, two types of issues have arisen concerning asylum. First, on occasion, controversial political figures have presented receiving countries with both national security and foreign policy challenges when they sought asylum. An example of this occurred in late 1998 when the leader of the Kurdish rebellion in Turkey, Abdullah Ocalan, requested asylum in Italy. Immediately after his arrest on warrants from Germany and Turkey, Ankara requested his extradition to stand trial on charges related to his activities as leader of the Kurdish Workers' Party (PKK), which was seeking independence for Turkish Kurds. The PKK urged Italy not to hand him over and threatened retaliation against Turkey. Ocalan's case presented Italy with a dilemma, squeezed between fellow NATO member Turkey's desire to try Ocalan and its own human rights positions and laws. Turkey charged that Ocalan was responsible for the deaths of 30,000 people over a fourteen-year period in his party's armed struggle for Kurdish autonomy. Human rights analysts estimate that 30,000–37,000 people had been killed on both sides of the conflict. Many Kurds consider Ocalan a freedom fighter and hero; however, human rights monitors have reported abuses committed under Ocalan's command. Italian law forbids extradition to countries with the death penalty, such as Turkey. Ocalan was on trial *in absentia* in Turkey on charges punishable with a death sentence: leading a terrorist organization, threatening the country's territorial integrity and ordering killings.

Italy refused to extradite Ocalan to Turkey, but Ocalan left Italy after an unsuccessful attempt to gain immediate asylum. The challenge became a wider European one, as the Kurdish leader sought asylum in various European countries. Kurds in various European countries demonstrated and at times took violent action to protest the treatment Ocalan received in

Europe. European states were greatly concerned about the adverse impact that this would have on both foreign relations and national security. Reportedly, Greece also refused to grant him asylum, but said that it provided him a place to stay in Kenya: 'The Greek government, in order to seek help and find a solution to the problem of Abdullah Ocalan on a European level, granted him a place to stay in Kenya where he had travelled after his efforts to find permission to reside in various European countries.' The Greek government denied that Ocalan had formally requested asylum but stated that he was not wanted in the country: 'If he came to Greece, the Kurdish cause would become part of Greek–Turkish differences and that would be no good' (BBC, 1999). The Kenyan authorities immediately arrested Ocalan and turned him over to Turkish authorities. In June, a Turkish court sentenced him to death. The death sentence has not, at the time of writing, been carried out.

A second type of impact on national security concerns the abuse of the asylum system by terrorists. The pre-eminent example of this occurred on 26 February 1993, when an explosive device detonated on the second level of the World Trade Center parking basement in New York City, killing six people and injuring more than a thousand. More than 50,000 people were evacuated from the World Trade Center complex during the hours immediately following the blast. Six perpetrators of this attack were ultimately arrested, tried, convicted, and each sentenced to 240 years in prison. Two of the perpetrators had sought asylum in order to enter or remain in the United States, including the mastermind, who, with a fraudulent Iraqi passport, claimed asylum based on persecution in Iraq. His asylum application was still pending when the attack occurred. Evidence at the trial showed that the terrorists' intent was to topple the city's tallest towers, amid a cloud of cyanide gas (Camarota, 2002).

Impact of restrictive asylum practices on international refugee protection

The vast majority of refugees try to find protection and assistance in the developing world. According to the *World Refugee Survey 2002*, between 13 and 14 million of the almost 15 million refugees worldwide reside in Africa, the Middle East and Asia. While only a limited number of refugees from these regions reach Europe, North America, or Australia, the asylum policies and practices in the developed world seriously affect the protection of the large numbers of refugees who remain in their regions.

When states in the developed world violate the core protection obligation provided by the Refugee Convention and Protocol – *non-refoulement* – states in the developing world imitate their misbehaviour. During the two-year period from 1992 to 1994, the official policy of the United States was to interdict Haitians on the high seas and return them directly to Haiti without considering any protection needs and rights they might have (Martin *et al.*,

1998). This was a period of political repression in Haiti, as the democratically elected government had been overthrown by a military coup. It was no surprise in 1996, then, when Côte d'Ivoire officials denied entry to a boat, the *Bulk Challenge*, carrying several thousand Liberian refugees. Despite a long tradition of generosity towards refugees from Liberia, Côte d'Ivoire did not hesitate to turn this boat away, knowing well that a key supporter of UNHCR had recently refouled thousands of Haitians on boats (USCR, 1997).

Even when developed nations stop short of such open refoulement but deny entry to their territory, the message is clear: find protection elsewhere. Australia adopted a new policy to address boat arrivals of asylum seekers in late August 2001, not long before national elections were to be held. Under the new policy, Australia refuses to allow such arrivals into Australian territory and sends them to other countries in the Pacific, where their refugee claims are assessed. After the number of boat arrivals increased in the late summer, Australia refused entry to a Norwegian freighter, the *Tampa*, carrying some 430 persons, most of whom claimed to be Afghans. The Australians negotiated temporary refuge for the passengers with the tiny Pacific nation of Nauru and New Zealand. Australia provided Nauru with an aid package worth the equivalent of US$10 million in return for hosting the asylum seekers. New Zealand said it would assess the asylum claims of those brought to its territory. The Nauru government asked UNHCR to screen the asylum seekers taken to Nauru, and UNHCR eventually agreed, but only for the group sent to Nauru. UNHCR expressed serious concern that Australia's actions could send a negative message to impoverished nations closer to conflict zones, which often take in hundreds of thousands of refugees (USCR, 2002).

Roadblocks to asylum, in fact, have become the rule rather than the exception in developed countries since the 1990s. Visa requirements, carrier sanctions, safe country of origin and safe third-country (STC) rules, expedited processing and removal, filing deadlines, detention and pre-inspection discourage or bar asylum seekers from receiving protection in developed countries. Many analysts believe that such tools lead asylum seekers into the hands of smugglers, making escape and finding protection far more risky. Such roadblocks are being also followed by countries now developing individualized asylum systems. In fact, developed countries such as Germany and the United States have advised countries such as Poland and South Africa how to replicate the developed country asylum system. In some instances, these new asylum countries are taking further restrictive measures. In implementing its Refugee Act of 1998, for example, South Africa has reportedly limited the number of asylum applicants simply by refusing entrance to the office building where applications must be filed (USCR, 2002).

Finally, it has become commonplace for the leading developed world nations to argue to developing countries that the South should act generously towards asylum seekers, at the same time that the North places significant restrictions in the way of those seeking asylum in the developed world. Given this contradictory approach, it is not surprising that the North's influence on international protection in the developing world has diminished. Developing countries with long traditions of generosity towards refugees, struggling to deal with continuing refugee crises in recent years, have chosen to follow what the North does as opposed to what it says.

Tanzania and Guinea, for example, have grown weary of large and continuous refugee influxes and are also increasingly concerned about security problems created by refugee warriors. Treatment of refugees after the passage of the 1998 Refugees Act became much more restrictive in Tanzania, for example, particularly with regard to freedom of movement. Analysts attribute this in part to the example set by the North. In fact, a perception exists that the North 'is "shifting" rather than "sharing" the responsibility and burden of hosting refugees to those unfortunate enough to be located near refugee-generating regions' (Kamanga, 2002; USCR, 2002).

Conclusions

To understand the impact of asylum on developed countries, it is first important to segregate asylum seekers from other types of migrants. The impact will vary depending on the proportion of the international migrants who are asylum seekers. While voluntary migration has generally risen steadily in the OECD countries since the 1980s, the movement of asylum seekers has come in ebbs and flows. The vast majority of migrants in the OECD countries are voluntary ones who migrate principally for employment or family reunification purposes. Of course, the proportion varies from country to country.

The impact will also vary depending on the proportion of the total resident population who are international migrants. Even in countries in which asylum seekers account for a significant share of international migrants, the total numbers in proportion to the native population are small. As a result, asylum seekers are unlikely to have significant demographic, labour market or other generalized impact on the society as a whole.

The most readily measurable impact of asylum is the cost to taxpayers to maintain an asylum adjudication process and to detain and/or care and maintain asylum seekers. Governments complain of these costs but relatively little documentation is available on the actual numbers. The limited studies available on the fiscal impact of asylum adjudications generally focus on gross expenditures, not taking into account possible contributions of asylum seekers and asylees to tax revenues and local economies. With regard to the latter, government policies regarding employment significantly affect the potential contributions of asylum seekers.

The economic impact of asylum turns on the government policies regarding eligibility for employment and welfare benefits, the education and skills characteristics of the asylum seekers and the capacity and willingness of labour markets to absorb new entrants. Again, as the policies vary considerably among the OECD countries, the impacts also vary. To the extent that asylum seekers and refugees are complements to the prevailing population in destination countries, the impact of asylum should be beneficial, particularly if refugees are able to enter the workforce.

While asylum impacts social, cultural and community relations in a variety of ways, perhaps the most important concerns the tensions that arise over the newcomers. Interestingly, the tensions arise most in the United States between newcomers and other minorities, while in Europe, the major friction occurs between newcomers and the majority population. Effective approaches addressing these tensions include: promoting tolerance through educational programmes, empowering migrants to participate in civic affairs, orienting new immigrants to the communities in which they live, mediating conflicts, prosecuting offences against racial and ethnic communities, establishing trust between migrant groups and law enforcement agencies and reducing anti-immigrant discrimination.

Asylum seekers have had important impacts on foreign policy and national security. States have intervened with force in order to prevent mass flows of refugees or address the human rights abuses that cause forced migration. When asylum seekers integrate into their host societies, they may exert considerable influence with regard to the host country's policies towards their country of origin. With respect to national security, asylum systems have been abused by terrorists who apply for asylum in order to enter or remain in their target country while their applications are pending.

Finally, the developed country's treatment of asylum seekers impacts the developing world's treatment of the vast numbers of such forced migrants. Refoulement in the North has been followed in the South. Restricting the entry and rights of asylum seekers in the developed world has been picked up and implemented in the developing world. When refugee protection has been weakened in economically strong states and asylum restrictions are perceived as burden shifting, international protection in the developing world where most refugees try to survive has been undercut.

Notes

1. Asylum seekers are excluded from the class of non-citizens allowed access to such assistance by Title 8 of the United States Code, §§ 1641–42 (2002). Persons granted asylum are eligible for cash and medical assistance during the first eight months after being granted status.
2. Title 8 of the Code of Federal Regulations, § 208.7(a) (2002).

References

Aldridge, F. and S. Waddington (2001). 'Asylum Seekers' Skills and Qualifications Audit Pilot Project', National Institute for Adult Continuing Education, www.niace.org.uk/projects/Asylum/Asylumreport.pdf.

Bach, R. and R. Carroll-Seguin (1986). 'Labor Force Participation, Household Composition and Sponsorship Among Southeast Asian Refugees', *International Migration Review*, 20(2): 381–404.

BBC (1999). 'Kurd Protests Sweep Europe' *BBC News Online* (17 February), news. bbc. co. uk/1/hi/world/europr/280355.stm.

Bennetto, J. (2001). 'Recruit Refugees to Scotland Yard, Says Police Chief', *Independent*, 25 June, www.unhcr.ch.

Bloch, A. (1999). 'Refugees in the Job Market: A Case of Unused Skills in the British Economy', in A. Bloch, and C. Levy (eds), *Refugees, Citizenship and Social Policy in Europe*, New York: Macmillan: 187–210.

Blos, M., P. Fischer and T. Straubhaar (1997). 'The Impact of Migration Policy on the Labour Market Performance of Migrants: A Comparative Case Study', *New Community*, 23(4): 511–35.

Borjas, G. (1982). 'The Earnings of Male Hispanic Immigrants in the United States', *Industrial and Labor Relations Review*, 35(3): 343–53.

Borjas, G. (1994). 'The Economics of Immigration', *Journal of Economic Literature*, 32(4): 1667–1717.

Brink, M. (1997). 'The Labour Market Integration of Refugees in the Netherlands', in P. Muss (ed.), *Exclusion and Inclusion of Refugees in Contemporary Europe*, Utrecht: European Research Center of Migration and Ethnic Relations, 187–203.

Camarota, S. (2002). *The Open Door: How Militant Islamic Terrorists Entered and Remained in the United States, 1993–2001*, Washington, DC: Center for Immigration Studies.

Card, D. (1990). 'The Impact of the Mariel Boatlift on the Miami Labor Market', *Industrial and Labor Relations Review*, 43(2): 245–57.

Christian, B. and S. Martin (1999). 'Transatlantic Perspectives on Improving Community Relations', Discussion Paper prepared for Transatlantic Learning Community: Migration Workgroup.

Fix, M. and J. Passel (1994). *Immigration and Immigrants: Setting the Record Straight*, Washington, DC: Urban Institute, www.urban.org/pubs/immig/setting.pdf.

Gott, C. and K. Johnston (2002). 'The Migrant Population in the UK: Fiscal Effects', RDS Occasional Paper, No. 77, London.

Hauff, E. and P. Vaglum (1993). 'Integration of Vietnamese Refugees into the Norwegian Labor Market: The Impact of War Trauma', *International Migration Review*, 27(2): 388–405.

Home Office (2001). *IND Annual Report 2000–2001*, http://194.203.40.90/default.asp?PageId=1210.

Home Office (2002). *Asylum Seeker Support – Estimates of Public Expenditure*, London, www.homeoffice.gov.uk/rds/pdfs/asylummodel1.pdf.

Husted, L., H. S. Nielsen, M. Rosholm and N. Smith (2000). 'Employment and Wage Assimilation of Male First Generation Immigrants in Denmark', IZA Discussion Paper, Bonn: Institute for the Study of Labour.

IADB (2002). *Remittances to Latin America and the Caribbean*, Inter-American Development Bank, Multilateral Investment Fund.

INS (2003). *2001 Statistical Yearbook*, United States Immigration and Naturalization Service, Office of Policy Planning.

IOM (2000). *World Migration Report 2000*, Geneva: IOM and UN.

Jandl, M. (1995). *Structure and Costs of the Asylum Systems in Seven European Countries*, Vienna: ICMPD.

Kamanga, K. (2002). 'International Refugee Law in East Africa: An Evolving Regime', *Georgetown Journal*, 3(1): 25–35.

Krahn, H., T. Derwing, M. Mulder and L. Wilkinson (2000). 'Educated and Underemployed: Refugee Integration into the Canadian Labour Market', *Journal of International Migration and Integration*, 1(1): 59–84.

Martin, S. and A. Schoenholtz (1999). 'Temporary Protection: US and European Responses to Mass Migration', ISIM Working Paper, Washington, DC.

Martin, S., A. Schoenholtz and D. W. Meyers (1998). 'Temporary Protection: Towards a New Regional and Domestic Framework', *Georgetown Immigration Law Journal*, 12(4): 543–87.

Migration News (2001). Latin America, 8(3), http://migration.ucdavis.edu/mn/entireissues/mar_2001mn.html.

Migration Policy Group *et al.* (1996). *The Comparative Approaches to Societal Integration Project*, Brussels: Migration Policy Group.

Migrationsverket (2002). *Facts and Figures 2001* (Norrköping), www.migrationsverket.se.

National Research Council (1997). *The New Americans: Economic, Demographic and Fiscal Effects of Immigration*, Washington, DC: National Academy Press.

OECD (2001). *Trends in International Migration: Continuous Reporting System on International Migration* ('SOPEMI'), Paris: OECD.

Schwartz, E. (2002). 'Practicing at Home What We Preach Abroad: Lessons on Refugee Policy from the Clinton Administration', *Georgetown Journal*, 3(1): 13–23.

Tress, M. (1998). 'Welfare State Type, Labour Markets and Refugees: A Comparison of Jews from the Former Soviet Union', *Ethnic and Racial Studies*, 21(1): 116–38.

UNHCR (2001). *Asylum Applications in Industrialized Countries: 1980–1999*, UNHCR Population Data Unit, Population and Geographic Data Section, www.unhcr.ch.

UNHCR (2002). *Number of Asylum Applications in 30 Industrialized Countries, 1992–2001*, www.unhcr.ch.

USCR (US Committee for Refugees) (1997). *World Refugee Survey 1997*.

USCR (2000). *World Refugee Survey 2000*.

USCR (2002). *World Refugee Survey 2002*.

UN Population Division (UNPD) (1999). *Population Ageing 1999*, UN Doc. No. ST/ESA/SER.A/179.

UN Population Division (2000). *Replacement Migration: Is it a Solution to Declining and Ageing Populations?*, UN Doc. No. ST/ESA/P/WP/160.

UN Population Division (2002). 'Overview', *International Migration Report 2002*.

Wooden, M. (1991). 'The Experience of Refugees in the Australian Labor Market', *International Migration Review*, 25(3): 514–35.

Zimmerman, W. (1995). 'Migrants and Refugees: A Threat to Security?', in M. Teitelbaum and M. Weiner (eds), *Threatened Peoples, Threatened Borders*, New York: W.W. Norton: 88–116.

6
Asylum Migration: Implications for Countries of Origin

Khalid Koser and Nicholas Van Hear

Introduction

There is a substantial literature on the implications for countries of origin of voluntary migration. In broad terms, there are three main approaches. One considers the effects of the absence of migrants, with a particular focus on the concept of 'brain drain', whereby the educated and skilled dominate outmigration (for example, Adepoju, 1991). Another considers the ways that migrants continue to interact with their country of origin from abroad, with a focus on economic remittances (for example, Lim, 1992). The third approach considers the potential benefits of return migration for countries of origin (for example, Diatta and Mbow, 1999).

In contrast, there has been little serious thought about the implications for countries of origin of *involuntary migration*. There are several reasons for this. One reason is lack of data: for example there is no systematic information on the skills and educational background of refugees, so it is impossible to assess to what extent the educated or skilled are disproportionately represented. A further reason is bias. Research and policy have overwhelmingly focused on the impacts of refugees on their country of asylum, with little consideration, for example, of the impacts of the absence of sometimes significant proportions of population on countries of origin. More broadly, research and policy have tended to frame refugees as 'problems' rather than considering their potential. For example, it is only recently that research, some of which is reviewed in this chapter, has shown how refugees can and do remit substantial amounts of money to their countries of origin. Still less is there work on the influence on their countries of origin of refugees who left their homeland more than a generation ago, except perhaps in terms in political lobbying (for example, Hungarians who fled Hungary in 1956, Czechs who fled after 1968, Chileans who fled in the 1970s and so on). Such work might give us clues as to the longer-term influence of refugees and asylum seekers on their homelands.

There is growing consensus among scholars that the distinctions between voluntary and involuntary migrants are not always as sharp as has often been assumed (for example, Koser, 1997; Van Hear, 1998), and this lends conceptual validity to a chapter that asks to what extent and how refugees should be incorporated in a field of study that has traditionally been the domain of economic migrants. There are also policy reasons for asking to what extent asylum seekers and refugees can make contributions to their countries of origin. First, their numbers appear to be increasing relative to other kinds of migrant. Second, as 'durable solutions' become increasingly elusive, many are staying outside their countries of origin for increasing lengths of time, and even after the end of conflict in the homeland. In these circumstances, it is important to consider to what extent and how involuntary migrants can contribute to post-conflict reconstruction and, in the longer term, development of the homeland.

The purpose of this chapter is to synthesize what is known about the influence of asylum migration on countries of origin. It combines an analysis of data, a review of the literature and empirical examples from our own research. In structure the chapter follows the logic of the 'refugee cycle'. We consider the effects of the absence of refugees on countries of origin, focusing on the scale of movements, the characteristics of refugees, where they go and their length of time in exile. We review the evidence about the influence of asylum seekers and refugees on their country of origin from exile, then we consider the implications for countries of origin of the return of asylum seekers and refugees. The conclusion acknowledges the limited state of current knowledge and draws out some policy implications.

The effects of exodus

Properly to understand the effect of the absence of refugees on their countries of origin would require detailed analysis of the scale of refugee flows, the characteristics of the refugees and how long they stay away. Data inadequacies greatly limit the extent to which such analysis is possible.

Scrutiny of the ratio of refugees to the total population in their countries of origin for the ten largest refugee populations in 2001–02 shows that refugee flows can deprive countries of a significant proportion of their population (see Koser and Van Hear, 2003). Thus an estimated one in seven Afghans, one in ten Bosnians, one in eleven Eritreans and one in thirteen Burundians lived outside their country as refugees in 2001–02. The implications of such significant proportions really depend on the demographic, economic and social characteristics of the refugees, and how their profile compares with that of the population remaining at home. In other words, are refugee flows depopulating particular sections of the society or undermining particular sections of the economy? Appropriate data to assess this simply do not exist on a systematic level. For example, UNHCR collates basic demographic data, but by country of asylum rather than by country of origin. Where a country of asylum predominantly hosts refugees from a single country of origin, these data can be extrapolated to provide a basic profile of refugees from that origin country.

Afghanistan is one for which country of asylum data can be extrapolated in this way. This is because the vast majority of refugees in Pakistan and Iran are from Afghanistan, and at the same time the vast majority of refugees from Afghanistan are located in those two countries. But even then, without comparable data on the population that remains in Afghanistan, it is hard to assess the impact of the absence of certain population cohorts. Afghanistan's refugees, for example, appear to be fairly evenly balanced between the sexes – 39 per cent of the refugees in Iran are female and 53 per cent in Pakistan (UNHCR, 2002). But a lack of data on the sex ratio within Afghanistan means that the extent to which refugee flows have disrupted the demographic profile in Afghanistan cannot be assessed.

Similarly, a significant proportion of Afghan refugees – 58 per cent in Iran and 37 per cent in Pakistan – are of an economically active age (in conventional terms, between 18 and 59) (UNHCR, 2002). Arguably their absence is depriving Afghanistan of a significant proportion of the labour force. On the other hand, since Afghanistan has a high unemployment (or underemployment) rate, it might be argued that refugee flows have reduced competition for scarce jobs and resources.

Afghanistan is exceptional in that the location of its main refugee populations allows some analysis of this kind. It is far harder to perform a similar exercise, say, for Sudanese refugees, many of whom live in countries such as Uganda and Kenya which host refugees from other countries too. Thus, we know that 45 per cent of refugees in Kenya are female (UNHCR, 2002), but we do not know what proportion of Sudanese refugees in Kenya is female.

It is not just conditions in the country of origin that can influence the effect of the absence of refugees, but also circumstances in exile. As is often the case among refugee populations, children (meaning those under 17) comprise an important proportion of Afghan refugees – 39 per cent in Iran and 59 per cent in Pakistan (UNHCR, 2002). Leaving aside arguments about the importance of children to the social fabric of a country, the economic impact of the absence of these children will depend on factors such as how long they are in exile and the extent to which they receive an education or training there. In other words, it may not be flight that necessarily deprives a country of origin of its potential, but continued absence as the refugee acquires new skills. This raises the significance of the return of asylum seekers and refugees, which is considered later in this chapter.

A related factor is where refugees go. It is broadly true that the majority of refugees seek safety within their regions, and that the majority of refugees are therefore located in the poorer countries of the world. We might describe these refugees as living in the 'near diaspora'. An increasing proportion, however, appear to be moving longer distances to more developed countries, and live in what we may term the 'wider diaspora' (Van Hear, 2003). It is these refugees in the 'wider diaspora' who are likely to be the particularly skilled or educated or better-off, simply by virtue of the entrepreneurial spirit – and, more mundanely, the money required to make journeys, especially as they appear to have become dominated by human smugglers (Koser, 2001). Similarly, it seems likely that it is these refugees who will have greater opportunity to enhance their skills or education. Finally, they may also be the refugees least likely to return home even after conflict. Even though they may be relatively small in number, refugees of this sort may well represent both the greatest immediate loss and the greatest potential for countries of origin.

Influence from exile

It has been increasingly recognized in recent years that asylum migrants enter other kinds of migration streams, joining those who move in search of employment, education, professional advancement, marriage or for other purposes. Given such 'mixed migration', asylum seekers form part of mixed communities of migrant origin in a given country of destination (Crisp, 1999). Moreover, a substantial proportion of asylum applications are by people already resident as students, visitors, tourists, or illegal immigrants (Crisp, 1999). Further, asylum seekers are often part of family or ethnically based networks that comprise disparate migrant categories. In these circumstances, it can be difficult to distinguish the influence of asylum migrants from other kinds of migrants on their countries of origin.

Given these considerable limitations, this part of the chapter reviews what the evidence shows about the influence of asylum seekers and refugees on their countries of origin. It starts by looking at data available on economic remittances and other transfers to migrants' countries of origin, and the part asylum seekers may play in these transfers. Next it looks at the deployment of remittances in conflict-torn countries. We then review recent evidence that suggests that asylum seekers and refugees can make contributions to their country of origin that extend beyond economic remittances. Finally in this section, we consider the obstacles and incentives for refugees and asylum seekers to contribute to the reconstruction or development of their countries of origin.

The scale of refugee remittances

The macro-level evidence for the contribution of asylum seekers to countries of origin is scanty. One important contribution for which there is some evidence is remittances, but for several reasons the conclusions that can be drawn are very limited. First, the data on remittances generally are very patchy, and that for countries in conflict and which produce asylum seekers are even more so since data collection in such countries is generally much more difficult. Second, such data that exist do not allow the contribution of asylum seekers to be disaggregated from that of other migrants. Third, asylum seekers in richer countries may remit both to the homeland and to neighbouring countries of first asylum to support their relatives, making their contribution more diffuse than that of other migrants. Nevertheless it is possible to draw some conclusions from the limited data available.

Remittances from abroad are now widely recognized to be crucial to the survival of communities in many developing countries, including many which produce asylum seekers and refugees. Estimated to total US$100 billion in 2000 (Martin, 2001), migrants' remittances represent a large proportion of world financial flows and amount to substantially more than global official development assistance or aid. To underline their importance for the developing world, 60 per cent of global remittances were thought to go to developing countries in 2000 (Gammeltoft, 2003).

Most of these remittances are sent by economic migrants rather than by asylum seekers and refugees. Moreover, countries in conflict and producing refugees are not among the main territories that receive remittances. Of the ten countries receiving most officially recorded remittances, two are low-income (India and Pakistan); six are lower middle-income (Philippines, Turkey, Egypt, Morocco, Thailand and Jordan); and two are upper-middle-income (Mexico and Brazil) (Gammeltoft, 2003). Although there are conflicts within some of these countries – in Pakistan, India and the Philippines, for example – they are not the world's most conflict-torn, nor are they the main producers of the world's refugees.

On the other hand, since remittance figures are missing for many countries in conflict and that have produced refugees, such countries may be more important recipients of remittances than the officially recorded figures suggest. Even on the basis only of available data on officially recorded transfers, Armenia, Azerbaijan, Colombia, Ethiopia, Myanmar, Rwanda, Sri Lanka, and Sudan – all countries that have experienced conflict and produced refugees in recent years – each received annual remittances totalling more than US$10 million in the later 1990s (Gammeltoft, 2003). In the case of Myanmar these receipts were more than US$100 million, in the case of Colombia more than US$650 million and in the case of Sri Lanka close to US$1 billion (Gammeltoft, 2003). While these remittances may largely originate from migrants who are not asylum seekers – labour migrants in the case of Sri Lanka, for example – at least some of the money transferred will have come from refugees. Moreover, since countries in conflict tend to receive less by way of other financial inflows, such as foreign direct investment (FDI) and development assistance, the inflow of remittances, like humanitarian aid, tends to assume greater proportionate significance.

When considering these transfers, the distinction introduced above between refugees and asylum seekers in the 'near diaspora' and in the 'wider diaspora' needs to be reinforced. With some exceptions, refugees in the 'near diaspora' seldom generate sufficient income to send money to their kin who have remained at home. They are more likely to be the conduits for resources transferred from refugees and asylum seekers in more affluent countries, particularly when formal means of money transfer, such as banks or remittance agencies, are unreliable or non-existent. This appears to have been the case with Afghan refugees in Pakistan in the 1990s: because of the lack of a functioning banking system in Afghanistan, transfers from refugees and others in the wider diaspora were routed through this near diaspora, and became an increasingly important source of income as aid dried up (Jazayery, 2003; Van Hear, 2003). This pattern of the near diaspora in neighbouring countries being the conduit for remittances from the wider diaspora may well be replicated elsewhere.

Scrutiny of particular countries from which asylum seekers originate appears to bear out some of these general observations. Two such countries are now examined, Sri Lanka and Somalia. Both have suffered from protracted conflict since the 1980s, and both have generated substantial diasporas which include many asylum seekers and refugees, but also other kinds of migrant.

The Sri Lankan diaspora

Sri Lanka has experienced complex forms of migration within and outside the country since the 1980s (McDowell, 1996; Fuglerud, 1999; Rotberg, 1999; Van Hear, 2002). At first this was largely economic migration, mainly to the Middle East; by the 1990s about 200,000 Sri Lankans went each year to work in the Middle East, as well as in South East and East Asia. Outmigration has also included a 'brain drain' of professionals and of people seeking educational advancement abroad. Since the civil war between the Sri Lankan armed forces and the Liberation Tigers of Tamil Eelam (LTTE) took off in 1983, a large outflow of asylum seekers, mainly Tamils, has taken place. While much of this movement was initially to Tamil Nadu in southern India, many Sri Lankan Tamils have sought asylum further afield, so that a far-flung diaspora has reinvigorated the prior dispersal of Sri Lankan migrants who left for the purposes of education or to take up professional positions abroad. By the 1990s, there were some 100,000 Sri Lankan refugees in southern India, and 200,000–300,000 in Europe and North America who joined earlier professional migrants.

The reach of the wider diaspora is substantial. Statistics are not always consistent, but the most important destinations for Sri Lankan asylum seekers and refugees in Europe and North America appear to be the United Kingdom, Canada, France, Germany and Switzerland. These countries are therefore significant bases from which mainly Tamil asylum seekers can influence Sri Lanka economically and politically.

It is impossible to disaggregate remittances sent by refugees and asylum seekers from those sent by other Sri Lankan migrants. However, some idea of the contribution of asylum seekers to total remittances, admittedly rather speculative, can be gleaned by looking at the available statistics in recent years. With the exception of the mid-1980s, remittances to Sri Lanka grew throughout the period of the war, from around US$150 million in 1980 to about US$1 billion in 2000; there were significant upward shifts in the early and mid-1990s – both times of intensified conflict (SLBFE, 1998). Remittances have eclipsed official development assistance (ODA) and humanitarian aid (Sriskandarajah, 2003). Most of the remittances recorded are sent by labour migrants in the Middle East. However, the share of remittances has shifted geographically, hinting at a greater contribution from refugees. Remittances from the Middle East fell from a peak of 85 per cent of total remittance inflows in the mid-1980s to just under 60 per cent in 1999. This proportionate decrease is partly due to the diversification of destinations for labour migrants – to south-east Asia, for example. But it is probably also due to increases in remittances sent by refugees in Europe and North America. Moreover the Tamil diaspora's contribution is almost certainly underestimated in these estimates, because much money is remitted through informal channels known as the *hundiyal* system (similar to the Somali *hawilad* system considered below). Furthermore, important outlays made by diaspora members on behalf of people at home, such as payment for overseas education or for migration abroad, are not technically recorded as remittances since they are not actually transferred to Sri Lanka. Like remittances proper, these may have significant impacts on the people left at home.

The Somali diaspora

Sri Lankan migration has many affinities with that of migrants from Somalia, another country that has suffered protracted conflict. (The term 'Somalia' is used here to refer to the territory still recognized internationally as such. In 1991, the northern part of Somalia was declared the independent Republic of Somaliland and a functioning administration was established there. However it is recognized by only a handful of countries. Some data nevertheless differentiates the two entities, and this is reflected in the text.) Since the 1970s there have been two main forms of movement out of Somalia, resulting in the formation of a large and influential diaspora which includes many asylum seekers. From the early 1970s, many Somalis went as migrant labourers to work in the Gulf states during the oil boom of that time; by the end of the 1980s up to 350,000 Somalis were working in the Middle East. The outbreak of civil war in 1988 and the interclan fighting after the fall of Siyad Barre in 1991 displaced hundreds of thousands of Somalis within the country and drove many others to leave to seek refuge in Ethiopia, Kenya, Yemen and other neighbouring countries, as well as to seek asylum further afield in the United Kingdom, Italy, the Netherlands, Scandinavia, Canada, the United States and other Western states. By 2000, there were thought to be some 400,000 refugees in eastern Africa and in Yemen, and more than 70,000 refugees in Western countries, out of a total diaspora in Western countries of perhaps 200,000 (UNHCR, 2000; USCR, 2000; Gundel, 2003).

Somalis are one of the most widely dispersed refugee populations in the world: in the late 1990s, asylum applications by Somalis were recorded in more than sixty countries. By then Somalis living in EU states were thought to number 120,000. The United Kingdom and Italy have the largest communities, based on historical and colonial ties: these long-established communities have been supplemented by more recent inflows of asylum seekers. In 2000, the United Kingdom received nearly half the asylum applications by Somalis in European countries, nearly 4,800 out of 10,900. The Netherlands and Scandinavian countries were the next most popular destinations for asylum seekers. These countries, together with Germany, to which asylum applications in recent years have been minimal, have substantial Somali populations, mainly based on asylum migration. North America also has substantial Somali populations: some 19,000 Somalis applied for asylum in Canada and 8,000 in the United States in 1990–98 (ECRE, 2000; USCR, 2001).

As the forms and destinations of Somali migration have diversified, so too have the sources of remittances. While figures are only rough estimates, from the late 1970s between US$300 million and US$400 million were remitted annually by Somalis abroad. Currently about US$500 million may be remitted to Somalia annually and perhaps the same amount to Somaliland (Ahmed, 2000; EIU, 2001). In the 1990s, the wider diaspora, partly formed by refugee outflows, accounted for a greater proportion of remittances (Ahmed, 2000).

Remittances from both economic migrants and refugees have become essential components of the economies of Somalia and Somaliland. For 2000, it has been estimated that aid totalled US$115 million and livestock exports US$125 million; both were eclipsed by remittance inflows. While they can only be guesstimates, statistics for earlier years show that remittances have almost always exceeded other financial inflows since the 1980s (Gundel, 2003).

The deployment of remittances in conflict-torn societies

Remittances from asylum seekers, refugees and other migrants abroad can help individuals and families to survive during conflict and to sustain communities in crisis. They do so both in countries of origin and in countries of first asylum. The limited evidence available suggests that these transfers are used in ways similar to those sent by economic migrants to people at home in more stable societies – for daily subsistence needs, health care, housing and sometimes education (Van Hear, 2002). Paying off debt may also be prominent, especially when there have been substantial outlays to send asylum migrants abroad, or when assets have been destroyed, sold off or lost during conflict or internal displacement. Asylum seekers and refugees may also fund the flight abroad of other vulnerable family members; this may not necessarily involve transfers of money home, but rather payments for tickets, to migration agents, for documents, for accommodation and to meet other costs incurred during and after travel.

There has long been debate about the impact of remittances by economic migrants (Massey *et al.*, 1998; Taylor, 1999). The pessimistic view is that they are 'wasted' on consumption, on luxuries, on social activities, or on housing, rather than being 'usefully' invested in productive enterprises. A more optimistic perspective is that investment of remittances in housing, health, education and social activities contributes to and in fact constitutes 'development'. Moreover, satisfying 'non-productive' demands may free up other surpluses for investment in more directly productive enterprises. 'Non-productive' use of remittances may also help to build the social capital on which productive activities are based. In conflict-torn societies and regions, the scope for investment in directly 'productive' enterprises may be very limited in conditions of great insecurity. Spending remittances on subsistence, housing, health, education and reducing debt take higher priority. But as in more stable societies, investment of remittances in social activities may be seen as the reconstruction of the social fabric, in which 'productive' activities are embedded. By facilitating the accumulation or repair of social capital, such investment may lay the foundation for later reconstruction and development (Goodhand *et al.*, 2000; Van Hear, 2002).

Other aspects of remittance transfers attenuate their beneficial influence on the countries from which asylum migrants come. First, the distribution of remittances is uneven: not all households receive them. Though not exclusively, remittances from economic migrants tend to go to the better-off households within the better-off communities in the better-off countries of the developing world, since these households, communities and countries tend to be the source of migrants. In the case of remittances from asylum migrants, the benefits are also selective, because asylum migrants also tend to come from the better-off households among those displaced. Furthermore, the distribution is likely to have become still more skewed in recent years because of the rising costs associated with asylum migration: long-distance mobility is increasingly the preserve of those who can afford to pay migration agents' inflated fees. A second tendency attenuating the benefits of remittances in the country of origin is that instead of contributing the local economy, the beneficiaries of remittances may well be absentee landlords and traders who siphon off a portion of them, and invest the proceeds elsewhere. Other leakages – notably payments to migration agents – also mean that a substantial part of remittances filter out elsewhere. Such leakages are magnified in the case of societies in conflict.

But perhaps the most serious charge is that remittances and other transfers from asylum seekers, refugees and others in the diaspora may help perpetuate conflict by providing support for warring parties. This negative view of diasporas, and by implication asylum seekers and refugees within them, has been advanced by several writers on the 'new wars' that have blighted many parts of the developing world in the 1990s. For Collier (2000), an influential voice in the research department of the World Bank, the existence of a large diaspora is a powerful risk factor predisposing a country to civil war, or to its resumption. Three other influential writers on the political economy of war – Anderson (1999), Duffield (2001) and Kaldor (2001) – hold similar views.

Kaldor and Duffield suggest several mechanisms by which diasporas contribute to warring parties. Diaspora assistance takes direct and indirect forms, Kaldor suggests. Direct forms include arms, money and other material assistance provided by the diaspora. Indirect forms include the appropriation by warring parties of remittances sent to individual families, converting a part of such remittances to military resources. This may be accomplished by various forms of taxation or extortion. The 'new wars' offer ample opportunities for such appropriation, not least through the checkpoints and blockades that are common features of these kinds of conflict, and which may be controlled by government forces, insurgents, warlords or freelances (Kaldor, 2001). Some diaspora members may also be conduits for the laundering of the proceeds of illicit trade and businesses controlled by warring parties (Duffield, 2001).

Again, scrutiny of particular cases bears out some of these general observations about the ambivalent impact of remittances in societies in conflict. In Sri Lanka, many households in the conflict areas have been sustained by remittances from those abroad, and could not have survived without them. On the other hand, resources from the diaspora have been extracted by the LTTE, through various forms of taxation and extortion (Davis, 1996; McDowell, 1996; Gunaratna, 1999). Furthermore, investment of transfers from abroad in productive activities in the conflict-affected areas has been minimal, given the destruction of much of the infrastructure during nearly two decades of conflict. Remittances in these areas have been mostly used to meet living costs, sometimes to fund education, and sometimes to finance migration for family members (Van Hear, 2002). This may change if the ceasefire signed early in 2002 between the government and the LTTE holds and consolidates into lasting peace. There is anecdotal evidence that since the ceasefire, Tamils abroad have been investigating the possibilities of reviving or investing in businesses in Jaffna and elsewhere. These 'green shoots' will need to be nurtured if peace, reconstruction and recovery are to be achieved.

Similar ambivalence is observable for Somali remittances. As elsewhere, the benefits of remittances in Somalia and Somaliland are uneven. Substantial sums of money are received by a relatively small proportion of households, largely because migrant workers and refugees generally come from better-off families who can afford to invest in sending someone abroad: in the late

1990s it cost about US$3,000 for an employment visa and ticket to the Gulf, and about US$5,000 for travel documents and a ticket to Europe or North America. Furthermore, the recipients of remittances are concentrated in urban areas (Ahmed, 2000). Even so, such transfers remain important flows at both the household and the aggregate level, and any threat to these flows could have dire consequences for family survival and for wider social stability, already fragile. Just such a threat arose late in 2001 in the wake of 11 September and the subsequent 'war against terrorism' when the main means by which Somalis transfer money home were seriously disrupted. The worldwide clampdown instigated by the United States on the Al Barakat *hawilad* (or money transfer network) in November 2001 underlined the wariness with which remittances to unstable regions were now perceived. Some of the implications for Somalis of the forced closure are now explored.

The Somali hawilad *system*

In the absence of a reliable formal banking system, Somalis have developed novel means of transferring money. The *hawilad* system makes use of the expansion and reduced costs of telecommunications since the 1990s. The system works very simply. If a Somali refugee or asylum seeker in London or Minneapolis needs to send money to a relative in Somalia or in a refugee camp in Kenya, s/he takes the money in pounds or dollars to the *hawilad* broker in the country of asylum, who then contacts the *hawilad* office in Somalia or Kenya by fax, telephone or email. Once identities have been checked and verified, the local currency equivalent is handed over to the recipient relative by the *hawilad* office in Somalia or Kenya. The system works on trust, and with commissions of around 5 per cent it is much cheaper and quicker than other forms of money transfer (Horst and Van Hear, 2002).

Until 2001 the two largest *hawilad* companies were Al Barakat and Dahabshil. Both were set up following the outbreak of the civil war in 1991 and the collapse of the formal banking sector. In November 2001, Al Barakat found itself on the list of organizations suspected of links with Osama Bin Laden and Al Qaeda. Al Barakat offices around the world were forcibly shut down, their assets confiscated and telecommunication lines cut as part of the 'global war against terrorism'. US officials justified these measures by claiming that tens of millions of dollars a year were moved by Al Barakat to Al Qaeda, but produced little evidence to support this allegation. Prior to the closure Al Barakat had the largest foreign branch network, operating in forty countries, and an extensive distribution network in Somalia (EIU, 2001). Terrorist networks may well have used the *hawilad* system, as have Somali warlords buying weapons and sponsoring war but, as UN agencies and others in Somalia have attested, the system is mainly used by ordinary Somalis, including refugees, with no such connections (Horst and Van Hear, 2002).

Although Somalis have been able to use other remittance companies, many of these companies relied on the infrastructure established by Al Barakat, and none of them had the latter's worldwide reach. The costs of transfer have increased and the ease of transfer has declined. The resulting curtailment of remittances led to real hardship; the UNDP attributed a worsening food crisis severely affecting 300,000 people and potentially a further 450,000 to a decline in remittances, as well as to drought and the continuing Saudi ban on imports of Somali livestock (EIU, 2001). However, the impact was more short-lived than many feared, since other *hawilad* companies filled the gap left by Al Barakat.

Other forms of contribution by asylum seekers and refugees

Research by Al-Ali *et al.* (2001), focusing on the participation of Bosnian and Eritrean refugees in post-conflict reconstruction in their countries of origin, suggests that their contributions extend beyond economic remittances alone.

Table 6.1 identifies the main activities found among the study communities. It distinguishes between those activities focused on the home country and those focused on the host country. Probably the most obvious activities that can contribute towards reconstruction in Bosnia or Eritrea are those with a direct impact in either country – for example, investments by refugees in land or businesses. At the same time, activities that sustain or support the society and culture of the home country within the exile community were considered by both communities to be equally important in shaping the home country's future. For example, among many Bosnian and Eritrean refugees there is a strong conviction that children born in host countries should learn their mother tongue, and share a national consciousness.

Table 6.1 also distinguishes between, and provides examples of, economic, political, social and cultural activities. The significance of economic remittances has already been considered in the preceding section: the findings from these and other case studies largely confirm those conclusions. In addition, it was found that refugees make significant political contributions in their country of origin. This was particularly the case among Eritreans, who were found to have participated in the political process in three main ways. First, it is estimated that over 90 per cent of all eligible voters in the Eritrean diaspora participated in the 1993 Referendum for Independence. Second, Eritreans in the diaspora were involved in the drafting and ratification of Eritrea's Constitution. Finally, the Constitution guarantees voting rights for the diaspora in national elections, rights which exiles appear actively to exercise (Koser, 2002).

It is not only people who travel between countries, but also ideas, values and cultural artefacts. These latter have been described as 'social remittances' (Levitt, 1998). In the study by Al-Ali *et al.* (2002), several Bosnian intellectuals and artists stated that they aimed to produce writing and art which could be distributed in both the host country as well as in Bosnia. Some journalists continue to work on a freelance basis for the Bosnian media, but others have either changed their profession or tried to establish themselves in the host country. Those who continue to write for newspapers, or work for

Table 6.1 Categorization of individual and community activities, by type and geographical focus

	Economic	Political	Social	Cultural
Home-country focus	• Financial remittances • Other remittances (for example, medicine, clothes) • Investments • Charitable donations • Taxes • Purchase of government bonds • Purchase of entry to government programmes	• Participation in elections • Membership of political parties	• Visits to friends and family • Social contacts • 'Social remittances' • Contributions to newspapers circulated in home country	• Cultural events including visiting performers from the home country
Host-country focus	• Charitable donations • Donations to community organizations	• Political rallies • Political demonstrations • Mobilization of political contacts in host country	• Membership of social clubs • Attendance at social gatherings • Links with other organizations (for example, religious and other refugee organizations) • Contributions to newspapers • Participation in discussion groups (e.g. Internet bulletin boards)	• Events to promote culture (e.g. concerts, theatre, exhibitions) • Education

Source: Al-Ali *et al.* (2001).

either radio or TV, stressed their aim to promote ideas of tolerance, a multi-ethnic Bosnia, democracy and freedom of speech. This was also true of artists, such as writers and painters, who were concerned with changing ideas in Bosnia as well as their host countries.

Little evidence was found of more formal channels for the transmission of 'social remittances' among either study community. In the Eritrean context, the greatest potential surrounds DEHAI, which is probably the leading website for the burgeoning 'virtual' Eritrean diaspora. DEHAI provides current news on Eritrea, links to other relevant websites and a bulletin board for discussion. It provides one example of how the construction of a new Eritrean nation is being discussed, and at times contested, by the diaspora – in this case in a 'virtual' environment. Constraints on Internet access in Eritrea limit the extent to which discussions are impacting upon that country directly, but they may well be shaping the ideas of the diaspora, which both formally – for example, through elections – and informally – through correspondence with friends and relatives in Eritrea – have a role to play in shaping the future of the country. Similar phenomena are manifested among other refugee diaspora groups. In the late 1990s, supporting to various degrees the LTTE's cause in Sri Lanka, there were reported to be fourteen active Eelam websites, sixteen media sites, five daily discussion groups, six human rights groups, five daily discussion groups, eight student organization home pages, sixteen link pages and a Tamil electronic library (Fuglerud, 1998). Jeganathan (1998) shows how visions of the Tamil aspirant homeland Eelam are constructed in various sometimes conflicting forms in 'webspace'.

Incentives and obstacles to contributing

As emphasized at the beginning of this section, it is increasingly hard to distinguish the contributions of asylum seekers and refugees from those of other conationals with whom they often reside. Much of what we have said about economic and other remittances applies across the range of migrant types. Indeed, what probably distinguishes asylum seekers in particular is that they may well face greater obstacles than most other migrants in making contributions to their countries of origin.

Table 6.2 is also taken from the research by Al-Ali *et al.* (2001). In investigating the capabilities of Bosnians and Eritreans to participate in relief and reconstruction in their home countries, they found an important distinction between individuals' *capacities* – or abilities – to participate, and their *desire* – or willingness – to participate. On the one hand, it is clear that where an individual is unemployed or earns only a low salary, s/he will often have little or no surplus money to contribute. In this case, unemployment, or a low salary, are factors influencing the *capacity* of the individual to participate. On the other hand, if an individual is in opposition to the government in the home country, and therefore does not want to support national reconstruction under that government, s/he may choose not to contribute despite being

Table 6.2 Factors increasing individual capabilities to participate in reconstruction in the home country

	Economic	Political	Social
Capacity	• Employment • Savings • Access to welfare and pensions from home country • Access to welfare and pensions from host country • Access to information • Access to banking facilities	• Secure legal status in host country • Positive attitude of host government and population towards ethnic–national diasporas • Political integration of diaspora by home government	• Freedom of movement within host country • Gender equality • Successful social integration in host country • Place of origin in home country
Desire	• Financial stability in host country • Economic incentives (or lack of disincentives) for remittances and investments in home country • Economic stability in home country	• Secure legal status in host country • 'Non-alienating' circumstances of flight • Positive attitude of home government towards diaspora • Political stability in home country • Lack of ethnic/religious discrimination in home country	• Links with family and friends in home country • Links with friends and family in other host countries • Integration within the diaspora in the host country • Positive attitudes towards home country • Desire to maintain 'national consciousness'

Source: Al-Ali *et al.* (2001).

able to afford to. In this case, political opposition to the government in the home country is a factor influencing the *desire* of the individual to participate. The crucial implication is that the capability of any one individual to contribute to their home countries is influenced by a combination of both capacity and desire to participate.

Building upon this distinction between capacity and desire, Table 6.2 combines two types of information. At one level, it indicates the main factors that influence both capacity and desire – distinguishing broadly between economic, political and social factors. At the same time these factors are qualified, to indicate the particular circumstances in which the capabilities of individuals to participate have found to be increased. Thus, for example, access to savings, a secure legal status in the host country and freedom of movement within the host country have all been found to increase the capacity of individuals to participate.

One advantage of presenting the factors in this qualified way is to stress that they are *dynamic*. The factors listed relate to the personal circumstances of individuals, such as their contacts with friends and family in the home country, who may themselves migrate, lose contact or die. They also relate to contextual circumstances in both the host country, such as the policies of the host government towards refugees, and the country of origin, such as economic or political stability there. Changes can occur in each of these locations.

In turn, an advantage of emphasizing that the factors influencing capabilities to participate are dynamic is that this highlights the role that policy inter- ventions can play in increasing capabilities. Many of the factors suggested to influence capacity in Table 6.2 are familiar from numerous other studies on the integration of refugees (for example, Wahlbeck, 1999). It is probably no surprise that better integration tends to empower refugees and increase their capacity to participate; still these findings provide yet another reason to support ongoing efforts in host countries to improve conditions for refugees. At the same time Table 6.2 implies that it is not only host governments that might usefully intervene. Obstacles to achieving many of the conditions shown to influence desire are more directly the responsibility of governments in the countries of origin – including, for example, removing economic disincentives for remittances and maintaining democracy. Finally, there are also implications for community organizations in the host countries – relating, for example, to factors such as social integration and gender equality within the diaspora.

Return and reconstruction: the tension between repatriation and remittances

While refugees can make substantial contributions to the homeland while abroad, as the previous section showed, the return of refugees can be a substantial force for development and reconstruction of the home country, not least in terms of the financial, human and social capital they may bring home with them (Stepputat, 1999). More cynically, as in the case of the protracted negotiations between UNHCR and the Eritrean government over the return of refugees from Sudan, returning refugees can also attract significant inputs of aid (McSpadden, 1999).

Governments of countries producing refugees have traditionally been suspicious of the loyalties of those who flee, for obvious reasons. However, governments of countries emerging from conflict are now increasingly coming to appreciate the potential that refugee diasporas hold, particularly in terms of the remittances they can send. This applies in particular to those in the wider diaspora. The Eritrean government was among the first to recognize this potential. After initial disappointment that Eritreans in the wider diaspora had decided not to return after independence, the government turned its attention to mobilizing – some might say exploiting – their potential (Koser, 2002). Since Independence, for example, every Eritrean in the wider diaspora has been asked by the government to pay 2 per cent of their income to the state, as a 'healing tax'. During the recent conflict with Ethiopia even greater demands were made of the diaspora, and there can be little doubt that their contributions paid for much of the conflict's costs.

More recently, the Afghan government has made similar overtures to the Afghan diaspora. Opening a seminar on trade and investment in July 2002, President Hamid Karzai appealed to 'all Afghans who are currently investing in other countries to come and invest inside the country, which is of national and personal benefit' (Fox, 2002). More than 1.8 million refugees have returned under assisted repatriation programmes (BAAG, 2002), and others under their own steam since the fall of the Taliban late in 2001, but it was unclear how many had gone back from the wider diaspora beyond Pakistan and Iran, and still less clear how many were prepared to invest in a country still beset by insecurity. Since late in 2002, the Afghanistan government has been planning to hold conferences in various parts of the world in an effort to woo expatriate Afghan businessmen back home (BBC News, 2002).

Moreover, mass return presents the dilemma that the flow of remittances to the home country will diminish. If the resolution of conflict or crisis is accompanied by large-scale repatriation, the source of remittances will obviously fall, raising potential perhaps for instability and further conflict. There may even be an argument against repatriation on these grounds. Such was the thrust of a series of appeals in the 1990s by the government of El Salvador for the US authorities to refrain from repatriating Salvadorans whose temporary protection in the United States was imminently expiring (Mahler, 2001).

Remittances to El Salvador grew from US$11 million in 1980 to US$1.34 billion in 1998. This huge increase was largely a consequence of El Salvador's civil war from 1979 to 1992, which displaced hundreds of thousands of people within the country and drove 1 million people abroad, mostly to the United States. Many of those in the United States sent money to support those left at home, so that by the end of the 1990s remittances were thought to sustain at least 15 per cent of Salvadoran households. Successive Salvadoran governments have pursued a number of strategies to maintain this important flow of income – from the very people its past actions have forced to flee. Perhaps the most bizarre of these interventions was the provision by the El Salvador authorities of legal assistance in the United States for Salvadorans to pursue or prolong asylum claims (Mahler, 2001).

The El Salvador and other similar cases highlight potentially damaging consequences for countries of origin if asylum migrants and refugees are repatriated *en masse*. The consequences include the possibility that a diminution of remittances may lead to hardship, instability, socioeconomic or political upheaval, and even the resumption or provocation of conflict – and then quite likely renewed outmigration. Repatriation of refugees may therefore imperil the very economic and political security – in broader terms, the human security – that the international community claims to want to foster. It follows that policies that purport to be oriented to migrants' countries of origin cannot afford to leave those abroad, especially those asylum seekers and refugees hosted by relatively affluent countries, out of consideration.

Conclusions

Following the logic of the 'refugee cycle', this chapter has reviewed what we know about the influence of asylum migration on countries of origin. Our conclusions focus on policy implications rather than those of a more conceptual kind.

Initially, we need both to acknowledge the limitations of the evidence presented and to guard against generalizations. There are at least three reasons why care is needed in interpreting our evidence. First, we have emphasized that the entire exercise has been hampered by insufficient data. We do not have the systematic data required properly to assess the impact of the absence of refugees from their country of origin; neither do we have complete data either on remittances sent by asylum migrants or on remittances to countries in conflict. A second, more conceptual problem has been trying to disentangle the influence of asylum seekers and refugees from that of other migrants and conationals overseas. What each of these observations reinforces, finally, is that there is simply not enough empirical research in this area. We have relied on a few, limited case studies, particularly among asylum seekers and refugees in the wider diaspora. We do not know to what extent findings here extend to others in the wider diaspora. And we know very little about the extent to which those in the near diaspora can influence their countries of origin.

Further research is important because the limited evidence available points to some potentially important implications for refugee policy. First, it indicates that exiled communities are not necessarily isolated communities. At least some asylum seekers and refugees are keen to maintain links with their countries of origin and try to engender change there, and at least some have considerable potential to effect change. The implication is that recent initiatives in both host countries and countries of origin to mobilize diasporas in the development process might be extended to refugees (see Van Hear and Sørensen, 2003). In industrialized countries, for example, there is renewed emphasis on the links between migration and development, one element of which is to include settled migrant communities in the process of development in their home countries. Similarly, a growing number of less developed countries (LDCs) are actively reaching out to diasporas to mobilize their resources and skills.

A second policy implication is that physical return is not the only way to integrate refugees in post-conflict reconstruction. This has been an assumption underpinning UNHCR's repatriation policy for many years – witness, for example, the insistence that in order to be eligible to vote in national elections refugees had to return to Cambodia, Mozambique and Namibia. In contrast, the evidence presented here suggests that refugees can contribute to democratization, reconciliation and reconstruction from a distance. It is a truism of the modern world that money, goods, ideas and votes can cross international borders more easily than people. This observation is only reinforced by the growing recognition that, for many refugees, return is not the preferred solution.

There is a final policy implication, upon which the preceding two rest. That is the need to empower rather than to marginalize asylum seekers and refugees. For asylum seekers and refugees to contribute to their countries of origin, the authorities of those countries should not view refugees as disloyal, and should accept that some refugees do not want to return. Equally as important, countries of asylum could help to enhance the potential of refugees, rather than putting costly barriers in their way in the form of a restrictive migration/asylum regime. Secure legal status and measures to overcome political, social and economic exclusion are among the initiatives that could help mobilize the potential of refugees to make a real difference. More broadly, the international community could galvanize refugees and asylum seekers in the wider diaspora: refugee participation in international forums, such as in donors' conferences and reconciliation and peace-building efforts, could be encouraged. This would allow resources from donors and from diasporas to be more coherently planned and coordinated for both reconstruction and development purposes. This is one area in which migration and development policies could be made more congruent and coherent, without subordinating the objectives of 'development' and conflict reduction to the imperatives of migration control.

References

Adepoju, A. (1991). 'South–North Migration: The African Experience', *International Migration*, 24(2): 205–22.

Ahmed, I. (2000). 'Remittances and Their Impact in Postwar Somaliland', *Disasters*, 24(2): 380–89.

Al-Ali, N., R. Black and K. Koser (2001). 'The Limits to Transnationalism: Bosnian and Eritrean Refugees in Europe as Emerging Transnational Communities', *Ethnic and Racial Studies*, 24(4): 578–600.

Anderson, M. B. (1999). *Do No Harm: How Aid Can Support Peace – Or War*, London: Lynne Rienner.

BBC News (2002). 'Afghanistan Woos Businesses Home', http://news.bbc.co.uk, 6 November.

British Agencies Afghanistan Group (BAAG) (2002). *BAAG Monthly Review*, December.

Collier, P. (2000). 'Economic Causes of Civil Conflict and Their Implications for Policy', Washington, DC: World Bank.

Crisp, J. (1999). 'Policy Challenges of the New Diasporas: Migrant Networks and Their Impact on Asylum Flows and Regimes', Working Paper, No. 7, Geneva: UNHCR.

Davis, A. (1996). 'Tiger International: How a Secret Global Network Keeps Sri Lanka's Tamil Guerrilla Organisation up and Killing', *Asiaweek*, 26 July.

Diatta, M. A. and N. Mbow (1999). 'Releasing the Development Potential of Return Migration: The Case of Senegal', *International Migration*, 37(1): 243–66.

Duffield, M. (2001). *Global Governance and the New Wars: The Merging of Development and Security*, London: Zed Books.

Economist Intelligence Unit (EIU) (2001). *Country Report: Somalia*, London: EIU.

European Council for Refugees and Exiles (ECRE) (2000). *Synthesis of the ECRE Country Reports for 2000*, London: ECRE.

Fox, D. (2002). 'Karzai Urges Afghan Businessmen to Invest at Home', Reuters, 18 July.

Fuglerud, O. (1998). 'Space and Movement in the Sri Lankan Conflict', SUM Working Paper, 1999.2, Oslo: University of Oslo, Centre for Development and the Environment.

Fuglerud, O. (1999). *Life on the Outside: The Tamil Diaspora and Long Distance Nationalism*, London: Pluto Press.

Gammeltoft, P. (2003). 'Remittances and Other Financial Flows to Developing Countries', in N. Van Hear and N. Sørensen (eds), *The Migration–Development Nexus*, Geneva: IOM: 101–32.

Goodhand, J., D. Hulme and N. Lewer (2000). 'Social Capital and the Political Economy of Violence: A Case Study of Sri Lanka', *Disasters*, 24(4): 390–406.

Gunaratna, R. (1999). 'The Internationalisation of the Tamil Conflict', in S. Gamage and J. B. Watson (eds), *Conflict and Community in Contemporary Sri Lanka*, New Delhi/ London: Sage.

Gundel, J. (2003). 'The Migration–Development Nexus: Somalia Case Study', in N. Van Hear and N. Sørensen (eds), *The Migration–Development Nexus*, Geneva: IOM.

Horst, C. and N. Van Hear (2002). 'Counting the Cost: Refugees, Remittances and the War Against Terrorism', *Forced Migration Review*, 14, September.

Jazayery, L. (2003). 'The Migration–Development Nexus: Afghanistan Case Study', in N. Van Hear and N. Sørensen (eds), *The Migration–Development Nexus*, Geneva: IOM.

Jeganathan, P. (1998). 'Eelam.com: Place, Nation and Imagi-Nation in Cyberspace', *Public Culture*, 10(3): 515–28.

Kaldor, M. (2001). *New and Old Wars: Organised Violence in a Global Era*, Oxford: Blackwell, and Cambridge: Polity.

Koser, K. (1997). 'Social Networks and the Asylum Cycle', *International Migration Review*, 31(3): 591–612.

Koser, K. (2001). 'New Approaches to Asylum?', *International Migration*, 39(6): 85–103.

Koser, K. (2002). 'From Refugees to Transnationals', in N. Al-Ali, and K. Koser (eds), *New Approaches to Migration*, London: Routledge: 138–52.

Koser, K. and N. Van Hear (2003). 'Asylum Migration: Implications for Countries of Origin', Discussion Paper, 2003/20, Helsinki: UNU–WIDER.

Levitt, P. (1998). 'Social Remittances: Migration Driven, Local-Level Forms of Cultural Diffusion', *International Migration Review*, 32(4): 926–48.

Lim, L. L. (1992). 'International Labour Movements: A Perspective on Economic Exchanges and Flows', in M. M. Kritz, L. L. Lim and H. Zlotnik (eds), *International Migration Systems*, Oxford: Clarendon Press: 133–49.

Mahler, S. (2001). 'El Salvador's Remittance Industry: A Crossroads of Conflict, Migration, Social Networks, Statecraft and the Global', Paper presented at the conference 'Living on the Edge: Conflict, Movement and State Formation on the Margins of the Global Political Economy', Copenhagen: Centre for Development Research, January.

Martin, S. (2001). 'Remittance Flows and Impact', Paper prepared for the Regional Conference on 'Remittances as a Development Tool', organized by the Multilateral Investment Fund and the IADB.

Massey, D., J. Arango, G. Hugo, A. Kouaouci, A. Pellegrino and J. Taylor (1998). *Worlds in Motion: Understanding International Migration at the End of the Millennium*, Oxford: Clarendon Press.

McDowell, C. (1996). *A Tamil Asylum Diaspora: Sri Lankan Migration, Settlement and Politics in Switzerland*, Oxford: Berghahn.

McSpadden, L. (1999). 'Contradictions and Control in Repatriation', in R. Black and K. Koser (eds), *The End of the Refugee Cycle?*, Oxford: Berghahn: 69–84.

Rotberg, R. (ed) (1999). *Creating Peace in Sri Lanka: Civil War and Reconciliation*, Washington, DC: Brookings Institution Press and the World Peace Foundation.

Sri Lanka Bureau of Foreign Employment (SLBFE) (1998). *Statistical Handbook on Foreign Employment 1998*, Colombo: SLBFE.

Sriskandarajah, D. (2003). 'The Migration–Development Nexus: Sri Lanka Case Study', in N. Van Hear and N. Sørensen (eds), *The Migration–Development Nexus*, Geneva: IOM: 259–86.

Stepputat, F. (1999). 'Repatriation and Everyday Forms of State Formation in Guatemala', in R. Black and K. Koser (eds), *The End of the Refugee Cycle?*, Oxford: Berghahn, 210–27.

Taylor, J. (1999). 'The New Economics of Labour Migration and the Role of Remittances in the Migration Process', *International Migration*, 37(1): 63–86.

UNHCR (2000). *The State of the World's Refugees*, Oxford: Oxford University Press.

UNHCR (2002). *Population Statistics (Provisional)*, Population Data Unit, 7 June.

US Committee for Refugees (USCR) (2000). *The World Refugee Survey 2000*, Washington, DC: USCR.

US Committee for Refugees (USCR) (2001). *The World Refugee Survey 2001*, Washington, DC: USCR.

Van Hear, N. (1998). *New Diasporas: The Mass Exodus, Dispersal and Regrouping of Migrant Communities*, London: University College London Press and Seattle: University of Washington Press.

Van Hear, N. (2002). 'Sustaining Societies Under Strain: Remittances as a Form of Transnational Exchange in Sri Lanka and Ghana', in N. Al-Ali and K. Koser (eds),

New Approaches to Migration: Transnational Communities and the Transformation of Home, London and New York: Routledge: 202–23.

Van Hear, N. (2003). 'From "Durable Solutions" to "Transnational Relations": Home and Exile Among Refugee Diasporas', Geneva: UNHCR Evaluation and Policy Analysis Unit, Working Paper, 83.

Van Hear, N. and N. Sørensen (eds) (2003). *The Migration–Development Nexus*, Geneva: IOM.

Wahlbeck, O. (1999). *Kurdish Diasporas*, London: Macmillan.

7
Illegal Immigration, Human Trafficking and Organized Crime

Raimo Väyrynen

Concepts and categories of migration

Human migration has been, and still is, intimately connected with the transformations of the world economy. Mass migrations were a common phenomenon in pre-modern world politics, in which they shaped the fates of empires and entire civilizations. Only in a rather late historical phase did the rise of territorial and national states start to impose constraints on migration flows (Koslowski, 2002).

The national borders continue to restrict international migration, but it may be that the process of economic globalization and the gradual decline of the territorial state are now accompanied by the growth of migration. In 2001, there were an estimated 175 million people living outside their country of birth; since 1975, the number has doubled. Most immigrants were living in Europe (56 million), followed by Asia (50 million) and North America (41 million). In developed countries, every tenth person is a migrant, while in developing countries one in seventy persons has this status (*International Migration*, 2002; *The Economist*, 2002a).

Illegal migration is a sub-category of international migration. Its distinguishing feature is the legal status that is defined by the rules adopted by national governments and intergovernmental organizations. The illicit status of migrants also has consequences for the mechanisms of cross-border movement and the personal position of migrants. In other words, illegal migration cannot be separated either from the larger dynamics of the global economy or the policies pursued by governments. Thus, although legal and illegal immigration differ in many crucial respects, they are both located at the interface of international economic and political systems.

Licit and illicit aspects of international migration can be depicted as a set of concentric circles. The largest circle covers all aspects of international migration, including illegal migration. Human smuggling is a special case of illegal immigration, while human trafficking is a sub-category of smuggling. Official definitions of these concepts are provided by the UN Protocol Against the Smuggling of Migrants by Land, Sea and Air and the UN Protocol to Suppress and Punish Trafficking in Persons, especially Women and Children. The Protocols are supplements to the so-called Palermo Convention or more specifically the UN Convention on Transnational Organized Crime adopted by the UN General Assembly on 15 November 2000 (UN A/55/383).

The Protocols define smuggling as 'the procurement, in order to obtain, directly or indirectly, a financial or other material benefit, of the illegal entry of a person into a State party of which the person is not a national or a permanent resident'. In that sense, the smuggling of individuals violates the rights of the state, while human trafficking amounts to the violation of human rights. Trafficking refers to the 'recruitment, transportation, transfer, harbouring or receipt of persons, by means of threat or other forms of coercion, of abduction, of fraud, of deception, of the abuse of power or of a position of vulnerability or of the giving or receiving of payments or benefits to achieve the consent of a person having control over another person, for the purpose exploitation'. The main forms of exploitation are prostitution, forced labour, slavery, or the removal of organs.

Migration, organized crime and the illicit economy

Illegal immigration, including human smuggling and trafficking, is just an element of the larger problem of organized crime and the illicit global economy. Organized crime refers to sub-national and transnational corporate agencies that operate systematically outside the purview of law with the intention of turning in profits for its members, especially the leaders. Organized crime is obviously illegal in nature, although it may have diverse connections with both the state agencies and legal markets.

It is useful to make a distinction between two key activities of organized crime groups; trafficking in illegal goods and the provision of protection and enforcement services, usually to other criminal businesses. The Russian case shows how the agencies (the *mafiya*), selling the use of force for protection, tend to form the core group of the criminal world. On the other hand, the position of organized crime involved in, say, marketing contraband has a more ambiguous position. The centrality of mafia-type organizations in Russia hinges on the fact that their activities compete directly with a key function of the state, the monopoly of force (Varese, 2001: 4–6; Volkov, 2002: 21–3). However, during Putin's reign the role of organized crime in the Russian economy and politics has declined.

However, even in the Russian case, one should not exaggerate the domestic protection function as the mafia is also extensively involved in transnational activities. In fact, organized crime has, in recent years, become more diverse in scope, more pervasive in its actions, and much more transnational in its reach. In sum, the 'transnational criminal today tends to be active in several countries, going where the opportunities are high and the risks are low' (Williams, 2001: 58–60). Not unlike terrorism, transnational organized crime makes efforts to benefit from the weak legal and bureaucratic capacity and flawed politics of weak or failed states (Williams, 2002: 169–74).

Organized crime is a key force of the illicit global economy that consists of transnational movements of goods or the type of activities criminalized by states. Illicit global economy is a more narrow concept than, for example, the underground economy or clandestine economy whose size is thus bigger, and the mixture of illicit and licit elements is different. However, not even the illicit economy operates entirely on its own; it interacts in a number of ways with the licit economy and public agencies (Friman and Andreas, 1999; for a description of the illicit global economy, see Naylor, 2002).

Indeed, the illegal and clandestine movement of people across national borders cannot be separated from their governmental control and law enforcement. Migration very easily becomes a deep political issue. Politicians tend to 'securitize' migration, and in particular illegal immigration, as a risk for the state that is regarded 'as a body or a container for the polity'. Immigration is often perceived as a danger for the integrity of the state and the nation, and thus a challenge to the principle of their sovereignty (Bigo, 2002: 66–8).

The sovereignty principle accords to states metapolitical authority to criminalize specific transnational activities and enforce provisions concerning them. However, states have seldom adequate capabilities fully to enforce restrictions on criminal activities; that is, their sovereignty is incomplete. This creates particular problems in areas where the market demand for illicit activities is high: 'The gap between the state's metapolitical authority to pass prohibition laws and its ability to fully enforce such laws is the space where clandestine transnational actors operate' (Friman and Andreas, 1999: 9–11; see also Williams, 2002).

A political economy approach to human smuggling would regard people as commodities; people are moved illegally for a payment across borders because they have profit value for the smuggler whose start-up costs in the business are small. People in traffic are often also in demand in the recipient country, primarily to fill gaps in the employment structure that needs cheap, irregular labour. In addition, the migrants turn themselves, often voluntarily, into transportable commodities because they expect to fetch a better price for their work in the target country. This creates a growing 'migration business' that has both legal and illegal elements. In fact, one may say, somewhat sarcastically, that people are a good commodity as they do not easily perish, can be transported over long distances and can be reused and resold (Salt and Stein, 1997; Ghosh, 1998: 21–3; Findlay, 1999: 75–7; Williams, 1999).

The focus on the economic models and business operations of illegal migration has its analytical merits, but it also distorts the reality in some significant ways. First, it abstracts the social and political environment in which the trafficking of the human beings takes place and overlooks the conditions and policies that fuel it. Second, the business or commodity approach pays inadequate attention to the exploitative aspects of human trafficking that deprives its objects of any legal protection (this aspect was explored early on by Warzazi, 1986). Third, human smuggling routinely gives rise to human rights violations that both traffickers and authorities have been known to carry out with impunity.

Obviously, in the international system of completely open borders, illegal population movements were a conceptual oxymoron. In a more specific way, one can say that the nature and degree of border control shapes the patterns of their crossing; the more coercive and stricter the control, the more difficult it is for undocumented migrants to enter the country (Kyle and Dale, 2001: 30–1).

This does not necessarily mean that the number of such migrants is reduced as a result, but that their border crossing becomes more costly and perilous. The experiences on the US–Mexican border show clearly how enforcement and smuggling have developed almost in a symbiotic relationship; each law enforcement move has provoked a law evasion counter-move, which in turn has been matched by more enforcement (Andreas, 2001: 122). The result is often a cat-and-mouse game between the smugglers/ traffickers and the law enforcement officers. The US–Mexican border also provides evidence on how Operation Gatekeeper and other crackdowns have put migrants in more peril as they try to enter the United States (Zeller, 2001; Sanchez, 2002).

In other words, illegal migration flows and state policies interact with each other; state boundaries and the intensification of their control by bureaucratic and paramilitary means increase the costs of entry to the migrants. To be able to cross the border, illegal immigrants may need the help of professional smugglers. The rise of entry costs and the growing size of groups mean, in turn, higher profits for the smugglers.[1] In sum, both the restrictive policies adopted by states and specific actions undertaken by the smugglers and traffickers affect the way in which the migration potential is actualized in international relations (Teitelbaum, 2001: 26–8). On the other hand, there is a variety of proactive and preventive policies by which the immigration flows can be regulated (Ghosh, 1998: 146–76).

In addition to facilitating cross-border movements, the Schengen Agreement has its own adverse effects. It has tightened up the outside borders of its parties, driving some cross-border activities underground and illegal immigrants into the hands of the smugglers. At the same time the attraction of the Schengen area has increased; if a migrant is able to enter the area, it is much easier to move around to other countries. This expands the scale in which the migrants are able to search for new opportunities (*The Economist*, 1999). The free mobility of people within the Schengen area has yet to be matched, however, by the harmonization of the EU legislation pertaining to immigration and asylum. The process was started in 1999 during the Finnish presidency, and the aim is to complete it during the Dutch presidency in the second half of 2004.

Migration, smuggling and trafficking

As noted above, illegal immigration, smuggling and trafficking are nested concepts. They all share the illegal character of the entry to a country, but they are quite different in terms of the specific economic intentionality and agency issues involved. Illegal immigration concerns voluntary transactions that are supposed to benefit the immigrant, his employer (a factory, a farm or a shop) and the third party (a temporary employment agency, a smuggler or a corrupt policeman).

Illegal labour flows are often countenanced by the target country because its economy needs the immigrants (and they are absorbed in the existing ethnic and family networks). There are even organizations that shelter illegal immigrants, providing them with humanitarian and legal assistance. For these reasons, illegal immigration can be, in reality, semi-legal and regular, and even tacitly accepted by the authorities.

The main intention behind illegal migration flows is economic in nature; people move across borders because of income differentials, in the hope of a more gainful employment. This does not mean, of course, that the regularized illegal immigration is without problems.[2] On the contrary, the migrant workers are often paid low wages, their living quarters are overcrowded, they receive hardly any health care services, and, in the absence of unions, labour laws are routinely violated. The working and social conditions of immigrant labour have received a lot of attention, especially in the ILO. In general, the human rights of migrants have been gaining increasing attention in international debates (Mattila, 2000).

Labour migration has been often modelled as a market transaction determined by supply and demand without considering the political economy of emigration (Ghosh, 1998: 34–43). However, regularized labour traffic may also be sponsored by 'migrant exporting schemes', to use the term coined by Kyle and Dale (2001). In such schemes there are agencies on the sending side that recruit and finance customers for the smugglers, who then assume the task of transporting them across the border. This has been called the 'mobilization phase' of the human smuggling chain (Salt and Stein, 1997: 479–81).

The exporting schemes may become human commodity chains that start from a local village and involve several intermediaries before the destination is reached. One careful study identifies seven different types of role in a smuggling operation which may require several years to complete (Icduygu and Toktas, 2002: 35–45; see also Salt, 2000: 44–5). These intermediaries are usually professionals, often small entrepreneurs, and they do not need to be members of any centralized crime syndicates.

The exportation of migrants is frequently initiated by the local entrepreneurs or elites who have connections with the smugglers and foreign employers. The 'en route' phase of migration and smuggling schemes can differ significantly in terms of its duration, mode of transportation and the degree of control, and of responsibility, that the smugglers have over their customers (Salt and Stein, 1997: 481–3). For all these reasons, it is justified to characterize at least a part of the human smuggling and trafficking as a 'network of locals' rather than an 'international mafia' (Salt, 2000: 42–3; Icduygu and Toktas, 2002: 45–7).

Exports of human labour can be contrasted with 'slave-importing operations' in which vulnerable people become prey to big-time criminal operators. In these operations, people are transported en masse, either clandestinely or with the help of bribed officials, to work in prostitution, plantations, sweat-shops or mines. The key feature of such an operation is that the migrants lose their freedom, and may become bonded labour and live in servitude (Kyle and Dale, 2001). History tells of several such slave importing operations by which people were moved by the millions from, for example, Africa to the United States, and from India to South Africa, Fiji and other places where a labour force was needed in mining and agriculture (Cohen, 1997: 57–79).

Both schemes described above may involve human trafficking, but their practical and moral character differs significantly from each other, with the slave importation scheme being the worst of the two. When in illegal migration the goal is only to find employment, the people moving have at least a modicum of freedom to decide whether they want to leave their country for a foreign destination. On the other hand, in the slave trade there is no such choice as it specifically targets those in the society who are weak, vulnerable and deprived (Bales, 1999: 10–11).

Human trafficking

The Protocols of the Palermo Convention make a clear distinction between human smuggling and trafficking. The latter refers to a process in which illegal and coercive means are used, both in the smuggling of the victims and being subject to an unfree or abusive status at the destination. Trafficking can be considered a form of international business (Salt and Stein, 1997: 470–1), which means that its borderline with human smuggling becomes blurred (Helminen and Kirkas, 2002: 21–2). The dilution of this borderline underestimates, however, the human rights violations that are involved in human trafficking (UNICEF, 2002: 2–4 and passim).

As a result, human trafficking is usually regarded as a nasty and repulsive business that receives almost universal moral condemnation, while illegal immigration, and even human smuggling, are understood because of the economic and humanitarian motives involved in them. The reason for this difference is that, in human trafficking, the focus is on the smuggler who is a criminal benefiting financially not only from the act of smuggling but also from the 'end use' of the victim. An illegal migrant is only a person who wants to improve his/her lot in the world, albeit by means defined as illicit by governments.

Yet illegal immigration and human smuggling, and even trafficking, are interrelated and result in a 'terrible paradox', as Miller (2001: 321) points out. The problem is that the more strictly the laws of immigration against the illegal entrants are enforced, the more sinister forms of criminality are used in human trafficking to overcome the barriers needed to make a profit. Ultimately, the intensity of the violence associated with the smuggling of human bodies and body parts has increased because of the 'aggressive extension of market values on the bodies of the vulnerable' (Truong, 2001: 11–14).

In other words, the higher the barriers of entry are to an attractive target country, the more complex become the methods and morality of human smuggling. The critical variable seems to be the interaction between the governments and organized crime syndicates. Phil Williams points out that 'organized crime both threatens states and exploit states'; it undermines the legality of states, but also uses its powers by corrupting officials and thus increases its own profits (Williams, 2002: 164–5, 174–8). Corruption is, indeed, a central element in human smuggling and trafficking, because it makes it easier to get the migrants across the borders.

Illegal immigrants may, of course, enter a country on their own, but often they need assistance from professional smugglers taking them in clandestinely. The interaction between authorities and smugglers/traffickers is more direct and corrupt when the latter provide the immigrants with fraudulent documents – such as passports, visas and job letters – or bribe the immigration officials. Belgian passports are notorious for their frequent use as impostor documents. There are several known cases in which the consulate officials of a country have been selling visas to the would-be migrants for a hefty fee. Travel agencies may also participate in such operations.

A special case in this context is the story of children sent by their parents through smugglers/traffickers to Western Europe in the hope that the parents will also be provided, in their childrens' wake, with the right to asylum. This practice is particularly common in Somalia where each month some 250 children are sent out with parents paying up to US$10,000 to get their teenagers, but sometimes only 4- to 5-year-olds, out of the country. These 'unaccompanied' children may eventually lead a decent life with their relatives, but equally they may be abandoned to prostitution and domestic slavery (www.irinnews.org/webspecials/Somalichildren, 19 January 2003). In France, young, unaccompanied immigrants often 'evaporate' from the official bureaucracy and find themselves in diverse conditions. There is only one reception centre for under-age immigrants (Tervonen, 2002).

In 2001 a total of 461, and in 2002 a total of 550 unaccompanied children went to Sweden; in 1999 the figure had been 236. The entrants were mainly Kurds from Northern Iraq, but they also came from Somalia, Serbia and Afghanistan. Swedish documentation shows that, in most cases, these children were assisted both by ethnic networks and by smuggling rings whose concern is money rather than a safe journey for their 'customers' (Kihlström, 2003a; Kihlström, 2003b).

It is commonly assumed that the role of the organized crime syndicates is pervasive in illegal migration. However, many comments tend to confuse illegal migration and human smuggling/trafficking in a less helpful way (this is done even by *Global Report* 1999: 223–5). In addition, empirical evidence points in a somewhat different direction; while organized crime is certainly involved in many illegal human transfers, they can also take place without the criminal contribution. Moreover, many smuggling rings are more like small enterprises run by a group of relatives or acquaintances.

If they *are* involved, crime syndicates tend to control the entire migration cycle in human trafficking, while in smuggling the main task is simply to take the person across a border for profit. Human trafficking may combine smuggling with other types of criminal activities, such as the drug trade and prostitution, which is possible because of the resources and networks of the organized criminal groups. In many cases these groups are tied together by ritual kinship relations that reaffirm their fraternal and operational common-alities (Paoli, 2001: 94–9).

For their operation, criminal networks become particularly relevant in the recruitment process in which the trafficker needs local contacts to find, either personally or through the media, new victims for the business. Human trafficking often involves coercion and violence, which are, how-ever, hardly effective means in the recruitment phase of the process. More important is the social access to the local communities and their willing-ness to provide human raw material for trafficking, because without that material the business would dry up (Koslowski, 2001: 347–9; Truong, 2001: 16–18).

Transnational mobility and borders

In political and legal terms, illegal immigration cannot be understood without considering its role in the wider category of transnational mobility and the nature of borders crossed by these flows. The relatively closed nature of borders can be contrasted with the increasingly free movement of goods, capital and technology across them. With the exception of the EU and a few other cases, where labour can move freely from one country to another, most people are contained by the current international regime within national borders. This also means that most workers continue to produce for the international market primarily from their home base. Capital and technology are much more mobile than productive activities *per se*. This creates a stark contrast between the global mobility of the rich and the immobility of the great majority of the poor (this contrast has been stressed by Bauman, 1998).

An additional factor is that much of the transnational mobility of the elite is licit in nature: tourism, business trips and temporary residence (or even multiple residences) in foreign countries. True, the masses also have access to legal routes of migration, though such migration has now become quite limited compared with the open embrace of immigrants of some hundred years ago in the United States and in the immediate post-Second World War period in Europe. In the 1950s and the 1960s, especially in Germany, Sweden and Switzerland, the liberal immigration regime was a result of the need for a semi-skilled labour force in the Fordist manufacturing system. These migration flows followed methodically the expansion of the industrial core of the world economy (Morawska and Spohn, 1997: 25–38).

Thus, in recent history, large-scale migration has been associated with the expansion of mass industrial production. Because of the demand for labour, immigration to Western Europe in the main remained legal in, and even assisted by, the recipient countries. However, the shift to more capital and technology-intensive modes of production has reduced significantly the need to import labour from the (semi-)peripheral countries. Instead, we find that capital is searching for new sites of production in which the combination of the costs and the productivity of labour is in the right proportion to relevant economic and political variables. These factors include access to the global and regional markets, and the character of governmental policy. The implication at the heart of this business logic is that it is in everybody's interest, for both economic and political reasons, to keep the peripheral labour force where it is now; that is, on the periphery.

These observations indicate that the globalization of capital is associated with the erection of economic and political barriers to the free flow of labour, especially between the periphery and the centre. The elites and masses of the core prefer to confine the exploitation of the low-paid labour force to the periphery. This barrier is often reinforced by the core govern-ments; for example, by closing the border for migration and imposing employer penalties (for an early analysis of this tendency, see Cohen, 1987).

It has often been noted, though, that in industrialized countries, the penalties for importing and employing illicit labour are weak and are enforced in a haphazard manner. However, in recent years, the control of borders has become stricter, largely because of the political backlash that the inflow of immigrants and refugees has fostered in several European countries. In reality, the issue is about the crisis of the asylum policy that represents both the complexity of the challenges of the new immigration and the ineptitude of the EU governments to deal with it (on the British situation, see *The Economist*, 2003).

In sum, the licit flow of unskilled (and even skilled) workers is now regulated increasingly by the core states, although the United States continues to be a partial exception in this regard. Core economies prefer to admit specialists, primarily in the information and biotechnology industries, who can add value to innovative and productive activities and thus contribute to the nation's competitive position in the world economy. Less skilled workers do not fit this economic image and are largely excluded by the core governments from the present immigration regime.

Brain drain from the periphery to the core has long existed, but today it seems to be more pronounced, and more selective, than before. While, in the past, university students could receive their basic education in decent colonial institutions, now they have to leave much earlier for Britain, France, and especially the United States, to claim their springboard for the future.

Restriction of movement is not limited only to the core; it is also used in the semi-periphery. Malaysia's recent crackdown on foreign workers is a good example. It had an estimated 800,000 legal and one million (some say 600,000) illegal foreign workers, most of them unskilled labourers from Indonesia. At the time of writing, half of the illegal workers have been deported and those caught after a grace period of four months will receive five years in prison and six strokes of a rattan cane. The motive of the government crackdown is mainly economic; by expelling illegal foreign workers, it hopes to provide jobs for native Malaysians, and promote more capital-intensive industry instead of relying on imported cheap labour (*The Economist*, 2002b; 2002c).

Occasional expulsion of foreign workers does not, of course, eliminate various low-paid and risky jobs in the core economies. Immigrant labour continues to be in demand simply because the prevailing polarized labour market needs underpaid workers, especially in the service sector. In addition, there are dirty and dangerous jobs that native-born workers try to avoid. Yet, to my knowledge, not a single industrialized country has a specific regime to admit labourers from (semi-)peripheral countries for menial jobs. Immigrants and refugees may end up working at such tasks, but this is seldom the stated purpose of their admission to a country. In part, this is because of the resistance of the trade unions which, if they accept immigration at all, demand equal wages and treatment for the foreign workers.

Legal immigration and asylum are, of course, still available options, although they are in many ways restricted. UNHCR has estimated that during 2001–02 the number of asylum seekers in twenty-eight industrialized countries dropped by 12 per cent. This reflects a common tendency to close borders, though it is by no means universal. EU countries Austria, Denmark, France, Germany and Sweden admitted 2,000 fewer asylum seekers than they had in 1990, while the absolute figure had grown in Belgium, the Netherlands, and in particular the United Kingdom. This variation in national statistics cannot, however, remove the fact that most of these countries have experienced an anti-immigrant backlash (Graff, 2002).

Some countries, such as Australia, have adopted particularly strict policies *vis-à-vis* asylum seekers. The number of immigrants and refugees Australia admits has declined steadily since the 1970s. The Howard government gained notoriety in August 2001 when its troops stormed a Norwegian ship, the *Tampa*, transporting over 400 Afghan refugees whom the ship had rescued from a sinking Indonesian ferry.

The government sternly refused to accept the Afghan asylum seekers into Australian territory; they became a test case for the determination of the government in general to keep illegal immigrants out of the country. The Afghans were turned away, instead, to Christmas Island and, later, to New Zealand and Nauru, to which Australia is providing funds to sustain the refugees. These moves were prompted by domestic politics, in which the Howard government was campaigning against One Nation, a rightist anti-immigrant party. In addition, these measures reflected a general anti-immigration tendency in Australian politics (Marsh, 2001; *New York Times*, 2001).

The European Union

In the EU, migration issues have recently dominated the political agenda. As early as February 1997, the Council adopted a joint action to combat the trafficking of human beings and sexual exploitation of children (97/154/JHA). A more comprehensive process was started in the Tampere European Council in October 1999. Its presidency conclusions reflect the duality of the EU's approach. On the one hand 'it would be in contradiction with Europe's traditions to deny freedom to those whose circumstances lead them justifiably to seek access to our territory'. This liberal principle was complemented, however, by the protective one; the 'common policies of asylum and migration' must provide 'consistent control of external borders to stop illegal immigration'. The Council paid particular attention to the need to tackle illegal immigration at its source (Tampere European Council, 1999).

The Tampere decisions were followed up by the Seville European Council (2002). The meeting aimed to speed up a common policy on asylum and immigration to integrate it with the Union's policies with the third countries. By using resources earmarked for trade expansion, development assistance and conflict prevention, the EU should aim, with third countries, at the joint management of migration flows, including compulsory return in the event of illegal immigration. The 'integrated, comprehensive and balanced policy' should also lead to the coordination of a visa regime and the establishment of a repatriation programme.

In July 2002, the EU Council adopted a Framework Decision on Combating Trafficking in Human Beings that defined common guidelines for the jurisdiction, the nature of offences, penalties and sanctions pertaining to human trafficking. The original aim of the Decision may have been ambitious, but the results remained limited as it was confined to 'the minimum required'. The minimum standard had to be enforced by member states by 'effective, proportionate and dissuasive criminal penalties, which may entail extradition' (European Union, 2002). To date, the penalties for human traffickers have varied between countries, but they have mainly been quite lenient. This fact has drawn organized crime into the business, in part from drug trafficking, in which penalties are higher (Moore, 2001).

Migration issues have recently gained a new urgency because of the admission to the Union in 2004 of several new member states. Fears have been growing that citizens of the new member states will start moving in great numbers to the territory of the present EU. Therefore, several old member states have imposed restrictions, lasting up to seven years, on the free movement of workers coming from the new member states. The immigration question has also been put on the political agenda by the nationalist-populist backlash against previous liberal immigration policies. In recent years, immigration issues have shaped domestic politics, especially in Austria, Denmark, France, Italy and the Netherlands.

A coalition of EU member states has decided to make a more forceful move against illegal immigration. Starting in 2003, Britain, France, Greece, Italy, Portugal and Spain have established two joint naval patrols; one in the Mediterranean and the other around the Canary Islands. The EU Council approved Operation Ulysses in September 2002 and in the future it may form an element of the common EU border guard. The task of the patrols is to intercept vessels that are assumed to be carrying illegal immigrants and take them to the nearest harbour.

It is estimated that the EU countries accept annually some 680,000 legal migrants from outside the Union. Rather than promising to increase the chances of legal immigration, the EU is putting more emphasis on preventing illegal immigration and integrating existing immigrants into the society. It has also taken steps to return refugees to countries such as Bosnia and Afghanistan, which are now considered safe for them. The level of legal migration can be compared with the estimated half a million illegal immigrants in the EU area who enter each year primarily from North Africa, the Middle East and Eastern Europe.

In a sense, the problem of illegal immigration is a result of political hypocrisy; governments ban or restrict the inflow of people who either deserve humanitarian protection or are needed to sustain economic activities. The common idea that an economy and its labour force can survive in fierce international competition by continuously ratcheting up its productivity and innovative activities neglects the simple fact that in every industrial country there are pockets of economic activity that can be maintained only by having access to cheap labour. In addition, the demographic trends in

Europe and Japan make it necessary to start importing foreign labour in increasing numbers in order to replace the greying population and provide adequate services for it.

The scale of human smuggling and trafficking

The exact number of illegal immigrants is impossible to estimate. This is not only because of the clandestine nature of the operations, but also the lack of common international standards about what 'illegal' exactly means. The estimates become even murkier if one adopts concepts such as 'irregular immigration'. The standard, and inexact, procedure is that the magnitude of illegal immigration is estimated on the basis of the number of border appre-hensions (Salt, 2000: 39–41). Official estimates indicate that in 1992 a total of 3.3 million irregular migrants have entered the United States, but current estimates are much higher, usually around 6–7 million. In Japan, in 1994, there were some 300,000 irregular immigrants, while for the EU a figure of 3 million irregulars is often quoted.

In the middle of the 1990s, an estimated 250,000–300,000 illegal migrants plus 700,000 asylum seekers arrived each year in Western Europe. Traffickers were used by 10–22 per cent; that is, 100,000–220,000 of the illegal entrants. By the end of the 1990s, the annual number of illegal immigrants entering the EU had increased to about half a million. However, the range of estimates for individual member states is usually so large that any total figure for illegal immigrants is at best a poor reflection of the reality. One reason for the poor quality of the data is that the definitions of the key concepts in illegal migration are inconsistent; this concerns in particular human smuggling and trafficking (Ghosh, 1998: 9–13; *The Economist*, 1999: 32; Salt, 2000: 37–9; Salt and Hogarth, 2000: 31–4).

The data problem is reflected by the fact that the estimates on the number of illegal immigrants in Germany vary from 0.5 to 1.5 million people (some 100,000 people are smuggled into the country each year, mainly through the Czech and Polish borders). In the Netherlands, there are an estimated 46,000 to 110,000 illegal immigrants, while in France the corresponding figure is said to be 400,000 (Cowell, 2002). A recent estimate is provided by the US Department of State, which has monitored human trafficking since 1994. It concludes that some 700,000 persons, especially women and children, are trafficked worldwide each year. Among them, 45,000–50,000 people are smuggled illegally into the United States (this figure seems to be on the low side).

In Europe, 1,500 women are said to be trafficked for prostitution into the UK each year, and the total number of people smuggled in is, of course, much higher. In the EU, in 1999, Belgium prosecuted 429, Germany 176, Italy 500 and Spain 1,008 cases of human trafficking. Although these figures cannot be strictly compared, they reinforce the general impression that the South European countries are the ones most exposed to human smugglers operating across the Mediterranean and the Aegean Sea (US Department of State, 2001).[3] Greece alone is assumed to have more than a million illegal immigrants, mainly from Turkey, Albania, Iraq and Romania. The figure seems high, and perhaps a figure of 300,000 illegal immigrants is closer to the truth (Cowell, 2002).

The smuggling and trafficking routes

Illegal immigrants enter Europe from well-known sources where political and social structures are fragmenting, the economy is deteriorating, laws are incomplete and poorly enforced, and criminal networks involved in trafficking are permitted to operate. The routes used for smuggling and trafficking people to Europe are not exactly clandestine in nature; they can be mapped quite well by combining various types of materials available. These routes overlap, in part, those used to smuggle drugs, cigarettes and stolen cars (for maps of smuggling routes, see Fabre *et al.*, 2000).

Turkey is one of the main gateways to Europe for immigrants from Iraq (especially Kurds), Iran, Afghanistan and many other Asian countries, including China. The number of smugglers arraigned in Turkey has risen from about a hundred in 1998 to 850 in 2000, while the number of illegal immigrants detained rose from 11,400 in 1995 to 29,400 in 1998, and to 94,000 in 2000. The increase in numbers has been said to show that Turkey, as a putative member of the EU, is taking the problem of human smuggling seriously. In 2001, 23,400 of the apprehended people came from Iraq, 8,500 each from Afghanistan and Iran, and 8,300 from Moldova (Icduygu and Toktas, 2002: 26–35).

Previously, smugglers crossing the Adriatic Sea used small boats, but the growth in the traffic has made it possible for them to rent dilapidated cargo ships that can take as many as 1,000 passengers, on a treacherous and sometimes deadly journey. The migrants usually pay US\$1,000–US\$3,000 to the smugglers depending on the route used. It is not unusual that the migrants are cheated of their money and left stranded in an unfamiliar place or, even worse, in the sea (Finkel, 2001a; Moore, 2001). Perils for the passengers are probably even worse in other parts of the world; for example, in 2001, a small wooden Indonesian ship on its way to Australia, carrying Middle Eastern asylum seekers, sank, taking some 300 people with it (Mydans, 2001).

A key argument of the so-called critical geopolitics is that the nature of space has been transformed in a major way; the territorial conception of space is complemented by spaces that are defined by various economic, legal and symbolic markers. They represent 'emerging spatial forms' that the disjuncture between the territorial system of nation states and the spatial structure of the global economy is creating (Agnew and Corbridge, 1995; see also Väyrynen, 2003). This disjuncture is characterized by various networks, gaps and enclaves.

Turkey is an example of a *juridical enclave* which so far has lacked appropriate legislation and enforcement mechanisms, which permits the human smuggling business to flourish. Such an enclave cannot usually exist without *social enclaves*, in which ethnic and other networks help the immigrants to find the right contacts and even to assume new identities. Juridical enclaves are established by governmental inaction, while social enclaves represent the societal aspect of transnational relations.

Increasingly, the business of human trafficking is conducted with the help of the Internet, when one can speak of a *virtual enclave*. The Internet has particular importance in the recruitment of women for sex trafficking, which joins drugs, gambling, pornography and terrorism as the fast-growing areas of illegal business (Sager, 2002). Territoriality has not disappeared altogether, however; there are also *territorial enclaves* that smugglers can safely use for their operations (Truong, 2001: 6–7). Patras in Greece, Sarajevo in Bosnia, Kiev in Ukraine, Zeebrugge in Belgium and Calais in France are examples of enclaves that are regularly used in human smuggling and trafficking (Fabre *et al.*, 2000: 51–2).

In other words, there are voids and gaps in the legal and territorial spaces as well as social and logistical networks that the crime syndicates can utilize in their search for quick profits from human trafficking. These enclaves are seldom connected by market-based economic ties, but they create a new kind of underground transnational system where interdependence is fostered by criminal networks that are looser and more informal in nature than is usually alleged (Paoli, 2001).

If one smuggling enclave, and routes linked to it, is closed, the interests of migrants and of intermediaries alike lead to the opening up of new routes. Thus, as the increased patrolling of the traffic across the nine-mile-wide Strait of Gibraltar has intensified, the flow of illegal immigrants from North Africa has been directed to the Canary Islands. In 1999, 875 illegal immigrants were detained there, but in 2000 the figure rose to 2,410, and in 2001 to 4,112. The immigrants are held in captivity for up to forty days after which they are formally deported, but in reality many of them find their way to Spain's mainland as illegal entrants (Daly, 2002).

From Turkey and Greece, illegal immigrants aim usually at Western Europe through various intermediary enclaves, among which Sarajevo and the Bosnian countryside, as way stations to the EU, are among the most popular. Estimates again vary considerably, but it has been assumed, somewhat conservatively, that in 2000 about 50,000 illegal immigrants either stayed in Bosnia or used it as their staging post to the EU. In the first half of 2001, a total of 11,000 people were allowed in at Sarajevo airport from a total of thirteen prime sources of migrants, while 4,000 people were refused entry. Out of the 11,000 entrants, only 3,000 departed the country legally, the others taking to the smuggling routes (Finkel, 2001b: 9).

As Bosnia is a landlocked country, the illegal migrants must continue their journey either by flying to other countries or moving through neighbouring countries, among which Croatia is a popular conduit. Bosnia and Croatia have, in all, 400 crossing points on their 900-mile land border, of which only fifty have been monitored so far. In Croatia, more than 20,000 illegal migrants are stopped annually by the police. Taking into account the porous nature of the border, the weakness of the central government in Bosnia, and the embedded corruption in the area, it is no surprise that the illegal crossing of the border is a widespread practice.

The situation has been changing slightly since 2001, when Bosnia finally established a State Border Service. In 2003, it had under control some two-thirds of the Bosnian–Croatian border. To stem the trafficking of illegal immigrants, the Bosnian central government has received external assistance from the EU and other sources. In addition, some countries, such as the UK, have established missions to Sarajevo to conduct pre-emptive monitoring of the illegal immigrants.

Those crossing the borders from Bosnia to neighbouring countries are often assisted by 'organizers' who have established among themselves networks within which the migrants are moved from one enclave to another. The 'organizers' also often have semi-permanent relations with the local authorities. Such relations are usually rife with corruption, as witnessed by the situation on the Bosnian–Croatian border. The infiltration into Croatia is not without risk, however; in 2000, some thirty people drowned when crossing the Sava River. From Croatia, some of the illegal immigrants continue their journey through Slovenia, whose officials report that 35,000 people crossed the border without permission. Some of those people move from there further on to Eastern and Central Europe (Buric, 2001; Finkel, 2001b).

Another route in the Balkans has been through Belgrade. The Milosevic regime developed close ties with China, whose citizens received numerous tourist visas in return for payments to the Yugoslav authorities. Many of the Chinese overstayed their visas in Belgrade, or continued their journey to various destinations in Western Europe. This pressure has been felt, among other places, on the Hungarian–Serbian border, where in one border section alone close to 3,000 illegal immigrants were apprehended in 2002, a figure that was 7–8 times higher than in 2001 (Buric, 2001; Wright, 2002).

Yet another route goes directly from Croatia, Slovenia (and especially Albania) to Italy, whose 4,800-mile-long coastline is impossible to close completely to illegal immigrants. In Italy, the destination is often the open coast of Apulia in its south-eastern corner. This area can easily be reached by speed boat from the other side of the Adriatic Sea, the shortest distance being some sixty miles. In 1997 alone, in the province of Lecce in Apulia, some 20,000 illegal immigrants were caught by the police. Most of them came from Albania (40 per cent), from the former Yugoslavia (24 per cent), Iraq (23 per cent), and Turkey (8 per cent) (*The Economist*, 1999: 32).

In Italy, Rome has become a gathering place for illegal immigrants from North Africa, the Middle East and South Asia (many of the latter from Bangladesh). The popularity of Italy among illegal immigrants is not only because of its exposed geographical location, but also because of the needs of the economy and government policy. Labour-intensive underground industries rely extensively on immigrant labour, whose wages are very low by European standards. This keeps the grey economy ticking over and obviates the need to export jobs abroad. The Italian government has also issued several mass amnesties to illegal immigrants who met some basic conditions. As a result, the illegals, estimated to number 230,000, live in the hope that there will again be a new amnesty (Juurus, 2001).

Because of large immigrant communities and the language, France is obviously another popular destination. It is also a way station to Britain, where the existing diaspora communities and the language also help the adjustment to new conditions. Eurotunnel (the 'Channel Tunnel') has become a popular, but perilous, route to the wonderland of Britain. At any one time, about a thousand asylum seekers and illegal immigrants have been waiting in the Red Cross compound in Sangatte on the French side that was opened in 1999.

The asylum seekers, night after night, made efforts to enter Britain through the rail tunnel. Others are packed in their dozens in the trucks and ferries that ply their business to Britain. In 2000, the British police and security guards intercepted about 5,000 people who were trying to reach Britain through the tunnel, but by the first half of 2001 the figure had risen to 18,500. In November 2002, after persistent demands by the British, the Red Cross closed the Sangatte camp to new arrivals, many of whom were Afghans.

There are harrowing stories of the risks the illegal immigrants are willing to take to arrive successfully in Britain. Some of them fail in this effort, as did 58 Chinese who were suffocated in a metal container in June 2000, and some two dozen who drowned in 2004 when harvesting clams. In the British view, France should tighten its policy because its authorities use no sanctions against those who try repeatedly to cross the Channel, whether via the tunnel or by sea. On the other hand, the French have criticized the British for having lax immigration rules that need tightening (Cowell, 2001; Richburg, 2001).

The end of the Cold War opened up the Eastern and Eastern Central European countries for migration flows to Western Europe. The most impoverished countries, such as Armenia and Romania, have become sources of immigrants, while others, such as the Czech Republic, have served more as conduits for immigrants coming from Eastern European countries or from outside Europe. Prague has become a very popular tourist city, and is hence increasingly international in flavour, which also allows illegal immigrants to 'melt' into the cosmopolitan urban environment and find ways to continue further into EU countries. The penalty for failure is small; the immigrant is returned to the Czech Republic, where the treatment of his/her asylum application continues uninterrupted (Branstein and Poolos, 2000).

Prostitution and slavery

As mentioned earlier, a central dimension of the illegal immigration concerns its intentionality. In one case, the human smugglers only undertake the task of transporting a person for a fee to a particular destination or way station, to be left there or to be delivered to another agent. Traffickers may do it 'honestly' or cheat the clients by leaving them in the lurch in an unfamiliar country without money, documents or contacts. These migrants tend to fall, sooner or later, into the hands of the asylum authorities in one of the countries en route.

If the smuggling takes place between two rather close points (say Albania and Italy, or Mexico and the United States) and if the routes are well known and tested, the traffickers may be more like family enterprises that do not need to have any deeper connections with organized crime. On the other hand, if the distance is great and the barriers to entry are high, organized crime syndicates are more likely to be involved, as is the case in the professional trafficking by 'snakeheads' of Chinese illegal immigrants to the United States that started in a big way in the 1980s.

The Chinese syndicates continue to control the lives of the migrants at their destination, disciplining them by force if necessary, and extract heavy payments for the services rendered, the smugglers holding their clients as virtual hostages until the fees have been paid. The average smuggling fee for illegal Chinese immigrants to the United States was US$27,000 in 1993, and it has obviously increased since then (for a detailed analysis, see Chin *et al.*, 2001: 138–47).

The second type of intentionality in human trafficking concerns the exploitation of a person in a particular end task that is usually prostitution or slavery; sometimes drug trafficking. The nature of employment is not decided by the victim, but is done by the agent hijacking him or her for profit or pleasure. The character of the job is not always known in advance, or the victim has only a vague idea about it. Victims lose their personal freedom and are thus unable to escape their predicament, or can do so only at great risk. The result is often physical and emotional harm. It is not unfounded to call trafficking 'a trade in human misery' (*Global Report*, 1999: 223).

The difference between these two different types of intentionalities is usually captured by using the concept of 'smuggling' to refer to illegal immigration in which an agent is involved for payment to help a person to cross a border clandestinely, and 'trafficking' to the use of coercion and victimization. This dichotomy has been emphasized in the UN-directed Vienna process on transnational organized crime. Its main implication is that 'smuggling' is a migration issue that has to be dealt with by legal and bureaucratic means, while 'trafficking' is a human rights issue and, as a consequence, the victim deserves protection (Salt and Hogarth, 2000: 20–3, 119–20).

This dichotomy is important for the reason that it removes a stigma associated with people who are trafficked for prostitution. If coercion and exploitation are involved, the migrant is not a criminal, but the victim of a crime. On the other hand, it has been argued that trafficking and exploitation are not synonymous, because trafficking can lead to different social outcomes depending on the target country (Pomodoro, 2001: 238–41).

Sex trafficking seems to be most common in Europe and South East Asia. A complete picture of the phenomenon is, of course, much more diverse; for example, there appears to be a continuing trafficking of women from the Dominican Republic to the Netherlands. Within Europe, most of the women working as prostitutes come from Russia and other countries of the former Soviet Union. The number of sex migrants in Europe is impossible to determine, but 100,000 is sometimes given as a conservative estimate.

A higher estimate is reached if one believes that 50,000 Russian women alone are lured every year into the sex business abroad. On that basis, one may even suggest that the number of foreign sex workers in the EU varies between 200,000 and half a million. Ukraine seems to be a major source of sex migrants, as 20 per cent of the trafficked migrants from there are women, while the corresponding figure for Lithuania is 7 per cent and Poland 9 per cent (*Global Report*, 1999: 225–7; Salt and Hogarth, 2000: 71–3; Weir, 2001). The higher standard of living and the Roman Catholic culture in Lithuania and Poland may explain the difference in numbers.

The estimation of the number of women trafficked for the sex industry is made even more difficult by the fact that women may come to a country for brief periods on a legal visa, go back home for a time, and return later. Those staying in the prostitution business for longer periods of time may have originally entered the country legally to work, nominally at least, as maids, entertainers, waitresses or secretaries (on problems of estimating trafficked migrants, see Salt and Hogarth, 2000: 29–43).

In Germany's red light districts alone, there are an estimated 15,000 Russian and other East European prostitutes. Moreover, according to Dutch evidence, over half of the women are below the age of 21. Even in Europe, it is not unusual, either, that children are trafficked for pornography and sex. In addition to Europe, women from Russia, Ukraine and elsewhere are trafficked to the United States, Japan, Macau and other places where there is a local or a tourist demand for sex services. For example, in South Korea, there are 6,000 illegal Russian female immigrants who make their living from prostitution (Caldwell *et al.*, 1999: 44–50).

In prostitution, there is also a Balkan route, not only into Western Europe, but also to Bosnia and Kosovo, where women are used, in addition to satisfying local demand, by international peacekeepers and civilian experts. In Bosnia, in 2001 there were an estimated 2,600 prostitutes, of whom 10 per cent were minors and 25 per cent claimed to have been trafficked. In Eastern Europe, prostitution grows out of poverty, which explains why 80 per cent of the women in Bosnia came either from Moldova or Romania (Dempsey, 2001).

The country origin of women working in prostitution in Kosovo is pretty much the same and they are, on average, 21 years old. Their history also illustrates another aspect of the transnational prostitution business; the women are usually sold on three to six times before arriving in Kosovo (Chausy, 2001). To address the problem, the Stability Pact for Southeastern Europe established in 2000 a Task Force on Trafficking in Human Beings that has developed a multi-year anti-trafficking action plan to enhance regional cooperation. South-eastern Europe provides vivid practical illustrations of how human trafficking has pervaded the zones of violent conflict, and how organized crime can operate with impunity in weak, flawed states (for a major study, see UNICEF, 2002).

The trafficking of women in South East Asia tells, if possible, an even more dismal story. In particular, there are many more minors in South East Asia than in Europe. UNICEF estimates – fortunately, it probably overestimates – that there are 800,000 child prostitutes in Thailand; 400,000 each in Indonesia and India; and 100,000 in the Philippines. In addition, the number is 300,000 for the United States, and varies between 500,000 and 2 million in Brazil (*Global Report*, 1999: 226; Hoffmann, 2001). In South East Asia, most of the child prostitutes are sold by their poverty-stricken parents or they are abducted from rural villages to work in urban brothels in their own countries. In Thailand, for example, the sale of young girls for prostitution is a common practice, sanctioned by prevailing religious beliefs (Bales, 1999: 34–79).

Thailand is both an exporter and an importer of migrant workers. In 1995, it was estimated that about 450,000 Thai nationals, of both genders, work outside their own country, and that 60 per cent of them – that is, 270,000 – were illegal migrants. Taiwan has been by far the most common destination for Thai migrant workers, who are mainly unskilled labourers (Phongpaichit, 1999: 77–9, 88–9). The exportation of women for prostitution and arranged marriages has also been a major element of this outward migration.

In Thailand, foreign sex workers, whose number has been increasing rapidly, usually come from Burma and Laos. There are an estimated 30,000 Burmese women working as prostitutes in Thailand who are brutalized by both the Thai and Burmese authorities, and in particular the military. On the unruly Thai–Burmese border, dotted with refugee camps, the smugglers work in tandem with the Thai border police, who coerce camp dwellers to recruit young girls for the traffickers and get paid for that help. These payments have become an 'informally institutionalized source of income for the police'. In the sex traffic across the Thai–Burmese border a financial premium is put on virgins that has resulted in the 'commodification of virginity' (Kyle and Dale, 2001: 40–7).

As illegal entrants, the trafficked Burmese girls have no protection and are at the mercy of the police and immigration officers. The situation is made worse by the Thai perception that the Burmese, especially the women, are culturally inferior and can be treated as if they were not even human beings. If a Burmese girl is deported to her own country, she faces imprisonment and hard labour there. The situation of the Laotian women in Thailand is slightly better because of the greater porosity of the Laos–Thailand border and a smaller cultural distance (Bales, 1999: 65–8; Phongpaichit, 1999: 90–2).

There is in Thailand a two-way street in the sex trade. In addition to the importation of prostitutes, many Thai women work in the sex business, especially in Japan, Germany and the United States. In Berlin alone there are an estimated 2,000 Thai prostitutes, while in 1995 their number in Japan was around 23,000 out of the total 100,000 sex workers in the country (many of the rest were Filipinas). In Germany, the women have usually entered the country legally, although they seldom have work permits. In Japan and the United States women have usually been brought in illegally and they are controlled by the agents with connections to criminal gangs. In the United States, these gangs are often Chinese or Vietnamese, holding female prostitutes as virtual slaves (Bales, 1999: 69–71; Phongpaichit, 1999: 8).

In South East Asia, Cambodia too is involved in sex traffic. The local sex industry expanded in the early 1990s with the end of the war and the arrival of international peacekeepers and other officials. There are now an estimated 80,000–100,000 prostitutes and sex slaves in Cambodia, most of them in Phnom Penh, while in 1990 the number was only about 1,000. The value of the sex industry is conservatively estimated at US$500 million per year. Cambodian girls are trafficked for prostitution mostly in Thailand, but also in Macau (thefuturegroup.org, 2001).

A distinction was made above between illegal migration, including smuggling, and human trafficking on the basis of the agencies and intentions involved in the process. It follows from this distinction that organized crime syndicates are involved primarily in human trafficking. As criminal organizations, these syndicates have no scruples about engaging in coercive and exploitative activities, because this is the way to make money.

Crime syndicates pursue both domestic and international activities that cannot always be separated from one other. Indeed, mafias are not only domestic organizations; they also have strong transnational ties – for example, in financial business and smuggling (De Brie, 2000). The Internet has become an increasingly important instrument for shady business deals. In the United States, it has been estimated that the value of underground business conducted online amounts to US$37 billion a year, which is about the same (at US$39 billion) as US consumers spend on legitimate Internet business (Sager *et al.*, 2002).

A new feature on the international crime scene is the rapid international-ization and mutual cooperation of organized crime syndicates originating from different countries. In addition to the Italian Mafia and Chinese triads, the Russian, Nigerian and Albanian crime syndicates, among others, have spread their tentacles across the world. These syndicates have also expanded their activities to new fields, so that they start resembling travel agencies as they provide documentation, transportation, accommodation and other necessary services for illegal migrants. As the supply of willing migrants continues to grow, the critical resources for an effective intermediary are contacts in the target area and enough money to cover start-up costs (Caldwell *et al.*, 1999: 50–61; Shannon, 1999: 30–3).

Criminal gangs, however, do other things that legal travel agencies do not do. They traffic women, by coercion if necessary, to brothel keepers for prostitution and are ready to seize them if they attempt to escape. An important aspect of the mafia operations is their involvement in debt collection, to make sure that the money borrowed by the trafficked person gets paid back from his or her work in prostitution or some other criminal activity. Sometimes this task is sub-contracted to the local mafia. In addition to the costs of trafficking, the victims have to pay for their keep, and for these expenses they can retain only part of the money earned from, say, prostitution (Caldwell *et al.*, 1999: 63–7; Shannon, 1999: 33).

Debt bondage of prostitutes and other slaves is particularly bad in South and South East Asia. The financial arrangements are so onerous that the slave has little chance of being released unless s/he becomes physically useless to the slaveholder. Often their debt burden accumulates over time despite all the free work performed by the slave for his/her holder (for details, see Bales, 1999).

The Albanian mafia is a good example of a criminal organization that specializes in smuggling human beings, drugs, cigarettes, alcohol, contraband and anything that has a market demand because of legal and political restrictions on their availability. As is well known, the Albanian mafia has penetrated to all levels of the country's government (Cilluffo and Salmoiraghi, 1999). The Kosovar mafia has extensive operations all over Europe. In London, Albanians and Kosovars control some 70 per cent of the massage parlours in Soho, where prostitutes are held as virtual slaves and treated with increasing violence. These groups have connections with immigration and prostitution rackets across Western Europe.

Conclusion

The pressures to migrate from the peripheral to the core countries are growing, on both the supply and demand sides. On the supply side, rampant political and economic crises, and the sheer lack of prospects of a more prosperous life, push people to move to the North where there is a need for a low-paid labour force in some industries and in the service sector. In fact, the present nature of global economic competition creates the need for both a high-skilled and low-skilled, expensive and cheap, labour force. The well-trained and productive component of the labour force produces for the international market, while the low-skilled part of it is geared more to meeting the domestic demand that helps to contain costs and check inflation.

The demographic gap between the South and the North creates further incentives to move. The EU countries alone, according to a UN estimate, need 1.6 million immigrants annually if they want to maintain, by 2050, their labour force at the current absolute level. Refugees seeking asylum are, as a rule, families with children, and in need of economic and humanitarian assistance and education before they can be gainfully employed.

'Economic migrants' are, in turn, usually young men who seek a better life and more money, part of which can be remitted to their families in their home country and thus pay the loans taken out to finance the journey to the North. These migrants seldom come from the most squalid conditions, but rather from families that own some land and other property. Often one of the older sons is financed by loans against this property to travel to the North and find a place there. Thereafter, other siblings and cousins have a better chance of following in his footsteps.

Human trafficking has expanded in tandem with the growing pressures of emigration and the closure of the borders, especially in the EU. In effect, there seems to be a direct correlation between the increasingly restrictive policies of the EU and its member states, and the level risks and fees associated with human smuggling. In other words, receiving states are creating by their policies a lucrative market for the traffickers. The destination of their 'commodity' is decided by the logistical ease by which it can be reached, but also by the prevailing political and legal conditions.

Usually, the countries that have lax immigration laws and small penalties for illegal immigrants and their traffickers, such as Italy and Spain, become popular targets and way stations. The EU has been trying to harmonize its immigration laws and asylum procedures, but so far practical progress has been limited. Human smugglers and traffickers tend to use entry points and routes where the risk of getting caught is lowest in comparison to the amount of money that can potentially be earned by using this particular juridical, social and territorial enclave.

Although illegal immigration and human trafficking are important political and social issues, their impact should not be exaggerated. First, in Europe, most illegal immigrants are not smuggled in by the traffickers; they usually arrive with a legal visa and simply overstay it. Few countries in the EU and in North America have reliable national systems to track those overstaying their visas (although the present war on terrorism has created various schemes of 'homeland security' to track illegal immigrants). These people often 'melt' into the local ethnic communities and the underground economy in which there is a demand for their unregulated labour force. One may even say that the highly regulated labour market in Europe has, perversely, increased the demand for illegal workers. Illegal immigrants do not always stay permanently, but they may well go home temporarily and then return again to earn more money.

One should not paint, however, too rosy a picture of illegal immigration. Many immigrants find themselves in desperate positions in major European cities and their flophouses, or in reception centres sited out in the countryside. They do not get asylum, either because of the strict legislation or delays in procedures, and thus do not have a chance to work or to move around. In particular, in cities they become prey to the organized crime gangs that may have smuggled them into the country in the first place.

Human trafficking can result in pernicious consequences. This is evidenced by severe human-rights violations, even slavery, in cross-border trafficking of women for prostitution. Especially in South East Asia, prostitution also involves very young girls who are physically and mentally destroyed by their sexual exploitation, while economically they fall in debt bondage. The situation is not much better in the case of those women who toil in sweatshops on practically every continent, but in particular in Asia. Their freedom and self-confidence have been stolen, and their bodies exploited for a quick profit.

Because of the nasty features of human smuggling and trafficking, there is a need for cooperative international measures. For good reasons, the World Commission on the Social Dimensions of Globalization (2004: 95–9) suggests that governments should establish a new multi-lateral framework for cross-border movement of people. In addition, a more effective dialogue is needed between labour-exporting and labour-importing countries.

Notes

1. The reality is revealed by an incident on the Mexican–US border. A truck driver sought to smuggle to the United States ninety-four illegal immigrants from Central America. He was caught and is now serving time in an overcrowded Mexican prison together with 4,000 other prisoners jailed on charges of immigrant smuggling. The driver was promised US$11,000 for the one-off operation, which is a considerable sum for a person whose weekly income is US$400 (which is itself very good by Mexican standards) (Thompson, 2001). If we estimate conservatively that each migrant paid US$700, the organizers pocketed about US$54,000 even though the operation failed. In Central America, over 300,000 migrants smuggled to the United States annually are handled by several hundred independent smugglers who often cooperate with the travel industry (US Government 2000: 47–8).

2. Ghosh (1998: 1–6) speaks of 'irregular migration' when referring to various aspects of illegal immigration. A problem with this concept is that much of the 'irregular' movement of people is a rather well planned and repeated activity.
3. The State Department prepared the report as a response to the Victims of Trafficking and Violence Protection Act (PL 106–386) passed by Congress in 2001. The report divided the countries into three tiers depending on how closely they complied with the minimum standards defined in the Act.

References

Agnew, J. and S. Corbridge (1995). *Mastering Space. Hegemony, Territory and International Political Economy*. London: Routledge.

Andreas, P. (2001). 'The Transformation of Migrant Smuggling Across the US–Mexican Border', in D. Kyle and R. Koslowski (eds), *Global Human Smuggling. Comparative Perspectives*, Baltimore, MD: Johns Hopkins University Press: 107–25.

Bales, K. (1999). *Disposable People. New Slavery in the Global Economy*, Berkeley, CA: University of California Press.

Bauman, Z. (1998). *Globalization. Human Consequences*, New York: Columbia University Press.

Bigo, D. (2002). 'Security and Immigration: Toward a Critique of the Governmentality of Unease', *Alternatives*, 27(1): 63–92.

Branstein, J. and A. Poolos (2000). 'East/West: Human Trafficking', 4 parts, www.rferl.org/nca/features/2000, September.

Buric, C. (2001). 'The Balkan Route in Illegal Migration', RFE/RL Balkan Report, 5(27) 13 April.

Caldwell, G., S. Galster, J. Kanics and N. Steinzor (1999). 'Capitalizing on Transition Economies: The Role of Russian Mafiya in Trafficking Women for Forced Prostitution', in P. Williams (ed.), *Illegal Immigration and Commercial Sex. A New Slave Trade*, London: Frank Cass: 42–73.

Chausy, J. P. (2001). 'Kosovo – Trafficking Report', Press Briefing Notes, IOM, 24 April.

Chin, K.-L., S. Zhang and R. J. Kelly (2001). 'Transnational Chinese Organized Crime Activities: Patterns and Emerging Trends', in P. Williams and D. Vlassis (eds), *Combating Transnational Crime. Concepts, Activities and Responses*, London: Frank Cass: 127–54.

Cilluffo, F. J. and G. Salmoiraghi (1999). 'And the Winner Is . . . the Albanian Mafia', *Washington Quarterly*, 22(4): 21–5.

Cohen, R. (1987). 'Policing the Frontiers: The State and the Migrant in the International Division of Labour', in J. Henderson and M. Castells (eds), *Global Restructuring and Territorial Development*, London: Sage: 88–111.

Cohen, R. (1997). *Global Diasporas. An Introduction*, Seattle: University of Washington Press.

Cowell, A. (2001). 'Britain Faces Flurry of Illegal Migrants Using Channel Tunnel', *New York Times*, 3 September: A10.

Cowell, A. (2002). 'Migrants Feel Chill in a Testy Europe', *New York Times*, 28 April: A14.

Daly, E. (2002). 'Squalid Dead End for Migrants' Hopes', *New York Times*, 30 May: A4.

De Brie, C. (2000). 'Etats, mafias et transnationales', *Le Monde diplomatique*, April: 4–5.

Dempsey, J. (2001). 'UN to Act on Prostitution in Bosnia', *Financial Times*, 28–29 July: 2.

Economist, The (1999). 'Europe's Borders: A Single Market in Crime', 16 October: 25–6, 32.

Economist, The (2002a). 'The Longest Journey. A Survey of Migration', 2 November: 5–6.

Economist, The (2002b). 'Malaysia: Threat of the Cane', 31 August: 44.

Economist, The (2002c). 'Malaysia's Foreign Workers: But Who Will Do the Dirty Work?', 16 February: 39.

Economist, The (2003). 'Asylum: Bordering on Panic', 1 February: 34–5.

European Union (2002). Council Framework Decision of 19 July on Combating Trafficking in Human Beings, 2002/629/JHA, Official Journal L 203, 1 August, Brussels.

Fabre, T. *et al.* (2000). 'La nouvelle économie du crime', *L'Expansion*, 632, November: 50–5.

Findlay, M. (1999). *The Globalisation of Crime. Understanding Transitional Relationships in Context.* Cambridge: Cambridge University Press.

Finkel, D. (2001a). 'A Road to Nowhere', *Washington Post National Weekly Edition*, 3–9 September: 9–10.

Finkel, D. (2001b). 'Balkans Are Open Door to West on Asylum Trail', *Daily Telegraph*, 7 September: 16.

Friman, H. R. and P. Andreas (1999). 'Introduction: International Relations and the Illicit Global Economy', in H. R. Friman and P. Andreas (eds), *The Illicit Global Economy and State Power*, Lanham, MD: Rowman and Littlefield: 1–23.

Ghosh, B. (1998). *Huddled Masses and Uncertain Shores. Insights into Irregular Migration*, The Hague: Martinus Nijhoff.

Global Report on Crime and Justice (1999). New York: UN Office for Drug Control and Crime Prevention/Oxford University Press.

Graff, J. (2002). 'Across the New Frontier', *Time*, 24 June: 24–33.

Helminen, M. and T. Kirkas (2002). 'Kauppatavarana ihminen', in T. Kirkas (ed.), *Eurooppa ja ihmissalakuljetus*. Helsinki: Suomen Pakolaisapu: 20–31.

Hoffmann, R. F. (2001). 'Zerstörte Kindheit', *Der Tagespiegel* (Berlin), 19 December: 7.

Icduygu, A. and S. Toktas (2002). 'How Do Smuggling and Trafficking Operate via Irregular Border Crossings in the Middle East'. *International Migration*, 40, 6, 25–54.

International Migration (2002). New York: United Nations Population Division (also www.unpopulation.org).

Juurus, K. (2001). 'Salaa Euroopassa', *Helsingin Sanomat*, Kuukausiliite, April.

Kihlström, S. (2003a). 'Barn smugglas hit från Afrika', *Dagens Nyheter* (Stockholm), 18 January: A1, A5.

Kihlström, S. (2003b). 'Fler ensamma barn söker asyl', *Dagens Nyheter* (Stockholm), 22 January: 6.

Koslowski, R. (2001). 'Economic Globalization, Human Smuggling, and Global Governance', in D. Kyle and R. Koslowski (eds), *Global Human Smuggling. Comparative Perspectives*. Baltimore, MD: Johns Hopkins University Press: 337–58.

Koslowski, R. (2002). 'Human Migration and the Conceptualization of Pre-Modern World Politics', *International Studies Quarterly*, 46(3): 375–400.

Kyle, D. and J. Dale (2001). 'Smuggling the State Back In: Agents of Human Smuggling Reconsidered', in D. Kyle and R. Koslowski (eds), *Global Human Smuggling. Comparative Perspectives*, Baltimore, MD: Johns Hopkins University Press: 29–57.

Marsh, V. (2001). 'Illegal Immigrant "Crisis" Lands Canberra in Hot Water', *Financial Times*, 12 December: 9.

Mattila, H. S. (2000). 'Protection of Migrants' Human Rights: Principles and Practice', *International Migration*, 38(1): 53–71.

Miller, M. J. (2001). 'The Sanctioning of Unauthorized Migration and Alien Employment', in D. Kyle and R. Koslowski (eds), *Global Human Smuggling. Comparative Perspectives*, Baltimore, MD: Johns Hopkins University Press: 318–36.

Moore, M. (2001). 'Human Cargo, Inhumane Conditions. Barely Seaworthy Ships Are Carrying Record Numbers of Illegal Immigrants into Europe', *Washington Post National Weekly Edition*, 4–10 June: 15–16.

Morawska, E. and W. Spohn (1997). 'Moving Europeans in the Globalizing World: Comparative Migrations in a Historical-Comparative Perspective (1955–1994 vs. 1870–1914)', in Wang Gungwu (ed.), *Global History and Migrations*, Boulder, CO: Westview Press: 23–61.

Mydans, S. (2001). 'Survivors Tell of Many Deaths in Sea Disaster Off Indonesia', *New York Times*, 24 October: A6.

Naylor, R. T. (2002). *Wages of Crime. Black Markets, Illegal Finance, and the Underworld Economy*, Ithaca, NY: Cornell University Press.

New York Times (2001). 'Australians Seize Ship to Keep Refugees at Sea', 30 August: A6.

Paoli, L. (2001). 'Criminal Fraternities or Criminal Enterprises?', in P. Williams and D. Vlassis (eds), *Combating Transnational Crime. Concepts, Activities and Responses*, London: Frank Cass: 88–108.

Phongpaichit, P. (1999). 'Trafficking in People in Thailand', in P. Williams (ed.), *Illegal Immigration and Commercial Sex. A New Slave Trade*, London: Frank Cass: 74–104.

Pomodoro, L. (2001). 'Trafficking and Sexual Exploitation of Women and Children', in P. Williams and D. Vlassis (eds), *Combating Transnational Crime. Concepts, Activities and Responses*, London: Frank Cass: 237–50.

Richburg, K. B. (2001). 'A Perilous Passage. Asylum-Seekers Take a Deadly Risk Crossing the Channel to England via the Eurotunnel', *Washington Post National Weekly Edition*, 10–16 September: 16.

Sager, I. (2002). 'The Underground Web', *Business Week*, 2 September: 67–74.

Salt, J. (2000). 'Trafficking and Human Smuggling: A European Perspective', *International Migration*, 38(1): 31–54.

Salt, J. and J. Hogarth (2000). 'Migrant Trafficking and Human Smuggling in Europe: A Review of the Evidence', in F. Laczko and D. Thompson (eds), *Migrant Trafficking and Human Smuggling in Europe*, Geneva: IOM: 11–164.

Salt, J. and J. Stein (1997). 'Migration as Business: The Case of Trafficking', *International Migration*, 35(4): 467–94.

Sanchez, T. (2002). 'Deadly Smuggling at the Border. A Crackdown on Mexican Migrants Has Resulted in Riskier Crossings', *Washington Post National Weekly Edition*, 19–25 August: 17.

Seville European Council (2002). *Presidency Conclusions*, European Union, 21–22 June.

Shannon, S. (1999). 'Prostitution and the Mafia: The Involvement of Organized Crime in the Global Sex Trade', in P. Williams (ed.), *Illegal Immigration and Commercial Sex. A New Slave Trade*, London: Frank Cass: 119–44.

Tampere European Council (1999). *Presidency Conclusions*, European Union, 15–16 October.

Teitelbaum, M. S. (2001). 'International Migration: Predicting the Unknowable', in M. Weiner and S. S. Russell (eds), *Demography and National Security*, New York: Berghahn Books: 21–37.

Tervonen, T. (2002). 'Lapsi etsii turvaa', *Suomen Kuvalehti*, 31: 24–7.

thefuturegroup.org (2001). 'The Future of Southeast Asia. Challenges of Child Sex Slavery and Trafficking in Cambodia', August, Canada: www.thefuturegroup.org.

Thompson, G. (2001). 'Big Money in Smuggling Migrants Is Tempting for Mexican Truckers', *New York Times*, 16 August: A1, A8.

Truong, T.-D. (2001). 'Human Trafficking and Organized Crime', *Working Paper Series*, No. 339, The Hague: Institute of Social Studies.

UNICEF (2002). *Trafficking in Human Beings in Southeastern Europe*, Belgrade: UNICEF.

US Department of State (2001). *Trafficking in Persons Report*, Washington DC: US Department of State, July.

US Government (2000). *International Crime Threat Assessment*, Washington DC: US Governmental Interagency Working Group, 15 December.
Varese, F. (2001). *The Russian Mafia. Private Protection in a New Market Economy*, Oxford: Oxford University Press.
Volkov, V. (2002). *Violent Entrepreneurs. The Use of Force in the Making of Russian Capitalism*, Ithaca, NY: Cornell University Press.
Väyrynen, R. (2003). 'Regionalism: Old and New', *International Studies Review*, 5(1): 25–51.
Warzazi, H. E. (1986). *Exploitation of Labour Through Illicit and Clandestine Trafficking. Subcommission on Prevention of Discrimination and Protection of Minorities*, E/CN.4/Sub.2/1986/6, New York: United Nations.
Weir, F. (2001). 'Russia Battles Its Sex Trade', *Christian Science Monitor*, 16 May.
Williams, P. (1999). 'Trafficking in Women and Children: A Market Perspective', in P. Williams (ed.), *Illegal Immigration and Commercial Sex. A New Slave Trade*, London: Frank Cass: 1–10.
Williams, P. (2001). 'Organizing Transnational Crime: Networks, Markets, and Hierarchies', in P. Williams and D. Vlassis (eds), *Combating Transnational Crime. Concepts, Activities and Responses*, London: Frank Cass: 57–87.
Williams, P. (2002). 'Transnational Organized Crime and the State', in R. B. Hall and T. J. Biersteker (eds), *The Emergence of Private Authority in Global Governance*, Cambridge: Cambridge University Press: 161–82.
World Commission on the Social Dimension of Globalization (2004). *A Fair Globalization. Creating Opportunities for All*, Geneva: International Labour Organization.
Wright, R. (2002). 'Tighter Security Fails to Deter Illegal Immigrants', *Financial Times*, 10 December: 10.
Zeller, T. (2001). 'Migrants Take Their Chances on a Harsh Path of Hope', *New York Times*, 18 March: 14.

8
Migration, Remittances and Growth*
Riccardo Faini

Introduction

In the nineteenth century, migration flows played a key role in fostering income convergence between Europe and the United States (O'Rourke *et al.*, 1996). In the present globalization episode, however, the role of migration is much more limited (Faini *et al.*, 1999). This is not because of lack of economic incentives. If anything, income differentials between sending and receiving countries are significantly larger than they were less than a century ago (Pritchett, 1997).

Restrictive immigration policies in the traditional receiving countries account largely for the more marginal role of migratory flows. Since 1974, immigration policies, particularly in Europe, have taken an increasingly restrictive stance, seeking both to discourage further immigration and to favour return migration.

Since the 1990s migration policies have taken a new turn. In response to the growing shortages of skilled labour, immigration polices have been geared increasingly to favouring the entry of skilled workers, while continuing to penalize unskilled flows.

Such trends raise major concerns among sending countries, on at least two counts. First, sending countries will be restricted substantially in their ability to rely on unskilled migration as an engine of growth and convergence. Second, the bias toward skilled flows risks exacerbating the brain drain and could well deprive such countries of their most skilled and talented people. On both counts, it is argued, growth prospects in emigration countries will be curtailed.

The link between migration and growth in sending countries is, however, quite complex. First, sustained migratory flows may be associated with an equally large flow of remittances that may help relieve the foreign exchange constraint in the home country. Second, migrants may return home after having acquired a set of productive skills, with a beneficial impact on the growth prospects of their home country. Finally, the policy bias in host

171

countries toward skilled flows may not necessarily penalize sending countries. As argued most recently by Stark *et al*. (1997, 1998), the incentive to acquire skills may be strengthened by the prospect of being able to migrate. Even in the presence of a brain drain, therefore, the average education level of those left behind in the home country may be higher than it otherwise might.

Accordingly, in this 'revisionist' approach to the analysis of the brain drain, skilled migration may turn into a 'brain gain' even if no account is taken of the potentially positive effects on the home country of remittances and return migration. Allowing for such factors would then further strengthen the case of the revisionist approach, to the extent, for example, that skilled migrants, because of their higher earnings, are likely to generate a larger flow of remittances.

As at the time of writing, however, the empirical evidence in support of the supposedly positive effects of skilled migration on the home country is, at best, limited. Moreover, even the theoretical predictions of the revisionist approach are not unambiguous. First, skilled migrants may have looser links with their home country – for example, because they are more likely to take their family to the host country and may therefore remit less rather than more. Second, prospective migrants may want to strengthen their chances of admission to the host country by pursuing their graduate studies there. The most talented individuals would then have an incentive to migrate at a relatively early stage in their school career, thereby definitely reducing the average enrolment ratio in the home country's educational system. Contrary to the revisionist approach, then, a higher probability for skilled workers to migrate may be associated with a decline in the home country's educational achievements. Moreover, as shown in the early contribution of Bhagwati and Hamada (1974), the brain drain may interact with domestic distortions so as to reduce welfare in the home country unambiguously. Finally, even the impact of return migration on home-country welfare may be less favourable than generally presumed (Constant and Massey, 2002).

The purpose of this chapter is to take a further look at the theoretical underpinnings and empirical evidence around the link between skilled migration, education and remittances. We find little support for the revisionist approach. On the contrary, our results suggest that the concerns voiced in sending countries about the economic impact of skilled migration are warranted. First, a higher skilled content of migration is found to be associated with a lower flow of remittances. As noted earlier, we interpret this result as indicating that skilled migrants tend to loosen their links with their home country. Second, we find little evidence suggesting that raising the skill composition of migration has a positive effect on the educational achievements in the home country. In contrast, the tertiary enrolment ratio in sending countries is associated negatively with the skilled content of migration.

The remainder of this chapter is organized as follows. In the next section, we present the simple static welfare computation of outward migration. We then assess how the skilled composition of migration affects education and remittances. We also consider the role of return migration before focusing on the existing institutional set-up for international labour flows, and conclude with some constructive suggestions.

The welfare impact of outmigration[1] without a brain drain

One unresolved issue in the analysis of international migration is whether the welfare of migrants should be attributed to the host or the home country. Presumably, the simple strategy would be to count temporary migrants that retain close links to their home country in the sending country population, and attribute permanent migrants to the receiving country. Yet this classification is fraught with difficulties, given that, by and large, the initial intention of migrants to move permanently or temporarily may not coincide with their final choice. Moreover, even permanent migrants retain some links with their country of origin. Overall, therefore, it seems more appropriate to analyse the welfare impact of migration separately for those left behind in the sending country; the migrants themselves; and the receiving country (Bhagwati and Rodriguez, 1975).

With these caveats in mind, we can turn to the standard representation of a two-country economy in Figure 8.1. Let A be the source country and I be the host country. Employment in country A (L_A) is measured from right to left, in country I (L_I) from left to right. The two schedules, MPL_A and MPL_I, measure the marginal productivity of labour in countries A and I, respectively, both

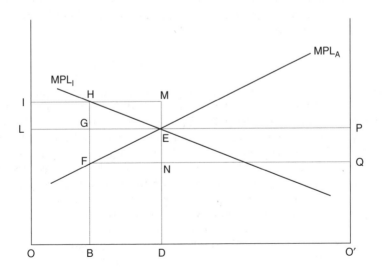

Figure 8.1 The welfare impact of international migration

as a declining function of their employment levels. The initial equilibrium is at point B. The post-migration equilibrium is at point D, with BD workers having migrated from country A to country I. It can easily be seen that those left behind in the home country suffer a welfare loss. The gains in labour income (the area NEPQ) are more than offset by the losses in income from capital (the area FEPQ). The net loss is equal to FEN. Conversely, the host country enjoys a net welfare gain (HGE). What about migrants? They are clearly better off; otherwise they would not have migrated. More crucially, the gains to migrants (FGEN) more than offset the losses of those left behind. Independently of whether migrants are classified in the home or the host country population, the key fact is that the gains from migration overwhelm the losses of those left behind. Migrants could therefore fully compensate the losers in their host country and still be better off. Moreover, while in most of the welfare literature, compensating income transfers typically are seen as merely a theoretical possibility, in the case of migration such transfers actually occur, in the form of remittances. Summing up, the net welfare effect of migration on the sending country is ultimately an empirical matter, and will depend on the way migrants are classified and on the amount of remittances. Interestingly enough, these two factors are likely to be closely interrelated to the extent that the propensity to remit may be larger for temporary migrants. On both counts, therefore, the welfare of the sending country should increase. Conversely, the flow of remittances from permanent migrants should be small. The home country will then lose out, both because migrants are no longer part of its welfare and because remittances are small.

But how large is the welfare effect of emigration? In a one-good, two-factor economy, the rough and ready formula for computing the aggregate welfare impact of migration (Borjas, 1995) is:

$$\Delta Q/Q = -(\alpha_L\, m^2\, \varepsilon)/2$$

where m is the outmigration rate, α_L is the income share of labour, ε is the elasticity of wages with respect to labour, and the welfare change (ΔQ) is measured as a ratio to initial GDP. Suppose that $\alpha_L = 0.7$, $\varepsilon = 1$,[2] and that 10 per cent of the home country population lives abroad ($m = 0.10$). The welfare loss from emigration would then be equal to less than four-tenths of 1 per cent of annual GDP – a relatively small effect. Would this effect be offset by remittances? Most likely yes, given the sheer size of remittances. Consider, for example, the case of Turkey, where the share of the population living abroad is fairly large, around 8 per cent (that is, $m = 0.08$). During the 1990s remittances averaged almost 2 per cent of GDP, thus dwarfing the welfare loss from emigration. Similarly, existing estimates suggest that slightly more than 7 per cent of Mexico's population lives abroad. According to our simple formula, welfare losses should be about three-tenths of 1 per cent of GDP. Remittances, on the other hand, account for more than 1 per cent of GDP, which more than offsets the loss from emigration.

These are simple, back-of-an-envelope calculations. To answer the question of whether the net effect of outmigration is positive after allowing for remittances we would need some firmer evidence on the relationship between remittances and the number of migrants abroad. If we simply assume that the GDP share of remittances (R) is a function of the percentage of the home country population living abroad,[3] with $R = \beta m$, the welfare effect of outmigration becomes:

$$\Delta Q/Q = -(\alpha_L \, m^2 \, \varepsilon)/2 + \beta m$$

Based on a simple cross-country regression, we take β to be equal to 0.3. This estimate is subject to errors, but appears to indicate that if m is not exceedingly large – that is, $m < \beta/\varepsilon\alpha_L \cong 0.43$ – the welfare impact of additional outmigration is positive.

The brain drain as a hindrance to welfare and growth

Apart from the brain drain, the welfare impact of emigration is likely to be small and more than offset by the flow of remittances. However, the calculations in the previous section assume labour to be homogeneous. Still, the most often voiced concern is that migration deprives sending countries of their most skilled and most entrepreneurial workers. Skilled workers may generate strong positive externalities in production (Lucas, 1990; Barro and Sala-i-Martin, 1995) and lead to faster growth. Moreover, the costs of education are typically borne by the home country, with its attendant benefits being lost to the country if the worker emigrates (Bhagwati, 1976). In terms of Figure 8.1, the marginal productivity schedule would shift inward as a result of the emigration of skilled workers and the dissipation of the related externalities. The size of such an effect would wipe out the second-order magnitude of the traditional Harberger triangle described in the previous section.

While, therefore, the 'old' development literature tended to see the brain drain as a significant hindrance to the economic prospects of developing countries, more recently these concerns have been amplified greatly by the emphasis in the new growth theory on human capital as a key engine of growth. In an interesting extension of the endogenous growth approach, Miyagiwa (1991) shows that the emigration of skilled workers will hurt mainly other skilled workers – those who did not migrate – that used to benefit relatively more from the scale externality associated with a large pre-brain-drain stock of skills. Contrary to conventional presumptions, unskilled workers would be relatively less affected.

The development literature also held that the brain-drain was a large-scale phenomenon. However, as acknowledged by Bhagwati (1976), the empirical evidence on the scale of the brain drain was at best patchy. Moreover, available data referred to flows rather than to stocks, and captured only gross flows with no information on reverse migration. Most of the evidence came from disparate and typically sources that were not comparable. In turn, lack of systematic evidence severely hampered empirical investigations in this field.

Still, the size of the brain drain has largely been undisputed. More recently, Stalker (1994) reports that sub-Saharan Africa lost 30 per cent of its skilled personnel between 1960 and 1987. The Caribbeans have also been hard hit, presumably because of the proximity to the United States and the relative ease in emigrating there. For example, Jamaica had to train five doctors in order to keep one. More recently, the presumption about the size of the brain drain has been confirmed by the excellent study by Carrington and Detragiache (1998). This was the first attempt to provide systematic and comparable evidence on the brain drain. The authors relied on the 1990 Census of the United States to estimate the educational attainments of migrants there. They then related these figures to the Barro–Lee data on educational levels in the source country to get migration rates for separate educational groups. Some selected results are reported in Table 8.1. The authors also compute total migration rates to the OECD by assuming that for each sending country the skill composition of OECD migration is the same as that to the United States. Obviously, this set of estimates is bound to be somewhat less reliable, particularly if migration to the United States only accounts for a relatively small share of total migration from a given country. In spite of all these caveats, the results are remarkable. First, migration rates are disproportionately large among educated people. Second, the absolute figures are substantial. For example, in Ghana, more than 15 per cent of the

Table 8.1 The brain drain: migration rates by educational attainments (percentages of host country's educational group)

Country of origin	To the United States		To the OECD	
	Secondary education (%)	Tertiary education (%)	Secondary education (%)	Tertiary education (%)
Korea	1.2	5.7	3.3	14.9
Philippines	4.4	6.6	6.0	9.0
Ghana	0.3	15.1	0.7	25.7
Uganda	0.6	15.4	0.6	15.5
Dominican Republic	29.7	14.2	30.5	14.7
Guatemala	29.1	13.5	29.1	13.5
Colombia	3.6	5.6	3.8	5.6
Mexico	20.9	10.3	20.9	10.3

Source: Carrington and Detragiache (1998).

home country population educated to tertiary level has migrated to the United States. Extending the analysis to the OECD raises the migration rate for this educational group to 25.7 per cent. This latter figure must, however, be interpreted with some caution, since only slightly more than 50 per cent of Ghana's migrants go to the United States. The figures for poorer countries in North America are equally impressive. More than 20 per cent of Mexicans with a secondary education live in the United States. For the Dominican Republic the figure rises to 29.7 per cent.

The revisionist approach to the brain drain

Is the brain drain a definite concern for sending countries? Or are there any mitigating factors? The traditional answer to the latter question is a cautious 'yes'. First, as noted earlier, migration may be associated with a substantial flow of remittances towards the home country. Under the plausible presumption that the earnings of skilled workers are relatively larger, we would expect the flow of remittances associated with the brain drain also to be more substantial. Second, skilled migrants may eventually return to their home country and bring with them valuable skills that will contribute to economic growth there. Third, and more recently, it has been argued that the prospect of migration by itself may foster domestic investments in education, provided that returns to skills are higher abroad. Stark *et al.* (1997, 1998), Mountford (1997) and Stark (2002) have all developed models where the possibility of emigrating may result in more education for those left behind. Beine *et al.* (2001) offer some empirical support to the claim that the brain drain may boost growth in the sending countries. By and large, therefore, the revisionist approach would hold that not only are there mitigating factors to the brain drain but also that the emigration of skilled workers may be beneficial for the home country. In Stark's words, the argument against the brain is then 'turned on its head'.

In what follows, we review the case for the revisionist approach. We assess separately the three main arguments in favour of the 'brain gain' discussed above on both theoretical and empirical grounds. We conclude that the case for the brain gain is at best unproved, and argue that the more traditional concerns about the negative impact of the emigration of highly skilled workers on the economic fortunes of sending countries remain valid.

Does the brain drain boost remittances?

IMF data for the mid-1990s calculated the total amount of remittances at US$65 billion. To put this figure in perspective, it is larger than the total flow of ODA. Remittances indeed play a critical role as a source of foreign exchange in several countries, as documented in Table 8.2. The key question, however, is how remittances are influenced by the skill composition

Table 8.2   Aid, exports and remittances, 1990–97 averages (percentages)

	Remittances GDP (%)	Aid GNI (%)	Exports GDP (%)
CE Europe and Central Asia	4.16	2.70	37.00
Turkey	1.96	0.33	17.82
East Asia and Pacific	1.05	3.41	42.88
Philippines	5.46	1.96	34.67
Indonesia	0.24	1.07	26.82
Latin America and Caribbean	2.17	4.56	27.54
Colombia	1.16	0.23	17.24
Mexico	1.19	0.09	21.92
Middle East and North Africa	7.19	3.07	32.20
Egypt	8.69	6.85	23.84
Morocco	6.68	2.76	26.08
South Asia	2.87	4.68	17.50
Bangladesh	3.05	4.49	9.19
India	1.59	0.64	9.70
Sub-Saharan Africa	3.71	15.06	27.42
Ethiopia	0.28	16.89	10.15
Nigeria	2.11	0.91	43.13
Senegal	3.04	12.99	28.84

of emigration. If skilled migrants tend to remit more, then the concern about the welfare impact of the brain drain may be diminished. Alternatively, the finding of smaller propensity to remit by skilled migrants would magnify such concerns.

Unfortunately, existing evidence on the propensity to remit of skilled workers is quite limited. Early evidence showed that remittances tend to increase with the level of education (Johnson and Whitelaw, 1974; Rempel and Lobdell, 1978). For the case of Philippines, however, Rodriguez and Horton (1994) found that the educational level of migrants has no effect on the amount of remittances. In addition to the limited and sometimes conflicting evidence, there is a more fundamental problem with this strand of literature. Suppose that skilled migrants tend to stay longer abroad,[4] because they are more willing to reunify with their families in the host country,[5] say, or face fewer constraints in their ability to do so. One typical finding of the literature is that the flow of remittances tends to decline with the length of the migrants' stay (Lucas and Stark, 1985). Therefore, even a positive coefficient of education on remittances cannot be taken as evidence that the brain drain is associated with a larger flow of remittances. The direct effect of skills may indeed be positive, but the overall effect, which controls for the longer propensity of skilled migrants to stay in the receiving country,

Table 8.3 Remittances and the skill composition of emigration

Dependent variable	REM/POP	REM/GDP
Explanatory variables		
Constant	91.4	0.07
	(62.2)	(2.00)
SM	10.8	0.28
	(4.82)	(2.02)
MSEC	−0.27	0.0007
	(0.43)	(1.42)
MTER	−0.93	−0.0005
	(1.84)	(1.95)
Y_{pc}	−9.76	−0.008
	(1.30)	(1.97)
R^2	0.53	0.33
NOB	33	38

Notes: REM: remittances; POP: working age population; SM: migrants abroad as a percentage of the home-country population; MSEC: percentage of population with a secondary education living abroad; MTER: percentage of population with a tertiary education living abroad; Y_{pc}: income *per capita* in the home country. NOB: number of observations. T-stats in parentheses.

may well be negative. By and large, therefore, it is difficult to draw any firm conclusions from the existing literature on the relationship between education and remittances.

Faini (2002) runs a simple set of regressions relating the ratio of remittances to GDP (or, alternatively, to the home country population) to a set of regressors that includes the stock of migrants, the income *per capita* in the sending country and, crucially, the skilled composition of migration. The latter variable comes from the Carrington–Detragiache data set.[6] There is no control for the length of migrants' stay in the host country. Hence, the coefficient of skills should capture the total impact of education on remittances. The results are shown in Table 8.3. Three facts stand out. First, as expected, remittances are an increasing function of the stock of migrants. Second, remittances decline with income *per capita* in the sending country, lending support to the altruistic motive for income transfers. Third, and more crucially, remittances decline as the share of migrants with a tertiary education goes up. The latter result is consistent with the notion that more migrants with higher levels of skills tend to move permanently to the host country. Their attachment to the home country becomes progressively weaker, and so does the propensity to remit. Additionally, the ease of family reunification that these migrants typically enjoy further weakens their willingness to remit. Overall, these effects obfuscate the more traditional channel where migrants with a higher education have larger earnings, and should therefore be more inclined to remit.

If confirmed by future research, these results are striking. Sending countries lose from migration on three grounds. First, there is the standard welfare loss, as shown in Figure 8.1. Second, the loss of skills attendant on the brain drain typically carries a negative externality. Third, skilled migration may lead to a smaller, rather than a larger, flow of remittances.

Does return migration mitigate the concern about the brain drain?

Return migration has a significant bearing on the impact of the brain drain. Returnees may take back home not only their original skills but also those they have acquired during their stay in the host country. The original loss to the home country may then be more than offset by the new and valuable skills the migrants was able to acquire abroad. Furthermore, as emphasized in the new migration literature, a temporary move abroad may be a key component of a strategy designed to overcome domestic market failures. For example, if because of credit market imperfections a home country resident is unable to undertake a profitable project, then a temporary stay abroad may allow him or her to accumulate sufficient capital to finance such project. Similarly, in the absence of complete insurance markets, a home-country household may be unwilling to undertake a high-return but high-risk project. Temporary migration, until the uncertainty about the project is resolved, may offer a way out. Indeed, the household may reduce its exposure to risk by having some of its members migrate to a country where returns are not perfectly correlated with the domestic economy. It may then be in a better position to take on additional risk and hence to implement the project.

On a more pessimistic note, returnees may be those that have not succeeded abroad. Migrants will typically return home if their initial expectations about wages and working conditions abroad are not met. In Duleep's (1994) definition, these are 'mistaken migrants'. Negative selection of returnees may also occur if skilled migrants are in a better position to acquire new skills – language proficiency, say – in the host country. To the extent that such skills are imperfectly rewarded in the home country, returnees will be those with more limited skills initially and lesser skills accumulation abroad. Moreover, as has already been noted, skilled migrants may be more willing to reunify with their families in the host country or face fewer constraints on their ability to do so. Once again, return migrants will be negatively selected.

Borjas and Bratsberg (1996) provide a fairly general model of return migration. They show that whether returnees will be positively or negatively selected cannot be determined on a-priori grounds. What can be said, however, is that, under fairly general conditions, return migration will tend to amplify the initial selection bias. If migrants were initially negatively selected, then returnees will be relatively more skilled. Conversely, if migrants were initially relatively skilled, then the least skilled are most likely to return to their home country. Intuitively, if the initial selection bias is positive with the more skilled also being more likely to migrate, then the least skilled will be the marginal migrants and will be more likely therefore to reconsider their initial decision. In this case, return migration will be negatively selected and, as a result, will do little to alleviate the negative welfare and growth impact of the brain drain.

There is considerable evidence about the negative selection bias of return migration. Solimano (2002) reports that, at least in science and engineering (S&E), a large fraction of Ph.D. graduates from developing countries tend to remain in the United States after graduating. National Science Foundation data show that, four years after graduation, 88 per cent of China's and 79 per cent of India's graduates in S&E are still working in the United States. More comprehensive evidence comes from Lindstrom and Massey (1994) for Mexican migrants; Reagan and Olsen (2000) for the United States; Bauer and Gang (1998) for Egypt; and Steiner and Velling (1994) and Schmidt (1994) for Germany. Rodriguez and Horton (1994) show that, in the case of the Philippines, returnees are somewhat less educated than those remaining abroad. Similarly, Knerr (1994) finds that, for Pakistan, skilled migrants tend to stay longer abroad than do unskilled workers. Finally, Borjas (1989) shows that the least successful foreign scientists are more likely to return home from the United States.

In apparent contrast, Jasso and Rosenzweig (1988) for the United States and Ramos (1992) for Puerto Rican migrants to the United States conclude that returnees tend to be more skilled. However, these findings are not inconsistent with the Borjas and Bratsberg model, to the extent that returns to skills are relatively high in Puerto Rico and the initial flow of migrants tend therefore to be negatively selected. Return migration, once again, tends to amplify the initial selection bias.

The bottom line of this literature can be best summarized as follows. Return migration will not provide much consolation to a country suffering from a brain drain problem. Only if initial migrants were mainly unskilled, as in Puerto Rico's case, will returnees be positively selected. Otherwise, the loss of human skills will at best be mitigated by return migration. There is also some evidence that returnees have difficulties in readjusting to the economic and social environment of their home country (Dustmann, 1996). Often, as observed by Knerr (1994) for Pakistan, skilled returnees tend to be unemployed for long periods.

Educational achievements and the brain drain

The revisionist approach holds that the brain drain may foster growth by raising the return to education. Stark (2002) and Beine *et al.* (2001) develop simple models where the sheer possibility of migration increases the return to education, thereby fostering further investments for skill acquisition and ultimately boosting growth. Beine *et al.* (2001) also provide some cross-country evidence in support of such claim.

From an analytical point of view, the conclusion that the brain drain will boost the incentive for education is not particularly new. The early literature on this issue fully acknowledged this possibility (Bhagwati and Hamada, 1974), but went further to assess the interplay between the brain drain and domestic distortions. Bhagwati and Hamada (1974), and Hamada and Bhagwati (1976), show that even in the case where skilled workers are involuntarily unemployed in the home country (and their marginal productivity is plausibly small, if not nil) the brain drain may be detrimental to the home country. Therefore, allowing unemployed or underemployed doctors, for example, to emigrate may not necessarily raise home welfare. First, in the absence of a possibility of emigrating, a doctor might have moved inland where his/her social marginal productivity was likely to be high. Second, the increase in the return to education may prompt more workers to seek education, more so if the wages of domestic skilled workers are tending to catch up with foreign levels. Skilled unemployment would then go up if the increase in the supply of skilled workers, combined with the fall in their demand, more than offsets the impact of skilled migration. Finally, the income *per capita* of those left behind would fall because of both the higher costs of education (which reduce home GDP) and the fall in skilled employment. Bhagawti and Hamada (1974) aptly conclude that 'in the society where welfare function depends on *per capita* income and unemployment rate, national welfare will quite possibly go down'.

On the empirical front, the evidence of Beine *et al.* (2001) is not conclusive. Their main finding is that, in relatively poor sending countries, educational levels are positively associated with migration. However, this result is not necessarily consistent with the revisionist view that skilled migration encourages more investment in education. Given that the authors use data on total migration rather than skilled migration alone, their result is also compatible with the very simple notion that migrants from relatively poor countries are mainly unskilled. Large outflows of unskilled migrants would almost automatically lead to a rise in the average skill level of those left behind in the home country. Hence the finding that (total) migration and human capital at home are positively correlated.

Aggregate migration data therefore cannot be used to discover whether skilled migration fosters education. To identify the effect of the brain drain correctly needs data on the skill composition of migration, and this is what the Carrington and Detragiache data set provides. Using this information, Faini (2003) estimated a simple equation relating educational achievements to a set of explanatory variables that include emigration. Rather than relying on the total migration rate – a fairly inadequate measure of the incentive to acquire skills – the Carrington and Detragiache data set is used to define an indicator of the migration probability for each educational group. These probabilities are, therefore, both country- and skill-specific. But these results do not support the conclusions of Beine *et al.* (2001). First, a higher migration probability for workers with a secondary education has no visible impact on the home country's secondary educational achievements. The coefficient has the 'wrong' sign but is not significantly different from zero. Second, a higher probability of migration for workers with a tertiary education has a significant and positive impact on the rate of secondary school enrolment. This finding suggests that increasing the return of higher (tertiary) education boosts the incentive to acquire lower (secondary) education. Third, and perhaps more surprisingly, the migration probability for workers with a tertiary education has a negative impact on tertiary enrolment. One way to interpret this result is to argue that prospective migrants may want to strengthen their chances of admission to the host country by pursuing their graduate studies there. The most talented individuals would then have the incentive to migrate at a relatively early stage of their school career, thereby definitely reducing the average enrolment ratio in the home country's university system. The evidence in the previous section about the large fraction of S&E doctoral graduates from developing countries still working in the United States four years after graduation is consistent with the notion that prospective migrants pursue their graduate studies abroad with a view also to strengthening their chance of being able to immigrate.

These results provide little evidence in support of the 'brain gain' argument. It is true that a higher probability of migration for individuals with a tertiary education seems to raise the return to secondary education. However, it is also associated with a lower level of tertiary enrolment. To assess the growth impact of these conflicting effects fully one would need to estimate a growth equation controlling for both secondary and tertiary education. In assessing the full effect of the brain drain, its impact on the flow of remittances would also have to be taken into account.

Conclusions and policy implications

We find little support for the optimistic view that the bias towards skilled migration in host countries may be beneficial for sending countries. Our results therefore add to the concern that the process of globalization may unduly penalize relatively poor countries. First, the bias against unskilled migration may deprive these countries of one of the most powerful engines of growth and convergence. Second, the growing preference for skilled migration may exacerbate the effects of the brain drain and further hamper growth prospects in sending countries. As well as the traditional case against the brain drain, I have highlighted in this chapter the possibility that skilled migrants may have, perhaps surprisingly, a lower propensity to remit. I have also shown that, while it is true that a more liberal policy towards skilled migration may raise the return to secondary education, this effect is to some extent negated by the unfavourable impact on tertiary enrolment. Finally,

I have argued that the evidence on the supposedly beneficial impact of return migration is far from conclusive.

Policy-makers have been preoccupied increasingly with the new round of trade negotiations and the global financial architecture. These concerns are fully warranted, given the need to expand and strengthen the multilateral trade system on the one hand and to prevent the recurrence of disruptive financial crises in emerging markets on the other. At the same time, however, little or no attention has been paid to the international labour market. A more symmetrical approach to global policy-making would then be required to define a multilateral framework for labour mobility (perhaps along the lines suggested by Rodrik, 2002; see also Solimano, 2001) and add labour standards to the existing proliferation of international codes. This would involve strengthening the 'fourth' international economic institution, in addition to the IMF, the World Bank, and the WTO: the International Labour Office. The ILO was created well before the other three institutions. As one of its senior officials stated, it relies mainly on 'persuasion' to convince member countries to adopt and implement its codes. It has limited resources and, as a result, a very much scaled down surveillance activity. Still, it is the recognized standard-setting agency of labour. Its role should be strengthened by broadening its mandate, to include, for example, the definition of a multilateral framework for migration, by expanding its surveillance role, and by providing it with additional resources. The new ILO would not work through sanctions, as does the WTO, or through conditionality, like the IMF. A closer cooperation with the World Bank should be envisaged, with a view to providing additional finance to countries that are genuinely intent on reforming their labour markets. The reform of the ILO along these lines should appear high on the international economic agenda.

Notes

* A first draft of this chapter was presented at the UNU–WIDER Conference in Helsinki on 'Poverty, International Migration and Asylum'. I am very grateful to Benedetta Cerciello and Cecilia Frale for their invaluable research assistance. The responsibility for any errors is solely mine.
1. This section draws on Faini (2002).
2. With CES production function, $\varepsilon = (1 - \alpha_L)/\sigma$, where σ is the elasticity of substitution. Then $\varepsilon = 1$ is consistent with $\alpha_L = 0.7$ and $\sigma = 0.3$.
3. This relationship is, however, likely to depend also on the skills composition of migration, the attachment of migrants to their home country, the wage differentials between the host and the source country and other complicating factors. A more accurate analysis of remittance behaviour is presented below.
4. More direct evidence on the positive relationship between education and duration of stay comes from Reagan and Olsen (2000) for the United States. Similarly, the intended duration of stay is found to rise with education in Germany (Steiner and Velling, 1994). This issue is more fully tackled in the next section.
5. Faini (2003) develops a simple model showing that high wage migrants have a larger propensity to reunify with their family in the host country.

6. Given the way the Carrington–Detragiache data set has been compiled, the sending countries for which the share of migration to the United States falls below 30 per cent – and for which, therefore, the data on the skills composition of migration are bound to be much less reliable – have been excluded from the sample.

References

Barro, R. and X. Sala-i-Martin (1995). *Economic Growth*, New York: McGraw-Hill.
Bauer, T. and I. Gang (1998). 'Temporary Migrants from Egypt: How Long Do They Stay Abroad?', *Discussion Paper*, No. 3, Bonn University: Institute for the Study of Labour.
Beine, M., F. Docquier and H. Rapoport (2001). 'Brain Drain and Economic Growth: Theory and Evidence', *Journal of Development Economics*, 64(1), February: 275–89.
Bhagwati, J. (1976). 'The International Brain Drain and Taxation. A Survey of the Issues', in J. Bhagwati (ed.), *The Brain Drain and Taxation. Theory and Empirical Analysis*, Amsterdam: North-Holland.
Bhagwati, J. and K. Hamada (1974). 'The Brain Drain, International Integration of Markets for Professionals and Unemployment: A Theoretical Analysis', *Journal of Development Economics*, 1(1): 19–42.
Bhagwati, J. and C. Rodriguez (1975). 'Welfare-theoretical Analyses of the Brain Drain', *Journal of Development Economics*, 2, September: 195–221.
Borjas, G. (1989). 'Immigrant and Emigrant Earnings: A Longitudinal Study', *Economic Inquiry*, 27: 21–37.
Borjas, G. (1995). 'The Economic Benefits from Immigration', *Journal of Economic Perspectives*, 9: 3–22.
Borjas, G. and B. Bratsberg (1996). 'Who Leaves? The Outmigration of the Foreign-Born', *Review of Economics and Statistics*, 78(1), February: 165–76.
Carrington, W. and E. Detragiache (1998). 'How Big is the Brain Drain?', *IMF Working Paper*, No. 98/102, Washington, DC: IMF.
Constant, A. and D. Massey (2002). 'Return Migration by German Guest Workers: Neoclassical Versus New Economic Theories', *International Migration*, 40: 5–38.
Duleep, H. O. (1994). 'Social Security and the Emigration of Immigrants', *Social Security Bulletin*, 57: 37–52.
Dustmann, C. (1996). 'Return Migration: The European Experience', *Economic Policy*, 22: 215–49.
Faini, R. (2002). 'Development, Trade, and Migration', *Revue d'Économie et du Développement*, Proceedings from the ABCDE Europe Conference, 1–2: 85–116.
Faini, R. (2003). 'Revisiting the Growth Effects of the Brain Drain', Mimeo, Rome: University of Tor Vergata.
Faini, R., J. de Melo and K. Zimmermann (1999). *Migration. The Controversies and the Evidence*, Centre for Economic Policy Research, Cambridge: Cambridge University Press.
Hamada, K. and J. Bhagwati (1976). 'Domestic Distortions, Imperfect Information and the Brain Drain', in J. Bhagwati (ed.), *The Brain Drain and Taxation. Theory and Empirical Analysis*, Amsterdam: North-Holland.
Jasso, G. and M. R. Rosenzweig (1988). 'How Well Do US Immigrants Do? Vintage Effects, Emigration Selectivity, and Occupational Mobility of Immigrants', in P. T. Schultz (ed.), *Research in Population Economics*, Vol. 6, Greenwich, CT: JAI Press.
Johnson, G. and W. Whitelaw (1974). 'Urban-rural Income Transfers in Kenya: An Estimated Remittances Function'. *Economic Development and Cultural Change*, 22, 473–9.

Knerr, B. (1994). 'Labour Migration from South Asia: Patterns and Economic Implications', in D. O'Connor, and L. Farsakh (eds), *Development Strategy, Employment and Migration. Country Experiences.* Paris: OECD Development Centre.

Lindstrom, D. and D. Massey (1994). 'Selective Migration, Cohort Quality, and Models of Immigrant Assimilation'. *Social Science Research*, 23, 315–349.

Lucas, R. E. (1990). 'Why Doesn't Capital Flow from Rich to Poor Countries?', *American Economic Review*, 80(2): 92–6.

Lucas, R. E. B. (1987). 'Emigration to South Africa's Mines', *American Economic Review*, 77(3): 313–30.

Lucas, R. E. B. (1997). 'Internal Migration in Developing Countries', in M. R. Rosensweig, and O. Stark (eds), *Handbook of Population and Family Economics*, Amsterdam: Elsevier Science.

Lucas, R. E. B. and O. Stark (1985). 'Motivations to Remit: Evidence from Botswana', *Journal of Political Economy*, 93(5): 901–18.

Miyagiwa, K. (1991). 'Scale Economies in Education and the Brain Drain Problem', *International Economic Review*, 32(3): 743–59.

Mountford, A. (1997). 'Can a Brain Drain be Good for Growth in the Source Economy?', *Journal of Development Economics*, 53(2): 287–303.

O'Rourke, K., J. Williamson and A. Taylor (1996). 'Factor Price Convergence in the Late Nineteenth Century', *International Economic Review*, 37(3): 499–530.

Pritchett, L. (1997). 'Divergence. Big time', *Journal of Economic Perspectives*, 11(3), Summer: 3–17.

Ramos, F. (1992). 'Out-migration and Return Migration of Puerto Ricans', in G. Borjas and R. Freeman (eds), *Immigration and the Work Force: Economic Consequences for the United States and Source Areas*, Chicago: University of Chicago Press.

Reagan, P. and R. Olsen (2000). 'You Can Go Home Again: Evidence from Longitudinal Data', *Demography*, 37: 339–50.

Rempel, H. and R. Lobdell (1978). 'The Role of Urban-to-Rural Remittances in Rural Development', *Journal of Development Studies*, 14(3): 324–41.

Rodriguez, E. and S. Horton (1994). 'International Return Migration and Remittances in the Philippines', in D. O'Connor, and L. Farsakh (eds), *Development Strategy, Employment and Migration. Country Experiences*, Paris: OECD Development Centre.

Rodrik, D. (2002). 'Final Remarks', in T. Boeri, G. Hanson and B. McCormick (eds), *Immigration Policy and the Welfare System*, Oxford: Oxford University Press.

Schmidt, C. (1994). 'The Country of Origin, Family Structure and Return Migration of Germany's Guest Workers', in G. Wagner (ed.), *Vierteljahrsheftzur Wirtschaftsforschung*, Berlin: Duncker and Humblot.

Solimano, A. (2001). 'International Migration and the Global Economic Order', *Policy Research Working Paper*, No. 2720, Washington, DC: World Bank.

Solimano, A. (2002). *Globalizing Talent and Human Capital. Implications for Developing Countries*, Oslo: ABCDE Conference for Europe.

SOPEMI (1995). *Trends in International Migration*, Annual Report, Paris: OECD.

Stalker, P. (1994). *The Work of Strangers. A Survey of International Labour Migration*, Geneva: International Labour Office.

Stark, O. (2002). The Economics of the Brain Drain Turned on its Head, Mimeo, Washington, DC: ABCDE Europe/The World Bank.

Stark, O., C. Helmenstein and A. Prskawetz (1997). 'A Brain Gain with a Brain Drain', *Economic Letters*, 55: 227–34.

Stark, O., C. Helmenstein and A. Prskawetz (1998). 'Human Capital Formation, Human Capital Depletion, and Migration: A Blessing or a "Curse"', *Economic Letters*, 60: 363–7.

Stark, O. and R. E. B. Lucas (1988). 'Migration, Remittances, and the Family', *Economic Development and Cultural Change*, 36: 465–81.

Steiner, V. and J. Velling (1994). 'Re-migration Behaviour and Expected Duration of Stay of Guest Workers in Germany', in G. Steinmann and R. Ulrich (eds), *The Economic Consequences of Immigration to Germany*, Heidelberg: Physica-Verlag.

Taylor, E. (1994). 'International Migration and Economic Development: A Micro Economy-wide Analysis', in E. Taylor (ed.), *Development Strategy, Employment and Migration*, Paris: OECD.

9
If People were Money: Estimating the Gains and Scope of Free Migration*

Jonathon W. Moses and Bjørn Letnes

> In the penultimate year of the Reagan presidency, the United States expelled over a million illegal aliens and was decidedly bullish about it. In the same year, the United States absorbed over two hundred billion dollars worth of direct foreign investment and was not even slightly sheepish about it. Australia, Great Britain, and, indeed much of the civilized and semi-civilized world has been doing much the same, albeit in a little less dramatic fashion, for the past decade or in some cases much more.
>
> The message is clear enough. Had immigrants been investments – had the people been money – their influx would have been welcomed with open arms. Instead, it was deeply resented and fiercely resisted.
>
> Robert E. Goodin (1992: 6)

'If people were money...': this is the provocative title to Robert Goodin's opening salvo in an edited collection entitled *Free Movement*. In raising this hypothetical question, Goodin's intent (and that of the edited volume that followed) was to provoke a moral debate about the way in which the developed world has been inconsistent in prioritizing international financial capital mobility while limiting international labour mobility.

It is, however, possible to raise Goodin's question in a different light. Rather than focus on the moral issues raised by the lack of international labour mobility, we might ponder the economic consequences of allowing people the same freedom of mobility that we now grant to money (or, for that matter, goods and services). This sort of pondering leads to two difficult and speculative questions that we address in this chapter: 'What sort of economic gains might the world expect to reap by liberalizing world labour markets?' and 'How realistic is the underlying framework used for estimating these gains?'

In raising these types of question, we do not wish to imply that a free-migration scenario is likely, or that answers are easily obtainable or non-controversial. We are fully aware of the practical, empirical and methodological difficulties involved in addressing such speculative questions. In spite of these difficulties, the questions remain important and relevant enough to warrant focused attention. Indeed, previous counter-factual analyses and historical studies suggest that the gains could be very significant.

The relevance of the question is clearly evident when we juxtapose the lessons of two research themes in contemporary political economy. On the one hand, there is an established literature that links contemporary globalization to increased global income divergence. On the other hand, there is a relatively new literature that links economic integration and real wage convergence during an earlier period (late nineteenth century) of globalization. When we recognize that the most striking difference separating these two periods of globalization is the degree of labour mobility, we are left to wonder: 'What if today's globalization was also characterized by free labour mobility?' The next section juxtaposes these two literatures.

The main body of the chapter expands on the findings of an applied equilibrium (AE) model originally produced for the UNU–WIDER conference on 'Poverty, International Migration and Asylum' (Moses and Letnes, 2004). Although the model is not designed to address the convergence question head-on, it generates estimates of the global economic gains we can expect from increased international migration. After a brief introduction of that model (and its results), we employ it to produce some new estimates with the aim of providing a 'reality check' for the model.

In short, AE models provide us with analytical skeletons of the relationship between international migration and economic growth. While these skeletons continue to develop, our immediate ambition is to hang some empirical 'meat' on them. In particular, we wish to expand on two implicit aspects of the estimates being generated: the actual number of migrants being generated by the various scenarios, and the per-migrant cost/benefit associated with each. These estimates can then be compared with contemporary migration flows and the findings of studies that analyse their economic impact.

The results of these comparisons suggest that our model tends to generate very large flows of migrants across international borders. Even in the most reasonable (1 per cent liberalization of labour restrictions) scenario, the model generates 44 million migrants (or about 5 per cent of the native population in the developed world). In addition, we find that the worldwide efficiency gains from this level of migration are also very large: indeed, they dwarf the anticipated impact of some of today's development strategies. Finally, the per-migrant gains generated by our model are much larger than those generated by an influential study of American conditions (Borjas, 1999).

These comparisons encouraged us to adjust the model so that it would generate lower per-migrant gains. In doing this, we found ourselves squeezed by empirical constraints on the input side of our model (with respect to the expected production efficiency differences separating rich and poor countries) and empirical constraints on the output side (that is, Borjas' estimates of per-migrant surpluses). The resulting model is a compromise that produces much smaller estimates for both migrant flows and efficiency gains. Even in this model, however, we find that the estimated efficiency gains from increasing migration are remarkably large.

We conclude by suggesting that the original model estimates are not unreasonable. If forced to decide whether we should rely on the empirically-grounded input estimates of the efficiency differences between richer and poorer regions (on the one hand), or tweaking the model to produce lower per-migrant gains, we would choose the former. As we adjust the model to produce lower estimates, the results become less plausible.

The puzzle

Two aspects of the literature in contemporary political economy provide the academic motivation for the question at hand. The first links globalization and global income inequalities; and the second attributes income convergence in the late nineteenth century to transatlantic migration flows. In juxtaposing the conclusions of these two disparate literatures, we are encouraged to consider the convergence effects of international migration.

We begin with the literature that examines the economic consequences of contemporary globalization. As late as 1820, *per capita* incomes were fairly similar around the world. Of course, they were low (ranging from about US$500 in China and South Asia to about US$1,000–1,400 in the richest countries in Europe); but they were comparable. Indeed, the World Bank has estimated that roughly three-quarters of the world's population then lived on less than US$1 a day (World Bank, 2000: 45).[1] Since then, however, *per capita* incomes have grown tremendously in the world's richest countries (for example, in Europe they have grown more than tenfold in real terms), while incomes for the world's vast majority stagnated (indeed, by some measures, these have actually declined). Not surprisingly, the result has been an increased spread in economic inequality.

Economic historians have long noted the growing income gap between rich and poor nations.[2] Kuznets' classic (1966) *Modern Economic Growth* focused on how a small but growing group of nations was able to combine industrialization, technical innovation and institutional and political developments to produce impressive records of economic growth. Later, Kuznets (1971) began to calculate the income differentials between rich and poor countries, finding a significant increase over time. Bairoch (1971, 1982) recorded similar findings. While the statistical material began to congeal, a consensus developed over the increasing income gap separating rich from poor.[3] As Glenn Firebaugh (1999: 1601) has suggested: 'Over the long haul, then – from the late eighteenth century through much of the twentieth – national incomes diverged. No one disputes that.'[4]

Influential international organizations (such as the World Bank, UNCTAD and the UNDP) have all referred to the growing international income gap, and placed it in the context of contemporary globalization. These institutions have relied on a number of indicators to prove their point – some more systematically than others. For example, the World Bank (2000: 51) reported that, in 1995, *per capita* GDP in the richest twenty countries was 37 times higher than that in the poorest countries – an increase from 18 times in 1960. In a similar fashion, UNCTAD (1997: 81) refers to an 'enormous increase in the income gap between the richest and poorest quintiles of world population'.[5]

The UNDP's 1999 *Human Development Report* is probably the most influential international report on income inequalities; and it is the provocative focus for the current flurry of statistical activity. While the UNDP report begins with a number of descriptive statistics, the measure of income inequality that has received the most academic attention is the UNDP's income ratio. Using the ratio between the income of the quintile of the world's population living in the richest countries, and the income of the quintile living in the poorest countries, the UNDP (1999: 3) found inequality increasing from 30:1 (in 1960) to 60:1 (in 1990), and to 74:1 (in 1997). This study has provoked a resurgence in interest regarding the question of income inequalities and its relationship to economic globalization, and a few critical voices have begun to emerge. Most notably, Sala-i-Martin (2002) is critical of the 'disturbing rise' in claims about global inequality.[6] The conclusions generated by this latest wave of research are less clear, as there are significant methodological and conceptual differences that separate the studies.[7] While these differences appear to be significant academically, their political significance can easily be exaggerated. Even the most optimist accounts of declining income inequalities show a very modest decline over time. In short, it is not necessary to go into the details of this debate to recognize that contemporary globalization is not generating substantial income convergence.

This brings us to the second thread of the literature that motivates the current project. This work engages explicitly the role of international labour mobility in the context of an earlier period of globalization, and makes frequent references to the similarities to, and differences from, contemporary globalization.

International labour mobility is one of the most striking differences that separates the character of contemporary globalization from that of an earlier era. While the degree of commercial and financial integration was relatively similar at the end of the nineteenth and twentieth centuries, the previous bout of globalization was inundated by enormous waves of voluntary migration across the Atlantic.[8] These migrants, totalling some 50 million in the century following 1820, were unhindered by national immigration controls or restrictions.[9] Recent work by Kevin O'Rourke, Jeffrey Williamson and Timothy Hatton links substantial income convergence to these waves of international migrants.

In *The Age of Mass Migration*, Hatton and Williamson (1998) document the ways by which mass migration contributed to the striking convergence of living standards found in the poor and rich countries on each side of the Atlantic.[10] Their comprehensive study addresses several aspects of the great Atlantic migration, but their most interesting finding (in the present context) is their conclusion that 'mass migration accounted for 208 percent of the real wage convergence observed in the Atlantic economy between 1870 and 1910' (1998: 227).[11]

This is not to ignore the important effects of other forms of market integration. In a related study, O'Rourke and Williamson (1999: 165) estimated that the effects of mass migration on wage convergence were more modest (just 125 per cent) in light of the influence of other international factors (for example, capital mobility). This study searches explicitly for the influence of other integration factors (that is, trade, finance and capital market integration), but with little success. They argue that, '[i]n theory, the forces of late-nineteenth-century convergence should have included commodity price convergence and trade expansion, technological catch-up and human capital accumulation, but in fact mass migration was the central force' (ibid.).

The effect of this potent cocktail of global factors is best illustrated in the remarkable Scandinavian catch-up at the beginning of the twentieth century. Scandinavia suffered from very high levels of emigration (especially from Norway), but it also enjoyed substantial inflows of international capital. As a result, real wages in Scandinavia grew at almost three times the rate of those in the European industrial core (O'Rourke and Williamson, 1999: 19).

While a 'capital-chasing labour offset' is an important component of the income convergence that characterized the Atlantic economy during the previous era of globalization, our focus will remain firmly trained on the dominant position played by labour migration. This focus reflects a practical compromise until a model can be produced where capital and labour flows reflect more accurately the historical record (that is, as complements, and not substitutes).[12] In the mean time, we take refuge in O'Rourke and Williamson's (1999: 166) observation: 'The convergence power of free migration, when it is tolerated, can be substantial given the late-nineteenth-century evidence. Convergence based on technological or accumulation catch-up in closed economy models miss the point. The millions on the move in the late nineteenth century did not'.

It is in the context of comparing the convergence effects from two different periods of globalization that the potential economic gains from increased international labour mobility become relevant. Of course, to agree that a question is relevant or important is not to agree about how to answer it. We suggest that a well-grounded AE model is a first step in the right direction.

Background analysis

In this section we introduce a model that produced our analytical point of departure. We then adjust the model to generate some new estimates – estimates that are more readily comparable with existing research in the field. In particular, we use the model to run five scenarios covering different levels of migration; we then generate estimates of the number of migrants and the economic costs/benefits associated with each of these scenarios.

In 1984, Hamilton and Whalley developed the first AE model for calculating the efficiency gains from increased international migration flows. This relatively simple model produced phenomenal results: finding that the annual gains from free labour mobility could exceed the (then) worldwide GDP. In particular, their unadjusted estimates produced gains that ranged from US$4.7 to US$16 trillion, at a time (1977) when worldwide GNP was just US$7.82 trillion (Hamilton and Whalley, 1984: table 4).

Conceptually, Hamilton and Whalley's argument can be divided into three parts. First, they assume there is a fixed supply of (worldwide) labour and full employment throughout the world. This labour supply, fully employed, produces a single output that is homogeneous across regions. Second, they use (regional) CES production functions to estimate differences in the marginal productivity of labour (MPL) across regions. These differences are assumed to be the result of barriers to mobility. Finally, they estimate how labour would reallocate in the absence of these barriers, and measure the associated efficiency gains. In short, Hamilton and Whalley assume that wage rate equalization is achieved through unimpeded international labour flows (not via the traditional factor price equalization theorem). An outline of their method is provided in Table 9.1.

Formally, Hamilton and Whalley generated marginal revenue product schedules directly from aggregate production functions for seven world regions. For each region they constructed a CES production function where they specified the substitution parameter, ρ_i. This implies a value for the elasticity of factor substitution in production for each region. To determine the weighting parameters, δ_i, they determined the first-order conditions for cost minimization, used observations on factor use and factor returns in each region, and assumed that factors were paid their marginal products before the immigration controls were removed. The scale parameter, γ_i, was then determined in the production function for each region. These estimated production function parameters were then used to calculate the change in labour allocation across regions after the removal of immigration controls. In the removal case, an

Table 9.1   Method for calculating global efficiency effects of modifying immigration controls

---

- For each region, an aggregate CES function is used:

$$Y_i = \gamma_i [\delta_i K_i^{-\rho_i} + (1 - \delta_i) L_i^{-\rho_i}]^{1/-\rho_i}$$

  where γ_i is a constant (defining units of measurement), δ_i is a weighting parameter, $\sigma_i = 1/(1 + \rho_i)$ is the elasticity of substitution between factor inputs, K_i and L_i are capital and labour service inputs, and Y_i is value added in region i.

- The elasticity of substitution, $\sigma = 1/(1 + \rho)$, is assumed to range from 0.5 to 1.5 (where ρ is the substitution parameter). As $\sigma \to 1$, the CES tends to the Cobb-Douglas function; and as $\sigma \to 0$ it tends toward the Leontief (fixed coefficient function). Obviously, where $\sigma = 1$ or $\sigma = 0$, the functions are undefined.

- From the assumption that factors receive their marginal product in each region in the presence of existing controls, values of δ_i are determined from the ratio of first-order conditions:

$$\delta_i = \left(\frac{K_i^{1/\sigma_i}}{L_i^{1/\sigma_i}} \right) \Bigg/ \left(1 + \left(\frac{K_i^{1/\sigma_i}}{L_i^{1/\sigma_i}} \right) \right)$$

- Units are assumed for the output produced in each region such that one unit sells for US\$1. The GDP value for the region, K_i, L_i, ρ_i, and δ_i are used to solve for γ_i.

- An iterative procedure is then used to calculate the change in labour allocation after a modification of immigration controls consistent with: (a) equalized MPL in all regions; and (b) full employment of the fixed labour supply.

Source: Moses and Letnes (2004).

equalized marginal revenue product of labour across regions was found, consistent with full employment of the fixed worldwide labour supply.

In a recent paper, we overhauled Hamilton and Whalley's analysis to provide more contemporary measures of the potential economic gain from liberating national labour markets.[13] In particular, we adjusted some of their underlying assumptions in the light of subsequent academic work, and extended the empirical coverage to include 1998 data. Like Hamilton and Whalley's original model, these global economic gains are derived from estimating the economic benefit from reallocating labour internationally. The new model and data was collected for three world categories or 'regions' (Low Human Development; Medium Human Development; and High Human Development) and used to estimate the efficiency and distributional gains from liberalizing world labour markets. This analysis showed that the gains to free migration are large, and similar to those produced by Ana María Iregui in Chapter 10 (though her model is more sophisticated and addresses different conceptual scenarios).

In particular, the world efficiency gains derived from a full relaxation of migration controls could be as high as US\$3.4 trillion. As world GDP in

Table 9.2 Comparison of annual worldwide efficiency gains from global removal of immigration controls, 1977–98, unadjusted and adjusted 3-region calculations (US$ trillions)

	Elasticities of substitution in production in all regions				
	1.5	1.25	1.0	0.75	0.5
No adjustments					
1977	8.50	7.97	7.19	5.93	3.69
1998	41.70	38.63	34.08	26.71	15.38
% gains relative to total real GDP					
1977	109.5	102.7	92.7	76.4	47.6
1998	118.1	109.4	96.5	75.6	43.6
Adjustments					
PW + EU3 & EU5					
1977	0.73	0.66	0.58	0.47	0.34
1998	4.33	3.91	3.39	2.75	1.97
% gains relative to total real GDP					
1977	9.4	8.5	7.5	6.1	4.4
1998	12.3	11.1	9.6	7.8	5.6

Notes: PW – population workforce adjustment; EU3 & EU5 – labour efficiency units correction using factors of 1:3 and 1:5 for the medium and low human development regions, respectively. *Source*: Moses and Letnes (2004).

1998 was substantially larger than in 1977, our diachronic comparison in Table 9.2 compares the unadjusted and adjusted results in terms of relative GDP. Here we see a substantial increase in efficiency gains over time, especially in the adjusted cases. Indeed, in our middle scenario – where elasticities of substitution were set to one in all regions – we find that the relative gains increased from 7.5 per cent to 9.6 per cent of world GDP over the intervening twenty-one years.

Another important result from this analysis is that the largest efficiency gains are made in the initial phases (or smallest levels) of migration. For example, a 10 per cent elimination of wage differentials (our surrogate for a 10 per cent increase in migration) generates about 22 per cent of the total potential gain.[14] This has enormous political significance, as it suggests that even a small liberalization of national labour market controls could bring substantial economic gain.

A new turn

The problem with AE analyses is that they remain hopelessly speculative. For example, the analysis sketched above provides no clear picture of how many migrants are being generated by the different scenarios, or (consequently) how the sizes of these flows relate to existing levels of international migration. As many of the adjustment mechanisms are internal to the model itself, there are few explicit reference points which the empirically-minded reader might grasp.

This section will develop two important aspects of the model. We begin by mapping the size of the migrant flows necessary for the model to generate the sorts of gains reported. Once quantified, we can compare these projections to current migration levels. With migration figures in hand, we can then estimate the per-migrant gains generated by the model (and how they are distributed), and these estimates can then be compared to others. By producing these kinds of estimates we hope to provide a better empirical reference point from which to evaluate the model.

To generate these new estimates, we consider five scenarios from our previous analysis. Considering that the relative size of the efficiency gain varies with the level of immigration, and that the largest gains are generated in the initial levels of migration, we focus on four potential scenarios that correspond to an increasing liberalization of migration controls (1 per cent, 10 per cent, 30 per cent and 100 per cent liberalization).[15] In addition, we add a baseline scenario that represents the level of international migration at the time of writing. Obviously, readers who are less inclined to speculation should focus on the first three scenarios (0 per cent, 1 per cent and 10 per cent increase).

In order to run these new scenarios, we fix the adjustable parameters in the model by relying on estimates grounded in the broader empirical literature. In particular, following Nadiri (1997: 109–10), we assume that the elasticities of factor substitution in production are equal to 1.00 in all three regions. We also adjust the model to consider variations in productivity and workforce size across all three regions. Thus, following Acemoglu and Zilibotti (2001), we assume that the productivity differences between the most and least developed regions are about 1:5 (and 1:3 between Medium and High regions); and, following the ILO (1998), we assume that the workforce represents 0.48, 0.41 and 0.41 of the High, Medium and Low Human Development region populations, respectively.

Migrant flows

The first step is to generate estimates of the size of the migrant flows associated with the different scenarios produced by the model. As noted earlier, these gains are made unevenly across migration levels: the largest efficiency gains (in relative terms) are for the initial units of migrating labour, since the marginal product differences are largest in the initial stages of development. In other words, we found that a substantial portion of total gains can be generated by a relatively small relaxation of international migration controls.

With the basic model in place, we ran four counter-factual scenarios, the results of which are presented in Table 9.3. The 0 per cent scenario takes the actual level of migration as its point of departure. These figures correspond to the UN Population Division's (UNPD, 2001: 139) estimate for the average annual net number (flow) of migrants over 1990–2000. Although the UNPD's regional categories do not overlap directly with our own, the discrepancy with our three-region aggregation is small.[16] This provides us with a good starting point for evaluating the size of the migrant flows under the various scenarios. The estimated number of migrants for each scenario and region are found on the left side of the table; on the right are the estimated efficiency gains. The figures in parentheses represent the reference ratio value: that is, the ratio of the regional population[17] and the regional GDP for each estimate.

So what do these figures tell us? Let us begin with the left side of the table. For a start we know that even a small increase in the migration level (1 per cent) corresponds to a phenomenally large increase in the number of migrants (given the benchmark figure of 2.48 million). In particular, the first (1 per cent) scenario depends on about 44 million people emigrating from the low and medium developed countries to the developed world. The second (10 per cent) scenario depends on 432 million people moving (divided roughly between low and medium sending countries). The practical obstacles associated with the 100 per cent scenario are clearly evident when we note that about two-thirds of the medium human development (MHD) population (*c.* 2.4 billion people) will find incentives to migrate in this scenario.

To contextualize these figures, we can estimate the size of the migrant flow as a percentage of a given region's population. Thus, today's immigrant stream into the high human development (HHD) world constitutes just 0.3 per cent of the domestic population in that region. With the 1 per cent scenario (44.15 million people) the relative size of the inflow remains fairly small: just 4.7 per cent of the population in the HHD world. In the 10 per cent scenario, however, the number of immigrants to the developed world is approaching half of the existing population, with the largest share of the sending country population coming from the poorest countries (nearly 30 per cent of the low human development (LHD) population is emigrating).[18]

Another measure of relative influence can be derived by returning to Goodin's hypothetical question: what if people were money? Following Goodin's approach, we can compare each region's relative reliance on foreign direct investment (FDI) with the relative size of the projected migrant flows in each scenario (Goodin 1992: 14). In this light, the number of migrants is rather large – even in the smallest (1 per cent) scenario. For example, the size of the FDI flow into the HHD region constitutes about 2.4 per cent of its real GDP (whereas the flows are only 0.9 per cent and 0.5 per cent in the MHD and LHD scenarios, respectively). In other words,

Table 9.3 Migrant size and efficiency gains, five scenarios

Scenario (%)	Number of migrants (millions)			Efficiency gains (billions)			
	LHD	MHD	HHD	LHD	MHD	HHD	Total
0	0.086	-2.48	2.39	0.0	-6.0	38.0	32.0
	(0.00016)	(-0.00072)	(0.003)		(-0.00046)	(0.040)	(0.001)
1	-24.86	-19.29	44.15	-22.0	-50.0	155.0	84.0
	(-0.034)	(-0.006)	(0.047)	(-0.023)	(-0.0038)	(0.007)	(0.003)
10	-214.96	-217.22	432.19	-198.0	-566.0	1 537.0	774.0
	(-0.290)	(-0.063)	(0.465)	(-0.211)	(-0.044)	(0.072)	(0.025)
30	-471.22	-752.93	1 224.15	-472.0	-2 014.0	4 465.0	1 978.0
	(-0.637)	(-0.219)	(10.316)	(-0.502)	(-0.156)	(0.208)	(0.063)
100	-702.67	-2 372.14	3 074.81	-820.0	-7 127.0	11 338.0	3 391.0
	(-0.950)	(-0.690)	(3.306)	(-0.872)	(-0.552)	(0.529)	(0.108)
Reference	740	3 440	930	940	12 920	21 450	31 310

Notes: HHD = high human development states; MHD = medium human development states; LHD = low human development states. Figures in parentheses are the relative ratios, based on the respective reference value (regional population) and each region's population and PPP GNP. The reference figures are (regional GDP). Values are rounded.

Source: Actual migrant figures (in the 0% scenario) come from the UNPD (2001); population and GNP figures are from Moses and Letnes (2004: table 2).

by adopting the 1 per cent scenario, the richest countries would be accepting a level of immigration that is relatively higher than its current reliance on foreign capital.[19] This volume of migration is also large in a historical context: for example, Simon (1999: 28) shows that working-age immigration to the United States, at its peak in 1910, represented only 2.8 per cent of the native population.[20]

We can now turn to the right side of the table, and consider the global economic gains associated with each scenario. It is our analytical ambition to map the gains that might be made by a relaxation of immigrant controls. In today's political context, however, a more reasonable scenario might be to consider the costs associated with closing off international migration completely. The first (0 per cent) scenario estimates the efficiency gains associated with today's level of international immigration (that is, 2.39 million migrants), and suggests that the existing situation benefits the world by about US$32 billion (or 0.1 per cent of world GDP). Should immigration be radically curtailed, it would appear that the largest losers would live in the richest countries, as it is here that the model generates the largest gains (US$38 billion).

In the other four scenarios, gains accumulate for the HHD region, and these are substantial at the higher migration scenarios. This is a function of the simple model employed. Still, this result is rather counter-intuitive, given the nature of much political debate about restricting immigration (and in light of the existing studies on the impact of immigration into developed countries). In the 1 per cent scenario, the world economic gain is estimated at US$84 billion, or 0.3 per cent of the world's (1998) GDP. The gains jump considerably when we consider the 10 per cent scenario – here, the world can expect to enjoy a US$774 billion windfall by allowing 432 million people to migrate.

How large are these gains relative to the impact of other development strategies? When we contrast the (US$84 billion) gain generated by the 1 per cent scenario against the estimated gains associated with alternative development strategies, the difference are both large and illuminating. For example, official development assistance from the OECD's DAC countries was estimated to be about US$51.4 billion in 2001,[21] and the IMF's current plan for debt relief will cancel just US$40 billion of debt (IMF, 2002)! If our estimates are correct, a small increase of international migration could produce economic gains that would surpass the target values of two important poverty relief strategies.

On the other hand, other liberalization schemes are expected to generate even larger effects – closer in size to those produced by our 10 per cent scenario. For example, the UNDP (2000: 4) suggests that developing countries lose annual agricultural export earnings to the tune of US$700 billion because of tariff and non-tariff barriers. In this context, a 10 per cent liberalization of migration controls might produce the same sort of economic gain as a full liberalization of agricultural trade. Finally, FDI to the developing world in the year 2000 totalled US$1.9 trillion (Letnes, 2002: 47), a significantly larger sum of money. In both of these latter examples, the gains are closer in magnitude to those produced by our 10 per cent scenario, but will probably have very different distributional consequences.

Per-migrant benefit

Now that we have estimated the size of the migrant flows and efficiency gains associated with each scenario, we can produce estimates of the costs/ benefits associated with each. These estimates can then be compared with estimates generated by other, related, studies. For our reference value, we rely on a formula used by Borjas (1995, 1999) in his work on the United States' 'immigration surplus':

$$-\tfrac{1}{2}sem^2 \qquad\qquad (9.1)$$

where s is labour's share of national income, e is the drop in native wages because of migration, and m represents the share of the labour force that is foreign-born (Borjas, 1995: 7).

Borjas estimates that the immigrant surplus for the United States was about US$10 billion at the end of the 1990s.[22] As this estimate relies on migrant stocks (that is, share of the foreign-born population), and not on annual immigrant flows, an estimate of the 'per-migrant' gain to the United States can be generated by dividing this surplus by the number of foreign-born residents (*c.* 25 million): a mere US$400 per immigrant.

To expand on the American example, we can employ the same percentage figure (that is, 0.1 per cent of GDP)[23] to the larger sample of HHD countries. By employing the same formula to comparable OECD data (where data are available), we can expect that the immigrant surplus for the OECD sample will be about US$23.4 billion.[24] As there were 56.7 million foreign-born residents in this sample group,[25] the per-migrant surplus for the developed (OECD) world can be estimated at US$413.

These estimates are very small compared to the sort of per-migrant gains generated by our model. The simplest way to calculate these figures is to divide the number of migrants generated in each scenario by its estimated efficiency gain. As Table 9.4 illustrates, these per-migrant gains can be broken down by region. From these figures it would appear that the relative gain/loss per migrant changes very little from scenario to scenario: the richest countries tend to benefit by about US$3,600 per migrant, whereas the middle-income and poorest countries tend to lose – about US$1,000 and US$2,700, respectively.

Despite the different results produced by these two approaches, they build on remarkably similar foundations. Central to each approach is the elasticity of factor prices for labour (that is, e in equation 1). From his research on the

Table 9.4 Per-migrant cost/benefit, four scenarios

Scenario (%)	Per-migrant cost (−) or benefit (+), US$		
	LHD	MHD	HHD
1	−885	−2 592	3 511
10	−921	−2 606	3 556
30	−1 002	−2 675	3 647
100	−1 167	−3 004	3 687

Table 9.5 Effect on labour and capital returns, four scenarios

Scenario (%)	Percentage change in wage rates to non-migrating labour			Percentage change in return to capital by region		
	LHD	MHD	HHD	LHD	MHD	HHD
1	1.1	0.2	−0.3	−2.3	−0.4	0.7
10	11.4	2.1	−3.1	−21.0	−4.4	7.2
30	37.3	8.0	−8.5	−50.2	−15.6	20.8
100	155.2	44.1	−17.6	−87.1	−55.2	52.8

US case, Borjas (1999: 91) estimated that a 10 per cent increase in immigrants would reduce the native wage by about 3 per cent.[26] This figure is remarkably similar to the estimates generated by our model, as evidenced in Table 9.5: in the 10 per cent scenario, our model generates a decline in wage rates to the non-migrant population of the HHD at 3.1 per cent. Perhaps the most surprising observation in Table 9.5, however, is the fact that a full liberalization of migration controls (which would unleash a migrant flow of about three billion people!) would only decrease HHD wages by 17.6 per cent! If accurate, this seems to be a relatively small price to pay for the sort of efficiency gains that are generated by the model.[27]

A new twist

Borjas' approach for estimating per-migrant surpluses suggests that our own estimates are too large: by almost nine times! In light of this observation, we thought it would be worthwhile to run our model with new efficiency adjustments in order to produce lower per-migrant efficiency gains. This model can then be used to generate new estimates of the migration flows and efficiency gains associated with each of the scenarios used above.

This strategy is not without difficulties, however.[28] First, it is important to recall that our own (original) efficiency adjustments were already grounded in the empirical literature. In particular, Acemoglu and Zilibotti (2001: 593)

202 Gains and Scope of Free Migration

find that the difference in output per worker between rich and poor countries in their sample ranges between 1:2 and 1:5 (most of the variance results from the different models being tested). On the basis of their study, we argued that the most reasonable efficiency adjustments between the HHD region and the MHD region would be 1:3; and between the LHD region and the HHD region: 1:5.[29] Thus, in order to produce the sort of per-migrant efficiency gains generated by Borjas' approach, we need to assume that the efficiency differences separating rich and poor countries of the world are much larger than is usually assumed (and verified empirically).

Worse, the model's interpretative utility sinks drastically when we try to amplify the efficiency differences sufficiently to produce estimates of the same magnitude as generated by Borjas' approach (that is, US$413). In fact, when these efficiency adjustments are raised too high, people in our model start migrating from the HHD to the MHD. This simply will not do![30] As a result, we have chosen to run the model with efficiency adjustments on the order of 1:5 and 1:10 (the HHD:MHD and HHD:LHD efficiency ratios, respectively). These are the largest efficiency adjustments that the model would embrace without producing implausible migration back-flow (from rich countries to poor countries).

With these new efficiency adjustments, our model produces per-migrant efficiency gains that are somewhere between the estimates generated by Borjas' approach (US$413) and those of our original model (see Table 9.6). For example, the per-migrant gains to the HHD world are generally about US$1,500, compared to the US$3,500 dollar gain in the original model (see Table 9.4). Note, however, that the per-migrant losses in both the LHD and MHD worlds have not changed much from the scenario depicted in Table 9.4.

These larger efficiency adjustments (and smaller per-migrant gains) correspond to much lower levels of international migration and smaller overall efficiency gains. Table 9.7 represents the equivalent of Table 9.3, but with estimates generated on the basis of the new efficiency adjustments. Compared to the original model, we see that an even larger share of the overall anticipated gain is generated at the initial stages of migration.[31] Equally significant is the fact that the 1 per cent scenario seems less politically

Table 9.6 Reduced per-migrant cost/benefit (efficiency correction 1:5 and 1:10)

Scenario (%)	Per-migrant cost (−) or benefit (+), US$		
	LHD	MHD	HHD
1	−905	−2 770	1 483
10	−895	−2 576	1 486
30	−932	−2 583	1 537
100	−1 033	−2 604	1 722

Table 9.7 Reduced migrant size and efficiency gains (efficiency correction 1:5 and 1:10)

Scenario (%)	Number of migrants (millions)			Efficiency gains (billions)			
	LHD	MHD	HHD	LHD	MHD	HHD	Total
0	0.086 (0.00016)	−2.48 (−0.00072)	2.39 (0.003)	0.0	−6.0 (−0.00046)	38.0 (0.040)	32.0 (0.001)
1	−11.05 (−0.015)	−1.08 (−0.0003)	12.13 (0.013)	−10.0 (−0.011)	−3.0 (−0.0002)	18.0 (0.0008)	5.0 (0.0002)
10	−104.75 (−0.142)	−11.88 (−0.003)	116.63 (0.125)	−94.0 (−0.100)	−31.0 (−0.002)	173.0 (0.008)	49.0 (0.002)
30	−264.60 (−0.358)	−46.61 (−0.014)	311.21 (0.335)	−247.0 (−0.263)	−120.0 (−0.009)	478.0 (0.022)	111.0 (0.004)
100	−559.71 (−0.756)	−223.17 (−0.065)	762.88 (0.820)	−558.0 (−0.594)	−581.0 (−0.045)	1 314.0 (0.060)	175.0 (0.006)
Reference	740	3 440	930	940	12 920	21 450	31 310

Note: See Table 9.3 and text for clarification and sources.

Table 9.8   Reduced effect on labour and capital returns (efficiency correction 1:5 and 1:10)

Scenario (%)	Percentage change in wage rates to non-migrating labour			Percentage change in return to capital by region		
	LHD	MHD	HHD	LHD	MHD	HHD
1	0.5	0.0	0.0	−1.1	0.0	0.1
10	4.9	0.1	−0.4	−10.0	−0.2	0.8
30	14.9	0.4	−1.0	−26.2	−0.9	2.2
100	50.7	2.1	−2.7	−59.3	−4.5	6.1

threatening – as it relies on just 12 million people moving to the developed world (or about 1.3 per cent of the HHD population). This relatively small number of people can be expected to generate an efficiency gain of about US$18 billion in the HHD region.

Obviously, these new efficiency adjustments produce much lower returns to both capital and labour across the range of scenarios – as evidenced in Table 9.8. In the 1 per cent scenario, the effect on factor returns is almost nil. Indeed, in all of these scenarios, the anticipated (negative) effect on wages is muted. This is a problem when we recall that Borjas finds a 10 per cent increase in emigration leading to a 3 per cent drop in the native wage in the HHD region (as did our original model). The new model's estimates are nowhere near this level of elasticity. Indeed, even in our 100 per cent scenario, workers in the developed world cannot expect that kind of fall in their wages. In return, workers in the poorest countries can expect a phenomenal (50.7 per cent) increase in *their* wages. Of course, the negative aspect of this reward is that domestic capital owners in the developing world experience an enormous decline in their expected rate of return.

In both versions of our model, the distributional shortcomings are clearly evident: all the efficiency gains are accrued in the developed world. Given the simple nature of the underlying model, this outcome is difficult to avoid. Nevertheless, we doubt that this is the case in practice. We can think of several reasons why emigration might improve economic conditions in the developing world – but the form of the current model does not give us much opportunity to incorporate them.[32] Future models will need to address this important shortcoming if we are to get to grips with the potential impact of migration on development.

Although our model focuses on the estimated efficiency gains from increased labour migration, it is important to remember that the underlying logic of the approach assumes dramatic international wage convergence. In this model, workers will continue to move as long is there is an international wage gap to exploit. This convergence alone will generate very important distributional consequences that are not particularly evident in our results.

Conclusion

We can now provide a provisional answer to Goodin's opening query. If people were money, and enjoyed the same freedom of mobility enjoyed by finance today, the world could expect an efficiency gain as high as US$3.4 trillion. This is an enormous windfall that could have phenomenal consequences for economic development and global income convergence. However, these consequences hinge critically on their distribution – an aspect of the model that remains underdeveloped.

The main objective of this chapter has been to try to provide the model with some better empirical grounding, from which we can evaluate the reasonableness of its estimates. In this context, our focus has been on two important aspects of the model: the number of migrants being generated by various scenarios, and the estimated per-migrant benefit associated with them. On both of these fronts, it appears that the model produces very large estimates. The number of migrants associated with each scenario makes even the smallest scenario politically untenable. And worse, the per-migrant gains being generated are almost nine times larger than those being generated by other studies.

Although the efficiency gains from the original model are large, they stand on reasonable empirical assumptions about the relative efficiency differences that separate rich and poor countries. When we modify the model to produce smaller per-migrant gains, we end up challenging these assumptions and generating migration flows that are clearly unreasonable (for example, from richer to poorer countries). In this light, we wonder if the original model is not producing better estimates of the anticipated gain. Seen from a different perspective, this might cast a shadow over the relatively small size of the immigrant surplus generated by Borjas' approach.

Even if we accept the modified model, in spite of its evident shortcomings, the estimated gains from increased migration remain significant (albeit lower). Liberalizing immigration restrictions may provide the fastest and easiest way of diminishing international wage gaps. We are, after all, talking about a significant amount of new wealth being generated by matching international supply with its potential demand. These are the same sorts of lessons as was the role played by labour migration during the previous era of globalization. To understand these lessons more clearly, we believe that a better AE model can be constructed – one built on more realistic foundations – in order to document the potential gains and their distribution.

Notes

* The authors would like to thank the anonymous reviewers and members of the IPE Forum at the Norwegian University of Science and Technology for useful comments on an earlier draft.
1. Figures are in constant 1990 United States dollars, adjusted for differences in purchasing power parity.

2. And, of course, the post-war convergence among rich countries, as in Gerschenkron (1952), Abramovitz (1979, 1986) and Maddison (1982, 1991).
3. For example, see Maddison (1995); Pritchett (1995); Sachs and Warner (1995) and Sheehey (1996). See also the overview in Firebaugh (1999: table 1).
4. There are two exceptions, of course: the post-war OECD and the Atlantic economy convergences. For the latter, see the discussion below.
5. See the foreword to Sala-i-Martin (2002) for an entertaining collection of what he sees as exaggerated claims in this area.
6. See Melchior *et al.* (2000) for an earlier and similar version of this argument.
7. In particular, those studies that rely on market or official foreign exchange rates tend to support the research conclusions of earlier scholars: there has been a growing increase in income inequalities since the 1960s. However, those who rely on purchasing power parity (PPP) exchange rate calculations have found a slight decrease in inequality since the 1960s. In addition, many of the conclusions in these studies hinge critically on whether or not China is included (and the weight it is given). For an overview and access to several relevant papers, see http://www.economist.com/inequalitypapers/.
8. For some explicit comparisons of the two periods of globalization, see Bordo *et al.* (1999); O'Rourke and Williamson (1999); James (2001).
9. This is not to deny that there were/are significant economic and social costs associated with international migration. The migration figure comes from Hatton and Williamson (1998: 7).
10. This experience stands in rough contrast to developments beyond the Atlantic economy. There appears to be no evidence of convergence when Central, South and East European countries are added. Nor does the evidence improve when China, Egypt, India, Turkey and the rest of Asia and the Middle East are added to the analysis (O'Rourke and Williamson, 1999: 25).
11. The percentage convergence explained is the counter-factual–actual ratio of change in ln[dispersion]. The large numbers are explained by the fact that the convergence effect of labour migration may be offset by the divergence effects of other factors. The total convergence effects will, of course, sum to 100 per cent. See Hatton and Williamson (1998: 228ff.) for a discussion.
12. The lack of capital mobility in this model probably exaggerates the returns/losses for labour and capital in both sending and receiving countries. Since we expect capital to follow labour (as it did in the previous era of globalization); the migration effect on the real wage in both regions will be attenuated. Similarly with respect to the returns on capital: in receiving countries, capital inflows will mute the rise in the return to capital; in sending countries, capital outflows will mute the fall in return to capital. See Hatton and Williamson (1994: 22ff.), for a description of these effects in the nineteenth century.
13. Moses and Letnes (2004). We refer the interested reader to this piece to trace the architecture and mechanics of the model employed below.
14. See Moses and Letnes (2004: table 6) [that is, elasticity of substitution in production in all regions = 1, population workforce adjustment and labour efficiency units correction (using factors of 1:3 and 1:5), adjusted 3-region calculation].
15. In fact, the model is simply producing estimates of the consequences of a 1 per cent, 10 per cent, 30 per cent and 100 per cent elimination of wage differentials. We use this as a surrogate for labour market liberalization.
16. A second caveat is in order. Our dataset contains only 120 countries, while the UN includes all the countries of the world. On both counts, the differences are

not large and should not affect the outcome of our estimations. A more detailed description of this, or any other, aspect of the analysis can be obtained by contacting the authors.

17. The total population is only 5.11 trillion, as we do not have data on all countries in the world.

18. An equal number of workers come from the MHD region in this scenario, but they only represent about 6 per cent of that region's population.

19. Of course, one can question whether this is the appropriate indicator. We are simply following, Goodin's (1992) lead, in using FDI *inflows*/GDP. If we consider the relative (FDI) *stock*, the share is much larger: 13.1 per cent (HHD), 6.0 per cent (MHD) and 4.7 per cent (LHD).

20. On the other hand, the reader will recall that the last period of globalization experienced 50 million Atlantic migrants (spread over a century), at a time when the world population was significantly smaller.

21. The Development Assistance Committee (DAC) is the principal body through which the OECD deals with issues related to cooperation with developing countries. DAC assistance accounts for at least 95 per cent of worldwide ODA. See OECD (2001a and 2001b).

22. In the United States' case, Borjas argues $s = 0.7$, $e = -0.3$ and $m = 0.1$, so that the US immigrant surplus is about 0.1 per cent of US GDP (which was *c*. 10 trillion dollars in 1998). See Borjas (1999: 87, 91).

23. We use the same percentage figure, as the labour share, wage effects and migrant share data are fairly similar in the broader OECD sample. In particular, if we assume that $s = 0.687$ (Gollin (2002), 2nd adjustment); $e = -0.3$ (the same as Borjas); $m = 0.07$ (Coppel *et al.* 2001: 10): we still end up with the same figure: 0.001. See Moses and Letnes (2004) for a justification of the choice of values.

24. Total GDP for this sample is US$23.4 trillion (OECD Main Economic Indicators).

25. Coppel *et al.* (2001: 10).

26. Borjas, in turn, builds on Hamermesh (1993).

27. To put this in a comparative context, the OECD estimates that the cumulative effects of an ageing population in the EU will reduce its living standards by about 18 per cent (Turner *et al.*, 1998). In other words, the developed world might expect an 18 per cent drop in living standards if immigration *does not* occur! See Coppel *et al.* (2001: 20ff).

28. An alternative strategy is to freeze the model and simply paste Borjas' per-migrant gains on to our model's estimates for the number of migrants in each scenario. This would produce lower, but still quite significant, efficiency gains. For example, in the 10 per cent scenario, the world efficiency gain would be estimated to be about US$178 billion (for example, 432,190,000 migrants, each generating US$413).

29. In the original Hamilton and Whalley (1984) piece, even smaller efficiency adjustments (1:2 and 1:3) were employed.

30. The model uses the efficiency factor to reduce the incentive to migrate as it increases the MPL in the MHD and the LHD regions. For this reason, these regions will – at certain efficiency factors – have higher MPLs than the HHD region. This explains the outmigration. It should be possible to redesign the model so that the increased efficiency factors will only reduce the efficiency gains – this would allow us to overcome this counter-intuitive result, and increase the efficiency adjustments even more. However, this 'solution' would not address the underlying

problem of adopting efficiency adjustments that are much larger than those justified by the empirical literature.

31. In the original model, a 1 per cent liberalization of migration secures 2.5 per cent of the total anticipated gain (see Table 9.3). In the new model, the 1 per cent scenario corresponds to a 2.9 per cent share of the anticipated gain. Indeed, 63 per cent of the total anticipated gain in the new model can be captured by only a 30 per cent liberalization.

32. As noted in Riccardo Faini's contribution (Chapter 8), some authors have argued that the incentive to acquire skills may be strengthened by the prospect of being able to migrate. On another front, the historical record is quite clear about the European wage-benefit associated with emigration in the late nineteenth century. Finally, it has been estimated that migrants send home, on average, about US$1,000 a year in the form of remittances (Harris, 2000: 98). If the level of remittances is this high, the per-emigrant gain to the sending country could be nearly as large as the per-migrant efficiency gain generated by the revised model (*c.* US$1,500). See Lucas (2004) for a recent survey of the literature that relates migration to development.

References

Abramovitz, M. (1979). 'Rapid Growth Potential and Its Realization: The Experience of the Capitalist Economies in the Postwar Period', in E. Malinvaud (ed.), *Economic Growth and Resources*, Vol. 1, London: Macmillan.

Abramovitz, M. (1986). 'Catching Up, Forging Ahead, and Falling Behind', *Journal of Economic History*, 46: 385–406.

Acemoglu, D. and F. Zilibotti (2001). 'Productivity Differences', *Quarterly Journal of Economics*, 116: 563–606.

Bairoch, P. (1971). *The Economic Development of the Third World Since 1900*, London: Methuen.

Bairoch, P. (1982). 'International Industrialization Levels from 1750 to 1980', *Journal of European Economic History*, 2: 268–333.

Bordo, M. D., B. Eichengreen and D. A. Irwin (1999). 'Is Globalization Today Really Different than Globalization a Hundred Years Ago?', NBER Working Paper, No. 7195, Cambridge, MA: National Bureau of Economic Research. Available at: www.nber.org/papers/w7195.

Borjas, G. J. (1995). 'The Economic Benefits from Immigration', *Journal of Economic Perspectives*, 9, Spring: 3–22.

Borjas, G. J. (1999). *Heaven's Door*, Princeton, NJ: Princeton University Press.

Coppel, J., J.-C. Dumont and I. Visco (2001). 'Trends in Immigration and Economic Consequences', OECD Economic Working Papers, No. 284, Paris: OECD.

Firebaugh, G. (1999). 'Empirics of World Income Inequality', *American Journal of Sociology*, 104, May: 1597–630.

Gerschenkron, A. (1952). 'Economic Backwardness in Historical Perspective', in B. F. Hoselitz (ed.), *The Progress of Underdeveloped Areas*. Chicago: University of Chicago Press.

Gollin, D. (2002). 'Getting Income Shares Right', *Journal of Political Economy*, 110: 458–74.

Goodin. R. E. (1992). 'If People Were Money...', in B. Barry and R. E. Goodin (eds), *Free Movement*, University Park, PA: Penn State University Press: 6–22.

Hamermesh, D. S. (1993). *Labor Demand*. Princeton, NJ: Princeton University Press.

Hamilton, B. and J. Whalley (1984). 'Efficiency and Distributional Implications of Global Restrictions on Labour Mobility: Calculations of Policy Implications', *Journal of Development Economics*, 14: 61–75.

Harris, N. (2000). 'Should Europe End Immigration Controls? A Polemic', *The European Journal of Development Research*, 12(1): 98.

Hatton, T. J. and J. G. Williamson (1994). 'International Migration 1850–1939: An Economic Survey', in T. Hatton and J. Williamson (eds), *Migration and the International Labour Market, 1850–1939*, London: Routledge: 3–34.

Hatton, T. J. and J. G. Williamson (1998). *The Age of Mass Migration. Causes and Economic Impact*, Oxford: Oxford University Press.

ILO (1998). *Yearbook of Labour Statistics*, ILO: Geneva.

IMF (1999). *Balance of Payments Statistics Yearbook*, Part I, Washington, DC: IMF.

IMF (2002). 'Debt Relief for Poor Countries (HIPC)', Fact sheet, Washington, DC: IMF. Available at: www.imf.org/external/np/exr/facts/povdebt.htm. Accessed 16 January 2003.

James, H. (2001). *The End of Globalization*, Cambridge, MA: Harvard University Press.

Kuznets, S. (1966). *Modern Economic Growth: Rate, Structure and Spread*, London: Yale University Press.

Kuznets, S. (1971). *Economic Growth of Nations*, Cambridge, MA: Harvard University Press.

Letnes, B. (2002). 'Foreign Direct Investment and Human Rights: An Ambiguous Relationship', *Forum for Development Studies*, 29(1): 33–62.

Lucas, R. E. B. (2004). 'International Migration Regimes and Economic Development', Report commissioned for the Swedish Foreign Ministry's Expert Group on Development Issues. Available at http://www.egdi.gov.se/.

Maddison, A. (1982). *Phases of Capitalist Development*, New York: Oxford University Press.

Maddison, A. (1991). *Dynamic Forces in Capitalist Development*, New York: Oxford University Press.

Maddison, A. (1995). *Monitoring the World Economy 1820–1992*, Paris: OECD Development Centre.

Melchior, A., K. Telle and H. Wiig (2000). 'Globalization and Inequality. World Income Distribution and Living Standards, 1960–1998', Studies on Foreign Policy Issues Report 6B, Oslo: Royal Norwegian Ministry of Foreign Affairs. Available at: odin.dep.no/archive/udvedlegg/01/01/rev016.pdf.

Moses, J. W. and B. Letnes (2004). 'The Economic Costs of International Labour Restrictions: Revisiting the Empirical Discussion', *World Development*, 32(10): 1609–26.

Nadiri, M. I. (1997). 'Some Approaches to the Theory and Measurement of Total Factor Productivity: A Survey', in E. N. Wolff (ed.), *The Economics of Productivity*, Vol. I, Cheltenham: Elgar: 95–135.

O'Rourke, K. H. and J. G. Williamson (1999). *Globalization and History*, Cambridge, MA: MIT Press.

OECD (2001a). 'Table 1: Net Official Development Assistance Flows in 2001', Paris: OECD. Available at: www.oecd.org/pdf/m00029000/M00029445.pdf. Accessed 16 January 2003.

OECD (2001b). 'A Mixed Picture of Official Development Assistance in 2001', Paris: OECD. Available at: www.oecd.org. Accessed 16 January 2003.

Pritchett, L. (1995). 'Divergence, Big Time', World Bank Policy Research Working Paper, No. 1522, Washington, DC: World Bank.

Sachs, J. and M. Warner (1995). 'Economic Convergence and Economic Policies', NBER Working Paper, No. 50389, Cambridge, MA: National Bureau of Economic Research.

Sala-i-Martin, X. (2002). 'The Disturbing "Rise" of Global Income Inequality', NBER Working Paper, No. 8904, Cambridge, MA: National Bureau of Economic Research. Available at: www.nber.org/papers/w8904.

Sheehey, E. J. (1996). 'The Growing Gap between Rich and Poor Countries: A Proposed Explanation', *World Development Report*, 24(8): 1379–84.

Simon, J. (1999). *Economic Consequences of Immigration*, 2nd edn, Ann Arbor, MI: University of Michigan.

Turner, D., C. Giorno, A. De Serres, A. Vourc'h and P. Richardson (1998) 'The Macroeconomic Implications of Ageing in a Global Context', OECD Economics Department Working Paper, No. 193, Paris: OECD.

UN Population Division (UNPD) (2001). 'World Population Prospects: The 2000 Revision. Vol. III'. Available at: www.un.org/esa/population/publications/wpp2000wpp2000volume3.htm.

UNCTAD (1997). *Trade and Development Report 1997*, Geneva: UNCTAD.

UNDP (1992). *Global Dimensions of Human Development. Human Development Report 1992*, Paris: UNDP.

UNDP (1999). *Human Development Report 1999*, New York: Oxford University Press for UNDP. Available at: www.undp.org/hdro/99.htm.

UNDP (2000). 'Linking Countries' International Policies to Poverty', *UNDP Poverty Report 2000. Overcoming Human Poverty*, ch. 4. Available at: www.undp.org/povertyreport/chapters/chap4.html. Accessed 15 January 2003.

World Bank (2000). *World Development Report 2000/2001: Attacking Poverty*, Washington, DC: World Bank.

10

Efficiency Gains from the Elimination of Global Restrictions on Labour Mobility: An Analysis Using a Multiregional CGE Model*

Ana María Iregui

Introduction

The classic economic argument in favour of labour migration is that people move in search of higher wages, thus increasing their own productivity.[1] However, as indicated by Layard *et al.* (1992), the decision to migrate also depends on other economic, social and political considerations. Among the economic aspects, migrants may take into account comparative wage levels (actual and expected); comparative unemployment rates and unemployment benefits; the availability of housing; and the cost of migration, which includes travel expenses, information costs, and the psychological cost of leaving friends and family. Weyerbrock (1995) also indicates that political instability and civil war may cause larger emigration flows than economic or demographic pressures.

Recent empirical studies on international migration have focused mainly on Mexico–United States migration patterns (Hill and Méndez, 1984; Robinson, *et al.* 1993; Levy and van Wijnbergen, 1994), and migration flows from Eastern Europe and the former Soviet Union into Western Europe (Layard *et al.*, 1992; Weyerbrock, 1995).

Hamilton and Whalley (1984) has to date been the only attempt to quantify the efficiency gains from the removal of global restrictions on labour mobility. They use a partial equilibrium framework, in which the parameters of a CES production function are estimated for a seven-region country classification. Then the estimated parameters are used to calculate the changes in labour allocation across regions after the removal of immigration controls. They assume that the worldwide labour supply is fixed, that full employment occurs in all regions, and that differences in labour's marginal product across regions arise from barriers to inward mobility of labour in high-wage countries. Hamilton and Whalley find large efficiency gains from the removal of immigration controls; in most cases, these gains exceed worldwide GNP generated in the presence of the controls. In addition, in labour-exporting regions, wage rates rise and capital owners become worse off; but on the other hand, in labour-receiving regions wage rates fall and capital owners become better off.

In this chapter I compute the worldwide efficiency gains from the elimination of restrictions on labour mobility. In contrast to Hamilton and Whalley (1984), I use a multi-regional general equilibrium model instead of a partial equilibrium approach, since the former provides an ideal framework to analyse the effects of policy changes on resource allocation and the structure of distribution, and thus on economic welfare. A distinctive feature of the analysis is that I consider a segmented labour market (that is, skilled and unskilled labour), which can be justified on the grounds that this factor is not homogeneous. The segmentation of the labour market jointly with the general equilibrium framework allows us to examine the distributional effects of migration between skilled and unskilled labour in each region, and between these two and capital.

According to the results, the elimination of global restrictions on labour mobility generates worldwide efficiency gains that could be of considerable magnitude, reaching 67 per cent of world GDP. With the introduction of a segmented labour market, welfare gains reduce to 59 per cent of world GDP, since the benefits and losses of migration are not evenly distributed within each country. And when only skilled labour migrates, worldwide efficiency gains are even smaller (11 per cent of world GDP), as skilled labour represents a small fraction of the labour force in developing regions.

The model

In a world economy characterized by countries with different levels of income, individuals have incentives to migrate to countries with higher wage rates. If labour were to be allowed to move from one country to another without restriction, it would do so until relative wages in the low-income country had risen sufficiently. Migration reduces the labour force in the low-income country (source region), leading to an increase in wages[2] and a reduction in the demand for labour. In addition, migration leads to a process of factor reallocation within the poor country: the remaining workers gain through higher wages, but capital owners lose, since labour is now scarce relative to capital. Conversely, in the high-income country (destination region) the labour force increases, which leads to a reduction in the wage rate (assuming no rigidities). This lower wage will increase the demand for labour and aggregate employment. During the transition, workers will lose through lower wages, and capital owners will gain, since labour is now less scarce relative to capital (see, for example, Layard *et al.*, 1992; Bhagwati *et al.*, 1998). This analysis is based on the assumption that labour is a homogeneous

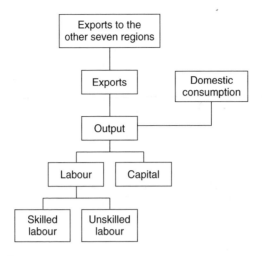

Figure 10.1   Production structure

factor of production. I shall show that the benefits and loses of migration are not distributed evenly within each country, as there are many types of labour.[3]

The structure of the model follows the standard specification of a multi-regional general equilibrium model. The model is static, and consists of eight regions, each with demand and production structures, linked through trade. Each region contains one industry that produces a single output, which is treated as heterogeneous across regions (Armington, 1969). There is a representative consumer in each region and, for simplicity, intermediate production is not considered.

Production in the model involves a CES value added function with capital (K) and labour (L) as primary inputs. There are two types of labour, skilled (Ls) and unskilled (Lu), and this labour market segmentation is a distinctive feature of our modelling exercise in comparison to previous work by Hamilton and Whalley (1984). Figure 10.1 presents the production structure of the model.

The model uses two-stage CES production functions, which are more flexible since they allow us to have different elasticity parameters at each stage of the production process. In the first stage, Ls and Lu are combined to produce the aggregate labour input (L); that is,

$$L^r = \phi^r \left(\pi^r Ls^{r^{(\varsigma^r-1)/\varsigma^r}} + (1-\pi^r)Lu^{r^{(\varsigma^r-1)/\varsigma^r}} \right)^{\varsigma^r/(\varsigma^r-1)} ,r = 1, ..., 8 \qquad (10.1)$$

where L^r is the aggregate labour input used in region r; Ls^r and Lu^r are skilled and unskilled labour inputs in region r; ϕ^r is a constant defining unit of measurement; π^r is a share parameter; and ς^r is the elasticity of substitution between skilled and unskilled labour in the production of the good in region r.

Labour demand functions for the two types of labour are obtained from cost minimization; that is, each industry selects an optimal level of Ls and Lu that minimizes the cost of producing L units of the aggregate input.

In the second stage, the aggregate labour input and capital are combined to produce value added. In each region the industry selects an optimal level of inputs that minimizes the cost of producing value added. Further, the commodity produced in each region can be transformed either into a commodity sold on the domestic market or into an export, according to a constant elasticity of transformation (CET) function. Then exports are allocated across regions according to a CET function.

Factors are non-produced commodities in fixed supply in each region. Factors of production are assumed to be internationally immobile, although this assumption is relaxed later on for L.

Turning to the demand side of the model, we assume that consumers within a region have identical homothetic preferences, which allows us to consider a representative consumer, endowed with all the labour and capital in the region. In this case, as there is only one good, the region's representative consumer demands a composite of domestically produced and imported goods subject to the region's budget constraint. Figure 10.2 presents the demand structure of the model.

The budget constraint in each region is given by income equal expenditure ($I^r = E^r$). The region's income is derived from ownership of factors of production, government transfers and the trade surplus (or deficit); that is:

$$I^r = P_{Lu,r}\overline{Lu}^r + P_{Ls,r}\overline{Ls}^r + P_{k,r}\overline{K}^r + TR^r + TB^r \qquad (10.2)$$

where $P_{Lu,r}$, $P_{Ls,r}$ and $P_{K,r}$ define the selling prices of the factors of production in region r; $\overline{Lu}^r$, $\overline{Ls}^r$ and $\overline{K}^r$ correspond to the region's endowment of unskilled labour, skilled labour and capital, respectively; TR^r represents transfers from the government; and TB^r corresponds to the region's trade surplus (or deficit). On the other hand, the region's expenditure includes the amount spent on goods as well as taxes paid:

$$E^r = P_r X^r + T^r \qquad (10.3)$$

where P_r and T^r correspond to the price and taxes paid by the consumer in region r, respectively.

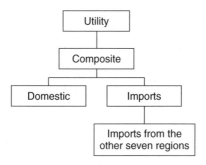

Figure 10.2 Demand structure

The model also incorporates trade and domestic tax policies. These include income, factor and consumption taxes, as well as import tariffs, all of which are modelled in *ad valorem* form. All tax revenues raised are assumed to be transferred back to consumers.

Finally, it is worth pointing out that some of the assumptions of the model may affect the outcome of the simulations. In global models it is usually assumed that capital is internationally immobile (see, for example, Whalley, 1985; and Shoven and Whalley, 1992). This assumption may not be very realistic, since international capital markets are becoming more integrated. However, this assumption is fundamental to the structure of the model; if all factors of production are allowed to move freely, the concept of region is no longer clear. Hence the need for a fixed factor in the specification of the model (in one of the extensions of the model, when capital is assumed to be internationally mobile, unskilled labour is the fixed factor in the model).[4]

Regarding labour, in the model it is assumed that differences in the marginal product of labour arise from barriers to inward mobility of labour in high-wage countries. Therefore, once barriers to labour mobility are eliminated, wage rates equalize across regions. The model also assumes that labour in one region is the same as labour in another, so that differences in labour quality or human capital per worker across countries are ignored. In the real world these differences are not only present but may also be significant. For example, Lucas (1990) indicates that production per worker in the United States is about fifteen times what it is in India; after correcting for differences in human capital, each American worker was estimated to be the equivalent of about five Indian workers. Another important factor that may affect labour productivity is the technology available in each region. Thus the elimination of restrictions on labour mobility may not ultimately eliminate differences in productivity across regions. As can be seen, some of the assumptions used in the specification of the labour market may be highly simplified; however, incorporating differences in the quality of labour across regions is severely constrained by data availability.

Once the model has been specified, it can be solved for an equilibrium solution. Equilibrium in the model is given by a set of goods and factor prices for which all markets clear. That is, demand–supply equalities hold in each goods and factors markets; zero profit conditions hold for each industry in each region; and each region is in external-sector balance (see Appendix A). Next we calculate the parameters of the model that are consistent with the benchmark dataset; these parameters allow us to reproduce the dataset as an equilibrium solution of the model. Then we compare counter-factual equilibria with the benchmark equilibrium generated by the data.

Empirical implementation

The model consists of eight regions, each of which engages in domestic and foreign trade activities. These regions were chosen to reflect world trade, and we use 1990 data for the United States (USA), Japan (JAP), the European Union (12-member EU), other developed countries (ODC), developing America (DAM), developing Africa (DAF), developing Asia (DAS), and developing Europe (DE).[5] Appendix B presents the grouping of individual countries.

We assume that each region produces one commodity, and that each region's domestically produced and imported goods are qualitatively different (Armington, 1969). We consider one commodity as our analysis focuses on the efficiency gains from the elimination of restrictions on labour mobility. The introduction of a segmented labour market is a very important feature of our model, so that we consider two types of labour: skilled and unskilled. This characteristic allows as to analyse the distributional effects that the migration of skilled labour has on unskilled labour, since the assumption of homogeneous labour implies that the benefits and losses of migration are distributed evenly within each region. Finally, the price of the commodity demanded by the consumer in USA is chosen as the numeraire.

Benchmark dataset

The benchmark dataset involves domestic activity data and external sector data for each region in 1990. Domestic activity data involve data on value added by component, the segmentation of the labour market and domestic taxes. External sector data includes data on foreign trade and import tariffs.

The size of the eight regions is given by their respective GDP in 1990 US dollars, consistent with the *World Tables* (World Bank, 1995). The benchmark dataset satisfies the equilibrium conditions of the model in the presence of the existing policies. I use data from national accounts as compiled by the United Nations, *World Tables* produced by the World Bank, and the IMF *Government Finance Statistics Yearbook* (IMF, 1996). Regarding foreign trade statistics, we use information from UNCTAD (1995) and the GATT *Trade Policy Review* (various years) for various countries.

The dataset used was based on one assembled previously by the author, in which each region produced three goods – namely, primary commodities; manufactured goods; and services. For the purpose of this chapter, these three goods were aggregated into a single commodity. We use information from (various issues of) the ILO's *Yearbook of Labour Statistics* to calculate the percentages of skilled and unskilled labour in each region. The percentages shown in Table 10.1 were obtained.[6]

As can be seen from the table, these percentages indicate that more than 17 per cent of the labour force in developed regions is skilled, while in developing regions this percentage is less than 16 per cent. National accounts, from which the wage bill is taken, report the remuneration of employees without distinguishing between types of labour. The percentages reported above are therefore important since they are used to split the wage bill into remuneration to skilled and unskilled labour in each region. The resulting wage bills are shown in Table 10.2 (figures in US$ billions).

Once the dataset has been assembled, some parameter values such as share parameters and scale parameters can be calculated directly from the equilibrium conditions of the model, following the procedure described in Mansur and Whalley (1984). Because of the functional forms used in the model, we need to specify parameter values for the elasticities of substitution and transformation that are not contained in the dataset. Once these parameters have been specified, share parameters can be obtained from

Table 10.1 Percentages of skilled and unskilled labour in each region

	USA (%)	JAP (%)	EU (%)	ODC (%)	DAM (%)	DAF (%)	DAS (%)	DE (%)
Ls	30.2	17.4	20.6	25.5	15.7	14.3	9.1	13.5
Lu	69.8	82.6	79.4	74.5	84.3	85.7	90.9	86.5

Notes: USA = United States; JAP = Japan; EU = 12-member EU; ODC = other developed countries; DAM = developing America; DAF = developing Africa; DAS = developing Asia; DE = developing Europe.
Sources: UNCTAD (1995); World Bank (1995); IMF (1996); GATT (various years/countries).

Table 10.2 Remuneration to skilled and unskilled labour (US$ bn)

	USA	JAP	EU	ODC	DAM	DAF	DAS	DE
Ls	999.8	281.0	643.5	297.7	61.4	10.2	48.6	110.6
Lu	2 313.8	1 330.8	2 473.0	871.7	330.2	60.8	485.8	706.8

Notes: As Table 10.1.
Source: As Table 10.1.

demand functions. On the supply side, share and scale parameters can be obtained from cost functions.

Elasticities

The key elasticities in our model are the skilled–unskilled labour substitution elasticity, as well as the elasticity of substitution between capital and the aggregate labour input. The degree of substitutability between skilled and unskilled labour determines the change in relative wages once a policy change is introduced. On the demand side of the model, the most important are the elasticities controlling substitution between import types in forming import composites, and those controlling substitution between comparable domestic goods and aggregate imports.

The majority of studies on labour–labour substitution use a disaggregation by occupation to separate the labour force; in particular, the disaggregation used most widely is between production and non-production workers, because of data availability. There does not seem to be consensus as to an approximate value for the labour–labour substitution elasticity, and this is reflected by the fact that there is a large range of variation in the elasticity estimates, from 0.14 to 7.5 (Hamermesh and Grant, 1979).[7] The big differences in the elasticity estimates can be the result of major methodological differences, such as the choice of estimating a cost or a production function, the choice of functional forms, the choice of data (time-series versus cross-section), and the disaggregation of the labour force according to various criteria, among others. The estimate of the elasticity of substitution between non-production and production workers was chosen as proxy for the elasticity of substitution between skilled and unskilled labour. We use a value of 0.9 in our central case, and this value is used for all regions, since individual estimates for each region were not available. Sensitivity analysis is performed around the value chosen in the range 0.5 to 2.5.[8]

In the case of the value added functions, the key parameters are the elasticities of substitution between the aggregate labour input and capital.[9] We use elasticities of factor substitution based on those used by Whalley (1985). Because of the lack of detailed regional data, our elasticities are almost identical across regions.

On the demand side of the model, two different types of elasticities are involved with the CES forms used: those controlling substitution between import types in forming import composites, and those controlling substitution between comparable domestic goods and aggregate imports. In this model, elasticities of substitution in consumption are not needed, because each representative consumer demands only one good, which is a composite of comparable domestic and imported (composite) goods.

Regarding trade elasticities, the most important are import-price elasticities and export-price elasticities. Substitution elasticities between import types making up any composite determine the export-price elasticities faced by regions. Substitution elasticities between import composites and comparable domestic products reflect import-price elasticity estimates in the literature, since it was not possible to find any econometric estimate of elasticities of substitution. The elasticities used in the model (central case) are presented in Table 10.3.

Calibration

Once the dataset has been assembled, and elasticity parameters have been specified, share and scale parameters can be calculated from the equilibrium conditions of the model, following the procedure described in Mansur and Whalley (1984).

The benchmark dataset provides information on equilibrium transactions in value terms. The first step of the calibration procedure involves the separation of these transactions into price and quantity observations. In order to do this, a units convention is widely used in which it is assumed that a physical unit of each good and factor is the amount that sells for one dollar. That is, both goods and factors have a price of unity in the benchmark equilibrium.

However, this approach is not applicable in the case of the labour market, because we assume different marginal products of labour, resulting from barriers to inward mobility of labour in high-wage countries (that is, wages

Table 10.3   Elasticities in the model

Elasticity	USA	JAP	EU	ODC	DAM	DAF	DAS	DE
ς	0.900	0.900	0.900	0.900	0.900	0.900	0.900	0.900
σ	0.830	0.800	0.820	0.840	0.850	0.860	0.840	0.840
π	0.920	0.930	0.859	0.948	1.263	1.019	1.546	2.715
ζ	0.990	0.930	0.919	1.130	0.544	0.572	1.227	1.410

Notes: For abbreviations, See Table 10.1.

ς is the labour–labour substitution elasticity.

σ is the elasticity of substitution between capital and the aggregate labour input; based on estimates presented in Whalley (1985).

π is the elasticity of substitution between domestic and imported goods. The values used are based on import price elasticities.

ζ is the elasticity of substitution between regional imports. The values used are based on export price elasticities.

Sources: For USA and JAP the source is Marquez (1990). For EU we use an average of the elasticities of Germany and the United Kingdom (Marquez, 1990); France, Belgium-Luxembourg, Denmark, Ireland, Italy and the Netherlands (Stern *et al.*, 1976); and Portugal (Houthakker and Magee, 1969). For ODC we use an average of the elasticities of Canada (Marquez, 1990); Austria, Finland, Norway, Sweden, Switzerland, Australia and New Zealand (Stern *et al.*, 1976). For DAM we use an average of the elasticities of Argentina, Brazil, Chile, Colombia, Costa Rica, Ecuador and Peru (Khan, 1974). For DAF we use an average of the elasticities of Ghana and Morocco (Khan, 1974). For DAS we use an average of the elasticities of Pakistan, India, Bangladesh and Sri Lanka (Nguyen and Bhuyan, 1977). For DE we use the elasticity for Turkey estimated by Khan (1974).

are different from one). In addition, we consider two types of labour, skilled and unskilled, each with a different productivity and, as a result, a different price within each region.

There is no agreement as to how to calculate the average wage rate. Here, we consider the wage bill (WB) for each region, as being taken from national accounts, and divide it by total population (TOTP), as taken from the *UN Demographic Yearbook 1994* (United Nations, 1996a). Total population, however, exceeds the workforce in each region. Therefore, as a second measure of the average wage rate we use the wage bill divided by the economically active population (EAP).[10,11]

Since there is labour market segmentation, we need to calculate the average wage rates of skilled and unskilled labour in each region. Given that in practice such data are not available, we use average earnings per worker in finance, insurance, real estate and business services as proxy for skilled labour wages, and average earnings per worker in wholesale and retail trade, restaurants and hotels as proxy for unskilled labour wages. The ratio between high and low wages is then used to infer the average wage rates for skilled and unskilled labour in each region. The resulting relative wage rates for the two types of labour are reported in Table 10.4. As can be seen, regardless of how the wage rates are calculated, USA, JAP, EU and ODC have higher wage rates than the developing world (that is, DAM, DAF, DAS and DE).

The final step in the calibration procedure is to use the price–quantity data to calculate parameters for demand and production functions from the benchmark equilibrium observations, given the required values of pre-specified parameters such as elasticities and tax rates. In order to do this, we use the equilibrium conditions together with first-order conditions (from utility maximization and cost minimization), to solve for function parameter values using equilibrium prices and quantities. Calibration allows the solution procedure to be tested, and ensures the consistency of agents' behaviour

Table 10.4   Relative wage rates, 1990 (US$)

Wage measures	*Regions*							
	USA	JAP	EU	ODC	DAM	DAF	DAS	DE
WB/TOTP								
Unskilled labour	91.3	96.3	60.2	72.9	6.7	1.0	1.5	13.8
Skilled labour	150.0	158.1	122.2	97.6	13.1	1.8	2.2	17.3
WB/EAP								
Unskilled labour	68.5	71.3	52.9	61.6	7.1	1.0	1.6	11.3
Skilled labour	112.6	117.0	107.5	82.4	13.8	1.8	2.3	14.1

Note: See Table 10.1 for list of abbreviations.

with the benchmark dataset. The model was solved using a routine written in the General Algebraic Modelling System (GAMS) software.

Model results

The model described above was used to calculate the worldwide efficiency gains from free mobility of labour. Two scenarios were considered: in the first, labour is a homogeneous factor of production; this scenario is included in order to compare the results with those obtained by Hamilton and Whalley (1984). In the second scenario, labour is classified as skilled and unskilled. In the latter scenario, we consider two cases: (i) both skilled and unskilled labour migrate; and (ii) skilled labour is the only factor that migrates. The case was not considered where unskilled labour is the only factor that migrates, since unskilled labour is usually involved in illegal migration and the model does not consider this type of migration.

The removal of restrictions on labour mobility modifies the market clearing condition that determines the equilibrium wage rate. In particular, when labour is homogeneous the equilibrium condition is given by

$$\sum_{r=1}^{8} L^r = \sum_{r=1}^{8} \overline{L^r} \tag{10.4}$$

where $\overline{L^r}$ corresponds to the region's endowment of labour. In the heterogeneous case we have

$$\sum_{r=1}^{8} Ls^r = \sum_{r=1}^{8} \overline{Ls^r} \tag{10.5a}$$

and

$$\sum_{r=1}^{8} Lu^r = \sum_{r=1}^{8} \overline{Lu^r} \tag{10.5b}$$

where $\overline{Ls^r}$ and $\overline{Lu^r}$ correspond to the region's endowment of the two types of labour.

In the model, international capital transfers are not considered, since it is assumed that migrant workers do not bring capital with them, nor send capital back home. Capital flows and transfers may alleviate the negative effects of migration on wages. In addition, the model assumes that all migrant labour enters the labour market (some migrants such as children and elderly people will not in fact work).

Once immigration controls are removed, labour migrates from low-wage to high-wage regions. The source regions are DAM, DAF, DAS and DE, while the destination regions are USA, JAP, EU and ODC. However, in the homogeneous labour case, DE becomes a destination region. When labour is heterogeneous, and both skilled and unskilled labour migrate, DE becomes a destination region for unskilled labour, and a source region for skilled labour. Regardless of whether labour is homogeneous or heterogeneous, the amount of the factor entering DE is not considerable.

Table 10.5 quantifies the effects of the removal of immigration controls on welfare, as measured by the aggregate equivalent variation.[12] In the homogeneous labour case, there is a reduction in production in all sectors in the source regions. This is accompanied by a reduction in exports and an increase in imports, which compensate for the reduction in domestic output. Conversely, in the destination regions, there is an increase in production in all sectors accompanied by an increase in exports and a reduction in imports from developing regions. In this case, there are large gains from the removal of global immigration controls, ranging from 54 per cent to 67 per cent of world GDP. These gains are not as large as those obtained by Hamilton and Whalley (1984), where in some cases the gains exceeded the worldwide economy GNP. The differences may be the result of the modelling frameworks (that is, partial equilibrium versus general equilibrium), the flows of labour leaving low-wage regions, or units of measurement, because Hamilton and Whalley (1984) used population, and I used units of labour.

Table 10.5 also presents the welfare effects of the removal of immigration controls when labour is a heterogeneous factor. In this case, as in the previous scenario with homogeneous labour, there is an increase in domestic output in developed regions, whereas output reduces in developing countries; the reduction in domestic output is accompanied by a reduction in exports and an increase in imports from developed regions. When both skilled and

Table 10.5   Welfare effects of the removal of immigration controls (equivalent variation as a percentage of world GDP)

Wage measures	Homogeneous labour	Heterogeneous labour	
		Both Ls and Lu migrate	*Only Ls migrates*
WB/TOTP	67	59	11
WB/EAP	54	48	9

Note: Ls and Lu denote skilled and unskilled labour, respectively.

unskilled labour migrate, efficiency gains range from 48 per cent to 59 per cent of world GDP. The gains are smaller than in the homogeneous case, as a result of the technological constraint imposed by the substitutability between skilled and unskilled labour. Thus, with a segmented labour market, skilled and unskilled labour have less opportunity to reallocate. When only skilled labour migrates, worldwide welfare gains are much smaller than in the previous two cases (from 9 per cent to 11 per cent of world GDP) because skilled labour represents a small fraction of the labour force in the source regions (that is, 14 per cent in DAM; 10 per cent in DAF; 5 per cent in DAS; and 14 per cent in DE).

The segmentation of the labour market also allows us to examine the distributional effects of immigration between skilled and unskilled labour in each region. Tables 10.6 and 10.7 present the distributional impacts of the

Table 10.6 Distributional impact of the removal of immigration controls: heterogeneous labour, both skilled and unskilled labour migrants (% change)

Wage measures	USA	JAP	EU	ODC	DAM	DAF	DAS	DE
WB/TOTP								
P_{LS}	−18	−22	0	26	837	6 671	5446	608
P_{LU}	−47	−50	−20	−34	620	4 697	3022	249
P_K	191	236	181	164	263	1 351	900	329
WB/EAP								
P_{LS}	−12	−15	−7	21	619	5 377	4246	604
P_{LU}	−40	−43	−23	−34	478	3 981	2467	263
P_K	145	179	142	129	363	1 130	755	312

Note: P_{LS} corresponds to the average wage rate of skilled labour; P_{LU} is the average wage rate of unskilled labour; and P_K refers to the return to capital. See Table 10.1 for list of abbreviations.

Table 10.7 Distributional impact of the removal of immigration controls: heterogeneous labour, skilled labour migrants only (% change)

Wage measures	USA	JAP	EU	ODC	DAM	DAF	DAS	DE
WB/TOTP								
P_{LS}	−60	−62	−51	−38	361	2 234	2 631	249
P_{LU}	24	55	48	40	117	217	189	129
P_K	27	60	51	42	115	211	184	128
WB/EAP								
P_{LS}	−52	−54	−50	−35	289	2 862	2250	281
P_{LU}	19	46	39	34	97	190	164	129
P_K	22	41	42	36	96	185	160	128

Note: See note to Table 10.6. See Table 10.1 for list of abbreviations.

removal of immigration controls. A priori one would expect labour migration from the source regions to increase the labour supply in the destination regions, reduce the average wage rate (assuming no rigidities), and benefit capital owners. In the source regions, the removal of immigration controls is expected to reduce the labour supply, thus increasing the average wage rate. As a result, capital is less scarce relative to labour, so that a reduction in the return to capital is expected.

When both skilled and unskilled labour migrate (see Table 10.6), average wages increase in the source regions because labour is less abundant relative to capital, and the return to capital decreases. The removal of immigration controls benefits skilled labour more than unskilled, because the former is a small proportion of the total labour force, and after migration this factor is scarcer in developing regions. In the destination regions, average wages reduce for both skilled and unskilled labour, since labour is now less scarce relative to capital, and the return to capital increases.

When only skilled labour migrates (see Table 10.7), there is a substantial increase in the remuneration of this type of labour in the source regions, since this factor of production is not abundant in these regions. The remuneration of unskilled workers and capital owners also increase, but by a considerably smaller percentage.

As to the destination regions, the inflow of skilled labour increases the supply of this type of labour, therefore reducing its average wage rate. As we would expect, both the average wage of unskilled labour and the return to capital increase, but skilled labour is worse off. The flexibility of wages allows the labour market to absorb labour immigration. Lower wages induce an increase in both labour demand and aggregate employment.

The amount of labour leaving the source regions amounts to over 50 per cent of the labour endowment of developing regions (see Table 10.8). A similar percentage change is observed when, in the heterogeneous labour case, both skilled and unskilled labour migrate. Changes are even greater when only skilled labour migrates (around 73 per cent of the skilled labour endowment of developing regions). Regarding migration costs, these are estimated at around 8 per cent of GDP when labour is assumed to be homogeneous, and

Table 10.8 Migration flows as a percentage of developing regions' labour endowment

Wage measures	Homogeneous labour	Heterogeneous labour	
		Both Ls and Lu migrate	Only Ls migrates
WB/TOTP	53	50	73
WB/EAP	51	48	72

Note: Ls and Lu denote skilled and unskilled labour, respectively.

when both skilled and unskilled labour migrate; see Table 10.9. These costs are clearly smaller than the welfare gains reported in Table 10.5. Conversely, when only skilled labour migrates, the estimated costs of migration are larger than the welfare gains, which can be explained by the fact that a much larger percentage of skilled labour leaves the developing regions. Thus the net welfare effects of the removal of restrictions on labour mobility are negative.

In summary, migration leads to factor reallocation, and during this process there are winners and losers. In the source regions, labour becomes scarcer relative to capital, and capital owners lose. However, not all workers are better off, since labour is a heterogeneous factor.

Emigration will benefit workers whose skills substitute those who migrate, whereas it will hurt those workers whose skills complement migrants. On the other hand, in the destination regions, labour becomes more abundant (less scarce) relative to capital, so that capital owners benefit. However, not all workers are worse off, because labour is a heterogeneous factor. Immigration will benefit those whose skills complement the immigrant worker, whereas immigration will hurt workers whose skills are a substitute to the immigrants.

A sensitivity analysis was also performed on the key elasticities of the model (these results are not reported here). In particular, in a first set of simulations, the elasticity of labour–labour substitution was varied from 0.5 to 2.5. This elasticity is very important in our model since it includes a segmented labour market, a feature that has not been considered in previous works. In a second set of simulations, the elasticities of substitution in the production of value added were set at values between 0.5 and 1.5 in all regions; this elasticity corresponds to the elasticity of substitution between the aggregate labour input and capital. We conclude that the results are

Table 10.9 Migration costs as a percentage of world GDP

Wage measures	Homogeneous labour	Heterogeneous labour	
		Both Ls and Lu migrate	Only Ls migrates
WB/TOTP	8	8	12
WB/EAP	8	8	11

Note and Source: Migration costs were calculated as the number of people migrating multiplied by the cost of moving. The number of people migrating is calculated as the economically active population in developing regions multiplied by the percentage of labour moving from developing to developed regions. As for migration costs, we use Conley and Ligon (2002) to obtain estimates of transport costs. They report airfares between countries' capitals as the cost of transporting embodied human capital and the cost of shipping a 20 kg express package between capital cities. We used their database, as taken from http://are.berkeley.edu/~ligon/papers/distance.tgz, to calculate an approximate average cost of moving from developing to developed regions. From the model it is possible to establish that people migrate from developing to developed regions, but not to which particular developed region.

robust to the elasticity choice, in the sense that the elimination of immigration controls generates worldwide efficiency gains. In addition, in the destination regions, capital owners benefit from labour immigration, and workers lose because of lower wages. In the source regions, capital owners are worse off and workers are better off. The sensitivity analysis also confirms that migration of skilled labour hurts unskilled labour in the source regions.

Model extensions

This section introduces three new features to the model: (i) transaction costs; (ii) international capital mobility; and (iii) selective labour mobility.

Transaction costs

This extension of the model seems appropriate, since migration is a costly process. There are costs involved in the process of moving from one region to another, such as transport costs, the costs of settling into the other region, the costs of finding a new job, and the costs of leaving behind friends and family. With the elimination of restrictions on labour mobility, labour will move until the marginal product of labour equals the cost of hiring labour; hence, a single market clearing wage no longer characterizes the equilibrium. Transaction costs thus drive a wedge between wages in developed and developing countries. These were modelled as a tax without revenue, whose rate is exogenously determined. The price received by owners of labour in each region corresponds to a percentage of the market clearing price when restrictions on labour mobility are eliminated. That is, the price of labour in each region is given by:

$$P_L^r = W(1 - TC^r) \tag{10.6}$$

where W corresponds to the world price of labour, and TC^r corresponds to regional transaction costs.

Transaction costs are difficult to quantify since there are no measures available. As mentioned earlier, there are costs associated with migration from low-wage to high-wage regions. In the case of developing regions, these costs can be very high. Taking into account the substantial differences in relative wages among the regions, we assume the following values for transaction costs: 0.9 for DAF and DAS; 0.8 for DAM; and 0.7 for DE. The transaction costs for developed regions (USA, JAP, EU and ODC) are assumed to be much smaller (that is, 0.1), since workers in these regions have little or no incentive to move to low-wage regions.

The introduction of transaction costs reduces migration flows (see Table 10.10). For example, when the average wage is measure as WB/TOTP and labour is homogeneous, migration reduces from 53 per cent of the developing regions' endowment of labour to 36 per cent. In the heterogeneous

Table 10.10 Migration flows in the presence of transaction costs (migration as a percentage of developing regions' labour endowment)

Wage measures	Homogeneous labour	Heterogeneous labour	
		Both Ls and Lu migrate	Only Ls migrates
Without transaction costs			
WB/TOTP	53	50	73
WB/EAP	51	48	72
With transaction costs			
WB/TOTP	36	32	53
WB/EAP	23	30	49

Note: Ls and Lu denote skilled and unskilled labour, respectively.

labour scenario, migration reduces from 50 per cent of the developing regions' endowment of labour to 32 per cent when the two types of labour are allowed to migrate, and from 73 per cent of the developing regions' endowment of skilled labour to 53 per cent when only skilled labour migrates. Welfare gains (see Table 10.11) and migration costs (see Table 10.12) are also smaller in the presence of transaction costs, because fewer people are moving from developing to developed regions.

Regarding the distributional effects, results not reported here indicate that when the labour market is segmented, skilled labour benefits relative to unskilled labour in the source regions; in the destination regions both types of labour lose, but unskilled workers are hurt even more when both skilled and unskilled labour migrate.

Table 10.11 Welfare effects of the removal of immigration controls in the presence of transaction costs (equivalent variation as a percentage of world GDP)

Wage measures	Homogeneous labour	Heterogeneous labour	
		Both Ls and Lu migrate	Only Ls migrates
Without transaction costs			
WB/TOTP	67	59	11
WB/EAP	54	48	9
With transaction costs			
WB/TOTP	31	26	6
WB/EAP	22	18	4

Note: See Table 10.8.

Table 10.12 Migration costs in the presence of transaction costs (as a percentage of world GDP)

Wage measures	Homogeneous labour	Heterogeneous labour	
		Both Ls and Lu migrate	Only Ls migrates
Without transaction costs			
WB/TOTP	8	8	12
WB/EAP	8	8	11
With transaction costs			
WB/TOTP	4	5	8
WB/EAP	4	5	8

Note: See Table 10.8.

Finally, migration, welfare gains and migration costs increase as the transaction costs for the developing regions are reduced (these results are not reported here). This is because transaction costs distort the labour market, especially in developing regions, and as the distortion is reduced, efficiency increases and the wage gap reduces.

Capital mobility

In the second elaboration of the model international capital mobility is introduced. Although this feature is usually ignored in global models (see for example, Whalley, 1985; Shoven and Whalley, 1992), it seems interesting to include it in the model, since capital markets are becoming more integrated internationally. In this case, the return to capital equalizes across regions. Therefore, a single market clearing rental rate characterizes the equilibrium; that is, the market clearing condition for the market of the capital factor is given by:

$$\sum_{r=1}^{8} K^r = \sum_{r=1}^{8} \overline{K^r} \tag{10.7}$$

that is, the sum of the demand for capital in each region must equal the global endowment of the factor.

Simulations were carried out for the scenario in which only skilled labour migrates, since a fixed factor is needed (in this case, unskilled labour). If all factors of production are allowed to move freely, the concept of region is no longer clear.

When the restrictions to skilled labour mobility are removed, we observe that labour moves from regions with low wages (DAM, DAF, DAS and DE) to regions with high wages (USA, JAP, EU and ODC); and capital moves from regions where it is abundant relative to labour (USA, JAP, EU and ODC) to regions where it is scarce relative to labour (DAM, DAF, DAS and DE). The effects on the remuneration of the factors of production are similar to those obtained when capital is not internationally mobile. A substantial increase is observed in the remuneration of skilled labour in the source regions, since this factor is not abundant in these regions, whereas unskilled labour and capital owners are worse off; in the destination regions, the remuneration of skilled labour falls and unskilled labour and capital owners are better off (see Table 10.13). The effects of capital mobility on the return to capital are smaller than the effects of skilled labour mobility on wages. This is explained by the fact that capital flows from developed to developing regions are smaller than labour flows from developing to developed regions. In particular, when wages are measured as the wage bill divided by TOTP, migration flows account for 56 per cent of the world endowment of labour, whereas capital flows account for only 7 per cent of the world endowment of capital.

In addition, aggregate welfare improves compared with the scenario without capital mobility (see Table 10.14). The improved welfare is the result of a better resource allocation with smaller distributional effects.

The previous results should be viewed with caution, since they are ruled by the specification of the capital market. That is, since we assume a competitive market, capital will respond to variations in its rate of return. However, as indicated by Layard *et al.* (1992), developing regions have low productivity, and it is possible that migration from DAM, DAF, DAS and DE to USA, JAP, EU and ODC would divert capital to developed regions that could be invested instead in developing regions.[13]

Selective labour mobility

The third elaboration of the model is the introduction of selective labour mobility. This extension seems interesting because some countries have

Table 10.13 Distributional impact of the removal of immigration controls in the presence of capital mobility (percentage change)

Wage measures	USA	JAP	EU	ODC	DAM	DAF	DAS	DE
WB/TOTP								
P_{LS}	−62	−64	−54	−42	332	3 018	2 454	226
P_{LU}	14	29	28	24	69	136	131	76
P_K	48	48	48	48	48	48	48	48
WB/EAP								
P_{LS}	−55	−57	−53	−39	263	2 663	2 092	255
P_{LU}	11	24	22	19	57	118	112	74
P_K	40	40	40	40	40	40	40	40

Note: See Table 10.1 for region abbreviations.

Table 10.14   Welfare effects of the removal of immigration controls in the presence of capital mobility (equivalent variation as a percentage of world GDP)

Wage measures	Only Ls migrates
Without capital mobility	
WB/TOTP	11
WB/EAP	9
With capital mobility	
WB/TOTP	13
WB/EAP	11

signed bilateral agreements with other countries that cover project-link work, seasonal work, work in border areas and guest workers.[14] We focus on the case where individuals in some particular regions in the developing world are allowed to migrate to developed regions. We consider the following seven possibilities:

  (i)   Workers in DAM migrate to USA, JAP, EU and ODC;
 (ii)   Workers in DAF migrate to USA, JAP, EU and ODC;
(iii)   Workers in DAS migrate to USA, JAP, EU and ODC;
 (iv)   Workers in DE migrate to USA, JAP, EU and ODC;
  (v)   Workers in DAM migrate to USA;
 (vi)   Workers in DAS migrate to JAP; and
(vii)   Workers in DAF and DE migrate to EU.

Each of these seven possibilities are analysed when labour is homogeneous; when labour is heterogeneous and both skilled and unskilled workers migrate; and when labour is heterogeneous and only skilled workers migrate. Under this elaboration, the average wage equalizes across the regions involved, whereas each of the excluded regions will have a market clearing condition for the labour market.

An aggregate welfare improvement was observed in all seven cases (see Table 10.15). The magnitude of the welfare gains depends on the size of the source region in terms of the labour market endowment. In particular, the highest welfare gains are obtained when workers in DAS are allowed to migrate to USA, JAP, EU and ODC, since DAS is the most densely populated region and has one of the lowest average wages. Conversely, the lowest welfare gains are obtained when DE is allowed to migrate to USA, JAP, EU and ODC; this result is not surprising, since DE is the third most populous region in the developing world, and the region's average wages are, in some cases, the highest in the developing world.

Table 10.15 Welfare effects of the removal of immigration controls in the presence of selective mobility (equivalent variation as a percentage of world GDP)

Migration flow/wage measures	Homogeneous labour	Heterogeneous labour	
		Both Ls and Lu migrate	Only Ls migrate
DAM → USA, JAP, EU, ODC			
WB/TOTP	5	5	2
WB/EAP	3	4	0
DAF → USA, JAP, EU, ODC			
WB/TOTP	11	11	3
WB/EAP	9	9	2
DAS → USA, JAP, EU, ODC			
WB/TOTP	47	52	9
WB/EAP	38	41	7
DE → USA, JAP, EU, ODC			
WB/TOTP	3	3	1
WB/EAP	3	3	1
DAM → USA			
WB/TOTP	4	4	1
WB/EAP	3	3	1
DAS → JAP			
WB/TOTP	15	24	4
WB/EAP	13	19	3
DAF, DE → EU			
WB/TOTP	10	11	3
WB/EAP	8	10	3

Note: → indicates the direction of the migration flow. See Table 10.1 for region abbreviations.

In terms of the amount of labour that moves between regions, the largest movement occurs when workers in DAS are allowed to migrate to USA, JAP, EU and ODC. In the homogeneous case, the proportion of labour that moves out of DAS is around 30 per cent of the world endowment of labour; and in the heterogeneous labour case, the proportion of labour that moves out of DAS is around 36 per cent of the world endowment of labour. Conversely, the smallest amount of migration occurs when the workforce in DE is allowed to migrate to USA, JAP, EU and ODC. These results suggest a positive relationship between the amount of migration and welfare gains.

As to the distributional impact of the removal of immigration controls, results not reported here indicate that the introduction of selective labour mobility does not affect the main conclusions (that is, workers in the source region and capital owners in the destination regions benefit from migration).

When both skilled and unskilled labour migrate, and workers in DAM migrate to USA, JAP, EU and ODC, skilled labour in ODC also migrates to the other developed regions because the remuneration of this factor is the lowest in the developed world. Skilled and unskilled labour are better off relative to capital in the source regions, and in DAM unskilled labour is better off relative to skilled labour. This result contrasts with the findings in the central case, and can be explained by the fact that more unskilled labour is migrating out of the region. In the other selective labour mobility cases, skilled labour is better off relative to unskilled labour and capital in the source regions, whereas in the destination regions unskilled labour is worse off relative to skilled labour, and capitalists benefit.

Finally, when we have a segmented labour market and skilled labour migration, skilled workers gain in the source regions relative to unskilled workers; and in the destination regions, both unskilled and skilled labour lose relative to capital, although unskilled labour loses less than skilled labour.

Concluding remarks

In this chapter we have computed the worldwide efficiency gains from the elimination of restrictions on labour mobility. One of the key features of our model is the introduction of a segmented labour market, as we consider two types of labour – skilled and unskilled. When labour is heterogeneous, the cases are considered where both skilled and unskilled labour migrate, and when only skilled labour migrates. In our analysis, wages differ across regions because of the existence of barriers to labour mobility, and wage rates are equalized as a result of the elimination of restrictions to labour mobility rather than free trade.

Our findings indicate that the elimination of global restrictions to labour mobility generates worldwide efficiency gains that could be of considerable magnitude (more than 50 per cent of world GDP). When only skilled labour is allowed to migrate, welfare gains are smaller (around 10 per cent), since skilled labour is a small proportion of the labour force in developing regions. The estimated costs of migration are smaller than the welfare gains when labour is homogeneous, and when both skilled and unskilled labour migrate.

Migration also leads to a process of factor reallocation in which there are winners and losers. In the source regions, labour becomes scarcer relative to capital, and capital owners lose. However, not all workers are better off, since labour is a heterogeneous factor. Emigration benefits workers whose skills substitute those of migrants, whereas it will hurt the workers whose skills complement migrants. On the other hand, in the destination regions, labour becomes more abundant (less scarce) relative to capital, and capital owners benefit. Again, not all workers in the destination regions are worse

off, because labour is a heterogeneous factor. Immigration will benefit workers whose skills complement the immigrant workers, while immigration will
hurt those whose skills are substituted by immigrant workers.

The model was then extended by including: transportation costs; capital
mobility and selective labour mobility. With the introduction of transaction
costs, wages fail to equalize across regions, migration flows reduce and in
consequence efficiency gains reduce as well. With capital mobility, global
welfare improves compared with the scenario without capital mobility, as
a result of a better resource allocation. With selective labour mobility, aggregate welfare improves and the magnitude of the gain depends on the size of
the region in terms of the labour endowment.

Finally, our results have shown that the elimination of global restrictions
on labour mobility generates considerable worldwide efficiency gains.
Despite these gains, the liberalization of worldwide migration is far from
realistic because of social and political tensions. High-income countries are
very reluctant to open their borders to free migration because they do not
want to become the destination of immigration of unskilled labour from
low-income countries. In the short run, countries regulate the flows of international migration by means of border controls and work permits, among
other means. In the long run, countries should concentrate their efforts in
the elimination of incentives to migrate, which could be accomplished by
reducing income disparities among regions.

Appendix A: equilibrium conditions of the model

Equilibrium is given by a set of goods and factor prices for which all markets
clear. That is, demand–supply equalities hold in each goods and factors
market; zero profit conditions hold for each industry in each region; and
each region is in external-sector balance.

In the goods markets, gross output equals final demand because intermediate
production is netted out; specifically, the model has the following blocks of
market clearing conditions:

- The supply of goods for domestic consumption must equal the demand
  for domestically produced goods;
- Exports from region *r* to region *s* must equal imports of region *s* from
  region *r*, because there are assumed to be no transfer costs (for example,
  transport) in shipping goods from one region to another;
- Total supply of composite commodities, which consists of the composite
  of similar domestic products and aggregate imports, must equal consumer's
  demand in each region; and
- In a segmented labour market, the supply of the aggregate labour input
  generated by the combination of *Lu* and *Ls*, must equal the demand for
  the aggregate labour input used in the production of value added.

In the factor markets we assume initially that all factors are internationally immobile. This assumption implies that factor prices are different in each region; this is an important assumption for the results of our model, since market clearing conditions in factor markets determine factor prices. Under this assumption, we have separate labour and capital equilibrium conditions in each region. That is, the region's endowment of capital and labour must equal factor use (that is, full employment occurs in all regions). In the second variant of the model, capital is assumed to be internationally mobile. This assumption implies that there is only one price for capital in the model, determined by the market clearing condition that factor use across all industries and regions must equal the world endowment of capital.

The zero profit conditions state that the total value of sales must equal the industry's costs, and they must hold in each region. In particular,

- In each region, the value of domestic output must be equal to the capital and labour costs of producing the good. At the same time, the value of domestic output equals the value of commodities sold in the domestic market plus the value of commodities sold as exports;
- The value of commodities sold as exports must equal the value of the sum of exports to the other seven regions;
- The value of total imports must equal the value of the sum of imports from the other seven regions;
- The value of the composite commodity demanded by consumers must equal the value of aggregate imports plus the value of domestically produced goods;
- The value of goods sold for domestic consumption must be equal to the value of the demand for domestically produced goods;
- The value of exports from region r to region s must be equal to the value of imports of region s from region r; and
- In a segmented labour market, the value of the aggregate labour input must be equal to the skilled and unskilled labour costs of producing the aggregate input.

Finally, the external sector balance condition indicates that each region is always on its budget constraint. In this case, we assume that in each region the value of exports minus the value of imports – that is, the trade surplus (or deficit) – remains fixed in real terms (the trade balance is not zero since this would involve adjusting the data). Formally, the external sector balance condition is:

$$P_M^r \ IMP^r + TB^r = P_X^r \ EXP^r$$

where $TB^r = TB_0^r \left(\dfrac{P_r X^r}{P_r^0 X^r} \right)$, P_r^0 is the benchmark consumer price (this price is equal to 1), TB_0^r is the benchmark trade surplus (or deficit), and the term in parentheses is a Paasche price index. We use this price index to take into account changes in prices in the new equilibrium.

Appendix B: regional classifications

Region 1: USA	United States			
Region 2: JAP	Japan			
Region 3: EU	Belgium	Denmark	France	Germany
	Greece	Ireland	Italy	Luxembourg
	Netherlands	Portugal	Spain	United Kingdom
Region 4: ODC	Australia	Austria	Canada	Finland
	Iceland	Israel	New Zealand	Norway
	South Africa	Sweden	Switzerland	
Region 5: DAM	Antigua & Barbuda	Argentina	Barbados	Belize
	Bolivia	Brazil	Chile	Colombia
	Costa Rica	Dominica	Dominican Rep.	Ecuador
	El Salvador	Grenada	Guatemala	Guyana
	Haiti	Honduras	Jamaica	Mexico
	Nicaragua	Panama	Paraguay	Peru
	St Lucia	St Kitts & Nevis	Suriname	Uruguay
	Trinidad & Tobago	Venezuela	St Vincent & the Grenadines	
Region 6: DAF	Algeria	Angola	Benin	Botswana
	Burkina Faso	Burundi	Cameroon	Cape Verde
	Central African Rep.	Chad	Comoros	Congo
	Côte d'Ivoire	Djibouti	Egypt	Equatorial Guinea
	Ethiopia	Gabon	Gambia	Ghana
	Guinea	Guinea-Bissau	Kenya	Lesotho
	Madagascar	Malawi	Mali	Mauritania
	Mauritius	Morocco	Mozambique	Namibia
	Niger	Nigeria	Reunion	Rwanda
	São Tomé & Principe	Senegal	Seychelles	Sierra Leone
	Sudan	Swaziland	Togo	Tunisia
	Uganda	Tanzania	Zambia	Zimbabwe
Region 7: DAS	Bahrain	Bhutan	Bangladesh	China
	Hong Kong	India	Indonesia	Iran (Islamic Rep.)
	Jordan	Kuwait	Laos	Lebanon
	Malaysia	Mongolia	Myanmar	Nepal
	Oman	Pakistan	Philippines	Qatar
	Rep. of Korea	Saudi Arabia	Singapore	Sri Lanka
	Syrian Arab Rep.	Taiwan	Thailand	Yemen
	United Arab Emirates			

Appendix B   (*Continued*)

Region 8: DE	Bulgaria	Croatia	Cyprus	Czech Rep.
	Estonia	Hungary	Malta	Poland
	Romania	Slovenia	Turkey	USSR (former)
	Yugoslavia (FR)			

Notes

* I would like to thank Chris Dawkins, Jesús Otero, Jeff Round and John Whalley for helpful comments and suggestions. I have also benefited from the comments of Jeff Crisp, George Borjas, the participants at the UNU–WIDER Conference on 'Poverty, International Migration and Asylum' held in Helsinki, and an anonymous referee. The views expressed in the chapter are those of the author and do not represent those of the Board of Directors of the Banco de la República (Central Bank of Colombia), or other members of its staff.

1. Layard *et al.* (1992) indicate that free trade and international capital mobility can also raise productivity, without labour migration.

2. The magnitude of the increase will depend on the elasticity of labour demand. The more elastic the demand for labour, the smaller the increase in wages.

3. For some trade theorists, the issue of the removal of restrictions on labour mobility may not be of great relevance because of the factor price equalization theorem, according to which factor prices will be equalized by free trade without internationally mobile factors (see Samuelson, 1948, 1949). However, this theorem is based on very restrictive assumptions, such as identical technologies in different countries, constant returns to scale, perfect competition, no factor intensity reversals, no specialization, and that the prices of the goods are equalized as a result of trade. Moreover, factor price equalization depends on the complete convergence of the price of the goods. In reality, the prices of the goods are not fully equalized because of both natural (for example, transportation costs) and artificial barriers to trade (for example, import tariffs, import quotas, voluntary export restraints). An additional reason why factor price equalization may not be achieved is that countries exhibit different technologies and resources, so they are unlikely to remain unspecialized (see, for example, Layard and Walters, 1978; Krugman and Obstfeld, 1994).

4. Instead of having a fixed factor, a non-tradable good could be introduced, so that all production factors could be interregionally mobile.

5. Initially, developing Oceania (which included Fiji, Kiribati, Papua New Guinea, Samoa, Solomon Islands and Vanuatu) was included as a ninth region. At the time of solving the model we encountered numerical problems because this region was very small compared to the others (in 1990 its GDP accounted for only 0.2 per cent of world GDP). Hence it was excluded from the analysis.

6. An appendix with the sources and the procedure followed to assemble the dataset is available from the author upon request.

7. Hamermesh (1993: 65), however, points out that the substitution relationship between production and non-production workers tells us little about the substitution between high- and low-skilled workers because 'there is a remarkably large overlap in the earnings of these two groups'.

8. The use of elasticity values greater than 2.5 were also tried, but numerical problems were encountered when solving the model.

9. Whalley (1985) points out that there is no consensus as to the quantitative orders of magnitude involved, since most time-series estimates of the aggregate substitution elasticity are in the neighbourhood of unity, and cross-section estimates are often around 0.5.
10. ILO (1996: 5) defines the economically active population as 'all persons of either sex who furnish the supply of labour for the production of goods and services during a specified time-reference period'.
11. Iregui (2003) also uses GDP *per capita* (PPP adjusted and unadjusted) as an alternative measure of the average wage rate, in order to compare the results of the model with those of Hamilton and Whalley (1984). The results obtained using these alternative measures are qualitatively the same and so are not reported here.
12. The equivalent variation (EV) is a measure of welfare change. It is defined as the amount of money equivalent to a particular change that has taken place between equilibria. In this case, an arithmetical sum of EVs, summed across regions, is used.
13. Lucas (1990) provides an alternative explanation.
14. For example, Germany has signed labour agreements with Hungary, Poland and the Czech Republic. Also Belgium, France and Switzerland have signed labour agreements with East European countries (Weyerbrock, 1995).

References

Armington, P. S. (1969). 'A Theory of Demand for Products Distinguished by Place of Production', *International Monetary Fund Staff Papers*, 16: 159–76.
Bhagwati, J., A. Panagariya and T. Srinivasan (1998). *Lectures on International Trade*, 2nd edn, Cambridge, MA: MIT Press.
Conley, T. and E. Ligon (2002). 'Economic Distance and Cross-country Spillovers', *Journal of Economic Growth*, 7: 157–87.
GAMS386 (1989). Washington: IBRD/World Bank.
GATT (various years). *Trade Policy Review*, various countries.
Hamermesh, D. and J. Grant (1979). 'Econometric Studies of Labor–Labor Substitution and their Implications for Policy, *Journal of Human Resources*, 14: 518–42.
Hamermesh, D. (1993). *Labour Demand*, Princeton, NJ: Princeton University Press.
Hamilton, B. and J. Whalley (1984). 'Efficiency and Distributional Implications of Global Restrictions on Labour Mobility. Calculations and Policy Implications', *Journal of Development Economics*, 14: 61–75.
Hill, J. and J. Méndez (1984). 'The Effects of Commercial Policy on International Migration Flows: The Case of the United States and Mexico', *Journal of International Economics*, 17: 41–53.
Houthakker, H. and A. Magee (1969). 'Income and Price Elasticities in World Trade', *The Review of Economics and Statistics*, 51: 111–25.
ILO (International Labour Office) (various issues). *Yearbook of Labour Statistics*, Geneva: ILO.
International Monetary Fund (1996). *Government Finance Statistics Yearbook*, Vol. 20, Washington, DC: IMF.
Iregui, A. M. (2003). 'Efficiency Gains from the Elimination of Global Restrictions on Labour Mobility: An Analysis Using a Multiregional CGE Model', WIDER Discussion Paper, 2003/27, Helsinki: UNU-WIDER.
Khan, M. (1974). 'Import and Export Demand in Developing Countries', *International Monetary Fund Staff Papers*, 21: 678–93.
Krugman, P. and M. Obstfeld (1994). *International Economics: Theory and Policy*, 3rd edn, New York: HarperCollins.

Layard, R. and A. Walters (1978). *Microeconomic Theory*. Maidenhead: McGraw-Hill.

Layard, R., O. Blanchard, R. Dornbusch and P. Krugman (1992). *East–West Migration. The Alternatives*. Cambridge, MA: MIT Press.

Levy, S. and S. van Wijnbergen (1994). 'Labour Markets, Migration and Welfare. Agriculture in the North-American Free Trade Agreement', *Journal of Development Economics*, 43: 263–78.

Lucas, R., Jr. (1990). 'Why Doesn't Capital Flow from Rich to Poor Countries?', *American Economic Review, Papers and Proceedings*, 80: 92–6.

Mansur, A. and J. Whalley (1984). 'Numerical Specification of Applied General Equilibrium Models: Estimation, Calibration and Data', in H. E. Scarf and J. B. Shoven (eds), *Applied General Equilibrium Analysis*. Cambridge: Cambridge University Press.

Marquez, J. (1990). 'Bilateral Trade Elasticities', *The Review of Economics and Statistics*, 72: 70–7.

Nguyen, D. and R. Bhuyan (1977). 'Elasticities of Export and Import Demand in Some South Asian Countries: Some Estimates', *Bangladesh Development Studies*, 5: 133–52.

Robinson, S., M. Burfisher, R. Hinojosa-Ojeda and K. Thierfelder (1993). 'Agricultural Policies in a US–Mexico Free Trade Area: A Computable General Equilibrium Analysis', *Journal of Policy Modelling*, 15: 673–701.

Samuelson, P. A. (1948). 'International Trade and the Equalisation of Factor Prices', *The Economic Journal*, 58: 163–84.

Samuelson, P. A. (1949). 'International Factor Price Equalisation Once Again', *The Economic Journal*, 59: 181–97.

Shoven, J. and J. Whalley (1992). *Applying General Equilibrium*, Cambridge: Cambridge University Press.

Stern, R., J. Francis and B. Schumacher (1976). *Price Elasticities in International Trade*, London: Macmillan.

UNCTAD (1995). *Handbook of International Trade and Development Statistics*, Geneva: UNCTAD.

United Nations (1996a). *Demographic Yearbook 1994*, New York: UN.

United Nations (1996b) *National Accounts Statistics: Main Aggregates and Detailed Tables*, New York: UN.

Weyerbrock, S. (1995). 'Can the European Community Absorb More Immigrants? A General Equilibrium Analysis of the Labour Market and Macroeconomic Effects of East–West Migration in Europe, *Journal of Policy Modelling*, 17: 85–120.

Whalley, J. (1985). *Trade Liberalisation among Major World Trading Areas*, Cambridge, MA: MIT Press.

World Bank (1995). *World Tables*, Washington, DC: World Bank.

Part III

Case Studies of Immigration and Asylum

11
The Economic Integration of Immigrants in the United States: Lessons for Policy

George J. Borjas

Concerns over the assimilation prospects of new immigrants to the United States have dominated the debate over US immigration policy since colonial days. Benjamin Franklin, for example, doubting the wisdom of German immigration, called the incoming migrants 'the most stupid of their own nation', and warned that 'through their indiscretion, or ours, or both, great disorders may one day arise among us'. But Franklin also appreciated the benefits of assimilation and even made specific policy recommendations about how to speed up the process: 'All that seems necessary is, to distribute them more equally, mix them with the English, establish English schools where they are now too thick settled' (*Observations Concerning the Increase of Mankind*, Pamphlet, 1751–5).

The most important *economic* feature of immigration in the post-1965 period has been a significant deterioration in the economic performance of successive immigrant waves. Relative to the native-born population, the 'new' immigrants are not as skilled or as economically successful as immigrants who came in earlier waves. The policy reaction to this trend would obviously differ if the entry wage disadvantage disappeared quickly, as the immigrants assimilated into the American economy and acquired skills and information valuable in the American labour market. As a result, there has been a great deal of interest in measuring and understanding the determinants of the rate of economic assimilation: the rate at which the disparities in economic opportunities (typically defined as earnings) between immigrants and natives narrow over time.

There is an important link between the notion of economic assimilation stressed in this chapter and the cultural issues that are traditionally emphasized in the debate over assimilation in the United States. In order to experience economic assimilation, an immigrant will often have to acquire skills that are valued by American employers, such as learning the English language, adopting the norms of the American workplace, and moving to economically vibrant areas that may lie outside ethnic enclaves. Each of these decisions helps to weaken the link between the immigrant's foreign past and his or her American future.

Many immigrants, therefore, face an important trade-off: in order to achieve economic progress they may have to discard the attributes, habits and characteristics that can hamper the chances of success in the American economy, and pick up the ones that enhance those chances. Put differently, economic assimilation and cultural assimilation will often complement each other: there will be more assimilation of one type when there is more assimilation of the other.

Before proceeding to a more conceptual discussion of the issues regarding economic assimilation, it is worth summarizing the extent to which this type of assimilation has in fact occurred in the past – both within a single generation, as the immigrants acquire labour market experience in the United States labour market, and across generations.

Economists often measure the rate of economic assimilation by calculating how the wage gap between natives and a specific wave of immigrants narrows over time (see Figure 11.1). Consider a group of immigrant men who arrived in the late 1960s at a relatively young age (they were 25–34 years old in 1970). These immigrants earned 12 per cent less than native workers of comparative ages at the time of entry. This wage gap had narrowed to about 3 percentage points by 1980, when both immigrants and natives were 35–44 years old. Overall, the process of economic assimilation reduced the initial wage disadvantage of these immigrants by 10 percentage points

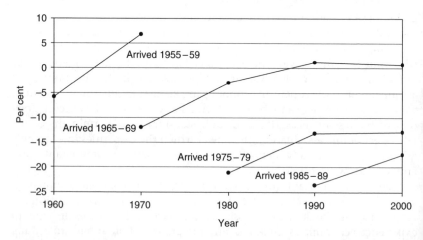

Figure 11.1   Economic assimilation within a generation: relative wage of immigrants arriving at 25–34 years old

over a thirty-year period, with much of the 'catch-up' occurring in the first ten years after immigration.

However, the young immigrants who arrived after 1970 face a much bleaker future – because they start out with a much greater disadvantage. Consider those who arrived in the late 1970s. By 2000, twenty years after arrival, those immigrants were still earning 13 per cent less than natives. But the situation is somewhat gloomier for those who arrived in the late 1980s: they started out with a 24 per cent wage disadvantage, but the wage gap had only narrowed to around 17 per cent by 2000. If this historical experience is used to extrapolate into the future, these cohorts should be able eventually to narrow the gap by about 10 percentage points, so these immigrants will earn much less than natives can throughout their working lives.

What factors determine the rate of economic assimilation? The acquisition of English language skills plays a crucial role in economic assimilation because it opens up many more job opportunities. In other words, immigrants earn substantially more if they understand and speak English. For example, Hispanic immigrants who speak English earn 17 per cent more than those who do not, even after adjusting for differences in education and other socioeconomic characteristics between the two groups. And as much as half of the wage narrowing that occurs between immigrants and natives in the first twenty years after the immigrants' arrival can be attributed to the gains from learning English.

The rate of economic assimilation also depends on whether immigrants live in an ethnic enclave. It is well known that immigrants tend to cluster in a small number of geographic areas. In 1990, a third of the immigrant population were living in only three metropolitan areas (Los Angeles, New York and Miami). This clustering gave rise to the large ethnic enclaves that are a distinct feature of many American cities. As a result, a disproportionately large number of Mexican immigrants live in Los Angeles; a disproportionately large number of Cuban immigrants live in Miami, and a disproportionately large number of immigrants from the Dominican Republic live in New York.

Although it is reasonable to suspect that this clustering affects the economic performance of immigrants, it is far from clear how this influence works. Some observers of the immigrant experience, particularly from a sociological perspective, argue that the geographical clustering of immigrants, and the 'warm embrace' of the enclave, helps immigrants to escape the discrimination they would otherwise encounter in the labour market. One could also argue, however, that the ethnic enclave creates incentives for immigrants *not* to leave and *not* to acquire the skills that might be useful in the larger national market, thus obstructing the move to better-paying jobs. The existing evidence tends to suggest that ethnic clustering impedes economic assimilation. In other words, the rate of economic assimilation of an immigrant group that is clustered in a small region of the country would rise substantially if that group were to be dispersed randomly over the United States.

In sum, it seems that immigrants who choose to enter the economic mainstream – by becoming proficient in the English language and by avoiding the 'warm embrace' of the ethnic enclave – are likely to become more fully integrated into American economic life.

It is well known that there is substantial dispersion in the relative wage of different ethnic groups in the first (that is, immigrant) generation. In 1998, for example, immigrants from the United Kingdom earned 20 per cent more than the typical native worker in the United States, while immigrants from the Dominican Republic earned 40 per cent less. How many of these ethnic differences persist into the second and third generations?

To answer this crucial question, one can track the economic performance of the children and grandchildren of the immigrants who arrived in the United States a century ago. Nearly 24 million people entered the country between 1880 and 1924. Not surprisingly, there were sizeable ethnic differences in economic achievement among the ethnic groups that made up the Great Migration. In 1910, for example, English immigrants earned 13 per cent more than the typical worker in the labour market at that time, Portuguese immigrants earned 13 per cent less, and Mexican immigrants earned 23 per cent less.

It appears that about 60 per cent of the wage gap observed between any two ethnic groups in 1910 persisted into the second generation, and that about a quarter of the initial wage gap persisted into the third generation. In rough terms, ethnic wage differences have a 'half-life' of one generation, so that roughly half of the wage gap between any two immigrant groups disappears between the first and second generations, and half of what remains in the second generation disappears between the second and the third.

The intergenerational 'stickiness' of ethnic wage differentials has important implications for any assessment of the long-run consequences of current immigration. In 1998, for example, Canadian immigrants earned 120 per cent more than Mexican immigrants, and 90 per cent more than Haitian immigrants. If the historical pattern holds, by around the year 2100 the third-generation descendants of today's Canadian immigrants will be earning about 25 per cent more than the descendants of today's Mexican or Haitian immigrants. Put simply, ethnicity matters in economic life, and it seems to matter for a very long time.

Many participants in the immigration debate typically assume that economic integration benefits not only immigrants, who are clearly better off as their economic situation improves, but also the native-born population. As a result, the United States should pursue policies that encourage and nurture the assimilation process.

Ironically, from a purely economic perspective, it is unclear that the native population is better off when immigrants assimilate rapidly. On the one hand, economic assimilation helps to narrow the economic gap between less skilled immigrants and natives, thus reducing the drain on many social services. The rapid assimilation of disadvantaged immigrants would also reduce the chances that this population, clustered in poor ethnic ghettoes, might become a new underclass, and the potential source of a great deal of social conflict. On the other hand, the economic gains from immigration arise from the *complementarities* that exist between immigrants and natives. For example, the immigration of less-skilled workers makes skilled native workers more productive, increases the profits of employers who use a less-skilled workforce, and reduces the prices of the goods and services produced by immigrants. In fact, economic theory implies that the economic gains from immigration are largest when the resources that immigrants bring into the United States, in terms of human and physical capital, most complement the resources that the natives already own. An obvious implication of this approach is that the quicker the immigrants become like American workers – in other words, the faster the rate of economic assimilation – the faster those gains vanish.

It is often argued, for example, that the current immigration of large numbers of less-skilled workers benefits the native population because the immigrants do jobs that the native population do not want to do. Less-skilled immigrants populate large parts of the low-paid service, manufacturing and agricultural industries. However, as economic assimilation takes place, and the skills of immigrants become more like those of natives, it will become less and less likely that the immigrants will want to do those jobs. After all, the assimilation process should open up better-paying opportunities for the immigrants. Hence the presumed gains from immigration vanish, and only a continuous replenishment of the low-skilled immigrant population can halt the deterioration of native economic well-being.

Although the theory may be ambiguous as to whether the United States benefits from assimilation, I suspect that the cost of addressing the social and economic problems created by a large underclass of immigrants (and their descendants) greatly exceeds the economic gains that arise from production complementarities between immigrant and native workers. After all, those productivity gains are quite small to begin with (probably less than US$10 billion annually). A simple cost–benefit calculation would then suggest that the United States would be better off encouraging rapid economic assimilation, thus making it easier for immigrants to acquire the skills and human capital that increase their marketability in their newly adopted country.

One key message of the historical evidence on economic assimilation is simple. The vivid metaphor of the melting pot – where all the economic differences across ethnic groups melt away in a relatively short time – is not entirely right. A better metaphor is one of a 'simmering pot', where the ethnic differences dissolve slowly.

The post-1965 resurgence of immigration has introduced many new ethnic groups into the American mosaic, and has also introduced substantial ethnic differences in skills and economic outcomes. How will the 'simmering pot' transform these differences over the course of the twenty-first century? As much as we would like to use the historical experience of earlier waves of immigrants to predict the future performance of current immigrants, I have come to believe that the historical record provides very little guidance. The assimilation of immigrant groups during the twentieth century was influenced by unique historical events and by social and economic circumstances that are difficult to replicate. Consider:

- The different waves of immigrants who entered the United States at the beginning and end of the twentieth century faced dramatically different economic conditions. The large immigrant flow in the early 1900s, composed mainly of less-skilled workers, helped to build the manufacturing sector. For example, three-quarters of the workers at the Ford Motor Company in 1914 were foreign-born, and over half of these immigrants came from the undeveloped areas of Southern and Eastern Europe. These manufacturing jobs evolved and eventually provided stable and well-paid economic opportunities to many immigrants and their descendants. The US manufacturing sector, however, stopped thriving long ago. As a result, the post-1965 immigrants, many of whom are again relatively low-skilled, have few well-paid job opportunities in that sector. In fact, the historic rise in the wages of high-skilled workers relative to that of low-skilled workers during the 1980s and 1990s indicates that the relative demand for low-skilled workers has fallen dramatically in recent decades. It is unclear, therefore, that the economic conditions facing the current flow of less-skilled immigrants will provide the same assimilation opportunities that the growing manufacturing sector offered to their counterparts a century ago.
- The expansion of the welfare state in recent decades has radically altered the set of economic incentives facing disadvantaged groups, and will probably slow down the rate of economic assimilation. Welfare programmes in the United States, though not generous by Western European standards, stack up pretty well when compared to the standard of living in many less developed countries. In 1997, for example, the typical two-child TANF household residing in California received around US$12,600 worth of assistance, including cash assistance, food stamps, Medicaid and other benefits. At the same time, *per capita* income in China and the Philippines was around US$3,500. These welfare opportunities may attract immigrants who would otherwise not have wished to migrate to the United States; and such a safety net may discourage immigrants who fail in the United States from returning to their countries of origin. In short, the welfare state creates a magnet that influences the migration decisions of people in the source countries, potentially changing the composition of the immigrant population in the United States in ways that may not be economically desirable. Although little is known about

the intergenerational transmission of welfare dependency, the income opportunities provided by the welfare state will obviously influence the immigrants' decision to acquire human capital in the United States, and affect the rate of economic assimilation of immigrants both within and across generations.

- There is less ethnic diversity among post-1965 immigrants than there was among early-twentieth-century immigrants. In particular, current immigration is much more dominated by a few ethnic groups than the Great Migration ever was. In 1990, for example, Mexicans made up almost 30 per cent of the immigrant population. In contrast, Germans and Russians – the two largest groups of the First Great Migration – accounted for only 15 per cent and 12 per cent of the immigrant population, respectively. The relative lack of ethnic diversity in post-1965 immigration may greatly reduce the incentives for assimilation by allowing the largest ethnic groups essentially to develop separate enclave economies and societies, interacting little with the economic mainstream. The available empirical evidence suggests that these ethnic enclaves impede the assimilation process. The lack of diversity among current immigrants, therefore, creates one additional obstacle on the road to economic assimilation.

- The political reaction to the social and economic dislocations associated with the Great Migration was swift and severe. In 1924, the United States adopted strict limitations on the numbers and types of people who could enter the country in any given year. This policy shift, combined with the poor economic opportunities available during the Great Depression, effectively imposed a moratorium on immigration. In the 1920s, for example, 4.1 million people entered the United States, but in the 1930s, only half a million people entered the country. The moratorium provided a 'breathing period' that may have fuelled the assimilation process by cutting off the supply of new workers to ethnic enclaves, and by reducing the economic and social contact between the immigrants and the various countries of origin.

- There is an important sense in which some of the large immigrant groups that arrived in the United States before 1924 were 'forcibly' assimilated by the changes in social attitudes that occurred as a result of the two world wars, and by the fact that some large ethnic groups originated in countries that were on the wrong side of these armed conflicts. Consider, in particular, the circumstances faced by German-Americans and Italian-Americans. The American reaction against German language and culture during the First World War was swift. For example, the *Harvard Encyclopedia of American Ethnic Groups* reports that 'by summer 1918 about half of the [US] states had restricted or eliminated German-language instruction, and several had curtailed freedom to speak German in public . . . The total number of German language publications declined from 554 in 1910 to 234 in 1920'. Similarly, it is hard to ignore General George Patton's colourful exhortation to his troops on the eve of the American invasion of Sicily on 9 July 1943:

> When we land, we will meet German and Italian soldiers whom it is our honor and privilege to attack and destroy. Many of you have in your veins German and Italian blood, but remember that these ancestors of yours so loved freedom that they gave up home and country to cross the ocean in search of liberty. The ancestors of the people we shall kill lacked the courage to make such a sacrifice and continued as slaves.

Surely these social circumstances and attitudes had a distinctive effect on the assimilation process experienced by Germans and Italians in the United States.

- Finally, the favourable ideological climate that boosted social pressures for assimilation and acculturation throughout much of the twentieth century has all but disappeared. Put differently, the consensus summarized by the motto of the United States seal, '*E Pluribus, Unum*' (From Many, One), no longer exists. It has now been replaced by such multicultural sound bites as 'Death by English' and 'Cultural assimilation, cultural acculturation . . . or cultural assassination!' The adverse impact of these attitudinal shifts on economic assimilation is compounded by government policies that encourage some immigrants to retain their ethnic and racial identities in order to qualify for particular benefits. For example, affirmative action programmes effectively require that members of a particular group (for example, a young black immigrant trying to gain admission to an elite college, or a Cuban entrepreneur who wishes to apply for minority set-asides) refrain from joining the economic mainstream in order to boost their chances of receiving the government-mandated assistance. Putting aside the obvious fact that these are not the grievances that the original framers of affirmative action programmes wished to redress, the programmes may exact a cost on the immigrant population by slowing down the economic assimilation of many qualifying ethnic groups.

Over the course of the twentieth century, the United States developed a highly nuanced immigration policy, making the immigration statutes almost as complicated and as long as the federal tax code. To a large extent, current policy awards most entry visas to people who have relatives who are already resident in the United States, with differential degrees of preference depending on whether the sponsor is a United States citizen or a permanent resident; and on whether the family connection is a close one (such as a parent, spouse, or child) or a more distant one (a sibling). Generally, these nuances help to determine the speed with which the visa is granted, with closer family connections typically leading to speedier entry.

Remarkably, the immigration statutes have nothing to say about assimilation. Not only are the assimilation prospects of a potential migrant ignored when awarding the entry visas, but the statutes do not contain any regulations that would either encourage or discourage economic assimilation after the immigrant enters the United States. Except for issues relating to the naturalization process, the reach of immigration policy over most immigrants ends once the immigrant enters the country.

The non-existence of an assimilation policy is almost unique among immigrant-receiving nations, where assimilation incentives are often built into the system that awards entry visas. An extreme example of this linkage is provided by New Zealand. In the late 1990s, New Zealand required that the 'principal' immigrant in the household be proficient in the English language, but allowed this principal immigrant to bring in family members who were not. However, a family member who could not pass the 'English standard' at the time of entry had to post a bond of $20,000 in the local currency (US$11,000). If this family member passed an English test within three months of arrival, the entire bond was refunded. If the family member failed this test at the three-month point but passed it within a year after arrival, the government refunded 80 per cent of the bond. If the family member failed to meet the English standard within a year after arrival, the family forfeited the entire bond.

As I have argued, it is unlikely that the social and economic conditions likely to face immigrants and their descendants in the next century will replicate those that boosted incentives for assimilation in the last century. As long as economic assimilation is perceived to be a desirable outcome of the immigrant experience, therefore, it seems prudent to reform entry policies so that preference is given to those immigrants who are more likely to have a successful assimilation experience, and to adopt policies that encourage economic assimilation directly.

Although it would be valuable to extend the reach of immigration policy to assimilation issues, it is unlikely that a political consensus can be created to design such policies, particularly since there is so much disagreement on whether assimilation itself is a goal that the United States should pursue. Consider, for example, the political implications of some of the policies that could easily increase the rate of economic assimilation. These policies include toughening the requirements for the civics and English language examination that immigrants take when they wish to become naturalized citizens; testing Benjamin Franklin's 1750s insights on assimilation by providing financial incentives for particular immigrant groups to resettle in non-immigrant areas; and overhauling the defective system of bilingual education that physically isolates the children of immigrant families in classrooms where they are taught in their native language for years. All these policy proposals are politically charged and highly contentious, and are unlikely ever to be implemented in the current social climate that values multiculturalism and derides the assimilationist ideology that dominated political debate for much of the twentieth century.

As a result, it would seem that the best chances for adopting policies that speed up economic assimilation lie in reforming the entry criteria so as to favour the entry of people who are the most likely to be economically successful in the long run. I have often argued that the native-born population of the United States would be better off if the country adopted a points system, similar to that used by Australia and Canada, which filtered the applicant pool on the basis of various socioeconomic characteristics. A points system would 'grade' the economic potential of potential migrants, using such variables as age, educational attainment, occupation and English language proficiency, and award entry visas to those applicants who most closely match the country's economic needs. The adoption of a points system that favoured the entry of skilled workers would probably also boost the chances for economic assimilation in the immigrant population.

In sum, the historical experience of past waves of immigrants provides little guidance for predicting the future assimilation prospects of current waves. The economic assimilation of the immigrants who arrived at the beginning of the twentieth century occurred under a unique set of historical, social and economic circumstances, and it is unlikely that these circumstances will be replicated in the twenty-first century. As a result, I suspect that the rate of economic integration of the current immigrants may not be as rapid as that experienced by their counterparts a century ago.

The post-1965 resurgence of immigration has already set the stage for ethnic differences in economic outcomes that are likely to be a distinctive feature of the American economy throughout the twenty-first century. These ethnic differences will almost certainly be a dominant feature of the social and political landscape in the United States, and will play a central role in the debate over social policy for many decades to come.

12
Development Cycles, Political Regimes and International Migration: Argentina in the Twentieth Century*

Andrés Solimano

Introduction

International migration is like a barometer of the economic and social conditions in home countries with respect to the rest of the world. Poor economic performance, lack of employment and of wealth-creation opportunities, and little respect for the civil and economic rights of the population prompt the emigration of nationals, while, good economic opportunities, jobs and open policies towards migrants act as a magnet for immigration from abroad.

The case of Argentina is a very interesting, albeit dramatic, story of a country that switched from being a net importer of people and capital in the first few decades of the twentieth century to being a net exporter of workers, professionals and financial capital to the rest of the world in the latter part of the century and the early twenty-first century.[1] Immigration and emigration patterns (particularly immigration flows from Europe) followed the long-run development cycle of growth and prosperity early in the century, followed by lagging growth performance and the recurrent crises that have characterized the Argentinean economy since at least the 1930s. Argentina has also lived through a pattern of volatile politics, with democracy and authoritarian regimes alternating from the 1930s to the 1980s. The phase of these political cycles current at the time of writing, which has lasted for more than twenty years (since 1983), has been characterized by the prevalence of democracy. Repeated economic crises, unstable growth and volatile politics have turned Argentina into a net emigration country in recent years.

This was in contrast with the last decades of the nineteenth and the early twentieth century, when Argentina received mass migration from Europe, chiefly from Italy and Spain, encouraged by the prospects offered by a country with vast unexploited land and ample opportunities for exporting grain, meat and other staples, coupled with a liberal policy towards international

251

migration. The flow of immigration from Europe to Argentina went through several phases during the twentieth century. It slowed down in the early inter-war period, resuming again in the mid-1940s until the early to mid-1950s when, given the recovery of Europe and the looming economic decline of Argentina, it virtually stopped.

Since the 1950s, immigration from Europe has been replaced by an influx of migrants from neighbouring countries such as Bolivia, Paraguay and the south of Chile. In the 1960s, 1970s and 1980s, and again in the early twenty-first century, there has been a steady rate of emigration of Argentinian professionals, scientists and intellectuals.

In an attempt to reverse poor economic performance, market-orientated reforms have been attempted since the mid-1970s, and with more intensity in the 1990s. In spite of hopes that these policies would re-create the prosperity that Argentina once enjoyed, efforts were often hampered by frequent macroeconomic and debt crises – for example, the collapse of the currency board experiment in 2001–02. This crisis left a legacy of output collapse, high unemployment, a fragile financial situation and a new wave of emigration, to Spain, Italy and other countries, a reverse of the immigration flows from Europe before the 1950s.

The purpose of this chapter is to look at the main economic and political determinants of migration flows to and from Argentina in the late nineteen and the twentieth century. The next section provides the main stylized facts of migration patterns, development cycles and political regimes in Argentina during the twentieth century, seen from an international perspective; then we look at the main conceptual issues regarding the economic and political determinants of international migration relevant to this study. An empirical analysis follows, of econometric estimates of net immigration equations for Argentina, based on time-series for various periods of the century, and this is followed, in turn, by the conclusion.

International migration to and from Argentina in the last century

The last 130 years or so of economic and political history in Argentina are a fascinating period for study of issues of international migration. Economic historians have labelled the period 1870–1914 as Argentina's *belle époque* (see Bunge and Garcia Mata, 1931; Diaz-Alejandro, 1970; Cortes-Conde, 1979; Taylor, 1994a). This was a period of rapid economic growth, large inflows of foreign capital and massive immigration from Europe. Emigrants came mainly from Italy and Spain, accounting for nearly 80 per cent of total migration to Argentina (see Bunge and Garcia Mata, 1931). Massive international migration in that period reflected the limited economic opportunities faced by populations in Spain, Italy and other European economies during those years. Argentina, in contrast, had abundant land, a scarcity of labour and entrepreneurs, and a dynamic export industry of grain and meat, orientated mainly towards the British market. Moreover, migration policies were open, to attract foreigners (mainly Europeans), a policy stance reflected in the constitution of 1853.

In addition to inflows of people, the country received significant flows of foreign capital, mainly from Britain through bonds that helped to finance the domestic infrastructure in the second half of the nineteenth century and up to 1914. Foreign capital provided the resources to build and upgrade railways, ports and roads. Foreign immigration, in turn, provided the labour and entrepreneurial capacity to seize these opportunities. During the period 1870–1914, the Argentine economy grew at a rate of 5.9 per cent per year, one of the highest of the world's economies at that time. The level of income *per capita* of Argentina was 33–38 per cent higher than that in Spain and Italy (see Table 12.1). However, over time this advantage was eroded as Italy (in the 1960s) and Spain (in the 1970s) caught up and overtook Argentina's living standards. The relative decline of Argentina's economy continued, and during 1975–2000 its GDP *per capita* was on average only 72 per cent of the level in Spain and 55 per cent of Italy.

Net annual immigration to Argentina in the period 1870–1914 averaged nearly 57,000 people per year, and the rate of net migration was nearly 15 per 1,000 (see Table 12.1). Interestingly, annual net migration in the period 1900–14 rose sharply, to 103,000 per year from around 34,000 in 1870–1900.

Net immigration fell sharply in the early inter-war years (1914–29) to around 40,000 per annum (nearly half of the number in the period 1900–14). The early inter-war years were highly disruptive for the world economy and Argentina was not immune to this. The First World War interrupted the process of global integration that had begun to develop in the first wave of globalization. In addition, world capital markets collapsed with the war, and reconstruction was a slow and erratic process. The disarray in world capital markets restricted Argentina's access to external financing.[2]

The 1930s were bad years for the Argentine economy. Average GDP growth declined to 1.5 per cent per annum.[3] Like other Latin-American economies, Argentina adopted an inward-looking development strategy in the early 1930s, raising tariffs on imports of intermediate and capital goods,[4] and restricting the allocation of foreign exchange to government-mandated priority goods. Argentina's economic decline also caused a sharp reduction in net European immigration flows, to 22,000 per year between 1930–40. Immigration from Europe resumed again from the mid-1940s to the mid-1950s (see Solberg, 1978), after which it virtually stopped. The human and economic devastation of the Second World War compelled many Europeans to leave their home countries, and Argentina was a natural destination because of previous ties and knowledge of the country gained during earlier waves of migration. However, as mentioned above, the rapid economic recovery in

Table 12.1 Argentina: economic periods and international migration, 1870–2000

Period	Net migration[a]		Total population (annual avg) (000s)	GDP growth in Argentina (annual avg)	Argentina (index 1990=100)	Argentina's GDP per capita						
						Ratio to GDP per capita						
	Annual average (000s)	Rate[b] (per 1,000 people)				USA	Spain	Italy	OECD	Bolivia	Chile	Paraguay
						(in 1990 Geary–Khamis dollars)				(in constant 1995 dollars)		
Global integration and rapid growth (belle époque)												
1870–1900	33 962.0	11.5	3037.8	6.2[c]	35.4[c]	0.58	1.17	1.28	0.78	n.a.	n.a.	n.a.
1900–14	103 786.7	17.0	6183.6	4.3	52.0	0.68	1.65	1.62	1.06	n.a.	n.a.	n.a.
1870–1914	56 957.9	15.1	4049.6	5.9[c]	41.6[c]	0.61	1.33	1.38	0.87	n.a.	n.a.	n.a.
Early inter-war years												
1914–29	40 436.5	4.4	9479.9	3.8	55.7	0.59	1.53	1.32	0.99	n.a.	n.a.	n.a.
Import substitution development strategy												
1930–40	21 945.0	1.7	13053.9	1.5	60.1	0.64	1.66	1.30	0.93	n.a.	n.a.	n.a.
1940–50	47 752.1	3.1	15 490.5	3.7	70.9	0.47	2.01	1.65	0.94	n.a.	n.a.	n.a.
1950–60	60 158.2	3.2	18 891.8	2.9	79.6	0.46	1.76	1.17	0.80	2.96	1.27	3.34
1960–70	32 969.3	1.5	22 277.1	4.7	95.4	0.45	1.27	0.83	0.68	3.37	1.29	3.63
1970–75	57 986.1	2.8	26 030.9	4.2	119.7	0.47	0.97	0.78	0.66	3.37	1.53	3.88
1930–75	41 268.5	2.3	18 280.7	3.3	81.4	0.50	1.58	1.19	0.82	3.19[d]	1.33[d]	3.56[d]

Early economic liberalization											
1975–90	−1387.5	−0.05	29 244.75	0.1	115.6	0.38	0.78	0.58	0.52	3.21	1.43	2.57
Intensive economic reform and liberalization											
1990–2000	−2 155.3	−0.1	34 732.1	3.6	122.2	0.32	0.62	0.48	0.44	3.47	0.97	2.53
1975–2000	−1 683.0	−0.05	31 439.5	1.6	119.0	0.36	0.72	0.55	0.49	3.33	1.25	2.57
1870–2000 average	9 865.0	6.4	18 503.3	3.9[c]	44.5[c]	0.50	1.37	1.11	0.80	3.26[d]	1.28[d]	3.05[d]

Notes: n.a. = not available; (a) net migration = immigration minus emigration; (b) net migration average/population of middle year of period; (c) since 1875; (d) since 1950.

Source: Solimano (2002).

Europe in the late 1940s and 1950s, alongside Argentina's lagging economic performance during the same period, steadily reduced incentives for immigration, as income gaps *per capita* between Argentina and European countries were closing (see Figures 12.1–12.3).

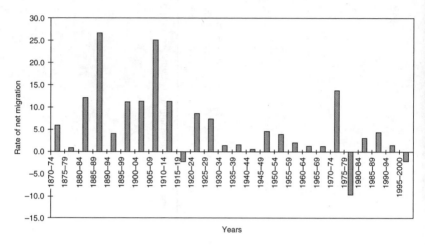

Figure 12.1   Rate of net migration, Argentina, 1870–2000 (per 1,000 people)
Source: GOA (1970) and ECLAC database (CELADE).

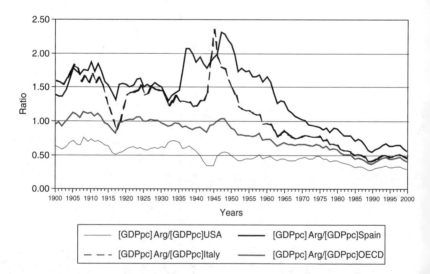

Figure 12.2   Ratio of Argentina's GDP *per capita* versus GDP *per capita* for the United States, Spain, Italy and OECD
Source: Maddison (2001) and IMF (2002).

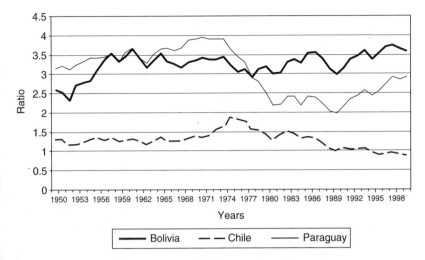

Figure 12.3 Ratio of Argentina's GDP *per capita* versus the GDP *per capita* of neighbouring countries
Source: Maddison (2001), and IMF (2000).

Immigration from Europe almost stopped in the late 1950s (see Table 12.2). But coinciding with this decline, there was an increase in migration (mainly of rural workers and unskilled urban labour) from neighbouring countries such as Paraguay, Bolivia and Chile (see Table 12.2). Paraguayans and Bolivians generally settled in the northern regions, while Chilean immigrants often went to work in the southern farms and oil fields of Patagonia. Since the

Table 12.2 Origins of immigration to Argentina, 1945–64 (thousands of people; 5-year totals)

Origins	1945–49	1950–54	1955–59	1960–64
Italy and Spain	256.3	276.1	73.9	3.9
Neighbouring countries:				
Paraguay	16.1	41.1	104.2	87.1
Bolivia	1.0	6.6	31.9	62.6
Chile	8.3	23.5	9.6	39.0
Brazil	4.7	9.5	1.4	6.7
Uruguay	−33.8	9.0	19.3	6.0
Sub-total, neighbouring countries	−3.7	89.7	166.4	201.4
Other countries	76.3	52.8	10.1	13.0
Total	328.9	418.6	250.4	218.3

Source: *Migration Facts and Figures* (1970: 2).

1930s, there has also been major internal migration from rural areas of Argentina to cities, associated with import-substitution industrialization, the growth of government and increasing urbanization. Thus immigrants from neighbouring countries performed the jobs in rural areas that rural Argentinian's had left to move to the cities.

Another important trend of the 1950s, 1960s and 1970s was the emigration of Argentinians, particularly professionals, highly-skilled people, scientists and intellectuals.[5] An important reason for this emigration of the country's professionals – in addition to the economic decline – lies in the policies of both the Perón administration that excluded non-Peronist intellectuals and professionals, and the open hostility of the military regimes towards dissent in the universities. This situation reached a critical point in 1967 under General Juan Carlos Onganía, when 1,305 faculty members from the University of Buenos Aires were expelled after government intervention (Lattes *et al.*, 1986). Furthermore, in addition to the direct expulsion of university staff, a 'brain drain' followed, as intellectuals began to leave because of the risk of being dismissed (or even imprisoned). Moreover, the military regime initiated large budget cuts which curtailed the country's development in research, teaching and culture.[6] Following an interlude of democratic government in the early 1970s (see Table 12.3 for the succession of governments), the political situation worsened again after the 1976 coup. The new military regime prompted a massive exile of scientists, professionals and students following the regime's overall repressive strategy in its attempt to reduce potential opposition.[7]

Table 12.3   Argentina: presidents and political regimes, 1874–2003

President	Period	Political regime
Nicolás Avellaneda	1874–80	Democratic
Julio Argentino Roca	1880–86	Democratic
Juarez Celman	1886–90	Democratic
Carlos Pellegrini	1890–92	Democratic
Luis Saenz Peña	1892–95	Democratic
Jose Evaristo Uriburu	1895–98	Democratic
Julio Argentino Roca	1898–1904	Democratic
Manuel Quintana	1904–06	Democratic
Figueroa Alcorta	1906–10	Democratic
Roque Saenz Peña	1910–14	Democratic
Victorino de la Plaza	1914–16	Democratic
Hipólito Irigoyen	1916–22	Democratic
Marcelo T. de Alvear	1922–28	Democratic
Hipólito Irigoyen	1928–30	Democratic
Jose E. Uriburu	1930–32	Authoritarian

Roberto M. Ortiz	1938–40	Democratic
Ramón S. Castillo	1940–43	Democratic
Pedro P. Ramirez	1943–44	Authoritarian
Edelmiro Farrel	1944–46	Authoritarian
Juan D. Perón	1946–51	Democratic[a]
Juan D. Perón	1951–55	Democratic[a]
Eduardo Lonardi	1955 Sept.-Nov.	Authoritarian
Pedro E. Aramburu	1955–58	Authoritarian
Arturo Frondizi	1958–62	Democratic
Jose M. Guido	1962–63	Democratic
Arturo H. Illia	1963–66	Democratic
Juan C. Onganía	1966–70	Authoritarian
Roberto Levingston	1970–71	Authoritarian
Alejandro Lanusse	1971–73	Authoritarian
Héctor J. Cámpora	1973 May-July	Democratic
Raúl A. Lastri	1973 July-October	Democratic
Juan D. Perón	1973–74	Democratic
María E. Martinez	1974–76	Democratic
Jorge R. Videla	1976–81	Authoritarian
Roberto E. Viola	1981 March-Dec.	Authoritarian
Leopoldo F. Galtieri	1981–82	Authoritarian
Reynaldo B. Bignone	1982–83	Authoritarian
Raúl R. Alfonsín	1983–89	Democratic
Carlos S. Menem	1989–95	Democratic
Carlos S. Menem	1995–99	Democratic
Fernando de la Rua	1999–2001	Democratic
Adolfo Rodriguez Saa	2001–02	Democratic
Eduardo Duhalde	2002–03	Democratic
Néstor Kirchner	2003–	Democratic

Note: [a] Partial, with restrictions.
Sources: Available at www.historiadelpais.com.ar.

In the last quarter of the twentieth century, Argentina became a country of *net emigration* to the rest of the world. Macroeconomic instability (higher inflation; slow and unstable growth) in the 1960s, 1970s and 1980s (see Table 12.4) clearly changed the earlier economic motives for immigration. In addition, the country's political history of populist–nationalist regimes and repressive military regimes (particularly in the late 1950s) with unstable and fragile democracy also conspired against sustained immigration from Europe.[8] Authoritarian regimes[9] that punished dissent and slashed budgets in universities induced the best-qualified (and hence more mobile) Argentinians to emigrate in significant numbers in the second half of the twentieth century (see Table 12.5). Immigration policies approved by the military regime in 1980 maintained preferences for European over Latin-American immigrants, and the treatment of immigrants was affected by considerations of 'national security'. In the early 2000s this legislation is being considered for reform.

Table 12.4 Main economic indicators, Argentina, 1950–2000

Year	Population (average, millions of people)	Rate of growth of GDP (annual average %)	Real GDP per capita[a] (annual average)	Rate of growth of GDP per capita (annual average %)	Average real wage index, 1995=100 (annual average)	Inflation, consumer prices (annual average %)
1950–54	18.0	2.5	5 045.4	0.5	101.8	20.2
1955–59	19.8	3.4	5 484.6	1.7	100.4	37.2
1960–64	21.5	4.6	5 883.0	3.1	99.9	24.0
1965–69	23.1	4.7	6 749.0	3.4	112.6	21.2
1970–74	25.0	3.9	7 918.0	2.4	125.6	62.4
1975–79	27.1	1.3	8 227.8	−0.2	113.0	206.4
1980–84	29.2	−1.6	7 606.1	−3.2	123.2	335.5
1985–89	31.4	−0.9	7 097.7	−2.5	114.5	1 105.1
1990–94	33.7	4.2	7 702.6	2.9	100.5	421.5
1995–2000	35.9	3.2	8 704.3	1.9	100.0	0.5
1950–59	18.9	2.6	5 261.6	0.8	100.8	30.2
1960–69	22.3	4.4	6 303.8	2.9	105.9	22.0
1970–79	26.1	2.9	8 058.3	1.4	117.6	130.0
1980–89	30.3	−0.7	7 384.1	−2.3	117.4	724.6
1990–2000	34.8	4.6	8 243.8	3.3	100.2	229.9

Note: [a] In 1990 Geary–Khamis dollars.
Sources: IMF (2002), March; Maddison (2001), and ECLAC database.

Table 12.5 Emigration of Argentinian professionals to the United States, 1950–70

Period	Medical doctors	Engineers	Scientists	Technicians	Total
1950	10	13	n.a.	25	48
1951	19	13	2	46	80
1952	19	34	11	60	124
1953	26	37	13	86	162
1954	20	51	11	100	182
1955	37	71	17	171	296
1956	89	135	34	232	490
1957	103	146	37	342	628
1958	70	53	17	273	413
1959	97	78	14	229	418
1960	74	77	25	267	443
1961	94	59	12	239	404
1962	116	96	36	391	639
1963	151	121	43	597	912

1964	140	88	27	496	751
1965	115	59	25	356	555
1966	126	90	31	238	485
1967	95	93	40	316	544
1968	42	42	6	221	311
1969–70	32	25	9	129	195

Source: Oteíza (1997).

Argentina's experience with foreign migration in international perspective

Argentina's *belle époque* and mass immigration coincided with a period of free trade, free capital mobility and ample international mobility of labour in the global economy. The prevailing monetary regime of the period was the gold standard.[10] Termed by economic historians as the *first wave of globalization*, it lasted from around 1870 to 1913.[11] These years were also accompanied by large flows of international migration and became known as the *age of mass migration* (see Hatton and Williamson, 1998). Around 60 million people migrated from resource-scarce, labour-abundant Europe to the resource-abundant, labour-scarce countries of the new world (Argentina, Australia, Brazil, Canada, New Zealand and the United States). Migrants came from Europe's 'core' countries such as Britain, Germany and France, and from 'peripheral' regions (for example, the Scandinavian countries, Spain, Italy and Portugal, Poland, Russia, Romania and the nations of the former Austro-Hungarian empire). The main destination country in Latin America was Argentina, but Uruguay, Cuba, Mexico and Chile also received considerable numbers of European migrants.

The First World War interrupted the process of economic interdependence and labour market integration across countries that had characterized the first wave of globalization. The year 1914 introduced nearly thirty years of economic instability and political turbulence: the First World War; high inflation in Europe in the 1920s; economic depression in the 1930s; and the Second World War in the first half of the 1940s. This turbulence led to increasingly restrictive policies for international migration in certain countries such as the United States, which, through immigration quotas in 1921 and 1924, limited the flow of people from Europe. Migrants then turned to Brazil and Argentina, and in the 1920s the latter accepted around three million European immigrants, although as many as two million later returned (see Chiswick and Hatton, 2002). At the same time, *emigration* restrictions were enacted in the Soviet Union, thus reducing Russia's share of the global migration flows to the Americas. The Soviet experience also indicates a positive correlation between emigration pressures and authoritarian regimes. The former Soviet Union in general suppressed exit (contrary to Argentina during its military regimes) or controlled exit selectively as expedient for getting rid of political dissidents.

The post-1970 period, the so-called *second wave of globalization*, has been characterized by constrained international labour markets. In fact, the increasing global integration in goods and capital markets of the second wave was not followed by an equal degree of integration in international labour markets, which operated under a far more constrained immigration policy framework than the one existing until 1913. The configuration of economic incentives for international migration to Latin America during the twentieth century was such that an inflow of people from Europe (until the 1950s, and mainly to Argentina) coexisted with an outflow from various Latin-American countries to the United States, Canada and other developed nations. It is interesting to note that, while most migrants to the United States in the nineteenth century were Europeans (slightly over 91 per cent of total migration in the period 1820–70, and 88 per cent in the period 1820–1920), this percentage declined to around 14 per cent during 1971–98. In contrast, during the same period immigration to the United States originated mainly from Latin America (46 per cent of the total, mainly from Mexico), followed by Asia (34 per cent).

An interesting contrasting case to Argentina is Ireland, a country that switched from net emigration to net immigration in a century and a half or so. In fact, Ireland since the middle of the nineteenth century (the famine years) until the 1970s was a country of emigration. In the 1990s, following a very dynamic period of rapid growth, inflow of foreign investment and job creation, the country has become a nation of net immigration. This is, of course, the reverse of Argentina's experience, as it became a net emigration country mainly in the last three decades of the twentieth century.

Main determinants of international migration

This section reviews the main economic and political determinants of international migration that can help to better understand the Argentinian experience. The following section presents the empirical analysis based on this discussion.

Economic and social determinants of migration

The economics of migration highlights the anticipation of higher incomes abroad compared to those earned at home (adjusted by the costs of moving) as a main determinant of the decision to migrate. There are, however, other variables that also matter in migration, such as the existence of differentiated economic cycles between sending and receiving nations, the influence of networks of nationals in the host country, migration policies, the political regime, and others.[12] Specifically, the magnitude and direction of international migration are often influenced by the following factors, some of a long-run nature and others cyclical:

(i)   *Per capita income or real wage differentials.* In general, people migrate from lower-wage (or lower *per capita* income) countries to higher-wage countries. Thus net immigration flows are positively correlated with the ratio between the real wage or *per capita* income in the destination country and in the country of origin;[13]

(ii) *Differentiated economic cycles between sending and receiving countries.* Cycles across countries are often not synchronized. The sending country may be in a recession and the receiving one in a boom. Clearly, this will induce migration from the former to the latter. In general, during periods of boom, rapid economic growth and labour shortage, receiving countries tend to absorb more migrants than during periods of sluggish growth and higher unemployment (moreover, in boom periods, the attitude of the public becomes more favourable to immigration). In contrast, recession and reduced economic possibilities in sending nations tend to encourage emigration to more prosperous nations;

(iii) *Network effects.* Empirical analyses of migration flows (Hatton and Williamson, 1998; Borjas, 2001) show that migrants tend to attach a high value to the existence of friends and relatives when they select their country of destination. In fact, family, friends and ethnic/nationals networks constitute an important support factor for obtaining information about jobs and other relevant national characteristics of the host nation, thus helping individual and family adjustment after migration;

(iv) *Policies toward immigration.* Economic incentives to migrate are often mediated by migration policies that can restrict or facilitate migration flows. Unfavourable migration policies in the host countries deter immigration, albeit not completely because of the phenomenon of illegal migration; in contrast, open policies to migration attract foreigners.

(v)   *Costs of migrating.* Emigrating entails several economic and emotional costs: travelling costs such as air tickets, shipping costs and living expenses in the host country, as well as the costs of job search. Unskilled and poor migrants are more affected by the economic costs of migration than high-skill migrants. The emotional costs of migrating are often associated with leaving behind relatives and friends.

(vi) *Cultural differences across countries.* Language, traditions and family relationships affect migration patterns. As these cultural traits are often different in the host country than in the sending nation, they tend to act as dampening factors to international migration; and

(vii) *Geographical distance and proximity.* In general, immigration to bordering countries (or countries of proximity) tends to be higher than immigration to countries located far away. Thus geography matters in the direction and size of emigration flows.[14]

Political determinants of migration

The list of determinants of migration would be incomplete without a reference to political factors that also affect migration. Prevailing political regimes – democracy or authoritarianism – in both the home and in the host country, also affect the decision to emigrate. This is very relevant in the case of Argentina, which in the twentieth century had frequent changes of political regimes, alternating democracy with authoritarian governments (see Table 12.2). In general, individuals prefer to live and work in countries where civil and economic rights are respected and protected, and that happens more often in democracies. In contrast, authoritarian regimes or dictatorships tend to curtail individual rights, and often engage in repressive activities.[15] The segment of migrants can be a target for those practices too. At an analytical level, Hirschman (1995) draws a distinction between a purely economic choice and collective action, and identifies exit as a predominantly economic choice and voice as a political action. In a market, if a customer is not satisfied with the quality of a product or its price, then she can promptly 'exit' the store and abstain from buying the item. In the realm of collective action, people exercise 'voice' in an attempt to change a situation through collective action. In turn, loyalty may lead people to avoid exit (and sometimes also voice). In non-democracies, the voice mechanism may be suppressed or become very costly to exercise, and individuals who are dissatisfied with the prevailing political and economic conditions, may choose to exit their home country.[16] This line of reasoning suggests a direct correlation between the emigration of nationals (or the repatriation of foreigners) and the existence of authoritarian regimes that suppress civil liberties in the host country. However, given the costs of migrating, it is likely that professionals, intellectuals, scientists and entrepreneurs (that is, human capital) are more likely to emigrate under regimes curtailing individual and economic rights than is unskilled labour, which is often less mobile internationally and faces financial constraints to migration.[17]

Econometric estimates of net migration equations for Argentina

In this section we present a time-series econometric analysis of a one-equation migration model incorporating insights of the previous discussion on economic and political determinants of net international migration to and from Argentina:

$$NM(t) = a + b\,\text{YPCGAP}(t) + c\,NM(t-1) + d\,\text{ECONCYCLE}$$
$$+ e\,\text{POLREGIME} + \text{random term} \qquad (12.1)$$

where $b < 0$, $c > 0$, $d < 0$, $e < 0$.

The variable $NM(t)$ represents the flow of net immigration (immigration minus emigration) in period t from the sending country to the recipient country. It is often recommended that the net immigration variable be normalized by population size (that is, rate of net immigration per 1,000 people or so). The variable YPCGAP(t) in period t denotes the ratio of the recipient country's real GDP *per capita* to that of the sending country (an alternative specification often used in the literature is to work with the ratio of the recipient country's real wage relative to the real wage in the sending country; see Hatton and Williamson, 1998). Here, we work with the GDP *per capita* variable as there is better availability of statistical information on GDP *per capita* than real wages for the sample period of this study, and since the migrants are not only labour, but also human capital and entrepreneurs whose income is not necessarily derived from real wages. The coefficient of the YPCGAP variable is expected to be positive, as an increase in the ratio of GDP *per capita* in the destination country relative to the home country is expected to increase the flows of immigrants. The lagged net migration flow, $NM(t-1)$, is intended to capture persistence effects, or path dependence, in the process of international migration.[18] Path-dependence is often associated with the relatives or friends effects already discussed above. The coefficient of this variable is expected to have a positive sign. The variable ECONCYCLE is an index of the economic cycle in the receiving country (this could also be extended to include economic cycles in the sending economies), capturing the short-term prospects for employment and income in the host countries for the migrants; the coefficient of this variable, measured as deviation of current from trend GDP, is expected to be positive. The variable POLREGIME is an index of authoritarianism or democracy in the recipient country. The sign of this variable's coefficient is expected to be negative when measured as an authoritarian regime. In other words, people are less inclined to migrate when there is an authoritarian regime in the host country. Similarly, nationals in non-democratic regimes may consider leaving for a given set of economic fundamentals.

Empirical results

The model of Equation (12.1) is estimated for Argentina by ordinary least squares correcting for serial-correlation and testing for cointegration. In all the specifications, the dependent variable is the rate of net immigration (immigrants minus emigrants per 1,000 people; see Box in the Appendix for details on the construction of the different variables). The model is estimated for three periods:

(i)   The period 1900–29, when large net flows of immigration went to Argentina, mainly from Europe;

(ii)   The period 1930–59, when there was a net slowdown in immigration flows; and

(iii) The period 1960–99, during which emigration from Europe was replaced by immigration from neighbouring countries. This was, as indicated before, also a period of emigration of professionals, scientists and intellectuals from Argentina, reflecting the country's economic decline, political instability and authoritarian regimes.

For the sake of completeness, we estimated the model for the entire twentieth century. In all specifications the dependent variable is the rate of net immigration (immigrants minus emigrants) per 1,000 people. The results of the estimations are reported in Tables 12.6–12.9.

Table 12.6 Argentina: dependent variable, rate of net immigration, 1900–29 (per 1,000 people)

	(1)	*(2)*	*(3)*
Constant	3.89	−14.86	−16.81
	(2.46)	(−3.96)	(−2.97)
Lagged net immigration (t–1)	0.63	0.20	0.20
	(6.20)	(1.74)	(1.43)
Log Argentina's GDP *per capita* over Europe's GDP *per capita*[a]		79.96	86.68
		(5.08)	(4.02)
Log cyclical output index in Argentina[b]			−11.16
			(−0.46)
R^2	0.40	0.76	0.76
h of (D − W)	0.62	1.10	1.71
No. of obs.	30	30	30

Notes: Rate of net immigration = immigration minus emigration per 1,000 people.
Method of estimation: OLS.
Values in parentheses correspond to t-statistics.
(a) (b) – see Appendix for definitions of these variables.

Table 12.7 Argentina: dependent variable, rate of net immigration, 1930–59 (per 1,000 people)

	(1)	*(2)*	*(3)*	*(4)*
Constant	0.55	0.07	0.64	0.90
	(1.33)	(0.16)	(1.83)	(2.43)
Lagged net immigration (t–1)	0.74	0.73	0.65	0.63
	(6.91)	(7.50)	(8.31)	(8.23)
Log Argentina's GDP *per capita* over Europe's GDP *per capita*[a]		5.58	2.74	2.97
		(2.69)	(1.59)	(1.77)
Log cyclical output index in Argentina[b]			22.86	21.32
			(4.51)	(4.27)
Index of political regime[c]				0.75
				(−1.70)
R^2	0.61	0.69	0.82	0.83
h of (D − W)	2.91	2.48	1.32	1.18
No. of obs.	32	32	32	32

Notes: Rate of net immigration = immigration minus emigration per 1,000 people.
Method of estimation: OLS.
Values in parentheses correspond to t-statistics.
(a) (b) and (c) – see Appendix for definitions of these variables.

Table 12.8 Argentina: dependent variable, rate of net immigration, 1960–99 (per 1,000 people)

	(1)	(2)	(3)	(4)	(5)	(6)
Constant	−20.51	−21.15	−25.31	−40.52	−58.85	56.08
	(−3.20)	(−3.44)	(−3.50)	(−4.98)	(−1.50)	(−1.36)
Log Argentina's GDP *per*	9.19	9.60	11.51	18.24	25.24	24.07
capita over GDP *per*	(3.13)	(3.41)	(3.51)	(5.01)	(1.67)	(1.52)
capita of Argentina's						
neighbouring countries[a]						
Log cyclical output index in		27.46	27.51	34.12	41.68	41.27
Argentina[b]		(1.81)	(1.85)	(2.36)	(1.92)	(1.85)
Lagged net immigration (*t*–1)			−0.27	−0.34	−0.34	−0.34
			(−1.38)	(−1.83)	(−1.80)	(−1.76)
Lagged net immigration (*t*–2)				−0.54	−0.49	0.50
				(−2.79)	(−2.23)	(−2.20)
Log Argentina's GDP *per capita*					6.49	−5.78
over Europe's GDP *per capita*[c]					(−0.47)	(−0.41)
Index of political regime[d]						0.60
						(0.38)
R^2	0.29	0.37	0.43	0.64	0.64	0.64
(D – W)	2.51	2.71	1.57[e]	(−1)[f]	(0.87)[f]	0.40[f]
No. of obs.	32	32	30	28	28	28

Notes: Rate of net immigration = immigration minus emigration per 1,000 people.
Method of estimation: OLS.
Values in parentheses correspond to *t*-statistics.
(a) (b) (c) and (d) – see the Appendix for definitions of these variables;
(e) h of Durbin–Watson;
(f) *t*-statistics of lagged resid(−1) education with respect to original education + resid(1).

Estimates for the period 1900–29

The regressions for this period (reported in Table 12.6) show a strong significance for the coefficient of the (log) of the ratio between the *per capita* income of Argentina and the *per capita* income of sending European countries (the largest weights in the average income *per capita* of Europe are given to those of Italy and Spain; see Appendix). Lagged migration, reflecting persistence and path dependence (for example, driven by the relatives and friends effects) is significant in the specification of column (2) in Table 12.6. A variable of cyclical output fluctuations in Argentina (log of ratio of current GDP over trend GDP, the latter estimated by the Hodrick–Prescott filter) appears to be insignificant in the regression. The variable reflecting authoritarian political regime has not been included, since this was a period of continuous democratic regimes up to 1930. The quality of the explanatory power of the regression R^2 is 0.76, a reasonably good fit.

Table 12.9 Argentina: dependent variable, rate of net immigration, 1900–99 (per 1,000 people; 3-year averages)

	(1)	*(2)*	*(3)*	*(4)*
Constant	3.76	5.55	6.41	6.27
	(3.30)	(7.33)	(8.11)	(5.52)
Log Argentina's GDP *per capita*	9.53	10.46	10.67	10.36
over Europe's GDP *per capita*[a]	(3.20)	(5.63)	(6.18)	(4.68)
Log cyclical output index in		55.43	54.24	53.48
Argentina[b]		(6.81)	(7.18)	(5.67)
Index of political regime[c]			−3.55	−3.39
			(−2.37)	(−2.00)
Lagged net immigration (*t*–1)				0.02
				(0.18)
R^2	0.26	0.72	0.77	0.76
(D – W)	0.92	1.64	1.99	0.16[d]
No. of obs.	31	31	31	30

Notes: Rate of net immigration = immigration minus emigration per 1,000 people.
Method of estimation: OLS.
Values in parentheses correspond to *t*-statistics.
(a) (b) and (c) See the Annex for the definitions of these variables;
(d) h of Durbin–Watson.

Estimates for the period 1930–59

The regressions of Table 12.7 show that both lagged net immigration and the log of the ratio of *per capita* income of Argentina with respect to the *per capita* income of Europe is statistically significant in explaining the rate of net migration to Argentina in this period. The index of cyclical output fluctuations in Argentina appears with a sign contrary to the one expected a priori. Interestingly, the variable denoting political regimes constructed as a dummy variable, with the value 1 for authoritarian regimes and 0 for democracy, appears with the expected sign – that is, negative. This supports the hypothesis that authoritarian regimes that curtailed civil liberties (and probably property rights) tended to deter immigration to Argentina over the sample period.[19] The variable is also statistically significant at 10 per cent significance levels in the sample period of this regression (1930–59).

Estimates for the period 1960–99

As noted earlier, since the 1960s the main origins of international migration to Argentina shifted from Europe to neighbouring countries, chiefly Bolivia, Paraguay and Chile (with some immigration also from Uruguay and Brazil).[20] To reflect this change in the main source countries, we replace the relative income variable of Argentina's GDP *per capita* with respect to Europe with the ratio of the log of Argentina's GDP *per capita* to the average GDP *per capita* of Bolivia, Paraguay and Chile. The estimated coefficient for this variable, shown in Table 12.8, is, in general, statistically significant and has the expected (positive) sign. Lagged migration (one and two years) is significant, although with the opposite sign. A little surprising is the result that the index of political regime appears to be insignificant and with the wrong sign in the period 1960–99 when there were several military dictatorships in the 1960s and 1970s (though not after 1983) that could be expected to deter immigration. This surprising result may relate to two factors:

(i)   Missing data on emigration during the military regimes in the later 1970s. As mentioned above, statistics on immigration and emigration flows were suspended for several years during 1976–81, when the country was ruled by military juntas, which apparently were not keen to show Argentina's emigration statistics; and

(ii)   When combined with the fact of missing data for the military periods, the share of the 40-year sub-sample – which corresponds to the authoritarian regimes – is not sufficiently large to influence the entire period.

The twentieth century: estimates for 1900–99

The final set of regressions covering the full sample period is reported in Table 12.9. To abstract from year-to-year fluctuations in net immigration flows, all the variables used in the regressions are three-years averages. Interestingly, the ratio of Argentina's GDP *per capita* to that of Europe (the main source of migration until the late 1950s) appears to be statistically significant in the whole period.[21] Lagged net migration is insignificant and the index of political regimes (authoritarianism) appears with a negative sign (as expected) and statistically significant for the full sample period, highlighting the importance of political regimes in immigration/emigration decisions.

Concluding remarks

This chapter has investigated the main patterns and determinants of international migration to Argentina in the twentieth century by looking at the main economic determinants of international migration as well as the influence of political regimes (democracy and authoritarianism) on migration flows.

Argentina is an interesting case of a country that was one of the leading economies in the world in the late nineteenth and early twentieth centuries, attracting massive inflows of people and capital from Europe. The rate of international migration was among the highest in the world in the early decades of the twentieth century. However, this situation started to change in the 1930s, as Argentina was hit by the world recession and, in response to the worsening external scenario, the country adopted inward-looking import substitution policies which remained in effect until the 1970s. From the 1930s to the early 1980s, Argentina lived through alternative periods of authoritarian regime and democratic government.

Consequently, because of the cumulative effects of a lagging growth and modest development performance noticeable since the 1930s, Argentina ceased to be the magnet it had once been for immigrants from Italy, Spain and other European countries. By the late 1950s, European migration to Argentina had virtually stopped, and immigrants came mainly from the neighbouring countries of Bolivia, Paraguay and Chile. At the same time, from the latter part of the 1950s through to the early 1980s, a considerable outflow of Argentinians left for other Latin-American countries (Venezuela and Mexico) and the United States and Canada as well as Europe. Argentina's modest and unstable growth rates, as well as the recurrent political crises during which democratic governments were often ousted by military coups that installed regimes curtailing civil rights, encouraged the emigration of (often well-educated) Argentinians. Emigrants included professionals, technicians and scientists, a fact that gave rise to concern about a brain drain. Needless to say, Argentina's internal circumstances also discouraged European immigration to the country, although the country still continued to receive immigrants from the neighbouring countries.

Our econometric estimates of net migration equations to Argentina find a positive, significant effect of the gap between the *per capita* income of Argentina (recipient country) and those of the sending countries (chiefly European nations until the mid-1950s), followed by neighbouring countries for the regressions covering the sub-periods 1900–29, 1930–59 and 1960–99.

The econometric estimates also show a statistically significant adverse influence of authoritarian regimes on international migration flows to Argentina, confirming the importance of political regimes on the decision to migrate. To summarize, the chapter finds that the two most important variables for explaining net international migration to and from Argentina in the twentieth century are the income *per capita* differential of Argentina versus the *per capita* income of the source economies, and the frequency of the country's authoritarian regimes.

Appendix

Construction of variables

Rate of net immigration
Immigration minus emigration per 1,000 people.

Argentina's GDP per capita
Argentina's GDP in millions of international 1990 Geary–Khamis dollars/Argentina's population in thousands at mid-year.

Europe's GDP per capita
GDP *per capita* is measured in millions of international 1990 Geary–Khamis dollars/population in thousands at mid-year.

i)   Europe's GDP *per capita* (1900–29, 1900–99) = 1/3 [1/6 of GDP *per capita* for Austria + for Belgium + for France + for Germany + for Switzerland + for UK] + 1/3 of GDP *per capita* for Spain + 1/3 of GDP *per capita* for Italy].
Changes in weights reflect decline in importance of Italy and Spain as sources of immigration to Argentina.

(ii) Europe's GDP *per capita* (1930–59, 1960–99) = 1/8 [GDP *per capita* for Austria + for Belgium + for France + for Germany + for Switzerland + for the UK + for Spain + for Italy].

GDP per capita for Argentina's neighbouring countries
GDP *per capita* is measured in millions of 1995 dollars/population in thousands at mid-year.
GDP *per capita* (1950–2000) of Argentina's neighbouring countries = 1/3 [Bolivia's GDP *per capita* + Chile's GDP *per capita* + Paraguay's GDP *per capita*].

Cyclical output index
Ratio of Argentina's GDP in millions of international 1990 Geary–Khamis dollars divided by GDP trend for Argentina in millions of international 1990 Geary–Khamis dollars.
GDP trend for Argentina was constructed using the Hodrick–Prescott filter.

Index of political regime
Dummy variable with the value 1 for authoritarian regime and 0 for democracy.

Notes

* Comments by Tim Hatton, George Borjas, Jeffrey Williamson and Roxana Maurizio are appreciated. Efficient research assistance provided by Claudio Aravena is greatly appreciated.
1. In 2002 Argentina went through (again) a very severe economic and financial crisis following the collapse of the currency board regime in place between 1991 and 2001. That crisis led to massive output collapse, a banking crisis, increased unemployment and massive emigration.

2. See Della Paolera and Taylor (1997); Della Paolera (1994) and Taylor (1995).
3. See Diaz-Alejandro (1970) and Della Paolera and Taylor (1997) for analyses of the impact of the 1930s on Argentina and its domestic policy response: see also Di Tella and Zymelman (1973).
4. Diaz-Alejandro (1970) and Taylor (1994b) have shown that the import substitution policies adopted in the 1930s in Argentina contributed significantly to an increase in the relative price of capital goods at home, thereby discouraging capital formation and growth.
5. See Lattes *et al.* (1986). See Table 12.5 for statistics of emigration of Argentinians to the United States in the period 1950–70.
6. The case of Cesar Milstein is telling. This outstanding Argentinian scientist emigrated from Argentina, went to work at the University of Cambridge and after a few years received a Nobel Prize for Medicine.
7. An empirical complication here, to understand the effect of this period on migration flows, lies in the fact that the military during the period 1976–81 largely stopped recording the outflows of Argentinians. It is worth noting that there were also military regimes in Bolivia and Paraguay during most of the period of emigration from these countries to Argentina.
8. These political features apparently, did not deter immigration from Bolivia or Paraguay, countries that also had authoritarian regimes.
9. Argentina has experienced considerable political instability and had frequent changes between democratic and authoritarian regimes from the early 1930s to the early 1980s. The cycle of replacing democratically elected governments by authoritarian regimes started with Jose Uriburu in 1930, following the last government of Hipólito Irigoyen, and ended with the military regime of General Galtieri in 1983, followed by the democratically elected president, Raúl Alfonsín, introducing more than twenty-years of uninterrupted democracy in Argentina (see Table 12.3).
10. See Eichengreen (1995) for an analysis of the gold standard in this and subsequent periods.
11. See Eichengreen (1995) and Solimano (2001a, 2001b).
12. Migration equations usually include the following variables as determinants: the ratio between real wage (or real *per capita* income) in the home country relative to the destination country, a lagged migration variable capturing persistence effects and friends and relatives effects (social network consi-derations), a two-decades lagged demographic variable representing population growth, and a variable denoting the degree of industrialization in the home country; see O'Rourke and Williamson (2000). See also Solimano (2001a, 2001b) for an analysis of the role of growth and international inequality on migration flows.
13. This simple specification can be amended to include the expected real wage differentials. Empirical evidence in the literature is reviewed in Hatton and Williamson (1998: chs 3 and 4), who undertake a detailed discussion of the impact of wage gaps on emigration flows from Europe to New World countries in the late nineteenth and early twentieth centuries. The real wage gap can be replaced by the *per capita* income gap between the sending and receiving countries if migrants also constitute human capital and entrepreneurs, whose income does not necessarily follow real wages.
14. See Markusen and Zahniser (1997) and Jasso *et al.* (1998) for analysis of immigration patterns to the United States in terms of skill composition.

15. See Olson (2000) for an insightful analysis of the economic consequences of democracies and autocracies.
16. For an interesting, albeit dramatic, account of how the German Democratic Republic used, as state policy, emigration of the most talented individuals during communism to get rid of active opposition and discontent, debilitating the country and contributing to its unexpectedly rapid demise after the end of the communist regime in 1990, see Hirschman (1995).
17. See Solimano (2004) for a discussion of emigration of human capital and its impact on developing countries and the global economy; also Pellegrino and Martínez (2001), and Hansen *et al.* (2002) for a discussion of emigration of scientists and professionals in the Latin American context. Earlier analyses of emigration of human capital and brain drain are Johnson (1964), Patinkin (1964) collected in Adams (1964). More recent treatment and empirical analyses of emigration issues are Haque and Kim (1994), Carrington and Detragiache (1998), Sutcliffe (1998), UNESCO (2001) and OECD (2002).
18. Another alternative is to use the stock of foreign migrants from previous years to capture network and persistence effects.
19. There were several episodes of authoritarian regimes in the 1930s, 1940s and 1950s (see Table 12.3) along with 'semi-democratic regimes' (that is, the two Perón governments ruling from the mid-1940s to the mid-1950s).
20. See Solberg (1978) and Tables 12.6 and 12.7.
21. We tried the ratio of GDP *per capita* of Argentina to the average of the GDP *per capita* of Bolivia and Chile since 1950 in the regression, but it was statistically insignificant.

References

Adams, W. (ed.) (1964). *The Brain Drain*. New York and London: Macmillan.
Borjas, G. (2001). *Heaven's Door*. Princeton, NJ: Princeton University Press.
Bunge, A. and C. Garcia Mata (1931). 'Argentina' in W. Willcox (ed.), *International Migrations*, Vol. 2. New York: National Bureau of Economic Research.
Carrington, W. and E. Detragiache (1998). 'How Big is the Brain Drain?', IMF Working Paper, No. 98/102. Washington, DC: IMF.
Chiswick, B. and T. J. Hatton (2002). 'International Migration and the Integration of Labor Markets', in M. Bordo, A. M. Taylor and J. Williamson (eds), *Globalization in Historical Perspective*, Chicago: Chicago University Press.
Cortes-Conde, R. (1979). *El Proceso Económico Argentino*, Buenos Aires: Editorial Sudamericana.
Della Paolera, G. (1994). 'Experimentos Monetarios y Bancarios en Argentina: 1861–1930', *Revista de Historia Económica*, XII(3) Universidad Carlos III.
Della Paolera, G. (1997). 'Finance and Development in an Emerging Market: Argentina in the Interwar Period', NBER Working Paper, No. 6236, Cambridge, MA: National Bureau of Economic Research.
Della Paolera, G. and A. Taylor (1997). 'Economic Recovery from the Argentine Great Depression: Institutions, Expectations and the Change of Macroeconomic Regime', NBER Working Paper, No. 6767, Cambridge, MA: National Bureau of Economic Research.
Diaz-Alejandro, C. F. (1970). *Essays on the Economic History of the Argentine Republic*, New Haven, CT: Yale University Press.
Di Tella, G. and M. Zymelman (1973). *Los Ciclos Económicos Argentinos*, Buenos Aires: Editorial Piados.

ECLAC database, Santiago: ECLAC. Available at: www.un.org/popin/regions/eclac.html.

Eichengreen, B. (1995). *Globalizing Capital: A History of the International Monetary System*, Princeton, NJ: Princeton University Press.

Ferenczi, I. and W. Willcox (1929). *International Migrations, Argentina*, Vol. I, Statistics. Cambridge, MA: National Bureau of Economic Research.

GOA (Government of Argentine) (1970). 'Government's National Direction of Migration, 1970 Census Argentina', *Demographic Bulletin 69*, Santiago: GOA.

Hansen, T., N. Agapitova, L. Holm-Nielsen and O. Vukmirovic (2002). 'The Evolution of Science and Technology: Latin America and the Caribbean in Comparative Perspective', Mimeo, Washington, DC: World Bank.

Haque, N. and S. A. Kim (1994). 'Human Capital Flight: Impact of Migration on Income and Growth', IMF Working Paper, No. 94/155, Washington, DC: IMF.

Hatton, T. J. and J. G. Williamson (1998). *The Age of Mass Migration. Causes and Economic Impact*, New York: Oxford University Press.

Hirschman, A. (1995). 'Exit, Voice and the Fate of the German Democratic Republic', in A. Hirschman (ed.), *A Propensity to Self-subversion*, Cambridge, MA: Harvard University Press.

IMF (International Monetary Fund) (2002). *International Financial Statistics*, Washington, DC: IMF: table 4.

Jasso, G., M. R. Rosenzweig and J. P. Smith (1998). 'The Changing Skills of New Immigrants to the United States: Recent Trends and Their Determinants', NBER Working Paper, No. 6764, Cambridge, MA: National Bureau of Economic Research.

Johnson, H. (1964). 'An "Internationalist" Model', in W. Adams (ed.), *The Brain Drain*, New York and London: Macmillan.

Lattes, A. E., E. Oteíza and J. Graciarena (1986). *Dinámica Migratoria Argentina (1955–1984): Democratización y Retorno de Expatriados*, Geneva: UNRISD, CNEP.

Maddison, A. (2001). *The World Economy. A Millennial Perspective*, Paris: OECD.

Markusen, M. and S. Zahniser (1997). 'Liberalization and Incentives for Labor Migration: Theory with Applications to NAFTA', NBER Working Paper, No. 6232, Cambridge, MA: National Bureau of Economic Research.

Migration Facts and Figures (1970). 'Immigration into Argentina from Neighbouring Countries', 74(2) (Statistical supplement to the International Catholic Migration Commission's Magazine).

O'Rourke, K. and J. Williamson (2000). *Globalization and History. The Evolution of a Nineteenth-Century Economy*, Cambridge, MA: MIT Press.

OECD (2002). *International Mobility of the Highly Skilled*, Paris: OECD.

OECD Observer (2002). 'The Brain Drain: Old Myths, New Realities'. Available at: www.oecdobsever.org.

Olson, M. (2000). *Power and Prosperity. Outgrowing Communist and Capitalist Dictatorships*, New York: Basic Books.

Oteíza, E. (1997). 'Emigración de profesionales, Técnicos y Obreros Calificados Argentinos a los Estados Unidos. Análisis de las Fluctuaciones de la Emigración Bruta Julio 1950 a Junio 1970', *Desarrollo Económico*, 39–40.

Patinkin, D. (1964). 'A "Nationalist" Model', in W. Adams (ed.), *The Brain Drain*, New York and London: Macmillan.

Pellegrino, A. and J. Martínez (2001). 'Una Aproximación al Diseño de Políticas sobre la Migración internacional Calificada en América Latina', Serie Población y Desarrollo, Santiago: CELADE-ECLAC.

Solberg, C. E. (1978). 'Mass Migration in Argentina, 1870–1970', in W. H. McNeill and R. S. Adams (eds), *Human Migration, Patterns and Policies*, Bloomington, IN: Indiana University Press.

Solimano, A. (2001a). 'International Migration and the Global Economic Order: An Overview', Policy Research Working Paper, No. 2720, Washington, DC: World Bank.

Solimano, A. (2001b). 'The Evolution of World Income Inequality: Assessing the Impact of Globalization', Macroeconomics of Development Series, No. 14, Santiago: ECLAC.

Solimano, A. (2002). 'Development Cycles, Political Regimes and International Migration: Argentina in the Twentieth Century', Paper presented at the UNU–WIDER development conference on 'Poverty, International Migration and Asylum' held on 27–28 September, Helsinki: UNU–WIDER.

Solimano, A. (2004). 'Globalizing Talent and Human Capital: Implications for Developing Countries', in *ABCDE-Europe, Development Economics*, Volume and Proceedings, World Bank. Also, Macroeconomics of Development Series, No. 15, Santiago: ECLAC.

Solimano, A., E. Aninat and N. Birdsall (eds) (2000). *Distributive Justice and Economic Development*, Ann Arbor, MI: University of Michigan Press.

Sutcliffe, B. (1998). 'Freedom to Move in the Age of Globalization', in D. Baker, G. Epstein and R. Pollin (eds), *Globalization and Progressive Economic Policy*, Cambridge: Cambridge University Press.

Taylor, A. (1994a). 'Three Phases of Argentine Economic Growth', NBER Working Paper Series on the Historical Factors in Long Run Growth, Historical Papers, No. 60, Cambridge, MA: National Bureau of Economic Research.

Taylor, A. (1994b). 'Mass Migration to Distant Shores: Argentina and Australia, 1870–1939', in T. Hatton and J. Williamson (eds), *Migration and the International Labor Markets, 1850–1939*, London and New York: Routledge.

Taylor, A. (1995). 'Peopling the Pampa: On the Economic Impact of Mass Migration to the River Plate: 1870–1914', NBER Working Papers Series on the Historical Factors in Long Run Growth, Historical Papers, No. 68. Cambridge, MA: National Bureau of Economic Research.

Timmer, A. and J. Williamson (1996). 'Racism, Xenophobia or Markets? The Political Economy of Immigration Policy Prior to the Thirties', NBER Working Paper, No. 5867, Cambridge, MA: National Bureau of Economic Research.

UNESCO (2001). *The State of Science and Technology in the World*, Montreal: Institute for Statistics.

13
Economic Integration and Migration: The Mexico–United States Case

Philip Martin

Introduction

Most regional and international regimes – systems in which national governments yield power to a supranational authority that grants member nations rights and imposes obligations on them – emerge from crisis. For example, after wars end, security regimes are often created: nations pledge mutual support via NATO and similar organizations to prevent or deal with future conflicts. Similarly, economic crises may be followed by trade regimes that require member states to lower barriers to goods from all member nations, as with the WTO. Finally, there can be financial regimes, such as the IMF establishing rules for fiscal and monetary policies before providing loans to governments.

Defence regimes are based on the expectation that mutual benefits will flow from peace, while economic regimes assume there will be increased output from comparative advantage and stable economic policies. The economic case for an international migration regime is weaker, and that established to deal with refugees struggled with a rising number of asylum applicants in the 1990s.[1] Most calls for an international migration regime imagine a system in which there would be fewer barriers to movement over national borders, and thus more migration. There are several speculative estimates of the gains from more international migration based on increased allocative efficiency – moving labour from lower to higher wage areas, with the wage gain reflecting the economic gain. Hamilton and Whaley (1984), in a general equilibrium modelling exercise, estimated that world GDP could double if barriers to labour migration were removed.

In a more incremental approach to estimating the gains from increased migration, the UNDP (1992) *Human Development Report* estimated that, if an additional 2 per cent of the 2.5 billion-strong labour force of developing countries were permitted to move to industrial countries – an additional 50 million migrants, and they earned an average US$5,000 a year, or a total of US$250 billion, and remitted 20 per cent of their earnings, or

US$50 billion a year, to their countries of origin, the extra remittances to their countries of origin would be equivalent to official development assistance.

According to the latest UN Population Division data, in the year 2000 there were about 175 million international migrants – people living outside their country of birth or citizenship for twelve months or more, up from 120 million in 1990. Some 70–80 million of the world's migrants are in industrial countries,[2] so adding another 50 million migrants – all in the developed countries – would almost double their numbers of migrants, and affect labour markets, employment patterns and wages in both sending and receiving nations. The United States has about 32 million foreign-born residents, including 15 million in the labour force, and their presence is estimated to add up to US$10 billion to the US$10 trillion GDP, or a tenth of 1 per cent, largely via wage depression. The sign of the migrant economic effect is positive, but its magnitude is small.

The labour force participation rates of migrants are lower in Europe. If we assume that migrants in all the industrial countries, which have a GDP of US$25 trillion, currently add a tenth of 1 per cent to GDP, the migrant gain is US$25 billion a year. If doubling the number of migrants doubled the gain, it would be US$50 billion a year. Adding US$50 billion to the GDP of industrial countries is about equivalent to their current ODA to developing countries. To put US$50 billion in perspective, if industrial country GDP grows by 2 per cent a year, it rises by US$500 billion, which means that doubling the number of migrants in the industrial countries has an economic impact equivalent to about one month's 'normal' growth.

These data suggest that the economic gains from current levels of immigration are relatively small, and that even a doubling of current levels would not add dramatically to growth. As with most economic activities, increasing migration highlights competition between competing goods – a faster-rising GDP may be coupled with more unemployment and/or inequality, *ceteris paribus*, for workers who compete with the additional migrants. Without social safety nets for such workers, which are rare in comparison to Trade Adjustment Assistance programmes for workers displaced by freer trade, these workers can be worse off, and social discontent could result. Furthermore, the process of admitting and integrating additional migrants can be costly.

I focus on the dynamics of change in two migration regimes: Mexico–United States migration in the 1990s, especially after NAFTA came into effect on 1 January 1994, and migration from Eastern to Western Europe in the 1990s, with a special emphasis on likely east–west migration after Poland and other Eastern and Southern European countries become full EU members with rights to freedom of movement. I conclude that it is easy to exaggerate the benefits and costs of migration. Economic integration is desirable for its own sake, and I conclude that the additional migration that sometimes accompanies economic integration is a 'reasonable price to pay' for the increased economic efficiency flowing from trade and investment that responds to comparative advantage. However, it is less clear that moving ex-farmers and their children over borders after they are displaced by economic integration is better than reintegrating them into growing home country economies and labour markets.

Thinking about migration

Migration is as old as humans wandering in search of food, but international migration is a relatively recent phenomenon: it was only in the early twentieth century that the system of nation states, passports and visas developed to regulate the flow of people across borders. Migration is the exception, not the rule, for two major reasons. The first and most powerful is inertia: most people lack the desire and drive to leave home and move away from family and friends. The second is the restriction of movement across national borders.

The growth in the number of nation states increases opportunities for international migration. There were 190 recognized nation states in the year 2000, up from forty-three in 1900, and each has a system of passports to distinguish citizens from foreigners, border controls to inspect people who want to enter, and policies that affect the settlement and integration of non-citizens. Most countries do not anticipate the arrival of foreigners who wish to settle and become naturalized citizens, and some positively discourage emigration.

There are five major immigration countries: the United States, Canada, Australia, Israel and New Zealand. Collectively, these countries accept 1.2 million immigrants a year. About 800,000 immigrants each year are admitted officially to the United States; 200,000 to Canada; 75,000 to Australia; 50,000 to Israel; and 35,000 to New Zealand. But these figures account for a small percentage of the estimated annual global immigration (see Table 13.1), which means that most people who take up residence in

Table 13.1   UN estimates of global migrants, 1965–2000

Year	Migrants (millions)	World population (billions)	Migrants (%)
1965	75	3.3	2.3
1975	85	4.1	2.1
1985	105	4.8	2.2
1995	148	5.7	2.6
2000	185	6.1	3.0

Source: UN Population Division (2001).

Table 13.2 Determinants of migration – factors encouraging individuals to migrate

Type of migrant	Demand-pull	Supply-push	Network/other
Economic	Labour recruitment, e.g. guest workers	Un- or under-employment; low wages, e.g. farmers whose crops fail	Job and wage information flows, e.g. sons following fathers
Non-economic	Family unification, e.g. family members join spouse	Flee war and persecution, e.g. displaced persons and refugees/asylum seekers	Communications; transportation; assistance organizations; desire for new experiences/ adventure

another country each year are not accepted as 'planned immigrants'. Instead, many foreigners move to join family members abroad or to seek asylum, are guest workers who are expected to depart after several years of work, or are unauthorized or illegal foreigners who enter and settle in defiance of immigration laws.

International migration is usually a major individual or family decision that is carefully considered. There are two broad categories of migrants: those who decided to migrate to another country primarily for economic reasons; and those who made the decision primarily for non-economic reasons (see Table 13.2). The factors that encourage a migrant to move are grouped into three categories: demand-pull; supply-push; and network factors. Economic migrants may, for example, be encouraged to migrate by demand-pull guest worker recruitment, while non-economic migrants might be motivated to cross borders to join family members settled abroad. A man living in rural Mexico, for example, may be offered a job in the United States by a recruiter, or hear about US job openings on the radio – a demand-pull factor. This potential migrant may not have a job at home, or may face crop failure, which make him willing to move: a supply-push factor. After obtaining information about US work and wages from a returned migrant, a network factor, he decides to migrate from Mexico to the United States.

The three factors encouraging an individual to migrate do not have equal weights, and the weight of each factor can change over time. Generally, demand-pull and supply-push factors are strongest at the beginnings of a migration flow, and network factors become more important as the migration stream matures. Thus the first guest workers are recruited, often in rural areas where jobs are scarce. But after migrants return with information about job opportunities abroad, network factors may become more important in sustaining migration, so that even employed workers in Mexico may migrate to the United States for higher wages.

These examples are illustrative. Individuals contemplating migration may be encouraged to move by one, two or all three factors. The importance of pull, push and network factors can change over time.

One of the most important non-economic motivations for crossing national borders is family unification – a father working abroad wants to have his wife and children join him, for example. In such cases, the anchor immigrant is a demand-pull factor for family chain migration. The migrant's immediate family may be followed by brothers and sisters, and then by *their* families.

Some migrants are impelled to cross national borders by war and political persecution. Some of these migrants qualify as refugees according to the 1951 Geneva Convention, which defines a refugee as a person residing outside his or her country of citizenship who is unwilling or unable to return because of 'a well-founded fear of being persecuted for reasons of race, religion, nationality, membership of a particular social group or political opinion'. Countries that signed the Geneva Convention pledged not to *refoul* or return persons to places where they could be persecuted.

Migration is a result of differences: in demographic growth, in incomes, and in security and human rights. These differences are increasing, so international migration is likely to increase in the twenty-first century. A comparison of the demographic evolution of Europe and Africa is instructive. In 1800, Europe had about 20 per cent of the world's one billion people, and Africa had 8 per cent. In 2000, the populations of these two continents were almost equal – Europe had 728 million residents and Africa 800 million, giving each 12–13 per cent of the world's population. If current trends continue, Europe will shrink to 660 million by 2050, or about 7 per cent of the world's nine billion residents, while Africa will expand to 1.8 billion – 20 per cent of the world's residents. Demographic trends north and south of the Mediterranean raise a migration question: will Africans migrate northwards, to a Europe that may have 'excess' infrastructure and housing for a smaller population? History suggests that the answer will be yes – some 60 million Europeans emigrated from a more densely settled Europe to the Americas and Oceania between 1800 and 1915. The issue for Europe and Africa will be how to manage what appears to be an inevitable south–north migration.

Economic trends provide a second example of differences that are likely to increase potential migration. The world's GDP was US$30 trillion in the year 2000, and is expected to double by 2030. Economic growth is expected to be fastest in developing countries, but higher incomes in the industrial democracies mean that many young people in developing countries will be able to earn in one hour abroad the equivalent of a day's wages at home. According to the World Bank, global *per capita* income averages

US$5,000, but *per capita* incomes in the twenty-five high-income countries averaged US$26,000 per person in 1999, and US$1,200 in the 175 poorer countries. This means that an average person moving from a poorer to a high-income country can increase his/her income twenty-two times; this large income gap explains why migrants often take huge risks to enter high-income countries.

There is a second dimension to economic differences between high-income and poorer countries that suggests increased international labour migration in the twenty-first century. The world's labour force in 1999 was 2.9 million, and 1.3 million or 45 per cent of the world's workers were employed in agriculture. In developing countries, incomes in agriculture are generally lower than in urban areas.[3] There is a 'great migration' away from the land in many developing countries that are integral components of the world migration system, including China, Mexico and Turkey, and this great migration will probably continue through the twenty-first century, with three implications:

- First, ex-farmers everywhere are most likely to accept so-called '3-D' jobs (dirty, dangerous and difficult) in urban areas inside their own countries, as can be seen in Chinese coastal cities, where internal migrants fill 3-D jobs, and abroad, where Chinese migrants are employed in industries ranging from services to sweatshops;
- Second, ex-farmers who must find new jobs and new sources of income often make physical as well as cultural transitions when they leave rural areas, making them more willing to go overseas if there is recruitment or a migration infrastructure that can help them to cross borders;
- Third, cities in developing countries have become nodes in the international migration infrastructure – cities are the places to which migrants go to get visas and documents for legal migration, or to make arrangements for illegal migration.

Demographic and economic differences, augmented by the flight from the land in developing nations, promise more migration in the twenty-first century. The third major difference that suggests more international migration involves security and human rights. As global conflicts such as the fight between capitalism and communism ended in the 1990s, local conflicts erupted in many areas, leading to separatist movements, new nations and migration, as in the former USSR and former Yugoslavia. The process of nation state creation continues: there were forty-three generally recognized nation states in 1900, 121 in 1980, and 193 in 1998. In most cases, creating new nation states leads to a reshuffling of population, as in South Asia and Europe after the Second World War. However, in some cases, the creation of nation states can produce migrants without any physical movement taking place, as with Russians in the Baltic States, for example, who were considered to be foreigners in Latvia or Estonia. The creation of migrants as borders move may become more common as independence movements spread – for example, in Indonesia.

Evolution of Mexico–United States migration

The largest-volume migration relationship in the world has moved about nine million of the 109 million people born in Mexico to the United States, half of them since 1990; an additional 1–2 million Mexicans work seasonally in the United States. There are about 15 million foreign-born workers in the US labour force of 142 million, including 5–6 million Mexican-born workers, most of them in formal sector jobs.

Mexico has a labour force of about 40 million, but many of those considered to be employed in Mexico are self-employed farmers, unpaid family workers, or in the informal sector – the usual indicator of formal-sector employment in Mexico is enrolment in the pension system, IMSS. In 2001, there were 12.4 million Mexican workers enrolled in IMSS, and their number was forecast to rise to 13.1 million in 2003, or about 350,000 a year (Estudios Económicos y Socio-Políticos de México, n.d.). Thus, about 30 per cent of the 18 million Mexican-born workers with formal-sector jobs are in the United States.

Migration has been the major relationship between Mexico and the United States for most of the twentieth century, and Mexican migrants were negatively selected – that is, those who left Mexico had less education and skills than had the average Mexican (Martin, 1993). The movement of Mexican migrants to the United States has often led to tensions that, on some occasions, slowed economic integration. For example, successive Mexican governments complained about the poor treatment of Mexican citizens in the United States, and the nationalism engendered by attacks on the United States is one reason why Mexico has refused to open its nationalized oil industry to foreign (US) investment. A standard treatment of Mexico–United States relations before the 1990s is entitled 'Distant Neighbours', reflecting the lack of a shared vision, and a common Mexican saying has been, 'Poor Mexico, so far from God, so close to the US'.

History helps to explain why Mexico–United States migration may have slowed economic integration. There was Mexico–United States migration throughout the twentieth century, but only during two periods – 1917–21 and 1942–64 – were there formal bilateral agreements to regulate the employment of most of the Mexican migrants in the United States. At the beginning of both the First and the Second World Wars, US farmers were able to persuade the United States government to make 'exceptions' to immigration rules to admit Mexican guest workers, and both guest-worker programmes ended after pressure from US labour and civil rights groups, who argued that the Mexican migrants depressed wages and increased unemployment for similar US workers.

Both guest-worker or Bracero programmes were followed by illegal Mexico–United States migration, as in particular rural Mexicans dependent on rain-fed farming learnt to go north for higher wages and more opportunities. At first it was very easy to cross the border – the US Border Patrol was not established until 1924, after the first Bracero programme ended. The Depression led to 'repatriations' of Mexicans to free up jobs for Americans, and practically stopped Mexico–United States migration, and there was little Mexican migration north during the 1930s, the era in which Midwestern Dust Bowl farmers moved to California hoping to start anew. They found instead large and labour-intensive factories in the fields that were accustomed to paying relatively low wages to seasonal workers who were available when needed, and John Steinbeck's 1940 novel, *The Grapes of Wrath*, gave an emotional impetus to the common economic prescription of the time, namely the break up of large farms that needed armies of seasonal workers and were viable only if workers were paid seasonally.

There was a great deal of sympathy for structural changes in farming to reduce the employment of seasonal workers, but low farm wages had been capitalized into higher land prices, and landowners unwilling to see land prices fall used the outbreak of the Second World War to lobby for a new Bracero programme (Craig, 1971; Martin, 1996: ch 2). During the Second World War, Braceros, prisoners of war, interned Japanese, and state and local prisoners were employed as farm workers, and their presence in the fields sent an unmistakable signal to US farm workers: economic mobility would require occupational and often geographic mobility; getting ahead in the US labour market would require getting out of the farm workforce.

After the Second World War had ended, the Bracero programme expanded. Farmers assumed that seasonal workers would continue to be available at US minimum wages, and they expanded the production of labour-intensive crops as the baby boom increased demand for fruits and vegetables, water became available to expand irrigated farming, and the interstate highway system lowered transportation costs between the west coast, which produced 40–50 per cent of fruits and vegetables, and the east coast, home to most consumers. The growth of labour-intensive agriculture in areas dependent on Braceros reflected both an expanded western agriculture and the displacement of eastern farmers. California became the number one farm state in 1950, displacing New Jersey as the garden state supplying fruits and vegetables to eastern population centres.

The Bracero programme ended in 1964, amid predictions that labour-intensive agriculture would shrink in areas that had been dependent on Bracero workers, and that commodities that had been picked by Braceros would have to be imported from Mexico. These predictions – by farmers and agricultural researchers – proved to be false. Farm wages rose sharply. Cesar Chavez and the United Farm Workers (UFW) won a 40 per cent wage increase for grape-pickers in 1966, increasing their wages from US$1.25 to US$1.75 an hour in the UFW's first contract. In response to this rise in wages, there was a wave of labour-saving mechanization, and there were predictions that the US seasonal farm labour market would soon be like construction labour markets, offering high hourly wages when seasonal work was available, and maximum unemployment insurance benefits when there was no work (Martin and Olmstead, 1985).

Mexico–United States migration was low during the late 1960s and early 1970s, and US farm workers had their 'golden age', with many in California employed under union contract and earning wages double the minimum wage. However, some of the ex-Braceros had become US immigrants – during the 1960s, a United States employer could issue a letter asserting that a foreigner was 'essential' to fill even a seasonal job, and a foreigner could use this offer of employment to become an immigrant. Some ex-Braceros became immigrants in this manner, and the immigrant visa, printed on a green card, made them green-card commuters – Mexicans who worked in the US seasonally, and then returned with their savings to Mexico.

As these green-card commuters aged, many sent their sons north, using false or altered green cards, or simply entering the United States illegally. A smuggling infrastructure soon evolved to move rural Mexicans to rural America, and this infrastructure was strengthened markedly by an attempt by the UFW, the dominant US farm worker union, to win 40 per cent wage increases in 1979, when wage-price guidelines called for maximum 7 per cent wage increases. Labour contractors hiring unauthorized workers broke many of the strikes, and competition between union hiring halls and labour contractors to supply seasonal workers to farmers were generally won by the contractors. The number of workers under UFW contract dropped from 60,000–70,000 in the early 1970s to 6,000–7,000 by the mid-1980s (Mines and Martin, 1984).

Mexico–United States migration rose in the early 1980s with peso devaluations that made work in the United States more attractive. One crude indicator of illegal Mexico–United States migration – apprehensions of Mexicans just inside the 2000-mile Mexico–United States border – reached their all-time peak of 1.8 million in 1986, meaning that the United States was apprehending an average three Mexicans a minute, twenty-four hours a day, seven days a week. In 1986, two events occurred that, contrary to expectations, led first to more Mexico–United States migration, and eventually closer economic integration:

- The United States enacted the Immigration Reform and Control Act (IRCA) of 1986 to prevent illegal immigration by imposing sanctions on US employers who knowingly hired unauthorized foreigners; and
- Mexico changed its economic policy from import substitution to export-led growth.

Both policy changes increased Mexico–United States migration. IRCA included two legalization or amnesty programmes – the theory was that Mexicans and other unauthorized foreigners who had developed an equity stake in the United States should be integrated rather than deported. However, the legalization programme for unauthorized farm workers – the Special Agricultural Worker (SAW) programme – was rife with fraud, and when it closed had allowed over 1 million Mexican men to become US immigrants. There were only about six million Mexican men in rural Mexico in the mid-1980s, and the SAW programme gave one-sixth of them immigrant visas. However, their families were deliberately excluded from the SAW programme, under the theory that SAWs would commute to seasonal farm jobs as green-card commuters (Martin, 1994). But the SAWs did not behave as expected. Many quickly left the farm labour force and moved to Californian cities, where their families joined them, and were replaced by unauthorized workers in the fields (see Figure 13.1).

US-trained economists achieved political power in Mexico and, under President Carlos Salinas, Mexico proposed the North American Free Trade Agreement (NAFTA) in 1990, after the Canada–United States Free Trade Agreement came into effect in 1989. In an ironic twist, the major opposition to NAFTA turned out to be in the United States, where Ross Perot won 20 per cent of the vote in his 1992 campaign for president in part predicting that NAFTA would lead to a 'giant sucking sound' of

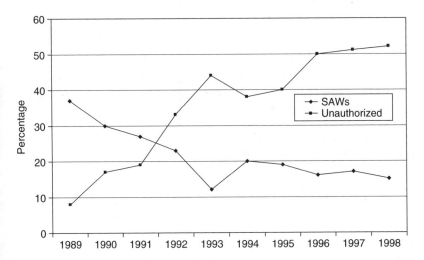

Figure 13.1 Shares of legalized and unauthorized US crop workers, 1989–98
Note: SAW = Special Agricultural Worker.
Source: National Agricultural Workers Survey (available at: www.dol.gov/dol/asp).

US jobs moving to Mexico. Despite strong opposition from Perot, US unions and environmental groups, NAFTA came into force on 1 January 1994.

NAFTA and the migration hump

NAFTA lowered barriers to trade and investment in Canada, Mexico and the United States, and was expected to spur job and wage growth in the three member countries. Most of the benefits of this freer trade were expected to accrue to Mexico, and most of the adjustments to freer trade were also expected in Mexico. The most frequently cited study of NAFTA's likely effects concluded that Mexican employment, projected to be 30 million in 1995, would be 609,000 (or 2 per cent higher) because of NAFTA. Mexican wages were projected to be 9 per cent higher with NAFTA, largely because foreign investment (and Mexican money staying in Mexico) was expected to raise the value of the peso relative to the dollar, thus reducing Mexican living costs (Hufbauer and Schott, 1992: 47–64).

Virtually all studies agreed that most of the additional jobs produced by NAFTA would be in Mexico. Some anticipated displacement in Mexico, and predicted additional migration, in part to urge the US and Mexican governments to create a North American Development Bank to create jobs in rural Mexico. For example, Hinojosa and Robinson (1991) estimated that NAFTA would displace about 1.4 million rural Mexicans, largely because of changes in Mexican farm policies and freer trade in agricultural products, and projected that 800,000 of those displaced would stay in Mexico and 600,000 would migrate (illegally) to the United States over 5–6 years. Hinojosa-McCleery (1992) developed a Computable General Equilibrium (CGE) and sketched three migration scenarios. In 1982, they estimated there were 2.5 million unauthorized Mexicans in the United States, the cost of migrating illegally was US$1,200 (smuggling costs and lost earnings), and the US earnings premium was US$3,000 a year (US$4,000 a year in the United States, and US$1,000 a year in Mexico). Their migration scenarios: no more unauthorized Mexico–United States migration; four million Mexican illegal workers; and five million Mexican illegal workers. They thought the middle scenario of these three could be achieved with a guest-worker programme (called by them 'managed interdependence').

Martin (1993) examined NAFTA's likely impacts on Mexican and US agriculture because most Mexican-born US residents came from rural areas in Mexico, and most had their first US job on farms. After examining how demand-pull factors in the United States would evolve after NAFTA, as well as supply-push factors in Mexico and networks that enabled Mexicans to find US jobs, he concluded that the flow of Mexicans to the United

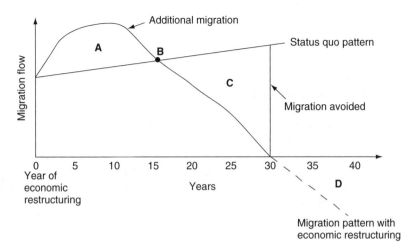

Figure 13.2 The migration hump

States, running at 200,000 settlers and 1 to 2 million sojourners a year in the early 1990s, would probably increase by 10 per cent to 30 per cent for five to fifteen years, producing a migration hump. However, Mexico–United States migration should then decline, for demographic and economic reasons. If a US demand-pull for migrants persisted even after Mexico–United States migration slowed, migrants might come from Central America, China or elsewhere – there has been a sharp upsurge in Central American migrants in rural America. The Clinton administration used the migration hump to argue that Congress should approve NAFTA because the additional migration – the hump – was a reasonable price to pay in the short run for less Mexico–United States migration in the long run.

The migration hump is pictured in Figure 13.2, where the straight line represents the status quo migration flow and the curved line depicts a migration hump, with the volume of migration on the y-axis and time on the x-axis. Economic integration leads to an increase in migration over the status quo trajectory, and this additional migration is represented by A. However, economic integration also speeds up economic and job growth, so that migration falls and the volume of migration returns to the status quo level at B. As migration continues to fall, area C represents the migration avoided by economic integration.

Trade theory and the migration hump

The critical policy parameters are A, B and C – how much does migration increase as a result of economic integration (A), how soon does this hump disappear (B), and how much migration is 'avoided or saved' (C)? Generally, three factors must be present for a migration hump: a continued demand-pull in the destination country with economic integration, an increased supply-push in the origin country as a result of economic integration, and migration networks that can move workers across borders. Comparative statics – before and after equilibrium points – usually ignore the process of adjustment to freer trade, and assume that trade is a substitute for migration in both the short and long term. The migration hump, by contrast, is a short-run relationship between migration and economic integration.

Standard trade theory allows trade and migration to be complements when basic assumptions – including identical production technologies; factor homogeneity; constant returns to scale; instantaneous adjustment; and perfect competition, full employment, and complete markets, are relaxed. In standard trade theory, if a country in the North (N) is capital rich, and a country in the South (S) is capital poor, the two countries share the same technologies or production functions, and the same two factors of production, capital and labour, are used in each country to produce two goods, free trade means that each country will export the good that is more intensive in the factor that is relatively more abundant – Country N will import labour-intensive goods from Country S, and Country S will import capital-intensive goods from Country N.

Stolper and Samuelson considered the effect on factor prices (wages and the return on capital) of an import tariff that increases the domestic price of the import-competing good relative to that of the export good. Under the Heckscher–Ohlin assumptions, plus the assumption that the underlying trade pattern is not altered by the tariff, an import tariff increases the real reward of the relatively-scarce factor and lowers the real reward of the other factor, or a tariff levied against labour-intensive imports in Country N will increase Country N's wages. Migration in response to international wage differentials means that protectionism in Country N should increase migration from the South, or the protection of capital-intensive industries in the South should spur emigration. Trade liberalization, on the other hand, shifts the production of labour-intensive goods to Country S and capital-intensive goods to Country N, which in turn puts upward pressure on Country S's wages, thus discouraging emigration.

However, if there are technology differences, trade and migration can be complements. Corn in Mexico has been highly protected; a guaranteed price of corn that was twice the world price was the social safety net in rural areas but, despite 2–4 million corn farmers in Mexico, 75,000 corn farmers in Iowa in the mid-1990s produced twice as much corn, at half the price, as did the Mexican farmers. The United States produced about ten times more corn than Mexico and, using herbicides and other capital inputs, can export corn to Mexico and undercut Mexican farmers, who use labour-intensive production methods. The Mexican corn example illustrates the fact that, if the basis for trade is differences in technology, then trade and migration may be complements, as, for example, trade in computers and software is accompanied by the migration of computer specialists.

Factor productivity differences between countries are one reason to trade, but *reasons* for productivity differences can help to explain migration behaviour. Suppose Mexican workers are more productive in the United States than they are in Mexico because of better public and private infrastructure. In such cases, migration can complement trade, as occurred when much of the Mexican shoe industry moved from Leon, Mexico to Los Angeles, California in the 1980s – shoes produced by Mexican workers in Los Angeles were then exported to Mexico. Migration, by converting less-productive Mexican workers into more-productive US workers, in this case discouraged the production a labour-intensive goods in Mexico, and encouraged migration to the United States.

A third assumption of the standard trade model is that (identical) production functions in the two countries exhibit constant returns to scale. However, if costs of production fall as output expands, especially in US industries that employ Mexican migrant workers, economic integration may expand US production, thereby increasing the demand-pull for migrants. This means that, when the basis of trade is economies of scale, migration and trade can be complements.

The fourth assumption of the standard trade model is that adjustments to changing prices and wages are instantaneous, and the process of adjustment does not affect the comparative-static equilibrium. With economic integration, workers are often displaced, but it may take time for them to find new jobs. For example, freeing up trade in corn may displace Mexican farmers, but there may be few jobs created by economic integration in the areas in which they are displaced. Furthermore, the new jobs created via economic integration may hire different types of workers than those that were displaced, as when older men are displaced from corn farming, but border-area *maquiladora* factories that expand with integration hire mainly young women. If the displaced Mexican men have better network connections and opportunities in the US labour market than in other Mexican labour markets, there may be more migration with more trade.

The fifth assumption of trade theory is that markets are perfect; there is full information, no risk, and no transactions costs. The new economics of labour migration is based on relaxing this assumption, showing that, for example, a family with a migrant abroad may experiment with a risky new crop, knowing that there will be remittances if the crop fails. Similarly, remittances that enable some families to buy television sets may encourage others to send a migrant abroad so that they can keep up with the neighbours.

Mexico–United States migration in the 1990s

The fact that relaxing the assumptions of the standard trade model can allow trade and migration to be complements, especially in the short term, is well appreciated, but there has been less effort to determine how much additional migration there is or is likely to be with economic integration. Mexico–United States migration rose in the 1990s with closer economic integration, and this section outlines Mexico–United States migration patterns and reasons for the upsurge in the 1990s.

NAFTA came into effect on 1 January 1994. There was an immediate political crisis in Mexico, as Zapatista rebels launched an armed campaign in the state of Chiapas. In March 1994, the leading presidential candidate was assassinated. In an effort to bolster the new candidate, the Mexican money supply was increased sharply in the run-up to July 1994 elections, enabling President Ernesto Zedillo to eke out a win over a very strong challenges from candidates on both the left and the right.[4]

Many economists urged outgoing President Salinas to devalue the peso, which was kept artificially high by the foreign portfolio investment pouring into Mexico, but Salinas resisted, wanting to be the first outgoing president not to devalue the currency. However, in December 1994, just as Zedillo was being sworn in, Mexican and foreign investors began to convert pesos into dollars at the fixed rate of 3.45 pesos to US$1, Mexico ran out of reserves to support the peso, and it fell to 6 pesos to US$1 (in July 2002, for example, it was trading at 10 pesos to US$1). The result was Mexico's worst economic crisis in decades. In the autumn of 1994, there were 10 million workers in formal-sector jobs (enrolled in IMSS); by the end of 1995, there were 9 million. Apprehensions of Mexicans just inside the US border surged: to 1.1 million in FY94; 1.4 million in FY95; 1.6 million in FY96; 1.5 million in FY97; and 1.7 million in FY98. The Mexican economy began to recover in 1996, and by 2001 the number of workers enrolled in IMSS surpassed 12 million, as both trade and foreign investment increased sharply.

Much of the growth in Mexico during the 1990s occurred in *maquiladoras* – foreign-owned plants in border areas that import components duty free, assemble them into goods, and then export the goods; the value added in Mexico – wages and utilities – is typically 10 per cent to 20 per cent of the value of the finished good. The *maquiladora* or Border Industrialization Programme was launched by the United States and Mexico in 1965 to provide jobs for former Braceros and their families that had moved to the border, and now had no source of income.[5] In line with its closed economy strategy of protecting local industries, Mexico required that *maquiladora* goods be exported, and as the finished goods entered the United States, duty was charged only on the value added by Mexican assembly operations.

The number of *maquiladoras* and their employment increased sharply after several peso devaluations in the 1980s. There were twelve maquiladoras employing 3,000 workers in 1965; 600 employing 120,000 workers in 1980; 2,000 employing 472,000 workers in 1990; and 4,000 employing a peak 1.3 million workers in the autumn of 2000 and *maquiladora* exports of US$53 billion surpassed oil as Mexico's leading source of foreign exchange in 1998. At the height of the *maquiladora* boom, when *maquiladora* workers were being paid US$1.50 to US$2 an hour (including benefits), the state of Baja California posted signs on the border advising migrants attempting illegal entry saying: 'Migrant Friend: Don't put yourself at risk. Baja Californians will give you a hand'.

Maquiladoras have been a major success in job-creation, but they never created jobs for former Braceros. The Braceros were young men, while most of the *maquiladora* workers were young women – over 60 per cent in the year 2000. *Maquiladoras* preferred to hire young women from the interior who were getting their first job to men, who had worked in the United States, or wanted to work in the US, believing that the young women were more likely to be satisfied with repetitive assembly-line work. Despite the preference for young women, *maquiladora* workers have very high turnover. A *maquiladora* must often hire two workers to keep one job slot filled, an annual turnover rate of over 100 per cent, which many analysts attribute to uniform wages and benefits – that is, to monopsony employer behaviour. *Maquiladora* wages in dollar terms in 2002 remain below 1994 levels.

During the late 1990s, the Mexican economy and Mexicans migrated northward with *maquiladora* expansion. It is very hard to sort out cause and effect between economic integration and Mexico–United States migration. Clearly, the economic integration symbolized by *maquiladoras* drew many Mexicans to the border area, but there is little smoking gun evidence of a trampoline effect or stepping stone migration, in which internal migrants to border areas become international migrants. The clearest smoking gun involves the 100,000-plus indigenous Mexicans, Mixtecs and Oaxacans from southern Mexico, who were recruited to work in Mexico's export-orientated vegetable industry in the northern part of the country. Their jobs end in the spring, just as the demand for farm workers in the United States increase, and some of them continued on to the United States. One survey of Mixtec workers in the United States in the late 1990s found that two-thirds had worked in northern Mexican export-orientated agriculture before arriving in the United States (Zabin *et al.*, 1993).

Mexico–United States migration in the twenty-first century

The migration hump has both an up- and a down-side. Many pessimists look at the 1990s upside of the Mexico–United States migration hump and see only continued Mexico–United States migration. But such migration might fall faster than expected for demographic and economic reasons. As a result, the US border control build up may be completed just as Mexico–United States migration begins to fall for other reasons, and enforcement may get the credit that demography and economics deserve.

Mexico's population of 100 million is growing by 2 per cent a year. In the late 1990s, legal Mexican immigration was 150,000 to 200,000 a year, and unauthorized Mexico–United States migration was even higher. Mexican population growth peaked at 3.3 per cent in 1970, but in 1974, the Mexican government launched a family planning programme that helped birth rates to fall sharply: fertility dropped from an average of seven children per woman in 1965 to 2.5 by 2000. Declining fertility reduces migration both directly and indirectly, because households with fewer children tend to keep them in education for longer, reducing the need for jobs for young people entering the labour market, and educated Mexicans are less likely to emigrate.

Mexico has a major job creation challenge, but the number of people turning fifteen, the age of labour force entry in Mexico, is projected to drop by 50 per cent between 1996 and 2010, from about one million a year to 500,000. According to the IMF, there is a 2:1 relationship between economic and job growth in Mexico; that is, 2 per cent economic growth is associated with 1 per cent job growth. The IMF includes all types of employment, and thus uses an employment base of 30 million, so that each 1 per cent job growth increases employment by 300,000, including 100,000 formal-sector jobs. If Mexico can achieve its economic growth target of 6 per cent a year, then the declining number of additional workers and the rising additional jobs X-curve will meet at some time in the next few years. The next challenge would be to upgrade jobs and wages (see Figure 13.3).

Conclusions

International migration has great potential for disrupting orderly relations between nations, despite the fact that the number of migrants is relatively small. In a world of six billion, the number of international migrants rose sharply in the 1990s, and led to efforts to reduce immigration in Europe by, *inter alia*, preventing the entry of asylum applicants, and to reduce welfare costs associated with immigrants in the United States by restricting their eligibility. All the industrial democracies increased expenditures on immigration control, and many joined regional forums to discuss migration issues.

With trade as a substitute for migration, economic integration should reduce economically motivated migration. However, in the short run, migration and trade can increase together, producing a migration hump when migration levels are viewed over time. The United States attempted to

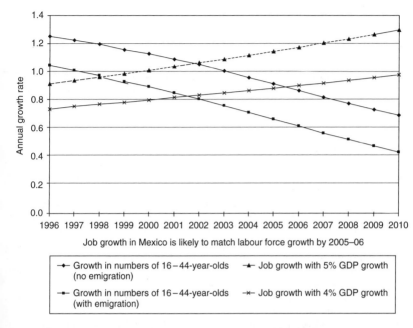

Job growth in Mexico is likely to match labour force growth by 2005–06

Legend:
- Growth in numbers of 16–44-year-olds (no emigration)
- Growth in numbers of 16–44-year-olds (with emigration)
- Job growth with 5% GDP growth
- Job growth with 4% GDP growth

Figure 13.3 Demographic and job growth in Mexico, 1996–2010

reduce Mexico–United States migration with trade, and NAFTA came into effect in January 1994 in part to enable Mexico to export tomatoes, rather than tomato pickers. However, during the 1990s, Mexico–United States migration increased sharply. Mexican economic growth was very uneven, economic integration added jobs for new labour force entrants, but not those displaced by trade, and the US economy boomed, providing a demand-pull for Mexicans with US contacts.

High levels of Mexico–United States migration between 1995 and 2005 should not obscure the fact that migration may soon diminish for demographic and economic reasons. A combination of the sharp drop in Mexican fertility in the 1980s and 1990s, economic and job growth, and the near completion of the exodus from agriculture should reduce Mexico–United States migration after 2005, just when the US build-up of protection along the border is nearing completion. If this occurs, analysts must be careful to credit the demographic and economic factors that reduce migration pressure, not the border controls whose completion happened to coincide with diminished migration flows.

The migration hump has three major policy implications. First, economic integration should be advocated as the best long-run policy to promote 'stay-at-home' development, but not sold as a short-term cure for unwanted migration. Second, there is a need for a better understanding of adjustment processes under economic integration, so that increases in migration can be anticipated and dealt with in a manner that does not slow increased trade and investment. Third, emigration countries that benefit economic integration could be expected to help manage the migration hump in light of the resistance to free trade in many ageing industrial democracies worried about unwanted immigration.

Notes

1. The 1951 Geneva Convention on refugees obliges signatory countries not to *refoul* or return to danger persons who are outside their countries because of a well-founded fear of persecution because of race, religion, nationality, membership of a particular social group or political opinion. As the number of asylum seekers – foreigners who arrived in industrial countries and asked not to be returned because they faced persecution at home – rose in the 1990s, the industrial countries spent an estimated US$10 billion a year caring for and processing applications of asylum seekers. Members of the EU have been struggling with the challenge of developing common standards and criteria for evaluating and handling applicants as well as for 'burden-sharing' – sharing the cost of processing asylum applications and supporting applicants while they await a decision.
2. The UN estimate is 150 to 200 million migrants in 2000. There is no country or regional breakdown, but in 1990, when the UN estimated 120 million migrants, 66 million (55 per cent) were in developing countries and 54 million (45 per cent) in developed countries.
3. This income gap encourages rural–urban migration, helping to explain why there are shanty towns around many cities in developing countries, and why the urban population of the low- and middle-income countries rose from 32 per cent to 41 per cent of these countries' population between 1980 and 1999.
4. The Institutional Revolutionary Party (PRI) was in power from 1930 to 2000, and Zedillo received 49 per cent of the vote in 1994, the National Action Party (PAN) 26 per cent, and the Democratic Revolution Party (PRD) 17 per cent.
5. Many Braceros moved to the border area to increase their chance of being selected. The US employer had to pay transportation from the workers' place of recruitment to the US job, and employers thus preferred border-area workers.

References

Boeri, T. and H. Brucker (2000). 'The Impact of Eastern Enlargement on Employment and Labour Markets in the Member States', *Financial Times*, 27 June: 15.

Craig, R. B. (1971). *The Bracero Program: Interest Groups and Foreign Policy*, Austin, TX: University of Texas Press.

Estudios Económicos y Socio-Políticos de México (n.d.). Available at: www.banamex.com/weblogic/svltC71930EstSE?LNG = 1&SEQ = 3&folio = 5.

Hamilton, B. and J. Whaley (1984). 'Efficiency and Distributional Implications of Global Restrictions on Labour Mobility', *Journal of Development Economics*, 14: 61–75.

Heckscher, E. (1949). 'The Effects of Foreign Trade on the Distribution of Income', in H. S. Ellis and L. A. Metzler (eds), *Readings in the Theory of International Trade*, Philadelphia: Blakiston.

Hinojosa-Ojeda, R. and R. McCleery (1992). 'US–Mexico Interdependence, Social Pacts and Policy Perspectives: A Computable General Equilibrium Approach', in

J. Bustamante, C. Reynolds and R. Hinojosa-Ojeda (eds), *US-Mexican Relations: Labor Market Interdependence*. Stanford, CA: Stanford University Press.

Hinojosa-Ojeda, R. and S. Robinson (1991). 'Alternative Scenarios of US–Mexican Integration: A Computable General Equilibrium Approach', Working Paper, No. 609, Berkeley, CA: Department of Agricultural and Resource Economics, University of California.

Hinojosa-Ojeda, R. and S. Robinson (1992). 'Labor Issues in a North American Free Trade Area', in N. Lustig, B. Bosworth and R. Lawrence (eds), *North American Free Trade: Assessing the Impact*, Washington, DC: The Brookings Institution.

Hufbauer, G. and J. Schott (1992). *North American Free Trade: Issues and Recommendations*, Washington, DC: Institute for International Economics.

Krauss, M. B. (1976). 'The Economics of the "Guest Worker" Problem: A Neo-Heckscher–Ohlin Approach', *Scandinavian Journal of Economics*, 78: 470–6.

Martin, P. L. (1993). *Trade and Migration: NAFTA and Agriculture*, Washington, DC: Institute for International Economics.

Martin, P. L. (1994). 'Good Intentions Gone Awry: IRCA and US Agriculture', *The Annals of the Academy of Political and Social Science*, 534, July: 44–57.

Martin, P. (1996). *Promises to Keep: Collective Bargaining in California Agriculture*, Ames, IA: Iowa State University Press.

Martin, P. L. and A. L. Olmstead (1985). 'The Agricultural Mechanization Controversy', *Science*, 227(4687): 601–6.

Massey, D. S., R. Alarcon, J. Durand and H. Gonzalez (1987). *Return to Aztlan: The Social Process of International Migration from Western Mexico*, Berkeley and Los Angeles, CA: University of California Press.

Mines, R. and P. L. Martin (1984). 'Immigrant Workers and the California Citrus Industry', *Industrial Relations*, 23(1): 139–49.

Mundell, R. A. (1957). 'International Trade and Factor Mobility', *American Economic Review*, 47: 321–35.

Ohlin, B. (1933). *Interregional and International Trade*, Cambridge, MA: Harvard University Press.

Riding, A. (1985). *Distant Neighbors: A Portrait of the Mexicans*, New York: Alfred A. Knopf.

Stolper, W. F. and P. A. Samuelson (1941). 'Protection and Real Wages', *Review of Economic Studies*, 9: 58–73.

UN Population Division (2001). 'World Population Prospects: The 2000 Revision. Vol III'. Available at: www.un.org/esa/population/publications/wpp2000wpp2000 volume3.htm.

US Commission for the Study of International Migration and Cooperative Economic Development (1990). '*Unauthorized Migration: An Economic Development Response*', Washington, DC.

Zabin, C., M. Kearney, D. Runsten and A. Garcia (1993). *A New Cycle of Rural Poverty: Mixtec Migrants in California Agriculture*, Davis, CA: California Institute for Rural Studies.

14

The Nature and Pattern of Irregular Migration in the Caribbean

Elizabeth Thomas-Hope

Introduction

Behind the anxiety relating to refugees and asylum seekers lies the issue of irregular migration. As with regular migration, irregular relocation in the Caribbean includes different types of movement. One is the illegal entry into the Caribbean of people from other regions. Currently, such immigrants are chiefly from China, entering the Caribbean countries with the intention of moving on to the United States. A second type of irregular migrant leaves the Caribbean countries to go directly to destinations outside the region, mainly the United States, Canada and countries in Europe. Finally, a third type of irregular migrant originates in the Caribbean and moves to other locations within the region. Thus irregular relocation affecting the Caribbean concerns both immigrant and emigrant, and is both intra- and extra-regional with regard to the source and destination of movement. In general, irregular migration parallels the patterns of regular migration flows, and could be considered to represent the 'informal sector' of the migration process.

Irregular migrants include:

- Those who illegally cross borders by evading border controls, including asylum seekers who are not deemed to be 'genuine refugees' (Castles and Miller, 1998: 289);
- Those who enter through the regular channels of entry but using illegal documents;
- Those who enter a country legally but over-extend the limits of their visas; and
- Persons whose residency or citizenship status is altered subsequent to their move, through changes in the laws and regulations governing the criteria for legal status.

As in many other parts of the world, irregular migration is increasing in the Caribbean. Migration continues to be identified by most Caribbean societies as the only alternative to the existing conditions in individuals' home countries. These range from minor frustrations or insecurity to major hardship and breaches of human rights. In addition, 'migrant' communities have already been established at the destinations of earlier movements of people, and these provide the means for reunification of families and the support needed to survive on arrival in the host country. This creates an important aspect of the dynamic that perpetuates the migration process. Under dire circumstances, and because legal channels for entry into potential immigration countries (particularly those in North America and Europe) remain selective on grounds of nationality, education and occupational status, there is likely to be a continuing flow of migrants trying to circumvent formal channels by resorting to informal ones.

Irregular migration itself creates its own momentum. The successive waves of migrants departing from communities and relatively small countries have a destabilizing effect that undermines confidence in the system, and lowers morale. There are various means for migrating outside the official system, but unfortunately many migrants, whether knowingly or inadvertently, become caught up in the web of trafficking and smuggling rings that operate within the region. This entangles irregular migration in a complex system of illegal activity with implications extending beyond the specific issue of migration.

This chapter offers an overview of irregular migration with respect to the Caribbean region, with particular reference to the patterns of movement, short-term implications, and wider underlying issues.

Caribbean irregular migration in context

Migration has been of major significance in the making and development of the Caribbean. Present-day Caribbean societies have largely been formed through immigration, both forced and free. Subsequently, emigration has played an increasingly important role, with continuing and overlapping episodes of emigration within the wider Caribbean, and also to other regions, notably Europe and North America.

Substantial Caribbean communities have become established at all the major relocation destinations. At the same time, there have always been currents of return migration to respective home countries, and circular movement between countries. Migrants and their home communities have adopted livelihood strategies that, over time, have become transnational in character because of the associated flows of people, information, goods and finance. Guest-worker programmes have also provided work for migrants, both in agricultural harvesting and the hotel industry in the United States and Canada. These activities provided a channel for the movement of large numbers of workers on a regular, seasonal basis.

The guest-worker schemes have been negotiated through bilateral arrangements between source and host governments. In some cases, the government of the sending country has been reimbursed by the government of the receiving country. For example, for many years the Dominican Republic paid the Haitian government for access to the Haitian labour force. Specifically, in 1980 US$2.9 million was paid for 16,000 workers (*braceros*) (French, 1991, cited in Castles and Miller, 1998) but this arrangement lapsed in 1986 after Jean-Claude (Baby Doc) Duvalier was forced out of office. Since then, the sugar industry in the Dominican Republic has relied on private recruiters to find the estimated 40,000 workers needed each year from November to May for harvesting (Preeg, 1985; Castles and Miller, 1998).

A number of overlapping movements also occur: Haitians go to cut cane in the Dominican Republic, while Dominicans go to other locations in the Caribbean and to the United States. Haitians and Dominicans are the largest and second-largest groups of Caribbean emigrants respectively, both in terms of intraregional and extraregional movements (see, for example, Marshall, 1979). Vincentians have traditionally travelled to Barbados to cut cane (Marshall, 1984), and Barbadians, along with Jamaicans, have gone to Florida or to other parts of the United States and Canada for fruit and tobacco harvesting (McCoy and Wood, 1982). Variations in migration flow, including the volume, characteristics of the migrants, reasons and strategies for achieving individual aims, are numerous. Furthermore, legal controls for managing these movements of people, either by encouragement or deterrent in the countries of origin and destination, have differed considerably. Migrations have also varied with regard to the duration of the stay abroad, and in the timing of movement between source and destination. In addition to long-stay migration, many movements have been transient in nature, with people engaged in varied forms of formal and informal business activities and trade. People return and leave again, establishing transnational communities between which there is ongoing movement of people, capital and goods.

Just as the characteristics of the movements have varied greatly, so have the reasons for migration. But the underlying explanations have remained fundamentally the same and have been reinforced with every passing generation (Thomas-Hope, 1992, 1999). Following the emancipation of slaves in the nineteenth century (with the exception of Haiti, where slaves freed themselves in a revolutionary upheaval at the end of the eighteenth century), migration was closely associated with the flight of former slaves from plantations, and the pursuit of full liberty from the plantation system that had dominated every facet of national life and individual livelihood. Movements continued throughout the twentieth century, increasing in volume from different Caribbean countries in successive decades, albeit continually changing in character over time.

In addition to migration being associated with the desire to escape the plantation system and the traditional constraints in favour of upward

555

mobility in post-colonial societies, small Caribbean countries have only limited physical and environmental resources. Other factors have contributed to the destabilization of many Caribbean societies since the 1980s, including poor economic performance, indebtedness to the international banks (particularly the World Bank and the IMF), demographic imbalance and major rural–urban shifts. In other countries of the region, notably Haiti, political instability and environmental disaster have added to the dismal picture (Castles and Miller, 1998). Countries that have been spared this negative development in the second half of the twentieth century have become the net receivers, rather than the senders, of both regular and irregular migrants. Thus, migration – by extending options and opportunities to a wider regional and global context – offered people the means of eluding conditions that range from restrictions on upward mobility to major hardship or abhorrent circumstances, including violence or the threat of it.

The dynamics of migration reflect the interplay of international, national, household and personal factors. People of all social classes migrate, but the international economic order and the division of labour, in conjunction with the level of social and physical capacity for absorption of specific island populations, create the conditions in which legislative control and inducement to the movement of labour across national borders are formulated and implemented. Economic, social, demographic and political realities, as well as the perception of these, influence immigration regulations and legislation, and thus determine people's access to migration. These same factors subsequently condition the method and process of entry of different national or ethnic groups into the 'host' society, and also affect the impact that migration has at the destination.

Contrary to the simplistic explanations often advanced, migration is not a passive reaction to internal 'push' or external 'pull' forces. Similarly, irregular migration is usually not a simple process of crossing international borders at the migrants' own volition. International decisions influence migration flows in a number of direct and indirect ways and, within the wider international and national context, migration is a part of a dynamic set of negotiations at all levels. Based on various geo-political motivations, nation states negotiate for the movement of labour through official or unofficial channels. This is evident in the comparative reception by the United States of Cubans granted asylum on political grounds versus Haitians who, applying on economic grounds, were refused entry (Boyle *et al.*, 1998). While there is no formal negotiation with respect to refugee and other irregular movements, various subtle mechanisms are used by the 'sending' country to exert pressure on other states to receive their nationals.

Thus 'forced migration' should not be conceptualized as necessarily the result of specific persecution that literally causes people to flee for their lives. Forced migration may also result from the institutional structure of the social, economic and political systems that make the peaceful sustaining of life and livelihood impossible. This can occur in combination with de facto circumstances whereby segments of the population, who cannot for one reason or another be 'managed' in or by the existing socioeconomic and/or political regime, are driven out or allowed to leave without hindrance to seek residence elsewhere. Thus, whether 'free' movement or refugee, formal or informal, there is a selective process of overt or covert transactions that operates at the interface of the needs of the immigration country on the one hand and the potential for migration in the emigration country on the other.

Ranging from the macro-level forces of global economic and political systems to the micro-level strategies and ambitions of the household and individual, there exists a variety of societal imperatives, perceptions and interactions that translate into the opportunities and tensions that trigger migration flows. Among these are the conditions that formally qualify an individual for passage across international borders, and are largely articulated in the criteria for entry established by prospective destination countries.

The criteria for gaining immigration priority status generally lead to the disproportionate selection of the educated, the highly skilled and the young to the exclusion of others. An exception is the criterion of a 'dependent relative' of an existing resident. It is to be noted that recruitment campaigns are mounted periodically by North American and European countries to attract selected migrants, of late specifically students, teachers and nurses.

In addition to those with criminal records who are excluded automatically, people from countries that are considered to be low-priority sources of entrants to North America, Europe or even other neighbouring Caribbean countries, generally do not meet the selection requirement for formal entry and landed immigrant status. Invariably, countries ranked with the lowest priority for immigration of nationals are the poorest, and within those countries the poorest and least educated sectors of the population are the least favoured groups. It is precisely from these countries that the motivation to emigrate is the greatest. The adverse perception of which they are victims is based on a number of factors generally associated with race and/or poverty. This negative image is also compounded by the very existence of irregular migrant movement itself. Thus, where people cross national borders without the sanction of the authorities or the formal socioeconomic system, or in excess of the environmental carrying capacity, it increases resistance in the host societies.

Irregular migration itself creates anxiety, sometimes bordering on hysteria, in the receiving countries, which results in the formulation of new regulations, or the more stringent enforcement of existing regulations, in an effort to reduce the number of future immigrants. This concern might be well-founded in very small island states, because in all probability the flow of people could exceed the capacity of the destination to absorb and settle the new population within the time-frame of migrant entry. After initial concern, long-term xenophobia follows. There is the danger of politicians exploiting or responding to public anxiety and hurriedly formulating poorly conceived policies and short-term decisions.

Trends in Caribbean irregular migration

The pattern of movement

The direction and volume of irregular movements reflect two interrelated hierarchies of opportunity based on economic conditions and distance. At one level, irregular migrants constitute the materially poor from the poorest countries to other nations within the Caribbean, and affect destinations within the shortest distances from the point of origin, as financial costs are generally commensurately lower for these places than more distant locations.

In addition to transport costs, opportunity cost is highest for the United States. The risk of being intercepted is lower in those countries of the region that can afford only rudimentary coastguard surveillance. For example, entry into the Turks and Caicos Islands since 1994 has been rather easier than into the Bahamas. In other territories where there is cooperation with the US Coastguard based in San Juan, surveillance is tight, as is the case of the US Virgin Islands. The selection of a destination therefore reflects a compromise on the part of the migrant between lower risk and costs versus preferred location.

The main flows of irregular migration are listed below (see also Figure 14.1).

Immigrants from outside the region

Most irregular migrants moving into the Caribbean currently are from China. An unknown number of Chinese migrants are smuggled annually by organized rings and syndicates into the area, including the United States. Many of those destined for the United States are landed first in the Caribbean, especially the islands of the eastern Caribbean or in Central America (CNN, 2001).

From the Caribbean to North America and Europe using formal routes

Migrants move from Caribbean countries to the United States and the European Union (EU) directly or via transit points (some of which become their final destinations). Regular airline routes and the use of false documents provide the means of entry. In recent years, major movements of this type have been from Jamaica to the United States, the United Kingdom or Canada. A second but similar corridor is from the southern Caribbean through Trinidad, and then to the United States and/or the United Kingdom.

Land border crossings

With respect to irregular migration, the only land border of relevance in the island Caribbean is between Haiti and the Dominican Republic. This has

302

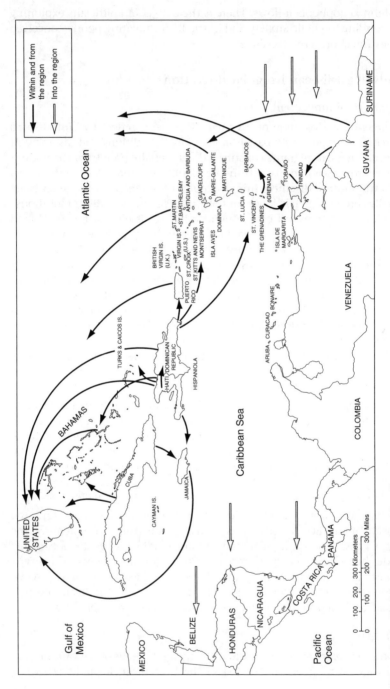

Figure 14.1 Caribbean irregular migration

been a long-standing crossing point for large numbers of regular migrants such as seasonal sugar-cane workers, as well as undocumented irregular migrants. Some of these remain, legally or illegally, in the Dominican Republic. On the part of Haitians, the seasonal movement across the border into the Dominican Republic, and the illegal extension of stay, continue.

Irregular movements by boat

Caribbean island states have long, heavily indented and poorly patrolled coastlines, offering many potential points for landing small craft. The movements usually involve relatively short distances (albeit at times in dangerous conditions), to the more remote locations of neighbouring countries. Travel can be a single journey from one territory to another, or involve multiple stages.

Currently, the main issue relating to irregular migration in the Caribbean, chiefly because of the large numbers involved, are the migrants who attempt to enter a Caribbean country or the United States by boat. The boats are undocumented and in many cases operated by smuggling rings. Large boats are used if direct travel to the United States is intended, but to reduce the risk of being observed and intercepted by the US Coastguard, the final leg of the journey is made in small boats, usually from archipelagos of the Bahamian, or Turks and Caicos Islands. Much smaller numbers of Haitians and Cubans travel by sea to Jamaica or Cayman and later attempt to move from there to the United States. Between mid-February and May 2004, over 500 Haitians arrived in Jamaica by boat (Jamaican Ministry of National Security, unpublished data). The majority filed applications for asylum, whereas 116 sought voluntary repatriation to Haiti, assisted by the International Organization for Migration (IOM) and the United Nations High Commissioner for Refugees (UNHCR).

Haiti, Cuba and the Dominican Republic are the major sources of these irregular movements. Haitians travel mainly to the Bahamas or the Turks and Caicos Islands, almost always with the intention of relocating to the United States, while Cubans prefer to travel directly to Florida. Haitians and Dominicans also travel eastwards to islands having a prosperous tourist industry, such as Antigua, or to the British Overseas Territory of Anguilla, or the French Departments of Martinique and Guadeloupe, including their offshore islands – Marie Galante and the Iles des Saintes. The British, Dutch and French colonial territories in the Caribbean are linked to the EU, and thus their economies are supported externally. Here, opportunities are better and the possibility of moving on to Europe exists.

The route of irregular migrants from the Dominican Republic has tradition-ally been – and continues to be – across the Mona Passage to Puerto Rico, with the aim of moving on to the United States. More recently, there has been movement from the Dominican Republic to the various Eastern Caribbean islands that could, in the eyes of the migrants, later provide possibilities for entry either to the United States or the EU. This movement is also characterized by smuggling rings involved in the trafficking of young women and girls destined for prostitution at locations in the Caribbean itself, especially in the former Netherlands Antilles, in countries of Central and South America, and in Europe (Kempadoo, 1999).

In the south-eastern part of the Caribbean, there is a small but significant (compared to the size of the countries concerned) movement from Guyana, Grenada, St Vincent and the Grenadines and Dominica, into Trinidad and Tobago and Barbados.

The volume of irregular migration

By virtue of the nature of irregular migration, there are no hard data on the number of illegal migrants in the countries of destination or transit. Relevant countries of entry collect data on the numbers of people caught, detained or deported. Rough estimates are also made of the number of migrants who in fact land at their various destinations, but there are no statistics available on illegal entry into the islands of the Eastern Caribbean.

The movement destined, either directly or through transit points, for the United States was dominated by Haitians over the period 1982 to 1994, and numbers peaked in 1992 with 31,438 people interdicted, followed by a decline after 1995 to less than 2,000 in any year (Alien Migrant Interdiction, 2002; see Thomas-Hope, 2003). In 1990 and 1991, there were over 1,000 Dominicans interdicted, and in 1995 and 1996 there were 4,047 and 5,430 interdicted, respectively, after which numbers fell once more, to 1,463 in 1997 and less than 1,000 each year thereafter. Between 1991 and 1994, the number of Cubans interdicted was also much higher than previously recorded, increasing from fewer than 4,000 in 1993 to more than 37,000 in 1994, after which numbers again declined (Alien Migrant Interdiction, 2002).

The Ministry of Foreign Affairs of the Bahamas and the authorities in the Turks and Caicos Islands also maintain records of irregular migrants apprehended by the security forces. The former reported that in the year 2000, 4,879 Haitians were intercepted, 6,253 in 2001, and during the first eight months of 2002, 4,077 were detained (Bahamian Ministry of Foreign Affairs, unpublished data, 2002).

In what is fast becoming a typical news story, the Jamaican press reported in August 2002 that, 'the Bahamian authorities had detained 204 Haitian migrants who were found crowded aboard a 40-foot sloop at sea in the southeastern Bahamas' (*The Daily Observer* (Jamaica) 14 August 2002: 16). The migrants were taken by the Coastguard to a location on the southern island of Inagua, where they were handed over to immigration authorities for processing and repatriation. In each case, the majority of migrants were male; fewer than 20 per cent were female.

Over the same period, authorities in the Turks and Caicos Islands apprehended 806 people in 2000, 2,038 in 2001 and 845 in the period January to

July 2002 (Turks and Caicos Islands, unpublished data, 2002). The trend towards increasing volume is similar to that seen in all parts of the region. Whether the increases in numbers apprehended represent greater vigilance by the authorities, or whether they reflect an increase in the volume of flow of Haitian irregular migrants, is an open question.

Strategies relating to irregular migration in the destination countries

Haitians who began to leave their country in large numbers for the United States between the 1970s and 1994 did not have preferential opportunities for asylum. Their attempts to obtain refugee status in the United States became more difficult with the practice of interdiction at sea in the 1980s. There are still an estimated one million internally displaced persons (IDPs) in Haiti.

In response to the mass migration of Cubans in 1980 and the increasing number of Haitians landing in the US, President Ronald Reagan, on 29 September 1981, issued Presidential Proclamation No. 4865 which suspended the entry to the US of undocumented migrants from the high seas. Since then, the American strategy has been to interdict irregular migrants at sea before they land in the United States, and this practice was intensified with the Haitian 'boat people' in 1991, after the coup that overthrew the elected president, Jean-Bertrand Aristide.

Following the coup in Haiti and the dramatic increase in the volume of irregular migration, migrants interdicted at sea by the US Coastguard were processed as asylum claimants first on ships and then at the US military base in Guantanamo Bay (GTMO) in Cuba. Those identified as leaving Haiti for economic reasons, as opposed to political persecution, were denied asylum and returned to Haiti. During this time, the camp at GTMO was operating at capacity, with more than 12,000 migrants (Alien Migrant Interdiction, 2002). When numbers increased beyond capacity, Washington ordered that all other interdicted persons be summarily repatriated without recourse to appeals for asylum.

In 1992, President George Bush issued Executive Order 12807, which enabled the US Coastguard to enforce the suspension of the entry of undocumented migrants by intercepting them at sea, and returning them to their country of origin or departure (Alien Migration Interdiction, 2002). In 1993, 'Operation Able Manner' was launched with the intent of concentrating Coastguard patrols in the Windward Passage (between Haiti and Cuba) in order to interdict Haitian migrants. This continued until a new government took over in Haiti in 1994. In that year, the Coastguard was involved in a massive operation responding to the movements first from Haiti and then from Cuba. Over 63,000 migrants were interdicted. At its peak, seventeen US Coastguard vessels were patrolling the coast of Haiti, while thirty-eight Coastguard vessels were in the Straits of Florida in connection with 'Operation Able Vigil'.

Some migrants are intercepted by the US Coastguard in US waters, in the Florida Straits, and often even in Haitian territorial waters. Others are intercepted in the Caribbean itself, a situation made easier for the US authorities by virtue of the Shiprider Agreements to which many Caribbean states are signatories. (These agreements permit US authorities to search and detain vessels within the coastal waters of certain Caribbean states.)

In addition to interception at sea, other strategies employed by destination countries, especially the United States, include diplomatic pressure on the countries of origin. This is exemplified by the case in 1991 of the Haitian 'boat people', after the coup, when the US president announced that US troops would invade Haiti unless the military coup leaders stepped down in favour of Aristide. The ensuing diplomatic negotiations led to an agreement; 20,000 American troops landed in Haiti, and a few weeks later, Raoul Cedras, the rebel leader, resigned (Weiner, 1995). This high-level response demonstrates the seriousness of the security risk perceived by the United States in the continued arrival of large numbers of irregular migrants seeking asylum. Within the very small states in the Caribbean, the notion of sovereignty and possible threats to this are ever-present.

The negative response to the refugee crisis in the region has been strongest on the part of the United States, but the rest of the Caribbean has reacted similarly within their respective capabilities. In particular, the Bahamas and the Turks and Caicos Islands, which are the principal Caribbean destinations of irregular migrants from Haiti, offer no asylum. The authorities of these countries – the Bahamas, an independent state; and the Turks and Caicos Islands, a dependent territory of the United Kingdom – prefer interception at sea, police round-up raids, detainment, and later repatriation.

Migrant communities, transnational environments and social capital

Substantial communities of migrants – mainly of Cubans, Haitians, Dominicans, Jamaicans and Trinidadians – exist at the destination points of major movements in the Caribbean, the United States, Canada and the EU states. Significant Haitian communities also exist in the Bahamas (see Marshall, 1984), and in the Turks and Caicos Islands. Newer communities of Dominican migrants have developed in the Turks and Caicos Islands as well as in the north-eastern Caribbean islands of St Martin, Antigua and Anguilla (a British dependent territory). These communities form the network providing the social capital that is invaluable for the protection and assistance needed to survive at the destination, obtaining legal status or finding opportunities to move on to the United States.

The transnational experience is not spatially delineated, but creates transmigrant perspectives of one's personal world and options, self-identity included. It has been suggested that, in the Haitian case, migrants have yet to articulate fully an identity that reflects their transnationalism (Schiller and Fouron, 1999), while others state that, 'They have created no language or identity that gives full voice to the complexity of their daily lives' (Basch *et al.*, 1994: 146).

The status of irregular migrants and the next generation

The status of migrants is largely determined by the mode of entry and policies relating to asylum, residency and citizenship.

Irregular migrants may regularize their residency in a country by applying for and receiving asylum; being granted a work permit; or obtaining the right to apply for citizenship through marriage with a national. These regulations can be changed at any time by the host government. Work permits and their annual renewal can cost a significant sum of money in relation to the low-level jobs of the irregular migrants. Furthermore, in most cases, work permits can be denied on any ground without recourse to impartial investigation. The same concerns citizenship status; once applied for, it can be denied, or finally granted after a protracted period of several years. The overall issue of migrants legalizing their status is not consistent from one country to another; there is no transparent process, it is costly to the applicant and subject to revision at any time.

Changes in the laws and regulations governing citizenship and rights to work and residency can suddenly change the status of a person without the individual departing or entering the country. This action by governments is particularly questionable when it concerns changes in the status of individuals who have been legally resident for some years in a country, or those who have children born in the host country, and who suddenly find themselves affected dramatically by new regulations governing the renewal of work permits or determining the citizenship of the children of immigrants. Usually citizenship is granted to an individual according to the country of birth, but this can vary, depending on the regulations outlining the rights of either the father or mother to transfer citizenship to the child.

In 1991, following democratic elections in Haiti and growing concern about the human rights of the Haitian workers in the Dominican Republic, the Dominican government expelled more than 10,000 Haitians, many of whom had lived for years in the country, or had been born there (French, 1991: 15, cited in Castles and Miller, 1993: 137). Further political events in Haiti, in particular the overthrow of Aristide in September 1991, led to a renewed emigration of Haitians attempting to reach the United States. Most were intercepted, detained and finally deported to Haiti.

The problem of stateless children has arisen in Anguilla and in the Turks and Caicos Islands in recent years. In July 2002, the issue became a scandal when the children of Haitian parents but born in the Turks and Caicos Islands were threatened with expulsion (termed 'repatriation') to Haiti. According to unofficial sources, some children had in fact been sent back, but were returned by the authorities on the grounds that they were not Haitian citizens. The children demonstrated with placards, using the publicity given to a protected species of reptile, the iguanas, which had been dubbed as 'belongers', in order to encourage their protection. The children of Haitian parents born in the same islands were now considered 'non-belongers' and in consequence were in danger of being expelled.

Implications of the movements

Cost to the migrants

To the migrant, the cost of illegal relocation is financial as well as physical and emotional. Travel by sea is usually by private boats, invariably operated by those engaged in human trafficking and drug-smuggling activities. These are not concerned with safety regulations and place their passengers in danger, both from the natural elements and the law. The risks and the costs are high, even though they are generally undertaken with the full knowledge of the migrants themselves.

Financial cost

The financial cost of irregular migration involves payments made for the journey from the home country to the destination, and for the documents needed for entry into the destination country. These services can generally only be secured at extortionate rates. In the early 1990s, fraudulent US visas were available in Jamaica and Trinidad and Tobago at a cost ranging from US$300 to US$5,000, respectively (IMP, 2001). In addition, there are often a number of indirect costs involved to ensure the means of remaining at the destination. These may include a series of payments to cover anything from the arrangement of a bogus marriage to supplying a work permit.

Physical and emotional cost

In all respects, migrants are highly vulnerable to the risk of official sanction (deportation or detention) as well as the risk of extortion and violence at the hands of smugglers and other agents with whom they enter into negotiations with regard to their movements.

In addition, individual opportunists prey on vulnerable migrants, transporting them in ill-equipped vessels to locations that are neither safe havens nor sometimes even the countries sought by the migrants. Stories abound of the total disregard for the safety or humanity of the irregular migrants, who have on occasion been left stranded in small craft at sea after paying large sums of money for passage to some agreed destination. As illicit landings invariably take place at night, many migrants have been led to believe that they have landed in the United States, only to discover later that they are on some uninhabited Caribbean island.

The risks to which the migrants are exposed are evidenced by the number of casualties recorded. The story in 1981 of the bodies of thirty Haitian migrants being washed ashore on Hillsboro Beach, Florida, may not be regarded as an isolated incident (Alien Migrant Interdiction, 2002). Further, and with increasing frequency in the Caribbean, as elsewhere in the world, people seeking migration opportunities have found themselves victims of international traffickers engaged in the sex industry, being forced into prostitution at the destination.

Cost to the countries of destination

Financial cost

Border controls and surveillance for the purpose of interdicting irregular migrants at sea are a significant cost to countries trying to control irregular migration. But, should the migrant succeed in landing, the costs of deportation to the country of origin, or social security support, are much greater. In those cases where migrants succeed in landing and later obtain work permits and are therefore permitted to remain legally, the host countries are faced with the cost of providing social services and education for the expanding migrant community. This is considered by some countries to make great demands on their national budgets.

Security

There are relatively small, but significant, groups engaged in smuggling, trafficking and other criminal activities, travelling within and outside the Caribbean to North America and Europe in pursuit of these illegal activities. In some cases, they are criminals and pose a threat to the countries in which they operate. Another group linked to criminality are the irregular migrants who, although without any prior criminal record, are forced by their impoverished economic and marginal social position at the transit location to become involved with the local criminal elements in an effort to survive before moving to their final destination. Transporters of irregular migrants, some of whom are a part of organized and well-armed criminal gangs, also pose a security risk on the high seas as well as to the states within which they operate.

Inclusion of irregular migrants into society at the destination

The migrants who reach a transit country must then negotiate with compatriots and other local residents for food, shelter and the means of obtaining a niche in the local economic and ethnic system. Finally, if onward migration is the goal, further negotiations must be effected, involving more 'middle men' at each stage of the process. At each level of negotiation, the irregular migrant is vulnerable to extortion and abuse. They also experience problems specifically associated with their irregular migrant status, especially in terms of access to housing, and medical and social services.

Health

The illegal status of the migrants at their destination means at best poor, and at worst no, access at all to services, in particular medical services. Added to this, the living conditions of illegal migrants lead to increased health risks, in particular with regard to infections and sexually transmitted diseases.

There is a high rate of HIV-Aids and tuberculosis in Haiti (UNDP, 2000). In the Turks and Caicos Islands, people applying for a work permit, which is reissued annually at varying costs, are subjected to a blood test. The work permit can be declined at any stage, based on the allegation (true or otherwise) that the individual's blood is 'not clean'. However, the fact that an immigrant seeking a work permit would be deported if found to be infected with HIV, tuberculosis or any other disease, serves to drive these individuals 'underground'. They remain untreated and pose a greater health risk to society than if the matter were dealt with openly.

Environment

The harmful effects of the journey are compounded by the equally unhealthy conditions in which many of the migrants are forced to live on arrival at their destination. They must remain under cover until they can regularize their status, and illegal migrants 'live rough', often without proper sanitation, clean water or adequate food. Others crowd in with friends and relatives who have legalized their resident status by obtaining work permits. Thus areas associated with migrant communities tend to comprise both legal and illegal residents. Invariably, these areas become environmentally degraded, adding to the unhealthy living standards of the migrants themselves, and to the prejudice against them.

Xenophobia and the image of the irregular migrant

Irregular migrants, in addition to being the victims of circumstances, usually also become the victims of negative societal attitudes at the destination, and this can contribute to the development of a vicious cycle of unfortunate events.

As discussed by Marmora (1999), the xenophobic attitude towards foreigners is not a new phenomenon. Underlying prejudice can manifest itself as violence or latent prejudice. Such feelings are based on cultural or ethnic differences within a society and become evident only under stress; for example, in situations of competition or perceived competition for jobs and services. These negative manifestations become part of the normal behaviour of one sector of society towards another and are generally tolerated by all. They may be based on negative feelings towards the 'outsider', the fear of losing privileges that stems from individual insecurity about one's own racial, social or economic standing. Black racial characteristics and poverty produce xenophobic attitudes towards Haitians by people who themselves are black and attempting to rise above poverty. The prejudice invariably represents a subconscious fear of the status or ideals of society being jeopardized, or at least compromised.

The xenophobic picture of the migrant groups easily becomes institutionalized in the host society's efforts to 'manage' these groups, and to establish policies to control their numbers and their privileges. Thus the distinction of the migrant groups may never fade, nor will their low social status improve. This phenomenon is reflected in the terminology – the 'belongers' and the 'non-belongers' – used in the Turks and Caicos Islands to distinguish 'true Turks' from Haitians, even those of the second and third generation. The effort to maintain the distinction is further reflected in the fact that it is not common for Turks and Caicos Islanders and Haitians to intermarry or have children together.

In stark contrast are the attitudes and behaviour of the Turks and Caicos Islanders towards the Dominicans, who are perceived as possessing attractive 'Latin' physical characteristics because of their *mulatto* or *mestizo* heritage. Migrant Dominican women are favoured for 'reception desk' positions in bars, clubs and restaurants to attract clientele. These images and perspectives become articulated, consciously or unconsciously, in society and have an impact on immigration policy.

Of all the countries in the region, Haiti is the most impoverished economically, politically and environmentally. The irony is that, because of this degradation, it is also the country with the least opportunities for legal or formal migration. Moreover, the persisting episodes of both regular and irregular migration contribute to the continued destabilization of the Haitian economy and society. The migrants themselves, even those who fail, feed the dynamics for future flows, perpetuating the process.

The wider issues: poverty and irregular migration

Although the selection criteria for regular emigration are complex and are not solely determined by simple economic or political forces, countries with the largest regular emigration are also the same as those with the highest rates of irregular emigration. Over the 1980s and 1990s, Haiti, the Dominican Republic, Jamaica, Grenada, St Vincent and St Kitts-Nevis experienced high net emigration, all with 15 per cent or more of the population emigrating in the 1991–92 fiscal year (CCPHC, 1994). The countries with net immigration are the Bahamas, the US Virgin Islands, the Turks and Caicos Islands and, in the 1990s, Antigua-Barbuda. The British Virgin Islands and Antigua have experienced high emigration levels but these have been exceeded by higher immigration levels, accounting for 26 per cent and 42 per cent of their populations, respectively.

GDP figures for selected Caribbean countries demonstrate the large divergence within the region. While the GDP *per capita* for the US Virgin Islands in the year 2000 was in excess of US$15,000, for the Bahamas US$13,871 and for Barbados US$8,266, it was only US$2,061 for the Dominican Republic, and less than US$2,000 for Jamaica, less than US$1,000 for Guyana and, even lower, less than US$400 for Haiti (World Bank, 2002). Furthermore, the discrepancy in the GDP *per capita* rates between Caribbean countries had increased progressively over the second half of the twentieth century. Thus the contrast between the economic levels of the major countries of emigration (regular and irregular) and those of immigration within the Caribbean is very great.

The disparities between the Caribbean countries in their material living standards can also be indicated by measures of human poverty. Haiti is worse off by far with a poverty index in excess of 46, ranking it seventy-first in the global order. Even in Caribbean terms, this is alarming, since the next highest poverty index is recorded for the Dominican Republic at a value of 20 per cent and in twentieth position worldwide (UNDP, 2000; see Thomas-Hope, 2003).

The limited access to basic human goods such as safe water, health services and sanitation reflects the relatively poor situation of many Caribbean countries but, above all, it confirms the particular plight of Haiti (Thomas-Hope, 2003). Similarly, literacy rates (at 73.5 per cent in 1998) and school enrolment in Haiti indicate low levels both in absolute and relative terms within the Caribbean. Fertility rates recorded in Haiti are the highest for the region, as are infant mortality and maternal mortality rates. Life expectancy and food security are the lowest for the region, and among the lowest worldwide. These demographic trends indicate an average annual population growth of 1.6 per cent (the highest in the region) and a young population (only 3.6 per cent of the population was 65 and over in 1998) that will continue to reinforce the size of irregular emigrant streams from that country for many years to come (UNDP, 2000).

Finally, in Haiti, as a consequence of the political and economic circumstances, environmental conditions deteriorated progressively throughout the 1980s and 1990s, exacerbating the migration situation even further. Haitian migrants have already been described as leaving their homes because their country has become an 'environmental basket-case' (Myers, 1993: 189, cited in Black, 1998: 24).

Regardless of which indicators are used to measure material and non-material human circumstances, there can be no doubt about the extent of the disparity that exists between Caribbean countries. The indicated data confirm the same absolute and relative picture of the Caribbean region in the global context, and of Haiti in the Caribbean context. Furthermore, the data reflect factors that cannot be measured by indicators, such as confidence in the future of one's country, and sense of security and self-esteem, all of which are desperately low.

Conclusion

There is no sign of the demand for migration abating in the Caribbean, and irregular movements will certainly continue and possibly increase. The trends show the emergence of new sources of large numbers of emigrants and new directions of movement when routes to preferred destination countries are blocked more effectively. It is evident that the urgent formulation of policies needs to focus not only on the short-term management of irregular migration through increased restrictions and policing, but also to prioritize on policies that face the challenge of finding enduring long-term solutions.

Based on current trends, and barring any sudden, dramatic events, Haiti, the Dominican Republic, Guyana and Jamaica will most probably continue to be the source of significant numbers of irregular migrants in the coming decades. The Bahamas, and the Turks and Caicos Islands constitute at present – and are likely to continue to be – the major transit countries for Haitians en route to the United States. Citizens of the Dominican Republic will continue to go to Puerto Rico in order to try to enter the United States; and to countries of the eastern Caribbean such as Dominica and St Lucia as the major stopping points to the French Departments of Martinique and Guadeloupe, and thence to mainland Europe. Similarly, people from the Dominican Republic and Jamaica will continue to move to Anguilla, Antigua, St Martin and other islands of the north-east Caribbean.

Policy

Policies concerned with the short- and medium-term issues relating to irregular migration are undoubtedly required. With respect to the Caribbean, these need to address principally border control management, social stability and national security, and the costs associated with retaining or deporting people. But the approach to be adopted for border management has not been universally agreed. In the first place, monitoring is required to ensure that countries and their agents abide by the international agreements concerning the rights and protection of refugees and other persons in need of protection. Efforts in border management and control of irregular movements must be handled with due regard for the human rights of the individuals concerned. Furthermore, according to a liberal democratic view, people should not be returned to their home country against their will. However, there was a dramatic reversal of this approach in US policy in 1994. At that time, Cubans seeking sanctuary in the United States were granted asylum in return for the Cuban government's promise to prevent others from leaving the country (Weiner, 1995).

Because of the complexity of the overall pattern of migration, there are implications for the entire Caribbean region. It is essential, therefore, that arrangements are put in place that will enhance cooperation between states on migration management. This should incorporate many aspects of the relocation operation, including the collection of accurate data on irregular migration and the need to share this information regularly with other countries in the region. The link between migrant transportation, and smuggling and trafficking rings makes it imperative that bilateral and multilateral agreements on the intelligence of these operations are strengthened. This would enable the enhancement of the networks and the establishment of focal points in each country to strengthen regional approaches for combating trafficking and smuggling, and for regularly exchanging information on this issue (IMP, 2001).

Regional efforts are not supported wholeheartedly, as each country is potentially at risk of suffering a negative impact by any change in the status quo with regard to regional migrants and North American immigration regulations. Besides, as efforts are intensified to curb illegal entries, countries will have to invest more resources into this effort. Similarly, deportation costs will continue to be a burden on the countries involved.

Part of the dynamics and the irony of irregular migration is the need for cheap, unskilled labour during periods of economic growth. Despite the claims of governments to be committed to stopping these movements, many of the factors that influence them are to be found in the very interaction that takes place between the countries of immigration and emigration.

At times, there is a demand to curtail immigration in the destination countries. As political pressure mounts, this leads to pressure being put ultimately on the governments of the sending countries, as evidenced by the US intervention in Haiti in September 1994, and the agreement with Cuba in 1995. But under normal circumstances the prevailing mood in the destination countries is less obvious, as illegal migrants and their legal compatriots provide valuable services in sectors that are shunned by nationals – and at wages lower than would be accepted by nationals. The presence of illegal migrants will therefore continue to be guarded by those who gain the most from their continued arrival.

Nevertheless, opportunities available to irregular migrants of escaping poverty and improving their economic position at the destination are eroded by their illegal status. This contributes to continued poverty at the destination as they are forced to survive on the lowest margins of existence. Caribbean countries are linked to each other, and to North American countries, not only because of past and present diplomatic relations, but also because existing migrant communities are connected in the system of transnational interactions and flows. Should the circumstances of the migrant communities deteriorate, this would provide additional fuel for national groups to lobby against the illegal migrants.

The impact of irregular migration on the countries of origin is outside the scope of this chapter. Yet it is here that efforts for a durable solution must ultimately lie. The problem of persistent poverty and the international and national structures that reinforce deprivation have to be confronted. A long-term approach must also include environmental solutions. When countries become as environmentally degraded and impoverished as Haiti, the implications for migration, whether regular or irregular, will undoubtedly intensify. Many Haitians are already environmental refugees and this number is likely to increase exponentially in the future (Alien Migrant Interdiction, 2002). Given this fact, the countries of the north will be faced with the challenge that new waves of asylum seekers claiming environmental refugee status may well be supported in their demands by international lobbyists.

References

Ahmed, I. (1997). 'Exit, Voice and Citizenship', in T. Hammar, G. Brochmann, K. Tamas and T. Faist (eds), *International Migration, Immobility and Development*. Oxford: Oxford International Publishers, Berg Imprint: 159–219.

Alien Migrant Interdiction (2002). 'US Coastguard'. Available at: www.uscg.mil/hq/g-l/mle/a,iostats1.htm.

Basch, L., N. G. Schiller and C. S. Blanc (1994). *Nations Unbound*, Amsterdam: Gordon and Breach.

Black, R. (1998). *Refugees, Environment and Development*, London: Longman.

Boyle, P., K. Halfacree and V. Robinson (1998). *Exploring Contemporary Migration*, London: Longman.

Castles, S. and M. J. Miller (1998). *The Age of Migration: International Movements in the Modern World*, 2nd edn, London: Macmillan.

CCPHC (Caribbean Community Regional Census Office) (1994). *Commonwealth Caribbean Population and Housing Census, 1991*, Port of Spain, Trinidad.

CNN (2001). 'Migration on Rise Worldwide', 2 November. Accessed on CNN.com.

IMP (International Migration Policy Programme) (2001). 'Irregular Migration and the Protection of Refugees and Other Persons in Need of Protection – Summary', Background paper, Module 5, presented at The International Migration Policy Seminar for the Caribbean Region, Geneva: UNFPA UNITAR IOM ILO: 8–9.

Kempadoo, K. (ed.) (1999). *Sun, Sex and Gold: Tourism and Sex Work in the Caribbean*, New York: Rowman and Littlefield.

Marmora, L. (1999). *International Migration Policies and Programmes*, Geneva: International Organization for Migration.

Marshall, D. (1979). *The Haitian Problem: Illegal Migration to the Bahamas*, Kingston, Jamaica: University of the West Indies, Mona, Institute of Social and Economic Research.

Marshall, D. (1984). 'Vincentian Contract Labour Migration to Barbados: The Satisfaction of Mutual Needs?', *Social and Economic Studies*, 33: 63–92.

McCoy, T. L. and C. H. Wood (1982). *Caribbean Workers in the Florida Sugar Cane Industry*, Occasional Paper, No. 2. Gainesville, FL: Center for Latin American Studies, University of Florida.

Preeg, E. (1985). 'Migration and Development in Hispaniola', in R. Pastor (ed.), *Migration and Development in the Caribbean: The Unexplored Connection*, Boulder, CO: Westview Press: 140–56.

Schiller, N. G. and G. Fouron (1999). 'Transnational Lives and National Identities: The Identity Politics of Haitian Immigrants', in M. P. Smith and L. E. Guarnizo (eds), *Transnationalism from Below*, New Brunswick, NJ: Transaction Publishers.

Thomas-Hope, E. (1992). *Explanation in Caribbean Migration: Perception and the Image – Jamaica, Barbados, St Vincent,* London: Macmillan.

Thomas-Hope, E. (1999). 'Emigration Dynamics in the Anglophone Caribbean', in R. Appleyard (ed.), *Emigration Dynamics in Developing Countries, Vol. III: Mexico, Central America and the Caribbean,* Aldershot: Ashgate: 232–84.

Thomas-Hope, E. (2003). *Irregular Migration and Asylum Seekers in the Caribbean,* Discussion Paper, No. 2003/48, Helsinki: UNU-WIDER.

UNDP (United Nations Development Programme) (2000). *Human Development Report 2000,* New York Oxford: Oxford University Press.

Weiner, M. (1995). *The Global Migration Crisis,* New York: HarperCollins.

World Bank (2000). *World Development Indicators 2000,* CD-ROM, Washington, DC: World Bank.

15

A Tale of Two Countries: Poverty and Income Distribution Among Immigrants in Denmark and Sweden Since 1984

Kræn Blume, Björn Gustafsson, Peder J. Pedersen and Mette Verner

Introduction

In recent decades, low-skilled immigration to the rich OECD countries has been of increasing importance. Many European OECD countries were open to immigration by people from outside the rich OECD area until the first oil price shock in the mid-1970s. At that time, many countries, including Denmark and Sweden, enacted legislation to stop the flow of guest workers, and this has been in effect since then.

In the Nordic area, there has been free mobility of labour since 1954. Furthermore, both Denmark and Sweden are members of the EU, which constitutes a broad area of free labour mobility. The cross-country net mobility of citizens, both intra-EU and intra-Nordic, has, however, been modest. A fairly new, but important, factor regarding international mobility is the relatively large net immigration of people from the less developed countries to many countries in the EU, Denmark and Sweden included. Because of the restriction on guest workers, this new wave of immigrants has consisted of 'tied movers'; that is, individuals moving for family reunification and of refugees. Highly specialized people from outside the rich OECD area can obtain a residence permit, but only for a job with a specific firm for a specialized vacancy. Thus a major change since the mid-1970s in many EU countries concerns the composition of immigration, from being work-related to becoming a difficult integration process into labour markets characterized by high skill requirements and relatively high minimum wages.

The difficulties of immigrants in integrating into the labour market are reflected in the ratios between unemployment rates for immigrants and for the native population; see OECD (2001, 2002). These ratios range from a level of 2–3 in a number of European countries, including Denmark and Sweden, and a level of about 1 in the USA and Canada. These major deviations are the net outcome of differences not only in labour market institutions, but most probably also in immigration policies. In Canada, for example, immigration permits are granted on qualitative criteria, which enable the person to enter a job quickly, while similar criteria for education, experience, financial status and so on are largely absent in the EU.

The increasing importance of net immigration from the less developed countries, compounded by the slow and imperfect integration into the host country's labour market that is obvious in many countries, is expected to have an impact on aggregate income distribution and on poverty rates. We expect the impact in the European welfare states to be greater on market income compared to disposable income. Consequently, we expect to find, in empirical studies, an increasing gap between the poverty levels among the native populace and immigrants from the less developed countries.

A small number of cross-sectional studies exist that illustrate the differences in poverty levels between immigrants and host-country citizens. Some of these results are surveyed briefly in the next section. Then, using fairly comparable panel datasets going back to 1984, we argue that Denmark and Sweden are relevant case studies for a comparative analysis of the development in poverty levels between immigrants and natives. We also discuss briefly a number of economic and institutional factors that make a country a relevant comparative case. The following section introduces our data and describes the construction of the poverty line used in the analysis before we review the development of poverty levels, as observed in Denmark and Sweden.

Some earlier studies on immigrant poverty

Earlier cross-sectional studies from 'classical' immigration countries show a substantial difference in poverty rates, depending on the country or region of origin. This fact is illustrated in Figure 15.1 with cross-sectional data for the United States from 1980, which show that the range of poverty levels is between 6 per cent and 37 per cent. These are summary cross-sectional data, and part of the difference could be a reflection of the changing arrival patterns over time and subsequent variations in the duration of time in the United States.

Based on cross-sectional data for 1991 for twenty-five ethnic groups in Canadian metropolitan areas (CMA), Kazemipur and Halli (2001) report similar results. Using the same data to illustrate regional variations, Kazemipur and Halli (2001) find a immigrant poverty-level pattern that fluctuates between 8 per cent and 32 per cent.

A regional variation of this magnitude is not observed for all residents of Canada, as is seen in Figure 15.2. It is evident that poverty levels are much higher for immigrants than for native-born citizens in all high-poverty regions. There is evidence that the economic upturn in the late 1990s resulted in

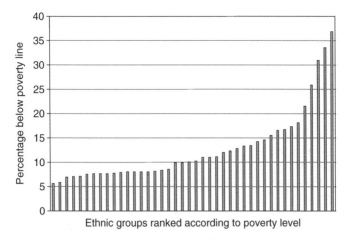

Figure 15.1 Percentage of immigrants in the USA below the poverty line, by origin of sending country, 1980
Source: Borjas (1990).

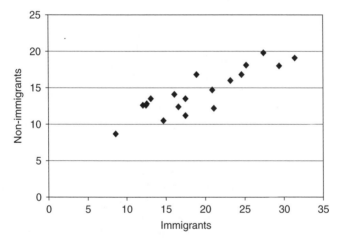

Figure 15.2 Poverty rates for immigrants and non-immigrants according to region (CMA), 1991
Source: Kazemipur and Halli (2001).

reductions in the poverty rates of recent immigrants, but there have been no changes in the situation for non-immigrants; see Smith and Jackson (2002).

In a number of studies, poverty in Canada – including its concentration on immigrants and the concentration of poverty and deprivation to urban areas – is considered similar to that found in the United States and Northern Europe. Ley and Smith (1997) compare the geographic concentration of poverty in three major cities in Canada for 1971 and 1991. They find increasing dispersion over this period with regard to metropolitan poverty. Immigrants, according to Ley and Smith, are just one group among those with limited opportunities. Ley (1999) discusses what is termed as 'the myth of the Canadian immigrant underclass'. Low-income problems are discussed, but Ley (1999) also highlights a broad range of mitigating factors in addition to the purely financial indicators. In Canada, as in Northern Europe, poverty and deprivation are concentrated to a large extent in neighbourhoods in which most of the housing is subsidized.

Ekberg (1994) focuses on Sweden, and reports that, in 1991, foreign-born families had a poverty rate of 14 per cent while the corresponding figure for the total population was 8 per cent. Poverty rates among foreign-born individuals are negatively related to the years since arrival in the host country. This finding also appears in other studies using data from approximately the same period (Gustafsson, 1997; Hammarstedt, 2001). To take two examples: while the cohort of 1988–90 arrivals, mainly refugees, have a poverty rate of 28 per cent, immigrants arriving before 1969, who were mainly work migrants, have a rate as low as 7 per cent: this is even slightly lower than that of the total population.

An earlier study, in 1996, which followed up the development of adults from the less developed countries immigrating to Sweden during the 1980s shows relatively large poverty rates (Gustafsson, 1999). For example, while 12 per cent of native male adults were classified as poor, the corresponding proportion for males originating from Poland was 22 per cent, from Turkey 46 per cent, and from Iran as high as 63 per cent (female rates are at the same levels). Results from an analysis of the risks of being poor in 1996 indicated that in addition to factors such as education and family type, the work history of the immigrant since arrival had strong predictive value.

Bell (1997), using data from the General Household Survey (GHS), and Berthoud (1998) with data from the British Household Panel Survey (BHPS) find that immigrants, on average, perform as well or even slightly better than natives, with regard to market income in the United Kingdom. The data in Berthoud (1998) are disaggregated on a small number of different immigrant groups, and this more disaggregated evidence indicates a considerable fluctuation in the average market income, from a high level for the first or second generation white immigrant population to a low level for first and second generation arrivals from Pakistan and Bangladesh. It is interesting to note that first as well as second generation arrivals from India have a similar average market income to the native-born white population. The gaps between high and low with regard to disposable income are only slightly smaller. Using data from the German Socioeconomic Panel (GSOEP) for the years 1994–98, Büchel and Frick (2004) found that in West

Germany the average market income for non-EU immigrants was around 70 per cent of the average level for the native-born German population. However, with regard to disposable income, this immigrant group earned 80 per cent of what was earned by natives.

The relevance of Denmark and Sweden as comparative cases

Denmark and Sweden share similar labour market and welfare state characteristics. But, at the same time, they differ considerably in cyclical profiles and immigration experience during recent decades, and this fact creates a unique case for comparative analyses. The labour market in both countries is characterized by a high level of unionization, high relative minimum wages, egalitarian wage distribution, the public sector as a major employer, and very high female participation rates. Both countries have experienced a secular shift from low-skilled industrial jobs towards service-sector jobs. Taxes are very high in both countries, and these are reflected on the expenditure side by the universal residence-based benefits for unemployment, housing, children and old age. At the same time, the public sector offers a wide range of services in the areas of education, health, and child and elderly care, either free or at a low cost.

Both countries have followed similar immigration policies; that is, immigration from low-income countries has been restricted to tied movers and refugees. But there have been big differences in both the stocks and flows in international mobility. The initial stock relative to the native population was much higher in Sweden, while in Denmark throughout the 1990s the relative increase in the number of immigrants was greater. Further, there are major differences in the composition of immigrant origins, both on the part of the stocks and the flows of arrivals. Although Denmark and Sweden have experienced major deviations with regard to cyclical profiles during the period analysed, both also had problems of high unemployment among immigrants from the less developed countries in the 1990s.

With regard to income distribution, both countries have very low levels of inequality in equivalent disposable incomes; that is, after the equalizing effects of the highly progressive taxes and regressive transfers have been eliminated. While the level of Gini coefficients and poverty rates are low in both countries, they have increased in Sweden (Gustafsson and Palmer, 2002), and decreased in Denmark during most of the period analysed.

Data and poverty line

Swedish data

The data used for Sweden in this study are from the so-called SWIP database, which consists of 10 per cent of the Swedish immigrant population covering the years 1968 to 1999, merged with a 1 per cent sample of the native population.[1] It is based on administrative registers and contains a large number of demographic, labour market and income variables. In the present study, we use observations for the years 1984–97, and immigrants in this sample are defined as persons born outside Sweden. This dataset has the same advantage as the Danish data; it includes a large number of foreign-born individuals compared to samples typically used to measure poverty. There is also the advantage of a panel property, which makes it possible to follow individuals over time and to apply an observation period longer than one year. However, the narrow definition of a family – defined as one or two adults and their children (a person is regarded as an adult on turning 18 years of age) – is a disadvantage. Most important, a young adult of 18 years and older but living with his/her parents is treated as a separate unit. Consequently, many young people reported to have high poverty rates might, in reality, be sharing income with their parents. This should be kept in mind when interpreting results for young adults, but as the definition of a family is similar in the datasets for Denmark, there should be no distortion in the cross-country comparison because of this.

Danish data

The Danish dataset is extracted from the Institute of Local Government Studies (AKF) panel database, which is built on administrative registers in Statistics Denmark and covers the period since 1984. The panel dataset contains a large number of demographic, labour market, income, taxes and benefits variables. The data include 100 per cent representation of the immigrants and their children, and a 10 per cent representative sample of the whole population. This sampling scheme thus involves an overlap between the representative population sample and the immigrant sample. The classification of people as immigrants, descendants and natives follows the definitions applied by Statistics Denmark; see Poulsen and Lange (1998). They differ, albeit only slightly, from the Swedish classification criteria; that is, being born in or outside Sweden.

The low-income measure

To construct our low-income line (or poverty line), based on the recommendations in Atkinson *et al.* (2002), we use 60 per cent of the median in the distribution of equivalence-adjusted disposable incomes as the cut-off point. We use the OECD equivalence scale applied to disposable household incomes (including child support and subsidies to housing) for conversion to individual incomes; that is, the weight is 1.0 for the first adult in household, 0.7 for other adults, and 0.5 for each child. The equivalent scale-adjusted household income is assigned to each household member, and each household is assigned a weight equal to the number of members irrespective of age. It should be noted that the low-income line is calculated from the income distribution for the full representative samples; that is, including individuals of all ages. In the analysis below, however, only individuals aged 18–65 are included.

The calculated poverty rates are based on income as reported in administrative registers. Work and earnings in the shadow economy are consequently not covered. Danish survey studies of participation in the shadow economy result in somewhat conflicting evidence regarding whether participation differs between natives and immigrants and refugees. The most recent evidence (in Rezaei, 2004) finds, however, very low hourly wages for immigrants in the shadow economy. Based on available evidence, we thus conclude that inclusion of incomes from the shadow economy would not influence reported poverty rates in any significant way.

Descriptive evidence

Recent immigration patterns

Since the mid-1980s, the number of immigrants in Denmark and Sweden has increased at a relatively stable rate. As seen from Figure 15.3, the stock of immigrants in Sweden has been much higher than in Denmark throughout the period. In 2001, the share of immigrants in the total population is 12 per cent in Sweden, whereas it is 5.5 per cent in Denmark; and the relative share of immigrants is significantly larger in Sweden.

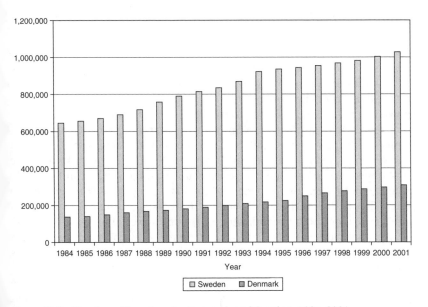

Figure 15.3 Number of immigrants, Denmark and Sweden, 1984–2001

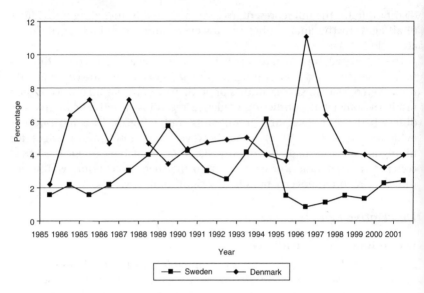

Figure 15.4   Relative changes in stock of immigrants, Denmark and Sweden (percentages)

The development in the stocks of immigrants appears to be fairly smooth. This, however, changes considerably when we look at the relative year-to-year trend in the two countries (Figure 15.4): the relative increase in the stock of immigrants has been higher in Denmark than in Sweden; 1989 and 1994 are exceptions.

Another major difference is noted when we look in more detail at the composition of the immigrant population by national origin. Based on the UN classification of more developed and less developed countries, we have the breakdown of the immigrant stock from these two country groups as shown in Figure 15.5. According to the UN classification, the more developed countries include all the European countries (except Turkey, Cyprus and a number of former Soviet republics) and the USA, Canada, Japan, Australia and New Zealand; see Poulsen and Lange (1998). At each point in time the share of people from the less developed country group is higher in Denmark, although both countries experienced an increasing share throughout the period. The fairly low share in Sweden is in part a reflection of the very high number of people from Finland, who constitute an exception to the otherwise relatively low level of cross-national migration flows between the Nordic countries. Between 1980 and 2000, the absolute number of immigrants from Finland dropped from 251,342 to 195,447, which in relative terms implies a decrease from 40.1 per cent to 19.5 per cent. A major part of the increase in the share of the less-developed-country immigrants in Sweden thus reflects return migration to Finland.

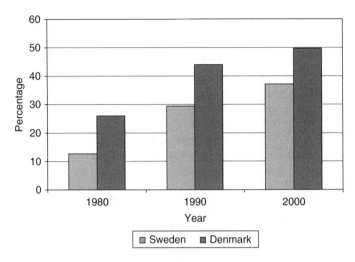

Figure 15.5 Relative percentage of immigrants, Sweden and Denmark, from less developed countries, 1980–2000

Table 15.1 Number of residents from major non-Western countries living in Sweden and Denmark, 2001

Sweden		*Denmark*	
FR Yugoslavia	73 274	Turkey	29 680
Iraq	55 696	Bosnia and Herzegovina	18 027
Bosnia and Herzegovina	52 198	Iraq	15 099
Iran	51 844	FR Yugoslavia	12 545
Poland	40 506	Lebanon	11 924
Turkey	32 453	Somalia	11 847
Chile	27 153	Iran	11 348
Lebanon	20 228	Poland	10 391
Syria	14 646	Pakistan	10 313

Differences in the composition of immigrant origin are highlighted in Table 15.1, which shows the number of immigrants coming from the nine non-Western countries with the largest expatriate communities in Sweden and Denmark. The poverty shares of these immigrant groups in Denmark and Sweden are shown in Figures 15.8 and 15.9. People from Bosnia and Herzegovina, however, are not included in the charts as they arrived in the two host countries only in the second half of the 1990s. Thus income data on their part are only for a short period. As can be seen from Table 15.1, ranking by country of origin is different for Sweden and Denmark. Sweden has a considerable community of former Chileans and Syrians, while Somali and Pakistani immigrants are well represented in Denmark.

Trends in the low-income incidence

Figure 15.6 shows the percentage of individuals in Denmark having an equivalent disposable income of less than 60 per cent of the median. The low-income incidence for native Danes appears to be very stable at around 10 per cent, with a very slight decrease in later years. For the immigrants as a whole, however, the picture is very different. From a level of less than 20 per cent at the beginning of the observation period, the low-income incidence increases steadily until the early 1990s, when it stabilizes. This levelling-off may be attributed partly to the more favourable business cycle in effect from 1994. When the immigrant population is divided into people from more developed and less developed countries, it becomes clear that the trend for all immigrants is largely driven by the group from the less developed countries. For immigrants coming from the more developed countries, the low-income share is less, below 15 per cent in 1984, but increasing to a level of just under 20 per cent by 1999.

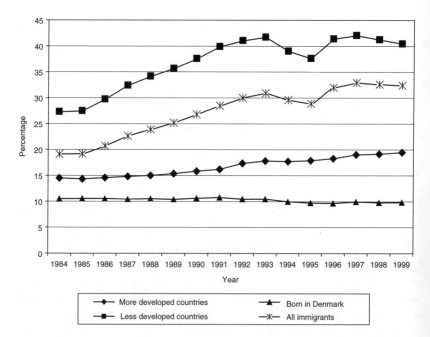

Figure 15.6 Percentage of individuals in Denmark with equivalent disposable income less than 60 per cent of the median

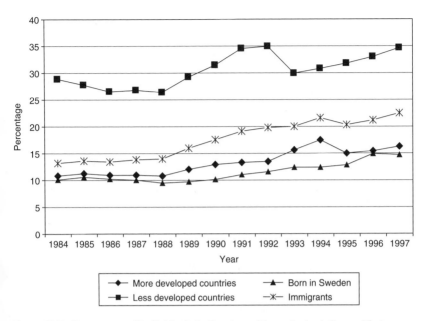

Figure 15.7 Percentage of individuals in Sweden with equivalent disposable income less than 60 per cent of the median

Figure 15.7 shows the picture for Sweden. Initially, the percentage of low-income individuals among the native population is very similar to the situation in Denmark, but the percentage steadily increased over the 1990s. In relative terms, the increase is 50 per cent, rising from 10 per cent to 15 per cent of the Swedish population. Among the immigrants, the low-income percentage increases in the late 1980s from about 14 per cent to approximately 23 per cent. This means that the poverty rates for immigrants in Sweden are lower than in Denmark for each year during the period analysed. We also find bigger differences in poverty rates for each year in the period for immigrants and natives in Denmark compared to Sweden. Finally, for both countries, a widening of the difference is observed between the poverty rates for natives and immigrants throughout the period.

In Figure 15.7, when immigrants to Sweden are separated into the two country groups (the more developed and the less developed countries), we see that immigrants from the more developed countries are on average only slightly more likely than the native-born to qualify as low-income individuals. This observation applies to the entire period studied. For immigrants from the less developed countries, the low-income share is around 30–35 per cent, with an increasing trend.

The aggregated numbers by origin given in Figures 15.6 and 15.7 do not identify the factors that would explain the differences in poverty levels between Swedish and Danish immigrants, nor can they explain the larger gap in Denmark in the poverty levels between the native population and immigrants. In this context, a number of factors are relevant. First, we have already observed that the relative increase in the stock of immigrants in Denmark was much higher than in Sweden during the period, indicating that immigrants in Denmark, especially in the 1990s, spent a shorter period, on average, in the host country. This implies a lower labour force attachment and consequently a lower level of market income. Another factor of potential importance is the difference in the composition of immigrants by ethnic background, as it is well documented that the ease with which immigrants integrate into labour markets differs between different groups (compare Table 15.1 and Figure 15.5). We explore this factor further later in the chapter.

Next, as mentioned earlier, the cyclical profiles have differed considerably between the two countries in the period analysed. Sweden had full employment, leading to excess demand for labour, until the late 1980s. This was followed by an extremely fast increase in unemployment and a decline in labour force participation in the first years of the 1990s. Looking at Figure 15.7, we find a fairly stable difference between the poverty level for immigrants and the native population until 1988, followed by a significant increase in this difference in the depression years around 1990. Finally, the difference stabilizes from the mid-1990s at a higher level than in the 1980s. In Denmark, unemployment increased from a high initial level between 1986 and 1993. Since then, unemployment has declined strongly. The poverty-level gap between immigrants and the native population increased throughout the period because of rising unemployment, but it stabilized once the cyclical situation improved again.

The factors mentioned here will, of course, interact in different ways. It should be emphasized, however, that the labour market integration of immigrants, both in its extent and its speed, is of fundamental importance when comparing the deviations in poverty rates between Denmark and Sweden, because in switching from market incomes to disposable incomes, taxes and benefits have, to a large extent, the same structure in both countries. Overall, according to OECD (2001, 2002), the ratio between the unemployment rate for immigrants and for the native population is slightly lower in Denmark than in Sweden. At the same time, labour force participation is higher for native Danes than for native Swedes, and participation rates in both countries have been low, and on average falling, for immigrants from the less developed countries during the 1990s. The bottom line of these arguments seems to be that the differences in poverty levels must, for the most part, be ascribed to variations in arrival patterns and national origin.

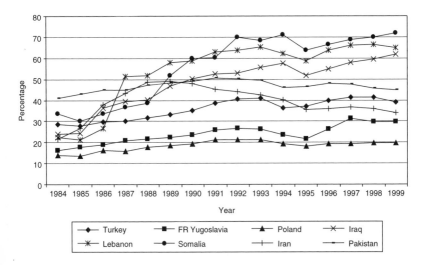

Figure 15.8 Low-income percentages for immigrants from selected countries, Denmark

From the previous figures, it is clear that immigrants from the less developed countries are exposed to a much higher risk of having low-income status. These low-income percentages are analysed in more detail in Figure 15.8. The low-income percentages are generally the lowest for immigrants from Turkey, Poland and FR Yugoslavia, and have followed similar patterns, although at different levels. For immigrants from Pakistan, the low-income percentage has been steady, at around 40–50 per cent. For immigrants from Iran, a peak was reached in 1989 and their low-income percentage has been decreasing steadily since then. On the part of immigrants from Lebanon, Iraq and Somalia, low-income percentages have shown an increasing trend throughout the period, with 1995 being the only exception.

We see in Figure 15.9 that in Sweden, immigrants from Poland and FR Yugoslavia have the lowest low-income percentage, as was the case in Denmark. Immigrants from Turkey, Iraq and Somalia (data only available after 1993) have the highest low-income incidence, with substantial variation around an increasing trend. The trend of immigration from Iran has been decreasing from relatively high levels. Fluctuations in levels and profiles over time in Figures 15.8 and 15.9 reflect, among other things, different arrival patterns and duration of residence in the two countries.

Looking more closely at the countries covered in Figures 15.8 and 15.9, some interesting new aspects appear. For people from FR Yugoslavia, we find in both countries an increasing trend in the percentage of low incomes, with a higher level in Denmark, except around 1994. We also find some interesting differences by decades for those from Iran: in the 1980s, the

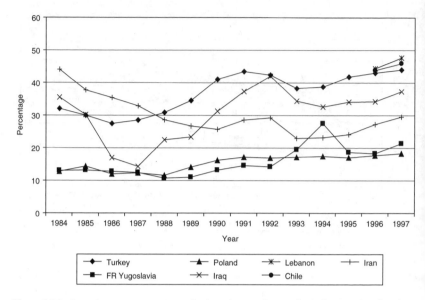

Figure 15.9   Low-income percentages for immigrants from selected countries, Sweden

low-income percentages increased in Denmark, but decreased in Sweden, while in the 1990s, the low-income percentage was stationary in Sweden, but falling in Denmark, reaching nearly the same level in both countries by the late 1990s. The low-income percentage for Polish immigrants has a similar profile in the two countries, but its level is higher in Denmark. The gap is closing, however, by the end of the period. Finally, it is interesting to take note of Turkey. This is the only group of immigrants with approximately the same absolute number of people residing in both Denmark and Sweden (see Table 15.1). The incidence of low incomes is very similar, but seems to have been higher in Sweden since the cyclical turning point in 1989. Thus, of the four countries compared most closely here, we find the low-income percentages are higher in Denmark, but the differences tend to decline towards the end of the period. All four countries are, or were, refugee countries, while immigrants from Turkey, the only country with a higher low-income percentage in Sweden, are guest workers and tied movers. To analyse these pairwise country differences would be an interesting topic for future study.

Poverty rates and years since immigration

The data above indicate a general trend of low-income incidence for immigrants compared to the native population. It is, however, important to recognize that these simple measures do not reveal important determinants, such as the number of years individuals have spent in the host country. Depending on the countries of origin, an integration period may be needed before a certain level of income is achieved. One way to examine this is to focus on 'arrival cohorts' and follow their development over time to determine whether low-income status is a transitory phenomenon from which it is possible to 'escape', or whether it is a more persistent problem. Furthermore, follow-up of the arrival groups makes it possible to examine whether some cohorts are doing better than others. This may, of course, be related to the immigrant composition in terms of country of origin, age and educational level. Further, there is the issue of return to the home country, or on-migration to a third country, meaning that some people leave the cohort and that this exit can be – and most probably is – selective. Historically, return-migration from Denmark and Sweden has been much greater among immigrants from the developed countries than from developing countries; see Jensen and Pedersen (2004).

Figure 15.10 shows the low-income percentages for four different immigrant cohorts coming from the more developed countries, based on the number of years spent in Denmark. It is striking that, for these immigrants, the low-income percentage steadily decreases with the years since arrival. All cohorts experience a low-income percentage of around 45 per cent in the first year after arrival, but after eleven years, the percentage is at or below 20 per cent. Though the pattern is very similar irrespective of the year of entry, it is noteworthy that low-income percentages for the 1984 immigrants

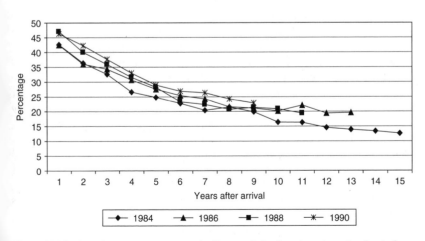

Figure 15.10 Low-income percentages in Denmark for four immigrant cohorts from the more developed countries, by years since arrival

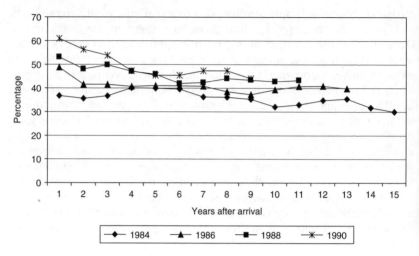

Figure 15.11 Low-income percentages in Denmark for four cohorts of immigrants from the less developed countries, by years since arrival

are generally the lowest, whereas the 1990 cohort is generally the highest. As can be seen from Figure 15.11, this latter point also holds for immigrants from the less developed countries, and for them it is even more pronounced. Compared to the more developed countries, the low-income shares decline much more slowly for immigrants from the less developed countries, and they tend to stabilize at a much higher level. Also, differences between the cohorts are generally larger, meaning that the various cohorts experience very different probabilities of having low incomes. This, of course, also reflects the differences in national background, as illustrated in Figure 15.8.

Figures 15.12 and 15.13 show similar data for Sweden for the same arrival cohorts. For the developed-country immigrants, the low-income percentage fluctuates on arrival between 27 per cent and 30 per cent for all four cohorts, and is thus lower than in Denmark. However, as in Denmark, we see a general decline in the low-income percentage as the period of residence increases. After eight years in Sweden, the low-income percentage stabilizes at around 20 per cent, a level similar to that found in Denmark. Also as in Denmark, the immigrants in the 1984 cohort generally had a lower risk of having a low income than the later-arriving cohorts.

In Figure 15.13, the trends for the cohorts of immigrants from the less developed country group tell a very different story than for the immigrants from developed countries. The low-income percentages in the first year after arrival vary considerably over the cohorts, and in spite of decreasing low-income rates in the very early years, they increase again after 3–6 years (depending on the arrival cohort). The level is significantly higher, especially

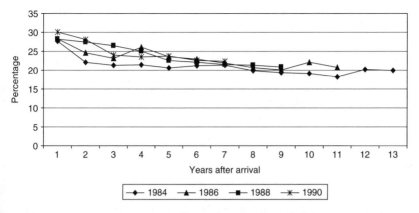

Figure 15.12 Low-income percentages in Sweden for four immigrant cohorts from the more developed countries, by years since arrival

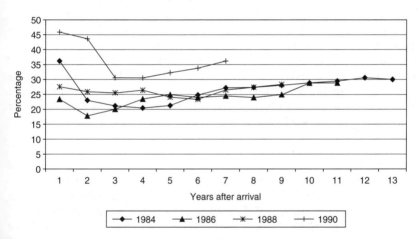

Figure 15.13 Low-income percentages in Sweden for four cohorts of immigrants from the less developed countries, by years since arrival

for the 1990 cohort, than for the other cohorts examined. It is interesting that the economic situation for immigrants coming from the less developed countries deteriorates over time, and it seems apparent that no assimilation in terms of income takes place. Compared to Denmark, this is also noteworthy because no such increasing trend is found, though low-income percentages were generally higher in Denmark. It is interesting to note that the 1984 and the 1986 cohorts seem to conform, from around 1990, to the general pattern for native Swedes of increasing low-income levels.

We thus find that later-arriving immigrant groups from the less developed countries have higher poverty rates when measured by the same number of years since entry into the host country as the early cohort in our study. Although occurring in both countries, this phenomenon is more pronounced for immigrants to Sweden, which may be a reflection of the macroeconomic shock faced by the country in 1990. This macroeconomic shock at the beginning of the 1990s might also be the reason why poverty rates among immigrants from the less developed countries increase with the years since arrival. Further, we find that poverty rates for immigrants from the less developed countries, after the same number of years of residence, are higher in Denmark than in Sweden.

An interesting modification to the picture of immigrant low-income percentages being higher in Denmark becomes obvious when the income-share profiles for the oldest cohort (those entering in 1984) from the two country groups are compared in Figure 15.14. The low-income percentage increased in the fifth year of arrival, with a cumulated increase of 10 percentage points up to 1997; that is, an increase of some 5 percentage points more than for Swedish-born people. At the same time, in Denmark, the low-income percentage declined by 5 percentage points.[2] Another interesting difference is apparent for the 1984 immigrant cohort from the more developed countries: the low-income share in Sweden was stationary at around 20 per cent (except for the two first years), while the share in Denmark decreased throughout the period, dipping below the 20 per cent level nine years after arrival and ending at 14 per cent in 1997; that is, only slightly above the level found for native-born Danes (see Figure 15.6).

Age differences

As mentioned earlier, the summary figures may conceal considerable variation in other personal characteristics of the individuals involved. One major determinant is the phase of the individual's life-cycle when the observation takes place. Figures 15.15–15.18 examine the fluctuations in the incidence of low income among the immigrants according to their age groups (19–25 years; 26–39 years, and 40–55 years).

Figures 15.15 and 15.16 represent Denmark. For immigrants from the more developed countries, the tendency is very clear: that is, the younger the individual, the higher the probability of having a low income, and this likelihood increased during the 1990s. Many of the immigrants in the 19–25 years age bracket from the more developed countries are likely to be students, and the number of foreign students increased over the period analysed. For individuals in their early working career (25–34 years), the low-income percentage also increased slightly over the years, whereas it was stable for the 40–55-year-olds, and at the same level as for native-born Danes.

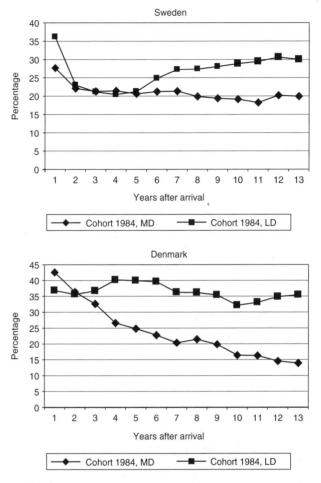

Figure 15.14 Low-income percentages for the 1984 cohort of immigrants from the more- and less developed countries, Sweden and Denmark

Figure 15.16 shows the trend for low-income percentages for immigrants from less developed countries. There was not much difference in the early part of the period across the age brackets, but over time, and especially in the early 1990s, differences increased, becoming very pronounced for the two younger age groups, which seemed to develop along with big shifts in the composition of immigrants from different national backgrounds.

Figures 15.17 and 15.18 focus on Sweden. Figure 15.17 shows that the trend for Sweden is similar to that for Denmark, although the level for young immigrants from the more developed countries is lower than in

336

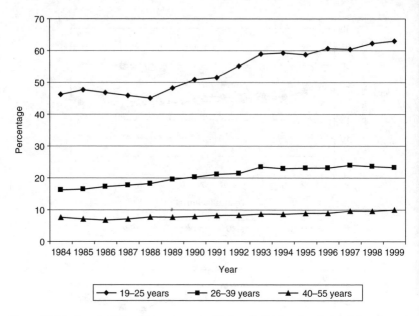

Figure 15.15 Low-income percentages in Denmark by age brackets of immigrants from more developed countries

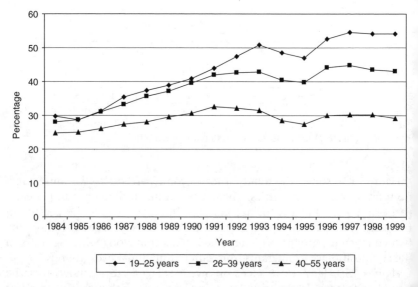

Figure 15.16 Low-income percentages in Denmark by age brackets of immigrants from less developed countries

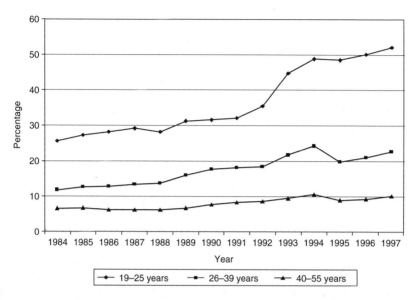

Figure 15.17 Low-income percentages in Sweden by age brackets of immigrants from more developed countries

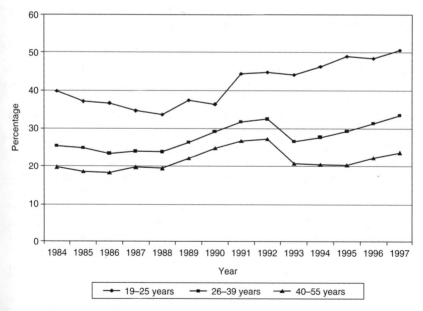

Figure 15.18 Low-income percentages in Sweden by age brackets of immigrants from less developed countries

Denmark. However, this difference decreased when Sweden was hit by the deep recession at the beginning of the 1990s. At the end of the period, around 50 per cent of Sweden's youngest immigrants from the developed-country group were considered to be poor; in Denmark the proportion was around 60 per cent. For immigrants from the less developed countries, the tendency, shown in Figure 15.18, was similar to that in Denmark, but there the differences across ages were smaller in the early part of the observation period.

Concluding remarks

In this chapter, we have reported estimates of the poverty rates for adult immigrants to Denmark and Sweden for the period from the mid-1980s to the end of the 1990s, and compared these with corresponding rates for the native population. The data, extracted from two large comparable databases, are similar, and we thus have good reason to believe that the differences observed across countries indicate true variances. We defined poverty or low income for both countries as a situation where the equivalent disposable income was less than 60 per cent of the median for the country and the year under study. The focus of the study was to examine the broad picture of the poverty rates among immigrants versus native citizens, and to lay the foundation for further research using the present databases.

A major conclusion of the chapter is that the difference in poverty rates between the native population and immigrants has increased in both countries. This can be traced, first to the fact that poverty rates among immigrants from the less developed countries have increased, and that the number of these immigrants has increased rapidly. At the end of the period studied, certain groups of immigrants from the less developed countries show fairly large poverty rates in both Denmark and Sweden. In contrast, few immigrants in the 40–55-year-old age group originating from developed countries were classified as poor.

Further, we have found that, while poverty rates among the developed-country immigrants decrease as the years since immigration grew, this was generally not the case for migrants from the developing countries. In Denmark, rates were found to be reducing very slowly, and in Sweden they tended to increase, in parallel with the general rise in the country's low-income percentages in the 1990s. Newly arrived groups from the developing countries have higher poverty rates than the earlier arriving cohorts after a similar number of years of residence. These patterns are common to both countries.

While much of the observed pattern is similar for both Denmark and Sweden, differences also exist. Most important, the bridge in the poverty rates of the immigrants and of the native population is larger in Denmark. Poverty rates among all immigrants to Denmark were higher than those for people settling in Sweden; this applied to all the years studied. While poverty rates for the native population were similar in Denmark and Sweden at the beginning of the period studied, they remained stable in the former but increased in the latter. Denmark was thus found to have the lowest poverty record among the native population, but the situation is reversed for immigrants to the country. The poverty levels also differ considerably among immigrants coming from different countries. The fact needs to be emphasized that in Denmark and Sweden the composition of the national background of the immigrant stocks is very different. For example, the only group of immigrants from the less developed countries with nearly the same number of residents in both countries is those from Turkey. All other national groups of immigrants are much larger in Sweden than in Denmark. The Turkish immigrants are thus an exception to our general observation, and the poverty rates for this group are higher in Sweden. Furthermore, the conclusion of generally lower immigrant poverty rates in Sweden is modified when we look at the group of immigrants for which our data provides the longest observation period – the 1984 cohort. In our future work, a cohort approach will be important in determining which parts of the observed cross-country differences are a reflection of compositional effects and which are true differences.

Notes

1. In the present study we restricted the analyses of Swedish data to the period ending in 1997 because a change in sampling strategy currently makes it difficult to include observations for 1998–99 in the analysis.
2. This is followed by another 5 percentage points decline from 1997 to 1999, not shown in Figure 15.14 in order to keep the periods the same in the two countries, but it does appear in Figure 15.11.

References

Atkinson, T., B. Cantillon, E. Marlier and B. Nolan (2002). *Social Indicators. The EU and Social Inclusion*. Oxford and New York: Oxford University Press.

Bell, B. D. (1997). 'The Performance of Immigrants in the United Kingdom: Evidence from the GHS', *Economic Journal*, 107(441): 333–44.

Berthoud, R. (1998). 'The Incomes of Ethnic Minorities', ISER Report, No. 98–1, Colchester: University of Essex, Institute for Social and Economic Research.

Borjas, G. J. (1990). *Friends or Strangers. The Impact of Immigrants on the US Economy*, New York: Basic Books.

Büchel, F. and J. R. Frick (2004). 'Immigrants in UK and in West Germany: Relative Income Positions, Income Portfolio, and Redistribution Effects', *Journal of Population Economics*, 17: 553–81.

Danish Economic Council (2001). *The Danish Economy Autumn 2001*, Copenhagen: Danish Economic Council (in Danish).

Ekberg, J. (1994). 'Är invandrare fattiga?' ('Are Immigrants Poor?'), *Ekonomisk Debatt*, 22(2): 169–77 (in Swedish).

Gustafsson, B. (1997). 'Invandrares försörjning' ('Income Maintenance of Immigrants'), in Statens invandrarverk (National Immigration Board), *Mångfald och ursprung.*

Norrköping: Rapport från ett multietiskt Sverige (Diversity and origin. Report from a multiethnic Sweden): 78–85 (in Swedish).

Gustafsson, B. (1999). 'Fattigdom och andra mått på inkomststandard' ('Poverty and Other Income Measures'), in Socialstyrelsen (The National Board of Health and Social Welfare), *Social och ekonomisk förankring bland invandrare från Chile, Iran, Polen och Turkiet* (Social and Economic Integration among Immigrants from Chile, Iran, Poland and Turkey), Series Invandrares levnadsförhållanden: 2 (in Swedish).

Gustafsson, B. and E. Palmer (2002). 'Was the Burden of the Deep Swedish Recession Equally Shared?', *The Review of Income and Wealth*, 48(4): 537–60.

Hammarstedt, M. (2001). 'Disposable Income Differences between Immigrants and Natives in Sweden', *International Journal of Social Welfare*: 117–26.

Jensen, P. and P. J. Pedersen (2004). 'To Stay or Not to Stay. Return Migration from Denmark', Mimeo, Aarhus: Department of Economics, University of Aarhus.

Kazemipur, A. and S. S. Halli (2001). 'Immigrants and "New Poverty": The Case of Canada', *International Migration Review*, 35(4): 1129–56.

Ley, D. (1999). 'Myths and Meanings of Immigration and the Metropolis', *The Canadian Geographer*, 43(1): 2–19.

Ley, D. and H. Smith (1997). 'Immigration and Poverty in Canadian Cities, 1971–1991', *Canadian Journal of Regional Science*, XX(1, 2): 29–48.

Ley, D. and H. Smith (2000). 'Relations between Deprivation and Immigrant Groups in Large Canadian Cities', *Urban Studies*, 37(1): 37–62.

Lundh, C., L. Bennich-Björkman, R. Ohlsson, P. J. Pedersen and D.-O. Rooth (2002). *Arbete? Var god dröj!* (A Job? Please wait!), Stockholm: SNS.

OECD (2001, 2002). *Employment Outlook*, Paris: OECD.

Poulsen, M. E. and A. Lange (1998). *Indvandrere i Danmark* (Immigrants in Denmark), Copenhagen: Statistics Denmark.

Rezaei, S. (2004). *The Dual Labour Market in a Welfare State Perspective – A Study of the Dilemma between Informal Economic Practice and the Socio-economic Integration of Immigrants*, Report, University Centre of Roskilde.

Smith, E. and A. Jackson (2002). *Does a Rising Tide Lift All Boats? The Labour Market Experiences and Incomes of Recent Immigrants, 1995 to 1998*, Ottawa: Canadian Council on Social Development.

16
Iraqi Asylum Migrants in Jordan: Conditions, Religious Networks and the Smuggling Process*

Géraldine Chatelard

The cumulative effect of ten years of European Union (EU) policies on migration has been an overriding emphasis on control at the borders, and beyond the borders, of EU states through a series of measures: carriers' liability, stricter visa requirements, readmission treaties with Central and Eastern European states, and electronically fortified borders. As several case studies have shown, trying to keep economic migrants out has had, among others effects, the result of allowing the development of networks of human smugglers (Koser, 1997; McDowell, 1997; Salt and Stein, 1997; Ghosh, 1998; Messe *et al.*, 1998; Morrison, 1998; Van Hear, 1998; Koslowski, 2000; Peter, 2000; Salt and Hogarth, 2000; Snyder, 2000). Migration control policies have affected asylum seekers in much the same way as other groups of migrants, forcing them to resort to illegal migration to reach Western Europe, and therefore criminalizing them in blatant contradiction of international law governing the status of refugees (Engbersen and van der Lun, 1998; Van Hear, 1998).

In 2000, the UN adopted a Protocol against human smuggling, testifying to the growing concern by state authorities and international organizations who view migrant smuggling and trafficking as undermining international collaborative efforts to produce ordered migration flows.[1] In the 1990s, the International Organization for Migration (IOM) conducted a vast policy-orientated research programme on the topic, which was also the subject of several academic studies (IOM, 1994; IOM, 1995; Ghosh, 1998; Meese *et al.*, 1998; Salt and Hogarth, 2000; Snyder, 2000). Salt and Stein (1997) even devised a model for analysing smuggling as a business, dividing it into three stages: the mobilization and recruitment of migrants in their countries of origin; their movement through the transit stages; and their integration into labour markets and society in the host countries. Despite contributing rich documentary and theoretical perspectives on a new field, the various approaches adopted in these studies have three major limitations. First, when considering the transit process of irregular migrants originating from developing countries, they are almost all located at the gateway of Western industrialized states, leaving the first stages of migration and smuggling in the shadows. Second, even the very few studies that document smuggling in a single transit country in the South take for granted that migrants from developing countries aim systematically from the beginning of their migration at reaching the West. Third, like the policies that allow smuggling rings to thrive and that criminalize migrants whatever their profile, these studies do not differentiate clearly between patterns of voluntary and involuntary migration. A few studies avoid this pitfall by looking specifically at the smuggling of asylum seekers. Unfortunately, they all concentrate on the last stage of irregular migration, either looking at transit across Central or Eastern European countries, or at smuggling between EU member states (Koser, 1997; McDowell, 1997; Morrison, 1998; Koslowski, 2000). Again, very little is revealed of the transit and smuggling processes of asylum seekers in their regions of origin or at other stages along the route.

Moreover, recent trends of studies on international migration emphasize their transnational character and point to the role played by social and economic networks in prompting, facilitating, sustaining and directing the movement of migrants, especially to industrialized countries, and their mobility between various regions of the world (Portes, 1995; Van Hear, 1998; Vertovec and Cohen, 1999). Applying these paradigms to the study of forced migrants, a few pioneering works now show that non-European refugees and asylum seekers have found it increasingly difficult to gain admission to industrialized countries unless they have been able to activate broad, transnational networks composed of individuals of different migrant categories, and in particular to pay for the services of smugglers (Koser, 1997; McDowell, 1997; Muus, 1997; Crisp and Van Hear, 1998; Koser and Lutz, 1998; Morrison, 1998; Doraï, 2002). Several of these studies emphasize the role of networks based on common affiliations such as ethnicity, kinship, residential proximity or religion. But again, because these studies are located at one end of the route, in the country of destination, they cast little light on transit: but it is an essential process providing a link to, and not a disruption of, migrants' trajectories and the architecture and dynamics of the various networks that sustain their movement.

In all cases, the first transit stage(s) of irregular asylum migration in countries of the South has not been explored in depth, and a series of questions still need to be asked. The first set of questions is related to the motivation of asylum migrants. What are the initial intentions of forced migrants when they leave their countries of origin? Why do a number of them prefer to seek asylum in an industrialized country rather than in a state closer to home? What about the treatment they receive in regional host countries, their socioeconomic conditions and legal status in first countries of reception, and the impact of these factors on migration strategies? In brief, does pointing at such 'pull' factors as lenient asylum policies or economic prosperity in industrialized countries explain current trends of asylum migration and the complex motivations of migrants who undertake long, costly and risky transcontinental journeys?

The second set of questions concerns the various means at the disposal of migrants to undertake long-distance and irregular moves. Is the functioning of the social networks that support their migration similar to that of voluntary migrants? In particular, can these networks operate between Western host countries and the country of origin (often being war-torn, politically unstable, under the grip of authoritarian governments, etc.)? In this context, what about the role of the first host country in providing a base for social networks to operate, and for allowing smuggling? Does the recruitment of migrants necessarily take place in the country of origin – implying that forced migrants take their original decision to move to the West at the beginning of their migration? In short, what does a study of transit in its first stage tell us about the nature, the functioning and the interrelations of the various networks that sustain the movement of asylum migrants?

This chapter looks at the case of Iraqi forced migrants in the Hashemite Kingdom of Jordan. More particularly, it will explore how the country's policy responses to this influx, which started with the 1991 Gulf War, had an impact on the migrants' decision merely to transit Jordan, their first host country, rather than to stay there long-term. In a context of extreme vulnerability, poverty and religious-based discrimination, it will also look at the support networks of migrants in Jordan, with a particular emphasis on religious ones. Finally, it will document the smuggling process as it takes place from Jordan, a country that, unlike Iraq, has a concentration of the prerequisites necessary for smuggling rings to operate.

Combining sociological and anthropological approaches, this chapter will argue that the structural context in the first regional host country plays a major part in shaping the strategies of forced migrants, in determining their transit, and in allowing for the development of smuggling and trafficking rings that intersect with migrants' social – in this case, religious – networks to allow for further emigration to Western industrialized countries. In passing, it will also challenge a number of accepted views on the distinctions between trafficking and smuggling, and about the so-called 'pull' of industrialized countries.

Background

Iraqi forced migrants

In 2003, 3–4 million Iraqis were reported to be living abroad, of whom over 500,000 were recognized (conventional or other) refugees.[2] In 2001, Iraqis were the third major refugee caseload in the world.

The majority of Iraqis currently living abroad as refugees or asylum seekers fled their country during the 1991 Gulf War or in the following decade.

344 Iraqi Asylum Migrants in Jordan

Most left Iraq in 1991–2, not so much as a direct consequence of the United States-led bombing of the country but rather because of two episodes of failed revolt against the regime of Saddam Hussein. In 1991, the Kurds in the northern provinces and the Shiites in the central area revolted, and both uprisings were crushed. Continued repression led to outmigration of members of both groups at a slow but steady pace until the fall of the dictator. Later in the 1990s, fighting between rival Kurdish factions in the northern autono-mous provinces and the drainage of the marshlands in the Shiite area of the Shatt el-Arab in the south were additional reasons for people to leave. Members of other social groups were also prompted to leave their country as the embargo imposed by the UN Security Council in 1991 contributed to the deterioration of the domestic economic situation. Additionally, continuous violations of human rights affected all kinds of opponents to the Ba'thist regime (USCR, 1991; LCHR, 1992; UNHCR, 1996; Amnesty International, 1997). Often, emigration was motivated by a mixture of economic and political factors, particularly for social groups such as the Shiites or the Kurds, who were collectively denied access to public resources. The outcome is that many people had no assurance either of physical security or the ability to sustain their livelihoods, a fact that blurs the traditional distinction between involuntary (or forced) migrants and voluntary (here, economic or labour) migrants.

Whatever their final destination, Iraqis had to move first by road to a neighbouring country, since the embargo prevented them from travelling directly to a more distant location by sea or air. Accessibility of neighbour-ing countries has been conditioned by the opening of borders, the treat-ment received at the hands of the authorities, other factors such as the presence of relatives, co-ethnics or co-religionists, or the location of the country en route to further emigration.

Over 300,000 Iraqis have requested asylum in a Western country since 1991. In most cases, they have reached their countries of final destination through irregular channels after transiting Turkey, Syria or Jordan.

Jordan's policy responses

In the wake of the 1991 Gulf War, Jordan, bordering Iraq on the west, received an influx of a million refugees of different nationalities fleeing Kuwait and Iraq. Among those, about 360,000 were Jordanian involuntary 'returnees'; that is, citizens of the Hashemite Kingdom, most of them of Palestinian origin, who had settled in the Gulf, in some cases decades before. Understandably, Jordan gave priority to the reception and integration of the 300,000 of these who decided to remain in the country (Van Hear, 1995).

Later in 1991, a wave of thousands of Shiite Iraqis went to Jordan after the uprising against Saddam Hussein by members of their sect was forcibly repressed. Since then, Iraqi migrants, voluntary or involuntary, have been arriving in Jordan in smaller, but steady numbers, entering the kingdom through the one open border point, fleeing both the regime and the embargo. A majority of these have not remained in Jordan, but have used the country as a gateway to other Arab or Western countries. In 1996, a UNHCR Background Paper on Iraqi Refugees and Asylum Seekers reported that, by some estimates, 1–2 million Iraqis had gone to Jordan since the Gulf War. According to the same source, the number of Iraqis remaining in Jordan was undetermined because most were transiting. The various sources, mainly reports from human rights groups, that mention Iraqi migrants in Jordan are no more precise (Amnesty International, 1997; USCR, 1991–2001; USDS, 1991–2001). Official figures are non-existent, and declarations by officials published in the Jordanian media are inconsistent, varying from 50,000 to 180,000. NGO sources may go up as high as 300,000. It is hard to make more than 'guesstimates' of the scale of Iraqi immigration in Jordan, not only because the authorities choose to be silent on the issue, but also because of the nature of the transit migration. The group is unstable, people's stays are transitory and new individuals arrive as others leave.

Jordan has adopted what can be deemed a 'semi-protectionist' policy towards Iraqi forced migrants; that is, letting them into the country but depriving them of any status, of protection and of any means of livelihood (Chatelard, 2002). The border with Iraq has always remained open, and until the situation was dramatically altered following the American-led invasion of Iraq in 2003, Iraqis could enter Jordan on a temporary visa and stay legally for up to six months. After that period, they became illegal aliens and were at risk of being returned to Iraq. Nevertheless, Jordan has always refrained from mass expulsion. On the other hand, the country is not a signatory of the 1951 Geneva Convention Relating to the Status of Refugees (henceforth, the 1951 Convention) but has allowed the United Nations High Commissioner for Refugees (UNHCR) to operate on its soil since 1991. But the UN agency's recognition rate of Iraqi asylum seekers is much lower than that of several industrialized countries and does not exceed 30 per cent, while recognized refugees have to be resettled in a third country. Jordan has also adopted a set of discriminatory social measures against Iraqi forced migrants, including those registered as asylum seekers: they cannot work legally, schooling for children has been made extremely difficult, almost no aid and relief is provided, and access to medical facilities is more expensive than for Jordanian nationals. Finally, most Iraqi forced migrants are Shiite, an Islamic sect with no indigenous members and no legal status in Sunni Jordan. Shiites have been unable to obtain recognition from the authorities and experience suspicion, if not open discrimination.

The motives behind Jordan's policy responses to the influx of Iraqi forced migrants have a historical basis, in particular in relation to the Arab–Israeli conflict that has left Jordan to deal with 1.6 million Palestinian refugees (in a population of 5 million), and to such current geopolitical realities as the UN embargo that has turned Jordan into the external border of Iraq, making it impossible to close the crossing point between the two countries. Jordan is also under severe economic strain, as 30 per cent of its labour force is unemployed. The authorities therefore argue the country's economic and societal incapacity to absorb large numbers of Iraqis. In many ways, Iraqi migration to Jordan is seen as a security issue that should not be publicized by adopting proactive measures (Chatelard, 2002).

Within the broader structural context of their official treatment, turning to the livelihood strategies of Iraqi forced migrants in Jordan allows us to understand two important dynamics in the transit process. One is how discriminatory practices, deficient administrative measures and the limited role of UNHCR deter migrants from staying in Jordan by making them an extremely vulnerable group. The other one is how, as a last recourse, they resort to social networks based on religious affiliations that first provide material and moral support, and are used eventually as channels to undertake further emigration linked to smuggling rings.

Methodology

At the time the fieldwork was carried out, Iraqi migrants across Jordan were in many ways 'invisible', neglected in the grey literature produced by international organizations, human rights groups and Jordanian public bodies or civil society organizations (NGOs, research centres and so on). They were the object of no specific study and usually mentioned only in passing. Moreover, Jordanian officials were not available to discuss the issue, and the Jordanian press was of limited use. Consequently, I had to adopt a multiple methodology to gather sociological data and background information.

Between 1999 and 2001, in order to assess the socioeconomic conditions of Iraqis in Jordan and their livelihood strategies, I undertook in-depth fieldwork based mainly on participant observation. I conducted about forty informal interviews with Iraqi forced migrants in Amman, mainly in their homes, and maintained regular, friendly relations with a number of families and individuals. I made regular visits to gathering places such as coffee shops and the so-called Iraqi market in Amman. I also attended religious meetings at churches and once accompanied a group of Shiites celebrating the religious festival of Ashura. This was an occasion, among other things, to meet religious leaders. Subsequently, I was able to maintain relations over the Internet with a number of individuals I had met in Jordan and who had migrated successfully to Western Europe, North America or Australia. At that stage, they were willing to provide me with details of the smuggling process, with little risk involved. During the summer of 2001, I visited some of them in the Netherlands and Denmark, where I was able to meet more Iraqis. I spoke to them about their migration and the way they were supporting the emigration of others still at that time in Jordan.

In May–June 2001, looking more specifically at those who claimed asylum while in Amman, the UNHCR allowed me to conduct a survey among a sample of 121 asylum seekers awaiting a final decision. During face-to-face interviews conducted in Arabic, seventy questions were asked to assess their socioeconomic profile, circumstances in Jordan, network of family relations in Iraq and abroad, channels of information about Jordan and the migration process, and future plans if their claim was rejected. I subsequently met some of them again outside the premises of the UNHCR where they gave me more details about their conditions and intentions. I estimate that the sample that served as a basis for this chapter comprises roughly 200 individuals, plus many more family members or friends of those interviewed, who provided more limited data.

Finally, at different stages over three years, I conducted several in-depth interviews with the representative and staff at UNHCR in Amman, had several meetings with members of a number of foreign and local relief and human rights NGOs operating in Jordan, and interviewed immigration officers in a number of Western embassies in Amman.[3]

Profile, conditions, livelihood strategies

To assess the migrants' socioeconomic profile, legal status and livelihood strategies in Jordan, I mainly, but not exclusively, made use of the survey conducted with asylum seekers at UNHCR in Amman. The aim of the survey was also to identify the pull factors that had made them choose Jordan as a first host country, the reasons why they did not want to stay, and their intentions for further emigration should their claim for asylum be rejected.[4]

Socioeconomic profile

Among respondents to the survey, 56.3 per cent were men, and 43.7 per cent women; 64.6 per cent of all respondents were between 25 and 39 years old, and 23.7 per cent were between 40 and 69 years old. The large female representation should not be taken as an indication that Iraqi migrant women are generally almost as numerous as migrant men. From other observations, it rather seems that women are over-represented among asylum seekers because they are more vulnerable than men and approach the UNHCR more frequently to provide some kind of status and protection.

A typical profile of an Iraqi forced migrant (who may not ask for asylum at the UNHCR) is a male between 25 and 45 years old who, if married, has left his family behind in Iraq until he finds an opportunity that will allow them move to Jordan. This will occur either if he gains recognition of his refugee status at the UNHCR, or if he migrates to another country and sends money for his family to move, first to Amman, or if his stay in Jordan lasts and he has enough income to have his family join him. It can thus be inferred that the proportion of Iraqi women in Jordan has increased since the second half of the 1990s as more Iraqi men have made it to the West, or as many have been stranded in Jordan for several years.

A large majority of the respondents were Shiites (66.8 per cent); followed by Christians (13.1 per cent); Sunnis (11.7 per cent); and Sabeans (8.4 per cent) (see the Appendix).[5] If Shiites represent roughly 55 per cent of the population of Iraq, Sunnis account for another 35 per cent, with the rest being mainly Assyro-Chaldean Christians while Sabeans represent less than 0.5 per cent. Among the respondents, the over-representation of Christians, Sabeans and Shiites, and the under-representation of Sunnis, are clear signs that religious minorities are leaving Iraq at a higher rate than the Sunni sociological majority that does not suffer from group persecution or discrimination.[6]

Of the respondents, 90.4 per cent defined themselves as ethnically Arabs. The rest answered that they were Assyrian, Kurd (on two occasions) and Turkmen (on one occasion). With regard to the Kurds, who represent 15 per cent of all Iraqi nationals, the fact that only few of them moved to Jordan is confirmed by further discussion and observation outside the strict limits of the survey. This is for geographical and sociopolitical factors: the proximity of Turkey or Iran to the north and north-east of Iraq, where most of the Kurds live, and the fact that, as a cross-border ethnic group, they prefer to travel to another Kurdish area.

Typically, Iraqi forced migrants who have approached the UNHCR to seek asylum are individuals with a secondary or university education (>90 per cent), who have held positions as civil servants (including doctors and engineers), teachers, traders or shopkeepers in Iraq (73.5 per cent). Women have an equally high rate of secondary and university education and roughly two-thirds were once employed in Iraq. Apart from those Shiites who come from the marsh-lands in the South (7.5 per cent of the total), or for village Assyrians from the North (4 per cent of the total), they have an urban background. Most migrants considered themselves to have once been reasonably well-off in Iraq, but had experienced a dramatic drop in income following the devaluation of the Iraqi dinar, or because they were dismissed from their employment in the public sector. They usually came to Jordan with savings, either after selling their belongings or property in Iraq, or with money lent by relatives.

This leads to two comments. First, the lower middle class or severely impoverished Iraqis do not have the financial means to undertake long-term emigration. If they do move to Jordan, they belong to that category of people who go back and forth and work mainly as street vendors in Amman. Second, the amount of money that forced migrants take with them, and the large proportion who have sold all their property, are signals that they are not planning to go back to Iraq in the near future, or even at all. This was the case with 67.8 per cent of the Christians and Sabeans, and a third of the Shiite respondents, who said that they had sold everything they had.

Socioeconomic situation in Jordan

As regards their socioeconomic situation in Jordan, only 7.2 per cent of the male respondents said they did not work at all. But of those working, only

2.3 per cent had a work permit, and 71.6 per cent said that they worked on and off as street vendors, cleaners, painters and at other petty jobs. The others, roughly 20 per cent, who had a steady job were cleaners, gardeners or office boys. Of the women, 74.5 per cent were totally unemployed, and those working were domestic workers or employed as seamstresses working from home. Only two had an illegal but steady clerical job.

The average monthly income respondents declared they were earning was 40 Jordanian dinars (JD)[7] for a single person and 70 JD for a household, irregular in 84.5 per cent of the cases. Those who had the highest standard of living benefited from the financial support of relatives abroad, and/or had only arrived recently in Jordan and were still living on their savings. In Jordan, the poverty line is estimated to be less than 100 JD a month for a household, and all the people interviewed, including those outside the survey sample, felt that they were experiencing a dire professional and social downfall and had been placed in a much lower social status than the one they belonged to in Iraq. As employment is scarce, irregular and not well paid, and as the cost of living in Jordan is up to ten times higher than in Iraq, migrants who come with savings spend them in a few months. After a period of being relatively well off, most survive on the margin of the Jordanian society, engaging in menial jobs in the informal sector, and facing an extremely precarious economic situation.

The migrants' situation is further aggravated by their housing conditions. Iraqi migrants congregate in the cities where they can live in a familiar environment, and hope to pass unnoticed, and to maximize their social and economic opportunities. While 87.4 per cent of the respondents lived in Amman itself, the remainder lived in urban areas within a radius of 40 km of the capital. Typically, they lived in unsanitary and overcrowded dwellings in the poverty belt of Amman, and in informal/squatter areas with a high Palestinian refugee population. These neighbourhoods can be equated to refugee camps, but without the legal status and the facilities (sewage system, electricity and water, health and educational systems).

Only three families among the 54.2 per cent who had school-age children were sending them to school, and they were all Christians benefiting from aid from a Catholic relief society. The others said they thought schools were not open to Iraqi children, or that they had tried to place their children in school but had been told to produce documents they had not brought with them from Iraq.

Finally, 41.3 per cent declared that they currently had, or had had, health problems while in Jordan, but only 9.8 per cent had consulted a doctor. In 67.3 per cent of the cases, at least one of the respondents' children currently had medical problems too, and 40.1 per cent of these had been taken to see a doctor. All those interviewed said that they gave priority to their children's health over their own. Of those who had reason to consult a doctor but had not been to a medical facility, 93.7 per cent said that it was too expensive.

Reasons for choosing Jordan

Open borders and anticipated work opportunities are the two main reasons respondents gave when asked why they had selected Jordan and not another neighbouring country such as Turkey, Syria or Iran. The possibility of approaching the UNHCR came only in fourth position after accessibility of third countries, either in the Arab world or in the West. Other frequent answers (there were multiple possibilities) included the fact that Jordan was an Arab State, and not a foreign country; the presence of relatives who had already moved there; or the fact that it was the less risky choice. This calls for a number of comments.

First, most people do not have the initial intention of crossing borders illegally, an important point to consider for future developments. Among the Shiites interviewed, the majority had close or distant relatives that were refugees in Iran, a country party to the 1951 Convention. Nevertheless, they took into account the fact that the Iraq–Iran border was closed to migrants and did not want to take the risk of being arrested or shot. It was a similar situation with the Assyro-Chaldeans, who could have attempted to cross irregularly into Syria, where a number of their co-religionists and family members were granted asylum under a UNHCR mandate at the beginning of the 1990s.

Second, as shown by other questions that were asked, an overwhelming majority of the migrants had a distorted vision of the economic situation in Jordan before they undertook to move there. Similarly, they had no accurate knowledge of the legal and socioeconomic conditions of Iraqi migrants. Compared to Iraq in the 1990s, Jordan looked to them like a wealthy country with a thriving job market. Besides, they expected the Jordanian authorities to demonstrate a degree of Arab solidarity with them and give them a legal status and a work permit.

This poses questions as to how information circulates between Jordan and Iraq. Those who go back and forth – for example, taxi or bus drivers, 'suitcase traders', street vendors or mobile labourers, do see Jordan as a place for economic gain. On the other hand, Iraqi forced migrants who are in Jordan and cannot or do not want to go back to Iraq have very limited means of passing on detailed information to relatives left behind. There is no postal service between the two countries, and Iraq forbids Internet access. Telephone lines are frequently tapped and conversations kept to a minimum. Letters sent with taxi drivers cannot tell much either, for fear that the Iraqi authorities might intercept them, and oral messages through these same intermediaries are necessarily brief. As a result, and despite the proximity of the two countries, Iraqis come to Jordan with expectations that are not met. These possibly derive from the fact that Jordan did once offer jobs to a good number of highly skilled Iraqis, and that is still the dominant image in Iraq today.[8]

Third, only a third of the respondents had come to Jordan with the idea of transit in mind. These migrants were mainly the ones who already had family members abroad and/or who no longer had any family members in Iraq. They had either come to seek family reunification through the UNHCR, or had initially expected to obtain an immigration visa easily in a foreign embassy based on being Iraqis who were fleeing the regime of Saddam Hussein. The situation is that, between 1991 and 1994, Western consulates offered a number of visas on humanitarian grounds, preferably to those who were skilled and already had relatives in the destination country. In this way, Iraqi Christians, who as a group had a long history of migration to Australia, Canada, the United States or Brazil, left in large numbers. Moreover, until 1998, doctors, engineers or teachers could hope to negotiate a work contract in Yemen or Libya through these countries' embassies in Amman. But all these possibilities have now sharply declined, if not totally disappeared.

Apart from those who were planning to transit Jordan rapidly, two-thirds of the respondents came to Jordan with the view of staying long-term, at least until the political situation at home improved enough to enable them to return. This fact is confirmed by numerous other people interviewed in other settings, who said that they would rather stay close to Iraq where they could still communicate with relatives, albeit in a limited fashion, or easily be reunited with them if the relatives had to leave. It is only as an ultimate choice that they are/were convinced to undertake further migration out of Jordan.

Finally, despite the fact that all the individuals in the sample survey were registered with the UNHCR as asylum seekers, only 17 per cent of them mentioned choosing Jordan because of the possibility of asking for asylum, and among those only a few had heard of the UNHCR's office in Amman before they left Iraq. The overwhelming majority learnt about the organization from other Iraqis in Jordan. While, on average, respondents had been in Jordan for 22 months (with a minimum of 4 months and a maximum of 51 months), most had waited for about a year before approaching the UNHCR, an issue to which I shall return later.

Legal documentation

Most forced migrants enter Jordan legally with a valid Iraqi passport. A minority is smuggled across the border or enters with a fraudulent passport because they were not able to secure an intelligence-approved travel document in Iraq. As stated above, most Iraqi forced migrants (that is, those who do not want, or cannot, return to Iraq), fall into illegality after six months of residence with the risk of being expelled by the authorities. This is only one aspect of the problem of legal documentation that Iraqis experience while in Jordan.

Illegal aliens cannot gain access to the official job market, nor most state-subsidized services such as health and education. While employers usually underpay their Iraqi labourers,[9] unscrupulous ones do not pay them at all, and Iraqis have no legal recourse. Also, as landlords have to register their foreign tenants with the police, proper housing is another a problem. Thus most Iraqis are confined to informal areas. Nevertheless, their rent is on average 1.5 times higher than that of their Jordanian/Palestinian neighbours, and there are no rental agreements, so tenants may be expelled at any time.

Finally, a number of migrants cannot obtain documents from their embassy for fear of Iraqi intelligence. When their passports expire, they cannot renew them, and they cannot obtain birth, marriage or death certificates. Some use middlemen to obtain these papers, but such services entail a cost that not all Iraqis can afford. As even Sunni religious courts do not want to register the marriages of Shiites, or their newborn children, or even to deliver a death certificate in a country where religious communities are in charge of personal and family status, many migrants find themselves deprived of any legal existence after a few months in Jordan.

But perhaps the worst aspect of the documentation problem concerns the fine for overstaying that most Iraqis are unable to pay. It amounts to 1.5 JD per day of overstay and detains in Jordan even those who at some point could decide to go back to Iraq. There is a possibility of being excused the penalty on exit, but in this case individuals would not be allowed to return to Jordan in the future, so they would be trapped inside Iraq or have to find another exit route – two very bleak prospects for most of those who have left their country with no desire to return under the current circumstances.

UNHCR and asylum

In view of the difficult situation they face in Jordan, Iraqi forced migrants have limited strategic choices available to them to improve their legal status. The most obvious one is to register as an asylum seeker with the UNHCR, even if some know that their claim is unfounded. In recent years, the UNHCR's recognition rate of Iraqi asylum seekers in Jordan was 20 per cent on average. Including those who have no hope of ever becoming 'legal' refugees, the registration card provided by the UNHCR, and the long delay in dealing with cases (up to two years in cases of appeal), allow migrants to gain a legal foothold in Jordan, avoiding possible expulsion, and to plan for the future. As a side effect, and since the UNHCR's staff are aware of this tactic, the number of non-bona fide asylum seekers devalues the asylum claim of those genuinely in need of protection as they are then all suspected of being bogus.[10]

In fact, a surprisingly small proportion of Iraqi forced migrants chose the UNHCR as an option. Between 1991 and 2000, only about 30,000 migrants had sought asylum through the UN agency.[11] There are a number of reasons that might account for this low figure. Some relate to a lack of knowledge of how the UNHCR's office functions. As most of the Iraqis are illegal aliens, they keep a very low profile and go into hiding, and are afraid to come out of hiding because they believe that they will be handed over to the Jordanian police for overstaying. Their view is that the UNHCR shares information on cases with the Jordanian authorities. A more serious concern is that Iraqi agents have infiltrated the UNHCR, and this fear deters many from approaching the organization. Another reason that might explain why relatively few Iraqis present themselves to the organization is their fear of seeing their claims rejected and of subsequently being deported to Iraq where, until recently, they would have incurred the death penalty for having claimed asylum abroad.

Finally, a number of those who seem to have genuine cases do not want to approach the UNHCR in Jordan, a country that offers temporary shelter but not asylum. They want to choose where they will settle, a difficult thing to do in a resettlement process where host states establish quotas in response to domestic interests, and where little scope is left for refugees to choose their final destination. In particular, several Shiite clerics I met had suffered serious persecution at the hands of the intelligence services in Iraq, but did not want to register with the UNHCR because their specific aim was to reach London, a major centre of Shiite learning where they had colleagues. They said they intended to seek asylum directly in the United Kingdom once they had succeeded in getting there through irregular channels.

Intentions of further emigration

Most Iraqi migrants do not achieve either economic or physical security and know that there is little prospect of any improvement in their situation. As their savings diminish rapidly, those for whom returning to Iraq is not an option start thinking of leaving Jordan for a better place. Of the respondents, 98.2 per cent stated that they wanted to leave Jordan as soon as possible, and gave as the main reasons their bad economic situation, living conditions and insecure status. Before leaving Iraq, only a minority initially viewed Jordan as a transit stage and had some accurate information about the means at their disposal to move on, but most respondents considered that they did not have realistic ideas about visa regulations or employment opportunities in Western countries before reaching Jordan. Once they have taken the decision to leave Jordan, they are no longer naïve, as they have had time to be advised by other migrants who have been there for a longer period.

One of the important sets of information circulating among migrants, and making up good part of their discussions, is the possibility of seeking asylum in Western countries. It is said, quite accurately, that in some European countries or in Australia the recognition rate of Iraqi asylum seekers is more than twice that of the UNHCR in Amman. Besides, in the case of a rejection of their claims, Iraqis also know that they can stay in Western states as illegal aliens and will not be returned to Iraq. They hope to find a job with the help of fellow nationals. On the other hand, they also learn that Syria or Lebanon will not offer them substantially better opportunities than Jordan. Generally, work and security, which they cannot find in Jordan or elsewhere in the Middle East, are available in Europe, in North America or in Australia.

Among the respondents to the survey, only 9.3 per cent had no family member, relative or close friend abroad. Of the remaining 90.7 per cent, two-thirds had family members, relatives or close friends in a Western country, of which 89.6 per cent were either asylum seekers or refugees. While those who had left people behind in Iraq had a low and irregular level of communication with them, all those who knew Iraqis settled in the West were maintaining a high level of communication by telephone, by post, or though the Internet. Together with details about emigration from Jordan gained from other Iraqi migrants in the country, those who intended to leave Jordan generally had an amazing knowledge of asylum procedures in the countries where they had connections. On the other hand, only 5.2 per cent of the respondents (exclusively Sabeans and Christians) said they had left nobody behind, even distant relatives. These were in fact the last groups of whole extended families to leave, with no prospect of ever returning. But for the 94.5 per cent remaining, relatives and family members constitute a pool of potential migrants who are very likely eventually to follow those who leave Jordan on their way to the West.

Networking for survival

Aid and relief from religious institutions and networks

There is no aid and relief provided by Jordanian public or private institutions, or by foreign NGOs, who are prevented by the authorities from setting up projects aimed at Iraqis. On the other hand, Jordan has a thriving, well-integrated local Christian community, and Church charities are the only ones allowed to provide aid to Iraqis, mostly in kind. The official possibilities offered by the Jordanian authorities to the Christian community so that it takes care of Iraqi co-religionists stem from the complementary relationship that historically has developed between the Hashemite state and the various Christian Church organizations (Chatelard, 1997). In this context, the religious affiliation of migrants is an important factor to take into account, to understand both their livelihood strategies in Jordan and their migration process out of Jordan. Just as religious affiliation is the main means through which Jordanian society discriminates against categories of Iraqi migrants, so religious affiliation becomes one of the main ways forced migrants use to avoid this discrimination.

Asked if they had approached institutions for help, and which ones (apart from the UNHCR), respondents to the survey answered that they had in only 15.4 per cent of cases. Catholic and Protestant charities, parish churches or the Italian Hospital (run by a Catholic religious community) were the only institutions they listed. These facilities are open officially on a non-denominational basis, yet all but four of their users were Christians or Sabeans. Generally, the Muslim respondents who knew of the institutions' existence, but had not approached them, justified their attitude by saying that these were reserved for Christians.

In practice, it is true that Christian charities offer some of their services more willingly to Christian than to Muslim Iraqis. Caritas, for example, is a Jordanian organization operating in Iraq, facilitating the movement of Iraqi Christians out of Iraq. Once in Jordan, it provides them with a number of social services, such as medical care and, on some occasions, schooling for children in Catholic schools. The organization also runs an income-generating project for Iraqi women in a mainly Christian-populated town near Amman. Church officials may also act as middlemen for the granting of visas to migrate to Western countries, or intercede in favour of detained illegal aliens.

For their part, Iraqi Shiites do not have any previous experience of accessing Christian hospitals or other social or educational facilities, also not uncommon among Jordanian Sunni Muslims. Moreover, the granting of aid to Iraqi migrants in Jordan seems to be used as an avenue by American missionary organizations. Iraqi Shiites do not differentiate between non-missionary and missionary Christian activities: they are deeply suspicious of all the relief services.[12] Whatever the reasons, the fact remains that, apart from Christians and Sabeans, most other Iraqi migrants do not turn to existing, local Christian charities.

The major Christian denominations present in Jordan have an official status that allows them to run social and medical facilities. On the other hand, Shiite Islam has no indigenous followers in Jordan, no official status and therefore no established social institutions or facilities – and no legal possibility of registering any. Sunni mosques and charities, *zakat* committees or medical facilities (such as the Islamic Hospital and various religious-based NGOs) may provide Sunni Iraqis with some relief, but these structures do not have networks of schools and cannot help migrants to gain access to Western consulates, or to protect them from expulsion. Moreover, they are not willing to aid the Shiites who, in turn, expect to be ill-received on the basis of their religious affiliation, which they cannot hide as they have a very distinctive way of praying. Because of all these factors, Shiite Iraqis, who form a majority of the forced migrants, and are therefore the most vulnerable group.

Despite the fact that the Jordanian authorities are suspicious of any informal Shiite religious gathering, semi-clandestine prayer rooms (*majlis*) have been opened in the apartments of young mullahs (clerics) who have left Najaf or Karbala, the major centres of Shiite learning in Iraq. These meeting places are reserved for men who gather on Fridays and during religious festivals (Ashura, Ramadan). *Majlis* have a religious role but also perform a major social function: migrants find moral support, newcomers bring news from relatives and the political situation at home, participants exchange information about available jobs and housing in Jordan and so on. Apart from the Iraqi market and a few coffee-shops in Amman, *majlis* are the only meeting places that are tolerated by the Jordanian authorities, which keep an eye on them, and occasionally close them. Permanent links are kept with the Shiite centres in the United Kingdom, Iran and Iraq through a circulation of individuals, information and money used for relief but also, as I shall show later, for undertaking migration to the West.[13]

Much more than the Iraqi Christians, therefore, the Shiite community remains at the margin of Jordanian society. Its members cannot achieve economic security in Jordan and have to cope with the negative image Jordanians have of them as both Iraqis and as Shiites. More than the Sunnis, who in many cases expect to return to Iraq sooner or later, or even to go back and forth on a regular basis and trade between the two countries, the Shiites make no long-term investment in Jordan. Moreover, the community is continually being reshaped: *majlis* can be closed by the police, mullahs can migrate to the West either as refugees resettled by the UNHCR or through irregular channels, new mullahs may arrive from Iraq, and other clerics and students also leave for the West while new ones come.

Iraqi migrants' needs are purely socioeconomic and their concerns revolve around personal security and work opportunities. Since the absence of a legal or religious status does not allow them to have a stable foothold or officially recognized representatives, they are not in a position to approach the Jordanian authorities to negotiate an improvement in their situation. Therefore, they have no public claim for recognition or integration, and can make no demands for the granting of collective rights. Their desire to leave Jordan grows as their stay extends, and as years pass they want to reunite with family members who have completed their migration successfully to a safer haven. Whatever their denominational affiliation, Iraqi forced migrants establish only temporary enclaves on the edge of Jordanian society.

The pull of social networks

Once they have taken the decision to emigrate from Jordan, Iraqis face a new set of difficulties as the immigration policies of Western countries in the 1990s resulted in a limitation of the legal possibilities of access and admission. Yet this reality does not seem to deter Iraqis who, with the help of smugglers and the support of social networks, find legal or illegal ways of skirting visa restrictions and increased border controls. There are clear patterns in the direction of Iraqi emigration, from the Middle East in general, and from

Jordan in particular. Their final destinations in Western Europe are mainly Germany, Norway, Sweden, Denmark, the Netherlands and the United Kingdom. Much further away, Australia has also become a favourite choice, together with Canada. One may therefore ask two main questions. One is, what are the pull factors that attract Iraqis to certain Western countries and not to others? And the other is, how they reach these destinations from Jordan, taking into account the considerable administrative and practical difficulties they encounter, and the amount of money such a journey implies? Concentrating on the migrants' efforts while they are still in Jordan, but already dragged into transnational dynamics, I shall attempt to give an analytical view of the choices available to them, and of the difficulties they face in taking the first step of their journey – that is, exiting Jordan.

The main reason for choosing a country of final destination in the West is, first and foremost, the presence of family members, friends or co-religionists. These often appear in conjunction as Iraqis have now been migrating in large numbers since the early 1990s, and formal communities or informal groupings of Iraqis have had time to develop, especially in the main reception countries. From the interviews I conducted, in both Jordan and in Western Europe, and from other scattered sources, it seems that both the ethnic and religious affiliations of Iraqi migrants determine the direction of their migration. Whereas, among Western states, Germany hosts the largest Iraqi community (over 50,000), relatively few of those I interviewed (15.7 per cent of the respondents to the survey) mentioned that they had relatives there. In fact, it is mainly the Kurds who move to Germany, as a number of studies on migrant communities in Europe have shown. The Shiites listed first the United Kingdom, then Denmark, the Netherlands and Sweden. As far as could be assessed from the scarce, non-academic literature available on Shiite communities in Western Europe, and from looking at religious sites on the Internet, all these countries have registered Shiite associations and mosques. Iraqi Christians, on the other hand, cited most frequently Australia, Canada, the United States or the United Kingdom, where they have a much longer tradition of emigration that pre-dates the current trend. In all these countries, there exist Assyrian and/or Chaldean associations and churches established before the 1990s (for the United Kingdom, and the only study devoted to the non-Kurdish Iraqi diaspora, see Al-Rasheed, 1998). There is no need to expatiate on the pull factor constituted by the presence of personal or other social networks, a dynamic that has been explored extensively in various studies on international migration (in particular, see Portes, 1995; Van Hear, 1998; Vertovec and Cohen, 1999; Faist, 2000).

'People die like flies nowadays.' This is how the immigration officer in the embassy of a Nordic country in Amman jokingly put it to explain how Iraqis were abusing humanitarian visas his country grants to foreigners who want to attend the funeral of a relative there. Iraqis, of course, almost never return, and increasing numbers come to the embassy and produce genuine death certificates established by the relevant authorities. They also have the proper documentation to prove their family connection with the deceased. Documents are not necessarily fake, as the number of Iraqis in Nordic countries today is large enough to explain the greater numbers that are dying there. But it illustrates that many Iraqis are ready to exploit every legal means to migrate, and every loophole in the legislation of which they are aware, and that social networks are essential means in this regard. These loopholes are numerous and it is not my aim here to list all those of which the Iraqis take advantage. They are very much the 'holes in the wall' that Bigo (1996) and other analysts of European security policies point at as being left deliberately by the authorities for a variety of economic reasons linked to the increased need for cheap labour.

But the types of legal loopholes put some Iraqis at a greater advantage than others. Australia and Canada have sponsorship schemes for refugees or immigrants. In the case of Canada, relatives settled there or groups with a maximum of five legal entities can submit a sponsorship application to the authorities, and have to prove that they can meet the financial needs of the sponsored for the following ten years. Cases rejected by the UNHCR can also reach the Canadian Immigration Board via sponsored files. These cases are dealt with at the embassy in Amman without consulting the UNHCR. Comparable schemes are also available for emigration to Australia. These benefit Iraqi Christians more than their Muslim co-nationals, for the simple reasons that Churches have both the financial and legal credentials to act as sponsors, they are alerted by Church communities in Jordan, or by the Iraqi Christian community in exile whose size is larger than that of the Muslims, and who have had time to organize, since their history of emigration to both countries is longer. Once again, it is the Shiites who are at a disadvantage, and those who are left with no other option than to resort to the services of smugglers in order to leave Jordan.

The smuggling process and social networks

The techniques and organizations Iraqi migrants resort to in order to reach the West despite the various visa requirements and police constraints are determined primarily by the very same constraints. As Koslowski expresses it:

> Just as states cooperate to control unwanted migration...unwanted migrants can cooperate as well to form social networks that facilitate international migration. Just as states deputize private sector actors, such as airlines, to enforce tougher migration controls and thereby change 'the gatekeeper' that confront the prospective migrant, migrants are employing non-state actors, smugglers, to foil restrictions imposed by states, and thereby transform the 'gatecrashers' from hapless peasants who may have never travelled abroad to teams of border crossers led by professionals, often using the latest technologies money can buy. (Koslowski, 2000: 205)

Albeit Iraqi forced migrants are in no way 'hapless peasants', paying for the services of smugglers or forgers is at the core of their migration strategies. In Jordan, as in other transit countries in the Middle East, it is impossible to obtain official data on the volume of migrants smuggled out of the country. One exception is Turkey, which has allowed the IOM to conduct a survey on transit migration on its territory showing that the overwhelming majority were Iraqi Kurds, and that very few non-Kurdish Iraqis were transiting that country (IOM, 1995). On the other hand, the rare studies devoted to refugees in Iran show that the Iraqi Arabs among them have received the best treatment of all refugees and are therefore less likely to undertake further emigration to the West (Rajaee, 2000; Le Roy, 2001; various UNHCR documents). Knowing that few opportunities exist for legal migration, all these elements point to Jordan as being the main smuggling route for Iraqi Arabs out of the Middle East.

Most of the Iraqi migrants I have talked to who had resorted to smuggling rings stated that they would rather have moved onwards legally than to break immigration laws and take risks.[14] They said that they only resorted to irregular migration in the absence of legal avenues, and that they could not grasp the motive behind the coupling of stringent border controls with liberal asylum laws. The fact that asylum seekers cannot use legal means to be admitted to countries offering them proper protection questions the very notion of 'smuggling' and the very concept of 'illegal' migration. Iraqi migrants themselves, if they do use the Arabic word for 'smuggling' (*tahrib*), sometimes simply refer to smugglers as 'middlemen', if not as 'saviours'. Morrison, in a report on trafficking and asylum seekers in the United Kingdom, argues that: 'There is no straight divide between humanitarian and commercial trafficking.... In some cases the 'agent'... is both a criminal and a saver of lives' (Morrison, 1998: 1). For social scientists, smuggling implies a reconceptualization of international migration, which is traditionally regarded as a relationship between migrants and a host government aiming at controlling access to its territory. Moreover, smuggling blurs the distinction between legal and illegal migrants, as smugglers may deliberately help to facilitate legal forms of migration at one stage or another in the migration process. For example, in international refugee law it is not considered criminal for asylum seekers to enter a country by illegal means. Smugglers, on the other hand, are able to obtain proper visas on legal passports, but with fake work certificates and invitation letters. At different stages, migrants thus drift in and out of legal status.

As for the Iraqis, their recruitment does not take place in Iraq, but in Jordan. The country is a nodal location because it concentrates the various prerequisites for smuggling to develop and function that are not available in Iraq: foreign embassies (Western and non-Western), Jordanian nationals or nationals of other countries whose passports can be bought or stolen, the necessary technology to forge documents, Internet and untapped telephone lines, a liberal banking system which allows the international transfer of money, an international airport with numerous flights in all directions, or, alternatively, open borders to Syria and then Turkey. Therefore, in Jordan, Iraqi prospective migrants to the West can obtain real or forged travel documents, they can access transportation to leave the country, obtain information on where best to leave to by calling their relatives who are already in the West, or get information on asylum procedures via the Internet. Finally, those who pay to be smuggled can have money transferred to them in Jordan. All these are things that cannot presently be done from Iraq, where few Western countries maintain diplomatic ties, it is under embargo and with no airport facilities, and has state-controlled banks and a heavy security apparatus.

It seems that, as has been documented in the case of Poland (Salt and Hogarth, 2000: 48), it is the demand for outmigration from Jordan that has created business opportunities that have been exploited by Jordanian individuals or organizations using existing structures or creating new ones. From a number of cases I looked at, it appears that several of the smuggling/ trafficking organizations are the heirs of Jordanian middlemen already performing cross-border activities, though usually in the direction of South East Asia. Some of the agencies that bring foreign domestic workers to Jordan, and have a wide knowledge of administrative requirements and travel documentation, carry out migrant smuggling as a supplementary area of business without specializing in it. Some bogus travel agencies have been set up in Amman, where they advertise openly in their shop windows travel visas or advice on how to emigrate to the West. Migrants are not deceived and know that these firms perform illegal activities even though they have an apparently legal front. Therefore, it is not so much the smugglers who need to approach the migrants, as the migrants who have learnt from others where to go to contact the smugglers, whose main function is to provide proper documentation or help in crossing to Syria to connect to the Turkish route. Trust is a very important element in the trade as it involves paying for a good part of the services in advance. As fees for transportation or documents are substantial and appear to be rising, migrants prefer to rely on those networks that have helped their relatives or friends to reach the West and can be seen to be honest.

Route patterns from Jordan to Europe are closely determined by Jordan's geographical situation and by the cost–benefit of the enterprise. A direct route by sea from Aqaba and the Suez Canal is impossible: Jordan does not have enough coastline to board migrants secretly, and ships are controlled in Suez. The main known route from the Middle East into Europe goes through Turkey, which acts as a hub where migrants, mainly from Iraqi Kurdistan, Iran and Afghanistan meet, and they then continue either by sea to Italy or by land to Greece and the Balkans. Because, from Jordan, this involves crossing several borders illegally or obtaining an equivalent number of fake documents and visas, and paying for each stage, the cost is high.

Estimates vary between US$4,000 and US$6,000, with risks at each and every step and months of travel to reach the final destination. A new route is now developing through Lebanon or Syria, where Iraqis board ships, but all these routes are considered extremely risky.

From Jordan to Western Europe, the safest and most direct route is by air. This implies a different set of conditions: a higher cost but greater security. Besides buying a plane ticket and often paying fees for overstay, correct travel documents are needed; namely, a valid passport and a visa or a falsified foreign passport. These can be obtained in Amman, where a trade in passports and forgery has developed. Stolen passports, with the substitution of photographs, can replace genuine Iraqi passports, especially if they come from a third Arab country, or from a Southern European state such as Greece or Portugal for reasons of verisimilitude. Visas may be fraudulent, but more frequently they are genuine and obtained after providing fake employment certificates in Jordan, letters of invitation to Europe by ghost companies, and genuine bank statements[15] – all documents that are secured through the local agents of the smuggling network in a 'travel agency'. Finally, passports may be collected on arrival by a member of the smuggling ring and sent back to Jordan for alteration and reuse.[16]

Whereas some of the networks that operate in Jordan with transnational ramifications do not seem to have connections with organized crime, and some Iraqis are involved at the highest level for humanitarian reasons, others are clearly connected to prostitution, as a number of interviews I was able to conduct with Iraqi women in Amman demonstrate. Bogus travel agencies offer to 'employ' Iraqi women who come to inquire about the costs of the trip as prostitutes until they have earned an amount of money considered sufficient to pay for their smuggling out of Jordan (and often also for family members). The number of work hours is determined in advance, and the money earned is held in trust by the pimp, who releases the women and provides them with travel documents only after they have found other women to replace them. There is no need for physical intimidation or isolation strategies as Iraqi women are already isolated, have nowhere to escape to, and cannot turn to the authorities. And they enter into these bonds 'voluntarily', in the absence of other survival means. From the literature on the trafficking of women, there is no other evidence of this debt-bondage being exerted in the transit country and none in the destination country. Generally, traffickers are said to exploit migrants *after* they are transported across the border, and in the case of prostitution, it is single young women who are involved (Salt and Hogarth, 2000: 62; Skeldon, 2000: 7). In Jordan, on the other hand, it is mainly women with children or ageing parents, and who are single heads of households.

The fact is that very few of those who have recourse to smugglers have the several thousands of dollars required. They have to borrow from friends and relatives who are already abroad, and not usually from a single source. Families can rarely support the cost for all their members at once, and a strategic choice has to be made of whom to send first. Frequently, male heads of households travel ahead of the family, not only for reconnaissance purposes but also because they leave their spouses and children as guarantees to the smugglers in Jordan until they are able to repay the entire cost of their trip. But some families chose to send the wife or a teenage child first, as they are the most likely to be able to obtain speedy recognition of their claim for asylum in the West and can then ask to be reunited with family members left in Jordan.

Because of the costs of irregular migration, Jordan is also a nexus of smuggling rings and social networks. All types of social networks support the move of asylum seekers into the West: kinship networks, political parties, co-ethnics, co-religionists and so on. In the illegal migration process, 'sending' and 'receiving' networks (Tilly, 1990) intersect, together with religious and smuggling networks who both have a transnational scope. I have explored more particularly those of the Shiite community, which might provide an example of how other transnational religious organizations support the movement of migrants. The Shiite *majlis* I mentioned above are places where information is exchanged on the best way to migrate to the West: how to buy a foreign passport or to get a Western visa, how much it costs, how to contact smugglers or forgers, which are the best countries to migrate to in terms of entry requirements and asylum procedures, what are the easi-est routes, and so on. Members who already have relatives in the West keep in contact with them by telephone or the Internet and pass on details to those attending the meetings. Young clergy play a pivotal role in mobilizing financial resources for the members of the community who wish to migrate. Financial networks have vast ramifications. Money might be collected through campaigns in Iran among Shiite co-religionists and relatives who have looked for asylum there. The two main Iraqi Shiite political parties in exile are based in Tehran, and so are several private foundations that channel funds to the United Kingdom, which has become, in the 1990s, a major centre of learning and cultural activity for the Shiites.[17] Funds are then either rechannelled to Jordan, or transferred directly to members of the smuggling ring in the West. The clergy have a priority in benefiting from financial help to migrate, in particular if they have no chance of obtaining refugee status through the UNHCR. But, like the women forced into prostitution, their departure is made conditional on the arrival of colleagues from Iraq to replace them to prevent the *majlis* disappearing. After being recipients of financial aid, members who have migrated to the West may remain in the networks by operating at a different level – gathering information and collecting funds.

The roles of social and smuggling networks are thus essential in facilitating and sustaining migration to the West. It is through these networks that migrants gather information, accrue money and bypass strict entry requirements. But the two types of network also overlap, either because relatives or co-ethnics are the smugglers, or because one or several elements (for example, money, documents) in the overall process are better obtained through a network other than via the one that organizes the smuggling.

Jordan is a first step that prepares migrants for their future situation in industrialized countries. It is both an antechamber and a training site. In Jordan, migrants will gain access to information about the situation in potential reception countries, and they will make a choice, plan a strategy. They will also get used to the problems they will face in the West, though less acutely: the restriction on free movement and integration in the job market; the quest for asylum; and illegality.

Conclusion

Changing focus to observe how and why asylum migrants merely transit in states neighbouring their home countries instead of using them as long term havens challenges the accepted views that migrants who move irregularly to industrialized states had the initial intention of doing so, and that mobilization and recruitment necessarily take place in the country of origin.

The case of Iraqi forced migrants transiting Jordan illustrates that, for a variety of cultural and practical reasons, a majority of asylum migrants who eventually reach the West via irregular means would rather stay in host countries close to their state of origin. It also shows that intercontinental trends of asylum migration cannot be fully understood without looking at a set of interrelated issues in the first countries of reception: their cultural proximity or distance from the country of origin of the migrants, geo-strategic concerns, domestic policies, administrative/legal deficiencies in the treatment of these migrants, discriminatory practices by the authorities or other social agents. These are all factors that can lead to poor socioeconomic and security conditions for migrants, and prompt them to continue their migration towards Western industrialized states, where they expect to receive better protection and opportunities.

Furthermore, ethnic and religious affiliations remain primary factors explaining both the discrimination and the survival strategies of asylum migrants in regional host countries in the Middle Eastern context, and further migration dynamics are strongly dependent on the functioning of transnational networks based on these affiliations that are not criminal by nature, even if smuggling is involved. The patterns of transit migration across Jordan confirm that 'international migrants travel along familiar avenues, circumscribed by strong linkages within or evolving within migration systems and by the example set by earlier movers and the support structures established by them' (Faist, 2000: 76). Social capital is Iraqi migrants' main asset, and among the various components of this capital, kinship and religious ties appear to be those mobilized first because they have already gained a transnational dimension. Interestingly enough, these are not activated so much from Iraq as from Jordan, which supports the idea that transnational social mechanisms need such vectors as globalized information, financial and transportation systems.

Once the mechanism is set in motion, it results in the type of chain migration described by Faist: 'The more immigrants of a given place stay in the destination region, the more want to come' (2000: 152–3). But this dynamic has to be supported by a readiness to migrate which, in the case of Iraqi forced migrants, is created not only by the sociopolitical conditions at home, but also by the type of reception they receive in neighbouring states in their region of origin.

Appendix: distribution of respondents by gender, age group and religious affiliation

Male	56.3
Female	43.7

Under 25 years old	*25 to 39 years old*	*40 to 69 years old*	*Over 69 years old*
9.1	64.6	23.7	2.6

Shiites	*Christians*	*Sunnis*	*Sabeans*
66.8	13.1	11.7	8.4

- Maximum level of education

	Illiterate/ No education	*Primary education*	*Secondary education*	*University graduate*
Male	0	8.2	34.5	57.3
Female	0.2	7.8	33.2	58.8

- Employment situation while in Jordan

	No work	*Unsteady job*	*Steady job*	*With work permit*
Male	7.2	71.6	18.9	2.3
Female	74.5	24.3	1.2	0

- Legal situation in Jordan at time of interview

	Entered illegally	*Over-stayer*	*Short-term resident*	*Long-term resident*
Male	4.5	86.8	6.4	2.3
Female	0	78.4	21.6	0

- Initial reasons for choosing Jordan

Open borders	83.4
Expected work opportunities	61.8
Accessibility of third country	31.3
Presence of UNHCR	16.8
Arab country	12.1
Presence of relatives	11.4
Less risky choice	9.5
Other	32.3

- Intentions at time of interview

Continue emigration	*Stay in Jordan*	*Go back to Iraq*
95.7	1.8	2.5

Notes

* I am grateful to the representative and staff of the UNHCR in Amman who have provided me with invaluable information, insight and access to some Iraqi asylum seekers. I also thank all the Iraqi respondents inside and outside UNHCR, the heads of various foreign NGOs in Amman who have answered my questions, the immigration officers in some Western embassies that have shared information with me, and the two anonymous reviewers who commented on a draft of this chapter. Fieldwork for this research, undertaken in 2000–01, was made possible by a series of grants from the Centre d'études et de recherches sur le Moyen-Orient contemporain (CERMOC), based in Amman. Writing was undertaken as a Jean Monnet Fellow at the Robert Schuman Centre, European University Institute, Florence.
1. There is often confusion between the concepts of human trafficking and smuggling. The UN anti-smuggling Protocol (2000) states that in trafficking, elements of coercion and exploitation (and often syndicates of organized crime) are involved. A smuggled migrant, on the other hand, is an individual who requests assistance to move into another state where s/he has no right of residence, and the smuggler's involvement goes no further than the crossing of the border (and the provision of relevant documentation). Salt and Hogarth, who have reviewed the various existing definitions, cite Belgium as having adopted one of the largest definitions of trafficking in its 'Alien Law' of 1980, which does not necessarily involve cross-border movement, though it is often linked to issues of irregular migration (2000: 20–3). 'Trafficking in persons' includes networks active in female prostitution (not necessarily cross-border), networks smuggling asylum seekers into Belgium, and those who exploit legal/illegal foreign employees. On the other hand, all smuggling networks do not have trafficking activities. Salt and Hogarth (2000: 22) list another definition proposed by Meese *et al.* (1998), according to which smuggling is a migration issue and has implications for the protection of the state, and smugglers can work for profit or for humanitarian reasons. On the other hand, trafficking in persons is a human rights issue, has implications for the individual as a victim, and traffickers work purely for financial gain.

Either process is a violation of migrant legislation in at least one of the countries involved (origin, transit or destination).

2. Unless indicated otherwise, all data in this chapter are taken from UNHCR statistics (www.unhcr.ch).

3. A paper by this author (Chatelard, 2002) deals with the issue of Iraqi refugees in Jordan from a policy perspective.

4. Questions about the 'push' factors that motivated the respondents' departure from Iraq were not asked as they were not relevant to this study and as I was careful not to be mistaken for a member of the UNHCR interviewing them to assess their claim to refugee status. I made a point of presenting myself clearly as an independent researcher. The sample was random and people were interviewed on a voluntary basis as they were coming to the UNHCR to renew documents, and not on a day when they were scheduled for an interview with UNHCR staff.

5. The Sabeans, or Mandaeans, are a sect dating back to the first centuries of Christianity and are followers of St John the Baptist. As Jews and Christians, they are recognized by Muslim tradition as 'Peoples of the Book'. The community is concentrated in Iraq and has no more than 20,000 members.

6. Sunnis are more numerous among those Iraqis who do not seek asylum in Jordan, and move back and forth between the two countries – such as suitcase traders, taxi drivers, illegal workers in agriculture or construction, and wealthy businessmen who have secured a permanent residence permit in Jordan.

7. At the time of writing, 1 JD = 1.42 euro or US$1.41.

8. The statements made in an IOM paper about the mechanisms of distorted information between migrants and those left at home do not seem to be applicable in the case under study: 'it is known that information received from family or friends is considered to be the most trustworthy. Ironically, however, information from this source has a tendency to be distorted – often including exaggerations or falsehoods about the informant's success... This often leads to a self-perpetuating network of informants who are reluctant to admit that they have not been successful in their migration attempts' (IOM, 1994: 18). In the case of Iraq, it is to a large extent the nature of the communication system(s) that accounts for the distortion.

9. A Sri Lankan house-maid gets 1.5 JD an hour, but an Iraqi woman performing the same job gets only 1 JD. Similarly, hourly rates are lower for Iraqi male labourers than for Egyptians.

10. To a certain extent, one wonders if several well-founded cases have not been rejected because of the prevailing atmosphere of suspicion against asylum seekers at the UNHCR. In fact, the recognition rate of Iraqis in Lebanon, who do not seem to have a profile that differs markedly from those in Jordan, is much higher: in 1998, while UNHCR Jordan recognized 13 per cent of the cases, UNHCR Lebanon recognized 50 per cent. But Iraqis are much less numerous in Lebanon, which they reach through Jordan and/or Syria.

11. It is interesting to notice where Jordan stands in the geography of Iraqi asylum. In 1998, it was the country that had received the second-largest number of applications by Iraqis (7,872), preceded by the Netherlands (8,300), and followed by Germany (7,435), and neither of these Western countries had a comparable population of Iraqis on their national territories.

12. In all likelihood, this is not without reason. The website of Servlife International, based in Houston, calls for a US$30 donation to provide 'an emergency relief packet with a Bible to Iraqi refugees in Jordan'. Another, CompassionRadio.com, asks for US$2 to 'help support a ministry providing Christian Day-Care [*sic*] for the [Iraqi] refugee children [in Jordan], where they will be taught the truth about Jesus and His love'. A couple of Shiite websites based in the UK denounce these sites, arguing that they are aimed at Muslim children.

13. An interesting aspect of these *majlis* is that they are attended by men who were not necessarily religious when in Iraq. Many were even close to the Communist Party. Once in Jordan, in the absence of any other network of support, they attend the *majlis* where they need first to gain religious respectability before applying for financial support.

14. For obvious methodological reasons, it is difficult to assess very clearly how the smuggling process works, who are the smugglers and/or traffickers, and how they are organized within Jordan and at the transnational level. Smuggled/trafficked individuals are often not aware of the overall functioning of the organization and can only contribute partial knowledge. Besides, they are reluctant to give details before undertaking their journey. It is therefore easier to collect information at the other end of the journey, when the migrants feel they have escaped the grip of the smugglers/traffickers, or of the border police, and can reveal information without risk. The best way was to contact migrants in Jordan and wait until they had completed their migration process to Western Europe or Australia to interview them face to face or via the Internet.

15. To provide a visa, most Western consulates ask for bank statements over several months. Therefore, migrants pay agents who open accounts in their names in a Jordanian bank and have it run for at least 3 to 4 months. The process is therefore a rather extended one to obtain all the necessary documents before the visa application can be made.

16. Migrants have to follow the routes set up by smugglers, but their final destination country is not necessarily the country of first arrival. For example, there is a route to Germany by air, but once there the Iraqi migrant manages on his/her own behalf, or with family members who come to meet him/her at the airport to reach Denmark, Sweden or the Netherlands, where asylum conditions are seen as being more favourable, or where s/he has relatives or friends. If the migrant is aiming at North America, s/he mainly uses the Jordanian facilities to buy a passport. The most expensive ones are, in decreasing order, those of Saudi Arabia, Greece and Cyprus, nationals of which are all permitted to travel to Canada without a prior visa application. Alternatively, the migrant does not need to resort to facilitators or smugglers within Jordan, but may need them later as s/he can travel to one of the Central American countries that have lax entry requirements and then reach the two main routes to the United States, either across Mexico or by boat through the Caribbean. Finally, those who prefer to go to Australia can fly from Amman to Malaysia or Indonesia. Both are Muslim countries and do not require visas from most nationals of Arab countries (although there have been some changes since the events of 11 September 2001: Australia has called on Indonesia to require visas for nationals from Iraq and Afghanistan). From these countries, migrants are smuggled by boat to Java and Australia. Those who fail can always turn to the UNHCR's regional office in Bangkok to seek asylum, or contact the smuggling

rings there that have specialized in providing high quality documents to Chinese migrants, often stolen from one of the 7 million tourists the country receives every year (Skeldon, 2000: 24).

17. In particular, this is the case of the Khû'i foundation, a welfare organization established in 1988 in Najaf (Iraq) by Ayatollah Khû'i, with branches in Iran. It transferred its headquarters to London in 1991 and has an important network of schools and charities all over the world, including a special welfare programme for refugees.

References

Al-Rasheed, M. (1998). *Iraqi Assyrian Christians in London: The Construction of Ethnicity*, Lewiston, NY: Edwin Mellen Press.

Amnesty International (1997). *Fear, Flight and Forcible Exile: Refugees in the Middle East*, London: Amnesty International.

Barth, F. (ed.) (1969). *Ethnic Groups and Boundaries*, Boston, MA: Little, Brown.

Bigo, D. (1996). *Polices en réseau, l'expérience européenne*, Paris: Presses de Sciences Po.

Chatelard, G. (1997). 'Les chrétiens de Jordanie: entre appartenance communautaire et identité nationale', *Les Cahiers de l'Orient*, quatrième trimestre, No. 48.

Chatelard, G. (2002). 'Incentives to Transit: Policy Responses to Influxes of Iraqi Forced Migrants in Jordan', Working paper, Florence: Robert Schuman Centre for Advanced Studies, European University Institute.

Crisp, J. and N. Van Hear (1998). 'Refugee Protection and Immigration Control: Addressing the Asylum Dilemma', *Refugee Survey Quarterly*, 17(3): 1–27.

Doraï, M. K. (2002). 'Palestinian Emigration from Lebanon to Northern Europe: Transnational Migratory Networks and Patterns of Solidarity', Paper presented at the Third Mediterranean Social and Political Research Meeting, Florence, 20–24 March, Florence: Mediterranean Programme, Robert Schuman Centre for Advanced Studies, European University Institute.

Engbersen, G. and J. van der Lun (1998). 'Illegality and Criminality: The Differential Opportunity Structure of Undocumented Migrants', in K. Koser and H. Lutz (eds), *The New Migration in Europe*, Basingstoke: Macmillan.

Faist, T. (2000). *The Volume and Dynamics of International Migration and Transnational Social Spaces*, Oxford: Oxford University Press.

Ghosh, B. (1998). *Huddled Masses and Uncertain Shores: Insight into Irregular Migration*, International Organization for Migration, The Hague: Martinus Nijhoff.

Gonzalez, N. L. and C. S. McCommon (eds) (1989). *Conflict, Migration and the Expression of Ethnicity*, Boulder, CO: Westview Press.

IOM (1994). *Transit Migration in Ukraine, Migration Information Programme*, Hungary: International Organization for Migration, August.

IOM (1995). *Transit Migration in Turkey, Migration Information Programme*, Geneva: International Organization for Migration, December.

Koser, K. (1997). 'Negotiating Entry into Fortress Europe: The Migration Strategies of "Spontaneous" Asylum Seekers', in P. Muus (ed.), *Exclusion and Inclusion of Refugees in Contemporary Europe*. Utrecht: ERCOMER: 157–70.

Koser, K. and H. Lutz (eds) (1998). *The New Migration in Europe*, Basingstoke: Macmillan.

Koslowski, R. (2000). 'The Mobility Money Can Buy: Human Smuggling and Border Control in the European Union', in P. Andreas and T. Snyder (eds), *The Wall Around the West: State Borders and Immigration Controls in North America and Europe*, Lanham, MD: Rowman & Littlefield: 203–18.

LCHR (1992). *Asylum under Attack. Report on the Protection of Iraqi Refugees and Displaced Persons one Year after the Humanitarian Emergency in Iraq*, New York: Lawyers Committee for Human Rights, April.

Le Roy, J. (2001). 'Statistical Outline of the Situation of the South Iraqi Refugees in Iran, including the Marsh Dwellers', in 'Iraqi Marshlands: Prospects', First drafts of papers presented at the Conference on the AMAR International Charitable Foundation, London, 21 May.

McDowell, C. (1997). *A Tamil Asylum Diaspora: Sri Lankan Migration, Settlement and Politics in Switzerland*, Oxford: Berghahn Books.

Meese, J., K. Van Impe and S. Venheste (1998). *Multidisciplinary Research on the Phenomenon of Trafficking in Human Beings from an International and National Perspective: A Pilot Study with Poland and Hungary*, Ghent: University of Ghent.

Morrison, J. (1998). *The Cost of Survival: The Trafficking of Refugees to the UK*, London: Refugee Council.

Muus, P. (ed.) (1997). *The Exclusions and Inclusions of Refugees in Contemporary Europe*, Utrecht: ERCOMER.

Peter, A. (2000). *Border Games: Policing the US–Mexico Divide*, Ithaca, NY: Cornell University Press.

Portes, A. (ed.) (1995). *The Economic Sociology of Immigration. Essays on Networks, Ethnicity and Entrepreneurship*, New York: Russell Sage Foundation.

Rajaee, B. (2000). 'The Politics of Refugee Policy in Post-Revolutionary Iran', *The Middle East Journal*, 54(1): 44–63.

Salt, J. and J. Hogarth (2000). *Migrant Trafficking and Human Smuggling in Europe: A Review of the Evidence with Case Studies from Hungary, Poland and Ukraine*, Geneva: International Organization for Migration.

Salt, J. and J. Stein (1997). 'Migration as a Business: The Case of Trafficking', *International Migration*, 35(4): 467–94.

Skeldon, R. (2000). *Myths and Realities of Chinese Irregular Migration*, Migration Research Series, Geneva: International Organization for Migration, January.

Snyder, T. (2000). 'Conclusion: The Wall Around the West', in P. Andreas and T. Snyder (eds), *The Wall Around the West: State Borders and Immigration Controls in North America and Europe*. Lanham, MD: Rowman & Littlefield: 219–27.

Tilly, C. (1990). 'Transplanted Networks', in V. Yans MacLaughlin (ed.), *Immigration Reconsidered*, Oxford: Oxford University Press: 79–95.

UNHCR (1996). *Background Paper on Iraqi Refugees and Asylum Seekers*, Center for Documentation and Research, Geneva: UNHCR.

United Nations (2000). *Protocol Against the Smuggling of Migrants by Land, Sea and Air*, Supplementing the United Nations Convention Against Transnational Organized Crime, United Nations, Geneva.

USCR (1991). *Mass Exodus: Iraqi Refugees in Iran*, Issue Brief, Washington, DC: US Committee for Refugees, July.

USCR (1991–2001). *Jordan Country Report*, Washington, DC: US Committee for Refugees.

USCR (1996). *World Refugee Survey. An Annual Assessment of Conditions Affecting Refugees, Asylum Seekers, and Internally Displaced*, Washington, DC: US Committee for Refugees.

USDS (1991–2001). *Jordan Country Report, Human Right Practices Reports*, Bureau of Democracy, Human Rights, and Labour, Washington, DC: US Department of State.

Van Hear, N. (1995). 'The Impact of the Involuntary Mass "Return" to Jordan in the Wake of the Gulf Crisis', *International Migration Review*, 29(2).

Van Hear, N. (1998). *New Diasporas: The Mass Exodus, Dispersal and Regrouping of Migrant Communities*. London: UCL Press.

Vertovec, S. and R. Cohen (eds) (1999). *Migration, Diasporas and Transnationalism*, Cheltenham: Edward Elgar.

17
Asylum Seekers as Pariahs in the Australian State
Claudia Tazreiter

The contemporary politics of asylum

The year 2001 marked the fiftieth anniversary of the United Nations Refugee Convention (hereafter the Refugee Convention), which articulates most directly the grounds for protection that should be offered to those fleeing persecution. The majority of countries in the world do have substantive obligations to people who claim to be refugees, as signatories to the Refugee Convention and its Protocol of 1967. In the fifty-year period since the establishment of the Refugee Convention, the idea of (some) rights being universal, thereby applicable to all of humanity rather than the members of a particular state, has been given political efficacy through the vehicle of human rights. Rights, such as those embodied in the Universal Declaration of Human Rights of 1948, privilege no particular concept of human life, or of cultural traits, beliefs or practices. The consolidation of human rights gathered momentum in the later half of the twentieth century through the proliferation of human rights institutions and the efficacy of the idea that protecting such rights is of intrinsic value across and between cultures and nations. The central pillars of human rights, including the Refugee Convention, continue to be important instruments for ensuring the protection of people in vulnerable, life-threatening circumstances. Yet at the same time, the persecution of individuals and groups has continued in various waves of violence in locations around the world, testing the practical efficacy of the universal norms embodied in human rights law. The grounds for persecution of particular individuals or groups continue to relate to those characteristics that differentiate people; characteristics such as race, religion, nationality, gender and, in particular, political affiliations. Yet we expect these very distinctions to be irrelevant, or at least suspended, when obligations to substantive human rights are tested, for example, as by the arrival of asylum seekers asking for protection under the Refugee Convention in a signatory state.

Notwithstanding the penetration of human rights as valued principles during the late twentieth century, geo-political shifts in the balance of political order from the early 1990s have resulted in an increase in localized conflicts, leading to humanitarian crises in many parts of the world. The dissolution of the Soviet Union ruptured the Cold War stand-off, which had maintained a modicum of international stability with the political polarization of the world around the camps of two superpowers, the Soviet Union and the United States. The effects of decolonization in Africa and Asia also continued to be felt into the 1990s, with both regional and local conflicts. Most recently the 'war on terror', first in Afghanistan and then in Iraq in the aftermath of the attack on the World Trade Center in New York and the Pentagon in Washington on 11 September 2001, has contributed to forced migration and to a Middle East region which continues to be politically volatile.

Paradoxically, it is the countries which themselves safeguard democratic principles, uphold the rule of law, and are the most vocal defenders of human rights around the globe that have felt the need to increase mechanisms of immigration control since the 1990s; these mechnaisms have in many cases been coercive, at times also employing violent means of control. Western democracies which have in the past benefited from immigration, whether through guest-worker programmes, or other planned immigration intakes, increasingly are concerned to guard their borders from the movement of people, including those claiming protection under the Refugee Convention, through various forms of internal and external deterrence. The movement of 'unauthorized arrivals' – those without a visa or other travel permit – has as a result become increasingly clandestine, with people-smugglers profiting from the trade in human cargo. Recent figures from the UNHCR point to a decline in asylum applications in most parts of the world (UNHCR, 2002). In the second quarter of 2002, for example, in the twenty European countries surveyed, applications fell by 8 per cent. Of course, such a decline can be an indication of the cessation of conflict and other refugee-producing phenomena. However, at a time in history when we know that the 'push-factors' that generate forced migration are not in decline, the drop in asylum applications, particularly in Western countries, indicates tougher border enforcement and other administrative techniques to deter asylum arrivals.

The 1951 Refugee Convention promises protection from *refoulement*; that those with genuine fears of persecution will not be returned to the source of their persecution. With this promise, however, receiver societies also bear the burden of providing for the needs of such new arrivals. It follows that addressing the 'root causes' of flight is in the long-term interest of receiver societies, ensuring that the numbers of unanticipated arrivals claiming protection are reduced. However, through the 1990s we have seen an emphasis on the part of Western states directed towards deterring such 'irregular' arrivals, and measures aimed at their removal, with less attention paid and resources allocated to initiatives seeking the resolution of refugee-causing conflict and violence. Measures aimed at deterring the arrival of asylum seekers have become a priority for states of the West, with an infusion of significant resources to fund internal and external measures to detect, detain, deport and in other ways discourage 'irregular' or 'unauthorized' arrivals, or 'aliens'.

Before exploring the case of the Australian response to asylum migration since 1999, I shall briefly outline the obligation to protect; an argument that begins with the assumption that borders must be porous enough for individuals to be able to claim protection in the first place.

Normative reasoning and the obligation to protect

The response to those who have fled their homes and seek protection elsewhere requires careful and detailed differentiation, highlighting the needs and the rights of residents as well as newcomers. Certainly, a tension exists between the 'needs of strangers' and the needs of citizens in either admitting or rejecting asylum seekers. Obligations to those seeking protection require a state properly to consider a protection application, ensuring that an impartial arbiter assess every claim for protection on its merits. A state that has acceded to international human rights conventions has 'special' obligations towards an individual who may be a refugee, no matter what his or her mode of entry. Such 'special' obligations pertain to the protection a refugee requires while the origin of persecution continues.

In practice, the application and validity of the Refugee Convention has been called into question as the movement of refugees has increased in scale and complexity in the post-Cold-War era. The provisions of international law, including the Refugee Convention as well as the UN Convention on Human Rights, indicate a contradiction in international cooperation in that the right to leave is provided with no complementary right to admission anywhere else. This contradiction has resulted in the prevalence of 'statelessness' and the phenomenon of 'refugees in orbit'.

The contemporary problem faced by the international community is to find a way to strike a balance between protection for those who genuinely require it, while ensuring that states are not overburdened with requests for protection by those who are not entitled. Borders must be porous enough not to disadvantage genuine cases, while the administrative systems for arbitrating on individual cases must be both *just* and *impartial*. The right of a state to turn away those not in need of protection must, in turn, be asserted if a robust international protection regime is to remain meaningful. I now move on to explore the tensions in instituting asylum systems, utilizing the case study of Australia. First, I examine briefly the refugee intake within the broader immigration system before moving to an analysis of the approach to asylum seekers in recent years.

A brief history of refugee migration to Australia

As a 'classic country of immigration', Australia proactively sets a yearly quota of immigrants, in similar fashion to other countries of immigration such as Canada and the United States. Those wishing to migrate can apply according to specified categories, such as skilled migration, family reunion, and humanitarian categories. Since the 1990s around 12,000 places per year have been set aside for the humanitarian intake, within an overall immigration intake that has oscillated around 100,000 per year. The humanitarian intake comprises various categories of refugees, or people in refugee-like situations.[1] The humanitarian programme has remained largely quarantined from controversy and had bi-partisan support. This 'off-shore' programme, where individuals who have been found to be refugees outside Australian territory are selected for resettlement by Australian immigration officials, is distinct from the 'on-shore' category of spontaneous asylum seeking arrivals who have not had their claim for protection heard by an authorized person. These on-shore arrivals have been the trigger for significant political turmoil in recent years. On-shore arrivals have been tied to the yearly immigration and humanitarian quota since 1996, shortly after the conservative Howard government was elected. This development has had the effect of setting an artificial cap on the number of asylum seekers that are able to be accommodated in the programme in any given year.[2] The number of such 'unauthorized arrivals' is thereby pegged to the humanitarian programme, with the result that when the number of asylum seekers successful in their applications exceed the quota set, the excess is taken from the humanitarian places offered for that year.[3] In other words, an artificial competition has been created between off-shore and on-shore arrivals.

I turn now to an analysis of the asylum debate in Australia in the period leading up to the *Tampa* crisis of August 2001 (see p. 380). I focus in particular on the administrative and policy developments in 'managing' asylum seekers, developments which generated, first, the policy of mandatory detention and, second, the introduction of a temporary protection visa (TPV). My aim is to show the way in which the management and treatment of asylum seekers from 1999 onwards, together with the way the issue was portrayed and debated in the public sphere, generated the conditions that enabled the *Tampa* incident and the political developments that followed to occur with overwhelming public support. Moreover, this policy approach is not a radical departure from past practices in the management of asylum migration in Australia, but rather indicates continuities with the past.

Detention: a uniquely Australian approach

No doubt the most contentious policy approach regarding asylum seekers has been the policy of mandatory and non-reviewable detention of those who arrive without documentation. Cambodian boat people who arrived in Australia from 1989 onwards, fleeing the Pol Pot dictatorship, were the first group of unauthorized arrivals subjected to mandatory and non-reviewable immigration detention in Australia. More than a decade later, this policy remains in place with a logic that can be traced to an over-emphasis on the idea of an immigration queue; a queue from which no individual should be exempt.

The response to boat arrivals from November 1989 marks a toughening in the approach to boat arrivals and other 'illegal' arrivals in Australia. The most significant recent 'wave' of boat arrivals began in 1999 and continued through the first half of 2001. All but the first wave of these arrivals, during the 1970s, have been subject to mandatory and non-reviewable detention. Though the numbers of boat arrivals in Australia were not significant until 1999, as indicated in Table 17.1, a widespread public perception of inundation, has fostered resentment towards asylum seekers. This perception of inundation and being unfairly overburdened, has in turn been fostered by successive governments in a bi-partisan fashion, along with a failure to communicate the dissonance between perception and reality. That is, Australia cannot be said to have been 'flooded' by boat people, as the figures indicate. We must search for other reasons to explain the continued legitimacy of mandatory detention as an appropriate response to asylum seekers.

Certainly, the bi-partisan support of mandatory detention had a significant bearing on the public acceptance of this policy through the 1990s. Successive Australian governments have long maintained that the detention regime is

Table 17.1 Non-citizens in Australia without authorization

Year	Arrivals by air	Arrivals by boat	Over-stayers
2000/01	1 508	4 137	53 000
1999/00	1 695	4 175	53 000
1998/99	2 106	921	53 143
1997/98	1 550	157	51 000
1996/97	1 350	365	45 100
1995/96	663	589	–
1994/95	485	1 071	–
1993/94	–	194	–
1992/93	2 448*	194	81 164
1991/92		78	–
1990/91		158	–
1989/90		224	–
Total	11 805	12 263	n.a.

Note: * Total arrivals by air, 1989–93.
Source: DIMIA Factsheet 74. www.immi.gov.au/facts/74unauthorised.htm

necessary for the maintenance of immigration control; that is, to 'uphold the universal visa requirement and to guard against unauthorized arrivals undermining the immigration program' (Mediansky, 1998: 126). However, there has also been an acknowledgement by the Department of Immigration, Multicultural and Indigenous Affairs (DIMIA), as well as by individual politicians, that the practice of mandatory detention is used as a deterrent to others who may arrive in this manner. This approach is contrary to the UNHCR recommendations on the justified application of detention of asylum seekers.[4]

In 1997 the running of Australia's immigration detention centres was opened to public tendering. The tender was won by Australasian Correctional Management (ACM), a subsidiary of the US Wackenhut Corporation, better known for developing privately run prisons in the United States. As well as being responsible for security within detention centres, ACM has been responsible for the delivery of social services, such as the accommodation, education, recreation, catering, health care, welfare and counselling, to detainees as well as for the infrastructure maintenance of the centres. One of the problems that has come to light from the privatization of detention management is the ability of the government to withhold information from the public on the grounds of commercial confidentiality agreements (Crock and Saul, 2002: 82). The result of this shift in responsibilities has been limited public scrutiny of detention practices and less transparent accountability procedures in the treatment of detainees. While access to the detention facilities in the urban centres of Sydney, Melbourne and Perth has been possible, though limited, for journalists and members of the public, access to the remote centres of South Australia and Western Australia has generally remained closed to the public, with journalists being admitted only for formal tours. Most recently, the Australian Audit Office has been critical of the running of detention centres by ACM, not least pointing to the high cost of detention falling on the Australian taxpayer (Australian Audit Office, 2004).

The public scrutiny of the detention issue has been inconsistent, though in recent years several public enquiries have focused the issue more clearly in the minds of the Australian public. The attention given to the detention issue by the Australian media has oscillated from periods of near silence to periods of daily scrutiny across media outlets. As Table 17.1 indicates, in the years 1999/2000 arrivals by boat did increase quite dramatically compared to earlier periods, though the number of unauthorized arrivals were small when compared to the number of annual asylum applicants arriving in the member states of the EU, in Canada and the United States. In this period, reports of riots and protests within detention centres, suicide attempts and actions of self-harm, including hunger strikes and the sewing-together of lips, were prominent in the popular media. For example, television footage during August 2000 showed ACM staff, assisted by South Australian police in full riot gear including helmets, batons and shields, quelling a protest consisting of around eighty detainees at the Woomera detention centre. Water cannon was also used to quell the riot (Mares, 2001: 35). These images were troubling to an Australian public unfamiliar with such scenes of violence and force within Australian territory. Other accounts began to emerge from detention centres of ACM officers utilizing what appeared to be excessive force against detainees. Video footage from the Villawood Detention Centre in Sydney showed detainees being assaulted and subsequently denied medical attention for their injuries (*Sydney Morning Herald*, 2 August 2001: 3). Unlike earlier periods, the media coverage of the detention issue after 1999 regularly highlighted the human suffering of detention, including psychological damage. In June 2001, the Australian Catholic Social Justice Council (ACSJC) characterized the treatment in detention centres as torture. During the same period the World Council of Churches (WCC) indicated that it was 'deeply troubled' about Australia's detention practices, particularly in the light of the small numbers of unauthorized arrivals arriving in Australia compared to other regions of the world (Reuters, 6 July 2001). The gathering weight of evidence, both local and international, became highly critical of the Australian government's practice of detention.

I turn now to an analysis of the policy of mandatory detention in Australia. I consider how such an approach had remained acceptable in a system welcoming of immigrants, including refugees under the humanitarian quota. Moreover, I explore some perhaps unanticipated consequences of detention.

The rationale for detention

The Australian state regularly and unapologetically utilizes the idea of deterrence as justification for the continued practice of mandatory and non-reviewable detention of asylum seekers in Australia. As already stated, since the early 1990s this has been a bi-partisan approach of the two major political parties in Australia, the Liberal/National coalition and the Labor Party. Detention is a policy decision and a strategic and administrative practice that is unambiguously about containment, separation and punishment. Detention reaffirms the security of the rest. Moreover, the association between detention and punishment, even in the case of asylum seekers, is neither an arbitrary nor an ambiguous association (Caloz-Tschopp, 1997: 166). While the nexus between security and punishment is often hidden in official accounts of detention practice and the rationale for such practices by governments, it becomes more visible through the testimony and circumstances of those detained (Human Rights and Equal Opportunity Commission, 2004).[5]

Western states have implemented a raft of deterrence measures since the 1990s. Such measures include carrier sanctions; special visa requirements on nationals from refugee-producing states; the placement of additional immigration officers at overseas ports; 'burden shifting' arrangements with other states; and the interdiction of refugees at frontiers as well as in international waters, ensuring that they cannot enter Western states and claim protection. The Australian state, however, remains unique among Western countries in the vigour with which it utilizes detention as a deterrence measure.[6] Other states tend to utilize detention for relatively short periods of time to establish health and security checks.

One well-documented side-effect of Australia's detention policy is the psychological trauma that detention causes: a phenomenon that is exacerbated when detention is prolonged, and of an indefinite period. Research conducted on the impact of detention on asylum seekers indicates that detention has the potential to re-traumatize people from a refugee background, many of whom experienced torture and trauma in their country of origin (Silove *et al.*, 1993; Silove and Steel, 1998). Torture and trauma counselling services have been reluctant to provide services to asylum seekers in detention, especially for those being detained for indefinite periods.

A growing concern among human rights groups in Australia in relation to the 'on-shore' arrivals, is the impact that detention has on the general well-being and mental health of detainees. Even for those living in the community, extreme anxiety is linked to delays in processing applications; the poverty resulting from a lack of entitlement to such items as work permits; racial discrimination and conflict with immigration officials; fears of being sent home; and separation from their families (Silove and Steel, 1998: 10–11).[7]

The most recent experiences of the self-harm of asylum seekers in detention, and the continuing concern over the physical and psychological development of children in detention has resulted in health professionals voicing their concern publicly (Silove *et al.*, 2000: 608–9). By August 2001, the Australian Medical Association (AMA) had become involved in the detention issue, with the federal president at the time, Dr Karen Phelps, speaking out against the health effects of detention (ABC Radio National, 13 August 2001).[8]

Creating 'second-class' asylum seekers with the temporary protection visa

One of the most significant changes in recent years to the status of individuals found to be genuine refugees is the introduction in October 1999 of a temporary protection visa (TPV, Visa Subclass 785). This change focuses on the documentary validity of entry to Australia as the determinant of the visa an individual may be granted once s/he has been found to be a refugee. The TPV grants a three-year temporary status, during which time no family reunion or access to other significant resettlement service is available. A TPV means an individual has no automatic right of return upon leaving

Australia and no eligibility for medical care, under Medicare.[9] On the other hand, those people who arrive in Australia with valid travel documents and subsequently apply for refugee status face an often arduous task in proving the legitimacy of their claims. That is, the bona fides of asylum seekers living in the community as individuals who have escaped some form of persecution are called into question even before the particulars of their situation can be investigated, because they had been in a safe enough position to avail themselves of travel documents from their government authorities and been able to purchase an air ticket to Australia.[10]

Two new categories of TPV were introduced into Australian law as a result of a raft of legislative changes under the Migration Amendment Bill 2001, soon after the *Tampa* incident of August 2001, and only weeks before the federal election of November 2001. I shall discuss the '*Tampa* incident' and the ensuing Migration Amendment Bill shortly. The earlier introduction of the TPV, in 1999, met with stiff opposition from NGO advocates, many of whom interpreted this measure as an erosion of Australia's commitment to its protection obligations and another indication of the development of a 'two-class' refugee system, where asylum seekers are stigmatized as 'queue jumpers', fraudulent and even criminal. The Refugee Council of Australia (RCOA), in a position paper on the TPV, argues that this new visa class is being used as a form of punishment for those who have circumvented Australian immigration control by their unauthorized entry, and to act as a deterrent to future arrivals. It lists the preclusion of family reunion as perhaps the most harmful limitation on TPV holders. In addition, the RCOA argues that Australia is acting in a manner contrary to its obligations under the Refugee Convention, which provides that contracting states shall 'not impose penalties, on account of their illegal entry' (Article 31), (RCOA, Position on Temporary Protection Visas, November 1999).

The policy and practice of mandatory detention, and the imposition of new regulations such as the TPV, were contested in a relatively narrow public debate until the period leading up to the *Tampa* crisis of August 2001. The *Tampa* crisis was in essence a relatively minor incident, involving the presence in Australian waters of a boatload of some 433 asylum seekers. However, this boatload and the Norwegian freighter, *Tampa*, which sought to rescue them at sea, became the justification for major changes to Australian immigration law and to the processing of asylum claims. This one incident also solidified public opinion firmly against asylum seekers. While there was nothing singular or conspicuous about the *Tampa* boatload of asylum seekers, the political and legislative responses of the Australian government to this particular boatload has become *the* caesura in the Australian public sphere and in the politics of asylum (Rundle, 2001; MacCallum, 2002). Coming as it did only a few weeks before the 11 September attacks on the World Trade Center in New York, the *Tampa* crisis marks a departure from more measured and considered policy development in earlier periods of Australian political life.[11]

The developments in the Australian handling of asylum claims, particularly since 1999, allow us now to consider the developments in the politics of asylum around the *Tampa* issue. Perhaps the developments leading up to *Tampa* go some way towards explaining the inflammatory response to this incident and the subsequent legislative changes. Widespread media scrutiny of detention, and particularly the issue of detaining children from 1999 to mid-2001, focused public attention on this issue in quite a new way. The central role of public opinion in the politics of asylum however crystallized in response to the '*Tampa* incident'.

Generating fear from one boatload of asylum seekers: *Tampa* and beyond

Events in late August 2001 demonstrated a dramatic escalation of the 'politics of asylum' and the ensuing treatment that those who seek protection in Australia faced. On 18 August, the *Sydney Morning Herald*, a major metropolitan broadsheet, carried the headline: 'PM calls for tighter law on asylum seekers'. The article began: 'The Prime Minister yesterday declared war on illegal immigrants, saying Australia must "redouble our efforts" to make it less attractive for them to come here.' On 26 August, a small boat, carrying 433 asylum seekers, who had embarked from Indonesia, was in distress and appeared to be on the verge of sinking some 140 km north of Christmas Island, which is part of Australian territory. A Norwegian commercial container ship, the MV *Tampa*, rescued the asylum seekers and, after initially seeking to return them to Indonesia, attempted to take them to Christmas Island.

The captain of the *Tampa*, Arne Rinnan, was refused access to Australian waters and was threatened with fines and the impounding of his ship. A stand-off ensued between the Indonesian, Norwegian and Australian governments on the question of responsibility for the asylum seekers. The Australian prime minister was interviewed by the national broadcaster, the ABC, on the evening of 27 August 2001. In response to a series of questions on Australia's response to the *Tampa* issue he stated:

> We are a decent, compassionate, humanitarian country, but we also have an absolute right to decide who comes to this country...It is an appalling human tragedy that people wander the world in search of a home. I understand that, but no country can surrender the right to decide who comes here and how they come here. We have an open, non-discriminatory immigration policy and obviously there are people who seek to exploit the generosity of Australia and what we are trying to do, as we have done at all points is [*sic*] strike a balance between our decency and our generosity, but also making certain that if people come here on the basis of being

refugees they are compared with all other people who are seeking to come here on the basis of being refugees. (ABC 7.30 Report, 27 August 2001)

Captain Rinnan broke the deadlock, insisting that the safety of his passengers should be the priority. As the *Tampa* made for Christmas Island, Australian Special Air Services (SAS) troops were ordered to board the ship and take control. Eventually, after multilateral negotiations, including the involvement of the UNHCR, the Australian government announced a new approach to unauthorized boat arrivals which was to become known as the 'Pacific Solution'. Prime Minister Howard insisted that the *Tampa* asylum seekers would not be allowed to lodge protection applications in Australia. After hasty negotiations with neighbouring Pacific Island nations, the *Tampa* asylum seekers, and all subsequent boat arrivals who have been intercepted by the Australian Navy, have been sent on to processing centres in the neighbouring Pacific states of Nauru and Manus Island of Papua New Guinea. The *Tampa* incident is estimated to have cost the Australian government US$120 million, and the 'Pacific Solution' is still proving to be a drain on Australia's financial resources, as Australia covers the cost of detention as well as 'friendship' payments to the nations that are hosting the asylum seekers who were 'pushed off' Australian territory to be processed in these neighbouring Pacific states.[12]

By mid-September 2001, the government had placed before the Australian Parliament a raft of legislative measures, which were passed with minor amendments before the federal election of 10 November 2001. The Migration Amendment Bill 2001 facilitates stricter border control and further restricts the rights of asylum seekers. The effect of the bill is to excise from the Australian Migration Zone the Australian territories of Christmas Island, Ashmore Reef, Cartier Reef and Cocos Island. As a result, boat arrivals landing their craft on these islands are not considered as being in Australian territory for the purpose of lodging a protection application. Further, the Border Protection Bill 2001 authorizes the removal of any vessel from Australian territorial water if it is deemed that the intention of the people aboard is to enter Australia unlawfully. Indeed, section 7A of the Act confirms the power of the government and its administration to act outside any legislative authority (Crock and Saul, 2002: 39). As part of this package of amendments, the Judicial Review Bill, first introduced to the Senate in December 1998, was passed. This mechanism restricts access to Federal and High Court judicial review of administrative decisions under the Migration Act 1958, such as the decisions of the Refugee Review Tribunal.[13]

In the time that has lapsed since the *Tampa* crisis, the effects of the political reaction to this one boatload of asylum seekers has not abated in the Australian public sphere. The diplomatic stand-off that ensued, as well as the raft of legislative changes that were passed through the Australian Parliament as a direct result of the *Tampa* crisis, are indeed disproportionate to the dilemma that 433 asylum seekers wishing to seek protection in Australia could be expected to generate. However, the *Tampa* crisis, coming as it did just two weeks before the terrorist attacks of 11 September on New York and Washington, has consolidated public opinion in Australia firmly in support of the governments actions. Public opinion polls reflected a ten-point surge in support of the government in the weeks leading up to the federal election of 10 November 2001, at the time the 'Pacific Solution' was being put in place (*The Australian*, 11–12 May 2002: 24–5).[14] It should be noted that a vocal minority within Australia rejects the government's approach to asylum seekers; the long-term detention of those who arrived before *Tampa* and the warehousing of the *Tampa* asylum seekers as part of the 'Pacific Solution'. National security and the maintenance of a control system of immigration – symbolized by an immigration queue – are the threads that bind the Howard government's administrative and legislative direction to public opinion. At the time of writing, the majority of the *Tampa* asylum seekers have been found to be genuine refugees and have been granted protection in states other than Australia.

In the weeks following the *Tampa* crisis, the asylum debate filled the front pages of national newspapers and was the key item in television and radio broadcasts with another asylum-seeker incident: the 'children overboard' affair. The government claimed that children had been thrown overboard by their parents from boats making their way to Australian waters in early September 2001, in an attempt to intimidate the Australian government:

> The Government reported that children wearing lifejackets were thrown into the sea after the vessel was stopped by HMAS Adelaide off Christmas Island yesterday. Adults, also in lifejackets, jumped overboard in what Mr Ruddock described as 'disturbing...planned and premeditated' action with the 'intention of putting us under duress'. The incident keeps the border control issue on centre stage, after last week's forcible removal of people from HMAS Manoora onto Nauru. (*Sydney Morning Herald*, 8 October 2001: 1)

The prime minister, John Howard, the immigration minister, Philip Ruddock, and the defence minister, Peter Reith, made much of the 'children overboard' incident, articulating repeatedly the bad moral character of people who were prepared to throw their children into the sea as a form of intimidation. On the influential talkback radio show hosted by Alan Jones, on 7 October 2001, prime minister Howard said: 'Quite frankly, Alan, I don't want in this country people who are prepared, if those reports are true, to throw their own children overboard. And that kind of emotional blackmail is very distressing' (Radio 2UE). Defence photographs were released, showing figures with lifejackets floating in the ocean, though identifying information was removed from the photographs. On the morning of the federal election, the asylum-seeker issue remained on the front page of all the country's major newspapers:

> Stories can be too good to be true. The tale of the Iraqi children thrown into the ocean off Christmas Island a couple of days after John Howard called the election was one such story. It always seemed too good to be true. Demonizing boat people was nothing new. Church leaders claim it had been under way almost since the 1998 election.
>
> The Howard Government has linked them with terrorists, tarred them with the Taliban brush, christened them 'illegals' and denounced them as abusers of the Australian court system. It was only another detail in this grim portrait to say they were the sort of people who would put their children's lives at risk to blackmail Australia into giving them asylum (*Sydney Morning Herald*, 10–11 November 2001: 27).

The Howard government won the 2001 election with an increased majority. A Senate inquiry after the election into the 'children overboard' incident took evidence from senior defence personnel and senior public servants. The inquiry findings indicate that in fact children were not thrown overboard; that the photographs the government released on the eve of the election, claiming that asylum seekers were seeking to blackmail the government, were instead saving their lives, as the vessel they were on was sinking. Rather than the asylum seekers behaving reprehensibly in putting their children's lives at risk, the evidence of the Senate inquiry has revealed a trail of obfuscation and at best a careful 'management' of the information at hand at the most senior levels of the defence force, the public service and among ministerial advisers (Weller, 2002).

It is pertinent, then, to ponder to what extent the *Tampa* incident is unique? Are there any connections with past practices? Though the political handling of the *Tampa* incident, and the resulting 'push off' policies that have been confirmed by legislation passed as part of the Migration Amendment Bill 2001, are clearly a new development in Australia's management of asylum seekers, the language of border protection – of 'queue-jumpers' and 'illegal aliens' – is not altogether a new development.[15] Rather, in this, as in other approaches to 'on-shore' arrivals, a bi-partisan approach is evident in the Australian political system, as I outlined earlier. This approach can be typified as privileging recruited migration as the only legitimate form of migration. This is an approach that only a 'resettlement' country such as Australia can adopt. Gerry Hand, the minister for immigration in the early 1990s in the Hawke Labor government made regular public pronouncements about 'illegals' and 'queue jumpers', utilizing derogatory labels as part of the legitimization of tougher legislative and administrative approaches.

While a continuity is evident between present-day and earlier approaches to asylum seekers, the developments that resulted from the *Tampa* crisis indicate a marked escalation in the deliberate use of a politics of fear, and drawing an unsubstantiated, yet powerful, link between asylum seekers and national security. Certainly such general fears are not unique to Australia. The extent to which legislative and administrative developments in Australia in relation to the protection of asylum seekers may be mirrored by other Western countries is doubtful. The Australian immigration minister visited Europe and Africa in August 2002, admitting that the asylum seekers who were; 'unable to pierce Australia's tough border protection system would inevitably look to Europe for alternative sanctuary' (*Sydney Morning Herald*, 24–25 August 2002). Certainly, as a proactive country of immigration which has in the past been held up as a successful model of harmonious multi-cultural coexistance between diverse ethnic, religious and other 'identity' groups, Australia's treatment of asylum seekers is sending a powerful signal to the world.

Conclusion

Concerns over security are by no means new phenomena in the logic that drives state responses to those seeking protection. However, heavy-handed responses to asylum seekers, or to those who have been 'ethnically profiled' as a terrorist risk, must engender a degree of unease for those who consider a robust international protection system an important marker of trans-national justice. The onus of proof for turning away asylum seekers should be with those who argue for the sanctity of territorial borders (that is, closed borders).

Policy-makers must be mindful that public opinion toward refugees and asylum seekers in various local settings, is shifting constantly and must be engaged and re-engaged with new incursions on the rights of refugees and those seeking protection in order to ensure the continued efficacy of inter-national human rights mechanisms and laws. Certainly, the interests of states must be fairly balanced against the needs of those wanting to enter. The issues around the entry of asylum seekers, particularly where they enter a country without authorization, are not straightforward, requiring a balance between needs and aspirations at the local level and the fulfilment of obligations that are held between states at the international level. Moreover, responses need to be nuanced and flexible to changing local and international conditions.

The 'security state' remains central in driving the political and social con-struction of refugees, and in particular of asylum seekers as 'irregular', and as a corollary, 'unwanted' arrivals. This picture re-emerges powerfully with the example of the Australian response to asylum seekers. Irregular arrivals are perceived as being a threat to the cohesion of the nation, while also providing a focus for resentment, readily exploited by politicians searching for simplistic ways of communicating about complex social and political problems to their constituents. For those countries such as Australia, who accept a certain number of Refugee Convention status persons for resettlement, the emergence of a 'two-class' system is possible, and indeed has emerged in recent years in the Australian case, with the introduction of the temporary protection visa (TPV). Those arriving spontaneously are more readily cast into a pot of 'non-authentic' or 'fraudulent' claimants, labelled 'queue jumpers', or, in the security-heightened environment of recent years, as 'criminals' or 'terrorists'.

The issue of people-smuggling and the illegal status of arrivals has caused enormous political tension in recent years, particularly as this form of entry is perceived as a security threat, no matter the veracity of someone's cause for such entry: the strength of a protection claim is immediately negated by the illegality of their arrival. However, despite the high levels of public anxiety in many Western countries, including Australia, the state has not lost control of immigration in the 1990s, and the categorization of 'crisis' with regard to the entry of 'unauthorized persons' in particular is much exaggerated (Zolberg, 1999). Numerous writers remind us of the continuity between past and present population movements (Joppke, 1998; Bade, 2000; Hollifield, 2000). Such continuity indicates that while the movement of people across borders has occurred in different 'waves' and for different reasons, some instigated from the source country, some from the country of destination, nevertheless, the 1990s has not witnessed what could be termed a crisis in the numbers of people moving, or attempting to move, to Western states for temporary or permanent protection. However, the response to asylum seekers by many Western states, including Australia, has had the effect of communicating a crisis.

As I have argued through an analysis of the developments in the Australian case, Western states face a dilemma in relation to how best to respond to unauthorized arrivals, setting in place legal and administrative measures to restrict the entry and the duration of stay of such arrivals, while at the same time maintaining a 'fair' and open system in relation to obligations at the national and international level. Certainly, Australia may not prove to be the yardstick for how Western states should respond to those arriving without authorization and subsequently seeking protection. However, the response of a state such as Australia, which has benefited from earlier waves of immigration and which, until recent years, was regularly invoked as a model of successful multicultural integration of newcomers, cannot be overlooked.

Notes

1. The Humanitarian Programme consists of three main categories: Refugee, Special Humanitarian and Special Assistance. In addition, in 1989, a new category called 'Women at Risk' was added to the refugee component for women who were deemed to be in particularly vulnerable situations. Between July 1989 and June

1997, 2,222 Women at Risk visas were issued. The establishment of the Women at Risk category came after considered and lengthy advocacy by Australian NGOs.

2. This numerical link, while officially not having an absolute ceiling, is nevertheless at least a potential psychological barrier to officers processing applications, making them aware that a certain absorption level has been preset.

3. The Australian government has not given any clear indication as to how it would proceed should the number of spontaneous arrivals exceed the total humanitarian quota.

4. The UNHCR guidelines on the detention of asylum seekers begin by stating that detention is inherently undesirable, particularly in the case of vulnerable groups, such as single women and children, unaccompanied minors and those with special medical or psychological needs. The guidelines assert that, as a general principle, the detention of asylum seekers should only be entered into in exceptional circumstances. The guidelines invoke Article 31 of the Refugee Convention, which asks contracting states not to apply restrictions to the movement of refugees, and not to punish them because of illegal entry.

5. The most recent HREOC report, *A Last Resort?*, investigates the circumstances of children in immigration detention in Australia. The report highlights the length of detention of children, with 90 per cent of children having been in detention for more than three months. One child was held in immigration detention for over four years before being assessed as a refugee. Over 90 per cent of children in detention were eventually recognized as refugees.

6. More recently, Australia has made a regional agreement with Indonesia, overseen by the International Organization for Migration (IOM), whereby Indonesian authorities, often the police, intercept and detain 'irregular' migrants bound for Australia. The Australian government shares the cost of caring for the detainees in Indonesia with the IOM until such time as they can be repatriated voluntarily, or resettled in a safe country. The majority of people detained in Indonesia who have been intercepted on their way to Australia are Afghani and Iraqi.

7. The report surveyed a group of Tamil asylum seekers in detention at the Maribyrnong Detention Centre in Melbourne. Of these detainees, 72 per cent reported having been tortured in their country of origin. The report poses the question of whether detention worsens the psychological symptoms of traumatized asylum seekers. On six measures, including depression, suicidal ideation, post-traumatic stress symptoms, anxiety, panic attack symptoms and physical symptoms, detainees were two to three times more likely to experience such adverse effects in detention compared to asylum seekers and resettlement refugees living in the community (Silove and Steel, 1998: 30).

8. It must be borne in mind that while many members of the medical profession in treating detainees have had significant concerns about the health of their patients, they are sworn to a confidentiality by an agreement with DIMIA when treating them.

9. More recent amendments to the TPV stopped any access to permanent residency status.

10. If successful in their claim, however, such entrants are granted permanent residency through a Visa Subclass 866, and have access to full social security benefits, to work permits and to 510 hours of English-language training.

11. The nexus between illegal boat arrivals and security has been a recurring theme utilized in a bi-partisan fashion to support detention policy, and used most recently by the Howard government to gain popular support for the actions and

legislative changes surrounding the *Tampa* crisis. Yet, notably in late August 2002, ASIO (the Australian Security and Intelligence Service) announced that, of the 6,000 asylum seekers to have arrived in Australia in the previous three years, none had been found to have posed any security risk to Australia (ABC Lateline, 22 August 2001).

12. In May 2004, the last detainee on Manus Island was released. He had spent the previous nine months in solitary detention, as all the other detainees had been released. This final nine months of his detention cost the country A$250,000.

13. This mechanism is known as a privative clause. On 4 February 2003, the High Court of Australia upheld the *Tampa* laws while affirming the 'right of any person from appealing against a decision of a public servant when they had made a "jurisdictional error" – for example, and error of law of bias' ('*Tampa* law loses its punch after ruling', *Sydney Morning Herald*, 5 February 2003).

14. Captain Arne Rinnan has received thirteen awards around the world for his actions in rescuing the asylum seekers, including an Australian human rights award, The Sailor's Prize for 2001, title of Captain of the Year by Lloyds' List and the Nautical Institute, and the King of Norway's Medal of Honour, 1st Class.

15. From February 2002, evidence of the Senate inquiry into the 'children overboard' affair emerged which indicated that senior government officials, including advisers to the prime minister, knew a few days after the official photographs released by the Royal Australian Navy depicting the incident were released in September, that they showed a rescue rather than were the result of children being thrown into the water. On 19 February 2002, the prime minister admitted that Peter Reith, the defence minister, told him three days before the election that there were doubts about the photos (*Sydney Morning Herald*, 20 February 2002: 1).

References

Australian National Audit Office (2004). *Management of the Detention Centre Contracts*, Auditor General Report No. 54, Canberra: Commonwealth of Australia.

Bade, K. J. (2000). *Europa in Bewegung. Migration vom späten 18. Jahrhundert bis zur Gegewart*, Munich: Verlag C. H. Beck.

Caloz-Tschopp, M. C. (1997). 'On the Detention of Aliens: The Impact on Democratic Rights', *Journal of Refugee Studies*, 10(2): 165–80.

Castles, S. (1996). 'Immigration and Multiculturalism in Australia', in K. J. Bade, *Migration, Ethnizität, Konflikt: Systemfragen und Fallstudien*. Osnabruck: Universitätsverlag Rasch: 251–72.

Crock, M. and B. Saul (2002). *Future Seekers. Refugees and the Law in Australia*, Annandale NSW: The Federation Press.

DIMIA (Department of Immigration, Multicultural and Indigenous Affairs) (1997). *Refugee and Humanitarian Issues: Australia's Response* Belconnen ACT, October.

Freeman, G. P. and J. Jupp (1992). *Nations of Immigrants. Australia, the United States, and International Migration*, Melbourne: Oxford University Press.

Hathaway, J. (1997). *Reconceiving International Refugee Law*, The Hague: Martinus Nijhoff.

Hollifield, J. F. (2000). 'The Politics of International Migration. How Can We "Bring the State Back In"?', in C. B. Brettell and J. F. Hollifield (eds), *Migration Theory. Talking Across Disciplines*, New York: Routledge: 137–86.

Human Rights and Equal Opportunity Commission (1998). *Those Who've Come Across the Seas: Detention of Unauthorised Arrivals*, Commonwealth of Australia.

Human Rights and Equal Opportunity Commission (2004). *A Last Resort? National Inquiry into Children in Immigration Detention*, Sydney: HREOC.

Ignatieff, M. (1984). *The Needs of Strangers*, London: Vintage.

Ignatieff, M. (1999). 'Human Rights', in C. Hesse and R. Post (eds), *Human Rights in Political Transitions: Gettysburg to Bosnia*, New York: Zone Books: 313–24.

Ignatieff, M. (2001). *Human Rights as Politics and Idolatry*, ed. and intro. by A. Gutman, Princeton, NJ: Princeton University Press.

Joppke, C. (1998). 'Why Liberal States Accept Unwanted Immigration', *World Politics*, 50(2): 266–93.

Kingston, M. (1993). 'Politics and Public Opinion', in M. Crock (ed.), *Protection or Punishment. The Detention of Asylum Seekers in Australia*, Sydney: The Federation Press: 8–14.

MacCallum, M. (2002). 'Girt by Sea. Australia, the Refugees and the Politics of Fear', *Quarterly Essay*, 5: 1–73.

Mares, P. (2001). *Borderline. Australia's Treatment of Refugees and Asylum Seekers*, Sydney: University of New South Wales Press.

Mediansky, F. (1998). 'Detention of Asylum Seekers: The Australian Perspective', in J. Hughes and F. Liebaut (eds), *Detention of Asylum Seekers in Europe: Analysis and Perspectives*, The Hague: Martinus Nijhoff: 125–39.

Parekh, B. (2000). *Rethinking Multiculturalism. Cultural Diversity and Political Theory*, Basingstoke: Palgrave.

Rundle, G. (2001). 'The Opportunist. John Howard and the Triumph of Reaction', *Quarterly Essay*, 3: 1–65.

Silove, D. and Z. Steel (1998). *The Mental Health and Well-Being of On-Shore Asylum Seekers in Australia*, Sydney: Psychiatry and Teaching Unit, University of New South Wales.

Silove, D., Z. Steel and C. Watters (1993). 'Retraumatisation of Asylum-Seekers', Unpublished paper.

Silove, D., Z. Steel and C. Watters (2000). 'Policies of Deterrence and the Mental Health of Asylum Seekers', *Journal of the American Medical Association*, 284(5): 604–11.

Taylor, S. (2000). 'Should Unauthorised Arrivals in Australia Have Free Access to Advice and Assistance?', *Australian Journal of Human Rights*, 6(1): 34–58.

Tazreiter, C. (2002). 'History, Memory and the Stranger in the Practice of Detention in Australia', *Journal of Australian Studies*, 72: 3–12.

Tazreiter, C. (2004). *Asylum Seekers and the State. The Politics of Protection in a Security-Conscious World*, Aldershot: Ashgate.

UNHCR (2000). *The State of the World's Refugees. Fifty Years of Humanitarian Action*, Oxford: Oxford University Press.

UNHCR (2002). 'Trends in Asylum Applications in Europe, North America, Australia, New Zealand and Japan' (January–June 2002), Population Data Unit/PGDS Geneva, 7 August. Available at http://www.unhcr.ch.

Viviani, N. (1996). 'The Indochinese in Australia, 1975–1995: From Burnt Boats to Barbecues', Oxford: Oxford University Press.

Weller, P. (2002). *Don't Tell the Prime Minister*, Melbourne: Scribe Publications.

Zolberg, A. R. (1999). 'Matters of State: Theorizing Immigration Policy', in D. Massey (ed.), *Becoming American, American Becoming*, New York: Russell Sage.

18

Controlling Asylum Migration to the Enlarged EU: The Impact of EU Accession on Asylum and Immigration Policies in Central and Eastern Europe*

Catherine Phuong

In May 2004, ten new Member States, namely Cyprus, the Czech Republic, Hungary, Malta, Poland, Slovakia, Slovenia and the three Baltic States (Estonia, Latvia and Lithuania) joined the EU. Around the year 2007, Bulgaria and Romania will probably also join. Previous enlargements have taken place,[1] but the accession of ten countries, mainly from Central and Eastern Europe, is unprecedented not only in terms of scale, but also for its political symbolism. For these states, EU membership confirms the success of their democratic and economic transition efforts and represents their (re-)integration to the European family after decades of political isolation.

Much has already been written about the impact of eastward enlargement on the EU's institutional framework and current EU policies.[2] This chapter deals with the recent measures implemented in candidate countries to control asylum migration to the enlarged EU. In particular, it assesses the impact of accession on the candidate countries' asylum and immigration laws and policies. In order to do so, I examine the ways in which candidate countries are responding to increasing asylum migration from the East and argue that recent changes in asylum and immigration laws in candidate countries have been affected by current EU efforts to devise a common immigration policy and a possible common asylum system. Instead of devising their own responses to asylum migration, candidate countries have merely aligned their asylum policies with EU practice and expectations.

Because of their geographical location, the new member states will now be responsible for policing the new eastern border of the EU and receiving asylum seekers travelling from further east. Cyprus and Malta are thus excluded from the analysis, which only examines candidate countries from Central and Eastern Europe. Current EU member states are very concerned about illegal migration from the east, and have put considerable pressure on candidate countries to set up efficient asylum systems and, more importantly, strict border controls. This chapter does not deal with issues of free movement of persons within the enlarged EU, but with the regulation of asylum migration from outside the EU. Until recently, most of the academic literature had concentrated on the emergence of EU immigration and asylum laws under the new Title IV introduced at Amsterdam in 1998,[3] and very little attention had been paid to the impact of these developments on candidate countries.[4]

Following a brief overview of the asylum situation(s) in candidate countries, the chapter demonstrates how the changes recently implemented in candidate countries may not be adapted to such asylum situation(s) because they result mainly from a policy transfer from EU member states that have totally different asylum situations. The EU strategy for controlling asylum migration to the enlarged EU can be broken down into several areas: setting up new asylum systems in candidate countries, restricting entry through the imposition of visa requirements, preventing illegal entry by reinforcing border controls, and facilitating returns with the signature of readmission agreements. Frequent reference will be made to Poland, because of that country's strategic importance in terms of controlling the future eastern border of the EU.[5] It is by far the largest candidate country, both in terms of area (313,000 km²) and population (38.6 million inhabitants in the year 2000). Moreover, Poland has a strategic position since it shares common borders with Germany to the west; Lithuania, Belarus and Ukraine to the east; and the Czech Republic and Slovakia to the south. It even has a common border with the Russian Federation, whose enclave around Kaliningrad is sandwiched between Poland and Lithuania, both future EU member states. Consequently, Poland shares borders with a number of countries that produce refugees (such as the Russian Federation, for example) on the doorstep of the future EU and/or for which EU membership is a very distant prospect. The EU is also extremely concerned about organized criminal networks operating in the former Soviet Republics, which may use Poland as an entry point into the enlarged EU. As a result, Poland constitutes a very important country in terms of controlling the 'main European migratory channel between a disintegrating East and an integrating West' (Jerczinski, 1999: 105), and thus for ensuring the EU's internal security. Finally, Poland has so far pursued dynamic policies towards its eastern neighbours, and the changes in asylum and immigration laws demanded by its new EU partners are likely to have a significant impact on these policies.

Recent and future asylum flows to Central and Eastern Europe

During the Cold War, the countries examined here were mainly refugee-producing countries. Nevertheless, Hungary received some refugees from neighbouring Romania in the late 1980s (Wallace, 2002: 609). Some asylum seekers from right-wing dictatorships also found refuge in the former communist states. In the early 1990s, Hungary also received asylum seekers from the FR Yugoslavia, but most of these returned to their country of origin as soon as the security conditions improved there. Since the mid-1990s, most candidate countries have become transit countries for people wanting to seek asylum further west. The number of asylum applications increased in most candidate countries, but there are substantial differences between countries. Indeed, the Baltic countries still receive a relatively low number of asylum applications, whereas countries such as the Czech Republic and Hungary have seen a dramatic increase in applications. Nevertheless, when compared to the numbers of applications lodged in Western European countries, candidate countries clearly do not face the same pressures.

To date, most asylum seekers in candidate countries have not in fact remained in these countries and have often attempted to move on to Western Europe. Since border controls have remained relatively strict between current EU member states and candidate countries, these asylum seekers often find themselves 'trapped' in candidate countries that have formed a buffer zone between Western Europe and poorer and less stable regions in Asia. The combination of migration pressure from the east following the disintegration of the Soviet Union and restrictive migration policies in the EU have led Central and Eastern European countries to become countries of destination. This phenomenon has been described as the 'closed sack' effect (Byrne *et al.*, 2002b: 28). With EU accession, more asylum seekers will target the new member states as countries of destination. To anticipate this change, and in order to gain EU membership, these countries were under considerable pressure to implement major changes to their asylum and immigration laws and policies.

The integration of Justice and Home Affairs issues in the enlargement process

The initial accession criteria did not refer explicitly to Justice and Home Affairs (JHA) issues, partly because the EU was only just getting involved in this area when enlargement was envisaged. The enlargement process finds its origins in the Association agreements, also called Europe agreements, which were signed between the EU and each country in the 1990s. The 1993 Copenhagen European Council confirmed that Central and Eastern European countries could at some point join the EU, and between 1994 and 1996, all of them formally applied for EU membership. However, EU member states refrained for a long time from giving specific dates for accession, and pressure was put on the EU by candidate countries to define a more specific pre-accession strategy.

Since 1993, the definition of the criteria for accession has been somewhat progressive and piecemeal. The basic condition for enlargement is contained in Article 49 TEU, which provides that any European state that respects the principles of democracy, human rights and the rule of law as set out in Article 6(1) TEU, may apply to become a member of the EU. When identifying more detailed accession criteria, the challenge was to enlarge the EU without diluting it – that is, without endangering the process of further integration. It was therefore crucial that new member states could be integrated without undermining the progress made since 1957. In addition, they had to be able to follow the current pace of integration without slowing it down.

The 1993 Copenhagen European Council identified three types of criteria. Candidate countries had to fulfil political criteria relating to the stability of institutions guaranteeing democracy, the rule of law, respect for human rights and minority rights. The importance of these criteria as essential prerequisites for opening accession negotiations was reaffirmed at the 1999 Helsinki European Council (Seiffarth, 2000: 62). Since one of the EU's primary aims remains the establishment of the internal market, candidate countries had to have a fully functioning market economy. Beyond these political and economic criteria, candidate countries also had to demonstrate their general ability to take on the obligations of membership, such as the adjustment of their administrative structures and a guarantee that EU legislation would be properly implemented.

In order to help candidate countries fulfil accession criteria, reinforced pre-accession strategies were defined for each country and updated regularly after 1997 on the basis of a Commission paper entitled 'Agenda 2000'. The reinforced pre-accession strategies were also based on the Europe agreements, the accession partnerships and national programmes for the adoption of the EU *acquis* (the draft accession treaty approved by the Council with the assent of the European Parliament and ratified by all current member states and the country concerned), and pre-accession assistance, which was allocated mainly through the Phare programme.[6] Since 1998, the Commission has produced annual reports on each candidate country, identifying the areas where progress was still needed before EU membership was possible.[7]

The 1997 Amsterdam European Council called for accession negotiations to start with a group of six states (Cyprus, Czech Republic, Estonia, Hungary, Poland and Slovenia) and negotiations were launched in March 1998. To this purpose, the EU *acquis* was divided into thirty-one chapters: a common negotiating position was adopted on each chapter by the Council and then put forward to each individual candidate country at bilateral inter-governmental conferences. Accession negotiations also started with another six countries (Bulgaria, Latvia, Lithuania, Malta, Romania and Slovakia) in February 2000. For ten of the twelve countries listed, negotiations were concluded on all thirty-one chapters, and negotiations are still taking place with Bulgaria and Romania. The first wave of accession took place in May 2004. For each country, accession was only possible once negotiations had been concluded on all chapters of the EU *acquis*.

When the EU's eastward enlargement was first envisaged, the main concern was about the economic gap between the existing EU economies and those of the candidate countries. Following the Balkan crisis in the first half of the 1990s, there was increasing awareness that non-economically related issues such as JHA issues also needed to be included in the accession negotiations in order to ensure the internal security of the enlarged EU. The Commission thus recommended that cooperation in JHA matters be more structured (Lavenex, 1998a: 284). One must recall that, before 1989, candidate countries did not have any immigration or asylum laws or policies, for the simple reason that there was no immigration to regulate (Grabbe, 2000: 529). With EU accession, these states are bound to become more attractive as countries of destination, and the Langdon Report released in 1995 emphasized the need to adopt measures against illegal immigration and to build efficient asylum systems in candidate countries (Lavenex, 1998a: 288). The inclusion of asylum and immigration matters in the accession negotiations was also made necessary by the transfer of these matters to the EC pillar at Amsterdam in 1998. In particular, the Schengen *acquis* became part of the EU *acquis* and, as such, also had to be adopted by candidate countries.

Cooperation between EU member states and candidate countries had already developed in the early 1990s. When Central and Eastern European countries acceded to the Council of Europe, EU member states took the opportunity to declare them safe third countries, despite their unsatisfactory asylum legislation. If these countries were considered to be safe third countries, asylum seekers who had travelled to the EU via these countries could be returned there without their application being examined in substance in any EU member state.[8] Similarly, some Central and Eastern European countries were also considered safe countries of origin where there was a presumption of protection: no genuine asylum seeker could come from such countries (Bouteillet-Paquet, 2001: 279–80).[9] In order to ensure returns to safe third countries and safe countries of origin in Central and Eastern Europe, a series of readmission agreements were concluded. In effect, EU member states are using these agreements to transfer the 'asylum burden' to Central and Eastern European countries.

The nature of the earlier cooperation between EU member states and candidate countries in the field of asylum and immigration set the tone of the current dialogue. As noted above, EU member states consider candidate countries to be a 'buffer zone' between themselves and countries further east. They also know that, in the medium to longer term, when complete freedom of movement of individuals is achieved within the enlarged EU, they will have to rely entirely on the new member states to control entry into the EU at the eastern border. The fear of crime and illegal immigration has prompted existing member states to demand strict border controls on the future eastern border, to ensure that the enlarged EU is as 'secure' as it has been so far. In practice, agreement on what constituted the EU *acquis* in the field of JHA was reached in May 1998 and was also referred to as the TAIEX list, which names all the texts to which candidate countries had to accede, introduce and/or live up to.[10] One could observe that this list contained a number of third-pillar instruments that are not legally binding upon existing member states, but which appear to have been presented as such to candidate countries (Lavenex, 2002: 703). As will be seen below, EU expectations go far beyond the mere adoption of the EU *acquis*: candidate countries also had to 'bring [their] institutions, management systems and administrative arrangements up to Union standards with a view to implementing effectively the '*acquis*', and in particular adopt and implement measures with respect to external border controls, asylum and immigration, and measures to prevent and combat organised crime, terrorism and illicit drug trafficking'.[11] Negotiations around Chapter 24 on JHA were concluded and it is already clear that the commitments undertaken by candidate countries in this field would be closely monitored before and upon accession. It is therefore a good time to review what measures candidate countries have undertaken in order to gain the confidence of their new European partners and, ultimately, EU membership.

Setting up asylum systems in candidate countries: the transfer of the EU asylum *acquis*

Before the end of the Cold War there was no need for asylum systems in the former communist states, so, when the first asylum seekers arrived in these countries in the early 1990s, the first generation of asylum legislation was hurriedly adopted. At the same time, all candidate countries became parties to the 1951 Geneva Convention on the Status of Refugees and its 1967 Protocol.[12] Nevertheless, the asylum systems initially set up in candidate countries did raise some problems in terms of refugee protection standards (Bouteillet-Paquet, 2001: 333). This was to be expected, since these countries had no tradition of asylum and/or lacked a human rights culture. When the EU realized this 'lack of humanitarian tradition, norms and institutions' (Lavenex, 1998a: 277), more attention was paid to asylum matters in the accession strategy. Initially, candidate countries adopted relatively generous policies towards asylum seekers because they had not yet realized the impact of future EU accession and also thought that the influx of asylum seekers was going to be temporary (Bouteillet-Paquet, 2001: 334). This attitude towards asylum seekers soon had to be modified, however, as all candidate countries found themselves under an obligation to adopt the EU asylum *acquis* and align their practices with the current restrictive EU policies. A second generation of asylum legislation was adopted in most candidate countries in the late 1990s in order to reflect these changes.[13] In addition, one project funded by the Phare programme started in April 1998 in order to help candidate countries adapt their asylum legislation and improve its implementation.[14]

EU assistance to candidate countries in the field of asylum has had two underlying objectives. First, it has been in the interest of current member states, most notably Germany, to improve asylum systems in candidate countries. Indeed, if these countries implement refugee protection standards that are equivalent to those of Western European states, such states will have less difficulty in justifying returns of asylum seekers because they will benefit from an equivalent level of protection in candidate countries. In other words, by improving protection capacities in candidate countries, member states are preparing them to receive returned asylum seekers, and hoping it will be possible to shift the 'asylum burden' eastwards (Byrne *et al.*, 2002b: 17). Although the motivation of member states can be seen as problematic, EU pressure to implement changes in the asylum systems of candidate countries has brought about some positive consequences. Asylum procedures have been adopted and/or improved, specialized administrative structures have been set up to deal with asylum seekers and refugees, support groups have been created and so on. It must be noted, however, that significant differences remain between the new member states, with the Czech Republic, Poland and Slovenia far ahead of the others. The second objective of EU efforts to modify asylum systems in candidate countries has been to ensure that these countries do not become too attractive to asylum seekers: they must therefore also adopt deterrence measures similar to those already in place in Western Europe.

One can wonder whether restrictive EU standards currently being imposed on candidate countries are adapted to the situations of those countries. A UNHCR officer has noted that 'some CEBS [Central Europe and Baltic States] have adopted notions they might not otherwise have contemplated introducing' (Petersen, 2002: 367). For example, accelerated procedures have been introduced in all candidate countries' asylum systems to deal with manifestly unfounded applications.[15] One may argue that, in some cases, these procedures have been introduced without the necessary procedural safeguards, and in any case, what candidate countries need are efficient, rather than accelerated, procedures. Indeed, the usefulness of accelerated procedures can be doubted for countries such as Estonia, for example, which receives fewer than thirty asylum seekers per year.[16] Candidate countries have also incorporated other well-established EU concepts such as 'safe third country'[17] and 'safe country of origin', whose conformity with international refugee protection standards may be in doubt (ECRE, 1998). As candidate countries are going through the transition from countries of transit where asylum seekers did not pause to lodge an application, to countries of destination, they must focus on establishing asylum procedures and reception conditions that are in full conformity with international human rights law and refugee law. They should not just import EU policies which may not be adapted to their current asylum situation and/or administrative structures and practices.

One of the main problems encountered by candidate countries relates to the fact that the exact content of the EU asylum provisions, which they are to adopt, is at the time of writing being defined by member states. There is thus uncertainty as to what norms must be implemented (the problem of the 'moving target') (Lavenex, 2002: 702–4). European asylum law has only emerged recently and is not yet very elaborate. At present, it is composed mainly of non-binding instruments adopted in the first half of the 1990s.[18] As noted earlier, these instruments were presented to candidate countries as binding and therefore to be implemented by them: there has thus been a 'hardening' of soft law, which is a cause for concern (Anagnost, 2000: 386). These instruments were supplemented by international conventions concluded outside the EU framework, such as the Dublin Convention on asylum and the Schengen Implementation Agreement, which contains some provisions dealing with asylum.[19] It was only as recently as 1998 that asylum became an EC competence under Article 63 EC, which envisages the adoption of legally-binding instruments in a number of areas by April 2004. To date, some instruments have been adopted and are now clearly part of the EU asylum *acquis* to be adopted by candidate countries.[20] Nevertheless, other proposed directives that also are important remain under negotiation, and candidate countries can only speculate as to what their final content will be.[21] At this point, when adopting new asylum legislation, they can try to anticipate EU developments and, if in doubt, may choose the most restrictive standards in order to demonstrate that they can stem the influx of asylum seekers as well as can current member states. What we have also witnessed is candidate countries amending their asylum and immigration legislation almost on a yearly basis in order to take into account recently adopted EU instruments; such frequent legislative changes create serious challenges to the stability and certainty of the law in candidate countries.

A more detailed analysis of the asylum provisions adopted by Poland in 1997 and 2001 illustrates how the EU asylum *acquis* was transferred to the legal system of a candidate country. Although Poland became a party to the 1951 Convention and its 1967 Protocol on 27 September 1991, there were no specific asylum procedures in place in the country.[22] At the time, Polish authorities seemed to believe that the sudden influx of asylum seekers would soon cease, and that no permanent bodies or procedures were necessary (Stainsby, 1990: 637). However, as a result of readmission agreements signed with EU countries, as well as an increase in direct arrivals, the numbers of asylum seekers in Poland continued to increase.[23] These asylum seekers were mainly from Russia, Romania, Armenia, Bulgaria and Azerbaijan (in order of decreasing numbers) (Mikolajczyk, 2002: 52). Moreover, it became increasingly clear that Poland would have to adopt the EU asylum *acquis* before accession. It was thus decided that Poland needed an asylum system in order to determine which asylum seekers should be granted refugee status.

It must be noted here that a large number of asylum seekers appeared to be people who have been returned from Germany under the readmission agreement signed on 29 March 1991 with Schengen countries, and the separate readmission agreement signed with Germany on 7 May 1993.[24] Under the safe third-country rule adopted by Germany, it is almost impossible to obtain asylum in that country if one has travelled via Poland (Grabbe, 2000: 529), and the overwhelming majority of asylum seekers in Germany have entered through the German–Polish border (Lavenex, 1998b: 140). In effect, Poland had become a de facto member of the Dublin Convention system as it received asylum seekers who have travelled to the EU via Poland, but it was not allowed to transfer asylum seekers to the EU (Lavenex, 1998b: 132–3). Poland was encouraged to sign the readmission agreement with Germany in exchange for funding of 120 million DM to improve its asylum systems and border controls (Bouteillet-Paquet, 2001: 292).

The 1997 Aliens Act constituted the first attempt to regulate comprehensively the situation of asylum seekers and refugees in Poland.[25] Chapter 5 of the Aliens Act dealt with refugee status. It appeared that the legislation introduced satisfactory procedural standards which included, for example, the right of asylum seekers to be informed in a language they understood (Article 33); the right to a personal interview (Article 40); and the right to contact the UN High Commissioner for Refugees' Office (UNHCR) (Article 49). Initial decisions on asylum applications were taken by the Ministry of Internal Affairs, and this responsibility has now been transferred to a specific body called the Office for Repatriation and Aliens, set up in 2001. Chapter 10 of the Aliens Act created a new institution to examine asylum appeals, the Refugee Board, established in 1999. Further appeals can be made to the Supreme Administrative Court, but only an extremely small number of decisions are reversed on appeal (Mikolajczyk, 2002: 55).

On paper, the laws and procedures adopted by Poland in 1997 appear to conform to international refugee and human rights standards,[26] but have been restrictively and/or not properly implemented. For example, time limits for lodging an application were initially interpreted quite strictly until the Supreme Administrative Court intervened (Chlebny and Trojan, 2000: 220–1). These time limits were removed in 2001. It was also reported that many initial interviews of asylum seekers were not conducted by qualified immigration officers (Monar, 2001: 42). This raises the more general problem of lack of resources, staff and training. Consequently, and despite the low number of applications compared with Western Europe, there is already a backlog of cases that were initially supposed to be decided within three months (Article 41). This period was extended to six months in 2001, but it is still shorter than the average time actually needed to obtain a decision on an asylum application. The recognition rate remains at just below 2 per cent, which is extremely low, even by Western European standards (Noll 2002: 322).[27]

Amendments to the 1997 Aliens Act were introduced in 2001, partly to meet EU requirements.[28] The two main changes in the field of asylum were the introduction of accelerated procedures (Article 41a) and the development of a temporary protection status (Chapter 6a). Nevertheless, while Article 53 provides that no persons can be deported if they would be exposed to a breach of the European Convention on Human Rights,[29] no subsidiary status currently exists in Polish law (Mikolajczyk, 2002: 73–4); failed asylum seekers (mainly Chechens) who cannot be deported are merely given a temporary residence permit and are not entitled to any support.[30] Some form of 'tolerated status' will be created to remedy this situation. The 1997 Aliens Act is to be replaced by two separate pieces of legislation on asylum and the regulation of immigration (entry, residence and exit). Every effort is made to ensure that the new legislation implements recently adopted EU standards without questioning the validity and conformity of these standards against international standards.

In drafting and amending the 1997 Aliens Act, most EU asylum standards contained in soft law instruments were largely 'taken into account' by Polish authorities; that is, they were implemented, as it was believed that these instruments would soon be adopted as legally binding. It is significant to note that, when assessing the conformity of the 1997 Aliens Act with EU standards, references were frequently made to soft law instruments. Negotiations on the Commission asylum proposals made under Article 63 EC were closely monitored, but it was clear that Poland could not amend its legislation each time a new directive or regulation was adopted by the EU.

EU influence has had some positive consequences on the treatment of asylum seekers in Poland. Unfortunately, Poland has also adopted a number of restrictive measures borrowed from EU practice. For example, in 1997, Poland adopted the concepts of safe country of origin and safe third country as defined in Articles 4(10) and 4(11) of the Aliens Act. However, these concepts were not always applied correctly: Article 35(3) of the 1997 Act provided that *access* to asylum procedures would be denied to anyone arriving from a safe third country to which she can return. This was an incorrect implementation of the EU soft law standards,[31] and the provision could not have been said to be in conformity with international refugee law standards. As a result, this provision was amended in 2001. In order to implement the 'safe country of origin' and 'safe third country' rules, the Polish government was required to adopt lists of safe countries under former Article 95. However, it failed to agree on such lists. In practice, these concepts could therefore not be applied (Mikolajczyk, 2002: 70). The requirement to adopt lists of safe countries was abandoned in 2001, and it seems that the two concepts can now be applied. In any case, although EU member states applied these concepts to candidate countries (Lavenex, 1998b), it seems unlikely that Poland would similarly be able to declare its eastern neighbours safe countries in order to send asylum seekers there. Nevertheless, Bulgarian and Romanian asylum seekers have seen their applications rejected on the basis that they were coming from safe countries of origin.[32] Poland may have been anticipating the application of the Protocol on asylum added by the Treaty of Amsterdam, which stipulates that 'Member States shall be regarded as constituting safe countries of origin'.[33]

Poland has also introduced accelerated procedures for manifestly unfounded applications (Article 41a), which are defined as applications not specifying any ground of persecution under the 1951 Convention or which are intentionally misleading. Manifestly unfounded applications include applications made by nationals of safe countries of origin. Article 41a constitutes a perfect example of the 1997 Act being amended to conform with a soft law instrument such as the 1992 London Resolution on manifestly unfounded applications for asylum (Mikolajczyk, 2002: 70). This non-binding Resolution invited EU member states to consider certain types of applications as manifestly unfounded and the introduction of accelerated procedures to examine such applications. One can note that Poland chose to consider as manifestly unfounded most types of applications mentioned in the Resolution.

For a country which currently 'only' receives fewer than 5,000 asylum applications per year, one can wonder how appropriate is the mere transposition of EU measures to the Polish legal system, and whether Poland would have adopted a similar asylum policy regardless of EU requirements. It may be argued that Poland would have adopted the same standards in any case: because of a lack of asylum tradition, it would have looked to its Western neighbours for models of asylum systems. On the other hand, EU standards and practice would not have been copied with the same zeal, and Poland could have developed its own asylum policy independently. Poland had little choice but to adopt the EU asylum *acquis* in its entirety before EU accession. Perhaps the alternative would have been for the Polish authorities to challenge parts of the EU asylum *acquis* whose conformity with international refugee law is in doubt. This could have made Poland an active partner in the shaping of the developing EU asylum system.[34]

Enlargement has provided an opportunity for candidate countries to establish comprehensive asylum systems and standards, with EU assistance and funding. On the other hand, the export of current EU asylum policies without reform simply entrenched restrictive practices which may not conform to international refugee and human rights standards. Nevertheless, while it appears that some EU member states put pressure on candidate countries to initiate some changes in their asylum systems, there is no doubt that they have been much more interested in investing in the improvement of border controls, which has been perceived as an essential requirement for ensuring the internal security of the enlarged EU.

Restricting entries: new visa requirements

One area that is likely to raise a number of problems is the EU's visa policy, which has become a central instrument of (asylum) migration control. Candidate countries had to adopt the EU's strict visa policy, which requires nationals of a long list of countries to apply for a visa in order to gain entry to the EU.[35] All refugee-producing countries are included in this list, and since it is not possible to lodge an asylum application from outside the country considering the application, visa requirements hinder access to asylum procedures. Most candidate countries had visa-free regimes with their eastern and southern neighbours. EU member states were especially concerned about restricting the entry of nationals of these new states resulting from the disintegration of the Soviet Union, all of which are included in the EU visa list (with the exception of the Baltic States). However, candidate countries were reluctant to impose visa requirements on the neighbours with whom they have often maintained close political and economic links (Jileva, 2002: 686–9). Moreover, some candidate countries wanted to allow national minorities living in neighbouring countries to have easy access to their territory. For example, up to 3 million ethnic Hungarians are living outside Hungary as a result of the 1920 Treaty of Trianon.[36] Finally, it must be noted that some of the former Soviet Republics are still refugee-producing countries, and the imposition of strict visa requirements would in effect contribute to denying persecuted individuals access to protection. It was recommended that the EU should consider the long-standing relationships between the candidate countries and their neighbours, and envisage special visa arrangements such as fast-track, multiple-entry visas, or single-country visas (House of Lords, 2000, para. 76). Hungary had also suggested special visa arrangements for ethnic Hungarians living abroad, but these proposals were abandoned (Grabbe, 2000: 531).

Poland terminated visa exemption agreements with a number of countries, mainly former Soviet Union Republics and other communist states.[37] However, the Polish authorities were much more reluctant to do the same with regard to its immediate eastern neighbours, namely Belarus, Russia and Ukraine: the introduction of visas for citizens of these countries posed a dilemma for domestic policy-makers, who wanted to protect close historical, cultural and economic links with them. There is, indeed, a concern that the new visa requirements pose a threat to economic activities in eastern areas (Anderson, 2000); such activities have partly been fuelled by 'shuttle migration' from Ukraine, for example (Iglicka, 2001: 8; Wolczuk, 2002: 245). Moreover, there are some Polish minorities living in Belarus (418,000) and Ukraine (220,000) who wanted to retain easy access to the Polish territory (IOM/ICPMD, 1999: 112). Finally, successive Polish governments have pursued dynamic foreign policies towards their eastern neighbours, in particular Ukraine, in order to stabilize the region (Wolczuk, 2001).

Measures introduced in 1998 to restrict entry from Belarus and Russia has already provoked strong protests from these countries (Grabbe, 2000: 530). This may explain why Poland delayed the introduction of visas for as long as possible. Visas were initially to be introduced in 2001 for these two countries, and in 2002 for Ukraine (Mikolajczyk, 2002: 60), but these dates were considered to be premature and visas were eventually introduced on 1 October 2003 for all three countries. Such new visa requirements are likely to have an impact on Chechen asylum seekers, who continue to be the most numerous among those seeking asylum in Poland.[38]

The introduction of visas contributes to a shift of responsibility for immigration control from border services to internal administrative services which will deal with an increased number of applications for residence permits (as migrants will use other means of entering and staying in the country) (Iglicka, 2001: 13) and external embassies dealing with visa applications. The implementation of the new visa regime required by the EU will not be cost-free, and embassies have to be staffed and equipped to deal with high numbers of visa requests. It is also to be expected that some asylum seekers will have to turn to illegal channels of migration as a result of the new visa requirements. In order to limit the negative impact of visas, it is crucial to ensure that the issuing of these remains as easy and as cheap as possible (IOM/ICPMD, 1999: 115). The Russian enclave of Kaliningrad raised some specific problems because it has found itself surrounded by EU member states: Russians transiting EU territory by land between Kaliningrad and the rest of Russia will now have to hold a passport and a transit visa.[39]

Preventing illegal entries: border controls at the EU's new eastern borders

During the 1990s, the EU's internal security agenda developed at a fast pace. One of the central elements of this agenda is external border controls that are becoming increasingly elaborate. Border controls are regulated within the Schengen framework, which has been integrated into the EU *acquis* since Amsterdam. The improvement of border controls in candidate countries was seen as an essential condition for accession. When visa requirements are imposed, illegal entry may constitute the only way of gaining access to asylum procedures, and border controls, which are reinforced to prevent illegal entry are therefore bound to have an impact on access to protection.

The Commission was keen to stress the 'need to strengthen border management, most urgently at future EU external borders, and to prepare for the participation in the Schengen Information System'.[40] Each of its yearly country reports focused on the need to improve border controls. This had thus become the main EU demand in JHA, and a priority area for EU aid. Indeed, many Phare projects on migration and border control have been funded in recent years. In particular, candidate countries need elaborate technological frameworks to enter the Schengen Information System, a computerized system storing information on people, stolen vehicles and other items, for use by the border control. Besides, the SIS requires the setting up of effective data protection mechanisms. Border services also need to invest in expensive surveillance equipment such as thermo/infrared cameras, x-ray units and police helicopters (House of Lords, 2000, para. 14). All in all, the adoption of the Schengen standards of border controls is not so much a problem of political will, but rather of resources, and it is already proving to be extremely expensive for the new member states.

Aside from the funding problem, a fundamental change of attitude has also been required from border guards, who now have to 'keep foreigners out rather than keep citizens in' (Grabbe, 2000: 529). The complete overhaul of border control mechanisms in candidate countries has thus required an important amount of human and financial resources, as well as training, and will not be achieved as promptly as member states would wish. Nevertheless, no concessions are being granted, and the Schengen *acquis* must be complied with in full,[41] even though it is well known that some earlier member states still did not comply with it (House of Lords, 2000, para. 25). In reality, there is doubt as to whether the candidate countries will be able to implement the Schengen *acquis* in full at the time of accession (House of Lords, 2000, para. 52). If this is the case, the problem remains that candidate countries are uncertain about what standards of border control, short of the Schengen standards, they are supposed to reach (House of Lords, 2000, para. 54). Considering how costly it is to upgrade border controls, there has also been uncertainty as to whether the borders with Bulgaria and Romania should be 'sealed' to the same extent as the eastern borders: since these countries are also to join the EU within the next few years, it would appear counter-productive to invest in border control infrastructures that would then have to be dismantled.

Poland has been a country of mass emigration since the mid-nineteenth century. Immigration to Poland has traditionally been negligible, hence the lack of immigration controls (Stola, 2001: 176). This lack of controls, particularly on the eastern border, has been a major source of concern for the EU because of the nature and location of the border. It is a 'green border' running through open country and mountains, so is difficult to police and has traditionally been relatively open, with many cross-border activities (Monar, 2001: 43). Poland shares more than 1,000 km of borders with Belarus, Ukraine and Russia, countries that are unlikely to join the EU in the near (or even distant) future, and they host criminal networks which try to smuggle goods and people into the EU.

Over the last few years, Poland has been under considerable pressure from the EU to adopt measures to establish and reinforce border controls. One must remember that, before 1989, there were no Polish border guards on the eastern border, only Soviet guards: most border controls took place on the western and southern borders (Monar, 2001: 44). The challenge was thus to organize a complete overhaul of the border guard service (Latawski, 1999). More crossing points were established on the eastern border, several thousand new staff were recruited and trained, equipment was purchased and so on. The EU, as well as individual member states such as Germany and the United Kingdom (House of Lords, 2000, para. 63), have invested considerable resources in the export of EU border control technology and staff training: it has been estimated that Poland received over 100 million euros of Phare funding to upgrade its eastern frontier controls (House of Lords, 2000, para. 61). Nevertheless, raising border controls to Schengen standards is proving to be extremely expensive, and EU funding is still insufficient to implement all the required changes (House of Lords, 2000, para. 60). Given the lack of funding, training border guards to deal with asylum seekers is probably not a priority. EU efforts focused on reinforcing controls at the Polish eastern border and extending the EU visa regime to its eastern neighbours. There is no doubt that EU accession has been 'the main stimulus for rebuilding the system of border control' (Mikolajczyk, 2002: 58).

Even though candidate countries have been under pressure to comply fully with the Schengen *acquis*, they are not a full part of Schengen upon accession. Indeed, free movement of citizens is not to be allowed in the years following accession. Transitional arrangements have been negotiated whereby free movement of workers will be guaranteed within seven years of accession.[42] This can be explained partly by the fear, notably in Germany and Austria, of a mass influx of migrants from the east similar to that witnessed in the final months leading up to the fall of the Berlin Wall in 1989 (Zielonka, 2001: 520). It follows that the new member states have to comply with the obligations arising from Schengen *before* benefiting from the advantages in terms of abolition of internal border controls and free movement of people.[43] In other words, tougher border controls must first be applied on the eastern borders of the new member states, and only then will concessions be made on their western borders (Grabbe, 2000: 527). It has been argued that the current EU demands on border controls 'might well be used as a pretext for postponing the free movement of labour and other persons for a long time' (Lavenex, 1998a: 293). It is ironic that, while Western states used to criticize communist states during the Cold War for imposing restrictions on the free movement of their own citizens, they now impose similar restrictions (Bouteillet-Paquet, 2001: 263), although the restrictions are obviously of a very different nature.

Facilitating returns: readmission agreements

There is no doubt that the most important obligation arising from the 1951 Convention to which all new member states are party is the obligation of *non-refoulement* (Article 33): state parties shall not return a refugee to a country where s/he would face threats to his/her life or freedom. The scope of this obligation has been extended beyond the refugee context by the Convention against Torture (Article 3)[44] and the ECHR case law on Article 3 (Lambert, 1999). Nevertheless, all candidate countries had started developing readmission agreements in order to facilitate the return of illegal immigrants and some asylum seekers.[45] When examining the text of some of these readmission agreements, it appears that they may not contain sufficient guarantees against *non-refoulement*.

As a result of the 1991 readmission agreement that allows Schengen countries to return to Poland anyone who has entered the Schengen area illegally via Poland, as well as rejected asylum seekers, an increasing number of people have been readmitted to Poland, particularly from Germany. With EU accession and entry into the Dublin Convention system, Poland can expect a further increase in the number of asylum seekers transferred from other member states, but it does not want to become the final destination for them. Consequently, it has endeavoured to negotiate and sign bilateral readmission agreements with its own neighbours: throughout the 1990s, Poland signed such agreements with all other candidate countries and some of its eastern neighbours.[46] It has also been negotiating readmission agreements with Armenia, Belarus, Kazakhstan, Russia and even countries further afield such as Vietnam. These readmission agreements are aimed at facilitating the transfer of illegal immigrants, which includes some asylum seekers, to other countries: Poland has, in effect, adopted the same strategy as the Schengen States to ensure that people do not stay in Poland.

The readmission agreements concluded by Poland with its neighbours are varied. Most of them cover not only nationals of both parties to the agreement, but also third-country nationals. One would expect Poland to conclude readmission agreements only with countries that are deemed to be safe for asylum seekers to be returned to, but it is debatable whether some countries, such as Bulgaria or Romania, can be regarded as safe for certain rejected asylum seekers of Roma origin.[47] Some agreements that cover asylum seekers do not contain any reference to the 1951 Convention, or even, in some cases, to any human rights instrument.[48]

One minimum prerequisite before signing a readmission agreement should be to ensure that the other party is at least a party to the 1951 Convention, which should guarantee that it is under the obligation of *non-refoulement*. However, it is worrying to note that a number of readmission agreements were signed with countries that were not parties to the 1951 Convention at the time of signature. For example, Poland signed readmission agreements with Estonia and Latvia in 1993, although both countries only became parties to the 1951 Convention in 1997. In most cases, Poland seemed to have waited until the other state party to the impending agreement had signed the 1951 Convention.[49] There is also a concern that Poland has signed, or is about to conclude, readmission agreements with countries that are still producing refugees and which figure among the list of the main countries of origin of asylum seekers in Poland.[50]

The readmission agreement concluded between Poland and Lithuania in 1998 was undoubtedly one of the most important to the extent that both countries are situated on one of the main migrant routes to Western Europe. It covered nationals of both countries and third-country nationals, including asylum seekers (Article 3). However, the agreement contained no reference to the 1951 Convention, nor did it guarantee access to asylum procedures:[51] the UNHCR expressed concern at 'the automatic return of asylum seekers to Lithuania without due consideration for the safety of the asylum seekers from *refoulement*, or the possibility of their entering the status determination procedure in Lithuania'.[52] As a result, the combination of the Dublin Convention, the application of the safe third-country rule and the conclusion of readmission agreements between Poland and its eastern neighbours can lead to 'chain deportations', sometimes all the back way to countries of origin (Byrne *et al.*, 2002b: 25).

It appears that some of the readmission agreements signed by the new member states with their neighbours do not contain enough guarantees that asylum seekers will not be removed by these states to yet another third country that may not be safe and/or may even be their country of origin. To some extent, the new member states have replicated the German strategy, which was to sign readmission agreements with all its eastern neighbours.[53] Nevertheless, Germany also attempted to engage in bilateral cooperation with these countries to reinforce their protection capacities: the new member states cannot offer the same level of support to their eastern neighbours as Germany did for *its* neighbours.[54]

Conclusion

The hard border regime imposed by the EU on candidate countries is likely to have an important impact on asylum seekers. When examining the asylum laws of the new member states, it appears that they are already providing, or will soon be, the same level of refugee protection as do current EU member states. Nevertheless, grave concerns must be expressed about the lack of strong guarantees against direct and indirect *refoulement*. Risks of *refoulement* have been increased by the introduction of strict immigration measures, and these risks are not being correctly evaluated because of the current lack of connection between migration control and asylum (ECRE, 1998, para. 5). Despite EU pressure, the new member states must not forget that they have international obligations not to return people to situations where their life or security would be at risk. This shows that EU demands were inconsistent to the extent that candidate countries had to demonstrate their commitment to democracy and human rights while, at the same time, adopting restrictive asylum and immigration policies towards foreigners. Candidate countries' adherence to international human rights law and refugee law is being tested, and it is important that domestic developments in the areas of immigration and asylum continue to be scrutinized.

Earlier EU developments in the field of immigration and asylum have already demonstrated the prioritization of security concerns over humanitarian ones and followed a strong logic of inclusion/exclusion as illustrated by strict border controls. Efforts to align candidate countries to EU policies followed the same logic. Recent developments, analysed above, also show the prioritization of security concerns over legitimate economic or foreign policy concerns. Not surprisingly, candidate countries became increasingly nervous about accession as they had realized that 'asylum and immigration are being instrumentalised by EU Member States in order to establish a filter or buffer zone between them and the countries of emigration' (Lavenex, 1998a: 290). With EU accession, the responsibility for ensuring border controls, tackling illegal immigration and dealing with asylum seekers falls disproportionately on candidate countries, which do not have the same financial and human resources. These countries were so keen to gain EU membership that they agreed to adopt most measures.

The EU is still under the illusion that efficient border control mechanisms can ensure its internal security. First, there is no such thing as perfect border controls, and migrants who are persistent will always find a way in. In any case, border controls alone cannot stem the flow of asylum seekers and other migrants or ensure the EU's internal security: the EU should address the causes of migration (poverty, human rights violations, armed conflict and so on) through its foreign and aid policies. It is also in the interests of the EU to ensure political stability in the region and maintain good relations with its immediate neighbours. It is thus important that it respects the new member states' special relationships with their eastern neighbours, instead of imposing its own policies on them without taking into account their foreign policy interests.

Notes

* Research for this chapter was partly based on a study trip conducted in Poland in June 2002 and funded by a grant from the Socio-Legal Studies Association (SLSA). I would like to thank Marek Szonert and Monika Prus (Office of Repatriation and Aliens), Irena Rzeplinska (Helsinki Foundation of Human Rights), Isabelle Rivière (Delegation of the European Commission in Poland), Katarzyna Cuadrat-Grzybowska (Office of the Committee for European Integration), Wladyslaw Czaplinski (University of Warsaw), Michal Kowalski (University of Krakow) and Christian Mahr (UNHCR London). I would also like to thank Ann Sinclair for her research assistance. An earlier version of this chapter was published as a paper in the *International and Comparative Law Quarterly* in July 2003. The author alone is responsible for the opinions expressed in this chapter.

1. Denmark, Ireland and the United Kingdom first joined in 1973; Greece in 1981; Spain and Portugal in 1986; and Austria, Finland and Sweden in 1995.
2. On issues of institutional reform in anticipation of enlargement, see, for example, Shaw (2001).
3. See, for example, Hailbronner (1998), O'Keefe (1999), and Simpson (1999), Guild and Harlow (2001).
4. For recent studies of asylum and immigration laws in candidate countries, see Byrne *et al.* (2002a) and Laczko *et al.* (2002).
5. The analysis is partly based on interviews conducted in June 2002 in Poland with government officials, NGOs dealing with refugees and asylum seekers, and academics.
6. The Phare programme was set up in 1989 to support the transition to a market-orientated economy in Poland and Hungary, and subsequently extended to other countries. It is now complemented by two other funds created in 2000, SAPARD (Special Accession Programme for Agriculture and Rural Development) and ISPA (Pre-accession Instrument for Structural Policies).
7. For the latest Progress Reports, see http://www.europa.eu.int/comm/enlargement/report2002/.
8. The 1990 Dublin Convention on the allocation of responsibility for examining an asylum application does not guarantee that an application will be examined by an EU member state and allows transfers of asylum seekers to safe third countries which are not parties to the Convention; see Article 3(5).
9. One must note that some EU member states do not always agree upon which Central European countries should be considered safe. Nevertheless, once candidate countries become EU member states, they will be covered by the 1998 Protocol on asylum for nationals of member states of the European Union (the 'Aznar Protocol') which states that all EU member states constitute safe countries of origin.
10. This list has been reproduced in van Krieken (2000: 104–14).
11. EU's initial position for the opening of negotiations with the first six countries, Document 6473/3/98 REV 3 JAI 7 ELARG 51, 25 May 1998, reproduced in Seiffarth (2000: 67–8).
12. Convention Relating to the Status of Refugees, 28 July 1951, 189 U.N.T.S. 1950 and Protocol Relating to the Status of Refugees, 31 January 1967, 606 U.N.T.S. 267. See UNHCR, State Parties to the 1951 Convention relating to the Status of Refugees and the 1967 Protocol as of 30 September 2002, at http://www.unhcr.ch. Hungary had since 1989 been a party to the 1951 Convention, for the reasons discussed.
13. See, for example, Czech Republic: Act No. 325 of 11 November 1999 on Asylum; Estonia: Law on Refugees of 18 February 1997; Hungary: Act CXXXIX of 9 December 1997 on Asylum; Poland: Aliens Law of 25 June 1997 (amended by the Act of 11 April 2001); Slovenia: Law on Asylum of 30 July 1999.
14. This Joint Support Programme on the Application of the EU *Acquis* on Asylum and Related Standards and Practices in the Associated Countries of Central and Eastern Europe resulted from cooperation between the Commission, UNHCR and the German Federal Office for the Recognition of Refugees, with the assistance of six other member states (Austria, Denmark, France, the Netherlands, Spain and Sweden). For more detail, see Anagnost (2000).
15. On accelerated procedures, see van der Klaauw (2001: 180–3).
16. On accelerated procedures, see, for example, Article 9 of the Estonian Law on Refugees of 18 February 1997; Articles 43–47 of the Hungarian Act CXXXIX of

9 December 1997 on Asylum; and Article 14(2) of the Lithuanian Refugee Law of 29 June 2000, No. VII-1784, No. 56–1651.

17. On the adoption of the safe third country concept by candidate countries, see Lavenex (1998b: 138).

18. See, for example, Resolution on manifestly unfounded applications for asylum, Resolution on a harmonised approach to questions concerning host third countries, Conclusions on countries in which there is generally no serious risk of persecution (London, 30 November and 1 December 1992), and Council Resolution of 20 June 1995 on minimum guarantees for asylum procedures, OJ 1996 C 274/13.

19. Convention determining the State responsible for examining applications for asylum lodged in one of the Member States of the European Communities, 15 June 1990 (hereinafter the Dublin Convention) OJ 1997 C 254/1, and Agreement on the Implementation of the Schengen Agreement of 14 June 1985 concerning the Gradual Abolition of Checks at their Common Borders, 19 June 1990 (1991) 30 ILM 84. For more detail, see Hailbronner and Thiery (1997).

20. Council directive No. 2001/55 of 20 July 2001 on minimum standards for giving temporary protection in the event of a mass influx of displaced persons and on measures promoting a balance of efforts between member states in receiving such persons and bearing the consequences thereof, OJ 2001 L 212/12; Council directive No. 2003/9 of 27 January 2003 laying down minimum standards for the reception of asylum seekers, OJ 2003 L 31/18; Council regulation No 343/2003 of 18 February 2003 establishing the criteria and mechanisms for determining the member states responsible for examining an asylum application lodged in one of the member states by a third-country national, OJ 2003 L 50/1.

21. Proposal for a Council directive laying down minimum standards for the qualification and status of third country nationals and stateless persons as refugees, in accordance with the 1951 Convention relating to the status of refugees and the 1967 Protocol, or as persons who otherwise need international protection, 12 September 2001, COM(2001) 510 final; Proposal for a Council Directive on minimum standards on procedures in member states for granting and withdrawing refugee status, 20 September 2000, COM(2000) 578 final.

22. Some amendments were made to the 1963 Aliens Act in 1991, but proved completely insufficient to deal with the situation, see Czaplinski (1994: 637).

23. A very high proportion of these applications (55 per cent in 1998) are discontinued as a result of the applicants disappearing, probably trying to enter the EU.

24. In 1998, there were 698 asylum applications lodged at the German–Polish border (Mikolajczyk, 2002: 53). To this figure one must add the number of applications lodged by asylum seekers readmitted from Germany within the country.

25. Aliens Act No. 114, 25 June 1997, OGRP, No. 739/1997. For more detail, see Chlebny and Trojan (2000).

26. Interview with Christian Mahr, UNHCR London, 29 September 2001.

27. Other candidate countries, such as Hungary and the Czech Republic, also have very low recognition rates, which puts them among the most restrictive countries in Europe.

28. See 2001 Regular Report on Poland's Progress towards Accession, SEC(2001) 1752, 13 November 2001: 87. I would like to thank Katarzyna Cuadrat-Grzybowska for providing me with an English translation of the amended 1997 Aliens Act.

29. European Convention for the Protection of Human Rights and Fundamental Freedoms, 4 November 1950, 213 U.N.T.S. 221.

30. Interview with Irena Rzeplinska, Warsaw, 11 June 2002.
31. See Note 17 above.
32. Telephone interview with Marek Szonert, Warsaw, 26 June 2002. In 2000, 308 people (members of the Roma community) from Bulgaria and 864 from Romania sought asylum in Poland (Mikolajczyk, 2002: 52).
33. Protocol on asylum for nationals of member states of the European Union, annexed to the EC Treaty (1998).
34. Email exchange with Michal Kowalski, 15 July 2002.
35. See Regulation No. 539/2001 of 15 March 2001 listing the third countries whose nationals must be in possession of visas when crossing the external borders and those whose nationals are exempt from this requirement, amended by Regulation No. 2414/2001 of 7 December 2001 (deleting Romania from the visa list).
36. See Zielonka (2001: 514) and Grabbe (2000: 531). See also the case of Romanian minorities in Moldova (*Le Monde*, 2002).
37. See 2001 Regular Report (Note 28 above): 85, and 2002 Regular Report, SEC (2002) 1408, 9 September 2002: 113–14.
38. See 2002 Regular Report, Note 37 above: 115.
39. See Communication from the Commission to the Council, The EU and Kaliningrad, COM(2001) 26 final, 17 January 2001: 5.
40. Making a success of enlargement, strategy paper and report of the European Commission on the progress towards accession by each of the candidate countries, 13 November 2001: 18.
41. See Article 8 of Schengen Protocol.
42. For the first two years, EU member states will apply national measures to regulate the employment rights of nationals from the new member states. For the next three years, they will be free to apply the EU *acquis* and remove obstacles to free movement. This transitional period can be extended for a further two years. In total, free movement of persons can thus be delayed by a maximum of seven years. Nevertheless, access to current member states' labour markets cannot be restricted from the time of accession and during the whole transitional period. In addition, preference will be given to nationals of the new member states over third country nationals.
43. See Commission, Note 39 above: 5.
44. Convention against Torture and Other Cruel, Inhuman or Degrading Treatment or Punishment, 10 December 1984, 23 *I.L.M.* 1027 and 24 *I.L.M.* 535.
45. See the full list of agreements concluded by candidate countries in Lavenex (2002: 708).
46. Poland has signed readmission agreements with Bulgaria (1993), the Czech Republic (1993), Estonia (1993), Hungary (1994), Latvia (1993), Lithuania (1998), Romania (1993), Slovakia (1993) and Slovenia (1996). It has also signed agreements with other countries such as Moldova (1994) and Ukraine (1993).
47. See Klaczynski (1997). The overwhelming majority of asylum seekers from these two countries do not obtain refugee status in Poland.
48. See the readmission agreements concluded between Poland and the Czech Republic, Slovakia or Ukraine (Bouteillet-Paquet, 2001: 362).
49. In the case of the readmission agreement signed with the Czech Republic, it was signed the day before the Czech Republic signed the 1951 Convention (10 and 11 May 1993, respectively).
50. See list of the main countries of origin for 1999–2000 in Mikolajczyk (2002: 52).

51. See the number of asylum applications lodged in Lithuania on readmission from Poland, in Sesickas *et al.* (2002: 238).
52. Background information on the situation in Poland in the context of the return of asylum seekers, UNHCR Geneva, November 1998, quoted in Mikolajczyk (2002: 62).
53. See list of agreements concluded by Germany in Lavenex (1998b: 133).
54. Interview with Christian Mahr, London, 29 September 2001.

References

Anagnost, S. (2000). 'Challenges Facing Asylum Systems and Asylum Policy Development in Europe: Preliminary Lessons Learned from the Central European and Baltic States (CEBS)', *International Journal of Refugee Law*, 12: 380–400.

Anderson, M. (2000). 'Border Regimes and Security in an Enlarged European Community: Implication of the Entry into Force of the Amsterdam Treaty', RSC Paper, No. 2000/8. Florence: Robert Schumann Centre, European Institute.

Bouteillet-Paquet, D. (2001). *L'Europe et le droit d'asile*, Paris: L'Harmattan.

Byrne, R., G. Noll and J. Vested-Hansen (eds) (2002a). *New Asylum Countries? Migration Control and Refugee Protection in an Enlarged European Union*, The Hague: Kluwer Law International.

Byrne, R., G. Noll and J. Vested-Hansen (2002b). 'Western European Asylum Policies for Export: The Transfer of Protection and Deflection Formulas to Central Europe and the Baltics', in R. Byrne, G. Noll and J. Vested-Hansen (eds), *New Asylum Countries? Migration Control and Refugee Protection in an Enlarged European Union*, The Hague: Kluwer Law International: 5–28.

Chlebny, J. and W. Trojan (2000). 'The Refugee Status Determination Procedure in Poland', *International Journal of Refugee Law*, 12: 212–34.

Czaplinski, W. (1994). 'Aliens and Refugee Law in Poland – Recent Developments', *International Journal of Refugee Law*, 6: 636.

ECRE (European Council on Refugees and Exiles) (1998). 'Position on the Enlargement of the European Union, in Relation to Asylum', London and Brussels: ECRE, September. Available at: www.ecre.org/positions/eu.pdf.

Grabbe, H. (2000). 'The Sharp Edges of Europe: Extending Schengen Eastwards', *International Affairs*, 76: 519.

Guild, E. and C. Harlow (eds) (2001). *Implementing Amsterdam: Immigration and Asylum Rights in EC Law*, Oxford: Hart.

Hailbronner, K. (1998). 'European Immigration and Asylum Law under the Amsterdam Treaty', *Common Market Law Review*, 35: 1047.

Hailbronner, K. and C. Thiery (1997). 'Schengen II and Dublin: Responsibility for Asylum Applications in Europe', *Common Market Law Review*, 34: 957.

House of Lords (2000). Select Committee on European Union, *Enlargement and EU External Frontier Controls*, HL Paper No. 110, London: The Stationery Office, 24 October.

Iglicka, K. (2001). 'Migration Movements from and into Poland in the Light of East–West European Migration', *International Migration*, 39: 3.

IOM/ICPMD (International Organization for Migration/International Centre for Migration Policy Development) (1999). *Migration in Central and Eastern Europe – 1999 Review*, Geneva: IOM.

Jerczinski, M. (1999). 'Patterns of Spatial Mobility of Citizens of the Former Soviet Union', in K. Iglicka and K. Sword (eds), *The Challenge of East–West Migration for Poland*, London: Macmillan: 105–19.

Jileva, E. (2002). 'Visa and Free Movement of Labour: The Uneven Imposition of the EU *Acquis* on the Accession States', *Journal of Ethnic and Migration Studies*, 28: 683–700.

Klaczynski, M. (1997). 'Re-admission Agreements Concluded by Poland', Available at: www.ujhrc.org/en/articles/klaczynski.htm.

Laczko, F., I. Stacher and A. K. von Koppenfels (eds) (2002). *New Challenges for Migration Policy in Central and Eastern Europe*, Geneva: IOM, ICPMD and TMC Asser Press.

Lambert, H. (1999). 'Protection Against Refoulement from Europe: Human Rights Law Comes to the Rescue', *International and Comparative Law Quarterly*, 48: 515.

Latawski. P. (1999). 'Straz Graniczna: The Mission, Structure and Operations of Poland's Border Guard', in K. Iglicka and K. Sword (eds), *The Challenge of East–West Migration for Poland*, London: Macmillan: 90–103.

Lavenex, S. (1998a). 'Asylum, Immigration, and Central–Eastern Europe: Challenges to EU Enlargement', *European Foreign Affairs Review*, 3: 275.

Lavenex, S. (1998b). 'Passing the Buck: EU Refugee Policies towards Central and Eastern Europe', *Journal of Refugee Studies*, 11: 126.

Lavenex, S. (2002). 'EU Enlargement and the Challenge of Policy Transfer: the Case of Refugee Policy', *Journal of Ethnic and Migration Studies*, 28: 701.

Le Monde (2002). 'A la frontière roumano-moldave', 9 June.

Mikolajczyk, B. (2002). 'Poland', in R. Byrne, G. Noll and J. Vested-Hansen (eds), *New Asylum Countries? Migration Control and Refugee Protection in an Enlarged European Union*, The Hague: Kluwer Law International: 48–77.

Monar, J. (2001). 'Justice and Home Affairs', in H. Wallace and A. Mayhew (eds), *Poland: A Partnership Profile*, OEOS Policy Paper, Brighton: University of Sussex, April.

Noll, G. (2002). 'Protection in a Spirit of Solidarity?', in R. Byrne, G. Noll and J. Vested-Hansen (eds), *New Asylum Countries? Migration Control and Refugee Protection in an Enlarged European Union*, The Hague: Kluwer Law International: 305–24.

O'Keefe, D. (1999). 'Can the Leopard Change Its Spots? Visas, Immigration and Asylum – Following Amsterdam', in D. O'Keeffe and P. Twomey (eds), *Legal Issues of the Treaty of Amsterdam*, Oxford: Hart: 271–88.

Petersen, M. (2002). 'Recent Developments in Central Europe and the Baltic States in the Asylum Field: A View from UNHCR and the Strategies of the High Commission for Enhancing the Asylum Systems of the Region', in R. Byrne, G. Noll and J. Vested-Hansen (eds), *New Asylum Countries? Migration Control and Refugee Protection in an Enlarged European Union*, The Hague: Kluwer Law International: 351–72.

Seiffarth, O. (2000). 'The Enlargement Process and JHA Cooperation', in P. J. van Krieken (ed.), *The Asylum Acquis Handbook*, The Hague: TMC Asser Press: 61–72.

Sesickas, L., V. Siniovas, M. Urbelis and L. Vyskiene (2002). 'Lithuania', in R. Byrne, G. Noll and J. Vested-Hansen (eds), *New Asylum Countries? Migration Control and Refugee Protection in an Enlarged European Union*, The Hague: Kluwer Law International: 226–66.

Shaw, J. (2001). 'The Treaty of Nice: Legal and Constitutional Implications', *European Public Law*, 7: 195.

Simpson, G. (1999). 'Asylum and Immigration in the European Union, after the Treaty of Amsterdam', *European Public Law*, 5: 91.

Stainsby, R. A. (1990). 'Asylum-seekers in Poland: Catalyst for a New Refugee and Asylum Policy in Europe', *International Journal of Refugee Law*, 2: 636.

Stola, D. (2001). 'Poland', in C. Wallace and D. Stola (eds), *Patterns of Migration in Central Europe*, London: Longman: 175–202.

UNHCR (2002). *Statistical Yearbook 2001: Refugees, Asylum-seekers and Other Persons of Concern – Trends in Displacement. Protection and Solutions*, Geneva: UNHCR.

van der Klaauw, J. (2001). 'Towards a Common Asylum Procedure', in E. Guild and C. Harlow (eds), *Implementing Amsterdam: Immigration and Asylum Rights in EC Law*, Oxford: Hart: 165–93.

van Krieken, P. J. (ed.) (2000). *The Asylum Acquis Handbook*, The Hague: TMC Asser Press.

Wallace, C. (2002). 'Opening and Closing Borders: Migration and Mobility in East–Central Europe', *Journal of Ethnic and Migration Studies*, 28: 603.

Wolczuk, K. (2001). 'Poland's Relations with Ukraine in the Context of EU Enlargement', Briefing note, No. 4/01, Brighton: ESRC One Europe or Several Programme.

Wolczuk, K. (2002). 'The Polish–Ukrainian Border: On the Receiving End of EU Enlargement', *Perspectives on European Politics and Society*, 3: 245.

Zielonka, J. (2001). 'How New Enlarged Borders Will Reshape the European Union', *Journal of Common Market Studies*, 39: 507.

Index